Atrocity Speech Law

More Praise for *Atrocity Speech Law*

"Professor Gregory Gordon's book, *Atrocity Speech Law: Foundation, Fragmentation, Fruition*, is an important contribution that will serve as a foundation stone for the future prevention of crimes against humanity.... [It] will be a very useful tool to all scholars seeking a more peaceful world.... [It] will offer new knowledge about a vital subject of stopping atrocity speech, which threatens the security of everyone." (*From the Foreword*)

Benjamin B. Ferencz, Nuremberg Prosecutor

"Holistic, authoritative, and comprehensive, Professor Gregory Gordon's masterful study of the relationship between expression and atrocity crimes sets out a framework for a delicate balance of competing objectives. It brings order to an area of international law that is fraught with fragmentation and contradiction."

William Schabas, Professor of International Law,
Middlesex University, London

"Professor Gregory Gordon compellingly argues that we need to re-conceptualize the jurisprudence of the international criminal law governing hate speech. He renames these principles 'atrocity speech law' and offers a trenchant critique of the inconsistent rulings of international tribunals. He proposes a resolution to the resulting conceptual uncertainties through a 'unified liability theory' that would harmonize the law on hate speech related to war crimes, genocide, and crimes against humanity. For those interested in effective prevention and punishment, this is a must read."

Professor Gregory Stanton, Founding President,
Genocide Watch, George Mason University, Arlington, VA

Atrocity Speech Law

Foundation, Fragmentation, Fruition

Gregory S. Gordon

Foreword by

Benjamin B. Ferencz
Nuremberg Prosecutor

OXFORD
UNIVERSITY PRESS

OXFORD
UNIVERSITY PRESS

Oxford University Press is a department of the University of Oxford. It furthers the University's objective of excellence in research, scholarship, and education by publishing worldwide. Oxford is a registered trademark of Oxford University Press in the UK and certain other countries.

Published in the United States of America by Oxford University Press
198 Madison Avenue, New York, NY 10016, United States of America.

Library of Congress Cataloging-in-Publication Data

Names: Gordon, Gregory S., author.
Title: Atrocity speech law : foundation, fragmentation, fruition /
Gregory S. Gordon ; foreword by Benjamin B. Ferencz.
Description: New York : Oxford University Press, 2017. | Includes bibliographical
references and index.
Identifiers: LCCN 2016044874 | ISBN 9780190612689 ((hardback) : alk. paper)
Subjects: LCSH: Hate speech—Law and legislation. | Atrocities—Law and legislation. |
Hate crimes—Law and legislation. | War crimes. | Genocide. | International law and human rights.
Classification: LCC KZ7177.A87 G69 2017 | DDC 342.08/53—dc23 LC record available at
https://lccn.loc.gov/2016044874

9 8 7 6 5 4 3 2

Printed by Edwards Brothers Malloy, United States of America

Note to Readers
This publication is designed to provide accurate and authoritative information in regard to the subject matter covered. It is based upon sources believed to be accurate and reliable and is intended to be current as of the time it was written. It is sold with the understanding that the publisher is not engaged in rendering legal, accounting, or other professional services. If legal advice or other expert assistance is required, the services of a competent professional person should be sought. Also, to confirm that the information has not been affected or changed by recent developments, traditional legal research techniques should be used, including checking primary sources where appropriate.

(Based on the Declaration of Principles jointly adopted by a Committee of the American Bar Association and a Committee of Publishers and Associations.)

To Annie,

Tiny traces of your love linger lightly on every leaf and none could have been written without you . . .

To Genevieve and Antonia,

The drive in drafting was the dream of dear daughters daring to do what's different—defiantly defending the damned like dad, in days after his deeds are done . . .

CONTENTS

PART THREE Fruition

FOREWORD

BY BENJAMIN B. FERENCZ
Nuremberg Prosecutor

Professor Gregory Gordon's book, *Atrocity Speech Law: Foundation, Fragmentation, Fruition*, is an important contribution that will serve as a foundation stone for the future prevention of crimes against humanity. It was 1947 when I served as Chief Prosecutor in one of the subsequent Nuremberg Trials (*Einsatzgruppen*) against twenty-two high-ranking and well-educated Nazi leaders. They were convicted of murdering over a million innocent victims, including thousands of children killed one shot at a time. In my opening statement, I referred to these acts as "genocide." The victims were slaughtered because they did not share the race, religion, or ideology of their executioners. I emphasized then, as I have done ever since, the right of all people to live in peace and human dignity regardless of their race or creed. One of the main reasons such horrendous crimes could be committed is attributable to the hatred generated by vicious Nazi propagandists such as Julius Streicher, the racist Nazi publisher, who was hanged in October 1946 for crimes against humanity.

The Nuremberg Principles recognized that crimes are committed by individuals and that the law must apply equally to everyone. These principles were universally hailed, yet remain largely unfulfilled. Curbing hate speech is a means to help prevent genocide and crimes against humanity. Failure to criminalize hate speech encourages fanatics such as those responsible for the 1994 genocide in Rwanda. Even today, many countries are still in the stage of development in which laws to prevent and punish hate speech have not yet been adequately developed. Professor Gordon's comprehensive and scholarly book shows us how that can be done.

Professor Gordon's book is always careful to show how, in regulating atrocity speech, liberty of expression can, nevertheless, be preserved. The First Amendment to the US Constitution that guarantees freedom of speech was never intended to justify the violation of fundamental human rights designed to protect everyone. One of the major contributions of this book is to identify and explain the historical treatment and relationship between speech and atrocity crimes. Hate speech, in fact, presents a clear and present danger to fundamental human rights everywhere that deserve protection by the rule of law.

We are moving in the right direction of substituting the rule of law instead of the use of armed force. Our limited ability to achieve peaceful goals is handicapped by the absence of any independent international enforcement mechanism, which is vital to settle disputes. There is no doubt that genocide can be incited by arousing public fears. Those who are prepared to kill and die for their own protection of perceived religious, political, economic, or other rights will produce a continuing state of terror throughout the world. We have still not recognized that you cannot kill an ingrained ideology with a gun.

Professor Gordon presents an analysis of international human rights and domestic laws governing speech that are already being applied to protect the citizens of many countries. His suggestions for how to incorporate this jurisprudence into the realm of international criminal law are necessary and timely. His "Unified Liability Theory" presents an original theory for improving this body of law. This, in turn, will help achieve meaningful deterrence and punishment of mass atrocity. Professor Gordon's book will be a very useful tool to all scholars seeking a more peaceful world.

What is fundamental is to have greater acceptance by the general public in all countries that law is better than war—no matter what. The current capacity to end all life on planet Earth now drains the resources required to eliminate some of the justified causes of conflict. We must teach tolerance, compassion, and willingness to compromise. It takes courage not to be discouraged. Since reason is frequently overruled by passion, and speech can incite mass murder as we have seen, I have sought to encapsulate my philosophy into a simple slogan: "Law Not War," as well as my advice to young people who will have to carry this torch forward since I am now in my ninety-seventh year. My advice is "Never Give Up." Studying Professor Gordon's book will offer new knowledge about a vital subject of stopping atrocity speech, which threatens the security of everyone.

PREFACE AND ACKNOWLEDGMENTS

In effect, this book developed in three separate stages. The first was during my formative years through college. As an eight-year-old boy, I was shown a graphic, arresting photo of a Nazi extermination center in a book on the Holocaust and it changed my life. I was always haunted by that image. And I had nightmares about it throughout my childhood. Even at such a young age, I felt I wanted to do something with my life that might contribute toward preventing such horrors from ever repeating themselves. For helping cultivate in me a sense of justice and the confidence that I could make a positive difference, I want to thank my parents, grandparents, and other family members, including my sister Corinne and Aunt Bunny. And I want to extend particular thanks to my mom for introducing me to travel and exploration and to my dad for giving me a great love of law and history. I am still trying to cope with my dad's recent passing and, in some ways, the publication of this book does not even seem real because he is not here to read the final version and give me his thoughts. Still, I hope he is looking down from heaven, proud of me.

I am also grateful to my old high school debate partner and friend, Dion Cominos, who helped sharpen my intellectual skills, and his mom, Joan, who sparked in me a passion for helping the underdog. In college, my dear friend Albert Latteur, and his son Dominique (and Dominique's wife Françoise), cultivated in me an appreciation for deep intellectual engagement and social justice. Gregory Colbert, the older brother I never had, helped me understand life's greater complexities and deeper rewards, and my good friend Marc Ballon became a fellow traveler in historical and geographical exploration. They deserve heartfelt thanks.

A second stage in the life of this book began after I earned my college degree at Berkeley. In law school, also at Berkeley, before the advent of the ad hoc tribunals in the early 1990s, I was studying the work of the attorneys at Nuremberg. I want to thank my girlfriend at the time, Amy Resner, for encouraging me to pursue and cultivate my interest in the subject of war crimes prosecution. A research project on the Nuremberg trials in Professor Bob Berring's class was critical in this regard, and I remain grateful to him for providing me this opportunity. Thanks are also due to the international law professor who mentored and inspired me the most, the incomparable David Caron.

During my early years in practice, including a clerkship with Federal District Judge Martin Pence in Honolulu, Hawaii, my knowledge and passion for international criminal law was deepened through a series of communications with Professor Cherif Bassiouni. At a time when the Nuremberg trials seemed only a distant relic of history, he inspired me to believe that international criminal law (ICL) would have a rebirth. And when that eventually happened, his great pioneering work inspired me to believe that ICL would be an essential tool in ending the culture of impunity. We still have a long way to go, but I believe the past two decades have borne that out.

Sadly, however, what brought about ICL's rebirth was a conflagration of intercommunal violence in the first part of the 1990s that I watched unfold in the media. I was shocked and appalled at the world's relative indifference to ethnic cleansing in the Balkans. But I was completely horrified by the commission of genocide in Rwanda in 1994 while the world stood by and did nothing. When the International Criminal Tribunal for Rwanda (ICTR) was established in 1994, I applied for a job with the Office of the Prosecutor and was fortunate to be hired. In this regard, I have to thank my dear friend Lovely Dhillon, who alerted me to the opportunity and encouraged me to apply. On arriving at the ICTR, I was assigned to the team responsible for investigating and preparing for prosecution of what would be known as the *Media Case*. I became Deputy Team Leader of this group of lawyers and police officers. We focused on preparing cases against the executives and announcers for the infamous Radio Télévision Libre des Milles Collines (RTLM), otherwise known as "Radio Machete," as well as journalists for other extremist media outlets, including the genocidal newspaper *Kangura*. I was eventually put on the trial team and helped prepare the cases for adjudication.

My being assigned to the *Media Case* team was luck of the draw, but it had a tremendous impact on my life. I realized how integral hate speech was to mass atrocity but at the same time always remained concerned about potential encroachments on liberty of expression. And there was a dearth of jurisprudence to guide us, what little existed coming from the Nuremberg judgments. So working on these cases required deep and creative thinking. And here I need to thank a slew of supervisors and colleagues who gave me great guidance and inspiration. My overall supervisor during case development strategy at the ICTR, Chief Prosecutor Louise Arbour, was exceptional in coordinating all the brainstorming. My immediate supervisors, Australian Army Colonel Craig McConaghy (Team Leader during the pretrial phase and then member of the Trial Team and now a close friend) and James Stewart (Trial Team Leader and currently Deputy Prosecutor of the International Criminal Court), were great mentors. Together we helped trace the contours of the key embryonic legal concepts and set the stage for successful prosecutions.

I would also like to thank other colleagues and friends during my time at the ICTR, including the great Alison Des Forges, who served as a consultant to our team, and other Office of the Prosecutor colleagues, including Brenda

Sue Thornton, Robert Petit, Michael Hourigan, Joshua Walker, Jacques Legros, Rosette Muzigo-Morrison, and Jim Lyons. Others connected to the work who made a significant positive impact on me were my supervisors at the US State Department (which, along with the US Department of Justice, seconded me to the ICTR), Gregory Stanton and David Scheffer, both of whose work continues to inspire me. I also learnt a great deal from my wonderful friend François-Xavier Nsanzuwera, Rwanda's Procureur de la République when the 1994 genocide began, as well as the courageous journalist Phillipe Dahinden, founder of Fondation Hirondelle, which sets up positive-message media outlets to counter hate radio in hotspots around the world.

My secondment with the ICTR ended before the *Media Case* went to trial, but it was gratifying to see that RTLM announcer Georges Ruggiu pled guilty and the three key media executives who went on trial, Ferdinand Nahimana, Jean-Bosco Barayagwiza, and Hassan Ngeze, were found guilty by an ICTR Trial Chamber and the convictions were affirmed on appeal. In the meantime, I had gone back to the United States to work with the US Department of Justice, as a white collar prosecutor in the criminal tax section (where I was eventually assigned to the Organized Crime Drug Enforcement Task Forces), while also doing a stint as a Special Assistant US Attorney for the District of Columbia (Sex Offense, Domestic Violence Section) and a detail with the Office of Overseas Prosecutorial Development Assistance and Training (OPDAT) (conducting a post–civil war justice assessment in Sierra Leone).

I eventually transferred to the Office of Special Investigations (OSI, now Human Rights and Special Prosecutions), the so-called "Nazi-Hunters" unit, where I prosecuted cases against persons who had collaborated in Nazi war crimes in Europe during World War II and had entered the United States hiding their dark pasts. The office eventually updated its mission to focus on modern war criminals, and I was again able to work on cases emanating from Rwanda and other parts of Africa. During my time at the Department of Justice, I gained crucial insights regarding the workings of domestic and international criminal law and human rights law, and I would like to thank my supervisors, Ronald Cimino (Criminal Tax), Eli Rosenbaum (OSI), and Carl Alexandre (OPDAT), for helping with my education. I would also like to thank fellow attorneys Melissa Schraibman Grinberg, Tom DiLeonardo, Charles O'Reilly, Karen Quesnel, Patrick Stokes, Jeff Nedrow, Audra Ibarra, and Adam Fels as well as IRS special agents Andrew Feldman and Brian Watson and OSI historians Robert Waite, Steven Rogers, and Jeffrey Richter. Stephen Rapp, who took over the trial team for the *Media Case* at the ICTR and eventually became US Ambassador-at-Large for War Crimes Issues, also gave me important support and guidance during these years. My thanks go to him as well.

While I was at the Department of Justice, the *Media Case* Trial Chamber judgment was issued, and I found myself re-engaged with the issues of incitement to genocide and persecution as a crime against humanity. I published an article in the *Virginia Journal of International Law* titled "*A War of Media, Words,*

Newspapers and Television Stations": The ICTR Media Trial Verdict and a New Chapter in the International Law of Hate Speech, 45 VA. J. INT'L L. 139 (2004). Around the same time, I was invited to guest lecture in the class of my former law school classmate and friend, Professor Cynthia Lee at George Washington Law to whom I also owe a big debt of gratitude. The experience of writing the article and teaching put an idea in my head: perhaps I might enjoy being a law professor.

Thus, the third stage in the development of this book began when I left the US Department of Justice and joined the legal academy. At the University of North Dakota School of Law, where I taught criminal and international law and served as Director of the Center for Human Rights and Genocide Studies (CHRGS), I had the chance to think more deeply about issues raised in my *Virginia Journal of International Law* (*VJIL*) piece. I then wrote a series of articles that, along with the *VJIL* article, laid the foundation for this book: (1) *From Incitement to Indictment? Prosecuting Iran's President for Advocating Israel's Destruction and Piecing Together Incitement Law's Emerging Analytical Framework*, 98 J. CRIM. L. & CRIMINOLOGY 853 (2008) (a symposium issue in which I was proud to have an article published alongside such luminaries as Cherif Bassiouni, David Scheffer, and another important colleague who has given me invaluable insights over the years and to whom I am very grateful, William Schabas); (2) *Music and Genocide: Harmonizing Coherence, Freedom and Nonviolence in Incitement Law*, 50 SANTA CLARA L. REV. 607 (2010); (3) *Formulating a New Atrocity Speech Offense: Incitement to Commit War Crimes*, 43 LOY. U. CHI. L.J. 281 (2012); (4) *Hate Speech and Persecution: A Contextual Approach*, 46 VAND. J. TRANSNAT'L L. 303 (2013); and (5) *The Forgotten Nuremberg Hate Speech Case: Otto Dietrich and the Future of Persecution Law*, 75 OHIO ST. L.J. 571 (2014).

I would like to thank my supervisors and colleagues at the University of North Dakota School of Law for their support of my scholarship during my time there. This would include Dean and Provost Paul LeBel and Dean Kathryn Rand, who gave me great moral as well as financial backing through summer research grants and excellence-in-scholarship fellowships. It also includes Professors Eric and Kit Johnson, Michael McGinniss, Patti Alleva, C. J. Vachon, Alex Sickler, Christine Fritze, Anne Mullins, and Tammy Pettinato. Indispensable as well to my scholarly output at UND were the library staff, including Director Rhonda Schwartz, the amazing Jan Stone (Head of Faculty Services), Carl Warrene (Systems Administrator), Kaaren Pupino (Head of Technical Services), Michael Hanson (Instructional and Support Technologist), Laurie McHenry (Cataloguing and Metadata), Jane Oakland (Circulation and Interlibrary Loan Manager), David Haberman (Head of Student Services), and Sherry Zeman (Office Manager). And I always benefitted from the support of other staff including Rob Carolin, Phylis Trelfa, Julie Simon, Trish Hodney, Cheri Tretter, Mark Brickson, and Karen Martin. I would also like to express my gratitude to all my awesome students over the years, including Michael Lopez, Rita Griguolaite, Mark Grainger, Stephenie Davis, Erik Escarraman, Sara Haselbauer, Tim Heise, Ali Jama, Meg

Morley, Dan Cooper, John Johns, Michael Lockhart, Evan Nelson, Amanda Grafstrom, Danielle O'Lochlainn, Shanna Brown, Benjamin Rowe, Jack Dwyer, Tracy and Jared Hines, Rachel Hoffman, and the Winnipeg Mafia (you know who you are!), who have completely engaged me intellectually and always inspired me to try harder. Let me also extend thanks to my colleagues at CHRGS, including Assistant Director Wilbur Stolt and members Rebecca Weaver-Hightower, Brian Urlacher, Kristine Paranica, and Victor Lieberman. I want to thank all our interns, especially Clarinda Solberg and Laurie Freid, and our great institutional supporter, Steve Hunegs, Executive Director of the Jewish Community Relations Council: Minnesota and the Dakotas. CHRGS would never have seen the light of day without the phenomenal support of Provost Greg Weisenstein and would not have thrived without the backing of President Robert Kelley and his inspirational wife, Marcia. You were all great supervisors and colleagues and are sorely missed.

But in 2014, I got a fantastic job offer I simply could not refuse. I picked up my family and relocated to Asia to take a law professor position with The Chinese University of Hong Kong Faculty of Law. Since the move, I have written two pieces whose ideas have found their way into this book: (1) *Speech Along the Atrocity Spectrum*, 42 GA. J. INT'L & COMP. L. 560 (2014); and (2) *Of War-Councils and War-Mongering: Considering the Viability of Incitement to Aggression, in* FOR THE SAKE OF PRESENT AND FUTURE GENERATIONS: ESSAYS ON INTERNATIONAL LAW, CRIME AND JUSTICE IN HONOUR OF ROGER S. CLARK (Brill-Nijhoff, S. Linton, G. Simpson, & W. Schabas eds., 2015). I have also gotten tremendous support from Dean Chistopher Gane and very helpful insights from my colleagues, Professors Michael Ramsden, Samuli Seppänen, Bryan Mercurio, Julien Chaisse, Bryan Druzin, Gonzalo Villata-Puig, Kevin Cheng, Stuart Hargreaves, Nina Jorgensen, Jyh-An Lee, Luke Marsh, Lutz Christian Wolff, Mimi Zou, Sandra Marco Colino, David Donald, and Michelle Miao. As well, I am grateful to the Chinese University of Hong Kong Law Library staff, John Barij, Iris Cheong, and Agnes Cheung. I would also like to give thanks to a great group of students here who have engaged me, inspired me, and supported me, including, but not limited to, Christina Ling, Charles Lo, Crystal Leung, Felicity Ng, Adrian Fong, Haley Jetson, Lloyd Meng, Noel Chan, LK Shiu, and all our amazing Research Postgraduate students [with a special shout-out to Daley Birkett for his research assistance].

A number of other people have played invaluable roles in making this book possible, and I want to thank them too. The Honorable Irwin Cotler, a giant in human rights advocacy and a former Minister of Justice and Attorney General of Canada, has been a great champion of my work and has invited me to present it to the Canadian Parliament. Dr. Charles Small, first at Yale and then as Director of the Institute for the Study of Global Anti-Semitism and Policy (ISGAP), has given me great encouragement and a forum to present my work at Yale, Harvard, and Columbia Universities, among other places. I have also appreciated the support of Ambassador Dore Gold, Israel's former Permanent Representative to the United Nations, who, in his capacity as Director of the Jerusalem Center for Public Affairs, has invited me to present my ideas at the United Nations and at the

British Parliament. I have also benefited from the encouragement and insights of Gasana Ndoba, Linda Melvern, Rakiya Omaar, Dr. Susan Allen, Professor Jonathan Busch, and Drs. Yaël Ronen, Elihu Richter, and Rony Blum. Other colleagues, who have inspired me and contributed to my professional development include William Dritsas, Becky Lenaburg, and Kari Erickson Levine.

Many other legal academics and practitioners have also made invaluable contributions to this book. My dear friend Laurie Blank has given me great advice related to both publishing and writing. Early drafts were vetted by other friends and colleagues, including Mark Drumbl, David Pimentel, and Barrie Sander. I have also gotten invaluable suggestions on the manuscript from Roger Clark, Gregory Stanton, Joseph Rikhof, Emma Irving, Suzannah Linton, Besmir Fedahic, Lisa Biersay, and Njahira Karanja. Over the years, I have gained great insights as well from other scholars who have written in this area, including Wibke Timmermann, Susan Benesch, Richard Wilson, and Carol Pauli. I extend my thanks to all of them. And I appreciate the many pearls of wisdom and words of encouragement given to me over time by my good friends and fellow academics/experts Michael Bazyler, Zachary Kauffman, William Merkel, John Barrett, Jean-Damascène Gasanabo, Natalie Pierce, David Simon, Bettina Ambach, Kris Kotarski, Margee Ensign, Craig Etcheson, Adam Birnbaum, Kathy Roberts, Sabrina Safrin, Mark Osiel, Cindy Buys, and Kevin Jon Heller. I also want to thank the incomparable Sandra Schulberg, an amazing friend whose Renaissance talents make important contributions to the fight against the culture of impunity.

Thanks as well to my stepfather and fellow attorney, George Montgomery, for his great guidance and belief in me all these years. My stepdaughter Antonia has also played such an important role in my life—she factors into these pages in so many ways. And I would like to thank other family members who have been there for me including my parents-in-law Charles C. and Linda Crenshaw, my brother-in-law Charles S. Crenshaw, step-sisters Laura and Megan Montgomery, my cousins Nicole Gump, Bobbie, Don and Ron Schwartz, Sheri and David Tornek, Maxine Rubin, Bina Contreras, Beth Rossmann Hite, Maureen and Howard Borden, and family friends Phil and Sarah Rabichow, Bill and Virginia Miranda, Carole Forrest, and Eve Cominos and Daniel Roemer. I am also grateful to the United Jewish Congregation of Hong Kong, in particular to Rabbis Stanton Zamek and Martha Bergadine.

Similarly, I am grateful to two organizations for which I have served as a consultant: the Sentinel Project for Genocide Prevention and the International Nuremberg Principles Academy (INPA). At the Sentinel Project, where I am on the advisory board, I particularly want to thank Executive Director Christopher Tuckwood, who, in spearheading Sentinel's technologically innovative projects, has helped me understand in a much deeper way the importance of using positive speech to combat hate speech. At INPA, I have had the good privilege of serving as a consultant on its Prevention and Accountability for Hate Speech Project, which has allowed me to appreciate the finer points of contextual analysis in situations of potentially genocidal or persecutory discourse. I am very grateful to INPA's former and current directors, respectively, Bernd Borchardt and Klaus Rackwitz, as well as the Head of the Interdisciplinary Research Unit, Marjana Papa, along with Project Officer and Assistant Researcher Kerry-Luise Prior. I also want to thank the Office of the Prosecutor of the International Criminal Court for welcoming me to present my scholarship and allowing me to consult—you have reminded me why this work is so important. I have also benefited from the support and insights of Adama Dieng, the UN Secretary-General's Special Adviser for the Prevention of Genocide, and Simona Cruciani of his office. A very special thank-you to them.

Benjamin Ferencz, the last living Nuremberg prosecutor, whose hard work and hunger for justice was singlehandedly responsible for prosecution of the *Einsatzgruppen* trial, has always been a hero. It is beyond an honor to have his Foreword open this volume. Thanks to his son Don too, a great scholar, lawyer and advocate for ICL causes. This book has also benefited tremendously from the invaluable insights of my ICL brother in arms, the great Prosecutor for the International Criminal Tribunal for the former Yugoslavia, Serge Brammertz. Thanks as well to ICTY Deputy Prosecutor Michelle Jarvis.

Through it all, I have had some incredible friends giving me encouragement, support, and editorial assistance for nearly all my professional and academic life. This would include Brent Austin, Kassi Berg and Jeff Barabe, Theodore Laufer, Mukesh Advani, Erik Zuckerbraun, Tim and Julie Clarkson and family, the Leichter clan, Ken Sargoy, Chris Van Gundy, Mary Newmayr, the Weaver-Hightowers, Suzanne de Lannoy, Mark Falzini, Diana Ohlbaum, Seth Greenberg, Pierluigi Congedo, Laura Bong, Julia Fineman Sauter, Danshera Cords, Jelani Jefferson Exum, Rada Bogdacenco, Dianna Moore, Anne Harringer, Kristen Allen, Eric Kelling, and Yvette Lapierre and Steve Finney. But more than anyone else, my closest friend, Dolph Hellman, has been there for me in so many important ways that this brief word of thanks here cannot do them justice. Suffice it to say that I am eternally grateful.

Finally, I have saved the best for last. I would like to express my appreciation to my editors at Oxford University Press, Blake Ratcliff, whose enthusiasm and support for this monograph from the beginning has been instrumental, and Alden Domizio, without whose generous assistance I could not have navigated through all the important post-manuscript-submission procedures and emendations. Thanks as well to Balamurugan Rajendran, Project Manager, Newgen Knowledge Works, who has been incredible to work with during the nitty-gritty editing phase. In all research connected to this tome, Jan Stone has been my eyes and ears, always forwarding me invaluable research whenever she came across it. I could not have done it without her. And I cannot thank her enough. Also indispensable has been my Research Assistant Icarus Chan—a brilliant student of the law whose work on this volume and many other projects fills me with great pride.

But I owe the deepest debt of gratitude to my wife, Annie, and my daugh ter, Genevieve, who generously gave me the space, time, and encouragement

I needed to realize this project, as well as the gift of love that helped inspire me through all the difficult moments. My wife is a partner in the truest sense of the word—I could not do this work without her. And my daughter is an inspiration every day. I will never forget what you have done for me. My love and thanks to both of you.

Introduction

> "Those who can make you believe absurdities, can make you commit atrocities."
>
> —Voltaire[1]

I. SETTING THE STAGE

In a broadcast during the week of April 6, 1994, at the beginning of the Rwandan Genocide, Hutu extremist station Radio Télévision Libre des Milles Collines (RTLM) falsely informed its listeners that Daniel Kabaka, a Kigali resident who happened to be a Tutsi, was a supporter of the Tutsi rebel group the Rwandan Patriotic Front.[2] Within twenty-four hours, Kabaka's house was attacked with a hand grenade and partially destroyed. Kabaka broke his leg in the blast and could not flee. While the rest of his family escaped, his twelve-year-old daughter, Chine, remained with him, saying she wanted to die with her father. Kabaka lay in the rubble of his residence until eight gendarmes arrived. Chine tried to save her dad by helping him move into the home's courtyard. But the gendarmes thoroughly searched the premises, found Daniel and Chine, and murdered them. The following week, an RTLM radio announcer on his way to work noticed hundreds

1. François-Marie Arouet (pen name "Voltaire"), *Questions sur Les Miracles*, *in* 8 Œuvres Complètes de Voltaire, 691 (Chez Furne 1836). The actual quotation is "Certainement qui est en droit de vous rendre absurde est en droit de vous rendre injuste." This would translate somewhat differently, but the above is the standard rendering of the quotation. *See*, *e.g.*, *Voltaire*, Wikiquote, https://en.wikiquote.org/wiki/Voltaire (last visited Sept. 12, 2016) (noting that this is the "widely used paraphrase"); Richard Dawkins, *NS Diary*, New Statesman, Jan. 30, 2006, at 8 (quoting Voltaire using the common paraphrase).

2. Prosecutor v. Nahimana, Case No. ICTR-99-52-T, Judgement and Sentence, ¶¶ 446, 467, 478 (Dec. 3, 2003).

of unarmed Tutsis—including numerous women and children—seeking refuge in Kigali's Islamic Cultural Center. Within an hour, RTLM announced that there were "cockroaches" in the center and falsely described them as armed. The next morning, the compound was encircled by soldiers and militia, who attacked and slaughtered the Tutsi civilians inside.[3] Broadcasts of this sort repeated themselves over the next ninety days until approximately 800,000 innocent victims had been murdered by the end of July.

Sadly, this kind of media communication was hardly unique during the decades that preceded the Rwandan Genocide—RTLM's transmissions merely representing the twentieth century's coda of genocidal discourse. About eighty years previously, the Ottoman propaganda weekly *Harb Mecmuasi*, "in order to justify [the Armenian genocide]," thoroughly prepared "the requisite propaganda material" in Istanbul.[4] Such propaganda contributed toward the murder of 1.5 million Armenian citizens by, among other things, convincing the Turkish people of "the need to 'rid ourselves of these Armenian parasites'" and identifying Armenians with "traditionally unclean animals such as rats, dogs, and pigs."[5] Two decades later, Nazi media organs, in particular *Der Stürmer*, helped mobilize the extermination of six million Jews in the Holocaust by labeling them "as germs and pests, not human beings, evil-doers, as disseminators of diseases who must be destroyed in the interest of mankind."[6] The twenty-first century has seen a perpetuation of this extermination rhetoric with Sudan's regime. In Darfur, South Kordofan, and the Blue Nile, atrocities have been "fueled by hate speech"—with the government using it to dehumanize blacks and spur the Janjaweed militia's genocidal violence against them.[7] Janjaweed have marched into liquidation operations chanting language such as the following:

> "Dog, son of dogs, we came to kill you and your kids."
> "Kill the black donkeys! Kill the black dogs! Kill the black monkeys!"
> "You blacks are not human. We can do anything we want to you."
> "We kill our cows when they have black calves. We will kill you too."
> "You make this area dirty; we are here to clean the area."
> "You blacks are like monkeys. You are not human."[8]

3. *Id.* ¶ 450.

4. Vahakn N. Dadrian, The History of the Armenian Genocide: Ethnic Conflict from the Balkans to Anatolia to the Caucasus 220 (2004).

5. David Livingstone Smith, Less Than Human: Why We Demean, Enslave and Exterminate Others 145 (2011).

6. Frank Chalk, *Radio Propaganda and Genocide*, Montreal Institute for Genocide and Human Rights Studies (Nov. 1999), http://migs.concordia.ca/occpapers/radio_pr.html.

7. Alexander Tsesis, *Inflammatory Speech: Offense v. Incitement*, 97 Minn. L. Rev. 1145, 1171 n.148 (2013).

8. David Livingstone Smith, *Dehumanization, Genocide, and the Psychology of Indifference*, Psychology Today (Dec. 2, 2011), http://www.psychologytoday.com/blog/philosophy-dispatches/201112/dehumanization-genocide-and-the-psychology-indifference-0.

These dark chapters in human history have established that dehumanization of the victims in the minds of the perpetrators—the key to overcoming instinctual and ethical compunctions against killing—is an often indispensable feature of mass atrocity. Dehumanization, in turn, is effected through the medium of speech, whether oral or written. And international law has come to recognize that. In fits and starts since the middle of the twentieth century, it has formulated a set of penal modalities to punish the mouthpieces of this toxic rhetoric: (1) direct and public incitement to commit genocide (prohibiting speech calling for genocidal acts regardless of whether those acts are committed); (2) persecution as a crime against humanity (forbidding discriminatory speech uttered as part of a widespread or systematic attack against a civilian population); (3) instigation (criminalizing speech that results in atrocity); and (4) ordering (outlawing commands to violate international law given in the context of a superior-subordinate relationship when the command is carried out).

Unfortunately, the piecemeal development of the law in this area has produced an unshapely and disjointed groups of crimes that, even on an individual basis, have not been applied in any systematic or coherent manner. Perhaps it comes as no surprise then, that the academic commentary surrounding this body of law has been equally fragmented. There have been articles and book chapters that have dealt with each of the crimes separately.[9] But nearly all of them focus on the crime of "incitement to genocide," or some aspect of it, to the exclusion of the other recognized crimes of persecution, instigation, and ordering. Moreover, no single treatise has looked at the overall chronology of the law's formulation and analyzed how each of the crimes has evolved individually over time or how each fits with one another given the doctrinal policy objectives.[10] In fact, the law's

9. *See, e.g.*, Catherine A. MacKinnon, *Prosecutor v. Nahimana, Barayagwiza & Ngeze*, 103 Am. J. Int'l L. 97 (2009); Robert H. Snyder, *"Disillusioned Words Like Bullets Bark": Incitement to Genocide, Music, and the Trial of Simon Bikindi*, 35 Ga. J. Int'l & Comp. L. 645, 673–674 (2007); Susan Benesch, *Vile Crime or Inalienable Right: Defining Incitement to Genocide*, 48 Va. J. Int'l L. 485 (2008) [hereinafter *Vile Crime*]; Audrey Golden, Comment, *Monkey Read, Monkey Do: Why the First Amendment Should Not Protect the Printed Speech of an International Genocide Inciter*, 43 Wake Forest L. Rev. 1149 (2008); Carol Pauli, *Killing the Microphone: When Broadcast Freedom Should Yield to Genocide Prevention*, 61 Ala. L. Rev. 665 (2010).

10. The only book in print that most closely fits this description is Wibke Timmermann, Incitement in International Law (2014). While that book considers the crimes of persecution and instigation, its primary focus, as its title suggests, is incitement. And it devotes considerable attention to the treatment of hate speech in international human rights law. The first three chapters are titled "The Harm in Incitement to Hatred," "Incitement to Hatred and the Right to Freedom of Speech," and "The Prohibition of Incitement to Hatred in Human Rights Law." Only the book's final two chapters, "Incitement to Hatred as Persecution" and "Criminalization of Incitement to Crimes," deal exclusively with international criminal law. And no chapter of the book is dedicated to dealing with the holistic reform of the entire body of law. Similarly, certain books have dealt more generally with hate speech or incitement, such as The Media and the Rwanda Genocide (Allan Thompson ed., 2007) (with chapters concentrating exclusively on the Rwandan genocide and only three touching specifically on legal issues, namely Charity Kagwi-Ndungu, *The Challenges in Prosecuting Print Media for Incitement to Genocide*;

programmatic goals have not been lucidly articulated vis-à-vis all of the offenses. Much of the scholarship focuses on the tension between free speech and nonviolence with regard to incitement to commit genocide, but very little has grappled with that conundrum as it applies to the crime of persecution.[11]

Similarly, within the context of adjudicating crimes arising from inflammatory rhetoric, the jurisprudence has failed to identify categories of hate speech that could help determine how to ease the friction between the competing goals of liberal expression of ideas and meaningful protection of victims.[12] The monolithic designation of "hate speech" does not give us any inkling of whether the words invite specific acts of violence or seek to provoke general feelings of animus. Nor does it reveal to whom the message is directed. And those details, within the greater context of the orator's milieu, could be crucial in determining whether to prosecute the speech or protect it.

Finally, the experts have not even managed to find an appropriate name for the entire body of law. Some refer to it as "international incitement law,"[13] but

Jean-Marie Biju-Duval, *"Hate Media"—Crimes against Humanity and Genocide: Opportunities Missed by the ICTR*, and Simone Monasebian, *The Pre-Genocide Cases against RTLM*); MICHAEL G. KEARNEY, THE PROHIBITION OF PROPAGANDA FOR WAR IN INTERNATIONAL LAW (2007); THE CONTENT AND CONTEXT OF HATE SPEECH: RETHINKING REGULATION AND RESPONSES (Michael Herz & Peter Molnar eds., 2012) (with only one atrocity speech chapter—on incitement to genocide—by Irwin Kotler). *See also* PROPAGANDA, WAR CRIMES TRIALS AND INTERNATIONAL LAW: FROM SPEAKERS' CORNER TO WAR CRIMES (Predrag Dojčinović ed., 2012). But there has not been one book devoted to a comprehensive analysis of the entire jurisprudential output and the relation of each of its parts to one another and to the whole.

11. There are a couple of exceptions. *See, e.g.*, Diane F. Orentlicher, *Criminalizing Hate Speech in the Crucible of Trial:* Prosecutor v. Nahimana, 12 NEW ENGLAND J. INT'L & COMP. L. 17 (2005) (dealing with persecution); Wibke Timmermann, *Incitement in International Criminal Law*, 88 INT'L REV. OF THE RED CROSS 823 (2006) (focusing almost entirely on incitement to genocide but containing some material analyzing the crime of instigation in relation to incitement); Gregory S. Gordon, *Hate Speech and Persecution: A Contextual Approach*, 46 VAND. J. TRANSNAT'L L. 303 (2013) [hereinafter *Hate Speech and Persecution*] (dealing comprehensively with the crime of persecution).

12. Susan Benesch has drafted a set of guidelines for monitoring inflammatory speech and evaluating its dangerousness, i.e., its potential for triggering intergroup violence. She calls such incendiary discourse "dangerous speech" and distinguishes it from "hate speech," which she characterizes as "too broad for successful early warning of mass atrocities . . ." Susan Benesch, *Dangerous Speech: A Proposal to Prevent Group Violence*, WORLD POLICY INSTITUTE (Jan. 12, 2012), http://www.worldpolicy.org/sites/default/files/Dangerous%20Speech%20Guidelines%20Benesch%20January%202012.pdf. Benesch's guidelines originated with her *Vile Crime* article, *supra* note 9, and were developed in the context of incitement to genocide. They do not necessarily deal with adjudicating hate speech as crimes against humanity (persecution). And they have been developed most recently in the context of atrocity prevention, not speech crime adjudication. In Chapter 9, this book will develop a typology of hate speech to assist in assigning liability for persecution.

13. *See, e.g.*, WIBKE TIMMERMANN, *supra* note 10. Tim Curry, *Review of Conference: "International Criminal Tribunals in the 21st Century"*, 13 No. 1 HUM. RTS. BRIEF 6, 7 (2005) ("Judge Navanethem Pillay, a former ICTR judge who is now a judge in the Appeals Division of [the] ICC, addressed the controversial decision in *Prosecutor v. Nahimana*, et al. (the *Media Case*)

that is too narrow and reflects the scholarly obsession with direct and public incitement to commit genocide at the expense of considering the other types of liability. Others have referred to it as "international hate speech law" or variations thereof, which does not adequately capture its relationship to particularly heinous or mass violence.[14] Indeed, the failure accurately to characterize this field of law has contributed to its fragmented and haphazard treatment in both the jurisprudence and the scholarship. So, at the outset, with a more holistic and accurate approach in mind, I propose a new name for this entire body of international rules and jurisprudence: "atrocity speech law."

II. AN OVERVIEW

Working with that new terminology, this book divides itself into three main sections dealing with the origins of atrocity speech law, its ultimate morphing into a disjointed state, and then proposals for a holistic fix. Those sections are titled as follows: (1) foundation; (2) fragmentation; and (3) fruition. Each of them shall now be considered in turn.

A. Foundation

1. A History of Speech and Mass Atrocity

The historical record is clear: instances of mass atrocity have always been accompanied by communications campaigns designed to demonize the intended victims and inflame the passions of would-be perpetrators.[15] Chapter 1 limns the chronology of speech and government-sponsored mass violence over the past one hundred years. It begins with the Ottoman genocide of the Armenians during World War I. In carrying out its murderous plan, the Young Turk government created the template for the modern genocidal propaganda campaign. It used the media and the wide dissemination of photographic images to depict

and its effects on *international incitement law* during the conference.") (emphasis added); H. Ron Davidson, *The International Criminal Tribunal for Rwanda's Decision in* The Prosecutor v. Ferdinand Nahimana et al.: *The Past, Present, and Future of International Incitement Law*, 17 Leiden J. Int'l L. 505 (2004).

14. *See, e.g.*, Stephanie Farrior, *Molding the Matrix: The Historical and Theoretical Foundations of International Law Concerning Hate Speech*, 14 Berkeley J. Int'l. L. 1, 7 (1996) ("One might ask whether *international hate speech law* has achieved the transformative potential to which the drafters aspired.") (emphasis added); Gregory S. Gordon, *"A War of Media, Words, Newspapers and Radio Stations": The ICTR Media Trial Verdict and a New Chapter in the International Law of Hate Speech*, 45 Va. J. Int'l L. 139, 149–153 (2004) [hereinafter *A War of Media*] (in his earliest scholarly pieces, even this author, admittedly, did not appreciate the entire scope of the law, in terms of a proper title for it).

15. *See, e.g.*, Mayo Moran, *Talking about Hate Speech: A Rhetorical Analysis of American and Canadian Approaches to the Regulation of Hate Speech*, *in* David Dyzenhaus & Arthur Ripstein, Law and Morality: Readings in Legal Philosophy 771 (2001) (referring to jurisprudence that links "hate speech to a history of genocide . . ."); Anthony Joseph Paul Cortese, Opposing Hate Speech 43 (2006) ("Instead, ethnic cleansing became normative through hate speech.").

Armenians as an impure, alien people collaborating with Turkey's enemies and bent on its destruction.

Less than two decades later, Nazi Germany and its *Reichsministerium für Volksaufklärung und Propaganda* (Reich Ministry of Public Enlightenment and Propaganda) availed itself of the Ottoman blueprint and went even further. Hijacking all communications media in Germany, including art, music, theater, films, books, radio, educational materials, and the press, the Nazis depicted Jews as disease-carrying insects or vermin, tumors, or tuberculosis that were infecting healthy Germans and thus had to be exterminated. By the time the Holocaust was being carried out, Nazi publications such as *Der Stürmer* were calling for Jewish annihilation "root and branch."[16]

Chapter 1 also reviews genocidal propaganda campaigns in the post–Cold War era with a particular emphasis on atrocity-triggering speech in the former Yugoslavia and Rwanda. Prior to the early 1990s outbreak of armed conflict in the former Yugoslavia, the Serbian Democratic Party (SDS), led by Radovan Karadžić, launched there an anti-"Bosniak" propaganda campaign.[17] They denigrated Muslims by referring to them, for example, as *balija* or "filthy gypsies."[18] They inculcated the Bosnian-Serb public with the message that Bosniaks were "malefactors," "cut-throats," and "terrorist diversionary groups." Eventually, this helped spark Bosnian-Serb violence against Muslims, which culminated in the genocide at Srebrenica.[19] Nearly parallel in time to this, Hutu extremists were using newspapers, such as *Kangura* and radio stations such as RTLM and Radio Rwanda to vilify Tutsis and inflame Hutu passions in preparation for genocidal massacres. These hate-media outlets characterized Tutsis as less than human—branding them *inyenzi* (cockroaches) and snakes—and used code words such as "go to work" to order their mass murder.

2. Hate Speech in International Human Rights and Domestic Law

In light of this compelling empirical connection between hate speech and mass atrocity, what laws, if any, criminalize the dissemination of such rhetoric? Chapter 2 begins to answer that question by examining international human rights instruments and domestic laws covering speech and violence. It notes preliminarily that there is an inbuilt clash in the principal human rights documents between the free expression prerogative and that of freedom from invidious

16. Erin Steuter & Deborah Wills, At War with Metaphor: Media, Propaganda, and Racism in the War on Terror 142 (2009).

17. Prosecutor v. Brđanin, Case No. IT-99-36-T, Judgement, ¶ 80 (Int'l Crim. Trib. for the Former Yugoslavia Sept. 1, 2004).

18. 2 John Oppenheim & Willem-Jan van der Wolf, Global War Crimes Tribunal Collection 148 (1997).

19. *Brđanin*, Case No. IT-99-36-T, Judgement, ¶ 80.

discrimination.[20] Such tension is apparent in the founding document of international human rights law: the Universal Declaration of Human Rights. Its Article 7, for instance, provides: "All are entitled to equal protection against any discrimination . . . and against any incitement to such discrimination."[21] Article 19, on the other hand, states: "Everyone has the right to freedom of opinion and expression."[22]

Regarding domestic jurisdictions, statutes dealing with hate speech can be placed in various categories along a spectrum. At the victim-protective end are nations like the Netherlands and Denmark, which promulgate and actively enforce robust hate speech laws. These countries are vigilant in terms of safeguarding the rights of vulnerable minorities based on the desire to uphold human dignity apart from and in addition to any interest in keeping public order.[23]

Chapter 2 then demonstrates that the United States is at the other end of the continuum. Universally deemed the most speech-protective jurisdiction, its Constitution's First Amendment stipulates that the government may "make no law . . . abridging the freedom of speech, or of the press."[24] Perhaps unlike any other nation, the United States has promoted freedom of expression, at the expense of regulation, in the hope that it could subject toxic messages to public scrutiny, relegate them to the margins, and safeguard and foster democracy in the process. As the United States has played a prominent role in developing the criminalization of atrocity speech on the global stage, and as its Supreme Court has often held forth on issues of speech liberty versus suppression, its domestic jurisprudence will be a particular focus of this chapter.

3. Nuremberg and the Foundational Atrocity Speech Law Instruments

Between these two competing policy objectives at odds in human rights instruments and municipal law—protection of free speech versus regulation of hate speech—international criminal law (ICL) would have to chart its own course. Chapter 3 considers the initial choices made by the newly formed body of ICL vis-à-vis atrocity speech. The framers of the Nuremberg International Military Tribunal (IMT) recognized straight away that Nazi barbarities were rooted in propaganda. Article 6 (c) of the IMT Charter permitted prosecutors to charge

20. *See* Gordon, *A War of Media, supra* note 14, at 145–147 (2004) (generally describing the conflict between and among the provisions of these international instruments).

21. Universal Declaration of Human Rights, art. 7, G.A. Res. 217A(III), U.N. GAOR, 3d Sess., Supp. No. 1, U.N. Doc. A/810 at 71 (1948).

22. *Id.*

23. *See* WvS Art. 137(d) (1881) (amended 1996), translated in The Dutch Penal Code, 133 (Louise Rayer & Stafford Wadsworth trans., Rothman & Co. 1997); The Danish Criminal Code §266(b), The Danish Criminal Code 107 (G.E.C. Gad. 1958).

24. U.S. Const. amend. I.

Nazi defendants with "crimes against humanity."[25] This was a novel offense that criminalized certain heinous acts committed against civilians that were outside the ambit of war crimes. Among those acts was "persecution" on political, racial, or religious grounds. Julius Streicher, editor-in-chief of the Nazi propaganda broadsheet *Der Stürmer*, was among those convicted of persecution based on his newspaper's hate speech directed against Jewish people.[26] Although the IMT acquitted Nazi Radio Division head Hans Fritzsche of the same charge, a subsequent tribunal in the American zone, pursuant to Control Council Law No. 10 (containing a crimes against humanity provision very similar to the IMT Charter's),[27] convicted Nazi Press Chief Otto Dietrich of persecution.[28]

Chapter 3 then considers the drafting and promulgation of the Convention on the Prevention and Punishment of the Crime of Genocide (Genocide Convention). In 1946, in the wake of the IMT's judgments and with the passage of Resolution 96(1), the UN General Assembly set to work on a treaty establishing genocide as a crime carrying individual accountability under international law.[29] It then adopted the 1948 Genocide Convention, Article II of which defined genocide as a series of acts (including, for example, killing and causing serious bodily or mental harm) committed with the intent to destroy, in whole or in part, a national, ethnic, racial, or religious group, as such. Article III then specified that a number of related acts committed in furtherance of Article II would also be punishable. That included "direct and public incitement to commit genocide."[30]

The chapter goes on to demonstrate that this provision was incorporated into the Statutes of the International Criminal Tribunal for Rwanda (ICTR) (at Article 2(3)(c))[31] and the International Criminal Tribunal for the former

25. Nuremberg Rules, in Agreement for the Prosecution and Punishment of the Major War Criminals of the European Axis art. 6(c), Aug. 8, 1945, 59 Stat. 1544, 1547, 82 U.N.T.S. 279 [hereinafter IMT Charter].

26. IMT Judgment, Oct. 1, 1946, *reprinted in* 22 The Trial of German Major War Criminals: Proceedings of the International Military Tribunal Sitting at Nuremberg Germany 501–502 (1946) [hereinafter Streicher].

27. Allied Control Council, Nuremberg Trials Final Report Appendix D: Control Council Law No. 10 (Dec. 20, 1945) [hereinafter CCL No. 10], *reprinted in* Telford Taylor, Final Report to the Secretary of the Army on the Nuremberg War Crimes Trials Under Control Council Law No. 10, at 250 (1949).

28. United States v. von Weizsaecker (Ministries Case), Judgment, in 14 TRIALS OF WAR CRIMINALS BEFORE THE NUERNBERG MILITARY TRIBUNALS: "THE MINISTRIES CASE" 308, 565–576 (1951).

29. G.A. Res. 96(I), U.N. GAOR, 6th Comm., 55th plen. mtg. at 189, U.N. Doc. A/64/Add.1 (1946).

30. Convention on the Prevention and Punishment of the Crime of Genocide, arts. II–III, G.A. Res. 260(III), U.N. GAOR, 3rd Sess., Part I, U.N. Doc. A/810 at 174 (1948).

31. Statute of the International Criminal Tribunal for Rwanda, S.C. Res. 955, art. 2(3)(c), U.N. Doc. S/RES/955 (Nov. 8, 1994) [hereinafter ICTR Statute].

Yugoslavia (ICTY) (at Article 4(3)(c)).[32] Each of those foundational instruments also contained a crimes against humanity (persecution) provision—Article 3(h) of the ICTR Statute and Article 5(h) of the ICTY Statute. Moreover, each had a provision for instigation and ordering—ICTR Statute Article 6(1)[33] and ICTY Statute Article 7(1), which list forms of individual criminal responsibility.[34]

Finally, in terms of key atrocity speech provisions in international criminal law, Chapter 3 looks at the Rome Statue of the International Criminal Court (ICC). Article 25(3)(e) of the Rome Statute criminalizes direct and public incitement to commit genocide, and Article 7(1)(h) proscribes persecution as a crime against humanity.[35] As no ICC decision has grappled with the contours of these atrocity speech crimes, these provisions are ripe for interpretation, and this book will offer guidance in that regard. In addition, Article 25(3)(b) criminalizes ordering, soliciting, and inducing of the statute's core crimes and will also be considered.

4. The Foundational Ad Hoc Tribunal Atrocity Speech Law Cases

In the meantime, the relevant ICTR/ICTY provisions were implicated in a series of important early cases. Those are covered in Chapter 4, which also lays out the elements of each offense as set forth in those decisions. Incitement was fleshed out in a string of ICTR judgments that broke down the crime into the following elements: (1) public; (2) direct; (3) *mens rea*; and (4) incitement. In *Prosecutor v. Akayesu* (1998), the Trial Chamber held that speech could be deemed "public" if addressed to "a number of individuals in a public place" or to "members of the general public at large by such means as the mass media, for example, radio or television."[36] And the communication could satisfy the "direct" criterion if, when considering the language "in the light of its cultural and linguistic content ... the persons for whom the message was intended immediately grasped the implication thereof."[37] The requisite *mens rea* bifurcates into a dual intent: (a) to provoke another to commit genocide, and (b) to commit the underlying genocide itself.[38] The Trial Chamber nominally indicated that causation was not a required element—put another way, to make out a prima facie case, the prosecutor need not prove the incitement resulted in genocide.

32. Statute of the International Criminal Tribunal for the Former Yugoslavia, S.C. Res. 827, art. 4(3)(c), U.N. Doc. S/RES/827 (May 25, 1993), *amended by* S.C. Res. 1166, annex, U.N. Doc. S/RES/116 (May 13, 1998) [hereinafter ICTY Statute].

33. ICTR Statute, *supra* note 31, art. (6)(1).

34. ICTY Statute, *supra* note 32, art. 7(1).

35. Rome Statute of the International Criminal Court arts. 25(e), 7(1)(h), July 17, 1998, 2178 U.N.T.S. 3 (entered into force July 1, 2002) [hereinafter Rome Statute].

36. Prosecutor v. Akayesu, Case No. ICTR-96-4-T, Judgement, ¶ 556 (Sept. 2, 1998).

37. *Id.* ¶¶ 557–558.

38. *Id.* ¶ 560.

The crime's most complicated and thorny feature involves its key defining element—"incitement" itself. In formulating this element, the ICTR had to grapple with distinguishing between legitimate exercise of free speech (regardless of how repugnant) and degradation of such discourse into criminal advocacy. The well-known 2003 decision in the so-called *Media Case* considered international human rights instruments and domestic laws and explicitly identified two analytic criteria to establish whether speech could be characterized as either lawful expression or illicit advocacy: its purpose[39] (embracing on one end of the spectrum, clearly lawful goals, such as historical research or distribution of news, and, on the other end, clearly unlawful ends such as explicit exhortations to violence) and its context.[40] The interval between these two poles of the continuum plainly calls for contextual scrutiny, and the ICTR suggested two evaluative factors: surrounding violence and the speaker's previous rhetoric.[41]

Chapter 4 also reviews the elements of persecution as a crime against humanity. Article 7 of the Rome Statute defines crimes against humanity as a series of acts, including persecution, when committed as part of a widespread or systematic attack directed against any civilian population, with knowledge of the attack.[42] Article 7(h) specifies that persecution must be against "any identifiable group or collectivity on political, racial, national, ethnic, cultural, religious, gender . . . or other grounds that are universally recognized as impermissible under international law."[43] Article 7(2)(g) then defines "persecution" as "the intentional and severe deprivation of fundamental rights contrary to international law by reason of the identity of the group or collectivity. . . ."[44]

In *Prosecutor v. Kupreskić* (2000), an ICTY Trial Chamber laid out a four-part test for resolving whether conduct can satisfy the *actus reus* requirement for persecution: (1) a gross or blatant denial; (2) on discriminatory grounds; (3) of a fundamental right, laid down in international customary or treaty law; and (4) reaching the same level of gravity as the other crimes against humanity enumerated in Article 5 of the ICTY Statute.[45] Also in 2000, the Trial Chamber in *Prosecutor v. Ruggiu* held that the offense of persecution as a crime against humanity through speech could be successfully consummated without the speaker explicitly urging violence.[46] The utterance of the words themselves,

39. Prosecutor v. Nahimana, Case No. ICTR-99-52-T, Judgement and Sentence, ¶¶ 1000–1006 (Dec. 3, 2003).

40. *Id.* ¶¶ 1004–1006.

41. *Id.* ¶ 1004 (speaking of massacres taking place surrounding the speaker's utterance) and ¶ 1005 (focusing on previous conduct to reveal purpose of text).

42. Rome Statute, *supra* note 35, art. 7.

43. *Id.* art. 7(h).

44. *Id.* art. 7(2)(g).

45. Prosecutor v. Kupreškić, Case No. IT-95-16-T, Judgement, ¶ 567 (Int'l Crim. Trib. for the Former Yugoslavia Jan. 14, 2000).

46. Prosecutor v. Ruggiu, Case No. ICTR-97-32-I, Judgement and Sentence, ¶ 22 (June 1, 2000).

in the context of a widespread or systematic attack directed against a civilian population, represented a deprivation of fundamental rights, such as liberty and humanity.

As well, Chapter 4 examines the elements of instigation. It consists of "prompting another to commit an offence."[47] In other words, the prosecution must demonstrate a causal connection between the instigation and the perpetrated offense.[48] This entails proving that the instigation "contributed" to the prompted person's commission of the crime.[49] The *mens rea* is double-layered—the intent to utter the speech and the intent for the target crime to be committed.[50]

Finally, Chapter 4 examines the elements of ordering. That crime requires a superior-subordinate relationship, issuance of a command to commit an international crime, an awareness that the order would likely lead to commission of an international crime, and a causal link between the order and the commission of the crime.[51]

Although these foundational statutes and cases have provided a rudimentary template for jurists to work with, upon deeper consideration of their text, some of their pronouncements are ambiguous and/or incomplete. Even when they are entirely clear, their subsequent application has been neither systematic nor consistent. They have also not been fleshed out in a way to ensure coherent application of the law going forward.[52] And that sets the stage for the next section of the book—"Fragmentation."

B. Fragmentation

Part Two of this book grapples with the disjointed and, as to a certain portion of the jurisprudence, disconnected aspects of the entire body of atrocity speech law. On the whole, these problems have given rise to what we may consider a "fragmented" jurisprudence. This disintegrated state has had its effects on each of the three core atrocity crimes in relation to hate speech—genocide, crimes against humanity, and the one that has not yet been referenced in this Introduction—war crimes.

47. Prosecutor v. Blaškić, Case No. IT-95-14, Judgement, ¶ 280 (Int'l Crim. Trib. for the Former Yugoslavia Mar. 3, 2000).

48. Prosecutor v. Bagilishema, Case No. ICTR-95-1A-T, Judgement, ¶ 30 (June 7, 2001).

49. Prosecutor v. Kordić, Case No. IT-95-14/2-T, Judgement, ¶ 387 (Int'l Crim. Trib. for the Former Yugoslavia Feb. 26, 2001).

50. Prosecutor v. Orić, Case No. IT-03-68-T, Judgement, ¶ 279 (Int'l Crim. Trib. for the Former Yugoslavia June 30, 2006).

51. Prosecutor v. Akayesu, Case No. ICTR-96-4-T, Judgement, ¶ 483 (Sept. 2, 1998).

52. *See* Gregory S. Gordon, *Music and Genocide: Harmonizing Coherence, Freedom and Nonviolence in Incitement Law*, 50 Santa Clara L. Rev. 607, 609 (2010) [hereinafter *Music and Genocide*].

1. The Problems with Incitement to Commit Genocide

Chapter 5 considers some of the problems that have arisen after initial formulation and application of the crime of direct and public incitement to commit genocide. For example, digging deeper into the *Akayesu* Trial Chamber judgment, we find that its treatment of the "direct" element is schizophrenically situated somewhere between Common Law and Civil Law conceptions. Moreover, the judges allude to the media through which "direct" speech could be disseminated, such as speeches or distribution of written material. But they have nothing to say about the quality of the speech itself. What might be its possible grammatical parameters or permissible degrees of metaphoric abstraction? Merely responding that such diagnostic inquiries are irrelevant as the overarching issue is whether the listener readily grasped the meaning of the discourse begs the question. Not furnishing future generations of jurists with insight as to the range of readily graspable phraseology represents a squandered opportunity.

Related to this, the incitement decisions are decidedly underinclusive with regard to the techniques of incitement they identify explicitly. Only a narrow focus on strictly linear and explicit exhortations factors into the surface judicial findings. But other, superficially less apparent but equally potent, incitement techniques are often employed by conflict entrepreneurs.[53] These methods—such as "accusation in a mirror" (when the speaker accuses the intended victim of wishing to perpetrate the kind of violence the speaker is requesting of third parties)[54]—can sometimes be read inferentially into court opinions, but that is all. This failure to provide a well-defined glossary of incitement techniques may also contribute to scattered, inconsistent, and potentially myopic jurisprudence going forward.

Nevertheless, as has been indicated, *Akayesu* provided important initial guidance regarding the "direct" and "public" facets of incitement. And the *Media Case* judgment offered limited but valuable guideposts for analyzing whether free speech rights have been abused to the point of criminality. Unfortunately, since the *Media Case* decision, these criteria have not been explicitly or systematically applied.[55] Chapter 5 will demonstrate that in the subsequent decisions of the Canadian Supreme Court in *Mugesera v. Canada* (2005)[56] and the ICTR in *Prosecutor v. Bikindi* (2008),[57] the judges failed to filter methodically the defendants' words through the "purpose" or "context" crucibles, or subject them to the contextual evaluative factors of surrounding violence or previous rhetoric.[58] That exercise would have bestowed the test with superior interpretive power and greater normative coherence. And the Tribunal's conclusions might therefore have been perceived as resting on less slender of a reed.

53. *Id.* at 638.

54. *See* Kenneth L. Marcus, *Accusation in a Mirror*, 43 Loy. U. Chi. L.J. 357, 359 (2012) (providing a description of the technique and its treatment in the law).

55. *Id.*

56. Mugesera v. Canada, [2005] 2 S.C.R. 100, 2005 SCC 40 (Can.).

57. Prosecutor v. Bikindi, Case No. ICTR-01-72-T, Judgement (Dec. 2, 2008).

58. *Id.*

Moreover, in *Bikindi* the Tribunal actually contaminated the overall analysis by adulterating its application of the "purpose and context" analytic criteria with application of the test it had previously formulated for consideration of the "direct" element of the offense.[59] This doctrinal mishmash has left much confusion in its wake.[60]

Additionally, courts squandered golden opportunities to flesh out the two existing analytic criteria for the incitement element. The *Media Case* Trial Chamber opinion suggested a base to which future decisions would return as a point of repair and build on as a platform for normative development.[61] Both the *Mugesera* and *Bikindi* decisions seemed oblivious to that reading of the *Media Case* judgment. In a nonsystematic way, they paid lip service to an element or two (primarily "context"), but that was all. And so only a skeletal set of scattered criteria and evaluative factors resulted from a string of decisions that could have been the foundation for doctrinal holism and heft.[62]

Finally, the existing case law has also created confusion regarding the issues of "causation" and the element of "public." With regard to the former, although the judges have held that causation is not a required element of incitement, they have also made inconsistent statements in that regard. The *Akayesu* judgment, for example, while holding that causation is not an element of incitement in the legal conclusions,[63] also asserted the need to prove "a possible causal link" between the relevant speech and subsequent violence in that case.[64] Moreover, the Tribunal went on to conclude that there was, in fact, a causal link between Akayesu's speech and the ensuing Tutsi massacres in Taba commune on April 19, 1994.[65] Such conflicting statements have engendered confusion as to whether there is a causation requirement for the crime of incitement.[66]

Regarding the "public" element, the problems it engenders are illustrated in the so-called "roadblock cases" at the ICTR. Even though inflammatory speech uttered at roadblocks was in a "public" place—because on public roads accessible to all citizens—the speech was held not to be "incitement" because "members of the public" were not present.[67] But if enough persons were present at the roadblock, then "members of the public" could be deemed in attendance and the

59. *Bikindi*, Case No. ICTR-01-72-T, ¶ 387.

60. Gordon, *Music and Genocide, supra* note 52, at 622.

61. *Id.* at 609.

62. *Id.*

63. Prosecutor v. Akayesu, Case No. ICTR-96-4-T, Judgement, ¶ 553 (Sept. 2, 1998).

64. *Id.* ¶ 349.

65. *Id.*

66. *See, e.g.*, Aurora Heller, *Wilson on Incitement*, Virginia Law Weekly (Apr. 19, 2013), http://www.lawweekly.org/?module=displaystory&story_id=3963&edition_id=231&format=html (reporting a scholar's view that "international criminal law inserts causality into the crime of inciting genocide.").

67. Prosecutor v. Nahimana, Case No. ICTR-99-52-A, Judgement, ¶ 862 (Nov. 28, 2007).

speech could be considered "incitement."[68] This is a distinction without principle and is exposed as unjustified from a policy perspective.

2. The Problems with Persecution, Instigation, and Ordering

Chapter 6 then exposes problems in the jurisprudence related to persecution, instigation, and ordering. It begins by demonstrating the fragmented approach to persecution law taken by the ad hoc international tribunals. In particular, the ICTR and ICTY have adopted polar opposite positions regarding the issue of whether hate speech not calling for violence can serve as an *actus reus* for persecution as a crime against humanity. For example, in judgments for *Prosecutor v. Ruggiu*[69] and the *Media Case*,[70] separate ICTR Trial Chambers found that hate-speech radio broadcasts not necessarily calling for action blatantly deprived the target ethnic group of fundamental rights and thus, even without proof of causally related violence, could be the basis for charging persecution.

In *Prosecutor v. Kordić* (2001),[71] on the other hand, an ICTY Trial Chamber found that the hate speech alleged in the indictment did not constitute persecution because it did not directly call for violence and thus failed to rise to the same level of gravity as the other enumerated crimes against humanity acts (such as murder and rape). Then, in the *Media Case* Appeals Chamber judgment,[72] the majority found that pure hate speech, if accompanied by separate calls for violence or actual violence, could give rise to persecution liability, but declined to rule on whether nonadvocacy hate speech, standing alone, is of a level of gravity equivalent to that of the other enumerated crimes against humanity offenses. And thus the law of persecution remains divided.

Chapter 6 also considers the fragmented approach to instigation. On one hand, it has been consistently confused with incitement, and this has exacerbated the muddled jurisprudence regarding causation in both bodies of law.[73] Moreover, there is no consistent approach to the crime's "contribution" requirement, and this has also led to a series of fragmented pronouncements regarding the degree of contribution.[74] And, at worst, it is arguably responsible for developing a "but for"

68. Prosecutor v. Ngirabatware, Case No. ICTR-99-54-T, Judgement and Sentence (Dec. 20, 2012).

69. Prosecutor v. Ruggiu, Case No. ICTR-97-32-I, Judgement and Sentence, ¶¶ 22, 24 (June 1, 2000).

70. *Nahimana*, Case No. ICTR-99-52-T, Judgement and Sentence, ¶¶ 1072–1073, 1092 (Dec. 3, 2003).

71. Prosecutor v. Kordić, Case No. IT-95-14/2-T, Judgement, ¶¶ 195, 198, 209 & nn. 271–272 (Int'l Crim. Trib. for the Former Yugoslavia Feb. 26, 2001).

72. *Nahimana*, Case No. ICTR-99-52-A, Judgement, ¶¶ 986–987, ¶¶ 446, 467, 478 (Nov. 28, 2007).

73. *See, e.g.*, Prosecutor v. Šešelj, Case No. IT-03-67-T, Judgement, ¶ 300, n.343 (Int'l Crim. Trib. for the Former Yugoslavia Mar. 31, 2016).

74. *See id.*

causation requirement in the jurisprudence.[75] Finally, contrary to precedent and sound policy, in the recent *Prosecutor v. Šešelj* judgment, an ICTY Trial Chamber, without any apparent justification, saddled instigation's *actus reus* element with a "different forms of persuasion" requirement. In other words, the traditional means of "urging" and "encouraging" would not be enough and other actions, such as threats, would be necessary to make out a prima facie case of instigation.[76]

Finally, Chapter 6 looks at the key problem in relation to the crime of ordering: the fact that it carries no inchoate liability. Given the high likelihood of an order being carried out due to the superior-subordinate relationship, criminal liability should attach to the superior by mere virtue of the fact that he issued the order. This is especially true since inchoate liability is a feature of incitement to genocide, but incitement does not suppose the existence of a superior-subordinate relationship.

3. The Absence of Incitement to Commit War Crimes

Chapter 7 demonstrates fragmentation in a different sense. In particular, one of the core constituent components of atrocity offenses—war crimes—remains detached from the main corpus of atrocity speech law. Put another way, there is a serious gap in international humanitarian law (IHL) regarding speech. Certain provisions related to speech do appear in the Geneva Conventions—but they focus quite narrowly on direct orders in connection with grave breaches.[77] But what if a commander does not give an order but rather subtly suggests violence against civilians *hors de combat* by dehumanizing them in speeches to his troops?

This chapter shows how such communication by officers, which cannot be considered an "order" but could very well lead to commission of atrocities, has been quite common in modern history.[78] Yet, no provision in IHL covers it. Even if it were an order, under the current schema, liability would attach only if atrocities were actually committed.[79] Again, what if the speech by a commander were uttered, the troops were prepared to massacre civilians, but just as the bloodbath was about to take place, enemy troops intervened and spared the civilians? Once

75. *Id.* ¶ 333 (observing that "the Prosecution was not able to marshal evidence that this speech would have been *at the root of* the departure of the Croats or the persecution campaign alleged by the Prosecution that was supposedly carried out in the locality after the speech.") (emphasis added).

76. *Id.* ¶ 295.

77. *See, e.g.*, Geneva Convention for the Amelioration of the Condition of the Wounded and Sick in Armed Forces in the Field art. 49, Aug. 12, 1949, 6 U.S.T. 314, 75 U.N.T.S. 31 ("The High Contracting Parties undertake to enact any legislation necessary to provide effective penal sanctions for persons committing, or ordering to be committed, any of the grave breaches of the present Convention defined in the following Article.").

78. *See* Gregory S. Gordon, *Formulating a New Atrocity Speech Offense: Incitement to Commit War Crimes*, 43 Loy. U. Chi. L.J. 281, 284–285 (2012) [hereinafter *Formulating a New Atrocity Speech Offense*].

79. *Id.* at 282.

again, pursuant to the law's current iteration, the commander would be let off the hook with respect to his incendiary and nearly murderous rhetoric.[80]

Further, recent history has shown that civilians may issue commands to military personnel or militias. Such was the case in Rwanda during the April to July period of 1994, when nonmilitary radio announcers exhorted soldiers and *Interahamwe* units to attack civilians. Such discrete pockets of media-fueled atrocity are carried out by military personnel, but the civilian source of the exhortations to commit the illicit violence would be exempt from prosecution according to IHL's present format.[81]

C. Fruition

Part Three of the book proposes remedies for these problems. It begins with suggestions for how to fix glitches within each of the offenses given the current structure of the law. It then considers how the overall formulation of the law might be reconfigured to promote greater coverage and holistic coherence.

1. Fixing Incitement to Commit Genocide

Fixing incitement law is the emphasis of Chapter 8. In light of the problems alluded to regarding the jurisprudence in this area, certain experts have called for new tests to replace the framework developed by the ICTR. Two are the focus of the chapter: the "Reasonably Probable Consequences" test and the "Communications Research Framework" test. However, as this chapter explains, these tests are, in various respects, either too rigid, ambiguous, or underinclusive. So they should not be used as wholesale replacements for the ICTR schema. That said, they provide many helpful suggested additions, and thus parts of them, especially their proposed evaluative factors for analyzing context, should be folded into the existing framework.

Thus, the balance of the chapter focuses on how to remedy the problems of the current ICTR approach. In addition to urging more systematic and detailed application of the existing criteria furnished by the ICTR jurisprudence, it proposes how those criteria can be fleshed out and expanded. As mentioned previously, the *Media Case* Trial Chamber judgment, through its subheadings, identified two criteria to be used for distinguishing legitimate expression from criminal advocacy—purpose of the speaker and context of the statement. Additionally, it provided two evaluative elements to consider for context—violence surrounding the speech and the speaker's previous rhetoric.

To begin, for purposes of expanding the existing criteria, deeper analysis of the *Media Case* judgment itself is a good starting point. This chapter identifies two additional criteria implicitly used by the *Media Case* Trial Chamber in framing its analysis: text and the relationship between speaker and subject.[82]

80. *Id.*

81. *Id.* at 283.

82. Gordon, *A War of Media*, *supra* note 14, at 172.

The Trial Chamber's discussion of the "text" element was an implicit part of its "purpose" subheading analysis.[83] Applying this element involved a parsing and exegetical interpretation of the key words in the speech.[84] Regarding speaker and subject, the Tribunal ruled that the analysis should be more speech-protective when the orator is part of a minority criticizing either the government or the country's majority population (and less so in other situations).[85]

Moreover, in considering Rwandan pop singer Simon Bikindi's liability for incitement regarding his music, two new analytic criteria suggested themselves: temporality and instrumentality.[86] The former considers whether speech is uttered contemporaneously with its publication and the latter whether the speaker is responsible for or instrumental in the speech's publication. These criteria are relevant in cases where speech is republished by a third party after initially being uttered by the original speaker.

Additionally, Chapter 8 proposes one other analytic criterion: channel of communication.[87] There are two reasons why this criterion should be added. First, from a temporal perspective, nonelectronic written communication media, such as newspapers, are much less apt to incite to mass violence than broadcast media, such as radio.[88] Second, the availability and circulation of the material should also be taken into account. A newspaper article, for instance, should be considered much less likely to incite in a country with a 90 percent illiteracy rate. Similarly, a text message should be treated more lightly in an extremely poor country with few smartphones or computers.

In the end, when these additional criteria are tacked on, the existing framework for determining whether hate speech constitutes incitement should consist of seven elements: (1) purpose; (2) text; (3) context (bifurcated into internal—related to the speaker—and external—related to facts surrounding the speech); (4) relationship between speaker and subject; (5) channel of communication; (6) temporality; and (7) instrumentality. Moreover, these criteria can be organized within the larger conceptual categories of "content" (purpose and text), "circumstances" (context and speaker-subject relationship), and "medium" (communications channel, temporality, and instrumentality). In turn, these categories can help us answer the what/why (content), who/where (context), and when/how (medium) questions related to the speech for determining whether it legally qualifies as incitement.

Further, within the context criterion, this chapter counsels adding into the mix additional evaluative factors. To begin, it would be helpful to bifurcate "context" into two separate subprongs—internal and external.[89] Internal context

83. Prosecutor v. Nahimana, Case No. ICTR-99-52-T, Judgement, ¶ 1001 (Dec. 3, 2003).

84. *Id.*

85. *Id.* ¶¶ 1006–1008.

86. Gordon, *Music and Genocide, supra* note 52, at 622–623.

87. *Id.* at 635–636.

88. *Id.* at 636.

89. Gordon, *Music and Genocide, supra* note 52, at 637–638.

would encompass characteristics of the speaker himself: his background and professional profile, his previous publication/broadcast history (which is largely similar to one of the evaluative factors in the ICTR *Media Case* judgment), and his personal manner of transmission (including tone of voice). External context would consist of the circumstances surrounding the speech. Here, a number of additional evaluative factors, some suggested in the alternative proposed tests alluded to above, could be considered. These would include political context, media environment, prior similar message, and the outbreak or imminent outbreak of international or noninternational armed conflict.

The chapter also proposes a typology of incitement techniques to deal with incitement's underinclusivity problem. In particular, based on a wide variety of fact patterns involving hate speech that spurred ordinary citizens to slaughter their neighbors by the thousands, the chapter articulates why future decisions should explicitly recognize the following as potentially chargeable forms of incitement: (1) direct calls for destruction; (2) predictions of destruction; (3) verminization, pathologization, demonization, and other forms of dehumanization; (4) accusation in a mirror; (5) euphemisms and metaphors; (6) justification during contemporaneous violence; (7) condoning and congratulating past violence; (8) asking questions about violence; (9) conditional calls for destruction; and (10) victim-sympathizer conflation.[90]

Chapter 8 also suggests a solution for dealing with the lingering causation issue in incitement law. Quite simply, it counsels courts against including consideration of resultant violence in the factual section of incitement judgments or ascribing any weight at all to causation as part of the factual analysis. Using this approach, along with crystal-clear language stating that causation is not an element and refraining from injecting equivocal and theoretical language regarding causation's role, this phantom element, which has caused so much confusion in the jurisprudence and academic literature, should disappear entirely. Causation should be a dead letter in incitement law—it is time to bury it and move on. And this makes sense from both a doctrinal and policy perspective: incitement is an inchoate crime for which liability attaches when it is uttered (assuming the other criteria can be satisfied). So resulting violence is irrelevant.

Finally, Chapter 8 explains how fixing the problem with incitement's "public" element is quite simple—eliminate it. Incitement can be just as effective, and lethal, if undertaken at a large "private" gathering as at a small "public" one (or through a disembodied voice on the airwaves). Any potential aggravating aspect of "public" incitement, such as its potential to cause wider destruction

90. *Id.* at 638. It is possible that, standing alone, depending on the facts of a particular case, certain of the less direct techniques, such as asking questions or victim-sympathizer conflation, would not provide sufficient evidence for bringing incitement charges. However, when multiple instances of speech are at issue, they could support separate charges of incitement when anchored to more egregious examples in the same indictment. Thus, victim-sympathizer conflation, on its own, may not rise to the level of incitement. But when considered in the context of direct calls and dehumanization, for instance, it might be included as a separate count of incitement.

because projected to a larger audience, could be taken into account at sentencing. Otherwise, there is no need for the "public" element as a liability factor, and it should be removed.

2. Fixing Persecution, Instigation, and Ordering

Chapter 9 ponders how the law might resolve the issues arising with respect to persecution, instigation, and ordering. First, the chapter considers how the law ought to harmonize the conflicting strands of persecution law. In particular, it explains why hate speech alone, not explicitly calling for violence, should qualify as the *actus reus* for crimes against humanity (persecution). In the first place, this is consistent with the logic and precedent of prior cases going as far back as the Nuremberg trials, especially the *Otto Dietrich* decision.[91] Second, it is impossible to ignore the legal context necessary to charge crimes against humanity in the first place. Such a charge presumes, per the crime's chapeau (or threshold elements), that the speech is uttered as part of a widespread or systematic attack directed against a civilian population.[92] The chapeau further requires that the defendant be aware that his speech is uttered as part of that attack. And the Rome Statute specifically requires that persecution be tied to one of the other enumerated crimes against humanity offenses (such as rape or extermination) or to another crime within the statute.[93]

As a result, the chapter will demonstrate that it is problematic to consider "hate speech" in a vacuum. Unlike incitement to genocide (an inchoate crime), which, as a legal matter, is not necessarily uttered in the context of simultaneous mass violence, hate speech as persecution must be legally tied to contemporaneous violence (based on the required "attack") in a context where the marketplace of ideas is shut down and speech thus loses its democracy and self-actualization benefits.[94] Thus, even when not explicitly urging violence, it should ordinarily satisfy the *actus reus* requirement of crimes against humanity. Nevertheless, given the defendant's strictly verbal conduct, as well as the fact that impingement on quasi-legitimate freedom of expression may be implicated, isolated or sporadic hate speech, as well hate speech uttered as part of low-level or geographically removed chapeau violence, should not qualify as the *actus reus* of hate speech as a crime against humanity.[95] Freedom of speech must be preserved to the greatest extent possible.

Thus, to help determine whether hate speech should be criminalized in this context, this chapter proposes considering it in greater depth by categorizing it along a spectrum. At one end, one would find the mildest forms of hate speech—general statements casting aspersions on a group.[96] Moving further along toward

91. *See* Gordon, *Hate Speech and Persecution, supra* note 11, at 359.

92. *Id.* at 347–349.

93. *Id.* at 347–348.

94. *Id.*

95. *Id.* at 365–369.

96. *Id.* at 341–346.

the other end of the spectrum, statements voiced directly at the victims could be categorized as "harassment." The next point in this direction along the continuum, incitement (not in the legal sense), entails advocacy directed toward third persons. Such incitement can be toward either hatred or violence. This is the most serious kind of hate speech and, all things being equal, is more likely to be found persecutory notwithstanding any freedom of expression concerns.

Chapter 9 will also discuss solutions for the problems that plague instigation and ordering. Regarding the former, future decisions must consciously, and unequivocally, acknowledge a strict doctrinal dividing line between legal "incitement" and "instigation." That, in turn, should also help put to rest the specious perception that causation is an element of incitement. At the same time, the chapter will recommend eliminating the new and unsupported "different forms of persuasion" *actus reus* requirement. And in the interest of establishing a clear and uniform guideline regarding instigation's relationship with the consummated crime, it will advise adoption of a "substantial contribution" standard.

With respect to ordering, the proposed nostrum is quite simple: expand its ambit to include inchoate liability. Regardless of whether the order is carried out, a superior should be brought to book for commanding his subordinate to commit criminal conduct as the nature of the relationship between speaker and listener betokens likely compliance.

3. Adding Incitement to Commit War Crimes

Chapter 10 is centered on a proposal related to speech in the context of armed conflict. As a logical response to the IHL speech-crime lacuna featured in Chapter 7, it recommends creation of a new offense: incitement to commit war crimes. This new delict would allow prosecution of atrocity-conditioning and atrocity-persuading commanders *before* their troops commit war crimes or even if they never commit such offenses. And it would expand IHL's reach to *civilians* who incite soldiers—always a distinct possibility in the modern world of mass-mobilization armed conflict. Chapter 10 will explain that the new crime would not unduly impinge on the free expression or operational communications prerogatives of officers and would serve an important IHL-compliance educational function.

4. A Unified Liability Theory for Atrocity Speech Law

Finally, Chapter 11 concludes the book's substantive analysis with a proposal for a "Unified Liability Theory" of atrocity speech law. It is not enough merely to offer limited remedies designed to fix the problems unique within each offense. Instead, a more holistic and global restructuring of atrocity speech law is in order. Why is this necessary? Unfortunately, the law governing the relationship between speech and atrocity has been formulated in dribs and drabs over the years. There has been no systematic or all-inclusive approach to creating a liability framework capable of capturing the full range of implicated verbal conduct.

Thus, when the Nuremberg framers crafted the IMT Charter, they did not consider that the important role played by hate speech in the Holocaust might necessitate formulation of a specific offense accounting for the unique characteristics of incendiary rhetoric in the atrocity context.[97] Rather, the IMT prosecutors simply shoehorned hate speech–related offenses into crimes against humanity (persecution) charges.[98] Similarly, when the drafters of the Genocide Convention considered speech, they did so uniquely within the context of a plan to destroy, in whole or in part, a national, ethnic, racial, or religious group, as such.[99] This narrow focus animated the drafting of Article III's incitement provision.[100] And that provision was merely cut and pasted into the ad hoc tribunal statutes without regard for its effect on other provisions that might be related to speech.[101]

In the same way, the instigation and ordering provisions in the ad hoc tribunal statutes were incorporated into the respective "Individual Criminal Responsibility" sections (Articles 6(1) ICTR and 7(1) ICTY, respectively) without taking into consideration how they might relate to or have a bearing on the incitement and persecution provisions located elsewhere.[102] And a similar textual fragmentation is reprised in the Rome Statute, with incitement limited to genocide and cabined in a subprovision not directly linked to instigation (solicitation/inducement in the Rome Statute) or ordering.

So this ungainly body of law, fused together on an ad hoc basis from disjointed parts, like a doctrinal Frankenstein's monster, is highly unlikely to be holistically effective or internally coherent. And, unfortunately, that is the present state of atrocity speech law. It engenders various problems such as reliance by governments on the vague atrocity law formulations for the suppression of legitimate speech[103] and inadequate notice to potential defendants as to what the law may

97. *See* Michael G. Kearney, The Prohibition of Propaganda for War in International Law 34–342 (2007) (indicating that the IMT Charter did not focus on speech per se but prosecutors read speech into the Charter and included it in charges of crimes against peace and crimes against humanity).

98. And, per Kearney, speech offenses were also inserted into crimes against peace charges. *Id.*

99. *See* Guido Acquaviva & Alex Whiting, International Criminal Law: Cases and Commentary 403–404 (describing the drafting history of the incitement provision in the Genocide Convention) (2011).

100. *Id.*

101. Gregory S. Gordon, *From Incitement to Indictment? Prosecuting Iran's President for Advocating Israel's Destruction and Piecing Together Incitement Law's Emerging Analytical Framework*, 98 J. Crim. L. & Criminology 853, 870 (2008).

102. *See* ICTR Statute art. 6(1), *supra* note 31, and ICTY Statute art. 7(1), *supra* note 32.

103. Joel Simon, Deputy Director of the Committee to Protect Journalists (CPJ), has warned that "[s]ome repressive countries could be emboldened" by the ICTR's jurisprudence. Joel Simon, *Murder by Media: Why the Rwandan Genocide Tribunal Went Too Far*, Slate (Dec. 11, 2003 12:54 PM), http://www.slate.com/id/2092372. In fact, according to Simon, "[m]any governments [in Africa] have exploited the perception that the violence in Rwanda was fueled by the media to impose legal restrictions on the press in their own countries." *Id.* Simon

proscribe, thus thwarting its preventive function. On the other hand, its anemic treatment of the range and specific characteristics of speech techniques (such as accusation in a mirror or predictions of violence) leaves it woefully underdeveloped and incapable of capturing the full range of liability inherent in atrocity speech.

But Chapter 11 proposes a solution. Much as the great physicist Albert Einstein sought to reconcile the interaction of gravity and electromagnetism into a unified field theory, the principles covered in this book can be reconciled to form a coherent and elegant body of law via the Unified Liability Theory for atrocity speech law.[104] The theory posits that we may detach the core crimes from their customary moorings. In other words, they must be separated from specific categories of criminal liability that have formed the traditional atrocity speech offenses—direct and public incitement to commit genocide, persecution as crimes against humanity, instigation, and ordering.

For example, the outstanding feature of incitement is its marrying inchoate liability with speech in reference to one crime only—genocide. However, if this type of liability itself were extracted, it could be applied to the other core crimes—that is, crimes against humanity and war crimes. Thus, incitement to commit crimes against humanity (and particular enumerated offenses could be specified—such as "incitement to commit extermination," for example) and incitement to commit war crimes would then be feasible offenses. There is no reason inchoate liability in reference to speech should be exclusively affixed to genocide.

Moreover, as part of taking a fresh look at incitement, and in light of its being applied to other offenses, it is recommended that the "public" element of the crime be removed in reference to all the target core crimes, including crimes against humanity. As demonstrated, "private" incitement may be no less lethal. And incitement to crimes other than genocide, in particular war crimes, is much less likely to be carried out in "public"—incitement to war crimes could be committed in a barracks, for example.[105] If the incitement were committed in "public," according to the traditional definition of that element, that could be taken into account as an enhancement factor at sentencing.[106]

concludes: "Since 2002, the Committee to Protect Journalists has documented nearly fifty such cases in at least a half-dozen countries . . . [including Rwanda] . . . where the current government has increasingly used allegations of ethnic 'divisionism' to silence critics, including those in the press." *Id.*

104. *See* Barry Parker, Einstein's Dream: The Search for a Unified Theory of the Universe 66 (2008) (". . . Einstein's unified field theory was to be the ultimate unified theory of the universe."). Although Einstein was not able to complete his work on the unified field theory during his lifetime, and science has not been able to finish it either, certain experts believe it is still viable. *See* Tim Folger, *Einstein's Quest for a Unified Theory*, Discover (Sept. 30, 2004), http://discovermagazine.com/2004/sep/einsteins-grand-quest#.UlrAxRC6eTU (". . . Einstein's last theory may have some life in it yet.").

105. *See* Gordon, *Formulating a New Atrocity Speech Offense*, *supra* note 78, at 303–304.

106. The word "direct" should also be removed from the title of the crime, although it should remain as a prima facie element for establishing liability.

With respect to hate speech as persecution, its defining characteristic is its being uttered *as part of* a widespread or systematic attack against a civilian population. Thus, it is speech that is noncatalytic and synchronous with, not anterior to, the target atrocity offense. In this sense it is different from incitement, instigation, and ordering, which criminalize pre-offense speech. But what if incendiary rhetoric were uttered *as part of* the destruction, in whole or in part, of a national, ethnic, racial, or religious group as such, that is, genocide (with the defendant being aware of that)? Or what if it were uttered *as part of* a massacre of innocent civilians by soldiers, that is, war crimes? In such cases, the speech would be secondary to a killing campaign that would entail its own liability. Nevertheless, the speech would be an important collateral but contemporaneous (and noninchoate) component of the campaign, deserving of liability in its own right. Thus, we could classify it as "speech abetting." And it could attach to both genocide and war crimes, as well as crimes against humanity.[107]

At the same time, instigation and ordering could continue to apply to all speech causally related to subsequent atrocity. It fits nicely within the new proposed framework, which would therefore consist of four separate categories of speech liability: (1) incitement; (2) speech abetting; (3) instigation; and (4) ordering. Thus, speech uttered in advance of atrocity (with the intent that such atrocity be committed), but not resulting in atrocity, would be charged as "incitement" to commit the particular atrocity at issue. This would be an inchoate form of liability. Moreover, speech delivered simultaneously with commission of an atrocity, with the knowledge that the speech was being delivered in this simultaneous fashion in support of the atrocity's commission, would be charged as "speech abetting." This would be a form of accomplice liability focused exclusively on speech (and made a separate offense given speech's central role in fueling atrocity). Further, speech pronounced with the intent to cause a particular atrocity and causally connected to that atrocity, would be charged as "instigation." This would also be a form of accessorial liability, but, in relation to speech abetting, graver given its catalytic nature.[108] Finally, in the context of a superior-subordinate relationship, if speech has a causal tie to subsequent violence, it would be charged as ordering, yet another type of accomplice liability. At the same time, as this book calls for such speech to be actionable regardless of whether the order is carried out, in such cases it would give rise to inchoate liability.

107. This is different from persecution, in that it does not entail depriving a protected group of a fundamental right based on the identity of that group. Persecution is a crime in itself. But speech abetting would be a mode of liability dependent on the commission of an independent crime. It should be noted, however, that speech abetting would not replace persecution. Rather, it would serve as another type of synchronous speech liability, with application to all the core crimes. Both or either could be charged, depending on the facts of the case and the charging strategy employed. This issue will be explored in greater detail in Chapter 11, "Restructuring: A Unified Liability Theory for Atrocity Speech Law."

108. Of course, one speech could give rise to charges with respect to more than one mode of criminal liability. This sort of scenario will be explored in depth in Chapter 11.

One could object that this elegant solution would nevertheless relegate the substantial body of atrocity speech law to a fringe criminal responsibility section of an international tribunal statute or a domestic universal jurisdiction law. To be clear, I propose that the international community enter into a treaty to operationalize the Unified Liability Theory: "The Convention on the Classification and Criminalization of Atrocity Speech Offenses." And, in accord with that treaty, Article 25 of the Rome Statute should be amended to include a new article, located at 25*bis* and titled "Liability Related to Speech." Far from marginalizing speech within the enveloping fold of generic inchoate or accomplice liability, the proposed plan for operationalization would recognize the important and unique role played by speech in the atrocity context. As it is, incitement, instigation, and ordering seem like scattered fragments inconspicuously buried within Article 25 of the Rome Statute. And persecution neither overtly contains, nor is explicitly identified with, speech.[109] The proposed Article 25*bis* would elevate speech to its proper station within the doctrinal constellation of atrocity law.

III. CONCLUSION

Reconciling free expression, mass violence prevention, and doctrinal coherence—that is the ultimate goal of a well-conceived and well-calibrated law of atrocity speech. And this book will demonstrate how that can be achieved. It will also suggest the possible consequences of the global legal community's failure to do so—a continued culture of impunity and renewed cycles of atrocity. And this could have adverse effects on more recent atrocity speech cases, including those arising in Sudan, Burma, and the areas controlled by the group known as the Islamic State.[110] But genocide, crimes against humanity, and war crimes can be eliminated if their root causes are addressed and dealt with properly. Perpetrator conditioning through speech is a *sine qua non* for mass atrocity. Dehumanization of and deceit about the victim group is the product of adroit verbal advocacy and legerdemain that has largely gone unpunished. Put an end to that and neighbors may no longer kill neighbors.

109. Although the proposed "speech abetting" and persecution are not exactly the same (with persecution being a crime implicating deprivation of a fundamental right and speech abetting being a mode of liability that does not), they both involve speech that is synchronous with atrocity and punished as such.

110. The Burma case, for example, involves Buddhist monks urging their coreligionists to attack Rohingya Muslims. *See* Roseanne Gerin, *Myanmar Minister Asks Mainstream Buddhists to Stop Hate Speech by Controversial Monk Group*, Radio Free Asia (July 13, 2016), http://www.rfa.org/english/news/myanmar/myanmar-minister-asks-mainstream-buddhists-to-stop-hate-speech-by-controversial-monk-group-07132016162445.html. Similarly, the Islamic State (ISIS) has engaged in a genocidal campaign against the Yazidis in ISIS-occupied territory and has used hate speech to help incite violence against them. *See, e.g.*, Raymond Ibrahim, *Yazidi Girl Exposes ISIS Rape Hellhole*, Gatestone Institute (May 12, 2016), https://www.gatestoneinstitute.org/8015/isis-rape-yazidi.

At the same time, perhaps the traditional focus on hate speech in relation to genocide, crimes against humanity, and war crimes is only a beginning. Other crimes should perhaps also be considered in reference to hate speech. This book will end with reflections on the prospects for expanding this area of international criminal law to cover other offenses such as aggression and terrorism. And it will suggest further paths of research, including in respect of sentencing and atrocity denial. The old adage that "words kill" likely applies with equal force to other offenses the global community may see fit to prosecute. And it should remind us that studying the relationship between speech and unspeakable acts of violence, as well as proposals for curbing it, should not end with this book.

PART ONE

Foundation

1

Speech and Atrocity

An Historical Sketch

> "The propagandists who lent themselves to this evil mission of instigation and incitement are more guilty than the credulous and callous minions who headed firing squads or operated the gas chambers."
>
> —Drexel A. Sprecher[1]

I. INTRODUCTION

One day in the summer of 1943, Erna Petri, a homemaker and wife of a senior German officer, was driving home from grocery shopping and noticed six frightened children, dressed only in shreds of clothing, crouching along the side of a country road. She had heard that a number of Jewish children escaped from a boxcar as they were being transported by train to Nazi death camps. She suddenly realized that she had come across a group of them. She told the frightened children, aged six to twelve, to come with her. She brought them into her home, and reassured and fed them. Then she led them into the woods by her house and shot each one of them in the back of the head.[2] Years later, when this German mother of two was asked how she could have committed such a heinous act, she replied:

> I am unable to grasp at this time how in those days that I was in such a state as to conduct myself so brutally and reprehensibly—shooting Jewish children. However earlier I had been so conditioned to fascism and the racial laws,

1. *See* Douglas Martin, *Drexel A. Sprecher, 92, US Prosecutor at Nuremberg, Dies*, N.Y. Times (May 8, 2006), http://www.nytimes.com/2006/05/08/us/08sprecher.html?_r=0.

2. Wendy Lower, Hitler's Furies: German Women in the Nazi Killing Fields 132–133 (2013).

Atrocity Speech Law. Gregory S. Gordon.

> which established a view towards the Jewish people. As was told to me, I had to destroy the Jews. It was from this mindset that I came to commit such a brutal act.[3]

Erna Petri's crime reminds us that, regardless of its mass dissemination, propaganda works on an individual and human level. And its lethal effects have been experienced over centuries. To situate the legal analysis that occupies the balance of this book, this chapter considers the historical link between hate speech and mass atrocity. Along the way, it provides a thumbnail sketch of many of the important actors, incidents, and cases that are described in greater detail in succeeding chapters.

The chapter begins with hate speech pre–World War II and then considers the toxic-message-ecosystem that conditioned Erna Petri to kill those children—the Nazi propaganda campaign against the Jews, the archetypal modern template for mass murder agitprop.[4] It then fast-forwards to the post–Cold War period and examines the role of speech in the atrocities committed in the Balkans and Rwanda in the first part of the 1990s. It concludes with a consideration of prominent post–Rwandan Genocide instances of hate discourse connected to large-scale human rights violations, including postelection violence fueled by media campaigns in Kenya and Côte d'Ivoire and extremist Buddhist rhetoric provoking the persecution of Muslims in Myanmar.

In tracing this history, two overarching rhetorical strategies become apparent—exclusion and threat. Regarding the former, those wishing to perpetrate mass atrocity typically attempt to convince fellow members of their "in-" group of the "otherness" of the victim "out-"group. In general, this is done via dehumanization, that is, equating members of the target group with animals, demons, vermin, or disease. Thus, they attempt to "exclude" the out-group from humanity.[5] This can also be achieved through invoking past wrongs allegedly committed by the out-group—in other words, incentivizing the in-group to seek revenge by settling past scores.[6]

3. *Id.* at 156.

4. "Agitprop" is defined as "propaganda that is designed to influence people by means of highly emotional, aggressive language about social problems . . ." William Rogers, Persuasion: Messages, Receivers and Contexts 88 (2007).

5. *See* John Haas, *Hate Speech and Stereotypic Talk*, *in* The Handbook of Intergroup Communication 135 (Howard Giles ed., 2012) ("[Speech] of this sort is designed to separate ingroup from outgroup members."); Alexander Tsesis, Destructive Messages: How Hate Speech Paves the Way for Harmful Social Movements 179 (2002) ("The very purpose of bigotry is to exclude weaker groups from political debate.").

6. *See* Richard Ashby Wilson & Christine Lillie, *Does Propaganda Incite Violence? Understanding the Effects of Hate Speech*, Institute for Advanced Study (Summer 2015), https://www.ias.edu/ideas/2015/wilson-lillie-propaganda ("We theorize that revenge speech disposes people to view the opposing group as lacking in any moral capacity, i.e., no longer made up of cognizant individuals capable of moral thought.").

With respect to the "threat" rhetorical strategy, the goal is to convince fellow members of the in-group that the out-group seeks to harm or eliminate the in-group or help the in-group's enemies in doing so.[7] These hate-rhetoric strategies are considered in greater depth later in the book, especially in regard to the different categories of incitement techniques in Chapter 8. For now, they are briefly referenced to help elucidate and contextualize the historical patterns that emerge in the chronology that follows.

II. PRE–WORLD WAR II: ANCIENT HATREDS AND THE ARMENIAN GENOCIDE

A. Pre–Twentieth Century

The link between speech and atrocity has an ancient lineage. Almost two millennia before the Common Era, Egyptian Pharaoh Amenemhet I is recorded as having incited against other ethnic groups in his region, whom he would ultimately slaughter and enslave, by describing them as animals. He is recorded as boasting: "I subdued lions, I captured crocodiles. I repressed those of Wawat, I captured the Medjai, I made the Asiatics do the dog walk."[8]

During the second century BCE, Roman politician Cato the Elder repeatedly, and explicitly, called for the destruction of Carthage (*Carthago delenda est*). Following these exhortations, "Carthage was destroyed . . . [with approximately] 150,000 out of 200,000 Carthaginians massacred by the Romans: proverbially, the Romans covered the ruins of Carthage with salt to prevent anything from ever growing."[9] The survivors, of whom 25,000 were women, were sold into slavery.[10] Roman historian Plutarch concluded: "The annihilation

7. Victoria Munro, Hate Crime and the Media: A History 56 (2014) (referring to hate speech in terms of creating "threat to status or resources [which] leads to increased prejudice against and rejection of the threatening out-group and support for punitive action" as well as "vilification of the source of the threat [promoting] aggressive solutions while heightening in-group solidarity.").

8. Muzhou Poo, Enemies of Civilization: Attitudes Towards Foreigners in Ancient Mesopotamia, Egypt and China 74 (2005). *See also* David Livingstone Smith, Less Than Human: Why We Demean, Enslave, and Exterminate Others 109 (2011). The Wawat and Medjai were Nubian people who lived in the area of modern-day Sudan, south of Egypt. *See* Richard Lobban, Historical Dictionary of Ancient and Medieval Nubia 404 (2004); William James Hamblin, Warfare in the Ancient Near East: Holy Warriors at the Dawn of History 416 (2006). *See also* William J. Hamblin, Warfare in the Ancient Near East to 1600 B.C.: Holy Warriors at the Dawn of History 419–420 (2006) (chronicling the atrocities—with reference to the Nubians: "I slaughtered Nubians and all the rest of Wawat . . ." and with reference to the Bedouins: "I destroyed the [nomadic] wild bow-people, the Sand-dwellers.").

9. William D. Rubenstein, Genocide: A History 2 (2004).

10. Ben Kiernan, *The First Genocide: Carthage, 146 BC*, 203 Diogones 27 (2004).

of Carthage ... was primarily due to the advice and counsel of Cato."[11] Ben Kiernan refers to Cato's grisly injunctions as possibly "the first recorded incitement to genocide."[12]

Moving closer to the modern era, Pope Urban II, in a sermon given at Clermont in 1095, stirred Crusaders to commit atrocities against Islamic residents of the Holy Land by telling them that Muslims "had ravaged the churches of God in the Eastern provinces, circumcised Christian men, violated women, and carried out the most unspeakable torture before killing them."[13]

And in the nineteenth century, Belgian King Leopold II used Catholic missionaries to help further his reign of terror in his "Congo Free State" colony. Native Congolese were essentially enslaved by Leopold's agents to harvest rubber from wild trees. Georges Nzongola-Ntalaja notes that this resulted in "the depopulation of entire villages and the heinous perpetration of crimes against humanity. . ."[14] Complicit in these crimes were Belgian missionaries, who helped subjugate the population on Leopold's behalf. Adam Hochschild explains that "Leopold subsidized the Catholics lavishly and sometimes used his financial power to deploy priests, almost as if they were soldiers, to areas where he wanted to strengthen his influence."[15] Kathryn Rountree adds that Leopold "used the Catholic missions to cement and extend his power in the Congo."[16] And he used hate speech to indoctrinate these agents before sending them to do his bidding in the colony. In one letter to them, he declaimed:

> Your principal objective in our mission in the Congo is never to teach the niggers to know God.... Your essential role is to ... protect your interests in that part of the world. For these things, you have to keep watch on disinteresting our savages from the richness that is plenty.... Evangelize the niggers so that they stay forever in submission to the white colonialists.... Convert always the blacks by using the whip. Keep their women in nine months of submission to work freely for us. Institute a confessional system, which allows you to be good detectives denouncing any black that has a different consciousness

11. A. E. Astin, Scipio Aemilianus 36 (1967).

12. Kiernan, *supra* note 10, at 27.

13. David Welch, *Atrocity Propaganda*, *in* Propaganda and Mass Persuasion: A Historical Encyclopedia, 1500 to the Present 23–24 (Nicholas J. Cull et al. eds., 2003).

14. Georges Nzongola-Ntalaja, The Congo: From Leopold to Kabila: A People's History 22 (2009).

15. Adam Hochschild, King Leopold's Ghost: A Story of Greed, Terror and Heroism in Colonial Africa 134 (1998).

16. Kathryn Rountree, Catholic Missionaries in Africa: The White Fathers and the Belgian Congo 1950–1955, Dec. 2009 (doctoral thesis, B.A. Louisiana State University), http://etd.lsu.edu/docs/available/etd-11102009-113627/unrestricted/THESIS_ROUNTREE_11102009.pdf.

> contrary to that of the decision-maker. Teach the niggers to forget their heroes and to adore only ours.[17]

Thus, modern propagandists have been able to mine deep veins of toxic rhetorical tradition to formulate effective dehumanization campaigns against their perceived enemies. The success of such campaigns will be seen in the sections that follow.

B. The Armenian Genocide

1. Background

More recently, hate speech was a major factor in the early twentieth century's most infamous atrocity—the Armenian Genocide. That tragedy had its roots in generations of Turkish persecution of Armenians as a Christian minority with "infidel" status in the Ottoman Empire's eastern Anatolia region.[18] During the nineteenth century, Russia, a Christian nation and the empire's direct regional neighbor to the north, advocated on behalf of the persecuted Armenians, taking up the case internationally that they be protected from discrimination and accorded more civil rights.[19] Despite making nominal efforts to improve the situation, the Ottomans resented this advocacy and eventually pushed back—intensifying persecution of the Armenians, especially after the tsar's victory in the Russo-Turkish War of 1877–1878.[20]

By 1915, the Ottoman sultan had been unseated and replaced by the leaders of the Committee of Union and Progress (CUP, and also known, more colloquially, as the "Young Turks").[21] World War I had broken out the previous year, and the Ottomans and Russians had faced off in battle yet again.[22] And, as before, the Russians claimed victory at Sarikamish in January 1915.[23] Stinging from defeat once more at the hands of tsarist forces, the Turks' hatred for the Armenians, who were naturally associated with the solicitous Russians, reached fever pitch. And it was within this context that the CUP launched its campaign of genocide against the Armenians.

17. Obvious Vengeyi, Aluta Continua Biblical Hermeneutics for Liberation: Interpreting Biblical Texts on Slavery for Liberation of Zimbabwean Underclasses 191 (2013).

18. Peter Balakian, *Armenians in the Ottoman Empire*, *in* 1 Encyclopedia of Human Rights 92 (David P. Forstythe ed., 2008).

19. *Id.*

20. *Id.*

21. *Id.* at 94.

22. *Id.* at 95.

23. *Id.*

2. The Ottoman Hate Speech Campaign

An integral part of that campaign involved conditioning the population to commit genocide via hate rhetoric. Such rhetoric originated within the ranks of the CUP leadership. Frightening evidence of it is found in a speech delivered to a CUP gathering in February 1915: "It is absolutely necessary to eliminate the Armenian people in its entirety, so that there is no further Armenian on this earth and the very concept of Armenia is extinguished."[24]

But to succeed in this gruesome enterprise, the CUP had to first indoctrinate ordinary Turks, and it did so via blanket dissemination of two general message types: (1) the Armenians were diseased parasites destroying the healthy body politic of the Ottoman Empire; and (2) the Armenians were Fifth-Columnists working on behalf of the empire's World War I enemies (particularly the Russians) to sabotage and attack the Ottomans from within.[25]

a. Dehumanization

Regarding the first message category, chief CUP propagandist, Ziya Gölkap, sought to spread the idea that "Turkey could only be revitalized if it rid itself of its non-Muslim elements."[26] Peter Balakian notes that this was an "[eerie] foreshadowing [of] the leading Nazi propagandists Alfred Rosenberg and Joseph Goebbels who propounded the central notion that Germany needed to be *Judenrein* [cleansed of Jews] if it was to revitalize itself."[27] Thus, "[anticipating] Nazi race-hygiene ideology, which depicted the Jew as a 'harmful bacillus' and 'bloodsucker' infecting the German nation from within," CUP ideology "envisioned the Armenian as an invasive infection in Muslim Turkish society."[28] Similarly, another Turkish official, regional governor Mehmed Reshid, "likened the Armenians to 'dangerous microbes,' asking rhetorically, 'Isn't it the duty of a doctor to destroy these microbes?' "[29]

24. G. S. Graber, Caravans to Oblivion: The Armenian Genocide 1915, at 87 (1996).

25. *See* Paul R. Bartrop & Steven Leonard Jacobs, Modern Genocide: The Definitive Resource and Document Collection 42 (2015) ("The characterization of Armenians as an internal enemy was strengthened by demonizing terms the CUP used to define the ethnic enemy as traitors, saboteurs, spies, conspirators, vermin, and infidels."); David Kupelian, How Evil Works: Understanding and Overcoming the Destructive Forces That Are Transforming America 190 (referring to Turks "accusing Armenians of being 'enemy collaborators'"); Fred J. Saato, American Eastern Catholics 41 (2011) ("Accusing the Armenians of stockpiling arms and munitions for a secessionist movement, the Turkish government began eliminating them on April 24, 1915.").

26. Peter Balakian, The Burning Tigris: The Armenian Genocide and America's Response 163–164 (2003).

27. *Id.* at 163.

28. *Id.* at 164.

29. *Id.*

b. Fabricating False Threats

The other central theme in Turkish anti-Armenian propaganda was connected to national security. Suzanne Moranian refers to such discourse as "a contrived argument of Armenian treachery."[30] This rhetoric unfairly painted Armenians as "traitors" who were arming for revolt.[31] Moranian explains:

> At widely scattered points, the Turks would announce the discovery of hidden arms, and then arrest thousands of Armenians for owning them. "The arms thus discovered," . . . were put on exhibition to arouse public indignation, and accomplished that purpose in spite of the fact that the number and character of the 'arms' were nowhere important enough to bother a local sheriff, and many were obviously [planted]. [A] case was thereby built up against the Armenians "in the minds of the common Turkish people, in preparation for the atrocities which were to follow . . . the situation was artificial and the accusations false."[32]

How was this extermination propaganda distributed? To begin, the CUP established a complex network of party branches on the provincial level with orders to launch "a program of nationalist indoctrination . . ."[33] Once this framework was put in place, it was reinforced by government-sponsored publications such as *Harb Mecmuasi* and others (e.g., *Tanin*).[34] Balakian explains that this message was disseminated "throughout the press from *Tâsvir-i-Ekfâr* and *Saba* . . . to opposition papers like *Ikdam* and *Zaman*."[35] And Vahakn Dadrian concludes that its purpose was to "justify" the Armenian Genocide.[36]

The Young Turks' genocidal rhetoric, what Hannibal Travis has described as "provocations and allegations of terrorism and revolution,"[37] was further spread through Muslim clerics preaching at prayer services and by town criers whipping up the masses at public gatherings.[38] According to Balakian, these initiatives "and other CUP militarization plans socialized the domestic population for a

30. Suzanne E. Moranian, *American Missionary Relief Efforts*, *in* America and the Armenian Genocide of 1915 191 (Jay Winter ed., 2003).

31. *Id.*

32. *Id.* (quoting Henry Harrison Riggs, *Turkey, 1910–1942, in* ABC Ms. History, vol. 31a, ch. III, pp. 3–5 (ABCFM Archives)).

33. Balakian, *supra* note 26, at 163.

34. Vahakn N. Dadrian, The History of the Armenian Genocide: Ethnic Conflict from the Balkans to Anatolia to the Caucasus 220 (2004).

35. Balakian, *supra* note 26, at 163.

36. Dadrian, *supra* note 34, at 220.

37. Hannibal Travis, *Turkey, Past and Future: Did the Armenian Genocide Inspire Hitler*, 20 Middle East Q. 27 (2013).

38. Frank Chalk, *Radio Propaganda and Genocide*, Montreal Institute for Genocide and Human Rights Studies (Nov. 1999), http://spectrum.library.concordia.ca/979957/1/A-MIGS__Occasional_Paper_Series__RADIO_PROPAGANDA_AND_GENOCIDE.pdf.

new kind of militancy and ethnic hatred."[39] There was, owing in large part to the propaganda campaign, what Jay Winter refers to as "the military, political and cultural space" in which genocide could be carried out.[40] In the spring of 1915, the liquidation plans were realized: throughout Turkey, Armenians were rounded up—able-bodied men were shot outright *en masse* while women, children, the infirm, and the elderly were sent on death marches into the desert.[41] Spanning the next two years, over one million Armenians were murdered in this way.[42]

III. THE HOLOCAUST

A. Background

Nazi Germany was a corrupt, toxic edifice built on hatred, lies, terror, and an obsessive personality cult.[43] It persecuted Jews, Roma gypsies, homosexuals, the mentally disabled, Seventh-Day Adventists, Jehovah's Witnesses, clergymen, Freemasons, and others.[44] But the brunt of its genocidal energy was directed toward Jews.[45] Their life under Nazi rule degraded during successive stages of dehumanization that began with civic exclusion and then progressed to dispossession, confinement, slavery, and, at the end, mass murder as part of the so-called "Final Solution to the Jewish Question."[46] The killing of six million Jews came to be known as the Holocaust, an essential component of which was systematic and pervasive hate speech.[47] Tonja Salomon explains:

> The first stage of genocide has always been the preparation and mobilization of the masses by means of propaganda. In Germany, the Nazis had started a long propaganda campaign against Jews long before they were deported

39. Balakian, *supra* note 26, at 163.

40. Jay Winter, *Under Cover of War: The Armenian Genocide in the Context of Total War*, *in* America and the Armenian Genocide of 1915, at 39 (Jay Winter ed., 2003).

41. Balakian, *supra* note 26, at 96.

42. *Id.* at 98.

43. *See generally* William Shirer, The Rise and Fall of the Third Reich: A History of Nazi Germany (2011).

44. Ellis Washington, *Social Darwinism in Nazi Family and Inheritance Law*, 13 Rutgers J.L. & Religion 173,181(2011); Jeffrey H. Barker, *Human Experimentation and the Double Facelessness of a Merciless Epoch*, 25 N.Y.U. Rev. L. & Soc. Change 603, 613 (1999).

45. Daniel Romanovsky, *Soviet Jews under Nazi Occupation in Northeastern Belarus and Western Russia*, *in* Bitter Legacy: Confronting the Holocaust in the USSR 232 (Zvi Y. Gitelman ed., 1997).

46. *The Nazi Holocaust, 1938–1945*, The History Place, http://www.historyplace.com/worldhistory/genocide/holocaust.htm (last visited Sept. 18, 2016) [hereinafter *The Nazi Holocaust*].

47. *The Holocaust: An Introductory History*, Jewish Virtual Library, https://www.jewishvirtuallibrary.org/jsource/Holocaust/history.html (last visited Sept. 18, 2016) [hereinafter *An Introductory History*].

> and murdered. They created "*Feinbild*" [face of an enemy] of Jews by using established anti-Semitic stereotypes. The Germans ultimately pictured Jews as "*Ungeziefer*" (vermin).[48]

As described in greater detail in an overview of the Holocaust:

> At the same time, a carefully orchestrated smear campaign . . . portrayed Jews as enemies of the German people. Daily anti-Semitic slurs appeared in Nazi newspapers, on posters, the movies, radio, in speeches by [Adolf] Hitler and top Nazis, and in the classroom. As a result, State-sanctioned anti-Semitism became the norm throughout Germany. The Jews lost everything, including their homes and businesses, with no protest or public outcry from non-Jewish Germans. The devastating Nazi propaganda film *The Eternal Jew* went so far as to compare Jews to plague carrying rats, a foreshadow of things to come.[49]

And thus, the Nazi regime expanded upon the Ottoman template and perfected the modern genocidal propaganda campaign. In the coming years, it would be used to great effect in execution of the Final Solution.

B. The Means of Carrying Out the Nazi Hate Speech Campaign

Exactly how was this hate speech project realized ? After taking power in January 1933, the Nazis pursued three broad strategic objectives to poison German minds and manipulate them to do Hitler's bidding regarding the Jews: (1) a steady stream of speechifying by the Nazi leadership; (2) establishment of a central communications apparatus—the Reich Ministry of Public Enlightenment and Propaganda (Propaganda Ministry), headed by Joseph Goebbels; and (3) destruction of the free press. Each of these shall be considered in turn.

1. Speeches by Nazi Leaders

The speeches of Nazi leaders, especially Hitler, were of first-order importance for the Nazis' rhetorical attack launched against the Jews. Jeffrey Herf explains:

> [Hitler] and some of his closest associates constituted an experienced core of anti-Semitic propagandists [but] Hitler remained the key storyteller and propagandist. His speeches were printed in the press, broadcast over the radio, and excerpted on hundreds or thousands of posters.[50]

48. Tonja Salomon, *Freedom of Speech v. Hate Speech: The Jurisdiction of "Direct and Public Incitement to Commit Genocide"*, *in* The Criminal Law of Genocide: International, Comparative and Contextual Aspects 141 (Ralph Henham & Paul Behrens eds., 2007).

49. *The Nazi Holocaust*, *supra* note 46.

50. Jeffrey Herf, The Jewish Enemy: Nazi Propaganda during World War II and the Holocaust 17 (2006).

As Hitler himself revealed at the outset of World War II, on the eve of unleashing his forces to commit atrocities across Europe: "I will provide a propagandistic *causus belli*. Its credibility doesn't matter. The victor will not be asked whether he told the truth."[51]

2. The Propaganda Ministry

The next major pillar in the Nazis' anti-Semitic propaganda structure was the work of the Propaganda Ministry. It was established on March 13, 1933, and charged with controlling and coordinating the content of Germany's press, art, film, music, and literature fields.[52] David Welch describes its writ as the "wholesale control of the mass-media."[53] Goebbels himself set as an objective for his new ministry to achieve "a mobilization of mind and spirit in Germany. It is therefore in the sphere of the mind what the Defence Ministry is in the sphere of defence."[54] The ministry started with 350 employees working in five divisions: propaganda, radio, press, motion pictures, and theater.[55] By 1941, it had mushroomed to over a thousand employees assigned to seventeen divisions, including art, music, periodicals, and literature.[56] It was primarily self-funded by radio license fees that were paid as a consequence of the Nazis manufacturing cheap transistor sets and distributing them to the masses.[57]

3. Destruction of the Free Press

To consolidate control over public discourse, the Nazis sought to eliminate any competing messages. The Weimar Republic already had control over German radio when the Nazis took power.[58] So the final, and very central, pillar of their

51. Robert B. Durham, False Flags, Covert Operations, & Propaganda 78 (2014).

52. *Propaganda and the Public*, German History in Documents and Images, http://germanhistorydocs.ghi-dc.org/sub_document.cfm?document_id=1579 (last visited Sept. 18, 2016).

53. David Welch, The Third Reich: Politics and Propaganda 29 (2002). Certain limited portions of the Nazi propaganda portfolio were simultaneously controlled by two other offices—the Party Central Propaganda Office and the Reich Chamber of Culture (*Reichskulturkammer*). *Id.* But these offices worked primarily at the behest and in support of the Propaganda Ministry. *Id.* at 29–30. Thus, not coincidentally, Goebbels was the president of the *Reichskulturkammer*. Randall L. Bytwerk, Bending Spines: The Propagandas of Nazi Germany and the German Democratic Republic 61 (2004).

54. Welch, *supra* note 53, at 29.

55. Bytwerk, *supra* note 53, at 61.

56. *Id.*

57. *Id.*

58. Keith Somerville, Radio Propaganda and the Broadcasting of Hatred: Historical Developments and Definitions 111 (2012) ("The Nazi takeover of radio broadcasting was simpler than the press . . . during von Papen's period as chancellor . . . radio was fully nationalized . . .").

propaganda campaign was destruction of the one media sphere not already controlled by the government—the free press.[59] Soon after Hitler's appointment as German chancellor in January of 1933, thousands of German journalists considered hostile to National Socialism, including Jews, liberals, conservatives, Social Democrats, and Communists, were forcibly removed from their jobs and many were arrested or chased out of the country.[60] Two hundred Social Democrat newspapers alone were shut down as well as thirty-five Communist publications—overall, this snuffed out a combined circulation of approximately two million.[61]

The harried scribes whose publications were not eliminated were replaced by Nazi loyalists.[62] In the end, only the most viscous anti-Semitic publications remained. Most notorious among these was *Der Stürmer*, established and run by a crude Nazi hatemonger named Julius Streicher, popularly known as "Jew Baiter Number One." Streicher's obscene tabloid has been described as:

> A major tool of the Nazis' propaganda assault. . . . At the bottom of the front page of each issue, in bold letters, the paper proclaimed, "The Jews are our misfortune!" *Der Stürmer* also featured cartoons of Jews in which they were caricatured as hook-nosed and apelike. The influence of the newspaper was far-reaching: by 1938 about a half million copies were distributed weekly.[63]

Finally, to cement its complete control over the press, on October 4, 1933, the Editorial Control Law formulated by Reich Press Chief Otto Dietrich placed all remaining newspaper and periodical editors under government control.[64] Thus was the Fourth Estate eviscerated in the Third Reich.

C. The Content of Nazi Hate Speech

1. Dehumanization

Now, with iron-fisted domination of the media apparatus, the Nazis embarked on an uninhibited anti-Semitic rhetorical persecution campaign. Much of it consisted of dehumanizing the Jews, reflective of Ottoman propaganda that had portrayed the Armenians as animals, diseases, and parasites. As David Livingstone Smith explains:

> The Nazis were explicit about the status of their victims. They were *Untermenschen*—subhumans—and as such were excluded from the system of

59. Herf, *supra* note 50, at 18.

60. *Id.*

61. *Id.*

62. *Id.*

63. *An Introductory History*, *supra* note 47.

64. Herf, *supra* note 50, at 18.

> moral rights and obligations that bind humankind together. It's wrong to kill a person, but permissible to exterminate a rat. . . . Jews were the main victims of this genocidal project. . . . Jewish people posed a deadly threat to all that was noble in humanity. [These] putative enemies of civilization were represented as parasitic organisms—as leaches, lice, bacteria, or vectors of contagion. . . . Sometimes the Nazis thought of their enemies as vicious, bloodthirsty predators rather than parasites.[65]

2. Fabricating False Threats

At the same time, the Nazis portrayed the Jews as enemies sworn to the destruction of Germany and German Jews, in particular, as internal enemies insidiously working to sabotage the "Fatherland" from within. Marvin Perry notes that Germans "were influenced by years of Nazi propaganda that consistently depicted Jews as Communists and fifth columnists, blamed them for causing the war in order to destroy Germany, and demonized them as an evil race, an alien *other* beyond the pale of caring."[66] And even as Jews all over Europe were being loaded into cattle cars for gassing in the death camps, "the Nazi propaganda machine was warning the German people of the demonic Jewish intention 'to exterminate all Germans.' "[67] The regime's ultimate message, that it was kill or be killed, was clear: "International law and international custom will be no protection against the Jewish will for total annihilation."[68]

D. The Key Nazi Propagandists

Apart from Goebbels and Dietrich, other Reich officials played leading roles in disseminating Nazi hate speech. For example, Robert Ley was the *Reichsorganisationsleiter* (Reich Organization Director) and, as such, was in charge of party training.[69] Alfred Rosenberg was the party's "theoretician," producing turgid and unreadable "philosophical" anti-Semitic tracts and, as Minister for the Occupied Eastern Territories, controlling propaganda in the occupied Baltic and Soviet regions.[70]

For the post-Holocaust justice project at Nuremberg, though, prosecutors focused on the hate speech of three Nazi propagandists in particular: Julius Streicher, radio personality Hans Fritzsche, and Press Chief Otto Dietrich. The International Military Tribunal (IMT) at Nuremberg convicted Streicher for crimes against humanity based on his poisonous screeds in *Der Stürmer*, which was published

65. Smith, *supra* note 8, at 15.

66. Marvin Perry, World War II in Europe: A Concise History 128 (2013).

67. Judith Woolf, The Memory of the Offence: Primo Levi's If This Is a Man 5 (2001).

68. *Id.*

69. Bytwerk, *supra* note 53, at 64.

70. *Id.* at 64–65.

through 1945.[71] Fritzsche was similarly charged owing to his work as head of the Radio Division of the Propaganda Ministry, but he was ultimately acquitted (problematically, as will be discussed later).[72] In the post-IMT US zonal trial known as the "Ministries Case," which prosecuted defendants in important posts in Nazi ministries in the center of Berlin,[73] Dietrich was charged with crimes against humanity in connection with his anti-Jewish hate speech as Reich Press Chief, and he was convicted.[74] The jurisprudence generated by the judgments in these cases will be considered in Chapter 3.

The effect of this Nazi hate speech policy was devastatingly effective: "[Nazi] propaganda campaigns created an atmosphere tolerant of violence against Jews [and] was likewise essential to motivating those who implemented the mass murder of the European Jews and of other victims of the Nazi regime."[75]

IV. POST–COLD WAR BALKAN ATROCITIES

A. Background

Yugoslavia emerged from World War II as the Social Federal Republic of Yugoslavia (SFRY), a well-integrated confederation of Serbs, Croats, Muslims, Slovenes, Albanians, Macedonians, and Montenegrins led by partisan hero Josip Broz Tito.[76] Nearly four decades later, the political union started falling apart.[77] First, Tito's death in 1980, and then severe economic decline leading to the internal erosion of communism (as in the rest of the region), weakened the glue that had held together Yugoslavia's various ethnic groups and political subdivisions for over four decades.[78] The country's actual disintegration started in May 1991, when Croatia and Slovenia announced they were separating from the Serbian-dominated central government in Belgrade.[79]

71. Antonio Cassese, Guido Acquaviva, Mary Fan, & Alex Whiting, International Criminal Law: Cases & Commentary 156 (2011).

72. Michael G. Kearney The Prohibition of Propaganda for War in International Law 42 (2007).

73. Larry May, Aggression and Crimes against Peace 171–72 (2008).

74. Sarabeth A. Smith, *What's Old Is New Again: Terrorism and the Growing Need to Revisit the Prohibition on Propaganda*, 37 Syracuse J. Int'l. L. & Com. 299, 319 (2010).

75. United States Holocaust Memorial Museum, *Nazi Propaganda*, Holocaust Encyclopedia, http://www.ushmm.org/wlc/en/article.php?ModuleId=10005202 (last updated July 2, 2016).

76. Robert J. Donia, Radovan Karadzic: Architect of the Bosnian Genocide 11 (2015).

77. *Id.* at 17.

78. *Id. See also* Branka Magas, The Destruction of Yugoslavia: Tracking the Break-Up 1980–1992, Introduction, xii–xiii (1993).

79. Roger P. Alford, *The Self-Judging WTO Security Exception*, 2011 Utah L. Rev. 697, 716 (2011).

Bosnia-Herzegovina, which was composed of 44 percent Muslims, 31 percent Serbs, and 17 percent Croats, followed suit nearly one year later when it declared independence in March 1992.[80] The Bosnian Serbs were represented by the Serb Democratic Party (SDS), under the leadership of Radovan Karadžić. In October 1991, Karadžić had issued a direct genocidal threat against Bosnian Muslims who might vote for independence: "This might lead Bosnia into a hell and [cause] one people to disappear."[81] Once Bosnia opted for independence, the Bosnian Serbs were able to carry out that threat. Better armed, given their support from the neighboring Serbian army, they refused to recognize the country's independence from Yugoslavia and went to war determined to take control of the state and wreak havoc on its non-Serb citizens.[82]

Bosnian Serb and Serbian armed forces, including militias, seized control of two-thirds of Bosnia-Herzegovina.[83] They then inflicted on the country's Muslim and Croatian population a reign of terror in an effort to expel them so as to "purify" the country.[84] Through this policy, which came to be known as "ethnic cleansing," Bosnian Serb forces drove Muslims from their homes, subjecting them to mass rape, confinement in concentration camps and genocide, most infamously at Srebrenica in July 1995.[85]

B. The Bosnian Serb Propaganda Campaign

To effectuate their ethnic cleansing plans, the Bosnian Serbs launched a propaganda campaign against the Muslims that created "mutual fear and hatred and particularly inciting the Bosnian Serb population against the other ethnicities."[86]

80. Paul Williams & Jennifer Harris, *State Succession to Debts and Assets: The Modern Law and Policy*, 42 Harv. Int'l L.J. 355, 385 (2001) (chronicling the date of Bosnia-Herzegovina's withdrawal from SFRY); Patrick Robinson, *The Interaction of Legal Systems in the Work of the International Criminal Tribunal for the Former Yugoslavia*, 16 ILSA J. Int'l & Comp. L. 5, 13 (2009) (detailing the ethnic breakdown in Bosnia-Herzegovina).

81. Kemal Kurspahic, Prime Time Crime: Balkan Media in War and Peace 97 (2003).

82. David Binder, *C.I.A. Doubtful on Serbian Sanctions*, N.Y. Times, Dec. 22, 1993, at A3 (reporting that the Serbian government supplied the Serbian forces which took control of over two-thirds of Bosnia).

83. *Id.*

84. Lindsay Peterson, *Shared Dilemmas: Justice for Rape Victims under International Law and Protection for Rape Victims Seeking Asylum*, 31 Hastings Int'l & Comp. L. Rev. 509, 512 (2008) ("In the late 1980s and early 1990s, Croatia, Slovenia, and Bosnia declared independence and Bosnian Serbs initiated a policy of ethnic cleansing to rid the nation of Croats and Muslims.").

85. *Id. See also* Aleksandar Marsavelski, *The Crime of Terrorism and the Right of Revolution in International Law*, 28 Conn. J. Int'l L. 243, 264 n.123 (2013) ("Perhaps the most notable example is the genocide in Srebrenica, which was committed in 1995 by the Bosnian Serbs . . .").

86. Prosecutor v. Brđanin, Case No. IT-99-36-T, Judgement, ¶ 80 (Int'l Crim. Trib. for the Former Yugoslavia Sept. 1, 2004).

According to the International Criminal Tribunal for the former Yugoslavia (ICTY) Trial Chamber in *Prosecutor v. Brđanin*:

> Within a short period of time, citizens who had previously lived together peacefully became enemies and many of them, in the present case mainly Bosnian Serbs, became killers, influenced by a media, which by that time, was already under the control of the Bosnian Serb leadership. The use of propaganda was an integral part of the implementation of the Strategic Plan and created a climate where people were prepared to tolerate the commission of crimes and to commit crimes.[87]

How was the Bosnian Serb leadership able to achieve this? Similar to the Nazis, the SDS wasted no time in seizing control of the Bosnian media apparatus, which in the early 1990s was television-focused (just as, for the Nazis, it was newspaper- and radio-focused).[88] So they took by force the Bosnian TV transmitters, starting in the summer of 1991.[89] In the lead-up to the war, on August 1, 1991, an SDS-supported paramilitary group known as the "Wolves of Vučjak," also backed by the Yugoslav Army, wrested control of the TV transmitter on Kozara Mountain between Banjaluka and Prijedor.[90]

Not long thereafter, Bosnian Serb paramilitary forces took over other transmitters in the towns of Plješevica, Doboj, Trovrh, Velež, and Vlašić, effectively establishing complete dominion over Bosnia's television airwaves.[91] In addition, reflective of the Nazi practice, Bosnian Muslim and Bosnian Croat TV station employees were fired and replaced by Bosnian Serbs.[92] Other media were also hijacked. At radio stations and most newspapers, as at the television stations, Serb journalists took over for sacked Muslim and Croat journalists.[93]

C. The Content of Bosnian Serb Hate Speech

This effectively deprived most of the Bosnian population from the mainstream Bosnian media message before the takeover that "had one constant line in the months leading to the war . . . their opposition to the war."[94] Instead, most Bosnians, many from ethnically mixed towns, heard the SDS message, consistent with that of

87. Kurspahic, *supra* note 81, at 97–98.

88. *Id.* at 98.

89. *Id.*

90. *Id. See also* Brđanin, Case No. IT-99-36-T, ¶ 81.

91. Kurspahic, *supra* note 81, at 98.

92. Brđanin, Case No. IT-99-36-T, ¶ 81.

93. *Id.*

94. Kurspahic, *supra* note 81, at 97.

the Yugoslav Federation's Serb president Slobodan Milošević, promoting the ideology of "all Serbs in a single state."[95] Kemal Kurspahić explains the effect of this:

> After that, it was all Milošević all the time. Constant war propaganda divided Serbs and Muslims who had lived together peacefully in Banjaluka, Prijedor, Sanski Most, Bosanski Novi, and dozens of other neighboring communities. Belgrade TV rhetoric concerning "threatened people" . . . "national survival," "the Croat-Muslim conspiracy," and "the Islamist threat" replaced the traditionally balanced reporting of Sarajevo TV, gradually separating longstanding neighbors and even close friends.[96]

Providing an even more graphic sense of the effect of this, Noel Malcolm explains in his history of Bosnia that "it was as if all the TV stations in the USA had been taken over by the Ku Klux Klan."[97]

These media messages were supplemented by speeches by SDS politicians that insulted and degraded Bosnian Muslims and Croats, "with the obvious aim of creating fear and hatred amongst the ethnic groups and inciting the Bosnian Serbs against other ethnic groups."[98] Over time, the hate rhetoric became increasingly aggressive. Media messages began to warn Bosnian Serbs that they were threatened with genocide by Bosnian Muslims and Croats and suggested that they needed to eliminate them before they were eliminated.[99] Ramping up the intensity of the propaganda , photos of mutilated soldiers were disseminated as were stories of crimes committed against Bosnian Serbs since the Ottoman occupation of the region in 1389.[100] Eventually, the indoctrination reached a fever pitch. Non-Serbs were threatened on the airwaves by being told they should move out or face unpleasant consequences. Finally, at its most extreme, Bosnian Serb media "openly incited people to kill non-Serbs."[101]

D. The Effects of Bosnian Serb Hate Speech

The ICTY Trial Chamber in *Prosecutor v. Brđanin* explained how the effects of this verbal persecution enterprise became even more dire.

> The propaganda campaign achieved its goals with respect to both the Bosnian Serb and the [non-Serbs]. While influencing the Bosnian Serb population to

95. *Id.*

96. *Id.* at 98.

97. Noel Malcolm, Bosnia: A Short History 252 (1996).

98. Brđanin, Case No. IT-99-36-T, ¶ 82.

99. *Id.*

100. *Id.*

101. *Id.*

> perceive and treat the non-Serb inhabitants as enemies and preparing the Bosnian Serb population for the crimes that were committed later, it also instilled fear among the non-Serb population and created an atmosphere of terror, which contributed to the subsequent mass exodus of non-Serbs.[102]

Tragically, this persecution program "culminated in the massacre of as many as 8,000 Bosniak men and boys at the town of Srebrenica in July 1995."[103] And "the attempt to eradicate the male Muslim population following the capture of Srebrenica represents the gravest and most obvious example of genocide during the wars in the former Yugoslavia."[104]

E. Other Hate Speech

1. Vojislav Šešelj in Serbia

Those responsible for instigating early-1990s massacres via hate speech in the Balkans were not limited to Bosnian Serbs. In Serbia itself, one of the most effective verbal promoters of ethnic cleansing was Vojislav Šešelj.[105] A prominent ultranationalist Serb politician (founder of the Serbian Radical Party) and paramilitary leader (organizer and leader, *inter alia*, of the Serb militia group known as the "White Eagles"), Šešelj is accused of summoning Serb fighters to commit ethnic cleansing of Croats, Muslims, and other non-Serb populations from large swathes of Croatian territory as well as areas in Bosnia and Herzegovina and the ethnically mixed Vojvodina region of Serbia.[106] Based on this hate speech and related violence, Šešelj was charged by the ICTY with involvement in a joint criminal enterprise and with counts of instigation and persecution as a crime against humanity.[107] On March 31, 2016, an ICTY Trial Chamber acquitted him but that verdict is being appealed by the prosecution.[108]

102. *Id.* at 83.

103. *Ethnic Cleansing*, History.Com, http://www.history.com/topics/ethnic-cleansing (last visited Sept. 18, 2016). *See also* Noreen L. Hertzfield, *Lessons from Srebrenica: The Danger of Religious Nationalism*, Kripke Centre Journal of Religion & Society, Supplement Series 2 (2007), http://digitalcommons.csbsju.edu/cgi/viewcontent.cgi?article=1003&context=theology_pubs (referring to "the ethnic cleansing that culminated in the massacre of Srebrenica . . .").

104. Helga Brunborg, Torkild Hovde Lyngstad, & Henrik Urdal, *Accounting for Genocide: How Many Were Killed in Srebrenica?*, 19 European J. Population 229, 232 (2003).

105. Bernard A. Cook, *Vojislav Šešelj*, *in* 2 Europe since 1945: An Encyclopedia 1135 (Bernard A. Cook ed., 2001).

106. Prosecutor v. Šešelj, Case No. IT-03-67-PT, Third Amended Indictment, ¶¶ 4–10 (Int'l Crim. Trib. for the Former Yugoslavia Dec. 7, 2007).

107. *Id.* ¶¶ 15–34; Gregory S. Gordon, *Šešelj's Provisional Release: Hate Speech, International Criminal Procedure and Transitional Justice*, Jurist (Feb. 7, 2015, 1:19 PM), http://jurist.org/forum/2015/02/gregory-gordon-seselj-release.php.

108. Marlise Simons, *Tribunal Acquits Serbian Nationalist of War Crimes*, N.Y. Times, Mar. 31, 2016, at A9.

2. Dario Kordić in Bosnian Croatia

Nor was hate speech in service of ethnic cleansing limited to ethnic Serbs. Dario Kordić, a prominent politician in the Bosnian Croat community, allegedly spewed forth venomous invective regarding his Muslim neighbors in the Lašva valley region. The ICTY prosecutor alleged that Kordić and others carried out the ethnic cleansing campaign against Bosnian Muslims by, *inter alia*, "encouraging, instigating and promoting hatred, distrust, and strife on political, racial, ethnic or religious grounds, by propaganda, speeches and otherwise."[109] For this speech activity, he was charged with persecution as a crime against humanity.[110]

Although convicted on other grounds, Kordić was acquitted on the speech-connected persecution charge because, according to the Trial Chamber, the hate speech at issue "does not rise to the same level of gravity as the other acts enumerated in Article 5 [i.e., the crimes against humanity provision of the ICTY Statute]" and "the criminal prohibition of this act has not attained the status of customary international law."[111] Later on in this volume, I will take issue with the Trial Chamber's legal conclusions. But the fact that hate speech took place in service of a Bosnian Croat ethnic cleansing campaign against Bosnian Muslims in this region is not in dispute.

V. THE RWANDAN GENOCIDE

The Rwandan Genocide is commonly associated with media incitement to mass violence.[112] And as much of the foundational jurisprudence of atrocity speech law derives from cases adjudicating guilt for speech crimes in connection with that cataclysm,[113] this section will delve a bit more deeply into the background of the genocide and the hate speech that helped fuel it.

A. Background to the Genocide

A former Belgian colony, Rwanda gained its independence in 1962 and was divided between the Hutu (84%) and Tutsi (15%) populations (the balance being

109. Prosecutor v. Kordić, Case No. IT-95-14/2-T, Judgement, ¶ 37 (Int'l Crim. Trib. for the Former Yugoslavia Feb. 26, 2001).

110. *Id.*

111. *Id.* at ¶ 209.

112. *See generally* William A. Schabas, *Hate Speech in Rwanda: The Road to Genocide*, 46 McGill L. J. 141 (2000–2001) (evidencing the perception of the link between media incitement and the genocide in Rwanda in 1994).

113. *See* Gregory S. Gordon, *From Incitement to Indictment?: Prosecuting Iran's President for Advocating Israel's Destruction and Piecing Together Incitement Law's Emerging Analytical Framework*, 98 J. Crim. L. & Criminology 853, 870 (2008) (describing the key role of ICTR jurisprudence in fleshing out the crime of direct and public incitement to commit genocide).

the Twa at 1%).[114] Hutus had come to resent and ultimately hate Tutsis given the way Belgium had governed the colony—largely empowering the latter and disenfranchising the former.[115] Once the majority Hutu population assumed governing functions in 1962, it unleashed a series of pogroms against the Tutsis that resulted in the massacre of thousands and a flood of refugees seeking safety in neighboring states.[116] These exiles thus created a diaspora in Central Africa's Great Lakes region.[117] In 1987, a group of those who had found safety in Uganda established the Rwandan Patriotic Front (RPF), which launched a military invasion of Rwanda in 1990.[118]

The invasion was checked with help from French and Belgian military units, but in the anti-Tutsi hysteria that surrounded it, a cottage industry of "hate media" began to spring up in Rwanda.[119] In this early period, one of the most prominent hate media mouthpieces was an extremist Hutu newspaper known as *Kangura* ("Wake Them Up" or "Wake It Up"). Described by Rwanda expert Alison Des Forges as "one of the most virulent voices of hate,"[120] it was founded by Hassan Ngeze in 1990 and "became a primary instrument in the preparation of the Hutu population of Rwanda for the genocide of the Tutsi population . . ."[121] Not long after the RPF invasion, *Kangura* printed in its pages "The Hutu Ten Commandments," which John Shattuck describes as "a venomous tract" that was

114. Goonhild Hoogensen & Bruce O. Solheim, Women in Power: World Leaders Since 1960, at 49 (2006) (noting that Rwanda achieved independence from Belgium in July 1962); Jared Cohen, One-Hundred Days of Silence: America and the Rwanda Genocide 11 (2007) (describing the ethnic breakdown of Rwanda).

115. *See* Howard B. Tolley, Jr., *Rwanda*, *in* 4 Encyclopedia of Human Rights 384 (David P. Forsythe ed., 2009) ("[Belgians] identified Tutsis as superior to Hutus and adapted the local feudal order for colonial rule."); Andrew Fitz-Gibbon, Positive Peace: Reflections on Peace Education, Nonviolence and Social Change 46 (2010) ("The Belgians utilized . . . the Tutsi minority to govern the . . . Hutu majority [and] after independence and Belgium's withdrawal from Rwanda, the Hutu majority wanted revenge on the Tutsi minority.").

116. Javaid Rehman, The Weaknesses in the International Protection of Minority Rights 66 (2003) (referring to the postindependence "massacre of approximately 20,000 Tutsi men, women and children."); Tolley, *supra* note 115, at 384 (noting that Rwanda's Hutu president was "mobilizing Hutus to drive more 'alien race' Tutsis into exile and [the] UNHCR estimated the number of Tutsi exiles in Burundi, Uganda, Tanzania and Zaire in 1964 at 400,000.").

117. Frank K. Rusagara, *The Spread of "Genocide Ideology" within the Great Lakes Region: Challenges for Rwanda*, *in* Rwanda Fast Forward: Social, Economic, Military and Reconciliation Prospects 218 (Maddalena Campione & Patrick Noac eds., 2004) (referring to the "Tutsi diaspora" in the region).

118. John Shattuck, Freedom on Fire: Human Rights Wars and America's Response 30 (2003).

119. *Id.*

120. Alison Des Forges, Leave None to Tell the Story: Genocide in Rwanda 77 (1999).

121. Samuel Totten & Paul Robert Bartrop, 2 Dictionary of Genocide: M-Z 306 (2008).

"published in Kigali and widely circulated throughout the country."[122] Noting that they "articulate a doctrine of Hutu militant purity,"[123] Philip Gourevitch provides a useful overview of the commandments:

> The first three commandments addressed the stubborn perception, constantly reinforced by the tastes of visiting white men and Hutus with status, that the beauty of Tutsi women surpasses that of Hutu women. According to Ngeze's protocols, all Tutsi women were Tutsi agents; Hutu men who married, befriended or employed a Tutsi woman "as a secretary or concubine" were to be considered traitors, and Hutu women, for their part, were commanded to guard against the Tutsi-loving impulses of Hutu men. From sex, Ngeze moved on to matters of business, declaring every Tutsi dishonest—"his only aim is the supremacy of his ethnic group"—and any Hutu who had financial dealings with Tutsis an enemy of his people. The same held for political life; Hutus should control "all strategic positions, political, administrative, economic, military, and security." Hutus were further commanded to have "unity and solidarity" against "their common Tutsi enemy," to study and spread "the Hutu ideology" of the revolution of 1959, and to regard as a traitor any Hutu who "persecutes his brother Hutu" for studying or spreading this ideology. . . . The eighth and most often quoted commandment said: "Hutus must stop having mercy on the Tutsis."[124]

John Shattuck describes the Hutu hardliner thinking regarding the genocidal implications of the eighth commandment:

> The eighth commandment's dictate, "Hutus should stop having mercy on Tutsis," was explained in graphic terms by one of the authors of this poisonous creed, Leon Mugesera, a friend of [Rwandan President Juvénal] Habyarimana: "We the people are obliged to take responsibility to wipe out this scum."[125]

122. Shattuck, *supra* note 118, at 30. The Ten Commandments were, in fact, a call for comprehensive exclusion of Tutsis from society and can be enumerated as follows: (1) Hutu males must not have close personal or work relations with Tutsi women; (2) Hutu women are superior to Tutsi women; (3) Hutu women must fraternize only with Hutu men; (4) Tutsis are dishonest and no Tutsi should conduct business with them; (5) all high-level positions in society should be occupied by Hutus only; (6) the education sector should be majority Hutus; (7) the military must be exclusively Hutu; (8) the Hutus should stop having mercy on the Tutsis; (9) all Hutus must have unity and solidarity; and (10) the ideology of the 1959 and 1961 revolution (when many Tutsis were disenfranchised, forced to leave Rwanda, or massacred) must be taught to Hutus at all levels. Totten & Bartrop, *supra* note 121.

123. Philip Gourevitch, We Wish to Inform You That Tomorrow We Will Be Killed with Our Families 87–88 (1998).

124. *Id.* at 88.

125. Shattuck, *supra* note 118, at 30.

Chilling as this was, from the RPF's perspective, the timing of the invasion, and the subsequent RPF military pressure exerted on Rwanda in its aftermath, was propitious. The Rwandan economy was quite weak,[126] and, over time, international donors were able to pressure President Habyarimana, to make peace with the rebel group.[127] Thus, the president's hardline-Hutu-dominated government reluctantly entered into a 1993 settlement with the RPF known as the Arusha Peace Accords, which envisioned a transitional power-sharing arrangement providing for RPF participation in both the government and military.[128] The Accords also stipulated the establishment of a UN peacekeeping mission, UNAMIR (UN Assistance Mission for Rwanda), that was tasked with monitoring implementation of the transitional regime.[129]

The hardliners in Habyarimana's clique (known as the *akazu*—"little house" in Kinyarwanda) loathed sharing power with the RPF and put the president in the impossible position of trying to quell internal dissenters while simultaneously placating the international community.[130] So he tried to temporize through glacial implementation of the accords and playing the various factions off one another.[131] But the strategy failed. Hutu extremists concluded Habyarimana was selling them out and that the Arusha Accords must be scuttled no matter what.[132] They took to the airwaves and the press to attack their greatest perceived enemies—the Accords, the international community (especially the Belgians),

126. *See* Caroline Thomas, Introduction, *in* Globalization, Human Security, and the African Experience 17 (Caroline Thomas & Peter Wilkin eds., 1999) ("The Rwandan civil war was preceded by the flare-up of a deep-seated economic crisis.").

127. Erin K. Baines, Vulnerable Bodies: Gender, the UN and the Global Refugee Crisis 134 (2004) ("Under international pressure and dependent on foreign assistance, Habyarimana agreed to sign the Arusha Peace Agreements . . .").

128. Julius Mutwol, Peace Agreements and Civil Wars in Africa: Insurgent Motivations, State Responses, and Third-Party Peacemaking in Liberia, Rwanda, and Sierra Leone 203 (2009).

129. *Id.*

130. *Id.* (noting that Hutu hardliners—represented by the CDR Party—were left on the sidelines and were resentful while international donors, such as the United States, the European Union, and Belgium insisted on implementation of the accords); Dean J. White, The Ignorant Bystander?: Britain and the Rwandan Genocide of 1994, 22 (2015) (". . . Hutu extremists close to Habyarimana, keen to retain their firm grip on power and control of the foreign aid money coming into the country, would not support the agreement.").

131. Andrew Wallis, Silent Accomplice: The Untold Story of France's Role in the Rwandan Genocide 78 (2013); White, *supra* note 130, at 22 ("In practice, the key step of transferring power to the transitional government was delayed repeatedly, usually due to the procrastination and stubbornness of Habyarimana.").

132. Paul J. Magnarella, *The Hutu-Tutsi Conflict in Rwanda*, *in* Perspectives on Contemporary Ethnic Conflict: Primal Violence or the Politics of Conviction? 119–120 (Santosh C. Saha ed., 2006) (observing that Hutu extremists could never accept the Accords and that they "cried treason and charged that the President himself had become an accomplice.").

and, most importantly, the Tutsis themselves.[133] And they devised a genocidal end-solution for dealing with their hated fellow countrymen.[134]

B. The Extremist Hutu Hate Speech Campaign

1. Radio

An essential part of that plan entailed establishing a broadcast platform dubbed "Radio Télévision Libre des Milles Collines" (or RTLM—later infamously known as "Radio Machete").[135] Hutu extremists also exploited the state-run radio station, "Radio Rwanda," to whip up hatred against the Tutsis.[136] In their genocidal broadcasts, these media outlets attempted to dehumanize the Tutsis by, among other things, referring to them as *inyenzi* (cockroaches). Alain Destexhe sees parallels between this genocidal media campaign and that of the Nazis against the Jews:

> Just as Hitler's grand plan was founded on an engrained European anti-semitism which he played on by singling out the Jews as the source of all Germany's ills, the Hutu radicals are the inheritors of the colonial lunacy of classifying and grading different ethnic groups in a racial hierarchy. While the Jews were described by the Nazis as "vermin", the Tutsis were called *inyenzi* ("the cockroaches that have to be crushed"). Anti-Tutsi propaganda presented them as a "minority well-off and foreign"—so similar to the image developed to stigmatise the Jews—and thus an ideal scapegoat for all Rwanda's problems.[137]

2. Print Media

This campaign was carried out on the airwaves but also in print. Most prominently, *Kangura* continued its hate speech campaign, disseminating both images and language meant to inflame ethnic hatred. Its November 1991 (Issue No. 26) cover, for instance, featured a photograph of Grégoire Kayibanda, Rwanda's

133. *Id.* at 120 ("Within days of the signing, Radio Milles Collines, a new, private station devoted to genocidal propaganda, began broadcasting anti-Accord and anti-Tutsi diatribes from Kigali."). *See also* Prosecutor v. Ruggiu, Case No. ICTR-97-32-I, Judgement and Sentence, ¶ 44 (vii) (June 1, 2000) (noting that RTLM announcer admitted to waging "a media war against the Belgians over the RTLM to attack the international policy adopted by the Belgian government towards Rwanda.").

134. Alain Destexhe, Rwanda and Genocide in the Twentieth Century 28–29 (1995).

135. Rachel Kerr & Erin Mobekk, Peace and Justice: Seeking Accountability after War 56 (2007).

136. Barbara Rylko-Bauer, Linda M. Whiteford, & Paul Farmer, Global Health in Times of Violence 52 (2009) ("Backed by Hutu Power extremists, proponents of a virulent Hutu-supremacist philosophy used officially sanctioned radio stations . . ."); Des Forges, *supra* note 120, at 84 ("RTLM announcer Kantano Habimana celebrated the transformation of Radio Rwanda from a "rival" to a "sister.").

137. Destexhe, *supra* note 134, at 28.

first postindependence president, who presided over the initial period of mass violence against Tutsis.[138] A machete was juxtaposed with the ex-president's image; and next to that a question was posed: "What shall we do to complete the social revolution of 1959?"—an allusion to the Hutu uprising that toppled the Tutsi monarchy and the attendant bloodshed.[139] The cover's ostensible goal was to prod *en masse* Tutsi butchery.[140]

Drawing from the ranks of disaffected youths, the Hutu hardliners also began to raise militias. The most prominent among these was attached to President Habyarimana's MRND Party (*Mouvement Révolutionnaire National pour le Développement*) and was known as the *Interahamwe* (meaning "those who work together" or "attack together" in Kinyarwanda).[141] The hardliners amassed an enormous cache of machetes and other weapons to arm the militias.[142] In turn, the militias, sufficiently indoctrinated and programmed for violence by, *inter alia*, the media outlets, started attacking and slaying Tutsis.[143] General Roméo Dallaire, chief of the UNIMIR contingent, was told by an anonymous informant that planned extermination was in store for the Tutsis.[144] His urgent dispatches to UN headquarters to this effect fell on deaf ears.[145] And his entreaties to confiscate arms caches were similarly ignored.[146] And so the stage was being set for genocide.

3. Hate Speech and Genocidal Dress Rehearsals

And there had been ominous warning signs involving hate propaganda even before Dallaire's discoveries. In fact, Hutu extremists had actually engaged in genocide "dress rehearsals" to test the effects of the lethal media-militia cocktail in a more focused manner. The most notorious of these occurred in 1992, in the Bugesera region, near the Rwandan capital of Kigali.[147] It was orchestrated by Ferdinand Nahimana, a former university professor who was then head of the government media agency ORINFOR (and later a principal founder of RTLM).[148] At Nahimana's

138. Larry May, *Incitement to Genocide and the Rwanda Media Case*, *in* Freedom of Expression in a Diverse World 103 (Deirdre Golash ed., 2010).

139. *Id.*

140. *Id.*

141. Destexhe, *supra* note 134, at 29.

142. *Id.*

143. *Id.* at 29–30.

144. Douglas W. Simon, *The Evolution of the International System and Its Impact on Protection against Genocide*, *in* Protection against Genocide: Mission Impossible? 56 (Neil Riemer ed., 2000).

145. *Id.*

146. *Id.*

147. Des Forges, *supra* note 120, at 79.

148. *Id.*

behest, Radio Rwanda aired an invented report declaring that the Tutsis had put together a "hit list" of persons supposedly targeted for murder by Tutsis in the Bugesera region.[149] This snippet of fiction was announced on Radio Rwanda to the militias as they were being trucked to that area.[150] In the immediate aftermath, enraged by the report, they murdered hundreds of innocent civilian Tutsis.[151] This well-choreographed blend of incendiary language and militia movement, followed by mass murder, was the blueprint for the one hundred days of genocide in April–July 1994. And it was repeated elsewhere. As reported by Alison Des Forges:

> [To] the accompaniment of virulent propaganda, radicals staged the practice for the catastrophe to come. The rehearsals took place in more than a dozen communities [involving attacks that] slaughtered some 2,000 Tutsi and dozens of [moderate] Hutu and established patterns for the genocide of 1994.[152]

Another hate speech red flag had popped up later that year, in November 1992, when Léon Mugesera, a leading member of the MRND Party, delivered a notorious oration advocating the annihilation of the Tutsis.[153] The speech was laced with murderous metaphors. For example, Mugesera infamously urged the audience to send the Tutsis "back to Ethiopia" by means of the Nyabarongo River, a non-navigable waterway used as a dumping ground for Tutsi corpses after postindependence massacres.[154] His verbiage also insinuated that Tutsis were outsiders, not genuine Rwandans but unwelcome aliens who came from the Horn of Africa region.[155] Mugesera's audience that day readily comprehended the significance of his words.[156]

So did the Rwandan authorities. They soon charged Mugesera with incitement, but he escaped to Canada, where an immigration case was filed against him.[157] Then, after years of proceedings and appeals in Canada, he was deported to Rwanda in 2012 to stand trial for his crimes and ultimately convicted in April 2016.[158]

149. Aimable Twagilimana, Historical Dictionary of Rwanda 123 (2007).

150. Linda Melvern, Conspiracy to Murder: The Rwandan Genocide 26–28 (2006).

151. *Id.* at 27.

152. Des Forges, *supra* note 120.

153. *Id.* at 39.

154. *Id.*

155. *Id.*

156. Narelle Fletcher, *Words That Can Kill: The Mugesera Speech and the 1994 Tutsi Genocide in Rwanda*, 11 Portal J. Multidisciplinary Int'l Studies 9 (2014).

157. Paul R. Bartrop, *Léon Mugesera*, *in* 4 Modern Genocide: The Definitive Resource and Document Collection 1769–1770 (Paul. R. Bartrop & Steven Leonard Jacobs eds., 2015).

158. *Id.* at 1770. On April 15, 2016, he was convicted, *inter alia*, of incitement to genocide and persecution as a crime against humanity, and sentenced to life in prison. *See* Robert

As violence intensified in the year following Mugesera's speech, Ferdinand Nahimana, who had been sacked from ORINFOR owing to his central role in orchestrating the Bugesera massacres, had taken the initiative with others in the extremist Hutu community to found RTLM, a private radio station.[159] To many, it appeared that RTLM was set up to accomplish explicitly what the government-controlled station, Radio Rwanda, could not—inflame the population against the Tutsis in preparation for the genocide.[160] And RTLM was the most important media outlet in terms of spreading the genocidal message against the Tutsis.[161] It is helpful, therefore, to look at the nature of RTLM messages both before and after the genocide.

C. Categories of RTLM Messages Pre-Genocide

In general, RTLM broadcast four types of messages before the genocide:

1. General efforts to create animosity toward Tutsis (for example, criticizing them for having too much wealth—a common anti-Semitic trope—or engaging in ethnic stereotyping regarding their physical characteristics);
2. Broadcasts that equated the terms *inyenzi* (cockroach) and *Inkotanyi* (a Kinyarwanda word meaning a violent warrior/killer from feudal times) with Tutsis in general;
3. Acknowledgments of RTLM's reputation as anti-Tutsi and inciting hatred toward Tutsis (for example, telling listeners that RTLM "sets people at odds with others," "creates tension," "heats up heads"); and
4. Specific verbal attacks against particular Tutsis (for example, a broadcast on April 3, 1994, specifically denounced a doctor in Cyangugu—and three days later he was burned alive in front of his house).[162]

And all of this, of course, was a precursor to the actual genocide. On April 6, 1994, Habyarimana's airplane, on its way back from talks in Arusha on implementing

Muriisa, *Rwanda: Suspect Gets Life Imprisonment for Genocide Related Crimes*, Imirasire (Apr. 16, 2016, 9:32 AM), http://eng.imirasire.com/news/top-news/in-rwanda/article/genocide-suspect-gets-life.

159. Twagilimana, *supra* note 149, at 122.

160. *Id.*

161. Des Forges, *supra* note 120, at 84 ("Before long, RTLM, with its greater drawing power, was displacing Kangura and other journals as the voice of extremism.").

162. Prosecutor v. Nahimana, Case No. ICTR-99-52-T, Judgement and Sentence, ¶¶ 345–355, 358–362, 363–368 (Dec. 3, 2003). *See also* Gregory S. Gordon, *"A War of Media, Words, Newspapers and Radio Stations": The ICTR Media Trial Verdict and a New Chapter in the International Law of Hate Speech*, 45 Va. J. Int'l L. 139, 161 (2004) [hereinafter *A War of Media*] (summarizing the types of pre-genocide RTLM broadcasts).

the accords, was shot down over Kigali.[163] Right away, Hutu extremists had roadblocks put up all over the Rwandan capital, and they dispatched death squads to murder high-profile Tutsi and moderate Hutu politicians.[164] A contingent of UNAMIR Belgian Blue Helmets were then murdered so as to incentivize Belgium and UNAMIR to withdraw from Rwanda.[165] Belgium did withdraw, and other countries, including the United States, followed suit.[166] The extremists were now ready to engage in mass killing across the country, and Rwanda was soon engulfed in a genocide that was being spurred on by RTLM's incendiary broadcasts. By the middle of July, close to one million Tutsis and moderate Hutus had been exterminated, many of them hacked to death with machetes.[167]

D. Categories of RTLM Messages during the Genocide

Supplementing the type of messages it disseminated pre-genocide, RTLM's post–April 1994 transmissions can be roughly divided into four new categories of incendiary speech: (1) calls for the extermination of all Tutsis, including dehumanization of Tutsis and use of code words such as "go to work"; (2) reporting that extermination had taken place and praising it; (3) calls for attacks on the remaining skeletal UNAMIR force; and (4) downplaying the extermination or urging the population to conceal traces of it so as to improve Rwanda's international image.[168]

An arresting instance of Category 1 is revealed in a June 4, 1994, broadcast by RTLM announcer Kantano Habimana:

> One hundred thousand young men must be recruited rapidly. They should all stand up so that we kill the *inkotanyi* and exterminate them . . . the reason we will exterminate them is that they belong to one ethnic group. Look at the

163. Marie-Helen Maras, Transnational Security 242 (2015).

164. Allan D. Cooper, The Geography of Genocide 176 (2009).

165. John A. Gentry, How Wars Are Won and Lost: Vulnerability and Military Power 111 (2012) ("For example, Rwandan extremists in April 1994 murdered 10 unarmed Belgian soldiers at the start of the genocide . . . . calculating correctly . . . that Belgium would . . . withdraw its troops from the UN mission in Rwanda if some of its soldiers died, thereby simplifying the task of perpetrating genocide.").

166. Frank Chalk et al., Mobilizing the Will to Intervene: Leadership to Prevent Mass Atrocities 30 (2010).

167. François Ngolet, Crisis in the Congo: The Rise and Fall of Laurent Kabila, at xiv (2011).

168. Prosecutor v. Nahimana, Case No. ICTR-99-52-T, Judgement and Sentence, ¶¶ 402–403, 419–424, 432–433 (Dec. 3, 2003). *See also* Gordon, *A War of Media, supra* note 162, at 162 (describing the types of speech disseminated by RTLM during this period). As will be described in Chapter 8, RTLM announcers communicated calls for genocide in other ways, including via posing questions, making predictions and falsely imputing to the Tutisis the same genocidal intentions harbored by the inciting extremist Hutus themselves (this incitement technique will be referred to as "accucation in a mirror").

> person's height and his physical appearance. Just look at his small nose and then break it.[169]

Georges Ruggiu, another RTLM broadcaster and the only white European convicted by the International Criminal Tribunal for Rwanda (ICTR), provided another example.[170] He urged listeners, especially the military and the *Interahamwe* militia, to finish off "the 1959 revolution."[171] Given the common parlance of ordinary Rwandans at that time, listeners would have interpreted this message as essentially saying: "Many were killed in 1959 but not all. We now need to finish the job. We must now massacre the entire Tutsi population."[172]

Categories of RTLM Messages before and during the Genocide are summarized in Table 1.1.

Table 1.1. CATEGORIES OF RTLM MESSAGES BEFORE AND DURING THE GENOCIDE

Before the Genocide	**During the Genocide**
1. Trying generally to create animosity toward Tutsis	1. Calling for the extermination of all Tutsis
2. Equating the terms *inyenzi* and *inkotanyi* with Tutsis in general	2. Reporting that extermination had taken place and praising it
3. Acknowledging its own reputation as anti-Tutsi and inciting hatred toward Tutsis	3. Calling for attacks on the remaining skeletal UNAMIR force
4. Launching specific verbal attacks against particular Tutsis	4. Downplaying or urging concealment of the extermination

E. The Effect of the Hate Speech and the ICTR Cases

What role did these media messages play in the genocide? ICTR judge Navanethem Pillay perhaps described it best and most evocatively in the *Media Case* Trial Chamber judgment:

> The Chamber accepts that this moment in time [the downing of the airplane on April 6] served as a trigger for the events that followed. That is evident. But if the downing of the plane was the trigger, then RTLM and *Kangura* were the bullets in the gun. The trigger had such a deadly impact because the gun

169. *Nahimana*, Case No. ICTR-99-52-T ¶ 396.

170. Gordon, *A War of Media, supra* note 162, at 153.

171. Prosecutor v. Ruggiu, Case No. ICTR-97-32-I, Judgement and Sentence, ¶ 44(vii) (June 1, 2000).

172. *See* WIBKE TIMMERMANN, INCITEMENT IN INTERNATIONAL LAW 177 (2014) (noting that when Ruggiu asked his listeners to "finish off the 1959 revolution," he "incited massacres of the Tutsi population.") Gordon, *A War of Media, supra* note 162, at 153.

> was loaded. The Chamber therefore considers the killing of Tutsi civilians can be said to have resulted, at least in part, from the message of ethnic targeting for death that was clearly and effectively disseminated through RTLM and *Kangura* before and after 6 April 1994.[173]

Given the close link between hate speech and genocide in Rwanda, the ICTR has served as a virtual laboratory for the development of atrocity speech law. Its work is encapsulated in a string of groundbreaking decisions: *Prosecutor v. Akayesu*[174] (ICTR's first incitement decision finding liability based on defendant's urging Hutu militia to slaughter town's Tutsi population); *Prosecutor v. Kambanda*[175] (incitement conviction against prime minister of rump genocide regime); *Prosecutor v. Ruggiu*[176] (Belgian RTLM announcer's incitement conviction included a count of crimes against humanity [persecution] based on hate speech); *Prosecutor v. Niyitegeka*[177] (incitement charges based on Rwandan minister's use of bullhorn directly after massacre to thank killers for "good work"); *Prosecutor*

Table 1.2. Overview of Key ICTR Cases

Cases	Description
1. *Prosecutor v. Akayesu*	ICTR's first incitement decision finding liability based on defendant's urging Hutu militia to slaughter town's Tutsi population
2. *Prosecutor v. Kambanda*	Incitement conviction against prime minister of rump genocide regime
3. *Prosecutor v. Ruggiu*	Belgian RTLM announcer's incitement conviction included a count of crimes against humanity (persecution) based on hate speech
4. *Prosecutor v. Niyitegeka*	Incitement charges based on Rwandan minister's use of bullhorn directly after massacre to thank killers for "good work"
5. *Prosecutor v. Nahimana, Barayagwiza & Ngeze*	Finding radio and print media executives guilty of incitement in connection with establishment of RTLM and dissemination of its genocidal broadcasts as well as founding and publishing of anti-Tutsi newspaper *Kangura*
6. *Prosecutor v. Bikindi*	Extremist Hutu tunesmith's liability based on code-word calls for murder directly before massacre, not on hate songs written before the genocide and disseminated by others

173. *Nahimana*, Case No. ICTR-99-52-T ¶ 953.

174. Prosecutor v. Akayesu, Case No. ICTR-96-4-T, Judgement (Sept. 2, 1998).

175. Prosecutor v. Kambanda, Case No. ICTR-97-23-S, Judgement and Sentence (Sept. 4, 1998).

176. Prosecutor v. Ruggiu, Case No. ICTR-97-32-I, Judgement and Sentence (June 1, 2000).

177. Prosecutor v. Niyitegeka, Case No. ICTR-96-14-T, Judgement and Sentence (May 16, 2003).

v. Nahimana, Barayagwiza & Ngeze[178] (finding radio and print media executives guilty of incitement in connection with establishment of RTLM and dissemination of its genocidal broadcasts as well as founding and publishing of anti-Tutsi newspaper *Kangura*); *Prosecutor v. Bikindi*[179] (extremist Hutu tunesmith's liability based on code-word calls for murder directly before massacre, not on hate songs written before the genocide and disseminated by others). These cases are summarized in Table 1.2 (and will be dealt with in greater depth in subsequent chapters).

VI. MORE RECENT CASES

A. Kenya

Since the Rwandan Genocide and the justice efforts that followed it, hate speech continues to play a seminal role in mass atrocity cases. Kenya is a prominent example. In the country's 2007–2008 postelection violence, for example, hate speech predominated on the airwaves and through other media.[180] One expert has noted that "Kenyan hate radio programs helped instigate violence between the Kikuyu and Luo peoples."[181] Kalenjin radio announcer Joshua arap Sang, who broadcast for KASS FM, was indicted by the International Criminal Court (ICC) in connection with his broadcasts dehumanizing political opponents.[182] He was accused of "whipping up ethnic hatred on the airwaves" that led to mass violence, including "the burning of a church near Edoret where ethnic Kikuyus were sheltering."[183] Arap Sang was charged with crimes against humanity (persecution), but the case was dropped given lack of evidence after reports of witness intimidation.[184]

B. Côte d'Ivoire

In Côte d'Ivoire, in the spring of 2011, while President Laurent Gbagbo insisted on maintaining power despite losing the presidency in a November 2010 election, radio broadcasters supporting him exploited the airwaves to demonize the

178. *Nahimana*, Case No. ICTR-99-52-T.

179. Prosecutor v. Bikindi, Case No. ICTR-01-72 T, Judgement ¶ 281 (Dec. 2, 2008).

180. *See Kenya: Spreading the Word of Hate*, IRIN News 5 (Jan. 22, 2008), http://www.irinnews.org/report/76346/kenya-spreading-the-word-of-hate.

181. Alexander Tsesis, *Inflammatory Speech: Outrage versus Intimidation*, 97 Minn. L. Rev. 1145, 1171 n.148 (2013).

182. *See* Gregory S. Gordon, *Setting the Record Straight on International Speech Crime Law*, Jurist (May 24, 2011, 8:00 AM), http://www.jurist.org/forum/2011/05/gregory-gordon-arap-sang.php [hereinafter *Setting the Record Straight*].

183. *At a Glance: Kenya Poll Violence Suspects*, BBC News (Jan. 7, 2015), http://www.bbc.co.uk/news/world-africa-12001281 (last visited Sept. 18, 2016).

184. Gordon, *Setting the Record Straight, supra* note 182; *ICC Throws Out Case against Kenya Deputy President Ruto and Journalist Sang*, Mail & Guardian Africa (Apr. 5, 2016, 5:20 PM), http://mgafrica.com/article/2016-04-05-international-criminal-court-to-rule-on-bid-to-throw-case-out-against-kenya-deputy-president-ruto.

supporters of Gbagbo's victorious opponent, Alassane Ouattara.[185] Partly owing to such hate speech, Gbagbo loyalists attacked pro-Ouattara civilians.[186] Gbagbo and his chief lieutenant Charles Blé Goudé have been charged by the ICC with crimes against humanity (persecution) and are now on trial in The Hague.[187]

C. Myanmar

More recently, in Myanmar (formerly Burma), as the country transitions from a long military dictatorship to a semblance of civilian rule, the Muslim minority has been subjected to religiously motivated violence by organized bands of Buddhist attackers. According to Human Rights Watch, in June 2012, dozens of Rohingya Muslims were killed and approximately 100,000 displaced after an attack by Arakan Buddhists.[188] Human Rights Watch reported that "the hostilities were fanned by anti-Muslim media accounts and local propaganda."[189]

Around that time, former US President Jimmy Carter expressed "'deep concern' over the recent inter-communal violence between Buddhists and Muslims and the use of 'hate speech' by some leaders."[190] The *BBC News* featured a sample of some of that hate speech, much of which allegedly emanates from a prominent Buddhist monk.[191] The monk is quoted as accusing "Muslim men of repeatedly raping Buddhist women, of using their wealth to lure Buddhist women into marriage, then imprisoning them at home."[192] As of yet, no criminal case has been brought in connection with this speech or the violence that has been triggered by it.

VII. CONCLUSION

At the writing of this book, hate speech continues to serve as a catalyst for atrocity in various hot spots around the world. A horrifying example is the ongoing

185. *See* Susan Benesch, *Ivory Coast in Speech-Fueled Catastrophe*, Voices that Poison (Apr. 2, 2011), http://voicesthatpoison.wordpress.com/2011/04/02/ivory-coast-in-speech-fueled-catastrophe/.

186. *Id.*

187. Press Release, *ICC Trial Chamber I Joins the Cases concerning Laurent Gbagbo and Charles Blé Goudé*, International Criminal Court (Mar. 11, 2015), https://www.icc-cpi.int/Pages/item.aspx?name=pr1097.

188. *"The Government Could Have Stopped This": Sectarian Violence and Ensuing Abuses in Burma's Arakan State*, Human Rights Watch (Aug. 2012), at 1, http://www.hrw.org/sites/default/files/reports/burma0812webwcover_0.pdf.

189. *Id.*

190. Paul Vrieze, *Jimmy Carter "Deeply Concerned by Sectarian Violence and 'Hate Speech'"*, The Irrawaddy (Apr. 6, 2013), http://www.irrawaddy.org/archives/31617 (last visited Sept. 18, 2016).

191. Jonathan Head, *What Is Behind Burma's Wave of Religious Violence?*, BBC News (Apr. 4, 2013), http://www.bbc.co.uk/news/world-asia-22023830.

192. *Id.*

genocide against the Yazidi people by the Islamic State of Iraq and Al-Sham (ISIS).[193] The Yazidis are a Kurdish religious group whose syncretic faith has ties to Zoroastrianism and ancient Mesopotamian creeds.[194] ISIS leaders have incited/instigated to genocide of the Yazidi referring to them via dehumanizing epithets such as "Satanists," denouncing them as not being "People of the Book," and defaming them as "polytheists."[195] Wiktor Pastucha and Aleksandra Spychalska elaborate:

> Dehumanization can be also clearly seen in the language used by Islamic State's media. Yazidis are picked as "devil worshippers", "Satanists" or "devil creed". . . . According to official [ISIS] fatwa, Yazidi woman can and should be sexually abused, because they are less than human . . . "Infidels" are described as a "cancer", as stealthy enemies that deserve only to be destroyed or become slaves.[196]

At the same time, South Sudan's warring parties, led, respectively, by President Salva Kiir, of the Dinka ethnic group, and Vice President Riek Machar, of the Nuer ethnic group, have used hate speech to fuel attacks against civilians from each side.[197] Among other media, this incendiary rhetoric has been disseminated via radio:

> In a country with an estimated 80 per cent illiteracy rate, South Sudanese are particularly reliant on radio as a means of getting news and of communicating information. . . . The Radio Bentiu FM station is a key source of news for the population [and rebels have] broadcast hate messages declaring that certain ethnic groups should not stay in Bentiu and even calling on men from one community to commit vengeful sexual violence against women from another community.[198]

193. Nick Cumming-Bruce, *ISIS Committed Genocide against Yazidis in Syria and Iraq, US Panel Says*, N.Y. Times (June 16, 2016), http://www.nytimes.com/2016/06/17/world/middleeast/isis-genocide-yazidi-un.html ("Islamic State forces have committed genocide and other war crimes in a continuing effort to exterminate the Yazidi religious minority in Syria and Iraq . . .").

194. Wiktor Pastucha & Aleksandra Spychalska, *How Islamic State Uses Propaganda in the Service of Genocide*, International Academic Forum (Apr. 4, 2016), http://think.iafor.org/islamic-state-use-propaganda-service-genocide/.

195. *Id.*

196. *Id.*

197. *Warring South Sudan Factions Used Media to Incite Public—Report*, Daily Nation (Oct. 29, 2015), http://www.nation.co.ke/news/africa/Warring-South-Sudan-factions--media-to-incite-public/-/1066/2934958/-/bv0v56/-/index.html.

198. Keith Somerville, *South Sudan: How Hate Radio Was Used to Incite Bentiu Massacres*, African Arguments (Apr. 24, 2014), http://africanarguments.org/2014/04/24/south-sudan-how-hate-radio-was-used-to-incite-bentiu-massacres-by-keith-somerville/.

Thus, ethnic hate propagandists continue to ply their trade with devastating effect. In the meantime, think tanks, nongovernmental organizations, academics, diplomats, bureaucrats, and statesmen have been strategizing regarding ways to combat and eventually silence these purveyors of division and mass violence.[199] Clearly, a multidisciplinary approach will be needed. And law, which evinces collective animosity toward, and provides the means to punish, speech meant to spark or sustain intergroup slaughter or persecution, is a central piece in the prevention mosaic. The following chapters will trace the origins of the relevant normative prescriptions, beginning with international human rights and domestic approaches and moving on to an examination of the related body of international criminal law.

199. *See, e.g., Hate Speech and Group-Targeted Violence: The Role of Speech in Violent Conflicts*, United States Holocaust Memorial Museum, http://www.genocidewatch.org/images/OutsideResearch_Hate_Speech_and_Group-Targeted_Violence.pdf (report of 2009 seminar that brought together academics, journalists, political analysts, policy professionals, and conflict analysts to examine the role speech acts play in genocide and related crimes against humanity).

2

International Human Rights and Domestic Law

"If liberty means anything at all, it means the right to tell people what they do not want to hear."

—George Orwell[1]

"[H]ate speech is both a calculated affront to the dignity of vulnerable members of society and a calculated assault on the public good of inclusiveness."

—Jeremy Waldron[2]

I. INTRODUCTION

In order to understand the development of atrocity speech law, a review of international and domestic laws regarding treatment of hate speech is imperative. Transnational regulation of hate speech is captured in a series of regional and global treaties that recognize the value of free speech but provide mechanisms to curtail it when used to promote hatred and/or violence. The domestic jurisdictions in most industrialized democracies follow this template. The exception is the United States, whose vigilance in protecting the dissemination of all speech, even the most virulently hateful, is unsurpassed in the world. Only reasonably likely imminent lawless violence, intended by the speaker, can result in government stifling or punishment of speech in the United States. As this chapter

1. John Rodden & John Rossi, The Cambridge Introduction to George Orwell 107 (2012).

2. Jeremy Waldron, The Harm in Hate Speech 5–6 (2012).

Atrocity Speech Law. Gregory S. Gordon.

demonstrates, Japan has largely followed the US lead. And Canada stands in the middle—somewhat ambivalent about bringing legal action against hatemongers but legally empowered to do so if the need arises. These different legal regimes, including the policy rationales that undergird them, are now to be explored.

II. PROTECTION OF FREE SPEECH VS. REGULATION OF HATE SPEECH AT THE INTERNATIONAL LEVEL

A. The Universal Declaration and Regional/International Treaties

Given the abuses of speech that paved the way for Nazi depredations—via suppression, deceit, degradation, and advocacy—the postwar international community was understandably eager both to protect its legitimate use and regulate its actionable abuse. It did so through a newly developing human rights law infrastructure, whose cornerstones were laid in 1948 with UN adoption of the Universal Declaration of Human Rights. The Declaration protects free speech through Article 19 but prohibits incitement to invidious discrimination through Article 7.[3] These two provisions illustrate the structural tension regarding speech inherent in human rights law—the desire to vindicate individual expression rights so as to promote democracy and self-actualization, set against the effort to stymie group-focused hate speech in order to foster equal protection and combat bigotry.[4]

That inherent dichotomy replicates itself in subsequent regional human rights instruments. The 1950 European Convention on Human Rights (ECHR), for example, contains a right to free speech in the first portion of Article 10, but it is tempered by follow-up language that specifies the right "carries with it duties and responsibilities, and may be subject to such . . . restrictions . . . as are necessary in a democratic society . . . for the protection of the reputation or rights of others. . . ."[5] This limitation has been interpreted to prohibit hate speech.[6]

In the Americas, the American Convention on Human Rights affords a significant freedom of expression guarantee, pursuant to Article 13, by ensuring the right to "seek, receive and impart information and ideas of all kinds" through any medium.[7] On the other hand, the treaty excludes hate speech from

3. Universal Declaration of Human Rights arts. 7, 19, Dec. 10, 1948, G.A. Res. 217 A(III), U.N. Doc. A/810, at 71 (1948) [hereinafter Universal Declaration].

4. *See* Stephanie Farrior, *Molding the Matrix: The Historical and Theoretical Foundations of International Law Concerning Hate Speech*, 14 Berkeley J. Int'l L. 1, 3 (1996) (discussing the tension in human rights law between freedom of expression and equality rights).

5. European Convention for the Protection of Human Rights and Fundamental Freedoms art. 10, Nov. 4, 1950, 213 U.N.T.S. 222, entered into force, Sept. 3, 1953 [hereinafter European Convention on Human Rights].

6. Farrior, *supra* note 4, at 4.

7. American Convention on Human Rights art. 13, Nov. 22, 1969, O.A.S.T.S. No. 36, 1144 U.N.T.S. 123 [hereinafter American Convention on Human Rights].

its protective ambit and mandates that states parties outlaw it. Paragraph 5 of Article 13 declares:

> Any propaganda for war and any advocacy of national, racial, or religious hatred that constitute incitements to lawless violence or to any other similar action against any person or group of persons on any grounds including those of race, color, religion, language, or national origin shall be considered offenses punishable by law.[8]

A similar clash is seen in treaties at the international level, which give teeth to the protections enshrined in the Universal Declaration of Human Rights but echo that document's dual treatment of speech. For instance, the International Covenant on Civil and Political Rights (ICCPR) begins with a freedom of expression guarantee in Article 19(2) but goes on to circumscribe it in Article 19(3).[9] Noting that the guarantee "carries with it special duties and responsibilities," subparagraph (3) permits the following restrictions on it if "provided by law" and "necessary": "(a) For respect of the rights and reputations of others; or (b) for the protection of national security or of public order (*ordre public*), or of public health or morals."[10] However, like the American Convention, the ICCPR goes further. Its Article 20(2) provides that "any advocacy of national, racial or religious hatred that constitutes incitement to discrimination, hostility or violence shall be prohibited by law."[11]

A comparable provision is found in the International Convention on the Elimination of All Forms of Racial Discrimination (ICERD). It is prefaced by the treaty's preamble, which declares that all human beings are entitled to protection "against any incitement to discrimination."[12] Then, Article 4 directs all states parties to "condemn all propaganda . . . based on ideas or theories of superiority of one race or group of persons of one colour or ethnic origin, or which attempt to justify or promote racial hatred and discrimination in any form, and undertake to adopt immediate and positive measures designed to eradicate all incitement to, or acts of, such discrimination . . ."[13]

8. *Id.* art. 13(5). The African Charter on Human and Peoples' Rights similarly provides for "the right to express and disseminate ... opinions within the law" but does not contain a direct corresponding limiting provision. African (Banjul) Charter on Human and Peoples' Rights art. 9, June 27, 1987, OAU Doc. CAB/LEG/67/3/Rev.5, 21 I.L.M. 58 [hereinafter African Charter]. However, Article 27(2) declares that "the rights and freedoms of each individual shall be exercised with due regard to the rights of others. . . ."

9. International Covenant on Civil and Political Rights art. 19, U.N.G.A. Res. 2200A (XXI), Dec. 16, 1966, 21 U.N. GAOR Supp. (No. 16) at 52, U.N. Doc. A/6316 (1966), 999 U.N.T.S. 171, entered into force Mar. 23, 1976 [hereinafter ICCPR].

10. *Id.* art. 19(3).

11. ICCPR, *supra* note 9, art. 20(2).

12. International Convention on the Elimination of All Forms of Racial Discrimination Preface, U.N.G.A. Res. 2106 (XX), Dec. 21, 1965, 660 U.N.T.S. 195, entered into force Jan. 4, 1969 [hereinafter ICERD].

13. *Id.* art. 4.

Article 4(a) goes on to criminalize "all dissemination of ideas based on racial superiority or hatred, incitement to racial discrimination, as well as all acts of violence or incitement to such acts against any race or group of persons of another colour or ethnic origin, and also the provision of any assistance to racist activities, including the financing thereof . . ."[14] Similarly, Article 4(b) requires states parties to "declare illegal and prohibit organizations, and also organized and all other propaganda activities, which promote and incite racial discrimination, and . . . recognize participation in such organizations or activities as an offence punishable by law."[15] Finally, Article 4(c) forbids "public authorities or public institutions, national or local, to promote or incite racial discrimination."[16]

It bears mention that the policy protecting citizens from the excesses of free speech is evinced as well in the derogation provisions of two key treaties. Both the ICCPR and the ECHR permit derogations from free speech rights in cases of public emergency "threatening the life of the nation" (ICCPR Article 4(1) and ECHR Article 15(1)).[17] Of course, derogations must be narrowly required by and restricted to the "exigencies of the situation" and not inconsistent with a state's other obligations under international law.[18] Interestingly, the body responsible for interpreting the ICCPR, the Human Rights Committee, has opined that Article 20, which forbids hate advocacy, may never be derogated from.[19] Although grounded in various policy considerations, this disparity of treatment regarding derogation as to protecting free speech versus prohibiting hate speech arguably suggests that, from a holistic perspective, the latter may raise greater public policy concerns for the global community than the former.[20] At the very least, concerns for safeguarding free speech rights cannot be presumed to easily trump anti-hate-advocacy measures on the international plane.

B. Case Law Interpreting the Treaties

1. Human Rights Committee Cases Interpreting the ICCPR

Jurisprudence interpreting these treaties provides helpful guidance for navigating between the competing policy objectives. In this regard, significant decisions have been issued by the Human Rights Committee, which is empowered

14. *Id.* art. 4(a).

15. *Id.* art. 4(b).

16. *Id.* art. 4(c).

17. ICCPR, *supra* note 9, art. 4(1); ECHR, *supra* note 5, art. 15(1).

18. ICCPR, *supra* note 9, art. 4(1); ECHR, *supra* note 5, art. 15(1). The ICCPR also mandates that derogations not "involve discrimination solely on the ground of race, colour, sex, language, religion or social origin." ICCPR, *supra* note 9, art. 4(1).

19. General Comment No. 29: States of emergency (art. 4), U.N. Doc. CCPR/C/21/Rev.l/Add.l (Aug. 31, 2001), ¶ 13(e).

20. Wibke Timmermann, Incitement in International Law 71–72 (2014).

by states that have ratified the ICCPR's First Optional Protocol to accept "communications" from individuals who, having exhausted local remedies, seek to vindicate their rights under the Covenant.[21]

The first of these implicating ICCPR Article 20(2), *J. R. T. and the W. G. Party v. Canada* (1983), was part of a trilogy involving government restrictions on anti-Semitic hate speech.[22] In *J.R.T.*, the principal complainant, John Ross Taylor, claimed the Canadian government impermissibly infringed on his Article 19(2) rights after it cut off his access to a telephone line being used to disseminate tape-recorded messages warning callers "of the dangers of international finance and international Jewry leading the world into wars, unemployment, inflation and the collapse of world values and principles."[23] In shutting down Taylor's operation, the Canadian government relied on the antidiscrimination provisions of its Human Rights Act. Although the Human Rights Committee deemed the communication inadmissible on exhaustion of remedies grounds, it did opine that the ICCPR imposed on Canada an obligation to enjoin Taylor's transmission of hate speech:

> [T]he opinions which Mr. Taylor seeks to disseminate through the telephone system clearly constitute the advocacy of racial or religious hatred which Canada has an obligation under article 20(2) of the Covenant to prohibit. In the Committee's opinion, therefore, the communication is, in respect of this claim, incompatible with the provisions of the Covenant, within the meaning of article 3 of the Optional Protocol.[24]

Thus, the Committee impliedly found no violation of Article 19(2) as the Canadian government's actions were necessitated pursuant to Article 20(2).

Thirteen years later, in *Faurisson v. France*, the Committee was confronted with a similar scenario after the communication's author was convicted in France for disseminating Holocaust denial speech, including casting doubt on whether gas chambers were used to mass murder Jews at Auschwitz and other Nazi extermination sites.[25] The French government justified its prosecution since Faurisson's challenging the reality of the Final Solution "incites his readers to

21. Optional Protocol to the International Covenant on Civil and Political Rights, G.A. Res 2200 (XXI), Dec. 16, 1966, U.N. GAOR, Supp. No. 16, at 59, U.N. Doc. A/6316 (1966) (entered into force Mar. 23, 1976).

22. International Covenant on Civil and Political Rights, Communication No. 104/1981: Canada (Jurisprudence), U.N. Doc. CCPR/C/18/D/104/1981 (J.R.T. & the W.G. Party v. Canada) (declared inadmissible Apr. 6, 1983).

23. *Id.* ¶ 2.1.

24. *Id.* ¶ 8(b).

25. International Covenant on Civil and Political Rights, Communication No. 550/1993: France (Jurisprudence) P 7.5, U.N. Doc. CCPR/C/58/D/550/1993 (1996) (*Robert Faurisson v. France*).

anti-Semitic behaviour" and threatens the "public order" given that it constitutes "racist" aggression.[26]

The Committee ruled in France's favor, finding that the French government had not violated Faurisson's right to free expression under Article 19. Indeed, it found the government's measures mandated under Article 19(3). In a concurring opinion, a Committee member found it crucial to "link liability with the intent of the author" and emphasized the "tendency of [Faurisson's] publication to incite to anti-Semitism."[27] To better discern this intent, the opinion homed in on certain textual clues, such as Faurisson's reference to "particularly Jewish historians" or "the magic gas chamber."[28] The opinion also noted the importance of the context in which the speech was uttered. For example, it focused on the text's casting doubt on firmly established historical facts while passing itself off as "impartial academic research that the victims of Nazism were guilty of dishonest fabrication."[29] Thus, the opinion found that the "restrictions placed on the author did not curb the core of his right to freedom of expression, nor did they in any way affect his freedom of research; they were intimately linked to the value they were meant to protect—the right to be free from incitement to racism or anti-Semitism."[30]

Moreover, although Faurisson had not been convicted of "incitement" per se, the opinion noted that ICCPR Article 20(2) was implicated by his conduct:

> However, there may be circumstances in which the right of a person to be free from incitement to discrimination on grounds of race, religion or national origins cannot be fully protected by a narrow, explicit law on incitement that falls precisely within the boundaries of article 20, paragraph 2. This is the case where, in a particular social and historical context, statements that do not meet the strict legal criteria of incitement can be shown to constitute part of a pattern of incitement against a given racial, religious or national group, or where those interested in spreading hostility and hatred adopt sophisticated forms of speech that are not punishable under the law against racial incitement, even though their effect may be as pernicious as explicit incitement, if not more so.[31]

In a decision from 2000, *Ross v. Canada*, the author of the communication was a schoolteacher who had published books and made public statements, outside

26. *Id.* ¶ 7.5.

27. *Id.*, Individual Opinion of Elizabeth Evatt and David Kretzmer, Co-Signed by Eckart Klein, ¶ 9.

28. *Id.*, ¶ 10.

29. *Id.*, ¶ 6.

30. *Id.*, ¶ 10.

31. *Id.*, ¶ 4.

of the classroom, attacking and denigrating the Jewish people.[32] On the basis of a parent's complaint against Ross alleging discrimination, and a subsequent investigation confirming the allegations, Ross was assigned a nonteaching position by the school board.[33] He appealed, but the Canadian Supreme Court upheld the finding of discrimination and the decision to remove Ross from the classroom.[34] Ross then submitted his communication to the Human Rights Committee, alleging that his removal from teaching duties violated his ICCPR Article 19 rights.

While the Committee found Ross's job reassignment amounted to a restriction on his free expression rights under Article 19(2), it concluded the government was justified in its actions pursuant to Article 19(3).[35] First, the restriction was provided by law (there was a legal framework for the proceedings that resulted in Ross's reassignment).[36] Second, it addressed one of Paragraph 19(3)'s aims—respect of the rights and reputation of others. In particular, as it was meant to curb Ross's anti-Semitic expression, it was ostensibly related to protecting the rights and reputation of Jewish students.[37] Third, given an apparent causal link between the authors' anti-Jewish publications and "the poisoned school environment" experienced by Jewish students in the district, the Committee found the restriction was actually necessary to achieve a legitimate purpose: again, to protect the rights or reputation of those of the Jewish faith—especially in the context of a school system with young students.[38]

2. European Court of Human Rights Cases Interpreting the ECHR

Similarly, in adjudicating individual complaints, the European Court of Human Rights has issued helpful guidance regarding application of Article 10 of the ECHR. In particular, the Court has had to find the right equilibrium between the free speech right guaranteed by Article 10(1) and the government's prerogative to restrict that right to protect individuals as well as various national interests pursuant to Article 10(2). Article 10(2) specifies three criteria to be considered in this regard: (1) whether the restrictions are prescribed by law; (2) whether their aim is legitimate; and (3) whether they can be considered necessary in a democratic society—in other words, as the European Court of Human Rights has opined,

32. International Covenant on Civil and Political Rights, Communication No. 736/1997: Canada (Jurisprudence) ¶ 2.1, U.N. Doc. CCPR/C/70/D/736/1997 (2000) (Ross v. Canada).

33. *Id.* ¶¶ 2.1–4.4.

34. *Id.* ¶¶ 4.5–4.8.

35. *Id.* ¶¶ 11.1–11.3.

36. *Id.* ¶¶ 11.3–11.4.

37. *Id.* ¶¶ 11.5.

38. *Id.* ¶ 11.6.

there must be a "pressing social need" and an intervention "proportionate to the legitimate aims pursued."[39]

a. *Jersild v. Denmark*

In contrast to the ICCPR Article 19/20 cases, these ECHR Article 10 decisions have, in the main, not been as sympathetic to government efforts to curb unpopular speech. Many of the ECHR cases have arisen out of speech restrictions imposed by the government in the national security context in Turkey. But one of them, the 1994 decision in *Jersild v. Denmark*, was precipitated by the hate speech–related conviction of a Danish journalist who had interviewed avowedly racist youths on a television program.[40]

As part of a "Sunday News Magazine" for the Danish Broadcasting Corporation, the journalist aired his discussion with three adolescent members of a homegrown skinhead movement known as the "Greenjackets."[41] The Court described the "Sunday News Magazine" as "a serious television programme intended for a well-informed audience, dealing with a wide range of social and political issues, including xenophobia, immigration and refugees."[42] During the interview, the teens made very offensive comments about immigrants and ethnic groups in Denmark, referring to some of them as "animals and using racial epithets."[43] Jersild was charged with, and convicted of, aiding and abetting the Greenjackets in violating a Danish law prohibiting "dissemination of ideas based on racial superiority or hatred, incitement to racial discrimination, as well as acts of violence or incitement to such acts against any race or group of persons of another color or ethnic origin . . ."[44] His conviction was upheld in the Danish courts of appeal.[45]

Jersild filed a complaint, alleging ECHR Article 10 violations, that was first addressed by the European Commission of Human Rights (which ruled in his favor) and then, after a referral by the Commission and Denmark, by the European Court of Human Rights, which published the decision at issue.[46] With respect to the first two criteria of the test under ECHR Article 10—basis in law

39. Jersild v. Denmark, App. 15890/89, Eur. Ct. H.R. (ser. A) 298 ¶¶ 29, 31 (1994), http://cmiskp.echr.coe.int/tkp197/search.asp?skin=hudoc-en (search Jersild v. Denmark in "Case Title" field).

40. *Id.*

41. *Id.* ¶¶ 9–11.

42. *Id.* ¶ 9.

43. *Id.* ¶ 11.

44. *Id.* ¶¶ 12, 19.

45. *Id.* ¶¶ 15–18.

46. *Id.* ¶¶ 1–8. When *Jersild* was decided, cases would be initially filed with the Commission, which would handle them in the first instance, and, if appropriate, refer them to the Court. But with the Council of Europe, under whose auspices the EHCR was drafted and adopted, welcoming approximately two dozen new states after the fall of the Soviet Union in the early

and legitimate aim—the Court observed that the Danish criminal code did indeed forbid the conduct of which Jersild was charged and convicted and that the prosecution was legitimately motivated by a desire to protect the reputation or rights of others as set forth in Article 10(2).[47]

Regarding the third Article 10(2) criterion—the necessity of the government action in a democratic society—the Court was not satisfied that Denmark had met its burden. Although the Court was sympathetic toward Danish efforts to combat racial discrimination and comply with its duties under the ICERD, it stressed that, in order to sustain the conviction, the speech at issue must appear "from an objective point of view to have had as its purpose the propagation of racist views and ideas."[48] It found that it did not. In this regard, the Court focused on the television program's introduction, which identified the youths as "racist" and "clearly dissociated [Jersild] from the persons interviewed."[49] In that segment, the Court noted, Jersild also described his guests as "extremist youths" and rebutted some of their statements.[50] Moreover, during the interview itself, Jersild posed questions suggesting that there were very accomplished black persons.[51] Thus, the Court found that Denmark's stated justifications for Jersild's conviction did not establish that the interference with freedom of expression was "necessary in a democratic society."[52]

1990s, a tremendous burden was placed on the system in terms of new cases needing adjudication under the ECHR. Thus, Protocol 11 to the Convention was adopted creating greater efficiency by abolishing the two-tier system of Commission and Court and allowing all cases to be filed with the Court directly. *See* William Ashby Powers, Note & Comment, *Hirst v. United Kingdom (No. 2): A First Look at Prisoner Disenfranchisement by the European Court of Human Rights*, 21 Conn. J. Int'l L. 243, 251 (2006) (explaining the background and mechanics of the reform effort). Other ECHR cases described in this chapter and filed pre-reform will be referred to as having been filed with the "European system."

47. *Id.* ¶ 27.

48. *Id.* ¶ 35.

49. *Id.* ¶ 34.

50. *Id.*

51. *Id.* ¶ 11.

52. It should be noted that two dissenting opinions would have upheld the conviction on the grounds that too little was said in the program to condemn the racist views of the Greenjackets. One dissenting opinion declared: "Neither the written text of the interview . . . nor the video film we have seen makes it clear that the remarks of the Greenjackets are intolerable in a society based on respect for human rights." *Id.*, Joint Dissenting Opinion of Judges Ryssdal, Berhhardt, Spielman, and Loizu, ¶ 3. The other dissent found that the statements, made "without any significant reaction on the part of the commentator, did indeed amount to incitement to contempt. . . . While appreciating that some judges attach particular importance to freedom of expression . . . we cannot accept that this freedom should extend to encouraging racial hatred, contempt for races other than the one to which we belong, and defending violence against those who belong to the races in question." *Id.*, Joint Dissenting Opinions of Judge Golkuklu, Russo, and Valticos.

b. The Turkish Cases

i. Incal v. Turkey

The cases from Turkey arise out of speech connected to Kurdish efforts to seek civil rights or autonomy that was prosecuted by Turkish authorities as criminal incitement on national security grounds. *Incal v. Turkey* (1998), for example, involved an attempt by the People's Labour Party (known as the "HEP") to distribute a leaflet in the Izmir constituency calling for the establishment of neighborhood committees to oppose the alleged official policy to remove Kurds from the city (through indirect acts, such as shutting down street traders).[53] After the party's executive committee requested permission from the Izmir security authorities to issue the leaflets, publication was enjoined and the leaflets seized on the grounds that they contained "separatist propaganda capable of inciting people to resist the government and commit criminal offences."[54] Moreover, in connection with their efforts to distribute the leaflets, a National Security Court convicted Incal, a member of the HEP executive committee, and other committee members, of "attempting to incite hatred and hostility through racist words" in violation of the "Prevention of Terrorism Act" and the "Press Act."[55] Incal filed a petition within the European system alleging, *inter alia*, that his criminal conviction violated ECHR Article 10.

Once again, the Court examined the speech infringement through the lens of the Article 10(2) criteria—that the infringement be "prescribed by law," that it be designed to carry out at least one of the public-weal aims laid out in Article 10(2), and that it be "necessary in a democratic society."[56] That the interference was prescribed by Turkish law was undisputed.[57] And the Court found that the aim of the law was to prevent disorder.[58]

But the Court held that the third criterion was not satisfied. It observed that Article 10 "is applicable not only to 'information' or 'ideas' that are favourably received or regarded as inoffensive or as a matter of indifference, but also to those that offend, shock or disturb; such are the demands of pluralism, tolerance and broadmindedness without which there is no 'democratic society.'"[59] Consequently, the Court concluded that the leaflet could be interpreted as trying to persuade the population to "band together to raise certain political demands."[60] And although the meaning of "neighborhood committees" was ambiguous, the

53. Incal v. Turkey, 29 Eur. H.R. Rep. 449, 480 (1998).

54. *Id.* ¶ 12.

55. *Id.* ¶¶ 15–16.

56. *Id.* ¶ 40.

57. *Id.* ¶ 41.

58. *Id.* ¶ 42.

59. *Id.* ¶ 46.

60. *Id.* ¶ 50.

Court ruled that the leaflet's advocacy could not be interpreted as "incitement to the use of violence, hostility or hatred between citizens."[61] This was especially true in this context, where an opposition party was speaking against the government—government suppression of speech in that context should be given "the closest scrutiny."[62] As a corollary, the Court appeared to be suggesting that, in the context of speech regulation, criticism of the government should be given extra latitude.[63]

ii. Arslan v. Turkey

In *Arslan v. Turkey*, the applicant wrote a book titled *History in Mourning, 33 Bullets*, which recounted an episode involving the massacre of Kurds that took place in Southeastern Turkey. [64] In the book, Arslan described the Turks as invaders and persecutors who had genocidal plans for the Kurds. He was convicted of the offense of disseminating separatist propaganda under the Prevention of Terrorism Act and sentenced to one year and eight months' imprisonment and a fine. He filed a petition in the European system challenging the conviction as being in violation of Article 10. In analyzing his petition, the Court referred to the Article 10(2) criteria and easily dispensed with the "prescribed by law" element.[65] Next, it found that, in light of the "sensitivity of the security situation" in southeast Turkey, the government had the legitimate goal of protecting national security and territorial integrity as well as preventing disorder in its restrictions of freedom of expression.[66]

As for the "necessary in a democratic society" criterion, the Court laid emphasis on the medium of communication—a literary historical narrative—as opposed to a mass media instrument that would be the more typical incitement vehicle.[67] And while the Court acknowledged the text did not contain a neutral depiction of facts, its criticism of the Turkish authorities could be characterized as political speech involving questions of public interest. As established in *Incal*, such speech must be given a wide regulatory berth, and there is little room for restricting it under Article 10. And even though the Court acknowledged that the book was written with a "hostile tone" and contained "acerbic passages" that painted "an extremely negative picture of the population of Turkish origin," it did not incite to violence or armed resistance.[68] That fact, along with the harsh

61. *Id.*

62. *Id.* ¶ 46.

63. *Id.*

64. Arslan v. Turkey, 31 Eur. H.R. Rep. 264, 287 (2001).

65. *Id.* ¶ 37.

66. *Id.* ¶ 40.

67. *Id.* ¶ 45.

68. *Id.* ¶ 48. But the Court did allow that, in cases of statements inciting to violence, there is a "wider margin of appreciation" for interference with freedom of expression. *Id.* ¶ 46.

prison term of one year and eight months, persuaded the Court that the conviction was "disproportionate to the aims pursued and accordingly not 'necessary in a democratic society.'"[69]

iii. The Sürek *Cases*

The next in this line of speaker-friendly cases was *Sürek and Özdemir v. Turkey* (1999).[70] The two applicants were, respectively, a major shareholder (Sürek) and editor-in-chief (Özdemir) of *Haberde Yorumda Gerçek*, a weekly review published in Istanbul, the Turkish capital. *Haberde Yorumda Gerçek* (The Truth of News and Comments) had published an interview with a leader of the Kurdistan Workers' Party (PKK), a political group that had been outlawed by the Turkish government. During the interview, the PKK leader explained the organization's origins and objectives, its rationale for turning to violence to realize its goals, and its resolve to continue waging war against Turkey as long as it resisted the will of the Kurdish people.

Sürek and Özdemir came under police scrutiny for their publication of the interview and were criminally charged with incitement-related offenses. A Turkish National Security Court ultimately found Sürek and Özdemir guilty of disseminating separatist propaganda and terrorist views, a violation of the Prevention of Terrorism Act of 1991.[71] A petition to the European system followed, and, as with the other cases, the Court found that the first two criteria of Article 10 were satisfied—the speech infringements were prescribed by law and they had the legitimate purpose of maintaining national security and public order.[72]

But, once again, the Court determined that the "necessary in a democratic society" criterion was not met. Alluding to the attendant requirement of a "pressing social need," the Court emphasized once more that Article 10(2) does not easily brook restrictions on political speech or debate on questions of public interest.[73] It then opined that the interview at issue could not be viewed as inciting to violence or hatred. Rather, it had a "newsworthy content which allowed the public [to] have an insight into the psychology of those who are the driving force behind the opposition to official policy in south-east Turkey...."[74] Therefore, Turkey could not show adequate justification for the substantial interference with freedom of expression.[75] On the other hand, following this analysis, the Court sounded a

69. *Id.* ¶ 50.

70. Sürek and Özdemir v. Turkey, App. Nos. 23927/94 and 24277/94 (Eur. Ct. H.R. 1999), http://cmiskp.echr.coe.int/tkp197/search.asp?skin=hudoc-en (search Surek and Ozdemir v. Turkey in "Case Title" field).

71. *Id.* ¶¶ 10, 12, 23.

72. *Id.* ¶¶ 47, 51.

73. *Id.* ¶ 60.

74. *Id.* ¶ 61.

75. *Id.*

cautionary note in dictum regarding the dangerous potential of the media to be used for illegal incitement:

> Particular caution is called for when consideration is being given to the publication of the views of representatives of organisations which resort to violence against the State lest the media become a vehicle for the dissemination of hate speech and the promotion of violence. At the same time, where such views cannot be categorised as such, Contracting States cannot with reference to the protection of territorial integrity or national security or the prevention of crime or disorder restrict the right of the public to be informed of them by bringing the weight of the criminal law to bear on the media.[76]

Moreover, in a concurring opinion, five judges of the Court counseled against assigning too much weight to the form of the words used and emphasized instead the importance of the general context in which the words were uttered and their probable impact. The central issues put forward by the concurring opinion boiled down to: (1) "Was the language intended to inflame or incite to violence?" and (2) "Was there a real and genuine risk that it might actually do so?"[77]

In contrast, in the 1999 companion case of *Sürek v. Turkey (No. 1)*, the Court concluded that limitations on hate speech and the "glorification of violence" did not run afoul of Article 10.[78] The applicant here was the same as the lead applicant in the *Sürek and Özdemir* case. The impetus for Turkish officials prosecuting this time was the review's publishing two letters to the editor critical of Turkish authorities' actions in the country's troubled southeast region. The first letter carried the title "Weapons cannot win against freedom" and alluded to two massacres alleged to have been methodically carried out by Turkish officials as part of a genocidal campaign to remove the Kurds from the region. The letter then reaffirmed Kurdish resolve to throw off the Turkish yoke and referred to Turkish officials as a "murder gang."[79] The second letter was styled "It is our fault," and it claimed that Turkish authorities, again characterized as a "murder gang," conspired to imprison, torture, and kill dissidents with the supposed goal of protecting democracy and the Republic.[80] As a result of these letters being published, Sürek was convicted of disseminating separatist propaganda under the Prevention of Terrorism Act of 1999, and thus he petitioned the European system alleging violation of his free speech rights under the ECHR.

As always, the first two criteria of the Article 10(2) test were checked off routinely, and the core of the Court's analysis lay in applying the "necessary in a democratic society" criterion. Here, the Court observed that the letters had the

76. *Id.* ¶ 63.

77. *Id.* Joint Concurring Opinion of Judges Palm, Tulkens, Fischbach, Casadevall, and Greve.

78. Sürek v. Turkey (No. 1), 1999-IV Eur. Ct. H.R. 353, 355.

79. *Id.* ¶ 11.

80. *Id.*

obvious goal of vilifying government officials via phrases such as "the Fascist Turkish army" and "the TC murder gang," along with words like "massacres" and "slaughter."[81] The inflammatory rhetoric of the letters, the Court added, amounted to "an appeal to bloody revenge by stirring up base emotions and hardening already embedded prejudices which have manifested themselves in deadly violence."[82] The Court also focused on the fact that the letters were published within the context of a grave national security crisis in southeast Turkey, the locus of Kurdish violent clashes and Turkish emergency rule.[83] With that backdrop in mind, the Court viewed the letters as "capable of inciting to further violence in the region by instilling a deep-seated and irrational hatred against those depicted as responsible for the alleged atrocities."[84] As well, the Court called attention to the fact that one of the letters identified individuals by name, thus potentially subjecting them to violence. The Court also observed that while government interference is impermissible for discourse that merely shocks or offends, this case surpassed that threshold as it entailed hate speech and a "glorification of violence."[85]

The Court also addressed the issue of Sürek's responsibility as a shareholder of the company that owned the review publishing the letters—not as a writer or member of the editorial staff. It found his not being a journalist did not affect his liability:

> While it is true that the applicant did not personally associate himself with the views contained in the letters, he nevertheless provided their writers with an outlet for stirring up violence and hatred. The Court does not accept his argument that he should be exonerated from any criminal liability for the content of the letters on account of the fact that he only has a commercial and not an editorial relationship with the review. He was an owner and as such had the power to shape the editorial direction of the review. For that reason, he was vicariously subject to the "duties and responsibilities," which the review's editorial and journalistic staff undertake in the collection and dissemination of information to the public and which assume an even greater importance in situations of conflict and tension.[86]

iv. Zana v. Turkey

The final Turkish case to consider from this series, *Zana v. Turkey* (1997),[87] takes the side of the government and seems to have informed the teaching of *Sürek*

81. *Id.* ¶ 62.

82. *Id.*

83. *Id.*

84. *Id.*

85. *Id.*

86. *Id.* ¶ 63.

87. Zana v. Turkey, 1997-VII Eur. Ct. H.R. 2533.

(No. 1). Like *Sürek (No. 1)*, the *Zana* Court ruled that free expression rights could be curtailed when the speech at issue would likely exacerbate an already tense security situation in southeast Turkey. However, somewhat different from Sürek's role as media company shareholder, Zana, a leader in the former Workers' Party of Turkey (TIP) and supporter of the Kurdistan Workers' Party (PKK), had served as the former mayor of Diyarkabir, the largest city in the Kurdish region of Turkey.[88] After the 1980 military coup in Turkey, Zana had been imprisoned, without being formally charged, as a Kurdish leader at a time when the government was trying to squash the budding Kurdish independence movement.[89] While incarcerated, he made the following remarks to journalists: "I support the PKK national liberation movement; on the other hand, I am not in favour of massacres. Anyone can make mistakes, and the PKK kill women and children by mistake . . ."[90] These remarks were published in the national daily newspaper and coincided with the killing of civilians by PKK militants.[91] Turkey's National Security Court found Zana guilty of violating the Criminal Code's prohibition on public incitement to hatred and hostility and its ban on belonging to armed groups or organizations.[92]

In reviewing the case, the European Court of Human Rights quickly dispensed with the first two Article 10(2) criteria employing the same analysis it had for the other Turkish national security incitement cases already examined—the criminal code section was easily identified and a public safety motivation was cited.[93] The Court then parsed Zana's statements to decide if the imposed speech restriction was necessary in a democratic society. It found that Zana's statements were inconsistent and ambiguous.[94] For example, Zana supported the PKK, a terrorist organization, but opposed massacres. Similarly, he disapproved of the massacre of women and children but also suggested that these were mistakes that anyone could make. What was most significant for the Court, however, was the fact that Zana's statements "coincided with murderous attacks carried out by the PKK on civilians in south-east Turkey."[95] Given that Zana was the former mayor of Diyarkabir, his supporting the PKK might be seen "as likely to exacerbate an already explosive situation" in the region. As a result, the Court found that Zana's conviction arose from a "pressing social need" and was proportionate to a legitimate aim.[96]

88. *Id.* ¶ 9.

89. Alan D. Cooper, The Geography of Genocide 224 (2009).

90. *Zana, supra* note 87, para. 12.

91. *Id.* ¶¶ 12, 50.

92. *Id.* ¶¶ 27, 51.

93. *Id.* ¶¶ 37, 41.

94. *Id.* ¶ 58.

95. *Id.* ¶ 59.

96. *Id.* ¶¶ 61, 62.

III. PROTECTION OF FREE SPEECH VS. REGULATION OF HATE SPEECH AT THE DOMESTIC LEVEL

In municipal jurisdictions, the degrees of protection of free speech versus regulation of hate speech can be charted along a spectrum, which is very speech tolerant at one end and much more restrictive at the other. The strongest bastion of speech protection is the United States legal system and Japan is not far behind. Alone among the wealthy liberal democracies of the world, neither of these countries has incorporated into its domestic statutes the anti–hate speech provisions of ICCPR Article 20(2) and ICERD Article 4. As well, the United States has signed these treaties subject to reservations regarding both of these provisions. What this means in terms of the domestic laws regarding hate speech in the United States and Japan will now be considered.

A. States that Have Not Incorporated ICCPR Article 20(2) and ICERD Article 4

1. The United States

a. The American Philosophy of Vigorous Speech Protection

The First Amendment to the US Constitution provides that the government may "make no law . . . abridging the freedom of speech, or of the press."[97] But what does this mean in practice? The nature and extent of the protection has been fleshed out and has evolved in a series of judicial opinions stretching back to the beginning of the twentieth century. Its underlying philosophy was expressed by Justice Oliver Wendell Holmes in his famous dissent in *Abrams v. United States*.[98] Holmes explained that the public communications space in the United States can be analogized to a "marketplace of ideas."[99] This is tantamount to an open discussion environment, where speakers offer competing ideas that vie for listener acceptance—with the supposition that the truth will emerge as the ideas are vetted against one another. Thus, the United States looks to freedom of expression, rather than suppression, to bring to light problematic ideas, banish or weaken them, and in the process reinforce democracy. Channeling the logic of John Milton's *Areopagitica* (1644) and John Stuart Mill's *On Liberty* (1859), Holmes encapsulated this philosophy in his seminal dissent:

> But when men have realized that time has upset many fighting faiths, they may come to believe even more than they believe the very foundations of their own conduct that the ultimate good desired is better reached by free trade in ideas—that the best test of truth is the power of the thought to get itself

97. U.S. Const. amend I.

98. Abrams v. United States, 250 U.S. 616 (1919).

99. *Id.* at 630.

> accepted in the competition of the market. . . . That at any rate is the theory of our Constitution. It is an experiment, as all life is an experiment.[100]

Taking a broader view, First Amendment scholar Thomas Emerson has identified four separate but interlinking rationales for America's vigorous protection of free speech rights: (1) the desire for self-fulfillment; (2) the advancement of truth; (3) social participation, in order to build "the whole culture"; and (4) the creation of a "stable community."[101] Professor Michel Rosenfeld offers four similar philosophical justifications, but slightly different in nuance, for America's free speech model: (1) the justification from democracy (without the freedom to convey and receive ideas, citizens cannot successfully carry out the task of democratic self-government); (2) the justification from social contract (in order to opt into the social contract (i.e., the establishment of the democracy), all citizens must be able to express their viewpoints to understand what is accepted and not accepted as part of the contractual relationship); (3) the justification from the pursuit of truth (discovery of truth is an incremental empirical process that relies on trial and error and that requires uninhibited discussion—essentially, the marketplace of ideas); and (4) the justification from personal autonomy (a rationale that is concerned with the self-expression/personal growth needs of individual speakers).[102]

Underlying these justifications is an even deeper existential link between maximum freedom for speech and the libertarian nature of the American psyche. As explained by Professor Rosenfeld:

> Freedom of speech is not only the most cherished American constitutional right, but also one of America's foremost cultural symbols. Moreover, the prominence of free speech in the United States is due to many different factors, including a strong preference for liberty over equality, commitment to individualism, and a natural rights tradition derived from Locke which champions freedom from the state—or negative freedom—over freedom through the state—or positive freedom. In essence, free speech rights in the United States are conceived as belonging to the individual against the state, and they are enshrined in the First Amendment to the Constitution as a prohibition against government interference, rather than as the imposition of a positive duty on government to guarantee the receipt and transmission of ideas among its citizens. Indeed, Americans have a deep seated belief in free speech as a virtually unlimited good and a strong fear that an active government in the area of speech will much more likely result in harm than in good.[103]

100. *Id.*

101. Thomas I. Emerson, The System of Freedom of Expression 6–7 (1970).

102. Michel Rosenfeld, *Hate Speech in Constitutional Jurisprudence: A Comparative Analysis*, 24 Cardozo L. Rev. 1523, 1532–1535 (2001).

103. *Id.* at 1529–1530.

Implicit in Rosenfeld's understanding of the conceptual foundations of free speech in the United States is the notion that Americans cherish the idea of governing themselves. For the great First Amendment scholar Alexander Meiklejohn, this is the key philosophical foundation of the First Amendment.[104] He contended that, absent self-governing citizens with access to information about matters of civic concern, democracy flounders.[105] According to Meiklejohn:

> We the people who govern, must try to understand the issues which, incident by incident, face the nation. We must pass judgment upon the decisions which our government makes upon those issues. And, further, we must share in devising methods by which those decisions can be made wise and effective or, if need be, supplanted by others which promise greater wisdom and effectiveness.[106]

b. The Evolution of the US Free Speech Legal Regime

Nevertheless, the robust protection offered public expression of inimical ideas in the United States was developed only gradually. During the early 1900s, the US Supreme Court struggled to define the boundaries of the First Amendment's free speech guarantee as it variously applied two competing tests—the more regulation-friendly "bad tendency" test, which gauged whether speech was permissible in reference to its tendency to yield criminal conduct and the more speech-protective "clear and present danger" test, which allowed restrictions only if speech presented a clear and present danger to the public order.

i. The Bad Tendency Test

In 1907, the Court first articulated the "bad tendency" test in *Patterson v. Colorado*.[107] In that case, with Justice Oliver Wendell Holmes writing for the majority, the Court upheld the contempt conviction of a newspaper editor who had questioned the impartiality of Colorado judges by linking them with local utility companies. Holmes noted that the First Amendment forbids "previous restraints" on publications but allows "the subsequent punishment of such as may be deemed contrary to the public welfare . . ."[108] He went on to opine that a publication impugning judicial integrity "would tend to obstruct the administration of justice."[109] Terry Eastland explains that "the Court was simply acknowledging

104. Matthew D. Bunker, Critiquing Free Speech: First Amendment Theory and the Challenge of Interdisciplinarity 9 (2001).

105. *Id.*

106. Alexander Meiklejohn, *The First Amendment Is an Absolute*, 1961 Sup. Ct. Rev. 245, 255 (1961).

107. Patterson v. Colorado, 255 U.S. 454 (1907).

108. *Id.* at 462.

109. *Id.* (emphasis added).

the continued validity of 'the bad tendency test'. . . . Part of the English common law of libel, which had been adopted in eighteenth century America, the test measured the legality of speech by its tendency to produce an illegal action."[110] Wilbur Miller describes this as a relatively "looser" test, under which, the "state did not have to prove that any illegal action resulted from the speech but merely demonstrate that the speech might have a tendency to cause illegal activity."[111]

ii. The Clear and Present Danger Test

Twelve years later, Justice Holmes formulated an alternative standard: the "clear and present danger" test. In *Schenck v. United States* (1919),[112] as the United States was fighting in World War I, the defendant, the general secretary of the American Socialist Party, produced and handed out 15,000 leaflets urging draftees to refuse conscription into the US armed forces.[113] Schenck was found guilty of violating, *inter alia*, the Espionage Act.[114] On appeal to the Supreme Court, he argued that his pamphlet communications were protected by the First Amendment.

Justice Holmes, authoring the majority opinion, acknowledged that "in ordinary times the defendants in saying all that was said in the circular would have been within their constitutional rights."[115] But he went on to stress the central role of context in evaluating the legality of problematic speech.[116] To illustrate, he famously postulated that even the "most stringent protection of free speech would not shield from liability a man who falsely shouted fire in a theatre and thereby caused a panic."[117] With this in mind, he explained that speech restrictions would be permissible only when "the words used are used in such circumstances and are of such a nature as to create a clear and present danger that they will bring about the substantive evils that Congress has a right to prevent."[118] Holmes went on to qualify this "clear and present danger" test by specifying that the issue is "[one] of proximity and degree."[119] In other words, in periods of heightened national security concerns, speech can be legally proscribed even though it might not be subject to censorship during more tranquil times.

110. Terry Eastland, Freedom of Expression in the Supreme Court: The Defining Cases, Introduction xxiii (2000).

111. Wilbur R. Miller, The Social History of Crime and Punishment in America (2012).

112. Schenck v. United States, 249 U.S. 47 (1919).

113. *Id.* at 49–51.

114. *Id.* at 48–49.

115. *Id.* at 52.

116. *Id.*

117. *Id.*

118. *Id.* at 52.

119. *Id.*

Later that year, in his dissent in *Abrams*, Justice Holmes elaborated on the contours of the clear and present danger test. In that case, by a 7–2 vote, the majority of the Court affirmed the conviction of five Russian anarchists, including the named defendant.[120] Justice John H. Clarke, writing for the majority, relied on the "bad tendency" test in ruling against the petitioners.[121] But in dissenting, Justice Holmes, joined by Justice Louis D. Brandeis, employed his newly minted clear and present danger test—this time with greater force. He specified that the government may criminalize speech only if it is "intended to produce a clear and imminent danger" and "it is only the present danger of immediate evil or an intent to bring it about" that confers on the government the authority to punish the speaker.[122]

Although this new standard was more speech-protective than the "bad tendency" test, it was still largely susceptible to government efforts to stifle speech. As Erin Guyton notes: "The clear and present danger test is a very broad, abstract standard to which proposed restrictions could easily be tailored."[123] And, in any event, over the next few years, the test was mostly shunted to the side while the Court continued to apply the "bad tendency" test.[124]

iii. Alternating between the Danger and Tendency Tests

For example, the bad tendency test was used in *Gitlow v. New York* (1925),[125] where a member of the "Left Wing Faction" of the Socialist Party of America was convicted of criminal anarchy under New York's Criminal Anarchy Law of 1902. The conviction stemmed from Gitlow's publishing a July 1919 tract titled the "Left Wing Manifesto" in *The Revolutionary Age*, a newspaper whose business manager was none other than Gitlow himself.[126] The Court affirmed Gitlow's conviction on the grounds that the government may suppress or punish speech that directly advocates the unlawful overthrow of the government. Justice Edward Terry Sanford's majority opinion embraced the bad tendency test, holding that "the general provisions of the statute may be constitutionally applied to the specific utterance of the defendant if its natural tendency and probable effect was to bring about the substantive evil which the legislative body

120. Abrams, 250 U.S. at 616.

121. *Id.* at 624.

122. *Id.* at 627 (Holmes, J., dissenting).

123. Erin D. Guyton, Comment, *Tweeting "Fire" in a Crowded Theater: Distinguishing between Advocacy and Incitement in the Social Media World*, 82 Miss. L.J. 689, 694 (2013).

124. In fact, a number of other cases involving prosecutions under the Espionage Act during World War I upheld convictions despite appeals on First Amendment grounds. *See, e.g.*, Frohwerk v. United States, 249 U.S. 204 (1919) (publication of twelve newspaper articles attacking the war); Debs v. United States, 249 U.S. 211 (1919) (single speech attacking United States' participation in the war); Schaefer v. United States, 251 U.S. 466 (1920) (publication of German language newspaper with allegedly false articles, critical of capitalism and the war).

125. Gitlow v. New York, 268 U.S. 652 (1925).

126. *Id.* at 655–656.

might prevent."[127] As Justice Sanford saw it: a "single revolutionary spark may kindle a fire that, smoldering for a time, may burst into a sweeping and destructive conflagration."[128] In dissent, Justice Holmes urged reliance on the clear and present danger test. And he used Justice Sanford's fire metaphor against him, noting that "eloquence may set fire to reason, but, whatever may be thought of the redundant discourse before us, it had no chance of starting a present conflagration."[129]

The Court applied the bad tendency test again in the 1927 case of *Whitney v. California*.[130] There, it upheld the conviction of the petitioner, a niece of former Supreme Court Justice Stephen Field. Her conviction under California's syndicalism law stemmed from her work in helping establish the Communist Labor Party of America.[131] Writing for the Court in support of California's position, Justice Edward Sandford held that the state may punish speech that is "tending to incite to crime."[132] In a famous concurrence, Justice Brandeis, joined by Justice Holmes, provided further conceptual succor to liberty of expression by concretizing Justice Holmes's more abstract "marketplace of ideas" trope. In attempting to flesh out the clear and present danger test, he linked the value of free speech with the healthy functioning of the democratic process.[133] In other words, to sustain meaningful democratic institutions, he indicated, citizens must be able to speak about and criticize the government without fear of retribution. In the immortal words of Justice Brandeis:

> Those who won our independence believed that the final end of the state was to make men free to develop their faculties, and that in its government the deliberative forces should prevail over the arbitrary. They valued liberty both as an end and as a means. They believed liberty to be the secret of happiness and courage to be the secret of liberty. They believed that freedom to think as you will and to speak as you think are means indispensable to the discovery and spread of political truth; that without free speech and assembly, discussion would be futile; that with them, discussion affords ordinarily adequate protection against the dissemination of noxious doctrine; that the greatest menace to freedom is an inert people; that public discussion is a political duty; and that this should be a fundamental principle of the American government.[134]

127. *Id.* at 671.

128. *Id.* at 669.

129. *Id.* at 673 (Holmes, J., dissenting)

130. Whitney v. California, 274 U.S. 357 (1927).

131. *Id.* at 364–365.

132. *Id.* at 371.

133. *Id.* at 375.

134. *Id.* at 375 (Brandeis, J., concurring).

As well, implicitly, Justice Brandeis moved beyond the clear and present danger test and indirectly formulated what has been called the "time to answer test": no danger flowing from speech can be considered clear and present if there is full opportunity for discussion. As expressed by Brandeis:

> Those who won our independence by revolution were not cowards. They did not fear political change. They did not exalt order at the cost of liberty. To courageous, self-reliant men, with confidence in the power of free and fearless reasoning applied through the processes of popular government, no danger flowing from speech can be deemed clear and present, unless the incidence of the evil apprehended is so imminent that it may befall before there is opportunity for full discussion. If there be time to expose through discussion the falsehood and fallacies, to avert the evil by the processes of education, the remedy to be applied is more speech, not enforced silence. Only an emergency can justify repression. Such must be the rule if authority is to be reconciled with freedom. Such, in my opinion, is the command of the Constitution. It is therefore always open to Americans to challenge a law abridging free speech and assembly by showing that there was no emergency justifying it.[135]

By 1951, however, the clear and present danger test had gained ascendency over the bad tendency test. But it still lacked teeth and proved vulnerable to aggressive government speech regulation, as demonstrated in *Dennis v. United States*.[136] During the early Cold War's draconian national security regime, and at the height of McCarthyism, Eugene Dennis, along with other high-ranking American Communist Party (CPUSA) leaders, were convicted of violating the Smith Act, which criminalized advocating the violent overthrow of the government or organizing/belonging to any group devoted to such advocacy.[137] Their convictions were based on their CPUSA membership and leadership status.

In prosecuting the defendants, the government did not allege that they were specifically plotting the violent overthrow of the government. Instead, the gravamen of the government's case was that it was an underlying goal of the CPUSA to violently overthrow noncommunist governments in general.[138] And the Court found that overarching motive sufficient to satisfy the clear and present danger test, holding that "that the words [clear and present danger] cannot mean that before the Government may act, it must wait until the putsch is about to be executed ... [if] the government is aware that a group aiming at its overthrow is attempting to indoctrinate its members and to commit them to a course whereby

135. *Id.* at 377.

136. Dennis v. United States, 341 U.S. 494 (1951).

137. Arthur H. Garrison, Supreme Court Jurisprudence in Times of National Crisis, Terrorism, and War: A Historical Perspective 179 (2011).

138. *Dennis*, 341 U.S. 494 at 509–510.

they will strike when the leaders feel the circumstances permit, action by the Government is required."[139]

iv. Brandenburg *and The Imminent Lawless Action Test*

The absence of imminence as a consideration in applying the clear and present danger test—so apparent in *Dennis*—is what prompted the Court to modify the test in the years that followed. *Yates v. United States* (1957)[140] was a harbinger of what was to come. In that case, fourteen lower-ranking CPUSA leaders were convicted of violating the Smith Act. The Court overturned the convictions, finding the Smith Act did not apply to mere "abstract doctrine of forcible overthrow, but of action to that end, by the use of language reasonably and ordinarily calculated to incite persons to such action."[141] Vis-à-vis *Dennis*, then, by implication, *Yates* "partially restored imminence" to the Holmes-Brandeis conception of the clear and present danger test.[142] In its next major First Amendment case in this area, the landmark decision of *Brandenburg v. Ohio* (1969),[143] the Court dispensed with this imprecise test altogether.

In *Brandenburg*, a Ku Klux Klan leader was appealing on First Amendment grounds his conviction under the Ohio Criminal Syndicalism statute for advocating violent means to effect political change. During a nighttime rally in an isolated area attended only by fellow Klansmen and a local television reporter (invited by the defendant and filming the event), Brandenburg addressed the gathering as the reporter recorded it with his motion picture camera. In the resulting film that was later shown in court as evidence, twelve hooded figures, some armed, could be seen.[144] The Klan members burned a cross and then Brandenburg gave a speech. He made derogatory and threatening remarks regarding Jews and African-Americans, including "Bury the niggers."[145] He then went on to say:

> This is an organizers' meeting. We have had quite a few members here today.... The Klan has more members in the State of Ohio than does any other organization. We're not a revengent organization, but if our President, our Congress, our Supreme Court, continues to suppress the white, Caucasian race, it's possible that there might have to be some revengeance taken. We are marching on Congress July the Fourth, four hundred thousand strong.[146]

139. *Id.* at 509.

140. Yates v. United States, 354 U.S. 298 (1957).

141. *Id.* at 316.

142. Jerome A. Barron & C. Thomas Dienes, First Amendment Law in a Nutshell, 76 (4th ed. 2008).

143. Brandenburg v. Ohio, 395 U.S. 444 (1969).

144. *Id.* at 445–446.

145. *Id.* at 446.

146. *Id.*

With this factual backdrop, the Court considered the legality of Ohio's Criminal Syndicalism statute against Brandenburg's First Amendment challenge. It began by alluding to *Whitney* (1927), which had sustained a conviction under a very similar California law.[147] The *Brandenburg* Court emphasized that *Whitney* "upheld the statute on the ground that, without more, 'advocating' violent means to effect political and economic change involves such danger to the security of the State that the State may outlaw it."[148] It then noted that *Whitney* had been "thoroughly discredited by later decisions."[149]

And that was its segue to announce a new test for deciding First Amendment advocacy cases: "[Constitutional] guarantees of free speech and free press do not permit a State to forbid or proscribe advocacy of the use of force or of law violation except where such advocacy is directed to inciting or producing imminent lawless action and is likely to incite or produce such action."[150] This "imminent lawless action" test, pursuant to which Brandenburg's conviction was overturned, finally restricted the government to the punishment of "direct incitement" and "instituted the immediacy requirement that [the US Supreme Court] had been building toward for decades."[151]

c. The Exceptions: Fighting Words, True Threats, and Group Libel

Through *Brandenburg*, the United States had promulgated the world's most speech-protective legal regime for repugnant advocacy. And that regime is still in place. But it is not without limitations. In particular, for our purposes, there are three categories of speech exempt from the advocacy shield of modern American free expression jurisprudence: fighting words, threats, and group libel.

i. Fighting Words

The US Supreme Court's "fighting words" rule was initially formulated in *Chaplinsky v. New Hampshire* (1942).[152] The defendant in that case, a Jehovah's Witness, had been convicted of violating a state law that forbade the use of offensive language against individuals in public places.[153] Chaplinsky had been distributing his sect's literature on the streets when he encountered a local law enforcement official who informed him that many citizens were complaining about him and suggested a riot could ensue.[154] The defendant then uttered the words that were the basis of his criminal charge and conviction: "You are a God

147. *Id.* at 447 (citing *Whitney*, 274 U.S. at 357).

148. *Id.*

149. *Id.*

150. *Id.*

151. Guyton, *supra* note 123, at 705.

152. Chaplinsky v. New Hampshire, 315 U.S. 568 (1942).

153. *Id.* at 569.

154. *Id.* at 569–570.

damned racketeer and a damned Fascist and the whole government of Rochester are Fascists or agents of Fascists."[155] On appeal to the Supreme Court, he argued that the government's case against him violated, *inter alia*, his First Amendment free speech rights.

Justice Frank Murphy wrote the opinion for a unanimous Court and rejected Chaplinsky's liberty of expression argument. He stated that "the right to free speech is not absolute at all times and under all circumstances."[156] He then described certain categories of expression that are not entitled to constitutional protection, including "the lewd and obscene, the profane, the libelous, and the insulting or 'fighting words.'"[157] He went on to define "fighting words" as "those which by their very utterance inflict injury or tend to incite an immediate breach of the peace."[158] They are exempt from the First Amendment because they "are no essential part of any exposition of ideas, and are of such slight social value as a step to truth that any benefit that may be derived from them is clearly outweighed by the social interest in order and morality."[159] In his dissent in *Rosenfeld v. New Jersey* (1972) Justice Lewis Powell described this mode of expression as "the willful use of scurrilous language calculated to offend the sensibilities of an unwilling audience."[160]

Nevertheless, *Chaplinsky*'s reach is rather limited as it does not cover offensive speech in general. In *Cohen v. California* (1972), a man who, while in a courthouse, wore a jacket with the words "Fuck the Draft" emblazoned on it was convicted of disturbing the peace by "offensive conduct."[161] In overturning the conviction, the US Supreme Court found that the phrase on the defendant's jacket did not constitute "fighting words" as it was "'clearly not directed to the person of the hearer,'"[162] and those in the courthouse "could effectively avoid further bombardment of their sensibilities simply by averting their eyes."[163] The Court concluded that, in bringing this case, local officials were attempting to act "as guardians of public morality."[164] And in this regard, they violated the First

155. *Id.* at 569.

156. *Id.*

157. *Id.* at 571–572.

158. *Id.* at 572.

159. *Id.* Murphy then found that the statute at issue had a legitimate aim—to preserve public peace—and was narrowly limited to specific conduct within the state power. And the words "damned racketeer" and "damned fascist" were likely to provoke retaliation in the person, causing a breach of the peace. *Id.* at 574. Thus, the statute and its application in that case passed constitutional muster.

160. Rosenfeld v. New Jersey, 408 U.S. 901, 905 (1972) (Powell, J., dissenting).

161. Cohen v. California, 403 U.S. 15, 16 (1971).

162. *Id.* at 20 (citing Cantwell v. Connecticut, 310 U.S. 296, 309 (1940)).

163. *Id.* at 21.

164. *Id.* at 22.

Amendment's guarantee of free expression by attempting to remove the jacket's offensive phrase "from the public vocabulary."[165] For, in the words of the Court "one man's vulgarity is another's lyric."[166] Additionally, and perhaps most significantly, the Court felt the conviction could not stand as it might help undermine the effective functioning of the marketplace of ideas: "[We] cannot indulge the facile assumption that one can forbid particular words without also running a substantial risk of suppressing ideas in the process."[167]

Chaplinsky's scope was further limited by *R.A.V. v. City of St. Paul, Minn.* (1992).[168] In that case, a group of teenagers allegedly burned a cross inside the fenced front lawn of the home of an African-American family, who lived across the street from where the petitioner was staying.[169] The petitioner was charged with violating a local bias-motivated criminal ordinance that prohibited the display of a symbol that aroused "anger, alarm or resentment in others on the basis of race, color, creed, religion or gender."[170] The local court dismissed the charge, the Minnesota Supreme Court reversed, and R. A. V. appealed to the US Supreme Court.[171]

In considering the case, the Court had to decide, *inter alia*, whether the ordinance fit into the "fighting words" category of First Amendment exemption.[172] R. A. V. argued that *Chaplinsky* should be read so as not to give constitutional sanction to the St. Paul ordinance on the grounds that it was "substantially overbroad."[173] But Justice Antonin Scalia, writing for the Court, did not rule on these grounds, concluding instead that even if all of the expression reached by the ordinance could be prosecuted as "fighting words," the ordinance was nevertheless facially unconstitutional given that it attempted to regulate fighting words on a selective basis.[174] As reasoned by Justice Scalia:

> Although the phrase in the ordinance, "arouses anger, alarm or resentment in others," has been limited by the Minnesota Supreme Court's construction to reach only those symbols or displays that amount to "fighting words," the remaining, unmodified terms make clear that the ordinance applies only to

165. *Id.* at 23.

166. *Id.* at 25.

167. *Id.* at 26. *See also* R.A.V. v. St. Paul, 505 U.S. 377, 414 (1992) (White, J., concurring) ("The mere fact that expressive activity causes hurt feelings, offense, or resentment does not render the expression unprotected.").

168. R.A.V. v. City of St. Paul, Minn., 505 U.S. 377 (1992).

169. *Id.* at 379–380.

170. *Id.* at 380.

171. *Id.* at 380–381.

172. *Id.* at 381.

173. *Id.*

174. *Id.*

> "fighting words" that insult, or provoke violence, "on the basis of race, color, creed, religion or gender." Displays containing abusive invective, no matter how vicious or severe, are permissible unless they are addressed to one of the specified disfavored topics. Those who wish to use "fighting words" in connection with other ideas—to express hostility, for example, on the basis of political affiliation, union membership, or homosexuality—are not covered. The First Amendment does not permit St. Paul to impose special prohibitions on those speakers who express views on disfavored subjects.[175]

ii. True Threats

The First Amendment also allows the government to prohibit "true threats." In *Watts v. United States* (1969),[176] the defendant was prosecuted for threatening the life of President Lyndon Johnson. As part of a small discussion group that broke off from a larger protest against police brutality near the Washington Monument in the nation's capital, the defendant, who was eighteen-years-old and had just been drafted into the military during the Vietnam War, stated: "If they ever make me carry a rifle the first man I want to get in my sights is L.B.J."[177] On the basis of the defendant's statement, a jury convicted him of the crime charged. The defendant petitioned to the US Supreme Court on First Amendment grounds, and the Court overturned the conviction. It found that the "political hyperbole" defendant engaged in must be distinguished from "true threats," which can be constitutionally criminalized.[178]

In *Virginia v. Black* (2003),[179] the Supreme Court specified the nature of "true threats":

> ["True threats"] encompass those statements where the speaker means to communicate a serious expression of an intent to commit an act of unlawful

175. *Id.* at 391. The case generated two concurring opinions. One by Justice Byron White, joined by three others, stressed that the majority opinion had complicated an otherwise simple case. He found the ordinance too broad because the capacity of speech to cause "hurt feelings, offense or resentment" does not render it unprotected. *Id.* at 414 (White, J., concurring). In a separate concurrence, Justice Blackmun expressed fear that the Court had been "distracted from its proper mission by the temptation to decide the issue over 'politically correct speech' and 'cultural diversity.'"

Id. at 415–416 (Blackmun, J., concurring). Justice Blackmun explained that neither of these factors was germane and the Court merely manipulated doctrine to avoid acknowledging that some fighting words are more deleterious for society than others. *Id.* at 415. In other words, lawmakers should have been permitted to focus on racially bigoted fighting words for special regulatory treatment. *Id.* Still, he agreed with Justice White that this particular ordinance reached beyond fighting words to speech protected by the First Amendment. *Id.* at 416.

176. Watts v. United States, 394 U.S. 705 (1969).

177. *Id.* at 705–706.

178. *Id.* at 708.

179. Virginia v. Black, 538 U.S. 343 (2003).

> violence to a particular individual or group of individuals. The speaker need not actually intend to carry out the threat. Rather, a prohibition on true threats protects individuals from the fear of violence and the disruption that fear engenders, as well as from the possibility that the threatened violence will occur. Intimidation in the constitutionally proscribable sense of the word is a type of true threat, where a speaker directs a threat to a person or group of persons with the intent of placing the victim in fear of bodily harm or death.[180]

In *Black*, the Supreme Court upheld a state statute that criminalized cross burning, if committed "with the intent of intimidating any person or group of persons."[181] The statute also provided that "[a]ny such burning of a cross shall be prima facie evidence of intent to intimidate a person or group of persons."[182] The Court, in an opinion authored by Justice Sandra Day O'Connor, extensively reviewed the history of cross burning in the United States and its longstanding link to intimidation of and violence against African-Americans by the Ku Klux Klan.[183] In upholding the statute, Justice O'Connor considered cross burning, although nonverbal, to be symbolic or expressive speech that constituted "true threats."[184] She went on to note that "[r]espondents do not contest that some cross burnings fit within this meaning of intimidating speech, and rightly so . . . the history of cross burning in this country shows that cross burning is often intimidating, intended to create a pervasive fear in victims that they are a target of violence."[185]

Moreover, Justice O'Connor found that the statute at issue was distinguishable from the one in *R.A.V v. City of St. Paul* because it did not implicate viewpoint discrimination—it punished all those who burned crosses with the intent to intimidate others.[186] It did not single out those, for example, whose intent was to intimidate based on race, gender, or religion. However, Justice O'Connor concluded that the "prima facie evidence" portion of the Virginia statute in *Black* was unconstitutional because it permitted prosecution solely on the basis of the cross burning itself, without reference to required extrinsic evidence of intent.[187]

iii. Group Libel

The other exempted category of speech is group libel. In *Beauharnais v. Illinois* (1952),[188] the Supreme Court upheld an Illinois law making it illegal to publish or

180. *Black*, 538 U.S. at 344.

181. *Id.* at 348.

182. *Id.*

183. *Id.* at 352–357.

184. *Id.* at 359–360.

185. *Id.* at 360.

186. *Id.* at 363.

187. *Id.* at 345–346.

188. Beauharnais v. Illinois, 343 U.S. 250 (1952).

exhibit any writing or picture portraying the "depravity, criminality, unchastity, or lack of virtue of a class of citizens of any race, color, creed or religion" and "exposes" them to "contempt, derision, obloquy, or which is productive of breach of the peace or riots."[189] The defendant was convicted of violating this law in connection with passing out leaflets "calling on the Mayor and City Council [of Chicago, Illinois] . . . to halt the further encroachment, harassment and invasion of white people, their property, neighborhoods and persons, by the Negro."[190]

The Court rejected Beauharnais's First Amendment challenge of the conviction. Writing for the Court, Justice Felix Frankfurter's opinion supported the Illinois statute based on twin rationales: (1) preventing violence and disorder;[191] and (2) proscribing libel, which is outside the ambit of First Amendment protection, even if directed against groups as opposed to individuals.[192] With respect to the statute's first rationale, Justice Frankfurter powerfully noted that "Illinois did not have to look beyond her own borders or await the tragic experience of the last three decades to conclude that willful purveyors of falsehood concerning racial and religious groups promote strife and tend powerfully to obstruct the manifold adjustments required for free, ordered life in a metropolitan polyglot community."[193]

Regarding the second identified rationale, Justice Frankfurter observed that it would be "arrant dogmatism" to deny that the government "may warrantably believe that a man's job and his educational opportunities and the dignity accorded him may depend as much on the reputation of the racial and religious groups to which he willy-nilly belongs, as on his own merits."[194] As a result, he found that "we are precluded from saying that speech cannot be outlawed if directed at groups with whose position and esteem in society the affiliated individual may be inextricably involved."[195]

Nevertheless, while still technically good precedent, *Beauharnais*'s influence has been stunted.[196] In fact, a federal appeals court in the so-called "Skokie case," *Collin v. Smith* (1978),[197] has suggested it may no longer be good law. In *Collin*, American Nazi Party (NSPA) members sought to march in their swastika-embroidered uniforms through the eponymous town's central artery, even though the Chicago suburb was predominantly Jewish and was

189. *Id.* at 251 (quoting the statute).

190. *Id.* at 252 (quoting the defendant's leaflet).

191. *Id.* at 259.

192. *Id.* at 254–258.

193. *Id.* at 258–259.

194. *Id.* at 263.

195. *Id.*

196. *See* Rosenfeld, *supra* note 102, at 1536 ("Beauharnais has never been explicitly repudiated, but it has been thoroughly undermined by subsequent decisions.").

197. Collin v. Smith, 578 F.2d 1197 (1982).

home to a substantial number of Holocaust survivors.[198] The petitioner, an NSPA leader, argued before the US Court of Appeals for the Seventh Circuit that the Skokie ordinances cited by town officials to justify nonissuance of the marching permit violated the First Amendment. Countering this argument, town officials cited the *Beauharnais* decision in support of their denying the permits.

The Seventh Circuit rejected the town's argument, asserting that the underlying rationales of *Beauharnais*—preventing speech that has a tendency to produce violence and proscribing group libel—did not apply in the case before it.[199] It also noted that, in light of cases decided since *Beauharnais* was handed down in 1952, the latter is likely no longer good law. Those cases include *Brandenburg*,[200] whose imminent lawless action standard implicitly calls *Beauharnais*'s continued validity into question, and *New York Times v. Sullivan* (1964),[201] which accorded some constitutional protection to defamatory statements made against public figures (only those made with "actual malice" could be the subject of legal prohibition).[202]

2. Japan

Although traditionally a rigidly regulated and hierarchical society without a long history of free expression prerogatives for its citizens,[203] modern Japan has been deeply impacted by American constitutional values that were instilled

198. *Id.* at 1199.

199. *Id.* at 1204–1205. On the facts presented, the Seventh Circuit's reasoning seems quite specious. Although the US Supreme Court denied certiorari in *Collin*, Justice Harry Blackmun felt the Court should have accepted the case "because the issue was so important and because the Seventh Circuit's decision seemed to conflict with the Court's precedent established in *Beauharnais v. Illinois*. . . . Blackmun thought that the case presented an opportunity to consider the proper limits—if any—on the exercise of free speech where a proposed demonstration was 'overwhelmingly offensive' to local residents. 'It just might,' he wrote, 'fall into the same category as one's 'right' to 'cry 'fire' in a crowded theater." Del Dickson, The Supreme Court in Conference (1940–1985): The Private Discussions Behind Nearly 300 Supreme Court Decisions 333 n.128 (2001).

200. *Brandenburg*, 395 U.S. at 444.

201. New York Times v. Sullivan, 376 U.S. 254 (1964).

202. *See* Kent R. Middleton & William E. Lee, The Law of Public Communication: 2016 Update 123 (2016) ("In *New York Times v. Sullivan*, the U.S. Supreme Court ruled for the first time that the First Amendment protects the publication of false statements that may damage an individual's reputation.").

203. *See* Joseph C. H. Chai, An Economic History of Modern China 98 (2011) (noting that during feudal times "Japanese society was hierarchic and rigidly controlled."). *See also* Ray A. Moore & Donald L. Robinson, Partners for Democracy: Crafting the New Japanese State under MacArthur 139 (2002) (pointing out that in postfeudal Japan, during the period of the *meiji* restoration, there was great government control over the lives of Japanese citizens and no free speech rights).

during the post–World War II American occupation.[204] In particular, Japan's 1947 Constitution contains Article 21, which is modeled on the American First Amendment, and provides: "Freedom of assembly and association as well as speech, press and all other forms of expression are guaranteed. No censorship shall be maintained. . . ."[205]

That said, perhaps reflecting Japanese tradition, the free speech guarantee is not as ironclad as in the United States. Article 12 of the Japanese Constitution contains somewhat of a clawback clause stating that "the people . . . shall refrain from any abuse of these freedoms and rights and shall always be responsible for utilizing them for the public welfare."[206] In the American legal system, no comparable provision can be found qualifying the US First Amendment.[207]

But even with Article 12 potentially diluting the free expression guarantee somewhat, Japan has not, in practice, promulgated legislation to curb hate speech or taken any criminal or civil action against public purveyors of such rhetoric. Unfortunately, at the same time, the country has experienced a contemporary wave of "racial slurs and threats of violence against ethnic minorities [primarily of East Asian origin]."[208] Moreover, in recent years, there has been "hate speech directed at foreigners in Japan . . . creating concerns about human rights problems. . . ."[209]

In particular, persons of Korean heritage have been the object of a hate speech campaign by a xenophobic group called *Zaitokukai* with especially virulent attacks occurring in the city of Osaka.[210] In 2013, outside of Osaka, in the largely ethnic Korean neighborhood of Shin-Okubo in Tokyo, hundreds of *Zaitokukai* members and supporters called Koreans "cockroaches," shouted "Kill Koreans," and threatened to "throw them into the sea."[211] As Japan considered ways of dealing with the problem, commentators pointed out that the country lacked any anti–hate speech laws, either on a municipal or national level, to deal with the

204. *See* Moore & Robinson, *supra* note 203, at 335 (2002) (referring to Supreme Allied Commander Douglas MacArthur's "victory in leading Japan to affirm a Western-style constitution as the basis for its new regime . . .").

205. Nihonkoku Kenpō [Kenpō] [Constitution], art. 21 (Japan).

206. *Id.*

207. Dan Rosen, *Policing Political Speech: Japan's Mistrust of the Marketplace*, 22 Mich. St. Int'l L. Rev. 799, 812 (2014) (The US Constitution, by contrast, includes no such duty. The difference is significant.").

208. Eric Johnston, *Osaka's Assault on Ethnic Invective Stalls*, Japan Times (June 15, 2015), http://www.japantimes.co.jp/news/2015/06/15/national/osakas-assault-ethnic-invective-stalls/#.VmJrFnYrK00.

209. *Id.*

210. Eric Johnston, *Hate Speech May Lack Clear Definition but Kansai Trying to Squelch It*, Japan Times (June 15, 2015), http://www.japantimes.co.jp/news/2015/06/15/national/hate-speech-may-lack-clear-definition-kansai-trying-squelch/#.VmF1jXYrK00.

211. *Osaka Court Upholds Ruling Banning Anti-Korean Hate Speech Outside School*, Japan Today (July 9, 2014), http://www.japantoday.com/category/national/view/osaka-high-court-upholds-ruling-banning-anti-korean-hate-speech-outside-school.

problem (apart from general tort law).[212] In 2015, Osaka attempted to pass a penal anti–hate speech ordinance but it met with great opposition and was tabled.[213]

Nevertheless, in a rare successful legal challenge brought by victims (not the government), a local court ordered *Zaitokukai* members to pay twelve million yen in civil compensation for tortious conduct directed at a Kyoto school, whose students are ethnic Korean, in connection with the defendants subjecting the students to verbal abuse during demonstrations in 2009 and 2010.[214] The court held that the group's activities met the ICERD's definition of racial discrimination and was beyond the pale of protected speech.[215]

Still, the legal action was isolated, rare, and of limited scope—consisting of civil tort actions against individuals. And, problematically, "the option of [the] usual civil trial [in tort] [creates] more economic, mental and timely burden on the victims."[216] In general, there has been little to no successful litigation against disseminators of public hate rhetoric in postwar Japan.[217] Thus, the UN Committee on the Elimination of Racial Discrimination, which interprets and enforces the ICERD, to which Japan is a signatory,[218] has strongly urged Japan to adopt measures to deal with racial discrimination and hate speech.[219] In a 2014 report, it recommended Japan take a series of steps to combat incendiary rhetoric, including investigating and, where appropriate, prosecuting individuals (including public officials and politicians), as well as organizations, who disseminate such verbal vilification and incitement to hatred.[220]

It is fair to conclude, then, that Japan, perhaps more than any other wealthy industrialized nation except the United States, puts great stock in the value of free speech as necessary for a healthy polity. Ronald Krotoszynski Jr. points out

212. *Id.* (commenting on the absence of "specific national laws banning racial discrimination").

213. Eric Johnston, *Osaka's Assault on Ethnic Invective Stalls*, JAPAN TIMES, June 15, 2015.

214. *Id.*

215. *Id.* This ruling was subsequently affirmed by the Japanese Supreme Court. *Id.*

216. *See* NGO Network for the Elimination of Racial Discrimination Japan (ERD Net), NGO Report on the Issue of Hate Speech in Relation to the Issue No. 10 of the List of Issues adopted by the Human Rights Committee, CCPR/C/JPN/Q/6, http://imadr.org/wordpress/wp-content/uploads/2014/07/Hate-Speech-in-Japan_ERD-NET_Human-Rights-Committe_111th-session.pdf. ("The lack of such laws becomes highly problematic in cases of hate speech targeting a group as a whole, e.g. Koreans, without specifying certain individuals, as provisions in the Penal Code or Civil Code, if any, can only be applied to the cases of individuals or specific organizations"). And ERD Net notes that "civil trials [usually take] two to three years, while the victims have to cover all the costs relating to the trial and legal representation . . ." *Id.*

217. *Id.* (noting that because of the burdens on a plaintiff to bring a civil action connected to hate speech "there have been [few] cases of hate speech . . . brought. . . .").

218. Japan entered a reservation with respect to Articles 4 (a) and (b) of the ICERD. *See* Ivan Hare, *Extreme Speech under International and Regional Human Rights Standards*, *in* EXTREME SPEECH AND DEMOCRACY 72 n.46 (Ivan Hare & James Weinstein eds., 2009).

219. Comm. on Elimination of Racial Discrimination, Concluding Observations of the Committee on the Elimination of Racial Discrimination: Japan, ¶¶ 8, 11, U.N. Doc. CERD/C/JPN/CO/7-9 (Aug. 2, 2014).

220. *Id.* ¶ 11.

that Japan's "clear and coherent vision of freedom of expression" largely "embodies Alexander Meiklejohn's vision of freedom of speech as a necessary corollary of democratic self-governance."[221] As a result, per Krotoszynski:

> The Japanese Supreme Court seems to share many of the same theoretical insights about the role and importance of free speech that the United States Supreme Court has articulated over the past half century. The Supreme Court of Japan, for example, has framed free speech questions in terms immediately familiar to students of the [American] First Amendment, routinely linking free speech values with the project of democratic self-government.[222]

B. States with Laws Incorporating ICCPR Article 20(2) and ICERD Article 4

When surveying the hate speech legal landscape around the world, the American model, as embraced by Japan, is rather anomalous.[223] That paradigm has developed with individualism and libertarianism as its lodestar.[224] On the other hand, communitarian values and other principles such as honor, dignity, and respect for religion have animated the formulation of jurisprudence governing protection of free speech versus regulation of hate speech in other nonauthoritarian states.[225] All of those states have laws on the books providing criminal or civil redress for victims of hate speech in conformity with the international agreements previously considered (i.e., ICCPR Article 20(2) and ICERD Article 4).

But they cannot be categorized monolithically. In particular, the US neighbor to the north, Canada, has struck a more finely calibrated balance between preservation of liberty and protection from hate. This "middle-ground" jurisdiction will be considered first.

1. The Middle-Ground Approach: Canada

Like the United States, Canada provides strong constitutional protection for freedom of speech through Article 2(b) of its Charter of Rights and Freedoms, which was enacted in 1982. That provision guarantees freedom of expression as follows:

> Everyone has the following fundamental freedoms:
>
> [(b)] freedom of thought, belief, opinion and expression, including freedom of the press and other media of communication.[226]

221. Ronald J. Krotoszynski, Jr., The First Amendment in Cross-Cultural Perspective: A Comparative Analysis of the Freedom of Speech 179 (2006).

222. *Id.* at 140.

223. Rosenfeld, *supra* note 102, at 1541.

224. *Id.*

225. *Id.*

226. Can. Const. (Constitution Act, 1982) pt. I (Canadian Charter of Rights and Freedoms), § 2(b).

But this language is tempered by Section 1 of the Charter, which sets out general parameters for balancing competing citizens' rights and governmental interests. It declares: "The Canadian Charter of Rights and Freedoms guarantees the rights and freedoms set out in it subject only to such reasonable limits prescribed by law as can be demonstrably justified in a free and democratic society."[227] It is further qualified by Section 27, which provides that the Charter "be interpreted in a manner consistent with the preservation and enhancement of the multicultural heritage of Canadians."[228] And Canada has found that one of the "reasonable limits" to free expression, consistent with preserving and enhancing its multicultural heritage, is regulation of hate speech. Traditionally, the regulatory effort has had two separate branches—one criminal and one civil.

With respect to the civil, Section 13 of the country's Human Rights Act empowered the Canadian Human Rights Commission to deal with complaints regarding the communication of hate messages by telephone or on the Internet.[229] The Commission was concerned with ensuring equality and rooting out discrimination as opposed to meting out punishment and thereby promoting deterrence.[230] But free speech advocates in Canada, who were concerned this law exerted an unacceptable chilling effect on legitimate expression, were able to convince the Canadian legislature to repeal it in 2013.[231] So now, at the national level, only criminal sanctions remain.[232]

Their origins can be traced back to the late 1960s, when Canada experienced an upsurge in racist activity and resultant pressure on the federal government to criminalize related hate speech.[233] Thus, as of 1970, the Canadian Criminal

227. *Id.* pt. I, § 1.

228. *Id.*, § 27.

229. Canadian Human Rights Act, R.S.C., ch. H 6, § 13 (1985) [Repealed, 2013, c. 37, s. 2]. In addition, Section 3(1) of the CHRA defines "the prohibited grounds of discrimination [as] race, national or ethnic origin, colour, religion, age, sex, sexual orientation, marital status, family status, disability and conviction for which a pardon has been granted." *Id.* § 3(1).

230. Kathleen Mahoney, *Hate Speech, Equality and the State of Canadian Law*, 44 Wake Forest L. Rev. 321, 341 (2009).

231. Michael Woods, *Hate Speech No Longer Part of Canada's Human Rights Act*, National Post (June 27, 2013), http://news.nationalpost.com/news/canada/hate-speech-no-longer-part-of-canadas-human-rights-act.

232. However, laws similar to CHRA § 13 remain on the books at the provincial and territorial levels. *See* Mahoney, *supra* note 230, at 327 ("The human rights codes of Alberta, British Columbia, the Northwest Territories, and Saskatchewan include provisions similar to [Section 13 of the Canadian Human Rights Act], with some minor variations, including provisions that prohibit signs, notices, and other representations that are likely to expose the members of an identifiable group to hatred or contempt.").

233. John Manwaring, *Legal Regulation of Hate Propaganda in Canada*, *in* Striking a Balance: Hate Speech, Freedom of Expression and Non-Discrimination v (Sandra Coliver ed., 1992).

Code includes two sections penalizing hate speech: (1) Section 318 criminalizes advocacy of genocide;[234] and (2) Section 319 outlaws incitement to hatred against any identifiable group "where such incitement is likely to lead to a breach of the peace" (Section 319 (1)) and willful promotion of hatred against a group identifiable on the basis of color, race, religion, or ethnic origin "by communicating statements, other than in private conversation" (Section 319(2)).[235] It is notable that Section 319(2) does not include explicit reference to inciting to violence.

The constitutionality of this provision was challenged in the leading case of *Regina v. Keegstra*.[236] The defendant there, a high school teacher in Eckville, Alberta, was prosecuted for unlawfully promoting hatred against an identifiable group pursuant to Section 319(2) of the Criminal Code.[237] The charges were based on Keegstra's classroom anti-Semitic statements, which vilified Jewish people. He told his students that Jewish people were "treacherous," "subversive," "sadistic," "money-loving," "power hungry," "child killers," who "created the Holocaust to gain sympathy."[238] And he notified his students that these anti-Semitic teachings were to be parroted by them in class and on tests lest their grades suffer.[239] Keegstra was convicted and appealed on the grounds that his Section 2(b) free expression rights under the Canadian Charter had been violated by application of Section 319(2) of the Criminal Code.

The Canadian Supreme Court rejected Keegstra's argument, finding that Criminal Code Section 319(2) was constitutional, as it was saved by Section 1 of the Charter, which permits infringement of rights via "reasonable limits prescribed by law as can be demonstrably justified in a free and democratic society."[240] The Court began its analysis by listing the rationales undergirding the free expression right and thereby reaffirming its strength: (1) seeking and attaining truth is an inherently good activity; (2) participation in social and political decision-making is to be fostered and encouraged; and (3) diversity in forms

234. Canadian Criminal Code, R.S.C. 1985, c.C-46, § 318.

235. *Id.* § 319.

236. R. v. Keegstra, [1990] 3 S.C.R. 697 (Can.). The constitutionality of Section 13 of the CHRA was also heard by the Canadian Supreme Court as a companion to the *Keegstra* case. *See* Canada (Human Rights Comm'n) v. Taylor, [1990] 3 S.C.R. 892 (Can.). In *Taylor*, the Court was split 4 to 3 over the issue of whether Section 13 was justified under Section 1 of the Canadian Charter of Rights and Freedoms, with the majority ruling that it was. *Id.* This is the case that would eventually be heard by the Human Rights Committee under the ICCPR. *See* International Covenant on Civil and Political Rights, Communication No. 104/1981: Canada (Jurisprudence), U.N. Doc. CCPR/C/18/D/104/1981 (J.R.T. & the W.G. Party v. Canada) (declared inadmissible Apr. 6, 1983) (discussed *supra* 22–24).

237. *Id.* ¶ 2.

238. *Id.* ¶ 3.

239. *Id.*

240. *Keegstra*, [1990] 3 S.C.R. at para. 96. For the same reason, the Court found that Section 13 of the CHRA passed constitutional muster. Taylor, [1990] 3 S.C.R. at ¶ 84.

of individual self-fulfillment and human flourishing ought to be cultivated in a tolerant and welcoming environment for the sake of both those who convey a meaning and those to whom meaning is conveyed.[241]

At the same time, the Court stressed the Canadian Constitution's commitment to multicultural diversity, group identity, human dignity, and equality. Thus, while any legislated restriction of speech amounts to an infringement of the free speech guarantee, the Court observed, infringements can be justified if they meet a two-pronged test under Section 1.[242] First, a valid governmental objective has to be established—in other words, the government must establish that the impugned state action furthers a goal of "pressing and substantial concern in a free and democratic society."[243] Per the Court: "Only such an objective is of sufficient stature to warrant overriding a constitutionally protected right or freedom."[244] Second, proportionality must be proved, and the analysis is broken down into three segments:

> First, the measures adopted must be carefully designed to achieve the objective in question. They must not be arbitrary, unfair or based on irrational considerations. In short, they must be rationally connected to the objective. Second, the means, even if rationally connected to the objective in this first sense, should impair "as little as possible" the right or freedom in question.... Third, there must be a proportionality between the effects of the measures which are responsible for limiting the Charter right or freedom, and the objective which has been identified as of "sufficient importance."[245]

The Court found Criminal Code Section 319(2) satisfied both tests. To begin, the government objective prong was satisfied because Canada was attempting to curb hate speech, which threatens "the self-dignity of target group members" and creates the very real possibility "that prejudiced messages will gain some credence, with the attendant result of discrimination, and perhaps even violence, against minority groups in Canadian society."[246]

Moreover, the proportionality prong was satisfied. First, the Court found that the means chosen to further this purpose—that is, criminal prosecutions—are

241. *Id.* ¶ 30. Based on this passage, Michel Rosenfeld notes that "the Canadian protection of freedom of expression, like the American, relies on the justifications from democracy, from the pursuit of truth and from autonomy [but the] Canadian conception of autonomy . . . is less individualistic than its American counterpart, as it seemingly places equal emphasis on the autonomy of listeners and speakers." Rosenfeld, *supra* note 102, at 1543.

242. *Keegstra*, [1990] 3 S.C.R. at ¶ 46 (citing R. v. Oakes, [1986] 1 S.C.R. 103, ¶¶ 73–74 (Can.)).

243. *Id.*

244. *Id.*

245. *Id.*

246. *Id.* ¶ 67.

rational in both theory and operation as they restrain defendants (without glorifying their actions), indicate the seriousness of hate speech, promote harmonious relations in society, and give comfort to victims.[247] Second, regarding the narrowly tailored criterion, while the suppression of hate propaganda via criminal action undeniably muzzles the participation of a few individuals in the democratic process, the Court found that the degree of this limitation is not substantial.[248] And the possibility of illegitimate enforcement is not sufficiently likely to raise constitutional concerns as the offense at issue suffers neither from overbreadth nor vagueness.[249]

Finally, as to element number 3, weighing of the importance of the state objective against the effect of limits imposed upon the Charter right, the Court concluded that Section 319(2) is "not a restriction of the most serious kind." It is a criminal statute suppressing hate speech, whose dissemination represents a weak right only tenuously connected with the values underlying the guarantee of freedom of speech.[250]

Overall, then, while lauding the value of free speech and showing admiration for its exalted station in the American legal firmament,[251] the *Keegstra* Court found that, considering "the special role given equality and multiculturalism in the Canadian Constitution" "a departure from the view, reasonably prevalent in America at present, that the suppression of hate propaganda is incompatible with the guarantee of free expression" was necessary.[252] It concluded that "values fundamental to the Canadian conception of a free and democratic society suggest an approach" different from that in the United States.[253]

Thus, Canada represents a bridge between the orthodox US liberty of expression stance and the pro-regulatory regimes in other Western democracies. And back-to-back analysis of the United States and Canada provides a fascinating historical and cultural point of reference given that they are "neighboring countries which were once British colonies and which are now advanced industrialized democracies with large immigrant populations with roots in a vast array of countries and cultures."[254] Indeed, Canada and the United States are much closer on the issue of free expression than even the *Keegstra* case suggests. As pointed out previously, Canadian free speech advocates have recently scored a big victory

247. *Id.* ¶ 102–108.

248. *Id.* ¶¶ 95, 137.

249. *Id.* ¶ 137.

250. *Id.* ¶¶ 139–140.

251. *Id.* ¶ 56 (referring to "the American experience" as "tremendously helpful" in reaching "conclusions regarding this appeal . . .").

252. *Id.* ¶ 60.

253. *Id.* ¶ 61.

254. Rosenfeld, *supra* note 102, at 1542.

in convincing the parliament to repeal Section 13 of the Canadian Human Rites Act. According to David Butt:

> Canadian freedom of expression law, like so many things Canadian, embodies compromise. In the United States, even the most hateful, virile and destructive speech is constitutionally protected. In many other countries, expression is suppressed if politically problematic. We walk between those extremes. Here you can be put in jail for hate speech. But before you condemn the prospect of jail for speaking your mind, consider the built-in limits to the hate speech law. There are seven of them, and together they pour a big pail of cold water on any over-zealous prosecutor intent on duct-taping your mouth. For a prosecution to go ahead, all of these conditions must be met: (1) the hate speech must be the most severe of the genre; (2) the hate speech must be targeted to an identifiable group; (3) it must be public; (4) it must be deliberate, not careless; (5) excluded from hate speech are good faith interpretations of religious doctrine, discussion of issues of public interest, and literary devices like sarcasm and irony; (6) the statements must be hateful when considered in their social and historical context; (7) no prosecution can proceed without approval of the attorney-general, which introduces political accountability because the attorney-general is a cabinet minister.[255]

2. Speech in Other Industrialized Democracies

In other industrialized democracies, there is little compunction to regulate content-based, group-focused hate speech.[256] For example, in the United Kingdom, an ideological kindred spirit of the United States as its former mother country,[257] hate speech that amounts to harassment of a target group or individual is a specific offense under various sections of the Public Order Act, 1986.[258] This is true in spite of the fact that the United Kingdom "recognizes a right to freedom of expression through its adherence to international covenants, such as the European Convention on Human Rights, and through commitment to constitutional values inherent in its rule of law tradition."[259] Other former British

255. David Butt, *Canada's Law on Hate Speech Is the Embodiment of Compromise*, The Globe and Mail (Jan. 19, 2015), http://www.theglobeandmail.com/globe-debate/canadas-law-on-hate-speech-is-the-embodiment-of-compromise/article22520419/.

256. *See* Moeen Cheema & Adeel Kamran, *The Fundamentalism of Liberal Rights: Decoding the Freedom of Expression under the European Convention for the Protection of Human Rights and Fundamental Freedoms*, 11 Loy. U. Chi. Int'l L. Rev. 79, 88–89 (2014) ("In fact, the United States appears to be the only Western state that allows such extended protection to hate speech.").

257. *Id.* at 89 (referring to the United Kingdom as "a state closest to the U.S. in terms of a shared political ideology").

258. Public Order Act, 1986, c. 64, §§ 5–6 (Eng.).

259. Rosenfeld, *supra* note 102, at 1544. The United Kingdom does not have a written constitution. *Id.*

colonies, *viz.*, South Africa,[260] New Zealand,[261] India,[262] and Australia all have laws regulating hate speech.[263]

Australia has a unique constitutional and legislative scheme. The Australian Constitution does not contain a bill of rights, and case law has carved out only a limited implied right of political speech.[264] Thus, free speech concerns provide little in the way of a bulwark against regulating hate speech. Indeed, a complex lattice of state and federal provisions, known as "antivilification laws," ban hate speech both criminally and civilly but flow from an administrative complaints-based mechanism.[265]

Pursuant to this scheme, which may vary from jurisdiction to jurisdiction, a person must initially lodge a hate speech complaint with the designated human rights office in the jurisdiction where the alleged offense took place.[266] That office then mediates a resolution between the parties, which typically consists of an apology or agreement to desist.[267] Only after this initial administrative remedy has been exhausted may a case be brought to a tribunal (in the case of state/territory jurisdictions) or federal court (in the case of the federal jurisdiction).[268] At the federal level and in Tasmania, only civil hate speech cases may be filed.[269] Western Australia, on the other hand, has enacted only criminal antivilification statutes.[270] And every other state and

260. *See* S. Afr. Const., 1996 art. 16(2)(b)–(c) (constitutional provision providing that freedom of expression does not extend to either the "incitement of imminent violence" or the "advocacy of hatred that is based on race, ethnicity, gender or religion, and that constitutes incitement to cause harm.").

261. *See* Human Rights Act 1993 §§ 61, 131 (N.Z.) (punishing any incitement of hostility or contempt against anyone in New Zealand or who may be arriving to New Zealand on the basis of color, race, or ethnic or national origin).

262. India Pen. Code ch. VIII, S153A (Dr. Sir Hari Singh Gour ed. 1990) (criminalizing promoting enmity between different groups on grounds of religion, race, place of birth, language, and other classifications).

263. *See* Adam Liptak, *Hate Speech or Free Speech? What Much of West Bans Is Protected in US*, N.Y. Times (June 11, 2008), http://www.nytimes.com/2008/06/11/world/americas/11iht-hate.4.13645369.html?pagewanted=all&_r=0.

264. Sarah Harding, *Kramer's Popular Constitutionalism: A Quick Normative Assessment*, 81 Chi.-Kent L. Rev. 1117, 1120 (2006).

265. *See* Tanya Katerí Hernández, *Hate Speech and the Language of Racism in Latin America: A Lens for Reconsidering Global Hate Speech Restrictions and Legislation Models*, 32 U. Pa. J. Int'l L. 805, 837 (2011).

266. *See* Katharine Gelber & Luke McNamara, *Private Litigation to Address a Public Wrong: A Study of Australia's Regulatory Response to "Hate Speech"*, 33 C.J.Q. 307, 307 (2014) (detailing these regulatory schemes).

267. *Id.*

268. *Id.*

269. *See Racial Discrimination Act* 1975 (Cth) §§ 18B–18F (on the federal level) and *Anti-Discrimination Act* 1998 (Tas) § 19 (for Tasmania).

270. *See* Criminal Code 1913 (WA), pt. II, ch. XI, §§ 76–80H.

the Australian Capital Territory have both criminal and civil antivilification laws.[271]

Outside of the Commonwealth sphere, similar treatment of hate speech predominates. Germany's constitutional guarantee of free expression, for example, is circumscribed by the competing fundamental value of human dignity (in contrast with the Canadian emphasis on multiculturalism). This limitation has great national significance for Germany given the historical context of the country's Hitler-era hate speech campaign against the Jews, which culminated in the Holocaust.[272]

Article 5 of the German *Grundgesetz*, the provision that protects freedom of speech, expressly permits limitation of the right "by the provisions of the general laws."[273] And the "general laws" include the Criminal Code. Thus, criminal liability can be imposed for incitement to hatred, or for attacks on human dignity against individuals or groups based on nationality, race, religion, or ethnic origin.[274] In particular, Article 130 of the *Strafgesetzbuch* (German Criminal Code) subjects to punishment "anyone attacking the human dignity of others by inciting hatred against a segment of the population, advocating the use of "violent or arbitrary measures against them," or exposing them to malicious slander.[275]

Elsewhere in Western Europe, a comparable statutory framework is found. French law, for example, criminalizes speech in the public domain that incites unlawful activity.[276] But France's original hate speech statute, dating back to the 1880s, was considered ineffectual at stemming a rising tide of racist rhetoric as immigrants arrived in greater numbers after World War II. In response, the country updated its hate speech legislation with a series of amendments collectively known as the "Pleven Law." The Pleven Law prohibits speech in both public and nonpublic places, whether published or spoken, that "provokes discrimination, hatred or violence against a person or a group of people" on account of ethnicity, nationality, race, or religion.[277] The Netherlands

271. *See, e.g.*, Anti-Discrimination Act 1977 (NSW) §§ 20B–20D, 38R–38T, 49ZS–49ZTA, 49ZXA–49ZXC; Anti-Discrimination Act 1991(Qld) §§ 124A, 131A; Racial Vilification Act (1996) (SA), Civil Liability Act (1936)(SA) § 73; Racial and Religious Tolerance Act 2001 (Vic); Discrimination Act 1991 (ACT) §§ 65–67.

272. *Id.* at 1548.

273. *Grundgesetz* [GG] art.5 (F.R.G.).

274. Rosenfeld, *supra* note 102, at 1551.

275. *Strafgesetzbuch* (StGB) § 130 (F.R.G.) *reprinted in* Juliane Wetzel, *Judicial Treatment of Incitement against Ethnic Groups and of the Denial of National Socialist Mass Murder in the Federal Republic of Germany, in* Under the Shadow of Weimar 105 n.12 (1993).

276. *See* Law of July 29, 1881 [hereinafter Law on Freedom of the Press], ch. 4, art. 23 (Fr.).

277. *Id.* art. 24.

has a similar statutory arrangement.[278] So do Austria, Belgium, Italy, and Switzerland.[279]

Not surprisingly, the laws in the Scandinavian countries adhere to the same principles. For instance, while freedom of expression is constitutionally guaranteed in Sweden, the *Riksdag* (parliament) may restrict it "to satisfy a purpose acceptable in a democratic society."[280] Sweden has found that such an acceptable purpose is suppression of hate speech, and the Swedish Penal Code specifically prohibits racist speech.[281] And fellow Scandinavian country Denmark is no different. The Danish Criminal Code criminalizes the dissemination of a statement by which a group of people are "threaten[ed], insult[ed], or degrad[ed] on account of their race, colour, national or ethnic origin, religion, or sexual inclination."[282] And we have already seen an application of this law in the *Jersild* case, analyzed above.[283]

Even outside of Europe, laws against hate speech have found purchase in countries as diverse as Cyprus, Nigeria, Israel, and Brazil.[284] In fact, Brazil is in no way a regional anomaly. For example, its neighbor Ecuador, through Article 212.4 of its Penal Code, punishes those who, through whatever medium, diffuse ideas based on racial superiority or racial hatred.[285] According to Tanya Katerí Hernández:

> In Latin America, like many countries in Europe, hate speech is prohibited . . . Latin American hate speech laws generally range from the criminal prohibition of the dissemination of ideas based on racial superiority to the criminal prohibition against inciting racial hatred. While the language of the statutes does vary across the region, the provisions are quite similar in their central focus on prohibiting the dissemination of messages of racial subordination and hatred without regard to whether violence is incited by the message.[286]

278. *See* WvS Art. 137(d) (1881) (amended 1996), translated in The Dutch Penal Code, 133 (Louise Rayer & Stafford Wadsworth trans., Rothman & Co. 1997).

279. *See* Thomas David Jones, Human Rights: Group Defamation, Freedom of Expression and the Law of Nations 189–224, 259–313 (1998).

280. *See Regeringsformen* [RF] [Constitution] 2:20(1)(Swed.). However, the restriction may never exceed what is necessary having regard to the purpose which occasioned it, nor may it be carried so far as to constitute a threat to the free formation of opinion as one of the foundations of democracy. *Id.* 2:22.

281. *Brottsbalken* [BrB] [penal code] 16:8 (Swed.).

282. *See* Straffeloven (Strfl) § 266 b (1).

283. *Jersild*, App. 15890/89 (Eur. Ct. H.R.), ¶ 12.

284. *See* Jones, *supra* note 279, at 189–224, 259–313.

285. Código Penal [Criminal Code] art. 212.4 (Ecuador).

286. Hernández, *supra* note 265, at 805, 827.

IV. CONCLUSION

Liberty to express ideas, even if repugnant or subversive, is a powerful foundation for any successful democracy. It helps promote self-governance and individual autonomy and exposes and marginalizes inimical ideas that might otherwise flourish in the shadows. But nearly all the world's liberal democracies have concluded that this liberty should not extend to extreme verbal vilification of groups based on race, religion, ethnicity, and other related group characteristics. Thus, consistent with the key international human rights treaties, they have fashioned laws seeking an equilibrium between speech rights protection and competing social concerns, such as equality and harmony among groups in multicultural societies and dignity of the individual being targeted by hate rhetoric. The contrasting vision of the United States, that there is important social utility in letting the hatemongers rant, offers a competing governance model that global legislators would need to consider when framing the very first laws governing atrocity speech. An account of the choices made and the resultant textual formulations now follows.

3

The Birth of Atrocity Speech Law Part 1

Nuremberg and the Foundational Statutes

> "The [Nuremberg] Charter also recognizes individual responsibility on the part of those who commit acts defined as crimes, or who incite others to do so . . . ."
>
> —Robert H. Jackson[1]

> "Incitement as a codified offence was unknown at Nuremberg . . . ."
>
> —Jens David Ohlin[2]

I. INTRODUCTION

The origins of modern atrocity speech law can arguably be traced to the dashed justice aspirations of diplomats in Paris in the aftermath of the Great War. In 1919, the Allies established the Commission on the Responsibility of the Authors of the War and on Enforcement of Penalties to assess liability for conflict-related crimes.[3] Among other things, the Commission's brief included reporting on "the facts as to breaches of the laws and customs of war committed [during the war] by the forces of

1. Robert H. Jackson, Chief of Counsel for the United States, Opening Statement Before the International Military Tribunal (Nov. 21, 1945), *in* Robert H. Jackson, The Nürnberg Case 30, 88–89 (1947).

2. Jens David Ohlin, *Incitement and Conspiracy to Commit Genocide*, *in* The UN Genocide Convention: A Commentary 210 (Paola Gaeta ed., 2009).

3. Yougindra Khushalani, The Dignity and Honour of Women as Basic and Fundamental Human Rights 11–12 (1982).

Atrocity Speech Law. Gregory S. Gordon.

the German Empire and their Allies . . ."[4] The Commission found that responsibility for initiating the conflict lay with the Central Powers,[5] which were liable for violations of the laws of war and humanity.[6] It advised that senior officials, including Kaiser Wilhelm II, be prosecuted for *ordering* those offenses, and having abstained from preventing them (essentially a protoversion of superior responsibility).[7]

But the Dutch government refused to surrender the Kaiser to the Allies, and thus the envisaged justice enterprise, along with its attendant "ordering" mode of liability, came into the world stillborn. The crime of "ordering" would eventually be codified in the statutes of the ad hoc tribunals after the Cold War.

As a result, the world would have to wait another twenty-six years for the true advent of atrocity speech law in the trial of the major Nazi war criminals after the Second World War. This chapter examines that history, starting with the crimes against humanity prosecutions of the propaganda defendants at Nuremberg, to the Genocide Convention, and then to attempts at codification of speech crimes by the International Law Commission in the Cold War years. It then considers the crimes as enshrined in the ad hoc tribunal statues as well as the Rome Statute for the International Criminal Court.

II. THE CRIME OF PERSECUTION AND THE ORIGINS OF ATROCITY SPEECH LAW AT NUREMBERG

The birth of the international human rights movement, and its efforts to stymie *future* government abuses, was one legal response to the inhumanity of the Second World War. But another juridical initiative focused on *past* government transgressions and sought to bring justice in respect of *individual* criminal responsibility. And so it was that representatives of the victorious Allied powers met in London in the summer of 1945 to organize trials of the top Nazi leaders.[8]

As detailed in Chapter 1, hate speech was an integral part of the Nazi genocide against the Jews. And the London summer of 1945 Allied negotiations took this into account. At a pivotal moment during the discussions, Chief US Prosecutor Robert Jackson alluded to the central role played by incitement in a colloquy with British representative Sir David Maxwell Fyfe:

> SIR DAVID MAXWELL FYFE: Mr. Justice Jackson, just to clarify the discussion, could your point be fairly put this way: that you want the entering into the plan to be made a substantive crime?

4. Violations of the Laws and Customs of War: Report of Majority and Dissenting Reports of American and Japanese Members of the Commission on Responsibilities, Conference of Paris, 1919, *reprinted in* 14 AM. J. INT'L L. 95 (Supp. 1920).

5. *Id.* at 107.

6. *Id.* at 114–115.

7. *Id.* at 129.

8. Brian K. Feltman, *Robert H. Jackson*, *in* 1 GERMANY AND THE AMERICAS: CULTURE, POLITICS AND HISTORY 571 (Thomas Adam ed., 2005).

MR. JUSTICE JACKSON: Yes. The knowing *incitement* and planning is as criminal as the execution.[9]

Indeed, in his historic opening statement before the International Military Tribunal, Justice Jackson emphasized the centrality of the role played by the "inciters behind the scenes" of the "Nazi conspiracy."[10]

A. The IMT Charter and the Hate Speech Prosecutions

Nevertheless, "incitement" was not separately criminalized with respect to Nazi atrocities in the final product of the Allied summer 1945 negotiations in London: the Charter of the International Military Tribunal (IMT) at Nuremberg (annexed to the August 8, 1945, "London Agreement").[11] Instead, criminal liability connected to hate speech was covered under the general rubric of "crimes against humanity."[12] It could also have been charged as "instigation" as Article 6 of the Charter provided for liability for "leaders, organizers, *instigators* and accomplices participating in the formulation or execution of a common plan or conspiracy to commit any of the foregoing crimes."[13]

Nevertheless, instigation was not the focus of charges for speech crimes at Nuremberg—it was crimes against humanity (CAH). In order to understand how speech was treated as a CAH in this regard, it is instructive to consider the general background of CAH and the specific subcategory of "persecution," under which speech-related offenses were charged.

As a legal term, "crimes against humanity" first found expression in an Allied communiqué to Turkish officials regarding the consequences of their mass slaughter of Armenians during the First World War. This joint message of France, Great Britain, and Russia explained that "in view of the crimes of Turkey against humanity and civilization" they would "hold personally responsible [for] these crimes all members of the Ottoman government and those of their agents

9. Robert H. Jackson, Report of Robert H. Jackson, United States Representative to the International Conference on Military Trials (Dept. of State 1945) 376 (emphasis added).

10. International Military Tribunal, 2 TRIAL OF THE MAJOR WAR CRIMINALS BEFORE THE INTERNATIONAL MILITARY TRIBUNAL 104 (1947) [hereinafter TMWC].

11. Margaret Eastwood, *Hitler's Notorious Jew Baiter: The Prosecution of Julius Streicher, in* PROPAGANDA, WAR CRIMES TRIALS AND INTERNATIONAL LAW: FROM SPEAKERS' CORNER TO WAR CRIMES 222–223 (2012) ("... incitement ... did not exist as a specific offense under the Nuremberg Charter ...").

12. *See* Diane F. Orentlicher, *Criminalizing Hate Speech: A Comment on the ICTR's Judgment in* The Prosecutor v. Nahimana, et al., 13 HUM. RTS. BRIEF 1, 3 (Nov. 2005), https://www.wcl.american.edu/hrbrief/13/hate_speech.pdf ("Two defendants before the IMT, Julius Streicher and Hans Fritzsche, were charged with crimes against humanity by virtue of anti-Semitic advocacy.").

13. Charter of the International Military Tribunal art. 6, Aug. 8, 1945, 59 Stat. 1544, 1547, 82 U.N.T.S. 279 [hereinafter IMT Charter] (emphasis added).

who are implicated in such massacres."[14] Unfortunately, the Allies never made good on their promise. Despite a postconflict war crimes commission report endorsing establishment of an international tribunal to prosecute the massacres as violations "of the laws of humanity," US representatives prevailed upon their coalition partners to omit reference to the offense because of its doctrinal novelty and imprecise definition.[15]

After the carnage of the Second World War, however, the offense came of age. Given the relatively narrow scope of war crimes, crimes against humanity was indispensable for punishing the Hitler regime's domestic depravity—Nazi atrocities against fellow Germans were not committed on battlefields, in prisoner-of-war camps, or as part of a foreign occupation.[16] And so it was that this new delict, crimes against humanity, was included in Article 6(c) of the Nuremberg Charter and defined as:

> [M]urder, extermination, enslavement, deportation and other inhumane acts committed against any civilian population before or during the war, or persecution on political, racial or religious grounds in execution of or in connection with any crime within the jurisdiction of the Tribunal, whether or not in violation of the law of the country where perpetrated.[17]

Parsing Article 6(c) reveals that it bifurcates into separate categories of crime: inhumane acts and persecutions on discriminatory grounds.[18] In appreciation of its novelty and considerable breadth, the Charter mandated that CAH be linked to one of the Charter's other principal crimes, for example, Crimes against Peace or War Crimes—this statutory yoking came to be known as the "war nexus."[19]

Armed with this new provision, Allied prosecutors at Nuremberg were able to bring before the IMT hate speech–centered cases against two defendants, Julius Streicher and Hans Fritzsche. These Nazi media figures were briefly introduced in Chapter 1. It is worthwhile here to consider in greater depth their respective crimes and trials.

14. Timothy L. H. McCormack & Gerry J. Simpson, The Law of War Crimes: National and International Approaches 45 (1997).

15. Harry M. Rhea, *Paris 1919 and Rome 1998: Different Treaties, Different Presidents, Different Senates, and the Same Dilemma*, 20 Transnat'l L. & Contemp. Probs. 411, 415–416 (2011); Stuart Ford, *Crimes against Humanity at the Extraordinary Chambers in the Courts of Cambodia: Is a Connection with Armed Conflict Required?*, 24 UCLA Pac. Basin L.J. 125, 137–138 (2007) [hereinafter CAH at the ECCC]; Beth Van Schaack, *The Definition of Crimes against Humanity: Resolving the Incoherence*, 37 Colum. J. Transnat'l L. 787, 779–798 (1999).

16. See Daniel Kanstroom, *Sharpening the Cutting Edge of International Human Rights Law: Unresolved Issues of War Crimes Tribunals*, 30 B.C. Int'l & Comp. L. Rev. 1, 9 (2007).

17. IMT Charter, *supra* note 13, art. 6.

18. Van Schaack, *supra* note 15, at 838 n.247.

19. *Id.* at 792 ("The war nexus allowed the drafters of the Charter to condemn specific inhumane acts of Nazi perpetrators committed within Germany without threatening the entire doctrine of state sovereignty.").

B. The *Streicher* and *Fritzsche* Persecution Cases before the IMT

1. Julius Streicher

Born on February 12, 1885, in the Upper Bavarian village of Fleinhausen,[20] Julius Streicher started his working life as a schoolteacher and then served in the German Army during the First World War. He was well regarded as a soldier and by war's end had earned, among other medals, the Iron Cross, First Class.[21] After Germany's defeat, Streicher took up the leadership mantle of the "German Socialist Party" (GSP) and was, at first, Adolf Hitler's political rival (with the GSP competing for members with Hitler's National Socialist German Workers Party).[22] But the rivalry was short-lived as the two rabid anti-Semites made common cause and fused their burgeoning fascist movements into one. Streicher became Hitler's loyal acolyte and rapidly accumulated high-profile posts during the Nazi rise to power, including general in the SA Storm Troopers, Gauleiter (district leader) of Franconia, and a member of the Reichstag.[23] Nuremberg prosecutor Drexel Sprecher wrote that "Streicher was known outside of Germany as the foremost anti-Semite of Nazi Germany . . ."[24]

In 1923, not long after merging his party with Hitler's, Streicher had established a virulently anti-Jewish newspaper called *Der Stürmer*.[25] Boasting 600,000 subscribers at its peak during Nazi rule, this vulgar tabloid demonized Jews with crude aspersions, false accusations, and grotesque caricatures.[26] Its influence was not limited to its subscription base, as towns around Germany displayed it on public bulletin boards in glass-covered cases. Over the next decade and a half, its poisonous rhetoric and images helped inflame the Reich's citizens against the Jewish minority. According to Nuremberg prosecutor Alexander Hardy:

> The full force and effect of [Streicher's] press propaganda on the masses is contained in an episode relating to the time when Streicher, as a Gauleiter, delivered a Christmas story to the children of Nuremberg. Reaching the climax of his Yuletide tale, which concerned a "little Aryan boy and girl," Streicher suddenly asked the children, do you know who the devil is?" And the little ones shrieked in chorus, "The Jew, the Jew."[27]

20. Randall Bytewerk, Julius Streicher: Nazi Editor of the Notorious Anti-Semitic Newspaper Der Stürmer 2 (2001).

21. *Id.* at 5–6.

22. Alexander G. Hardy, Hitler's Secret Weapon: The "Managed Press" and Propaganda Machine of Nazi Germany 82 (1967).

23. *Id.*

24. Drexel A. Sprecher, Inside the Nuremberg Trial: A Prosecutor's Comprehensive Account 919 (1999).

25. Ann Tusa & John Tusa, The Nuremberg Trial 504 (1983).

26. Hardy, *supra* note 22, at 82.

27. *Id.* at 83.

As part of the IMT indictment, Streicher was included in Counts One ("Common Plan or Conspiracy) and Four ("Crimes against Humanity").[28] The *actus reus* of the CAH charge against him, although not explicitly described in the indictment itself, was the second prong of the crime, that is, "persecution of political, racial and religious groups."[29] During presentation of the case-in-chief, it became apparent that there was a lack of evidence regarding Streicher's participation in preparing and planning the aggressive war.[30] Thus, the prosecution turned exclusively on the CAH count and Streicher's inflammatory propaganda against the Jewish community. In introducing his case, British prosecutor Mervyn Griffith Jones informed the Tribunal:

> For the course of some 25 years, this man educated the whole of the German people in hatred and . . . he incited them to the persecution and to the extermination of the Jewish race. He was an accessory to murder, perhaps on a scale never attained before.[31]

Over fifty documents were entered into evidence against Streicher, with more than twenty quotations extracted from his anti-Semitic speeches and articles published in *Der Stürmer.*[32] The documents tended to show that, from the beginning, Streicher called for the elimination of Jews from German society.[33] And his writings supported the escalation of the Nazi persecutory policies toward the Jews. For example, evidence of his writings showed how he prepared the groundwork for, and then later supported, the infamous 1935 "Nuremberg Laws" that stripped Jews of their German citizenship and deprived them of their core civil and political rights.[34] Such texts included reinforcing the blood libel, dehumanization via animal and microbe metaphors (comparing Jews to snakes and bacillus, for example), accusations of theft, rape, and an overall Jewish conspiracy for world domination, including the ultimate murder of non-Jews.[35] Later on, as the Final Solution was being implemented, the prosecution demonstrated that, "even with . . . knowledge of actual genocide unfolding, Streicher's propaganda . . .

28. 2 TMWC, *supra* note 10, at 29–41.

29. Eastwood, *supra* note 11, at 204.

30. *Id.* at 205.

31. 5 TMWC, *supra* note 10, at 91.

32. Eastwood, *supra* note 11, at 206.

33. *Id.* at 208 ("[The prosecution's case] sought to stress that, from his earliest political involvement, Streicher had engaged in propaganda that identified Jews as unwanted within Germany and/or perhaps more widely, claimed their existence represented [a form] of oppression against the freedom of German citizens that required the expulsion of this group.").

34. *Id.* at 208–209.

35. *Id.* at 209–211.

openly advocated, urged, supported and demanded extermination of the Jewish people."[36]

A key component of the prosecution's case was to demonstrate that Streicher was aware of the implementation of the Final Solution while he continued to churn out murderous anti-Semitic jeremiads in his newspaper. This was effectively demonstrated in Griffith-Jones's cross-examination of Streicher:

> The prosecution sought to show how he had copied an article, verbatim in *Der Stürmer*, from the *Israelitisches Wochenblatt*, dated August 27, minus the references made to the number of Jews missing and murdered. After writing "The Jewish reservoir of the East which was able to counterbalance the force of assimilation in the West no longer exists," the original text from the *Israelitisches Wochenblatt* then went on to say: "three million dead, the same number outlawed; many thousands, all over the world, mentally and physically broken . . ." This evidence demonstrated that Streicher had definitely read one particular copy of the *Israelitisches Wochenblatt*. Despite this damning evidence the defendant was not prepared to admit that he believed what was printed in a foreign Jewish newspaper. After this exchange of words, it appeared that Griffith-Jones' cross-examination strategy had been successful.[37]

In adjudicating Streicher's culpability, the IMT appeared to have little difficulty accepting the prosecution's interpretation of the evidence. Its judgment began by acknowledging the defendant's anti-Semitic rhetoric and reputation: "For his twenty-five years of speaking, writing, and preaching hatred of the Jews, Streicher was widely known as 'Jew-Baiter Number One.'"[38]

The judgment considered a plethora of pre- and postwar pieces Streicher himself authored advocating the destruction, "root and branch," of the Jewish people.[39] It stated that "[i]n his speeches and articles, week after week, month after month, he infected the German mind with the virus of anti-Semitism and incited the German people to active persecution."[40] The Tribunal also stressed that the defendant penned and published many of these eliminationist messages knowing that, at the same time, Jews in Eastern Europe were being liquidated. Thus, the judgment concluded: "Streicher's incitement to murder and extermination at the time when Jews in the East were being killed under the most horrible conditions clearly constitutes persecution on political and racial grounds in connection with war crimes as defined by the Charter, and constitutes a crime against humanity."[41]

36. *Id.* at 213.

37. *Id.* at 215.

38. *See, e.g.*, United States v. Goering, Judgment, Streicher (Int'l Mil. Trib. Sept. 30, 1946), *reprinted in* 6 F.R.D. 69, 161–163 (1946) [hereinafter Streicher Judgment].

39. *Id.*

40. *Id.*

41. *Id.*

2. Hans Fritzsche

Hans Fritzsche was born in Bochum, in Germany's Ruhr area, in 1900.[42] His later reputation as a sophisticated, erudite radio broadcaster stood in contrast to his humble origins:[43] his father was a civil servant and his educational career was in no way exceptional.[44] Like Streicher, he enlisted in the German army during World War I, serving as a private in the infantry. After the war, without completing a degree, he studied liberal arts at universities in Griefswald and Berlin.[45] Despite his failure to earn a diploma, he was able to transition into a journalism career. He started as a correspondent for the *Hamburg Press*[46] and eventually became the editor of the *Preussische Jahrbűcher*, a monthly journal. He then served as an editor for the *Telegraphen Union* news agency and the International News Service—part of Alfred Hugenberg's media empire.[47] After working for Hugenberg, Fritzsche "educated himself in the use of radio in mass media" and ultimately secured a post as head of the Weimar Republic's *Drahtloser Dienst* (Wireless News Service) in 1932.[48]

But he was an ardent German nationalist and had become disenchanted with his paymaster, the Weimar government. "Swayed by the oratory of Adolf Hitler," on May 1, 1933, he joined the National Socialist Party and was appointed to its Propaganda Ministry staff. [49] By 1938, he had worked his way up the Propaganda Ministry ranks to the position of chief of the German Press Division.[50] As part of this job, on a daily basis, he imposed Nazi propaganda "press directives," or *Tagesparolen*, on newspaper editors.[51] This was tantamount to giving the press its marching orders in terms of the content it would publish that day.[52] The IMT described the press directives, as "instructions [directing] the press to present to the people certain themes, such as the leadership principle, the Jewish problem, the problem of living space, and other standard Nazi ideas."[53] From this powerful position, Fritzsche was again elevated and became head of the Radio Division in 1942. As part of his duties in this new post, he hosted a daily radio program called "Hans Fritzsche Speaks."[54]

42. Leslie Alan Horvitz & Christopher Catherwood, Encyclopedia of War Crimes and Genocide 159 (2006); C. N. Trueman, *Hans Fritzsche*, The History Learning Site (Apr. 2012), http://www.historylearningsite.co.uk/nazi-germany/nazi-leaders/hans-fritzsche/.

43. Trueman, *supra* note 42.

44. Robert S. Wistrich, Who's Who in Nazi Germany 39 (2002).

45. *Id.* at 68.

46. Horvitz & Catherwood, *supra* note 42, at 159.

47. Trueman, *supra* note 42.

48. Hardy, *supra* note 22, at 87.

49. Trueman, *supra* note 42.

50. *Id.*

51. *Id.*

52. Wistrich, *supra* note 44, at 52.

53. *See* United States v. Goering, Judgment, Fritzsche (Int'l Mil. Trib. Sept. 30, 1946), *reprinted in* 6 F.R.D. 69, 186–187 (1946) [hereinafter Fritzsche Judgment].

54. Hardy, *supra* note 22, at 87.

Segments from this radio show were the basis of the CAH charges against Fritzsche during the IMT trial. Evidence presented at trial demonstrated that he had used his radio program to espouse the general policies of the Nazi regime, which "aroused in the German people those passions which led them to the commission of atrocities."[55] These broadcasts were "full of provocative libels against Jews, the result of which was to inflame Germans to further atrocities against Jews."[56] For example, on December 18, 1941, as *Einsatzgruppen* were murdering entire Jewish communities in Soviet occupied territories, Fritzsche declared:

> The fate of Jewry in Europe has turned out as unpleasant as the Führer predicted in the case of a European war. After the extension of the war instigated by Jews, this unpleasant fate may also spread to the New World, for you can hardly assume that the nations of this New World will pardon the Jews for the misery of which the nations of the Old World did not absolve them.[57]

While testifying on his own behalf at trial, though, Fritzsche was able to blunt some of the evidence presented against him during the prosecution's case-in-chief with self-serving statements and naked denials. For example, when asked by his counsel if he was aware of the fate of the Jews by war's end, he selectively referred to a conversation with a high-ranking SS officer who, as the Nazi regime was teetering on the brink of collapse, mentioned that Heinrich Himmler ordered that Jews not be harmed because he looked at them "as a kind of hostages."[58] But cross-examination by Chief Soviet Prosecutor Roman Rudenko did not probe this point further and let stand Fritzsche's assertion that his knowledge of the Jews' fate by war's end was limited to the contents of this conversation.[59] In fact, the entirety of the cross-examination was ineptly handled and merely allowed Fritzsche to deny allegations put to him without any further probing or attempts at impeachment. The following exchange, at the very outset of the cross-examination, demonstrates Rudenko's ineffective approach:

> GENERAL R. A. RUDENKO (CHIEF PROSECUTOR FOR THE U.S.S.R.): I should like to begin the cross-examination in determining the role which German propaganda played in the criminal activity of the Hitler Government. Tell me, do you admit that German propaganda disseminated racial theories and introduced into the minds of the

55. Fritzsche Judgment, *supra* note 53, at 186–187.

56. *Nuremberg Trial Defendants: Hans Fritzsche*, JEWISH VIRTUAL LIBRARY, https://www.jewishvirtuallibrary.org/jsource/Holocaust/Fritzsche.html (last visited Sept. 18, 2016).

57. *Id.*

58. International Military Tribunal, Nuremberg Trial Proceedings Volume 17, One Hundred and Sixty-Sixth Day, Friday, 28 June 1946, Morning Session, Dr. Heinz Fritz (Counsel for Defendant Fritzsche), 179, http://avalon.law.yale.edu/imt/06-28-46.asp (last visited Sept. 18, 2016).

59. *Id.*

German people the ideas of the superiority of the German race—that means, the idea of the "master race"? Do you admit that?

FRITZSCHE: The question touches upon two problems. May I reply to both of them? I admit that German propaganda spread the racial theory, but I deny that German propaganda spread the theory of the "master race."

GEN. RUDENKO: You do not admit it?

FRITZSCHE: No.

GEN. RUDENKO: Very well. You admit that the German propaganda incited in the German people racial hatred toward the Jews and propagated the necessity of their extermination?

FRITZSCHE: Once again two problems are contained in this question. May I answer to both?

GEN. RUDENKO: I beg your pardon, you do not have to emphasize this. Just answer the question; if there are two, answer two.

FRITZSCHE: I admit, as I have done in my answer to your first question, that German propaganda spread the racial theory but I deny most emphatically that German propaganda, had made preparations for, or had called for, the mass murder of Jews.

GEN. RUDENKO: But you do not deny that German propaganda preached to the German people racial hatred toward Jews? You do not deny that?

FRITZSCHE: I cannot even affirm that without reserve. That is the reason why, in my answer to the second question, I made a slight distinction. German propaganda, and under that I understand official German propaganda, did not even preach racial hatred. It only spoke about racial distinctions, and that is something quite different; but I will admit that there was a certain type of German propaganda which went beyond that and which did preach the clear-cut and primitive racial hatred.

GEN. RUDENKO: You will admit that the activity of German propaganda was also directed against the Church?[60]

As demonstrated in this passage, Fritzsche was able simply to deny any damaging facts without being pressed further. Most significantly, he flatly denied that Nazi propaganda incited hatred toward the Jews and the necessity of their extermination. Rudenko let that stand. And when Fritzsche admitted that there was a certain type of German propaganda "which did preach the clear-cut and primitive racial hatred," Rudenko did no follow-up whatsoever.

In light of these efforts, not surprisingly, the Tribunal acquitted Fritzsche, because it concluded his anti-Semitic tirades did not directly advocate persecution of the Jews and "his position and official duties were not sufficiently important . . . to infer that he took part in originating or formulating propaganda campaigns."[61]

60. *Id.* at pp. 194–195.

61. Fritzsche Judgment, *supra* note 53, at 186–187. Of course, this holding contradicts the Nuremberg principle that superior orders may not absolve a defendant from criminal liability.

Nuremberg prosecutor Alexander Hardy later revealed that evidence not yet found by the time of the IMT trial would have undoubtedly resulted in a finding of Fritzsche's guilt at a subsequent Nuremberg trial:

> [His work as chief of the German Press Division] was far more important than the task of venting his golden voice . . . [Later found press directives] brought the lie to Fritzsche's denials, during his trial before the IMT, of knowledge of such crimes as the extermination of the Jews and atrocities in concentration camps. He not only knew of them but played an important part in bringing them about.[62]

However, on February 4, 1947, Fritzsche was put on trial by a West German government *Spruchkammer*, or Denazification Court.[63] There, his culpability was established and he was sentenced to eight years, the maximum punishment such courts could mete out.[64]

C. The *Dietrich* Crimes against Humanity Case before the NMT

Follow-on cases against relatively inferior Nazi administrators before the Nuremberg Military Tribunals (NMTs), prosecuted exclusively by the Americans in their occupation zone, were governed by Control Council Law (CCL) No. 10,[65] which essentially duplicated the IMT Charter's CAH provision.[66] There were two principal differences: (1) the "war nexus" was deleted; and (2) the set of inhumane acts was enlarged with the addition of imprisonment, torture, and rape.[67]

62. Hardy, *supra* note 22, at 87. Dietrich ordered all written copies of the *Tagesparolen* be destroyed by the editors who received them. By the time of Nazi Press Chief Otto Dietrich's subsequent trial, prosecutors had found two editors who had not destroyed their copies. Those had not been discovered by the time of the IMT's judgment. *Id.* at 40–41.

63. Trueman, *supra* note 42.

64. Hardy, *supra* note 22, at 85.

65. Allied Control Council Law No. 10, Punishment of Persons Guilty of War Crimes, Crimes against Peace and Against Humanity, Dec. 20, 1945, *reprinted in* Telford Taylor, Final Report to the Secretary of the Army on the Nuremberg War Crimes Trials Under Control Council Law No. 10, at 250 (1949) [hereinafter CCL No. 10].

66. *See* Ford, *CAH at the ECCC, supra* note 15, at 147. Article II of CCL No. 10 reads: "1. Each of the following acts is recognized as a crime . . . (c) Crimes against Humanity. Atrocities and offenses, including but not limited to murder, extermination, enslavement, deportation, imprisonment, torture, rape, or other inhumane acts committed against any civilian population, or persecutions on political, racial or religious grounds whether or not in violation of the domestic laws of the country where perpetrated." Article II.1(c) also includes the terms "atrocities and offenses," but this turned out to be the exclusive terminology of CCL No. 10 and an historic anomaly—neither the IMT Charter nor subsequent international criminal law instruments containing CAH provisions has employed this language. CCL No. 10, *supra* note 65, art. II.1(c).

67. *Id.*

Given the relatively later time of his arrest and the fact that he was ostensibly subordinate to Joseph Goebbels, Otto Dietrich was not included in the IMT dock with the major Nazi war criminals.[68] Instead, he was brought to justice as part of the penultimate American NMT proceeding—the so-called *Ministries Case*, also known as the *Wilhelmstrasse Case*, or *United States v. Ernst von Weizaecker, et al.*[69] The eleventh of the twelve NMT trials, the twenty-one defendants in the case held senior positions in various Reich ministries or were high-ranking bankers or armaments officials.[70]

Like the other two Nuremberg propaganda defendants, Dietrich came from humble origins—born in 1897 in the western German city of Essen—and served in the German army during the First World War.[71] And, like Streicher, he was decorated for his combat service, earning the Iron Cross, First Class.[72] In 1921, he earned a doctorate in political science and then eventually broke into the newspaper business.[73] He started as a deputy editor of the Essen *Nationalzeitung* and then was hired as business manager for the *Augsburger Zeitung*, a German-national evening paper.[74] He became more prominent after marrying the daughter of a wealthy newspaper magnate (owner of the influential *Rheinisch-Westfälische Zeitung*). Through his father-in-law, he established good relations with important Rhineland industrialists and, after joining the Nazi Party in 1929, he gave Hitler access to them.

This helped forge a strong bond between the two men, and the Nazi leader reciprocated by making Dietrich party press czar.[75] With Hitler seizing power in 1933, Dietrich eventually assumed the same role on the state

68. Of course, Fritzsche, an IMT defendant, was also subordinate to Goebbels. But Fritzsche was put in the dock at the IMT at the insistence of the Soviet Union, which had in its custody significantly fewer IMT defendants than the other allies, especially the Americans. *See How Did Hans Fritzsche Avoid the Noose?*, The Propagander, http://grwa.tripod.com/050.html (last visited Sept. 18, 2016). Fritzsche was one of only two high-ranking Nazis captured by the Soviets (the other being Raeder). *Id.* They felt Fritzsche's inclusion would help balance the inequality regarding IMT defendants vis-à-vis the other allies. So his prosecution before the IMT, as opposed to a subsequent trial in the Russian zone, was motivated largely by incipient Cold War political considerations. *Id.*

69. United States v. Ernst Weizsaker (*Ministries Case*), *in* 12 Trials of War Criminals before The Nuremberg Military Tribunals under Control Council Law No. 10, 498 (1951) [hereinafter Ministries Case]. It is also known as the *Wilhelmstrasse Trial* because the German Foreign Office, where a number of the defendants worked, was located on the Wilhelmstrasse in Berlin.

70. United States Holocaust Memorial Museum, *Subsequent Nuremberg Proceedings, Case #11, The Ministries Case*, Holocaust Encyclopedia, http://www.ushmm.org/wlc/en/article.php?ModuleId=10007082 (last updated July 2, 2016) [hereinafter Holocaust Encyclopedia].

71. Roger Moorhouse, Introduction to Otto Dietrich, The Hitler I Knew: Memoirs of the Third Reich's Press Chief (1955), at ix (2010).

72. Wistrich, *supra* note 44, at 39.

73. *Id.*

74. *Id.*

75. Hardy, *supra* note 22, at 50.

level.[76] In this position, he exerted complete control over the German press in two principal ways.

First, as Fritzsche had, he held daily "press conferences" with editors of all German newspapers, orally providing them with the *Tagesparolen*, or daily press directives, as described above.[77] Second, Dietrich regulated newspaper content through the "Editorial Control Law," a directive that he was responsible for drafting.[78] The law mandated membership for all newspaper and periodical editors in the "Reich League of the German Press."[79] Dietrich was chairman of the Reich League and, in that capacity, operated courts that fined, punished, and removed editors whose newspapers published material inconsistent with Nazi doctrine.[80]

In this position, Dietrich's central role in the conditioning of the German people for persecution of the Jews was explained by former Nuremberg prosecutor Alexander Hardy:

> It was Dietrich, the *Poisoned Pen*, who led the press propaganda phases of the program which incited hatred and conditioned public opinion for mass persecutions on political, racial, and religious grounds. Heretofore, Dietrich's role has been ignored by historians, but actually he, more than anyone else, was responsible for presenting to the German people the justification for liquidating the Jews. . . . Dietrich had at his disposal not only Streicher's paper, but more than 3,000 other publications in the newspaper field and 4,000 publications in the periodical field with a circulation of better than 30,000,000 to disseminate anti-Semitism in a vastly more comprehensive manner. And, he did just that![81]

Based on this conduct, Dietrich was convicted on Count Five of the indictment for crimes against humanity.[82] In issuing its judgment, the NMT did not explicitly state that Dietrich was being convicted of crimes against humanity (persecution) specifically in connection with his hate speech directed at the Jews.[83] In fact, the title of Count Five of the indictment, the only count on which Dietrich was convicted, lumped together war crimes and crimes against humanity, without mentioning persecution or associated language.[84]

76. *Id.* at 52.

77. *Id.* at 40–44. Fritzsche Judgment, *supra* note 53, at 186–187.

78. Jeffrey Herf, The Jewish Enemy: Nazi Propaganda during World War II and the Holocaust 18 (2006).

79. *Id.*

80. *Id.*

81. *Id.* at 189.

82. Ministries Case, *supra* note 69, at 39–40 .

83. *See* Gregory S. Gordon, *The Forgotten Nuremberg Hate Speech Case: Otto Dietrich and the Future of Persecution Law*, 75 Ohio St. L.J. 571, 606 (2014) ("the decision never explicitly found Dietrich guilty of persecution for his speech activities.").

84. *Id.*

III. GENOCIDE AND THE CRIME OF INCITEMENT

A. Rafael Lemkin and the Formulation of a New Legal Concept

Hovering around the question of Nazi guilt at Nuremberg was the nascent concept of genocide. Although not a codified crime at international law when the IMT proceedings began, the term had been presented to the world in Polish jurist Rafael Lemkin's 1944 book *Axis Rule in Occupied Europe*.[85] "Genocide" was a combination of Greek and Latin root words—"genus" (Greek for race or tribe) and "cide" (Latin for killing).[86] Lemkin, who was himself a Holocaust survivor and refugee in the United States,[87] described genocide as follows:

> [A] coordinated plan of different actions aiming at the destruction of essential foundations of the life of national groups, with the aim of annihilating the groups themselves. The objectives of such a plan would be disintegration of the political and social institutions of culture, language, national feelings, religion and economic existence of national groups, and the destruction of the personal security, liberty, health, dignity, and even the lives of the individuals belonging to such groups. Genocide is directed against individuals, not in their individual capacity, but as members of the national group.[88]

In his book, moreover, Lemkin suggested the centrality of speech in carrying out genocide campaigns. In his view, it was not enough to punish only individuals who committed, or gave and executed orders to commit, genocide. The formulation of any anti-genocide law needed to include criminal liability for those who incited others to commit genocide by "whatever means," including "the formulation and teaching of the philosophy of genocide."[89]

B. Genocide at Nuremberg

At Nuremberg, the term "genocide" was alluded to in the IMT indictment, which referenced the Nazis' "deliberate and systematic *genocide*, viz., the extermination of

85. Jonathan A. Bush, *The Prehistory of Corporations and Conspiracy in International Criminal Law: What Nuremberg Really Said*, 109 Colum. L. Rev. 1094, 1178 (2009) (referring to "Raphael Lemkin, the refugee scholar who famously coined the term "genocide" in his 1944 book, Axis Rule in Occupied Europe.").

86. Rafael Lemkin, Axis Rule in Occupied Europe 79 (1944). *See generally*, Matthew Lippman, *The Drafting of the 1948 Convention on Prevention and Punishment of the Crime of Genocide*, 3 B.U. Int'l L.J. 1 (1985).

87. *Genocide Timeline*, Holocaust Encyclopedia, *supra* note 70, http://www.ushmm.org/wlc/en/article.php?ModuleId=10007095.

88. Lemkin, *supra* note 86, at 79.

89. Lippman, *supra* note 86, at 3.

racial and national groups, against the civilian population of certain occupied territories in order to destroy particular races and classes of people and national, racial, or religious groups, particularly Jews, Poles, and Gypsies and others."[90] In his closing argument, British Prosecutor Sir Hartley Shawcross charged that the defendants had "used various biological devices . . . to achieve genocide."[91] French Prosecutor Champetier de Ribes, for his part, argued that the defendants' crimes were "so monstrous, so undreamt of in history throughout the Christian era up to the birth of Hitlerism, that the term 'genocide' has had to be coined to define it and an accumulation of documents and testimonies has been needed to make it credible."[92]

Similarly, in the American NMT proceedings, the term "genocide" had no legal function but was used in court statements and documents (including some of the indictments and judgments) "to describe the Nazis' systematic persecution of various groups."[93] For example, in connection with the *Justice Case* CAH conviction of Oswald Rothaug (public prosecutor at the Nazi "People's Court"), the Tribunal found the defendant was furthering "the national program of racial persecution," and thus "participated in the crime of genocide."[94]

C. Drafting of the Genocide Convention and the Crime of Incitement

The momentum of the justice enterprise at Nuremberg, including a burgeoning awareness of the concept of genocide, carried over to the end phases of the trials. During that time, Lemkin spearheaded an effort to draft a convention to legislate against the offense internationally.[95] And the fruit of his labors, the 1948 Convention on the Prevention and Punishment of the Crime of Genocide (Genocide Convention), defines the offense, at Article II, as follows:

> [G]enocide means any of the following acts committed with intent to destroy, in whole or in part, a national, ethnical, racial or religious group, as such:
> (a) Killing members of the group;
> (b) Causing serious bodily or mental harm to members of the group;
> (c) Deliberately inflicting on the group conditions of life calculated to bring about its physical destruction in whole or in part;

90. 1 TMWC, *supra* note 10, at 43–44 (emphasis added) (referencing genocide in the context of the charge of war crimes (Count III)).

91. *Id.* Vol. 19 at 497–498.

92. *Id.* at 531.

93. Kevin Jon Heller, The Nuremberg Military Tribunals and the Origins of International Criminal Law 249–250 (2011).

94. United States v. Altostoetter (Justice Case), 3 Trials of War Criminals before the Nuremberg Military Tribunals under Control Council Law No. 10, at 1156.

95. *See* Samantha Power, A Problem from Hell: America and the Age of Genocide 52–54 (2002) (recounting Lemkin's efforts in drafting and securing support for adoption of the Genocide Convention).

(d) Imposing measures intended to prevent births within the group;
(e) Forcibly transferring children of the group to another group.[96]

Article III goes on to declare that the following acts, constituting or relating to genocide will be punishable:

(a) Genocide;
(b) Conspiracy to commit genocide;
(c) Direct and public incitement to commit genocide;
(d) Attempt to commit genocide;
(e) Complicity in genocide.[97]

Article II(c) criminalizes "direct and public incitement to commit genocide." But how did this provision find its way into the final draft of the Convention? To find out, it is necessary to consider the Convention's drafting history. A prelude to that history, which helps put the Convention's *travaux préparatoires* into context, is found in the immediate aftermath of the IMT judgment at Nuremberg.

D. The *Travaux Préparatoires* and Incitement's Development

What was the precise sequence of events that culminated in the drafting of the Genocide Convention? To chronicle it, one must rewind the clock two years. In November 1946, concerned by the mere incidental references to genocide during the IMT proceedings and its complete absence in the IMT judgment, Cuba, Panama, and India offered a draft resolution related to genocide at the first session of the General Assembly.[98] The document ostensibly had two goals: (1) present a declaration to the world that genocide was a crime that could be committed in peacetime as well as in time of war; and (2) acknowledge that genocide was subject to universal jurisdiction and could thus be prosecuted by any state, even without a territorial or personal link.[99]

General Assembly Resolution 96 (I), which was adopted on December 11, 1946, declared "that genocide is a crime under international law which the civilized world condemns."[100] But it failed to meet the objectives that motivated Cuba, Panama, and India to draft it in the first place.[101] In particular, it omitted any

96. Convention on the Prevention and Punishment of the Crime of Genocide, 3 U.N. GAOR, G.A. Res. 260A(III) art. II (1948), 78 U.N.T.S. 277 (1951) [hereinafter Genocide Convention].

97. *Id.* art. III.

98. Lippman, *supra* note 86, at 5.

99. William A. Schabas, *Introductory Note: Convention on the Prevention and Punishment of the Crime of Genocide*, United Nations Audiovisual Library of International Law, http://legal.un.org/avl/ha/cppcg/cppcg.html (last visited Sept. 18, 2016) [hereinafter *Introductory Note*].

100. G.A. Res. 96 (I), U.N. Doc. A/64/Add.1, at 189 (1946).

101. Schabas, *Introductory Note, supra* note 99.

reference to commission of the crime in peacetime.[102] Moreover, despite describing genocide as a crime "of international concern," it was silent as to the subject of jurisdiction.[103] Nevertheless, Resolution 96 (I) mandated preparation of a draft convention on the crime of genocide and thus it paved the way for more meaningful normative developments.[104]

Drafting of the Convention itself occurred in three distinct phases. Initially, the UN Secretariat presented a preparatory text that was written with the aid of three law professors—Raphael Lemkin, Vespasian Pella[105] (a pioneering Romanian jurist who, during the interwar years, was an advocate for establishing an international tribunal to try atrocity crimes), and Henri Donnedieu de Vabres[106] (France's principal judge for the Nuremberg IMT and a great international law expert in his own right).[107] This was not so much an actual draft document as it was "a compendium of concepts meant to assist the General Assembly rather than any attempt to provide a workable instrument or to resolve major differences."[108] In the second phase, the Secretariat's preparatory document was the basis of redrafting by an Ad Hoc Committee established under the aegis of the Economic and Social Council (ECOSOC).[109] In the third phase, in late 1948, the Ad Hoc Committee's reworked document was the springboard for negotiations in the Sixth Committee of the General Assembly.[110] That group agreed upon the final text of the Convention and submitted it for formal adoption to the plenary General Assembly.[111]

1. The Secretariat's Draft

The subject of speech as a core facilitating factor in the genocide process featured prominently in each stage of the drafting process. For example, in the Secretariat's draft, Article II stipulated that genocide included various inchoate conduct including attempts, preparatory acts, conspiracy, and direct public incitement. In particular, Article II(II)(2) criminalized "direct public incitement

102. *Id.*

103. *Id.*

104. *Id.*

105. *See generally In Memoriam: Vespasian V. Pella, 1897–1952*, 46 Am. J. Int'l L. 709 (1952) (chronicling the main achievements of his life).

106. *See* Jonathan A. Bush, *The Good, The Bad, and the Ugly—A Review of* The Nuremberg Trials: International Criminal Law Since 1945, 45 Colum. J. Transnat'l L. 899, 906 (2007) (book review) (referring to "the French judge at Nuremberg" and "the best known scholar in the field [of international criminal law] from the 1920s through the 1950s").

107. Schabas, *Introductory Note, supra* note 99.

108. *Id.*

109. *Id.*

110. *Id.*

111. *Id.*

to any act of genocide whether the incitement be successful or not."[112] The commentary pointed out that the "lightly or imprudently spoken word of a journalist or speaker himself capable of doing what he advises will be taken seriously by some of his audience who will regard it as their duty to act on his recommendation."[113] Judges "will have to weigh the circumstances and show greater or lesser severity according to whether his incitement is premeditated or merely represents thoughtless words."[114]

In addition, per Article III, all types of public propaganda tending to promote genocide were also criminalized. More specifically, Article III prohibited "all forms of public propaganda tending by their systematic and hateful character to provoke genocide, or tending to make it appear as a necessary, legitimate or excusable act . . ."[115] The commentary clarifies that Article III was meant to outlaw such "general propaganda as would, if successful, persuade those impressed by it to contemplate the commission of genocide in a favourable light."[116] It goes on to note that propaganda of this nature persuades members of the public "that the existence of the human group designated as the victim of genocide is a very great evil, that this group represents error and perversion, that it imperils society . . . [and] that it is an obstacle to progress. . . ."[117]

The commentary also alludes to the "public" nature of Article III's "propaganda"—such discourse must be addressed to the "public."[118] There is also insight regarding the propaganda content that is proscribed. In particular, the group that is the target of the propaganda "must be represented in an odious light [with] the propaganda . . . necessarily . . . heavily charged with hatred and . . . systematic, that is to say, repeated methodically."[119]

States were invited to provide commentary to the Secretariat's draft, and only the United States offered views regarding the hate speech aspects of the document. First, in general, the United States advocated removing "preparatory acts," such as studies or research.[120] Similarly, it requested that hate propaganda be excluded. It reasoned that these matters were too remote from the offense itself.[121]

112. 4 U.N. ESCOR at 7, U.N. Doc. E/447 (1947).

113. *Id.*

114. *Id.* at 31.

115. *Id.* at 32.

116. *Id.* at 7.

117. *Id.*

118. *Id.* at 33.

119. *Id.*

120. U.N. Doc. A/401.

121. *Id.*

2. The Ad Hoc Committee

After state comments were received, the second phase of drafting began. In early 1948, the matter was referred to ECOSOC, which created an ad hoc drafting committee (Ad Hoc Committee) consisting of China, France, Lebanon, Poland, the Soviet Union, the United States, and Venezuela.[122] To begin, certain Committee members, including the Soviet Union, submitted alternative draft conventions or documents espousing principles favored by the submitting state. The Soviet document, titled "Basic Principles of a Convention on Genocide," stressed that prohibiting genocide ought to encompass repression of incitement to racial hatred as well as sundry preparatory or preliminary acts, including study and research designed to develop techniques of genocide.[123] The United States, France, and China, for their parts, also submitted alternative draft conventions.

The Committee spent much of its time, during April and May 1948, debating the Soviet Principles document and the Chinese alternative convention draft.[124] It ultimately adopted a new draft based primarily on the Chinese version as modified during the Committee's spring sessions.[125] And this was then sent to the Sixth Committee of the General Assembly for final modification and adoption of the convention by the General Assembly.[126]

Ad Hoc Committee draft, Paragraph 3 of Article III, dealing with direct and public incitement to commit genocide, was considered controversial and was much debated. In some senses, it served as a minicrucible for the playing out of Cold War tensions as the Soviet Union and the United States were at loggerheads regarding its inclusion and scope. The United States wanted it deleted, fearing it would impermissibly infringe on freedom of expression.[127] It argued that incitement sufficiently direct to create danger of an imminent commission of genocide would be encompassed by, and be a part of, an attempt, or of an overt act of conspiracy to commit genocide.[128] Both of these, the United States contended further, were already prohibited under Article IV of the Ad Hoc Committee draft Convention obviating the need to include a separate incitement provision.[129]

122. ESC Res. 117(VI); U.N. Doc. E/734. *See* U.N. Doc. E/SR.139±140; U.N. Doc. E/AC.7/SR.37; U.N. Doc. E/663 (with the UK amendment, E/AC.7/65); and U.N. Doc. E/662/Add.1.

123. U.N. Doc. E/AC.25/7.

124. *See* William A. Schabas, Genocide in International Law: The Crime of Crimes 61, 63–64 (2000) [hereinafter Crime of Crimes] (outlining the stages and substantive points considered in connection with the Ad Hoc Committee's drafting).

125. *Id.* at 63–64, 69.

126. *Id.* at 69.

127. *Id.* at 73.

128. Ad Hoc Committee on Genocide Report to the Economic and Social Council on the Meetings of the Committee Held at Lake Success, New York, from 5 April to 10 May 1948, 7 U.N. ESCOR Supp. (No. 6) at 21, n.11, U.N. Doc. E/794 (1948) [hereinafter cited as the Ad Hoe Committee Report].

129. *Id.*

The Soviet Union, on the other hand, wanted it expanded by including an additional act of genocide that was in the Secretariat draft: "All forms of public propaganda (Press, radio, cinema, etc.) aimed at inciting racial, national or religious enmities or hatreds or at provoking the commission of acts of genocide."[130] As with so many other Cold War eventualities, the United States ultimately prevailed in blocking the proposed Soviet enlargement.[131]

Other Soviet attempts to expand the scope of genocidal acts to include speech-related conduct similarly came to naught. In particular, a proposed Soviet amendment was defeated that would have had states parties pledging to disband and prohibit organizations that incite racial hatred or the commission of genocidal acts.[132] Likewise, the Soviets unsuccessfully proposed inclusion of a provision on "preparatory acts" that included criminalizing "studies and research for the purpose of developing the technique of genocide; setting up of installations, manufacturing, obtaining, possessing or supplying of articles or substances with the knowledge that they are intended for genocide; *issuing instructions or orders and distributing tasks with a view to committing genocide.*"[133]

3. The Sixth Committee of the General Assembly and the Final Draft

In the end, after all the debates and the editing, only the provision on direct and public incitement to commit genocide survived in the final draft as submitted to the Sixth Committee of the General Assembly.[134] During the Sixth Committee deliberations, the United States, reprising its position during the Ad Hoc Committee process, attempted to persuade the other states that "incitement to commit genocide" should be punishable only if the incitement created an imminent threat of genocide.[135] In such cases, it contended, incitement would be punishable either as an attempt to commit genocide or as an overt act of a conspiracy to commit genocide.[136] Thus, a separate and dedicated incitement provision would be redundant and should not be included.[137] In advancing this point,

130. U.N. Doc. A/C.6/215/Rev.1.

131. Schabas, Crime of Crimes, *supra* note 124, at 74. Schabas helps put this rejection in context: "It should be borne in mind that, when the debate took place, the Committee had already agreed to include genocide of political groups within the text, a decision it later reversed. This context undoubtedly influenced attitudes towards the hate propaganda amendment." *Id.*

132. U.N. Doc. A/C.6/SR.105 (eighteen in favor, two against, with fifteen abstentions). The Ad Hoc Committee had rejected a similar proposal. Schabas, Crime of Crimes, *supra* note 124, at 76.

133. U.N. Doc. A/C.6/215/Rev.1 (emphasis added). *See also* Schabas, Crime of Crimes, *supra* note 124, at 74 (chronicling the failure of the Soviet proposal).

134. Lippman, *supra* note 86, at 45.

135. 3 U.N. GAOR C.6 (84th mtg.) at 213 (1948), Mr. Maktos (United States).

136. *Id.*

137. *Id.*

the US representative, John Maktos, asserted that the draft's incitement language was so broad that:

> [Any] newspaper article criticizing a political group, or suggesting certain measures with regard to such group for the general welfare, might make it possible for certain States to claim that a Government . . . was committing an act of genocide; and yet such an article might be nothing more than the mere exercise of the right of freedom of the press.[138]

In response, the Polish representative, Manfred Lachs, contended that, in light of the magnitude of the crime of genocide, early legal intervention was necessary. In other words, acts that might seem innocuous in ordinary circumstances must be criminalized in the context of preparing for genocide.[139] Yugoslavia's representative underscored that point by noting that incitement was the first step in the commission of genocide.[140] As for freedom of the press, Haiti's representative stated that the seriousness of the offense of genocide mandated that "the interests of the victims of genocide should take precedence over the interests of the Press."[141] The Soviet representative added that "freedom of speech could never be confused with the freedom to incite people to commit genocide."[142] In the end, the US position was rejected and incitement remained in the draft.[143]

The Sixth Committee transmitted the final draft to the General Assembly on December 6, 1948.[144] The latter made no changes to the Sixth Committee's draft Convention.[145] Thus, on December 9, 1948, at its one hundred and seventy-ninth meeting, the General Assembly unanimously adopted Resolution 260(A)(III), the International Convention on the Prevention and Punishment of the Crime of Genocide.[146] And so, with it, the crime of direct and public incitement to commit genocide was codified at international law.

IV. DEVELOPMENT OF ATROCITY SPEECH SOFT LAW DURING THE COLD WAR

As the 1940s came to an end, the international criminal law (ICL) developments sparked by Allied anti-Nazi solidarity began to peter out. The Cold War defined

138. *Id.*

139. *Id.* at 215, Mr. Lachs (Poland).

140. *Id.* at 216, Mr. Bartos (Yugoslavia).

141. *Id.* at 217, Mr. Demesmin (Haiti).

142. *Id.* at 220, Mr. Morozov (Union of Soviet Socialist Republics).

143. Lippman, *supra* note 86, at 46.

144. 3 U.N. GAOR, U.N. Doc. A/760 (1948).

145. Lippman, *supra* note 86, at 57.

146. 3 U.N. GAOR (179th plen. mtg.) at 851 (1948). The resolution was adopted by a vote of 56–0. *See* Lippman, *supra* note 86, at 57.

the new geopolitical reality—a bipolar world in which the consensus required for normative progress was sorely lacking. Nevertheless, during the early years of the US-Soviet twilight struggle, the ICL-development project was kept on life support by two doctrinal projects—codification of the so-called Nuremberg principles and creation of a draft Code of Offences against the Peace and Security of Mankind.

Both of these projects were spearheaded by the International Law Commission (ILC), which had been established by the UN General Assembly in 1948 for "the promotion of the progressive development of international law and its codification."[147] As a prelude to this, in 1946, the General Assembly had adopted Resolution 94 (I), creating the "Committee on the Codification of International Law" consisting of seventeen eminent experts in the field of international law.[148]

On the same day, the General Assembly also issued Resolution 95 (I), affirming the principles of international law recognized by the Charter of the Nuremberg IMT.[149] The resolution also directed the Committee on Codification of International Law "to treat as a matter of primary importance plans for the formulation, in the context of a general codification of offences against the peace and security of mankind, or of an International Criminal Code, of the principles recognized in the Charter of the Nuremberg Tribunal and in the judgment of the Tribunal."[150] Subsequently, the Codification Committee recommended establishing the ILC, which could then more formally, and definitively, draft a set of Nuremberg principles as well as (and consistent with) a "Code of Offences against the Peace and Security of Mankind."[151]

The ILC was then established, and it went to work drafting a set of Nuremberg principles, which it issued in 1950. For purposes of the development of atrocity speech law, of particular relevance is Principle VI, which reaffirms that crimes against humanity, and persecution in particular, "are punishable as crimes under international law."[152]

147. Statute of the International Law Commission, G.A. Res. 174 (II), Annex, art. 1 (Nov. 21, 1947) [hereinafter ILC Statute], http://legal.un.org/docs/?path_../ilc/texts/instruments/english/statute/statute.pdf&lang_EF, *amended by* G.A. Res. 485 (V) (Dec. 12, 1950); G.A. Res. 984 (X) (Dec. 3, 1955); G.A. Res. 985 (X) (Dec. 3, 1955); G.A. Res. 36/39 (Nov. 18, 1981).

148. G.A. Res. 94 (I), at 3, U.N. Doc. A/RES/94 (I) (Dec. 11, 1946).

149. Affirmation of the Principles of International Law Recognized by the Charter of the Nuremberg Tribunal, G.A. Res. 95(1), U.N. GAOR, 1st Sess., U.N. Doc. A/236 at 1144 (Dec. 11, 1946).

150. *Id.*

151. Report of the Committee on the Progressive Development of International Law and Its Codification, U.N. Doc. A/332 (July 21, 1947). The Committee further advised that "the implementation of the principles of the Nuremberg Tribunal and its judgment, as well as the punishment of other international crimes which may be recognized as such by international multipartite conventions may render desirable the existence of an international judicial authority to exercise jurisdiction over such crimes." *Id.* This marked the first step in the United Nations on the path toward development of a permanent international criminal court.

152. Principles of International Law Recognized in the Charter of the Nuremberg Tribunal and in the Judgment of the Tribunal, Documents of the Second Session Including the Report

Even more relevant is the Draft Code of Offences against the Peace and Security of Mankind, issued in 1954.[153] Article 2 of the Draft Code lists a number of punishable acts, including aggression, terrorism, genocide and crimes against humanity (including persecution), and war crimes.[154] The CAH provision, codified at Article 2(11), proscribes: "Inhuman acts such as murder, extermination, enslavement, deportation or persecutions, committed against any civilian population on social, political, racial, religious or cultural grounds by the authorities of a State or by private individuals acting at the *instigation* or with the toleration of such authorities."[155] So the Draft Code contemplates criminalizing instigation in the context of crimes against humanity and narrowly focuses on authorities exhorting private individuals to commit such offenses.

More importantly, Article 2(13)(i) criminalizes "direct incitement to commit any of the offences in the preceding paragraphs of this article."[156] Thus, the ILC included CAH (persecution), instigation (as to CAH), and, quite significantly, incitement to commit *all* the enumerated crimes—going beyond mere incitement to genocide. The ILC's updated 1996 version of the Draft Code similarly extended incitement to all of that version's enumerated crimes.[157] However, curiously, this version of the document stipulated that direct and public incitement "is limited to situations in which the other individual actually commits that crime."[158] Put another way, according to the 1996 Draft Code, liability attaches for this mode of responsibility only when an individual "directly and publicly incites another individual to commit such a crime *which in fact occurs*."[159]

V. DEVELOPMENT OF ATROCITY SPEECH STATUTORY LAW POST–COLD WAR

A. The Ad Hoc Tribunal Statutes

As described in Chapter 1, atrocities in the former Yugoslavia and in Rwanda in the first part of the 1990s resulted in the creation of ad hoc international criminal

of the Commission to the General Assembly, [1950] 2 Y.B. Int'l L. Comm'n 13, U.N. Doc. A/CN.4/SER.A/1950/Add.1.

153. Draft Code of Offenses against the Peace and Security of Mankind, [1954] 1 Y.B. Int'l L. Comm'n 1, U.N. Doc. A/CN.4/R.6.

154. *Id.* art. 2.

155. *Id.* art. 2(11).

156. *Id.* art. 2(13)(ii).

157. Rep. of the Int'l Law Comm'n, *Draft Code of Crimes against the Peace and Security of Mankind*, 48th Sess., July 17, 1996, U.N. Doc. A/CN.4/L.532; U.N. GAOR 51st Sess., Supp. No. 10, art. 2.3(f), *reprinted in* [1996] 2 Y.B. Int'l L. Comm'n 17.

158. *Id.* at 22.

159. *Id.* art. 2.3(f).

tribunals to bring perpetrators to justice. The first of these, the International Criminal Tribunal for the former Yugoslavia (ICTY) was the result of certain UN Security Council initiatives taken in 1992 and 1993 as violence raged among Yugoslavia's different ethnic groups and territories, particularly in Bosnia and Herzegovina.

In August 1992, with the international community failing to intervene, the Security Council issued Resolution 771, describing and condemning international law violations, including "ethnic cleansing," occurring in the former Yugoslavia.[160] This was followed by Resolution 780, on October 6, 1992, through which the Council established a Commission of Experts to analyze the crimes referred to in Resolution 771.[161] The Commission then conducted its investigation and recommended, in February 1993, establishment of an ad hoc war crimes tribunal,[162] which the Security Council created on May 25, 1993, through Resolution 827.

Per the resolution, the Security Council was setting up "an international tribunal for the sole purpose of prosecuting persons responsible for serious violations of international humanitarian law committed in the territory of the former Yugoslavia between 1 January 1991 and a date to be determined by the Security Council upon restoration of peace. . . ."[163] The statute of the Tribunal, together with a report from the Secretary-General, was included in an annex to the resolution.[164]

As the Security Council was establishing the ICTY, genocide was being planned in Rwanda. It was executed from April through July 1994, as the international community stood idly by during the slaughter of hundreds of thousands of innocent Tutsis by extremist Hutus. But the world did take cognizance of the mass killing via reports of the Special Rapporteur for Rwanda[165] and the

160. S.C. Res. 771, U.N. SCOR, 47th Sess., 3106th mtg. at 2, U.N. Doc. S/RES/771 (1992).

161. S.C. Res. 780, P6, U.N. SCOR, 47th Sess., 3119th mtg. at 2, U.N. Doc. S/RES/780 (Oct. 6, 1992) ("Requests the Secretary-General to establish, as a matter of urgency, an impartial Commission of Experts to examine and analyse the information submitted pursuant to resolution 771 (1992) and the present resolution, together with such further information as the Commission of Experts may obtain through its own investigations or efforts, of other persons or bodies pursuant to resolution 771 (1992), with a view to providing the Secretary-General with its conclusions on the evidence of grave breaches of the Geneva Conventions and other violations of international humanitarian law committed in the territory of the former Yugoslavia. . . .").

162. UN Security Council, Commission of Experts, Interim Report of the Commission of Experts Established Pursuant to Security Council Resolution 780 (1992), ¶ 55, U.N. Doc. S/35374 (Feb. 10, 1993).

163. S.C. Res. 827, U.N. SCOR, 48th Sess., 3217th mtg., U.N. Doc. S/RES/827 (1993).

164. Statute of the International Tribunal for the Prosecution of Persons Responsible for Serious Violations of International Humanitarian Law Committed in the Former Yugoslavia Since 1991, U.N. SCOR, 48th Sess., Annex, U.N. Doc. S/25704 (May 3, 1993), reprinted in 32 I.L.M. 1159, 1169–1201 (1994) [hereinafter ICTY Statute].

165. U.N. Doc. S/1994/1157, annex I and annex II.

preliminary report of a Commission of Experts that was established in circumstances similar to the one set up for the former Yugoslavia.[166]

In its October 1994 report, the Expert Commission for Rwanda, consistent with the one for the former Yugoslavia, recommended that perpetrators be brought to justice before an international criminal tribunal.[167] And once again the Security Council followed that advice. On November 8, 1994, the Security Council adopted Resolution 955, creating an "international tribunal to prosecute those responsible for genocide and other serious violations of international humanitarian law committed in Rwanda between 1 January 1994 and 31 December 1994."[168] Its statute is nearly identical to that of the ICTY; however, its war crimes provisions are different given that the Rwandan Genocide took place as part of an armed conflict that was strictly internal.

For purposes of the law of atrocity speech, the key provisions of the ICTY and International Criminal Tribunal for Rwanda (ICTR) statutes are the ones criminalizing instigation/ordering, genocide, and crimes against humanity (persecution). And, in that respect, they are identical.

With regard to instigation and ordering, ICTY Statute Article 7(1), under the rubric of "Individual Criminal Responsibility," provides that a person "who planned, *instigated, ordered*, committed or otherwise aided and abetted in the planning, preparation or execution of a crime referred to in articles 2 to 5 [i.e., war crimes, genocide, and CAH] of the present Statute, shall be individually responsible for the crime."[169] Article 6(1) of the ICTR Statute is a clone of ICTY Article 7(1).[170]

As for genocide, Article 4 of the ICTY Statute (and Article 2 of the ICTR Statute) declares:

1. The International Tribunal shall have the power to prosecute persons committing genocide as defined in paragraph 2 of this article or of committing any of the other acts enumerated in paragraph 3 of this article.
2. Genocide means any of the following acts committed with intent to destroy, in whole or in part, a national, ethnical, racial or religious group, as such:
   (a) killing members of the group;
   (b) causing serious bodily or mental harm to members of the group;

166. *See* Schabas, Crime of Crimes, *supra* note 124, at 100; Preliminary Report of the Commission of Experts Established Pursuant to Security Council Resolution 935 (1994), U.N. Doc. S/1994/1125; Final Report of the Commission of Experts Established Pursuant to Security Council Resolution 935 (1994), U.N. Doc. S/1994/1405.

167. *Id.*

168. Statute of the International Criminal Tribunal for Rwanda, S.C. Res. 955, U.N. Doc. S/RES/955 (Nov. 8, 1994) [hereinafter ICTR Statute].

169. ICTY Statute, *supra* note 164, art. 7(1) (emphasis added).

170. ICTR Statute, *supra* note 168, art. 6(1).

(c) deliberately inflicting on the group conditions of life calculated to bring about its physical destruction in whole or in part;
(d) imposing measures intended to prevent births within the group;
(e) forcibly transferring children of the group to another group.

3. The following acts shall be punishable:
(a) genocide;
(b) conspiracy to commit genocide;
(c) direct and public incitement to commit genocide;
(d) attempt to commit genocide;
(e) complicity in genocide.[171]

A quick glance at this provision quickly reveals that it incorporates verbatim the exact language of Articles II and III of the Genocide Convention. Why is such a key section of the statute strictly a cut-and-paste of a forty-five-year-old treaty provision? The answer is quite simple—those who drafted the statute:

> [Were] concerned with establishing an overlap between applicable international law and the law in force within the territory of the former Yugoslavia. They proposed that the crime of genocide be included within the statute because it had also been introduced in the domestic legislation of Yugoslavia.[172]

Thus, a central portion of the statute's subject matter jurisdiction was determined by the exigencies of the specific situation confronting its framers—the state of the law in the former Yugoslavia. As we will see, given the ripple effect this statute has had on subsequent iterations of the law, the impact of this ad hoc formulation was significant indeed.

Regarding the crimes against humanity (persecution) provision in the respective statutes, it is contained in Article 5 of the ICTY Statute and Article 3 of the ICTR Statute. ICTY Article 5 declares:

> The International Tribunal shall have the power to prosecute persons responsible for the following crimes when committed in armed conflict, whether international or internal in character, and directed against any civilian population:
> (a) murder;
> (b) extermination;
> (c) enslavement;
> (d) deportation;
> (e) imprisonment;
> (f) torture;
> (g) rape;

171. ICTY Statute, *supra* note 164, art. 4; ICTR Statute, *supra* note 168, art. 2.

172. Schabas, Crime of Crimes, *supra* note 124, at 98.

(h) persecutions on political, racial, and religious grounds;
(i) other inhumane acts.[173]

Similarly, Article 3 of the ICTR Statute stipulates:

> The International Tribunal for Rwanda shall have the power to prosecute persons responsible for the following crimes when committed as part of a widespread or systematic attack against any civilian population on national, political, ethnic, racial or religious grounds:
> (a) murder;
> (b) extermination;
> (c) enslavement;
> (d) deportation;
> (e) imprisonment;
> (f) torture;
> (g) rape;
> (h) persecutions on political, racial, and religious grounds;
> (i) other inhumane acts.[174]

While there are differences in the chapeau portions of these provisions—the ICTY incorporates an armed conflict nexus and the ICTR adds reference to a widespread attack based on discriminatory grounds—the *structure* of the two provisions is essentially identical. They both have a chapeau referencing jurisdiction to try certain offenses when those offenses are directed against a "civilian population." Moreover, each provision preserved "persecution" as a separate offense and eliminated the bifurcation of CAH between persecution and inhumane acts. Avitus Agbor notes that "the ICTY and ICTR have treated the definitions of crimes against humanity in the respective Statutes as synonymous."[175]

And what was the drafting of these provisions based on? Since the close of the Nuremberg proceedings, crimes against humanity, unlike genocide, had not been the subject of a treaty. So both ad hoc tribunal CAH provisions were modeled on the formulations from the Nuremberg versions of CAH.[176] Also, as with the genocide provisions, the CAH provisions were drafted to deal with the exigencies of the respective situations in the former Yugoslavia and Rwanda. The ICTY provision reflects the armed conflict context of the atrocities in the former Yugoslavia whereas the ICTR provision evidences the context of genocide in Rwanda.

173. ICTY Statute, *supra* note 164, art. 5.

174. ICTR Statute, *supra* note 168, art. 3.

175. Avitus A. Agbor, Instigation to Crimes against Humanity: The Flawed Jurisprudence of the Trial and Appeals Chamber of the International Criminal Tribunal for Rwanda, Foreword xxiv (2013).

176. *See* Gregory S. Gordon, *Hate Speech and Persecution: A Contextual Approach*, 46 Vand. J. Transnat'l L. 303, 310 (noting that the ICTY and ICTR formulations were based largely on CCL No. 10); Charles Garraway, *Courts and Tribunals*, Crimes of War, http://www.crimesofwar.org/a-z-guide/courts-and-tribunals/ (last visited Sept. 18, 2016) ("The Statutes of the Tribunals were based strongly on the Nuremberg precedent.").

Two other points about the ICTY Statute bear mentioning. First, in general terms, it was modeled on the Nuremberg IMT Charter.[177] Second, it was drafted in relative haste as it was meant to respond to an unfolding threat to international peace and security. Theodor Meron explains that:

> [Unlike] the International Criminal Court, the ICTY is not the product of a treaty resulting from extended negotiation. Rather the Tribunal was created by the Security Council of the United Nations pursuant to its powers under Chapter VII of the UN Charter to respond to threats to international peace and security. . . . [The] Tribunal's governing Statute [was] drafted quickly.[178]

And, significantly, the ICTY Statute largely served as the basis for the ICTR Statute.[179]

B. The Rome Statute

Similarly, the Rome Statute for the International Criminal Court takes its genocide provision directly from the Genocide Convention and bases the structure of its CAH provision on the ICTY and ICTR statutes.[180] A glance at the relevant provisions confirms this. Article 6 of the Rome Statute, covering genocide, declares:

> For the purpose of this Statute, "genocide" means any of the following acts committed with intent to destroy, in whole or in part, a national, ethnical, racial or religious group, as such:
> (a) Killing members of the group;
> (b) Causing serious bodily or mental harm to members of the group;
> (c) Deliberately inflicting on the group conditions of life calculated to bring about its physical destruction in whole or in part;
> (d) Imposing measures intended to prevent births within the group;
> (e) Forcibly transferring children of the group to another group.[181]

177. *See* Robert Cryer, Hakan Friman, Darryl Robinson, & Elizabeth Wilmshurst, An Introduction to International Criminal Law and Procedure 123 (2d. ed. 2010) ("[The ICTY Statute was] modelled in some ways on the Nuremberg IMT's charter . . . .").

178. Theodor Meron, The Making of International Criminal Justice: A View from the Bench 116–17 (2011).

179. *See* Cryer et al., *supra* note 177 ("[The] ICTR Statute was drafted by the members of the Security Council, following closely the model of the ICTY Statute."). The implications of the hasty drafting and cut-and-paste approach will be explored further in Chapter 11.

180. *See* Sven Bernhard Gareis, The United Nations: An Introduction 198 (2d ed. 2012) ("[The] provisions of Article 6 correspond largely with those of the 1948 Genocide Convention; Article 7, on crimes against humanity, is based on the provisions in the ICTY and ICTR statutes . . . .").

181. Rome Statute of the International Criminal Court art. 6, July 17, 1998, 2178 U.N.T.S. 3 (entered into force July 1, 2002) [hereinafter Rome Statute].

Moreover, although not appearing directly after this enumerated list (the modes of liability having been folded into Article 25), the incitement provision is essentially identical. Article 25(3) stipulates that "a person shall be criminally responsible and liable for punishment for a crime within the jurisdiction of the Court if that person.... (e) In respect of the crime of genocide, directly and publicly incites others to commit genocide . . ."[182] Mark Klamberg notes that Article 25(3)(e) is "in substance identical to Article III(c) of the 1948 Convention on the Prevention and Punishment of the Crime of Genocide, and the ICTY and ICTR Statutes."[183] Moreover, as in the ICTY and ICTR statutes, genocide "is the only international crime to which public incitement has been criminalized."[184]

As noted previously, the ICC's CAH provision also is structured similarly to that of the ICTY/ICTR provisions. Article 7 of the Rome Statute provides:

1. For the purpose of this Statute, "crime against humanity" means any of the following acts when committed as part of a widespread or systematic attack directed against any civilian population, with knowledge of the attack:
   (a) Murder;
   (b) Extermination;
   (c) Enslavement;
   (d) Deportation or forcible transfer of population;
   (e) Imprisonment or other severe deprivation of physical liberty in violation of fundamental rules of international law;
   (f) Torture;
   (g) Rape, sexual slavery, enforced prostitution, forced pregnancy, enforced sterilization, or any other form of sexual violence of comparable gravity;
   (h) Persecution against any identifiable group or collectivity on political, racial, national, ethnic, cultural, religious, gender as defined in paragraph 3, or other grounds that are universally recognized as impermissible under international law, in connection with any act referred to in this paragraph or any crime within the jurisdiction of the Court;
   (i) Enforced disappearance of persons;
   (j) The crime of apartheid;
   (k) Other inhumane acts of a similar character intentionally causing great suffering, or serious injury to body or to mental or physical health.
2. For the purpose of paragraph 1:
   (a) "Attack directed against any civilian population" means a course of conduct involving the multiple commission of acts referred to in

182. *Id.* art. 25(3)(e).

183. Mark Klamberg, *Rome Statute Article 25(3)(e) Commentary*, Case Matrix Network, https://www.casematrixnetwork.org/cmn-knowledge-hub/icc-commentary-clicc/commentary-rome-statute/commentary-rome-statute-part-3/ (last visited Sept. 18, 2016).

184. *Id.*

paragraph 1 against any civilian population, pursuant to or in furtherance of a State or organizational policy to commit such attack;

(b) "Extermination" includes the intentional infliction of conditions of life, *inter alia* the deprivation of access to food and medicine, calculated to bring about the destruction of part of a population;

(c) "Enslavement" means the exercise of any or all of the powers attaching to the right of ownership over a person and includes the exercise of such power in the course of trafficking in persons, in particular women and children;

(d) "Deportation or forcible transfer of population" means forced displacement of the persons concerned by expulsion or other coercive acts from the area in which they are lawfully present, without grounds permitted under international law;

(e) "Torture" means the intentional infliction of severe pain or suffering, whether physical or mental, upon a person in the custody or under the control of the accused; except that torture shall not include pain or suffering arising only from, inherent in or incidental to, lawful sanctions;

(f) "Forced pregnancy" means the unlawful confinement of a woman forcibly made pregnant, with the intent of affecting the ethnic composition of any population or carrying out other grave violations of international law. This definition shall not in any way be interpreted as affecting national laws relating to pregnancy;

(g) "Persecution" means the intentional and severe deprivation of fundamental rights contrary to international law by reason of the identity of the group or collectivity;

(h) "The crime of apartheid" means inhumane acts of a character similar to those referred to in paragraph 1, committed in the context of an institutionalized regime of systematic oppression and domination by one racial group over any other racial group or groups and committed with the intention of maintaining that regime;

(i) "Enforced disappearance of persons" means the arrest, detention or abduction of persons by, or with the authorization, support or acquiescence of, a State or a political organization, followed by a refusal to acknowledge that deprivation of freedom or to give information on the fate or whereabouts of those persons, with the intention of removing them from the protection of the law for a prolonged period of time.

3. For the purpose of this Statute, it is understood that the term "gender" refers to the two sexes, male and female, within the context of society. The term "gender" does not indicate any meaning different from the above.[185]

185. *Id.* art. 7.

"Persecution" is included among the list of inhumane acts at Article 7(1)(h) and includes an expanded list of target groups and a requirement that the act of persecution be connected to "any act referred to in this paragraph or any crime within the jurisdiction of the Court."[186] Further, it is defined in Article 2(g) as "the intentional and severe deprivation of fundamental rights contrary to international law by reason of the identity of the group or collectivity." Overall, though, this provision is essentially "equivalent" to the ICTY/ICTR provisions but with a "more elaborate definition."[187] Avitus Agbor opines that the common core of the ICTR/ICTY provisions was "effectively adopted by the Rome Statute of the International Criminal Court."[188]

And, as with the ad hoc tribunal statutes, "instigation" (implicitly translated to "solicitation" or "inducement") and "ordering" are generally assigned to the section on "Individual Criminal Responsibility." Article 25(3)(b) assigns liability to an individual who "orders, solicits or induces the commission of such a crime which in fact occurs or is attempted. . . ."[189]

VI. CONCLUSION

Having considered the genesis of atrocity speech law, some important observations can be made regarding the drafting history. First, statutory provisions relating to persecution and incitement were formulated pursuant to the immediate needs and political realities confronting the various framers. Second, from the Nuremberg provisions and the Genocide Convention through the Rome Statute, each successive generation of drafting bears the structural signature of the preceding generation—in other words, each new version is organizationally, and in some cases verbally, repetitive of the previous version.

Finally, with the exception of the Draft Code of Offences against the Peace and Security of Mankind, which extended incitement to all core crimes but was never operational, at no point along the way did the drafters appear to consider the potential resonances or linkages between and among the speech-related provisions. Incitement was siloed within genocide. Crimes against humanity (persecution) was in no facial way connected to speech and was structurally, as well as conceptually, separated from incitement. And, vis-à-vis the other speech-related provisions, instigation and ordering were treated as free-floating modes of

186. *Id.* art. 7(1)(h).

187. Jonas Nilsson, *Rome Statute Article 7(1)(h) Commentary*, Case Matrix Network, http://www.casematrixnetwork.org/cmn-knowledge-hub/icc-commentary-clicc/commentary-rome-statute/commentary-rome-statute-part-2-articles-5-10/#c1975 (last visited Sept. 18, 2016).

188. Agbor, *supra* note 175, at Foreword xxiv.

189. Rome Statute, *supra* note 181, art. 25(3)(b).

individual criminal responsibility. We will consider the larger doctrinal implications of all this in Chapter 11.

In any event, regardless of a lack of holistic intentionality or harmonization in the drafting of these texts, they were, on an individual basis, only bare-bones statutory provisions, bereft of judicial interpretation (with the exception of some limited Nuremberg judicial gloss for CAH (persecution)). But a series of ad hoc tribunal judgments from the late 1990s and early 2000s would help flesh out these provisions. It is to these cases that we now turn our attention.

4

The Birth of Atrocity Speech Law Part 2

The Foundational Ad Hoc Tribunal Cases and Offense Elements

> "Every idea is an incitement . . . Eloquence may set fire to reason."
>
> —Oliver Wendell Holmes[1]

> "It is my conviction that the contents of *Der Stürmer* as such were not incitement. During the whole 20 years I never wrote in this context, 'Burn Jewish houses down; beat them to death.' Never once did such an incitement appear in *Der Stürmer*."
>
> —Julius Streicher[2]

I. INTRODUCTION

As we have already seen, in the first part of the 1990s, mass internecine violence engulfed the former Yugoslavia and Rwanda. The drafting and adoption of the ad hoc tribunal statutes identified the crimes that would be charged internationally in connection with that violence. But the scope and elements of those transgressions were yet to be determined. By the second half of the decade, though, the tribunals started issuing judgments and providing invaluable insights into the relevant offenses. Among the charges considered by the tribunals were direct and public incitement to commit genocide, crimes against humanity (persecution), instigation, and ordering.

1. Gitlow v. New York, 268 U.S. 652, 673 (1925) (Holmes, J., dissenting).

2. International Military Tribunal, Nuremberg Trial Proceedings Volume 12, One Hundred and Sixteenth Day, Monday, 29 April 1946, Morning Session, Dr. Hanns Marx (Counsel for Defendant Streicher), p. 320, http://avalon.law.yale.edu/imt/04-29-46.asp (last visited Sept. 18, 2016).

Regarding incitement, the foundational cases of *Prosecutor v. Akayesu* (1998) and *Prosecutor v. Nahimana* (the so-called *Media Case*) (2003) laid out the essential elements of the crime: (1) direct; (2) public; (3) incitement; and (4) *mens rea*. And they provided other important insights about it, including the fact that causation was not an element. Those two judgments bookended a series of other incitement decisions that elucidated various incitement techniques, including speaking in code words and using metaphors.

Charging hate speech as crimes against humanity (persecution) has much deeper jurisprudential roots. Originating as an Allied reference to Turkish atrocities during World War I, crimes against humanity was included in the Nuremberg Charter. And one of its variants, persecution, was applied to a wide range of discriminatory actions, including use of hate speech perpetrated against a victim group when it effects a deprivation of fundamental rights. Building on this, in *Prosecutor v. Ruggiu* (2000), an International Criminal Tribunal for Rwanda (ICTR) Trial Chamber established that hate speech not calling for violence could qualify as persecution—the speech itself effected deprivation of a fundamental right.

Finally, jurisprudence also developed around the crimes of instigation and ordering. The cases specified that instigation involved calls for violence when the violence actually occurred and the charged speech made a contribution thereto. Ordering, for its part, was characterized by a superior-subordinate relationship between the speaker and the listener, where the latter actually carried out the crime.

In much greater depth, the balance of this chapter considers the doctrinal growth of each of these offenses, including their background and required elements.

II. DIRECT AND PUBLIC INCITEMENT TO COMMIT GENOCIDE

The ostensible link between verbal conduct and atrocity in Rwanda meant that speech-related international crimes would play a key role in cases before the ICTR. The offense of direct and public incitement to commit genocide, having been first codified after Nuremberg, was at last applied in an actual legal proceeding as the bloody twentieth century drew to a close. On September 2, 1998, ICTR Trial Chamber 1, composed of Judges Laïty Kama, Presiding, Lennart Aspegren, and Navanethem Pillay, found former Taba commune mayor Jean-Paul Akayesu guilty of various counts of genocide, direct and public incitement to commit genocide, and crimes against humanity.[3] It is an historic decision given that it is "the first conviction for genocide following the signing of the Genocide Convention in 1948."[4] But it is also the first post–Genocide Convention

3. Prosecutor v. Akayesu, Case No. ICTR-96-4-T, Judgement (Sept. 2, 1998). Akayesu was charged with incitement in Count Four of the indictment. *Id.* ¶ 1.2.

4. Fred Grünfeld & Anke Huijboom, The Failure to Prevent Genocide in Rwanda: The Role of Bystanders 20 (2007).

finding of guilt for the crime of direct and public incitement to commit genocide.[5] Given that the *Akayesu* case laid the legal groundwork for incitement, it is necessary to examine closely its facts and as well as the Tribunal's judgment.

A. *Prosecutor v. Akayesu* (1998)

1. The Facts

Akayesu was born in Taba commune, Gitarama Prefecture, in 1953. He became a pillar of the community—an active member of the local football team as a youth and a local schoolteacher and then school district inspector as an adult. He raised a family of five children and developed a reputation as a man of high morals, intelligence, and integrity.[6] He entered the political arena in 1991 as a founding member, and then president, of the local branch of the opposition party called the "Democratic Republican Movement" (*Movement Démocratique Républicain* in French, or MDR). Initially reluctant to run for public office, he ultimately campaigned for *bourgmestre* (mayor) of Taba and, with the support of key figures in the commune, won the election. He served as mayor from April 1993 until June 1994 and was, in effect, the supreme village leader, with stewardship over the local economy and law enforcement.[7] As explained by Samuel Totten and Paul Bartrop:

> [Akayesu] had control of the communal police and was responsible for the maintenance of order, but his authority extended beyond these formal limits. In Rwanda, a considerable degree of informal dominion devolved upon the role of mayor, who acted as a kind of father figure within the commune.[8]

In the early days of the Rwandan Genocide, Akayesu initially managed to shield Taba's Tutsis from the mass killing, forbidding the militia from carrying out their murderous mandate. But after an April 18 meeting of mayors with the rump government leaders then carrying out the genocide, Akayesu had a change of heart.[9] He reckoned that it was in his best interests to comply with their eliminationist demands and, in a gesture both practical and symbolic, exchanged his business suit for a military jacket. Townspeople then witnessed him urging the

5. *See* Charity Kagwi-Ndungu, *The Challenges in Prosecuting Print Media for Incitement to Genocide*, *in* The Media and the Rwanda Genocide 338 (Alan Thompson ed., 2007) ("In the first conviction of the ICTR, for direct and public incitement to commit genocide, the Trial Chamber described the essential elements of the crime. . . .").

6. Dianne Williams, Race, Ethnicity and Crime: Alternative Perspectives 184 (2012); Alexander Laban Hinton, Annihilating Difference: The Anthropology of Genocide 315 (2002).

7. Hinton, *supra* note 6, at 315.

8. 2 Samuel Totten & Paul R. Bartrop, Dictionary of Genocide 6 (2008).

9. Williams, *supra* note 6, at 184.

public to join in the liquidation of Tutsis and transform former places of safe-haven into centers of mass rape, torture, and murder.[10]

But with the Rwandan Patriotic Front winning the war and the genocidal regime retreating, Akayesu fled to Zaire (now the Democratic Republic of the Congo) and then to Zambia, where authorities arrested him in October 1995. Akayesu was initially charged with twelve counts of genocide, direct and public incitement to commit genocide, crimes against humanity, and war crimes.[11] The basis of the incitement count was an Akayesu speech made on April 19, 1994, in Taba commune. While leading a gathering of more than one hundred people assembled around the dead body of a young Hutu, Akayesu urged the population to unite in order to eliminate what he referred to as the "sole enemy": the accomplices of the *Inkotanyi*—a derogatory reference to Tutsis.[12]

2. The Trial Chamber's Judgment

In considering Akayesu's guilt for incitement, the Trial Chamber preliminarily noted that, "at the time the Convention on Genocide was adopted, the delegates agreed to expressly spell out direct and public incitement to commit genocide as a specific crime, in particular, because of its critical role in the planning of a genocide."[13] Related to this, the USSR's representative had observed that it was "impossible that hundreds of thousands of people should commit so many crimes unless they had been incited to do so and unless the crimes had been premeditated and carefully organized."[14] The Trial Chamber then quoted the Soviet diplomat lamenting that "in those circumstances, the inciters and organizers of the crime [were] allowed to escape punishment, when they were the ones really responsible for the atrocities committed."[15]

With this in mind, the Trial Chamber considered Akayesu's culpability for incitement. Primarily relying on Article 91 of the Rwandan Penal Code, it defined incitement as "directly provoking another to commit genocide through speeches at public gatherings, or through the sale or

10. *Id.*

11. Maria Eriksson, Defining Rape: Emerging Obligations for States under International Law? 366 (2011). The indictment was later amended to include charges of sexual violence. *Id.* Another groundbreaking, and historic, aspect of the case was the Tribunal's finding that rape could be the *actus reus* of genocide. Anne-Marie L. M. de Brouwer, Supranational Criminal Prosecution of Sexual Violence: The ICC and the Practice of the ICTY and the ICTR 80 (2005).

12. Prosecutor v. Akayesu, Case No. ICTR-96-4-T, Judgement, ¶ 673 (Sept. 2, 1998). *See also* Gregory S. Gordon, *"A War of Media, Words, Newspapers and Radio Stations": The ICTR Media Trial Verdict and a New Chapter in the International Law of Hate Speech*, 45 Va. J. Int'l L. 139, 150 (2004) [hereinafter *A War of Media*].

13. *Akayesu*, Case No. ICTR-96-4-T, Judgement, ¶ 551.

14. *Id.*

15. *Id.*

dissemination of written or audiovisual communication."[16] Moreover, it considered the crime to have been committed even if the incitement were not successful.[17]

Next, the Trial Chamber considered the crime's *mens rea*. It found that it consists of the intent directly to prompt or provoke another to commit genocide. In other words, the individual who incites others to commit genocide must herself have the specific intent to commit genocide, *viz.*, the intent to destroy, in whole or in part, a national, ethnic, racial, or religious group, as such.[18] In light of the circumstances surrounding Akayesu's acts, the Trial Chamber concluded the *mens rea* element was satisfied.[19]

The Chamber also considered the "public" element of the crime. It found that this criterion should be analyzed in light of two factors: (1) the place where the incitement occurred; and (2) whether or not "assistance" was "selective" or "limited."[20] It then cited the Civil Law treatment of incitement wherein words would be considered "public" when "spoken aloud" in a place that was public "by definition."[21] It added to the analysis by quoting the International Law Commission, which defined public incitement as "a call for criminal action to a number of individuals in a public place" or to "members of the general public at large by such means as the mass media, for example, radio or television."[22]

As for the "direct" element, the Trial Chamber ruled that it "should be viewed in the light of its cultural and linguistic content."[23] In other words, even if a speech

16. *Id.* ¶ 553. Interestingly, the Trial Chamber's reference to "provocation" was lifted from the Civil Law tradition and thus entailed verbal advocacy to commit a crime that actually results in commission of the target crime. The Trial Chamber went on to note that, for the Civil Law crime of provocation, "the prosecution must prove a definite causation between the act characterized as incitement, or provocation in this case, and a specific offence." *Id.* ¶ 557. This is quite odd since, at the same time, the Chamber acknowledged that incitement is an inchoate crime wherein causation is not a required element. As a result, William Schabas points out that the Chamber's analysis mixing consideration of incitement with provocation is "puzzling . . . [because] direct and public incitement is by its nature inchoate or incomplete, it is impossible to prove such a causal link." William A. Schabas, *Hate Speech in Rwanda: The Road to Genocide*, 46 McGill L.J. 141, 161 (2000). The negative consequences of this unfortunate loose analysis mixing consideration of incitement with provocation will be considered in later chapters, in particular, Chapter 5.

17. *Akayesu*, Case No. ICTR-96-4-T, Judgement, ¶ 553.

18. *Id.* ¶ 560.

19. *Id.*

20. *Id.* ¶ 556. The Trial Chamber did not provide a definition of the term "assistance." But another Trial Chamber, in the case of *Prosecutor v. Ruggiu*, substituted the word "assistance" with the word "incitement." Prosecutor v. Ruggiu, Case No. ICTR-97-32-I, Judgement and Sentence, ¶ 17 (June 1, 2000). However, the Chamber did not explain what it meant by referring to "selective" incitement, ostensibly since in both *Akayesu* and *Ruggiu*, the "public" criterion of the offense was not at issue. *Id.*

21. *Ruggiu*, Case No. ICTR-97-32-I, Judgement and Sentence, ¶ 17.

22. *Id.*

23. Prosecutor v. Akayesu, Case No. ICTR-96-4-T, Judgement, ¶ 557 (Sept. 2, 1998).

could be considered "direct" in one locale, it might not be in another, given the cultural and linguistic mindset of the audience.[24] Thus, the Trial Chamber found that an individualized factual inquiry would be necessary in each case. And, it added, "incitement may be direct, and nonetheless implicit."[25]

The inquiry the Trial Chamber had in mind would entail discerning "whether the persons for whom the message was intended immediately grasped the implication thereof."[26] In conducting this examination in *Akayesu*, the Trial Chamber considered both expert and fact witness testimony. With respect to the former, based on several Rwandan publications and broadcasts by Radio Télévision Libre des Milles Collines (RTLM), linguistics expert Dr. Mathias Ruzindana testified that the term *Inkotanyi* would be perceived by Rwandans as meaning "RPF sympathizer" or "Tutsi."[27] As for the fact witnesses, several backed Dr. Ruzindana by affirming on the stand that when the defendant prevailed upon the audience to "eliminate" the *Inkotanyi*, it was perceived as a call to kill all Tutsis.[28] In light of all this evidence, the Chamber found that that in the context of the time, place, and circumstances of Akayesu's speech, "Inkotanyi" meant "Tutsi" generally.[29]

Overall, then, each element had been satisfied. So based on his April 19, 1994, speech, the Chamber found Akayesu guilty of the crime of direct and public incitement to commit genocide.[30]

B. The Decisions between *Akayesu* and the *Media Case*

1. *Prosecutor v. Kambanda* (1998)

Genocidal rump regime Prime Minister Jean Kambanda was the next ICTR defendant to be convicted of incitement.[31] The case was also historic as Kambanda represented the first head of government in history to be convicted of genocide (and incitement to commit genocide, for that matter).[32] For his crimes, he was sentenced to life imprisonment.[33]

24. *Id.*

25. *Id.*

26. *Id.* ¶ 558.

27. *Id.* ¶¶ 147, 340.

28. *Id.* ¶¶ 333–347.

29. *Id.* ¶¶ 361, 709.

30. *Id.* ¶ 674.

31. Tonja Salomon, *Freedom of Speech v. Hate Speech: The Jurisdiction of "Direct and Public Incitement to Commit Genocide"*, *in* The Criminal Law of Genocide: International, Comparative and Contextual Aspects 145 (Ralph Henham & Paul Behrens eds., 2007).

32. *Id.*

33. Prosecutor v. Kambanda, Case No. ICTR-97-23-S, Judgement and Sentence, pt. IV (Sept. 4, 1998).

Kambanda hailed from Mubumbano in the Butare Prefecture. He held a university degree in commercial engineering and had been a bank executive and leader of the local branch of the MDR political party prior to 1994.[34] Married with two children but only thirty-nine years old at the time of the genocide, he was plucked out of relative obscurity and appointed as interim government prime minister soon after the massacres began. He remained in the position through the end of the genocide.[35]

Kambanda was arrested in Nairobi, Kenya, on July 18, 1997, and transferred to the custody of the ICTR, where he was charged with, among other counts, genocide and direct and public incitement to commit genocide. The incitement portions of the indictment were contained in counts 3.12–3.14 and 3.19. As Kambanda confessed to them in their entirety and the Trial Chamber relied on the facts contained therein to find him guilty of incitement, they are fully reproduced as follows:

> 3.12 In addition, on or about 21 April 1994, in his capacity as Prime Minister, **Jean Kambanda,** clearly gave his support to the *Radio Télévsion Libre des Mille Collines* (RTLM), with the knowledge that it was a radio station whose broadcasts incited the killing, serious bodily or mental harm to, and persecution of Tutsis and moderate Hutus. On this occasion, speaking on this radio station, Prime Minister **Jean Kambanda** encouraged the RTLM to continue to incite the massacres of the Tutsi civilian population, specifically stating that this radio station was "an indispensable weapon in the fight against the enemy".
>
> 3.13 Following the numerous meetings of the Council of Ministers between 8 April and 17 July 1994 in Kigali, Gitarama and Gisenyi, **Jean Kambanda** and Ministers of his Government incited, aided and abetted the *Préfets, Bourgmestres,* and members of the population to commit massacres and killings of civilians, in particular Tutsis and moderate Hutus. Furthermore, between 24 April and 17 July 1994, **Jean Kambanda** and Ministers of his Government visited several prefectures, such as Butare, Gitarama (Nyabikenke), Gisenyi, Kibuye, and Cyangugu, to incite and encourage the population to commit these massacres, including by congratulating the people who had committed these killings.

34. The MDR was one of the parties that sprang up in Rwanda after Habyarimana's MRND Party lost its monopoly on political power after opposition parties were legalized. *See* 2 Totten & Bartrop, *supra* note 8, at 291–292. A section of it, consisting of extremist Hutus who ultimately embraced the genocidal project, broke off and formed within the party the "MDR-Power" branch. *Id.* Kambanda belonged to this faction within the party. *Id.* The Arusha Accords had called for the prime minister position to be held by the MDR (but it was contemplated this would be by someone from the mainstream branch of the party). *See* Krysten Sinema, Who Must Die in Rwanda's Genocide?: The State of Exception Realized 10–11 (2015). That is why the rump government offered it to Kambanda. *Id.*

35. *Kambanda*, Case No. ICTR-97-23-S, Judgement and Sentence, ¶ 45.

> 3.14 **Jean Kambanda** and Ministers, including Pauline Nyiramasuhuko, attended a large rally in Butare on 19 April 1994, during which the President of the interim Government, Theodore Sindikubwabo, delivered an inflammatory speech that incited the population to begin the killings. By personally taking the floor at this rally, **Jean Kambanda** showed that he agreed with the inflammatory remarks made by the President.
>
> . . .
>
> 3.19 Between 8 April and 17 July 1994, in several prefectures, such as Butare, Kibuye, Kigali, Gitarama and Gisenyi, many Ministers, *Préfets, Bourgmestres,* Government civil servants and military personnel ordered, incited, aided and actively engaged in actions wilfully intended to massacre and exterminate the Tutsis and moderate Hutus. **Jean Kambanda** knew or should have known that his subordinates were about to commit crimes or had done so and failed to prevent or punish the perpetrators thereof.[36]

In accepting Kambanda's plea, the Trial Chamber issued a judgment and sentence. Given the guilty plea posture of the case, the judgment did not focus on doctrinal application or development. And, in light of Kambanda's overwhelming guilt with respect to his nonverbal conduct as prime minister of a government that carried out genocide, incitement did not factor heavily into the Trial Chamber's analysis.

That said, the judgment did provide valuable insights regarding the scope of incitement. In particular, in addition to referencing the conduct related in the relevant counts of the indictment, it alluded to a document Kambanda submitted to the Trial Chamber that provided more factual detail regarding the defendant's incitement.[37] For example, in it, Kambanda "acknowledges the use of the media as part of the plan to mobilize and incite the population to commit massacres of the civilian Tutsi population."[38] Moreover, pursuant to Paragraph 39(x) of the judgment:

> Jean Kambanda admits that in his particular role of making public engagements in the name of the government, he addressed public meetings, and the media, at various places in Rwanda directly and publicly inciting the population to commit acts of violence against Tutsi and moderate Hutu. He acknowledges uttering the incendiary phrase which was subsequently repeatedly broadcast, "*you refuse to give your blood to your country and the dogs drink it for nothing.*" (Wima igihugu amaraso imbwa zikayanywera ubusa).[39]

36. *Kambanda*, Case No. ICTR-97-23-S, Indictment, ¶¶ 3.12–14, 3.19 (Dec. 16, 1997) (emphasis in original).

37. The document was titled "Plea Agreement between Jean Kambanda and the OTP" and was signed by both the defendant and his counsel. *Kambanda*, Case No. ICTR-97-23-S, Judgement and Sentence, ¶ 39(6).

38. *Id.* ¶ 39(vi).

39. *Id.* ¶ 39(x) (emphasis added).

Overall then, regarding the range of incitement to genocide, the judgment implicitly teaches as follows: (1) encouraging incitement within the context of ongoing incitement as mass violence is taking place can itself constitute an independent act of incitement (here, Kambanda's encouragement of RTLM on the RTLM airwaves); (2) congratulating genocidal killers after they have killed (and implicitly may kill again) falls within the scope of incitement; (3) incitement can be effected via warnings that violence will be visited upon the audience by the intended victims unless the audience acts first and eliminates the intended victims before they can strike (in reference to Kambanda's implicit warning through reference to drinking blood that it was kill or be killed—we will refer to this incitement technique later as "accusation in a mirror"); and (4) metaphors not phrased in the imperative (in other words, Kambanda's law-of-the-jungle allusion to drinking blood) can constitute incitement.

2. *Prosecutor v. Ruggiu* (2000)

The next foundational incitement decision is *Prosecutor v. Ruggiu* (2000).[40] The defendant in that case, Georges Ruggiu, was a Belgian national and the only European indicted by the ICTR.[41] He had been a social worker who served in the Belgian Social Security Administration. In 1990, after meeting some Rwandan expatriates, he developed an interest in the country. By 1992, he had established a large network of Rwandan acquaintances living in Belgium, including students, political figures, officers, diplomats, and government officials.[42] Owing to his newfound passion for Rwanda, Ruggiu helped found, and became an active member in, the *Groupe de réflexion rwando-belge*, which published several articles about the Rwandan political situation, some of which were critical of the Arusha Accords.[43]

After traveling to the Land of a Thousand Hills in 1992 to attend a friend's wedding, Ruggiu's involvement in Rwandan politics intensified.[44] He became a central figure in the Belgian Rwandan-expatriate community and took part in major political debates. By early 1993, he had transformed into a radical opponent of the Rwandan Patriotic Front (RPF) and become an even more zealous advocate for the Rwandan government. On several occasions in May 1993, he was personally invited by Rwandan President Juvénal Habyarimana himself for meetings. At one of those encounters, Habyarimana asked Ruggiu for his opinion on how to improve the image of Rwanda and its government.[45]

40. Prosecutor v. Ruggiu, Case No. ICTR-97-32-I, Judgement and Sentence, ¶ 17 (June 1, 2000).

41. Gordon, *A War of Media, supra* note 12, at 153.

42. *Ruggiu*, Case No. ICTR-97-32-I, Judgement and Sentence, ¶ 38.

43. *Id.* ¶ 39.

44. *Id.* ¶ 40.

45. *Id.* ¶ 41.

In November 1993, Ruggiu finally transplanted himself to his new adoptive country to start a family and work for Habyarimana's political party. Using his influence with RTLM Director Ferdinand Nahimana, the Rwandan president then facilitated Ruggiu's hiring at the Hutu extremist radio station.[46] Ruggiu worked as an RTLM announcer, broadcasting anti-Tutsi and Belgian hate screeds from January 6, 1994, to July 14, 1994. As the RPF swept through Rwanda, Ruggiu fled with the génocidaires to the camps in Zaire and eventually found his way to Kenya.[47] He was arrested there on July 23, 1997, and transferred to ICTR custody.[48] On May 15, 2000, he pled guilty to the two counts of the indictment that had been issued against him—direct and public incitement to commit genocide and crimes against humanity (persecution).

Upon taking his guilty plea, and considering his expressed remorse, cooperation with the prosecution, and other mitigating factors, the ICTR sentenced him to twelve years' imprisonment.[49] Similar to *Kambanda*, as it was also in the context of a guilty plea, the *Ruggiu* judgment itself was neither an occasion for systematic doctrinal application nor the proper forum for significant jurisprudential development. Nevertheless, in contrast to *Kambanda*, the judgment did make reference to the elements considered in *Akayesu*, identifying and defining the *mens rea* and "public" prongs as well as acknowledging and explaining the absence of causation.[50]

As with *Kambanda*, the judgment also provided helpful jurisprudential gloss that built upon the *Akayesu* foundation. In particular, consistent with *Kambanda*, the Trial Chamber indicated that incitement can consist of indirect exhortations, including using code words. For example, Ruggiu's incitement was found to encompass: (1) regularly using the term *inyenzi* (literally "cockroach," in Kinyarwanda) in his broadcasts, which in the sociopolitical context of the time "[designated] the Tutsis as 'persons to be killed' ";[51] (2) telling his listeners that "the 1959 revolution ought to be completed" (the "1959 Revolution" refers to a period when Hutus took power in Rwanda and thousands of Tutsis were massacred);[52] (3) encouraging the public to "go to work," which, in the then-prevailing sociopolitical climate, was coded vernacular for "go kill the Tutsis and Hutu political opponents of the interim government";[53] and (4) thanking

46. *Id.* ¶ 42.

47. Thierry Cruvellier, Court of Remorse: Inside the International Criminal Tribunal for Rwanda 61 (2010).

48. *Id.*

49. *Ruggiu*, Case No. ICTR-97-32-I, Judgement and Sentence, ¶¶ 53–81.

50. *Id.* ¶¶ 14–17. Curiously, the Trial Chamber failed to make reference to the "direct" element. This is a preview of the problems that will arise in subsequent judgments in terms of lack of consistent identification and proper application of the required elements.

51. *Id.* ¶ 44(iii).

52. *Id.* Exhortations to "finish off the 1959 Revolution" were understood as calls for genocide against the Tutsis.

53. *Id.* ¶ 44(iv).

and congratulating perpetrators after massacres and reinforcing that the killers "were having a 'good time.'"[54]

3. *Prosecutor v. Niyitegeka* (2003)

The ICTR next had occasion to consider the parameters of direct and public incitement to commit genocide in the case of *Prosecutor v. Niyitegeka* (2003).[55] Defendant Eliézer Niyitegeka was a journalist who presented the news on Rwanda's government-run media outlet, Radio Rwanda. He was also a member of the MDR, chairman of the MDR in Kibuye Prefecture from 1991 to 1994, and a member of the national political bureau. He was sworn in as minister of information of the genocidal interim government just after the start of the planned massacres, on April 9, 1994.[56]

In 1996, Niyitegeka was indicted by the ICTR on charges of crimes against humanity, war crimes, and various genocide-related offenses, including incitement.[57] The incitement count was based primarily on three incidents during the genocide:

1. On April 13, 1994, in Rugarama (Bisesero region), Niyitegeka told a group of militia engaged in violence against the area's Tutsis "to go back 'to work.'"[58]
2. After the large-scale attack on May 13, 1994, at Muyira Hill, Niyitegeka held a meeting at Kucyapa for the purpose of planning the following day's massacres in Bisesero. He thanked the murderers for their participation that day and commended them for "a good work." He told them "to share the people's property and cattle, and eat meat so that they would be strong to return the next day to continue the "work." The next day, the Tutsis in Bisesero were pursued and slaughtered.[59]
3. On or about June 17, 1994, Niyitegeka held a meeting in which he told the region's *bourgmestres* to tell able-bodied men in the population to participate in the killing of Tutsis and said he would be personally present at the attack.[60]

In considering the defendant's incitement liability for these incidents, the Trial Chamber reviewed the *Akayesu* precedent. This time, the judges alluded to each

54. *Id.* ¶ 44(v).

55. Prosecutor v. Niyitegeka, Case No. ICTR-96-14-T, Judgement and Sentence (May 16, 2003).

56. *Id.* ¶¶ 5, 6.

57. *Id.* ¶ 7.

58. *Id.* ¶ 432.

59. *Id.* ¶ 433.

60. *Id.* ¶ 434.

factor analyzed by *Akayesu* (as opposed to the *Ruggiu* Chamber, which, as we have already seen, did not consider the "direct" criterion): (1) the "public" element; (2) the "direct" element (including the fact that "incitement may be direct, and nonetheless implicit"[61]); (3) *mens rea*; and (4) the lack of a causation requirement given that incitement is an inchoate crime.[62]

The Trial Chamber then applied these elements[63] and found that Niyitegeka's calls for the militias to "go to work" "were understood by his audience as a call to kill the Tutsi, and that the Accused knew his words would be interpreted as such."[64] It also indicated that in "thanking, encouraging and commending [the militia] for the 'work' they had done, 'work' was "a reference to killing Tutsi . . ."[65] And thus retrospective praise for past genocidal killing in the context of ongoing genocidal killing was determined to be an implicit form of incitement.[66]

4. *Prosecutor v. Kajelijeli* (2003)

Just two days before issuing its historic decision in the *Media Case*, the ICTR had occasion to revisit the incitement offense in *Prosecutor v. Kajelijeli* (2003).[67] Juvénal Kajelijeli, was the former *bourgmestre* of Mukingo commune, Ruhengeri Prefecture.[68] The evidence adduced at trial established that:

> [On] the morning of 7 April 1994, the Accused instructed the *Interahamwe* at Byangabo Market and incited the crowd assembled there to "[k]ill and exterminate all those people in Rwankeri" and to "exterminate the Tutsis". He also ordered the *Interahamwe* to dress up and "start to work".[69]

In its judgment, the Trial Chamber engaged in a relatively comprehensive review of the incitement jurisprudence to date. In the main, this consisted of trotting out the elements considered by *Akayesu*—public, direct, *mens rea*, and absence of causation—and characterizing them in identical fashion (primarily

61. Prosecutor v. Akayesu, Case No. ICTR-96-4-T, Judgement, ¶ 557 (Sept. 2, 1998).

62. *Niyitegeka*, Case No. ICTR-96-14-T, Judgement and Sentence, ¶ 431.

63. It should be noted that the application was not done in a systematic way—one element at a time. Rather, the facts were analyzed after consideration of the elements. And one can glean application of the elements in light of the facts discussed.

64. *Niyitegeka*, Case No. ICTR-96-14-T, Judgement and Sentence, ¶ 435.

65. *Id.* ¶ 436.

66. *Id.* The Trial Chamber did not explicitly state this, but it can be inferred from the text. *See* Gregory S. Gordon, *Music and Genocide: Harmonizing Coherence, Freedom and Nonviolence in Incitement Law*, 50 Santa Clara L. Rev. 607, 612 (2010) (noting that the ICTR found that thanking genocide perpetrators for their "good work" was "in part, the basis of the incitement conviction").

67. Prosecutor v. Kajelijeli, Case No. ICTR-98-44A-T, Judgement and Sentence (Dec. 1, 2003).

68. *Id.* ¶ 6.

69. *Id.* ¶ 856.

by quoting directly from the *Akayesu* judgment).[70] In light of the unusually explicit language used by the defendant on the occasion in question, applying the required incitement elements was implicit in the unequivocal finding of guilt on this count. As Sonja Salomon explains:

> As Kajelijeli used clear and non-ambiguous phrases there was no need to exhaustively analyse his speeches. There simply is no clearer phrase to constitute direct incitement than to ask people to go and exterminate people. A phrase like this can without doubt be subsumed under the legal definition developed by the Tribunal in the *Akayesu* decision.[71]

C. *Prosecutor v. Nahimana* (The *Media Case*) (2003)

Two days later, on December 3, 2003, ICTR Trial Chamber I issued its landmark decision in *Prosecutor v. Nahimana*, et al., commonly referred to as the *Media Case*. The Trial Chamber convicted the three defendants in that case—RTLM founders Ferdinand Nahimana and Jean-Bosco Barayagwiza, as well as Hassan Ngeze, editor-in-chief of the equally infamous newspaper *Kangura*. The counts of conviction included direct and public incitement to commit genocide as well as genocide, conspiracy to commit genocide, and crimes against humanity (extermination and persecution). This is arguably the most important incitement decision in international law so it will be broken down here in meticulous detail, starting with in-depth information about the role of the individual defendants and the charges against them and concluding with the Trial Chamber's analysis in its judgment.

1. The Defendants

a. Hassan Ngeze

Described by one expert as a "Hutu Power racist propagandist,"[72] Hassan Negeze was born on December 25, 1957, in Rubavu commune, Gisenyi Prefecture. He began working as a journalist in 1978.[73] By 1990, when the Rwandan Patriotic Front launched its first invasion into Rwanda, Ngeze was a reporter for the independent newspaper *Kanguka*.[74] Philip Gourevitch describes the origins of *Kanguka* and the paper it helped spawn, *Kangura*.

> Back in 1987, a newspaper called *Kanguka* began [and it] was critical of the Habyarimana establishment. Its originality lay in presenting an analysis of

70. *Id.* ¶¶ 850–855.

71. Salomon, *supra* note 31, at 146.

72. Peter Hadreas, A Phenomenology of Love and Hate 116 (2007).

73. Prosecutor v. Nahimana, Case No. ICTR-99-52-T, Judgement and Sentence, ¶ 7 (Dec. 3, 2003).

74. *Id.* ¶ 124.

> Rwandan life based on economic rather than ethnic conflict. *Kanguka*'s courageous staff faced constant harassment, but the paper was a hit with the small public who could read it. So in early 1990, Madame Agathe Habyarimana [the Rwandan president's wife] secretly convened several leaders of the *akazu* [a group of elite, powerful Hutu extremists] with the idea of launching a rival publication. [And] as their editor they hired a small-time hustler and big-time self-promoter named Hassan Ngeze, a former bus fare collector who had established himself as . . . a humourous man-on-the-street correspondent for *Kanguka*. The paper Ngeze produced, *Kangura*—"Wake It Up"—billed itself as "the voice that seeks to awake and guide the majority people." It [used] an identical format [to *Kanguka*] that tricked readers into buying it.[75]

Kangura began in May 1990, and its last issue, No. 59, was published in March 1994, one month before the start of the Rwandan Genocide. By the time the genocide began, *Kangura* was widely considered the best known and most widely read newspaper in Rwanda. In many ways, its lifespan and content embodied the preparation period for the genocide.[76]

In Chapter 1 we looked at the origins of *Kangura* and its role as the key print media outlet for Hutu extremists leading up to the genocide. We examined some of the more notorious content of the newspaper, including the Issue No. 26 cover depicting Rwanda's first president (who had presided over some of the worst ethnic massacres in the country's history) and a machete with the caption: "Which weapons are we going to use to conquer the *Inyenzi* (cockroaches) once and for all?"[77] We also considered the infamous apartheid manifesto "The Hutu Ten Commandments,"[78] which Totten and Bartrop observe "could in many respects have been adapted directly out of the Nazi Nuremberg Laws."[79] Totten and Bartrop conclude that "their repetition through the pages of *Kangura* served as an important means in the ongoing conditioning of the Hutu against the Tutsi of Rwanda."[80]

Another illustrative example of the newspaper's standard anti-Tutsi hate message is found in a February 1993 article in *Kangura* No. 40, entitled "A Cockroach Cannot Give Birth to a Butterfly." The article describes Tutsis as biologically

75. Philip Gourevitch, We Wish to Inform You that Tomorrow We Will Be Killed with Our Families 85 (1998).

76. *See* 2 Totten & Bartrop, *supra* note 8, at 306 (*Kangura* "became a primary instrument in the preparation of the Hutu population of Rwanda for the genocide of the Tutsi population that took place following the one hundred days that followed April 6, 1994.").

77. Larry May, *Incitement to Genocide and the Rwanda Media Case*, *in* Freedom of Expression in a Diverse World 103 (Deirdre Golash ed., 2010).

78. 2 Totten & Bartrop, *supra* note 8, at 306.

79. 1 Samuel Totten & Paul R. Bartrop, Dictionary of Genocide 238 (2008).

80. *Id.*

different from Hutus and intrinsically inclined toward "malice and wickedness."[81] Indeed, *Kangura* always returned to the same coarse and denigrating tropes—all Tutsis were cunning beasts—scheming, underhanded, avaricious, power-hungry, and violent. Tutsi women were sexual predators supposedly in a vast conspiracy with Tutsi men to use their superior looks to ensnare Hutu men into relationships to help promote Tutsi ethnic supremacy over Hutus.[82] The bigoted message was conveyed not only via text but also through crude, pornographic cartoons (much in the same way Julius Streicher debased Jews in *Der Stürmer*).[83]

Kangura published only five issues in 1994. The Trial Chamber characterized them as dealing primarily with the RPF military threat rather than the typical message of pure ethnic hatred.[84] But one aspect of *Kangura* in 1994 bears highlighting and establishes a connection between *Kangura* and RTLM. In March 1994, one month before the start of the genocide, *Kangura* launched a competition in Issue Nos. 58 and 59. The newspaper's readers were asked to identify which back issues contained specific portions of text. The competition's goal was described as "sensitizing the public, who loves the newspaper, to its ideas."[85] Some of the prizes that participants could win could "be seen at RTLM."[86] Readers were also asked to rate various RTLM announcers.[87] Further, in March 1994, RTLM publicized the competition and encouraged listeners to purchase *Kangura* as soon as possible so they could be sure to participate in the competition.[88]

b. Ferdinand Nahimana

Ferdinand Nahimana has been described as "a leading propagandist for the radical Hutu cause against the Tutsi minority prior to and during the Rwandan Genocide of 1994."[89] Born on June 15, 1950, in Gatonde commune, in the northern Ruhengeri Prefecture, he began his career in 1977 as an assistant lecturer of history at the National University of Rwanda,[90] where he became "involved in Hutu supremacist politics."[91] In that regard, Nahimana "developed a number

81. Prosecutor v. Nahimana, Case No. ICTR-99-52-T, Judgement and Sentence, ¶¶ 179–180 (Dec. 3, 2003).

82. *Id.* ¶ 963.

83. *Id.* ¶¶ 207–201.

84. *Id.* ¶ 230.

85. *Id.* ¶ 248.

86. *Id.* ¶ 247.

87. *Id.* ¶ 250.

88. *Id.* ¶¶ 251–252.

89. Paul R. Bartrop, A Biographical Encyclopedia of Contemporary Genocide: Portraits of Evil and Good 224 (2012).

90. *Nahimana*, Case No. ICTR-99-52-T, Judgement and Sentence, ¶¶ 5, 690.

91. Bartrop, *supra* note 89, at 224.

of theories concerning the racial origins of the Rwandan population—theories he was later to popularize when promoting the cause of ethnic Hutu superiority over the Rwandan airwaves."[92]

He quickly rose to prominence through a series of early and rapid promotions at the National University—Faculty of Letters Vice Dean (1980), Faculty of Letters Dean (1981), President of the Administrative Committee (1981), and then Assistant Secretary-General (1983).[93] Having come to the attention of powerful government leaders in Kigali, in 1990 he was tapped to become director of the Rwandan Office of Information (known as ORINFOR—an agency that ran the national radio station, Radio Rwanda). He served in that position until 1992, when, as described in Chapter 1, he was sacked in connection with the broadcasts he authorized that provoked the Bugesera massacres.[94]

Soon after his termination, Nahimana began contemplating the establishment of a private radio station that could broadcast a message more compatible with Hutu-hardliner thinking—this would eventually lead to the creation of RTLM.[95] He used his widespread network of contacts within the MRND to organize a *Comité d'initiative* or "Steering Committee"—consisting of six people, including Barayagwiza and Nahimana himself—and to secure the necessary financing. The funds were provided from a group of founding members—financial contributors and shareholders—who comprised a good cross-section of Rwanda's conservative and extremist Hutu elite. They included, among their ranks, leaders and members of the MRND, Coalition for the Defense of the Republic (CDR), and leaders of the *Interahamwe* militia.[96] Once the seed money was procured, the steering committee, which Nahimana acknowledged was a "provisional Board of Directors,"[97] named him chair of the Technical and Programming Committee.[98] Thus, in this position, he molded the station's journalistic content.[99]

92. *Id.*

93. *Nahimana*, Case No. ICTR-99-52-T, Judgement and Sentence, ¶¶ 5, 690.

94. *Id.*

95. *Id.* ¶¶ 490–491. Nahimana averred in court that he formed the plan to establish RTLM because he felt at that time Radio Rwanda was being controlled by the MDR and thus President Habyarimana's MRND party stances were not garnering ample coverage on the government-controlled national radio. *Id.* ¶ 490.

96. *Id.* ¶ 494. President Juvénal Habyarimana ultimately became RTLM's largest shareholder with two hundred shares. Colonel Théoneste Bagosora, considered to be the genocide's central plotter and behind-the-scenes leader also became a shareholder. *Id.* ¶ 508.

97. *Id.* ¶ 498. RTLM never held an election for a permanent board of directors. As a result, the "steering committee" continued to function as a board of directors for RTLM until the station closed down at the end of the genocide. *Id.*

98. *Id.* ¶ 491.

99. In addition, evidence at trial established Nahimana's control over RTLM banking, corporate management, and public relations. *Id.* ¶¶ 506–508. Thus, he played a central role in the establishment and management of the radio station.

And, as demonstrated in Chapter 1, RTLM content was noxious and murderous from the start. Pre-genocide, there was negative stereotyping of Tutsis (referring to them as devious, disproportionately wealthy, violent, and bloodthirsty, among other things), dehumanization (via animal/insect metaphors), and verbal attacks directed at particular individuals (that sometimes resulted in those individuals being physically harmed). During the genocide, this kind of discourse continued but was intensified by direct calls for liquidation of the Tutsis as well as retrospective praising of mass murder operations and appeals to the population to conceal the evidence of genocide.[100]

Nahimana claimed he merely initiated the RTLM project but lost operational control of it well before the genocide began. But the evidence at trial belied his claims. A whole slew of witnesses testified to dealing with and perceiving Nahimana in the pre-genocide period as the "main brain" behind RTLM or its "leader."[101] Still, the RTLM founder asserted that he had nothing to do with the radio station once the genocide began. He stated that after April 6 the steering committee ceased to exist, RTLM was taken over by the army and made into a "tool for killing," and that he took refuge in the French embassy and was eventually evacuated to Bujumbura, Burundi.[102]

However, once again, the evidence at trial painted a different picture. In a late April 1994 radio interview, as Tutsi mass graves were being filled in Rwanda, Nahimana described himself as an RTLM founder, who was happy the station was "instrumental" in "awakening the majority people." He also confessed that "today's wars are not fought using bullets only, it is also a war [*sic*] of media, words, newspapers and radio stations." Alluding to RTLM and Radio Rwanda, he added, "We were satisfied with both radio stations because they informed us on how the population from all corners of the country had stood up and *worked* together with our armed forces, the armed forces of our country with a view to halting the enemy."[103] Moreover, during the genocide, one witness, a journalist, testified that Nahimana held himself out as a political adviser to genocide-regime President Théodore Sindikubwabo. During a meeting with the journalist, Nahimana (with Barayagwiza present) volunteered that RTLM operations were to be moved from Kigali to Gisenyi. When the journalist stated that he was looking to set up a radio station in the region, Barayagwiza joked that the radio station would compete with RTLM—Nahimana did not contradict this.[104]

Another witness testified that, in early May 1994, Nahimana was seen entering the Ministry of Defense in the company of RTLM Provisional Director Phocas

100. *Id.* ¶¶ 402–403, 419–424, 432–433. *See also* Gordon, *A War of Media, supra* note 12, at 162 (describing the types of speech disseminated by RTLM during this period).

101. *Id.* ¶¶ 509–530.

102. *Id.* ¶ 541.

103. *Id.* ¶ 539 (emphasis added). Of course, as we have seen, in April 1994 Rwanda, "to go to work," in the context of the genocide, meant to kill Tutsis.

104. *Id.* ¶ 542.

Habimana. Even more damning, testimony established that a French diplomat asked Nahimana to have RTLM stop threatening UN Assistance Mission for Rwanda (UNAMIR) General Roméo Dallaire (and UNAMIR itself). Nahimana promised to intervene. And immediately after his pledge, the on-air attacks directed against Dallaire and UNAMIR came to an end.[105]

c. Jean-Bosco Barayagwiza

Counted among RTLM'S management team of "hatemongers,"[106] Jean-Bosco Barayagwiza, like Ferdinand Nahimana, was born in northern Rwanda in 1950—in Mutura commune, Gisenyi Prefecture—and became a lawyer through studies in the Soviet Union.[107] In 1992, he helped found the "Coalition for the Defense of the Republic," or CDR, the most extreme of the parties established by Hutu supremacists.[108] Also like Nahimana, he was a member of the *Comité d'initiative* while simultaneously holding the post of Director of Political Affairs in Rwanda's Ministry of Foreign Affairs.[109] With his attorney background, Barayagwiza acted somewhat as RTLM's in-house counsel, chairing its Legal Committee and drafting its articles of association. And, with Nahimana, he shared responsibility for RTLM banking, corporate management, and public relations.[110] RTLM editor-in-chief Gaspard Gahigi identified Nahimana as the media outlet's "top man" and Barayagwiza as "number two."[111]

Barayagwiza also contributed to RTLM broadcasting. On December 12, 1993, for example, he told RTLM listeners about his personal experience growing up as a Hutu in colonial Rwanda:

> A Hutu child . . . let me take my own example, for I was born a Hutu. [My parents] are Hutus. They brought me up as a Hutu, I grew up in Hutu culture. I was born before the 1959 revolution; my father did forced labor. . . . My mother used to weed in the fields of the Tutsis who were in power. My grandfather paid tribute money. I saw all those things, and when I asked them why they go to cultivate for other people, weed for other people when our gardens were not well maintained, they would tell me: "That is how things are; we must work for the Tutsis." The Tutsi had to be brought up knowing that he

105. *Id.* ¶ 543.

106. Moghalu Kingsley, Rwanda's Genocide: The Politics of Global Justice 87 (2005).

107. *Id.* ¶ 6; Dina Temple-Raston, Justice on the Grass: Three Rwandan Journalists, Their Trial for War Crimes, and a Nation's Quest for Redemption 31 (2005).

108. Prosecutor v. Nahimana, Case No. ICTR-99-52-T, Judgement and Sentence, ¶ 6 (Dec. 3, 2003); Howard B. Tolley, Jr., *Rwanda*, *in* 4 Encyclopedia of Human Rights 385 (David P. Forsythe ed., 2009).

109. *Nahimana*, Case No. ICTR-99-52-T, Judgement and Sentence, ¶ 6.

110. *Id.* ¶¶ 491, 494, 495, 506.

111. *Id.* ¶ 511. This was in an August 1993 interview. *Id.*

> was the chief, that the Hutu child was under his authority. . . . No Hutu would share his meal with a Tutsi; that was forbidden. It was inculcated in the Tutsis never to eat with the Hutus and we were told to fear the Tutsis.[112]

Also like Nahimana, there was ample evidence of Barayagwiza's association with and control over RTLM after April 6, 1994. While serving as an adviser to President Sindikubwabo during the genocide, Barayagwiza told a reporter (with Nahimana also present) that RTLM would be moving from Kigali to Gisenyi. As noted above, he also stated in a humorous manner that if the reporter were to set up a radio station in the region, which the reporter was hoping to do, that it would compete with RTLM.[113] Thus, Barayagwiza spoke as if he were still associated with and part of RTLM management.

2. The Arrests, Charges, and the Trial

Within three years after the end of the genocide, Hassan Ngeze, Ferdinand Nahimana, and Jean-Bosco Barayagwiza had each been arrested and surrendered to the ICTR. In a police raid conducted by Cameroonian authorities, Nahimana and Barayagwiza were apprehended in Yaoundé in March 1996 and transferred to ICTR custody in January 1997. For his part, Ngeze had ended up in Nairobi, Kenya, and, in July 1997, was snared in a multisuspect arrest operation carried out by Kenyan police.[114] He was then promptly surrendered to the custody of the Arusha Tribunal.[115]

The ICTR charged Ngeze (owing chiefly to his *Kangura* conduct—although other conduct was implicated, including acts on behalf of the CDR), Nahimana (almost entirely as a result of his RTLM activities), and Barayagwiza (based on his RTLM and CDR acts), pursuant to Articles 2 and 3 of the Tribunal's statute, with seven counts: conspiracy to commit genocide; genocide; direct and public incitement to commit genocide; complicity in genocide; and crimes against humanity (persecution, extermination, and murder).[116] Their cases were consolidated. And

112. *Id.* ¶ 345.

113. *Id.* ¶ 542.

114. Kingsley, *supra* note 106, at 167.

115. *Id.*

116. *Nahimana*, Case No. ICTR-99-52-T, Judgement and Sentence ¶ 8. Additionally, Barayagwiza was charged with two counts of serious violations of Article 3 common to the Geneva Conventions and of Additional Protocol II, pursuant to Article 4 of the statute. *Id.* ¶ 9. And Ngeze was charged with individual responsibility for the crimes charged under Article 6(1) of the statute. He was also charged with superior responsibility under Article 6(3) with respect to all but one of the crimes—conspiracy to commit genocide. *Id.* ¶ 10. Similarly, Nahimana was charged under Article 6(1) of the statute for his crimes. However, he was charged with superior responsibility under Article 6(3) only with respect to direct and public incitement to commit genocide and crimes against humanity (persecution), not for genocide. *Id.* ¶ 8.

the joint trial opened on October 23, 2000, and ended, after 230 trial days, on August 22, 2003.[117]

3. The Judgment

As noted previously, in addition to direct and public incitement to commit genocide, the Trial Chamber variously convicted the defendants of genocide, conspiracy to commit genocide, and crimes against humanity (extermination and persecution).[118] For our purposes here, we will limit the analysis to the Chamber's verdicts regarding the incitement charges.

Given that the incitement charges stemmed uniquely from media speech activity, the Trial Chamber considered it necessary to consider whether the defendants had legitimately exercised free speech rights or, conversely, engaged in illicit hate advocacy. To do so, it turned to existing international and domestic jurisprudence on this subject and framed its inquiry in terms of resolving the innate friction between freedom of speech and freedom from discrimination.

a. Review of the International Jurisprudence

As we saw in Chapter 2, the domestic jurisprudence largely bifurcates between the fiercely speech-protective American model (also followed to a large degree by Japan) and the rest of the world (as reflected in the decisions of the international adjudicative bodies). American lawyer John Floyd III, who represented Ngeze, strongly urged the Chamber to adopt the former standard. But the judges opted instead to be guided by the discrimination-sensitive international model. As they observed: "The Chamber considers international law, which has been well developed in the areas of freedom from discrimination and freedom of expression, to be the point of reference for its consideration of these issues, noting that domestic law varies widely while international law codifies evolving universal standards."[119]

A review of the international jurisprudence then followed. The Trial Chamber began by going over cases decided under the International Covenant on Civil and Political Rights (ICCPR). In doing so, it implicitly considered the collision

117. *Id.* ¶ 94.

118. *Id.* ¶¶ 1092–1094. Nahimana was found not guilty of crimes against humanity (murder) and complicity in genocide. *Id.* ¶ 1092. Ngeze was acquitted of the same charges. *Id.* ¶ 1094. And so was Barayagwiza except that he was also acquitted of the war crimes charges. *Id.* ¶ 1093.

119. *Id.* ¶ 1010. The judges went on to point out, though, that even American law accepts the core principles enshrined in international law and has established that incitement to violence, threats, group libel, false advertising, obscenity, and child pornography are not entitled to First Amendment protection. *Id.* ¶ 1010. As well, it noted that in the contemporaneous case of *Virginia v. Black*, 538 U.S. 343 (2003), the US Supreme Court found the First Amendment would brook bans on cross burning with the intent to intimidate. And in the area of US immigration law, the Trial Chamber stressed that defendants who had espoused Nazi doctrine before coming to US shores had been stripped of citizenship and deported from the United States on the basis of their anti-Semitic writings. *Id.* ¶ 1010. *See, e.g.*, United States v. Sokolov, 814 F.2d 864 (2d Cir. 1987).

between ICCPR Article 19 (protecting freedom of expression) and Article 20 (forbidding incitement to national, racial, or religious discrimination). As we saw in Chapter 2, *Ross v. Canada*[120] and *J. R. T. and the W. G. Party v. Canada*[121] dealt with that clash in the context of government suppression of anti-Semitic speech under ICCPR Article 19. The Trial Chamber considered those cases first.

In *Ross*, as summarized by the *Media Case* Trial Chamber, the Human Rights Committee upheld disciplinary action taken against a Canadian schoolteacher for remarks that were held to have "denigrated the faith and beliefs of Jews. . . ."[122] Similarly, in *J.R.T.*, the alleged Article 19 violations arose from the government's refusal to allow use of a phone service to convey messages warning of the dangers of "international Jewry" leading to wars, unemployment, inflation, and the collapse of world values and principles. The *Media Case* Trial Chamber emphasized that the complaint's inadmissibility was based on the fact that the telephone messages sought to disseminate "advocacy of racial or religious hatred."[123] Thus, the Chamber concluded, "there was no scope to consider the complaint under the Article 19 right of a state to restrict freedom of expression because . . . the restriction was required under Article 20 of the ICCPR."[124]

Lingering on the implications of ICCPR Article 20, the Trial Chamber next considered *Robert Faurisson v. France*,[125] where the Human Rights Committee contemplated the definition of "incitement" in Article 20(2).[126] As we saw in Chapter 2, Faurisson challenged his conviction in a French court for publishing doubts regarding the existence of gas chambers at Nazi concentration camps. The *Media Case* Trial Chamber focused on the Committee's conclusion that Faurisson had incited "his readers to anti-semitic [*sic*] behaviour" and thus the French decision had not run afoul of Article 19's free expression guarantee.[127] The ICTR judges also drew attention to a concurring opinion that supported the finding of an anti-Semitic purpose by noting Faurisson's references to terms such as "particularly Jewish historians" or the "magic gas chamber."[128] The *Faurisson* concurring opinion, the ICTR panel pointed out, also stressed the context of the

120. International Covenant on Civil and Political Rights, Communication No. 736/1997: Canada (Jurisprudence) U.N. Docs. CCPR/C/70/D/736/1997 (2000) (Ross v. Canada) [hereinafter *Ross*].

121. International Covenant on Civil and Political Rights, Communication No. 104/1981: Canada (Jurisprudence), U.N. Docs. CCPR/C/18/D/104/1981 (J.R.T. & the W.G. Party v. Canada) (declared inadmissible Apr. 6, 1983).

122. *Nahimana*, Case No. ICTR-99-52-T, Judgement and Sentence, ¶ 986.

123. *Id.* ¶ 987.

124. *Id.*

125. Robert Faurisson v. France, Communication No. 550/1993, International Covenant on Civil and Political Rights, U.N. Doc. CCPR/C/58/D/550/1993 (1996).

126. *Nahimana*, Case No. ICTR-99-52-T, Judgement and Sentence ¶ 988.

127. *Id.*

128. *Id.* ¶ 989.

complainant's messages—a challenge to well-documented historical facts with the implication that "under the guise of impartial academic research . . . the victims of Nazism were guilty of dishonest fabrication."[129]

As well, the Trial Chamber scrutinized cases decided under the European Convention on Human Rights, which, as we have seen, has developed jurisprudence balancing a free speech right (per Article 10(1)) with a state prerogative to circumscribe expression for purposes of national security or protecting the rights and reputations of others (per Article 10(2)).[130] On one hand, cases such as *Jersild v. Denmark* (1994)[131] overturned the conviction of a journalist who interviewed members of a racist youth group.[132] Although, the *Media Case* Trial Chamber stated, the journalist did not explicitly condemn the interviewees, the European Court of Human Rights alluded to segments of the interview in which Jersild characterized the group's members as "racist" and "extremist youths." The ICTR judges then quoted the European Court as concluding that the journalist "clearly disassociated him[self] from the persons interviewed."[133]

On the other hand, the *Media Case* Trial Chamber noted,[134] in *Zana v. Turkey* (1997), the European Court upheld the conviction of former mayor Mehdi Zana, from the Kurdistan region, which was under emergency rule as the result of violent clashes that had erupted between Turkish government security forces and Kurdish separatists.[135] As will be recalled from Chapter 2, in a widely circulated Turkish newspaper, Zana was reported as commenting that he supported the separatists and seemingly condoned their massacres by stating that "anyone can make mistakes."[136] The *Media Case* Trial Chamber concluded:[137] in light of the violence raging about him, the European Court found that the comments of Zana, as a former mayor in the region, "had to be regarded as likely to exacerbate an already explosive situation in that region."[138]

The *Media Case* Trial Chamber also considered the other Turkish national security cases dealing with speech-related convictions of Kurds. For example, it reviewed *Incal v. Turkey* (1998), which involved a Kurdish labor party distributing leaflets advocating creation of neighborhood committees to counter the supposed Turkish government policy of removing Kurds from the city (through indirect

129. *Id.*

130. *Id.* ¶ 991.

131. Jersild v. Denmark, App. 15890/89, Eur. Ct. H.R. ¶¶ 29, 31 (1994).

132. *Nahimana*, Case No. ICTR-99-52-T, Judgement and Sentence, ¶ 992.

133. *Jersild*, App. 15890/89, ¶ 34; *Nahimana*, Case No. ICTR-99-52-T, Judgement and Sentence, ¶ 993.

134. *Nahimana*, Case No. ICTR-99-52-T, Judgement and Sentence, ¶ 994.

135. Zana v. Turkey, 1997-VII Eur. Ct. H.R. 2533.

136. *Id.* ¶ 12.

137. *Nahimana*, Case No. ICTR-99-52-T, Judgement and Sentence, ¶ 994.

138. *Zana*, 1997-VII Eur. Ct. H.R. 2533 ¶¶ 667, 670.

acts, such as closing the businesses of street merchants).[139] As we saw in Chapter 2, the government prosecuted one of the party members, Incal, for "attempting to incite hatred and hostility through racist words" in violation of the "Prevention of Terrorism Act." The ICTR judges expressed interest in the European Court's finding that given the *context* of the party's efforts to distribute the leaflets, the latter were best described as efforts to persuade fellow Kurds to "band together to raise certain political demands."[140] And although the meaning of "neighborhood committees" was ambiguous, the Court ruled that, given the context of the situation in that locality, the leaflet's advocacy could not be interpreted as "incitement to the use of violence, hostility or hatred between citizens."[141] This conclusion was bolstered by another aspect of the context—an opposition party expressing dissent against the government establishment—government suppression of speech in that context should be given "the closest scrutiny."[142]

Next, the Trial Chamber looked at the European Court's decision in *Arslan v. Turkey*.[143] It will be recalled that in *Arslan*, the complainant authored a book called *History in Mourning, 33 Bullets*, which chronicled a massacre of Kurds in southeastern Turkey. Arslan characterized the Turks as invaders and persecutors who wished to liquidate the Kurds. A Turkish court convicted him of the crime of disseminating separatist propaganda under the Prevention of Terrorism Act. In finding Arslan's conviction violated ECHR Article 10, the European Court emphasized that the medium of communication in that case was a literary historical narrative, and not the sort of mass media vehicle with an account of contemporary events that would be more likely used to incite violence.[144] And, as in *Incal*, the European Court considered this political speech entitled to a greater presumption of legitimacy and thus less susceptible to restriction under Article 10.[145]

The Trial Chamber also broke down the holding in *Sürek and Özdemir v. Turkey* (1999).[146] In Chapter 2, we saw that case involved a Kurdish newspaper publishing a Kurdistan Workers' Party (PKK) leader's interview wherein the leader explained

139. Incal v. Turkey, 29 Eur. H.R. Rep. 449, 480 (1998).

140. *Id.* ¶ 50.

141. *Id.*

142. *Id.* ¶ 46. *Nahimana*, Case No. ICTR-99-52-T, Judgement and Sentence, ¶ 995 (Trial Chamber highlighting the particular importance of protecting the freedom of expression of political parties, and the need for "the closest scrutiny" in cases involving opposition parties).

143. Arslan v. Turkey, 31 Eur. Ct. H.R. 264, 287 (2001); *Nahimana*, Case No. ICTR-99-52-T, Judgement and Sentence, ¶ 996.

144. *Arslan*, 31 Eur. Ct. H.R. ¶ 45.

145. *Id.* ¶ 48. *Nahimana*, Case No. ICTR-99-52-T, Judgement and Sentence, ¶ 996 ("the Court again noted that there is little scope for restrictions on political speech or on debate on questions of public interest and that criticism of the Government must be given more latitude.").

146. Sürek and Özdemir v. Turkey, App. Nos. 23927/94 & 24277/94, (Eur. Ct. H.R. 1999); *Nahimana*, Case No. ICTR-99-52-T, Judgement and Sentence, ¶ 997.

the party's use of violence to achieve its objectives and its desire to continue its "war" against Turkey. Sürek and Özdemir, editor and shareholder, respectively, of the newspaper, were found guilty by a Turkish National Security Court of disseminating separatist propaganda and terrorist views.[147] The European Court did not interpret the interview at issue as inciting to violence or hatred—instead, it had a "newsworthy content which allowed the public [to] have an insight into the psychology of those who are the driving force behind the opposition to official policy in south-east Turkey...."[148] Nevertheless, the Court offered an admonition:

> Particular caution is called for when consideration is being given to the publication of the views of representatives of organisations which resort to violence against the State lest the media become a vehicle for the dissemination of hate speech and the promotion of violence. At the same time, where such views cannot be categorised as such, Contracting States cannot with reference to the protection of territorial integrity or national security or the prevention of crime or disorder restrict the right of the public to be informed of them by bringing the weight of the criminal law to bear on the media.[149]

Still, a concurring opinion advised against focusing too much on the words used and stressed instead the significance of the general context in which the speech was uttered and its probable impact. Per the concurring opinion, the key issues to resolve were: (1) whether "the language intended to inflame or incite to violence?" and (2) whether "there was a real and genuine risk that it might actually do so."[150]

The *Media Case* Trial Chamber then contrasted *Sürek and Özdemir* with *Sürek v. Turkey (No. 1)* (1999)—the latter involving only the newspaper shareholder from the previous case.[151] In *Sürek v. Turkey (No. 1)*, the European Court found that convictions arising from publication of letters to the editor alluding to Turkish "massacres" and "torture" against the Kurds and describing Turkish officials as a "murder gang," did not violate Article 10 because their incendiary language constituted "an appeal to bloody revenge by stirring up base emotions and hardening already embedded prejudices which have manifested themselves in deadly violence."[152] This was especially the case given the context—the letters were published in a region beset by violent clashes and Turkish emergency rule.[153]

147. *Sürek and Özdemir*, App. Nos. 23927/94 & 24277/94, ¶¶ 10, 12, 23.

148. *Id.* ¶ 61.

149. *Id.* ¶ 63.

150. *Id.* Joint Concurring Opinion of Judges Palm, Tulkens, Fischbach, Casadevall, and Greve.

151. Sürek v. Turkey (No. 1), 1999-IV Eur. Ct. H.R. 353, 355; *Nahimana*, Case No. ICTR-99-52-T, Judgement and Sentence, ¶ 999.

152. *Sürek (No. 1)*, 1999-IV Eur. Ct. H.R. 353 ¶ 62.

153. *Id.*

The Court also noted that one of the letters "identified persons by name, stirred up hatred for them and exposed them to the possible risk of physical violence."[154]

In reviewing *Sürek v. Turkey (No. 1)*, the *Media Case* Trial Chamber emphasized the European Court's assigning responsibility to Sürek as a shareholder, even though he was not responsible for editorial content.[155] As noted by the European Court, and cited by the *Media Case* Trial Chamber: "While it is true that the applicant did not personally associate himself with the views contained in the letters, he nevertheless provided their writers with an outlet for stirring up violence and hatred."[156]

b. Elements Derived from the International Jurisprudence

Having considered the general principles undergirding the international jurisprudence, the Trial Chamber turned to how those principles could relate to analysis of the crime of direct and public incitement to commit genocide. From the Human Rights Committee and European Court cases, the Chamber distilled two criteria through which adjudicators could determine whether speech could be analyzed as legitimate expression or criminal advocacy: purpose and context.

i. *Purpose*

First, the finder of fact must consider the object of the speech. The Trial Chamber set out examples of legitimate speech purpose: historical research, the dissemination of news and information, and the public accountability of government authorities.[157] At the other end of the gamut, overt appeals for violence would evince a clearly illegitimate objective.

In its discussion of "purpose," the Trial Chamber suggested the value of examining the speech's text itself, which could help reveal its object.[158] The Chamber observed, for instance, that in the *Faurisson* case,[159] the UN Human Rights Committee viewed the expression "magic gas chamber" as indicating the complainant sought to express anti-Semitic views rather than promote historical truth.[160] This could be contrasted with the *Jersild* case,[161] where the interviewer distanced himself from the hate speech by characterizing his interviewees as "racist" and "extremist youths." According to the *Media Case* Trial Chamber,

154. *Id.*

155. *Nahimana*, Case No. ICTR-99-52-T, Judgement and Sentence, ¶ 999; *Sürek (No. 1)*, 1999-IV Eur. Ct. H.R. 353 ¶ 63.

156. *Id.*

157. *Nahimana*, Case No. ICTR-99-52-T, Judgement and Sentence, ¶ 1001.

158. As will be explained later, this should be considered a separate criterion and analyzed independently from "purpose." *See* Chapter 8, Section III.D.1.

159. Robert Faurisson v. France, Communication No. 550/1993, International Covenant on Civil and Political Rights, U.N. Doc. CCPR/C/58/D/550/1993 (1996).

160. *Nahimana*, Case No. ICTR-99-52-T, Judgement and Sentence, ¶ 1001.

161. *Jersild*, App. 15890/89, ¶¶ 29, 31.

this exegesis permitted the *Jersild* Court to reason that the interviewer's objective was news dissemination, rather than validation of racist views.[162]

With respect to the Turkish national security cases, the *Media Case* Trial Chamber highlighted the European Court's distinguishing between "language that explains the motivation for terrorist activities and language that promotes terrorist activities."[163] The Chamber then cited *Sürek (No.1)*, where the European Court had found the newspaper shareholder liable for printing readers' letters that represented "an appeal to bloody revenge by stirring up base emotions and hardening already embedded prejudices."[164]

The *Media Case* Trial Chamber then contrasted this with *Sürek and Özdemir*.[165] In that case, the European Court affirmed the right of the very same newspaper to publish an interview with a PKK leader, wherein he expressed his goal of opposing the Turkish government by violent means, because the text itself could be considered newsworthy as opposed to "hate speech and the glorification of violence."[166] "The sensitivity of the Court to volatile language," the *Media Case* Trial Chamber stressed, "goes to the determination of intent, as evidenced by one of the questions put forward in a concurring opinion in this case: 'Was the language intended to inflame or incite to violence?' "[167]

ii. Context

Next, the Chamber instructed, the analysis should focus on context. Put another way, the judges explained, the situation external to and surrounding the speech at issue must be examined in order to appreciate the speech's import.[168] In the words of the panel:

> The Chamber also considers the context in which the statement is made to be important. A statement of ethnic generalization provoking resentment against members of that ethnicity would have a heightened impact in the context of a genocidal environment. It would be more likely to lead to violence. At the same time the environment would be an indicator that incitement to violence was the intent of the statement.[169]

162. *Nahimana*, Case No. ICTR-99-52-T, Judgement and Sentence, ¶ 1001.

163. *Id.* ¶ 1002.

164. Sürek v. Turkey (No. 1), 1999-IV Eur. Ct. H.R. 353 ¶ 62.

165. Sürek and Özdemir v. Turkey, App. Nos. 23927/94 & 24277/94, Eur. Ct. H.R. (1999).

166. *Id.* ¶ 61.

167. *Nahimana*, Case No. ICTR-99-52-T, ¶ 1002; *Sürek and Özdemir*, App. Nos. 23927/94 & 24277/94, Joint Concurring Opinion of Judges Palm, Tulkens, Fischbach, Casadevall, and Greve.

168. *Nahimana*, Case No. ICTR-99-52-T, ¶ 1004.

169. *Id.* ¶ 1022.

To flesh out this criterion and provide a more nuanced analysis, the Chamber turned to the *Faurisson* case,[170] where the Human Rights Committee had observed that, in context, the effect of challenging the existence of gas chambers—a well-documented historical fact—would encourage anti-Semitism. Similarly, in the *Zana* case,[171] the European Court of Human Rights considered the former mayor's statement about massacres in the context of the violence taking place at that time, which in the European Court's view, made the statement "likely to exacerbate an already explosive situation. . . ."[172]

The *Media Case* Trial Chamber went on to consider another important dimension of context. In particular, it explained that the actual denotation of words themselves may be belied by the context in which they are uttered.[173] For example, in *Incal*, the facial contents of the leaflets distributed that informed the population of Turkish plans to remove the Kurds may have seemed superficially innocuous. However, the *Media Case* Trial Chamber added:

> [The European Court of Human Rights] acknowledged the theoretical possibility that such expression might in fact be intended to inflame terrorist activity taking place elsewhere in furtherance of the aims of Kurdish independence. It is a question of evidence and judicial determination of the actual intent or the expression, taking the context into account.[174]

The Chamber made some additional significant observations regarding context. First, it stressed the jurisprudence's concern with protection of political expression, "particularly the expression of opposition views and criticism of the government."[175] According to the Chamber:

> The dangers of censorship have often been associated in particular with the suppression of political or other minorities, or opposition to the government. The special protections developed by the jurisprudence for speech of this kind, in international law and more particularly in the American legal tradition of free speech, recognize the power dynamic inherent in the circumstances that make minority groups and political opposition vulnerable to the exercise of power by the majority or by the government. . . . The special protections for this kind of speech should accordingly be adapted, in the Chamber's view, so

170. Robert Faurisson v. France, Communication No. 550/1993, International Covenant on Civil and Political Rights, U.N. Doc. CCPR/C/58/D/550/1993 (1996).

171. Zana v. Turkey, 1997-VII Eur. Ct. H.R. 2533 ¶ 670.

172. *Id.* ¶¶ 667, 670.

173. *Nahimana*, Case No. ICTR-99-52-T, Judgement and Sentence, ¶ 1005.

174. *Id.*

175. *Id.* ¶ 1006. Again, as will be explained later, this factor—opposition speaker—should be taken out of the "context" rubric and considered as a separate criterion.

> that ethnically specific expression would be more rather than less carefully scrutinized to ensure that minorities without equal means of defence are not endangered.[176]

On the opposite side of the balance sheet, however, "where there are issues of national security and where statements incite to violence, a 'wider margin of appreciation' is given to the discretion of authorities to restrict freedom of expression."[177] Finally, the Chamber indicated that, in the case of oral communication, the tone of the speaker in uttering the words would help put the speech into its proper context:

> In the Chamber's view, the accuracy of the statement is only one factor to be considered in the determination of whether a statement is intended to provoke rather than to educate those who receive it. The tone of the statement is as relevant to this determination as is its content. That Nahimana was aware of the relevance of tone to culpability was evidenced by his reluctance to acknowledge the text of the broadcast, "they are the ones who have all the money", when he was questioned on it.[178]

c. Application of the Elements

Using these criteria, the Trial Chamber went on to differentiate permissible speech from illegal incitement in the cases of *Kangura* and RTLM. The Chamber observed, for example, that certain articles and broadcasts introduced into evidence by the prosecution transmitted legitimate messages—for example historical information, political analysis, or advocacy of ethnic consciousness regarding the inequitable distribution of privilege in Rwanda. Regarding the latter, the Chamber highlighted Barayagwiza's December 12, 1993, broadcast in which he described the discrimination he experienced as a Hutu child.[179]

Using the Tribunal's two analytic criteria, the purpose of the speech appeared to be advocacy of ethnic consciousness. Bolstering this conclusion, the text itself employed language depicting historical inequities and not incitement. Moreover, the context at that point was not that of widespread genocide, as would be the case after April 6, 2004, but a period of social instability and political debate. Also, in terms of context, Barayagwiza related his experience as a member of the politically dispossessed criticizing the establishment of that era. And there were no national security implications. In concluding that Barayagwiza's broadcast was a permissible exercise of free speech, the Trial Chamber characterized it as "a moving personal account of his experience of discrimination as a Hutu."[180]

176. *Id.* ¶ 1008.

177. *Id.* ¶ 1006.

178. *Id.* ¶ 1022.

179. *Id.* ¶ 345.

180. *Id.* ¶ 1019.

In contrast to Barayagwiza's raising of ethnic consciousness, the Trial Chamber expressed disapproval of "harmful ethnic stereotyping" such as an RTLM broadcast where the announcer stated that the Tutsis "are the ones who have all the money." In this instance, the text itself does not withstand scrutiny. The Trial Chamber contrasted it with a broadcast that informed RLTM listeners that persons belonging to the Tutsi ethnicity owned 70 percent of the taxis in Rwanda.[181] This was strictly informational in nature as opposed to asserting that Tutsis "have all the money," which the Trial Chamber described as "a generalization that has been extended to the Tutsi population as a whole."[182] This textual analysis permitted the Trial Chamber to deduce that the speech had an improper purpose.

That conclusion was reinforced by the context of the speech. First, the "tone of the broadcast . . . conveys the hostility and the resentment of the journalist, Kantano Habimana."[183] In addition, "a statement of ethnic generalization provoking resentment against members of that ethnicity would have a heightened impact in the context of a genocidal environment. It would be more likely to lead to violence."[184] Finally, although the Trial Chamber did not explicitly point it out, the speaker was a member of the majority supporting the government then in power. And he was criticizing members of the minority. Overall, then, applying the Trial Chamber's analytic criteria, this would not be considered protected speech.[185]

At the far end of this spectrum is *Kangura*'s December 1990 publication of the "Ten Commandments"[186] and a June 4, 1994, broadcast by Kantano Habimana urging listeners to exterminate the *Inkotanyi*, who could be distinguished by height and physical appearance. Habimana then concluded this chilling exhortation by stating: "Just look at his small nose and then break it."[187] The purpose and text of this radio transmission clearly qualified as illicit incitement to ethnic

181. *Id.* ¶ 1021.

182. *Id.*

183. *Id.*

184. *Id.* ¶ 1022.

185. Even if this could not be considered "incitement," the Trial Chamber explained that less virulent forms of hate speech can qualify as the crime against humanity of persecution. *Id.* ¶ 1072. The Trial Chamber instructed that hate speech is as serious as the other acts enumerated as crimes against humanity under Article 3(h) of the ICTR Statute. *Id.* It also suggested that the *Kangura* article "A Cockroach Cannot Give Birth to a Butterfly," while not rising to the level of incitement, would constitute persecution as a crime against humanity. *See id.* ¶ 1037. *See also* Recent Cases, *The Media Case*, 117 HARV. L. REV. 2769, 2773 n.37 (2004) (describing the article as "discriminatory but not exhortatory.").

186. Prosecutor v. Nahimana, Case No. ICTR-99-52-T, Judgement and Sentence, ¶¶ 138–139.

187. *Id.* ¶ 396. The Trial Chamber explicitly characterized this broadcast as fitting into the "incitement" category. *Id.* ¶ 1032.

violence. Significantly, the speaker in no way attempted to distance himself from the message. In this regard, the Trial Chamber noted:

> In cases where the media disseminates views that constitute ethnic hatred and calls to violence for informative or educational purposes, a clear distancing from these is necessary to avoid conveying an endorsement of the message and in fact to convey a counter-message to ensure that no harm results from the broadcast. The positioning of the media with regard to the message indicates the real intent of the message, and to some degree the real message itself. The editor of *Kangura* and the journalists who broadcast on RTLM did not distance themselves from the message of ethnic hatred. Rather they purveyed the message.[188]

Moreover, Kantano Habimana was Hutu, a member of the majority ethnic group, and he was supporting government policies, while attacking the minority ethnic group, Tutsis. Further, the key contextual feature was an ongoing genocide.[189] There was no doubt then, that Habimana's June 4, 1994, broadcast constituted direct and public incitement to commit genocide.

d. Causation

The *Akayesu* Trial Chamber had ruled that the crime of direct and public incitement to commit genocide could be committed regardless of whether the incitement resulted in genocidal conduct.[190] As previously noted, though, a vital component of the Trial Chamber's factual findings involved showing a "causal relationship" between Akayesu's speech and the massacres that followed. The Trial Chamber concluded that there was such a causal link.[191]

As a result, *Akayesu* left the door open to the argument that direct and public incitement to commit genocide required demonstrating violence precipitated by the incitement. The *Media Case* judgment ostensibly closed that door in its legal findings: "The Chamber notes that this causal relationship is not requisite to a finding of incitement. It is the potential of the communication to cause genocide that makes it incitement."[192]

Nevertheless, its factual findings continued to suggest causation was being considered. For example, in reference to certain radio transmissions made in and around the period of April 6, 1994, the Trial Chamber found:

> RTLM broadcasts engaged in ethnic stereotyping in a manner that promoted contempt and hatred for the Tutsi population and called on listeners to seek

188. *Id.* ¶ 1024.

189. It should be pointed out that *Kangura*'s publication of "The Ten Commandments" was not within the context of the April–July genocide in Rwanda. In this sense, the illegal nature of the article is arguably somewhat diminished.

190. Prosecutor v. Akayesu, Case No. ICTR-96-4-T, Judgement, ¶ 553 (Sept. 2, 1998).

191. *Id.* ¶ 674.

192. Prosecutor v. Nahimana, Case No. ICTR-99-52-T, Judgement and Sentence, ¶ 1015 (Dec. 3, 2003).

> out and take up arms against the enemy. The enemy was defined to be the Tutsi ethnic group. These broadcasts called explicitly for the extermination of the Tutsi ethnic group.... A specific causal connection between the RTLM broadcasts and the killing ... has been established.[193]

D. Conclusion: Summary of Incitement's Foundational Elements and Principles

By the end of 2003, the ICTR cases adjudicating the offense of direct and public incitement to commit genocide had made significant progress in laying a foundational groundwork to analyze the crime. Through *Akayesu* and the *Media Case*, the following elements had been identified and defined: (1) direct (whether the persons for whom the message was intended immediately grasped the implication thereof—thus it can be implicit); (2) public (a call for criminal action to a number of individuals in a public place or to members of the general public via mass media); (3) incitement (illicit advocacy to genocidal action to be determined by reference to purpose and context); and (4) *mens rea* (the intent to incite and the intent to destroy, in whole or in part, a national, ethnic, racial, or religious group, as such).

At the same time, although not systematically integrated into the analysis, important insights into the nature and scope of incitement were provided by the decisions in *Kambanda, Ruggiu, Niyitegeka*, and *Kajalijeli*: (1) encouraging incitement within the context of ongoing incitement in a context of mass violence can itself constitute an independent act of incitement (in *Kambanda*, encouragement of RTLM on the RTLM airwaves); (2) congratulating and praising genocidal killers (and telling them that they are "having a good time") after they have killed (and implicitly may kill again) falls within the scope of incitement (*Kambanda, Ruggiu, Niyitegeka*); (3) incitement can be effected via warnings that violence will be visited upon the audience by the intended victims unless the audience acts first and eliminates the intended victims before they can strike (e.g., Kambanda's implicit warning through reference to drinking blood that it was kill or be killed); and (4) metaphors not phrased in the imperative (in other words, Kambanda's law-of-the-jungle allusion to Tutsis drinking the blood of dogs) can constitute incitement.

Further, and related to this, the jurisprudence to this point established that the use of code words could constitute incitement as follows: (1) Ruggiu regularly using the term *inyenzi* (literally "cockroach," in Kinyarwanda) in broadcasts, which in the sociopolitical context of the time designated the Tutsis as "persons to be killed"; (2) telling listeners that "the 1959 revolution ought to be completed" (the "1959 Revolution" referring to a period when Hutus took power in Rwanda and thousands of Tutsis were massacred); and (3) encouraging the public to "go to work," which, in the then-prevailing sociopolitical climate, was coded language for "go kill the Tutsis and Hutu political opponents of the interim government."

193. *Id.* ¶ 949.

Finally, the judgments suggest in their legal findings that, in light of incitement being an inchoate crime, causation is not an element. Nevertheless, the factual findings of the decisions show the judges considering causation nonetheless.

III. PERSECUTION AS A CRIME AGAINST HUMANITY

Persecution is considered an atrocity speech offense because hate speech may qualify as its *actus reus*. To understand why, we must first examine the development of the persecution offense generally, which reveals it covers a capacious range of conduct.

A. The Development of the Persecution Offense Generally

We saw in Chapter 3 that the term "crimes against humanity" (CAH) was first used in connection with the Armenian Genocide as the Allies attempted to put the Ottoman Empire on notice that it would be brought to justice for the massacres. It surfaced again at Nuremberg as a key part of the International Military Tribunal (IMT) Charter and then was the basis of charges against the propaganda defendants—Julius Streicher and Hans Fritzsche. It was also incorporated into Control Council Law No. 10 and was used to prosecute Otto Dietrich before the *Ministries* Nuremberg Military Tribunal (NMT). While IMT and NMT prosecutors were bringing the propaganda defendants to justice for this crime, they were also preparing cases against other defendants for the same charge.

One expert has observed that, in its global account of Nazi persecution of the Jews, the IMT centered on "the passing of discriminatory laws; the exclusion of members of an ethnic or a religious group from aspects of social, political, and economic life; and the creation of ghettos."[194] The Tribunal also convicted various defendants of persecution charges based on a broad assortment of activities. The gravamen of the persecution charge against Hermann Goering, for instance, consisted of his economic assaults on Jews, especially his post-*Kristallnacht* imposition of a billion mark fine against them.[195] Baldur von Schirach was found guilty of CAH (persecution) chiefly in connection with his deportation of Jews from Vienna in his role as that city's Gauleiter (regional branch Nazi leader).[196]

194. Mohamed Elewa Badar, *From the Nuremberg Charter to the Rome Statute: Defining the Elements of Crimes Against Humanity*, 5 San Diego Int'l L.J. 73, 128 (2004).

195. *See* United States v. Goering, Judgment (Int'l Mil. Trib. Sept. 30, 1946), *reprinted in* 6 F.R.D. 69, 148–149 (1946) (describing how Goering's interest in raising the billion mark fine was "primarily economic—how to get their property and how to force them out of the economic life of Europe"); *see also* Badar, *supra* note 194, at 129 ("[T]he finding of the Nuremberg Tribunal characterizing certain acts of economic discrimination as persecution support the conclusion that economic measures of a personal, as opposed to an industrial type, can constitute persecutory acts.").

196. *Goering*, 6 F.R.D. at 172–173.

And, as we have already seen, Julius Streicher was convicted of persecution as a crime against humanity in connection with his vicious verbal broadsides against the Jews in *Der Stürmer.*[197]

Taking the baton from the IMT, American judges in the course of the NMT Trials conducted under Control Council Law (CCL) No. 10 went even further in broadening the persecution offense's behavioral scope. For example, in *United States v. Altstoetter* (*Justice Case*), the NMT ruled that employment of a legal system to effectuate discriminatory policies amounted to persecution.[198] In *United States v. von Weizsaecker* (*Ministries Case*), the Nuremberg Military Tribunal held:

> The persecution of the Jews went on steadily from step to step and finally to death in foul form. The Jews of Germany were first deprived of the rights of citizenship. They were then deprived of the right to teach, to practice professions, to obtain education, to engage in business enterprises; they were forbidden to marry except among themselves and those of their own religion; they were subject to arrest and confinement in concentration camps, to beatings, mutilation, and torture; their property was confiscated; they were herded into ghettos; they were forced to emigrate and to buy leave to do so; they were deported to the East, where they were worked to exhaustion and death; they became slave laborers; and finally over six million were murdered.[199]

ICTR Judge Mohamed Shahabuddeen, in his partial dissent in the *Media Case* Appeals Chamber judgment, noted in reference to the above finding in *Ministries*: "it is clear that there were acts of mistreatment not involving violence and that such acts were admissible as evidence of persecution."[200] He added that this particular portion of the *Ministries* judgment "may be accepted as reflective of customary international law."[201]

Also in the post–World War II period, various domestic jurisdictions similarly charged Nazi war criminals with persecution.[202] But those courts failed to

197. *Id.* at 161–163.

198. *See* United States v. Altstoetter (Justice Case), Opinion and Judgment, in 3 Trials of War Criminals Before the Nuernberg Military Tribunals under Control Council Law No. 10: "The Justice Case" 954, 1063 (1951) (observing that Nazi judges' application of law against Poles and Jews represented "deliberate contributions toward the effectuation of the policy of the Party and the State").

199. United States v. von Weizsaecker (Ministries Case), Judgment, in 14 Trials of War Criminals Before The Nuernberg Military Tribunals under Control Council Law No. 10: "The Ministries Case" 308, 471 (1951).

200. Prosecutor v. Nahimana, Case No. ICTR-99-52-A, Judgement, ¶ 13 (Nov. 28, 2007) (Shahabuddeen, J., partly dissenting).

201. *Id.*

202. *See, e.g.*, Trial of Hans Albin Rauter (Netherlands Spec. Ct. at s-Gravenhage (The Hague) May 4, 1948 and Neth. Spec. Ct. of Cassation Jan. 12, 1949), *in* 14 Law Reports of Trials of

formulate a clear-cut definition of the crime or provide insights into its breadth. Moreover, as compared to genocide and war crimes, jurists never codified CAH in an international agreement. As a result, before creation of the ad hoc tribunals for the former Yugoslavia and Rwanda, CAH-persecution had "never been comprehensively defined."[203]

Still, some experts offered helpful insights. In his seminal CAH treatise, M. Cherif Bassiouni noted that "[t]hroughout history, the terms 'persecute' and 'persecution' have come to be understood to refer to *discriminatory practices resulting in physical or mental harm, economic harm*, or all of the above."[204] He added that international criminal jurists have commonly defined persecution as "[s]tate action or policy leading to the infliction upon an individual of harassment, torment, oppression, or discriminatory measures, designed to or likely to produce physical or *mental suffering or economic harm*, because of the victim's beliefs, views, or membership in a given identifiable group (religious, social, ethnic, linguistic, etc.)."[205]

Likewise, the International Law Commission, in its commentary on the 1991 Draft Code of Crimes against the Peace and Security of Mankind, imparted valuable perspective regarding the doctrinal bounds of the persecution offense:

> Persecution may take many forms, for example, a prohibition on practising certain kinds of religious worship; prolonged and systematic detention of individuals who represent a political, religious or cultural group; a prohibition on the use of a national language, even in private; systematic destruction of monuments or buildings representative of a particular social, religious, cultural or other group.[206]

Nevertheless, from a case law perspective, the definitional void was soon filled. Much of the jurisprudence originated from the International Criminal Tribunal for the former Yugoslavia (ICTY). For example, in *Prosecutor v. Tadić* (1997), an

War Criminals 89 (U.S. War Crimes Comm'n ed., 1949) (finding S.S. officer guilty of offenses against the Dutch civilian population, including persecution of Jews); Attorney General of Isr. v. Eichmann, 36 I.L.R. 277 (Isr. 1962) (convicting of CAH-persecution, among other charges, S.S. officer who implemented Final Solution); Fédération Nationale des Déportés et Internés Résistants Et Patriotes v. Barbie, 78 I.L.R. 125 (Fr. Cass. 1985) (assigning, *inter alia*, CAH-persecution liability to Lyon Gestapo chief).

203. Prosecutor v. Kupreškić, Case No. IT-95-16-T, Judgement, ¶ 567 (Int'l Crim. Trib. for the Former Yugoslavia Jan. 14, 2000).

204. M. Cherif Bassiouni, Crimes Against Humanity in International Criminal Law 326–327 (2d rev. ed. 1999) (emphasis added).

205. *Id.* at 327 (emphasis added) (internal quotation marks omitted).

206. Draft Code of Crimes Against Peace and Security of Mankind, art. 21, at 9, in Rep. of the Int'l Law Comm'n, 43d Sess., Apr. 29–July 19, 1991, U.N. Doc. A/46/10; GAOR, 46th Sess., Supp. No. 10 (1991).

ICTY Trial Chamber set forth three essential requirements: (1) the occurrence of a discriminatory act or omission; (2) a discriminatory basis for that act or omission on one of the listed grounds, specifically race, religion, or politics; and (3) the intent to cause and a resulting infringement of an individual's enjoyment of a basic or fundamental right.[207]

Subsequently, a four-part test for determining whether conduct can satisfy the *actus reus* requirement for CAH-persecution was formulated in *Prosecutor v. Kupreškić*: (1) a gross or blatant denial; (2) on discriminatory grounds; (3) of a fundamental right, laid down in international customary or treaty law; and (4) reaching the same level of gravity as the other crimes against humanity enumerated in Article 5 of the ICTY Statute.[208]

To put the fourth prong of the test into context, the Trial Chamber referenced the NMT judgment in *United States v. Flick*, focusing on a passage that distinguished between crimes against property and crimes against the person.[209] Within the terms of CCL No. 10, per the Tribunal, Nazi expropriation of *industrial* property from Jews was not of sufficient gravity in relation to various crimes against the person.[210]

That said, the *Kupreškić* Chamber recognized that crimes against property could be serious enough to constitute CAH-persecution.[211] In particular, it noted that in the *Flick* case, the Nazis had expropriated the *industrial* property of Jewish citizens.[212] However, the *Kupreškić* Chamber emphasized, an NMT judgment that followed, *United States v. Krauch (I.G. Farben Case)*,[213] indicated that, as distinct from the holding in *Flick*, crimes involving *personal* property, such as dwellings, household furnishings, and food supplies, could be deemed adequately grave for CAH-persecution purposes.[214] Thus, a reasonable inference can be drawn that, within the CAH context, crimes committed directly against the person (including those

207. Prosecutor v. Tadić, Case No. IT-94-1-T, Opinion and Judgment, ¶ 715 (Int'l Crim. Trib. for the Former Yugoslavia May 7, 1997).

208. *Kupreškić*, Case No. IT-95-16-T, ¶ 621.

209. *Id.* ¶ 619 n.897 (citing United States v. Flick, Opinion and Judgment, *in* 6 Trials of War Criminals Before the Nuernberg Military Tribunals under Control Council Law No. 10: "The Flick Case" 1187, 1215 (1952) [hereinafter *Flick*]).

210. *Flick*, at 1215.

211. *See Kupreškić*, Case No. IT-95-16-T, ¶ 619 n.897 (holding that crimes against personal property, in contrast to industrial property, might qualify as an "assault upon the health and life of a human being" in contravention of international law).

212. *Id.*

213. *See* United States v. Krauch (I.G. Farben Case), Testimony of Defense Witness Huenermann, *in* 7 Trials of War Criminals Before the Nuernberg Military Tribunals under Control Council Law No. 10: "The I.G. Farben Case" 1122, 1129–1130 (1952).

214. *Kupreškić*, Case No. IT-95-16-T, ¶ 619 n.897.

involving *personal* property) should be deemed sufficiently serious in accordance with the fourth prong of the *Kupreškić actus reus* test.

Finally, as part of piecing together this test for *actus reus*, and as a means of explaining it more fully, the *Kupreškić* Chamber offered some crucial insights as to the meaning and extent of the persecution offense: (a) "a narrow definition of persecution is not supported in customary international law"[215] and was understood by the IMT to "include a wide spectrum of acts . . . ranging from discriminatory acts targeting . . . general political, social and economic rights, to attacks on [the] person";[216] (b) persecution also includes acts such as murder and other serious acts on the person; (c) it is "commonly used to describe a series of acts rather than a single act," as "[a]cts of persecution will usually form part of . . . a patterned practice, and must be regarded in their context"; and (d) "[a]s a corollary to [(c)], discriminatory acts charged as persecution must not be considered in isolation" and "may not, in and of themselves, be so serious as to constitute a crime against humanity"—for example, curtailing rights to participate in social life (such as visits to public parks, theaters, or libraries) must not be considered in isolation but examined in their context and weighed for their cumulative effect.[217]

Citing this precedent, the Trial Chamber in *Prosecutor v. Brđanin*[218] ruled that "'the denial of fundamental rights to Bosnian Muslims and Bosnian Croats, including the . . . right to proper judicial process, or right to proper medical care' [constitute] persecutions." Crucially, the Trial Chamber refused to accept the defense argument that "any conviction [for a violation of any of these four rights] violates the principle of legality."[219] It explained:

> The Trial Chamber finds that this argument is misconceived as the Accused is obviously confusing the underlying acts or violations with the actual crime charged, namely that of persecution. The underlying acts (and corresponding violations) alleged are encompassed by the crime of persecution . . . . Any possible conviction would be for this crime and not for the underlying acts or violations. . . . The Trial Chamber reiterates its view that there is no list of established fundamental rights and that such decisions are best taken on a case by case basis. In order to establish the crime of persecution, underlying acts should not be considered in isolation, but in context, looking at their cumulative effect. The Trial Chamber considers that it is not necessary to examine the nature of each right individually, but rather to examine them

215. *Id.* ¶ 615.

216. *Id.* ¶ 597.

217. *Id.* ¶ 615.

218. Prosecutor v. Brđanin, Case No. IT-99-36-T, Judgement, ¶¶ 1029–1031 (Int'l Crim. Trib. for the Former Yugoslavia Sept. 1, 2004).

219. *Id.* ¶ 1030.

as a whole. It is appropriate, therefore, to look at the cumulative denial of the rights to employment, freedom of movement, proper judicial process and proper medical care in order to determine if these are fundamental rights for the purposes of establishing persecution.[220]

B. CAH-Persecution and Speech at the ICTR

As we saw in Chapter 3, dating from its incorporation in the IMT Charter and indictment, hate speech has been the object of CAH prosecutions. At Nuremberg, Nazi newspaper owner Julius Streicher was convicted of CAH-persecution based on his rabidly anti-Semitic harangues in *Der Stürmer.*[221] Hans Fritzsche, head of the Radio Division in Joseph Goebbel's Propaganda Ministry, was also prosecuted at Nuremberg for CAH-persecution, but acquitted.[222] And Reich Press Chief Otto Dietrich, based on "a well thought-out, oft-repeated, persistent campaign to arouse the hatred of the German people against Jews" was convicted of crimes against humanity pursuant to CCL No. 10 as part of the *Ministries Case.*[223]

Almost fifty years later, the ICTR picked up where the Nuremberg judgments left off—concluding that hate speech could qualify as the *actus reus* for CAH-persecution. The first case to do so was *Prosecutor v. Ruggiu.*[224] As we have seen, Georges Ruggiu was an RTLM announcer who verbally attacked Tutsis, moderate Hutus, and Belgians in the period leading up to and during the 1994 Rwandan Genocide.[225] The Trial Chamber that took his guilty plea described Ruggiu as playing "a crucial role in the incitement of ethnic hatred and violence" against both Tutsis and Belgian residents in Rwanda.[226] In addition to direct and public incitement to commit genocide, he pled guilty to CAH-persecution.[227]

In sentencing him, the Trial Chamber had occasion to review the Nuremberg jurisprudence regarding this offense. It began its analysis with the *Streicher*

220. *Id.* ¶¶ 1030–1031.

221. *See* United States v. Goering, Judgment (Int'l Mil. Trib. Sept. 30, 1946), *reprinted in* 6 F.R.D. 161–163 (1946).

222. *Id.* at 186–187.

223. United States v. von Weizsaecker, Judgment, *in* 14 Trials of War Criminals Before the Nuernberg Military Tribunals under Control Council Law No. 10: "The Ministries Case," at 565–576 (1950).

224. Prosecutor v. Ruggiu, Case No. ICTR-97-32-I, Judgement and Sentence, ¶¶ 18–19 (June 1, 2000).

225. *See* Bartrop, *supra* note 89, 280 ("[Ruggiu's] programs consistently incited his listeners to commit murder or serious attacks against the physical or mental well-being of the Tutsis and constituted acts of persecution against Tutsis, moderate Hutus, and Belgian citizens.").

226. *Ruggiu*, Case No. ICTR-97-32-I, ¶ 50.

227. *Id.* ¶¶ 10, 42–45.

decision, observing that the IMT in that case "held that the publisher of a private, anti-Semitic weekly newspaper '*Der Stürmer*' incited the German population to actively persecute the Jewish people."[228] The Chamber then averred that "[t]he *Streicher* Judgment is particularly relevant to the present case since the accused, like Streicher, infected peoples' minds with ethnic hatred and persecution."[229]

Referencing the ICTY judgment in *Kupreškić*,[230] the *Ruggiu* Trial Chamber then laid out the elements of CAH-persecution: "(a) those elements required for all crimes against humanity under the ICTR statute, (b) a gross or blatant denial of a fundamental right reaching the same level of gravity as the other acts prohibited under Article 5, and (c) discriminatory grounds."[231] Regarding element (a), the Chamber elaborated on the CAH *mens rea*, which it found to be the intent to commit the underlying offense, combined with the knowledge of the broader context in which that offense occurs.[232] In regard to the latter, the Chamber held:

> The perpetrator must knowingly commit crimes against humanity in the sense that he must understand the overall context of his act [. . .] Part of what transforms an individual's act(s) into a crime against humanity is the inclusion of the act within a greater dimension of criminal conduct; therefore an accused should be aware of this greater dimension in order to be culpable thereof. Accordingly, actual or constructive knowledge of the broader context of the attack, meaning that the accused must know that his act(s) is part of a widespread or systematic attack on a civilian population and pursuant to some kind of policy or plan, is necessary to satisfy the requisite *mens rea* element of the accused.[233]

As for the final two elements, the Chamber observed:

> The Trial Chamber considers that when examining the acts of persecution which have been admitted by the accused, it is possible to discern a common element. Those acts were [direct and public radio broadcasts all aimed at singling out and attacking the Tutsi ethnic group and Belgians] on

228. *Id.* ¶ 19.

229. *Id.*

230. Prosecutor v. Kupreškić, Case No. IT-95-16-T, Judgement, ¶ 627 (Int'l Crim. Trib. for the Former Yugoslavia Jan. 14, 2000).

231. *Ruggiu*, Case No. ICTR-97-32-I, ¶ 21.

232. *Id.* ¶ 20.

233. *Id.* (alteration in original) (internal quotation marks omitted) (quoting Prosecutor v. Kayishema, Case No. ICTR-95-1-T, Judgement, ¶¶ 133–134 (May 21, 1999)).

> discriminatory grounds, by depriving them of the fundamental rights to life, liberty and basic humanity enjoyed by members of wider society. The deprivation of these rights can be said to have as its aim the death and removal of those persons from the society in which they live alongside the perpetrators, or eventually even from humanity itself.[234]

Two essential points emerge from consideration of these dicta. First, the judges plainly indicate that the crime of CAH-persecution through speech can be successfully consummated without the speaker explicitly urging violence. In referencing *Streicher*, for example, the Trial Chamber implies that the offense was carried out through the defendant's inciting the German population to "persecute" the Jewish people. But "persecution" does not necessarily include physical violence within its ambit. *Oxford Dictionaries* defines persecution as "hostility and ill-treatment, especially because of race or political or religious beliefs; oppression."[235] This inference is reinforced by the ICTR's allusion to the offense as involving Streicher's infecting "peoples' minds with ethnic hatred and persecution."[236]

Any doubt regarding this interpretation of the ruling is removed when the Trial Chamber goes on to characterize the persecution in *Ruggiu* as consisting of radio broadcasts that "singled out" and "attacked" Tutsis and Belgians. Put another way, the words themselves assaulted the victims—they were not strictly a means through which to inspire others to commit violent acts apart from the words.[237] The consequence of the words represents a deprivation of fundamental rights, such as liberty and humanity (even if these are uttered with the intent of ultimately causing death or removal from society).

Second, in accord with offense's *mens rea* requirement, the offender must utter the words knowing that they are "part of a widespread or systematic attack on a civilian population and pursuant to some kind of policy or plan." This signifies that the speech is not an isolated case of hate-mongering, wholly severed from physical violence or inhumane treatment—it must be tethered to such violence or ill-treatment. As a result, the speech ought not be deemed merely "bad speech" or garden-variety "hate speech" in a normal societal context. In light of the *mens rea* requirement, any such discourse is indissolubly connected to a massive or well-planned attack on civilians.

234. *Id.* ¶ 22.

235. *Persecution*, Oxford Dictionaries, http://oxforddictionaries.com/definition/english/persecution (last visited Sept. 18, 2016).

236. *Ruggiu*, Case No. ICTR-97-32-I, ¶ 19.

237. A Trial Chamber of the ICTR later left no doubt about this interpretation. Prosecutor v. Nahimana, Case No. ICTR-99-52-T, Judgement, ¶ 1072 ("The denigration of persons on the basis of their ethnic identity or other group membership in and of itself, as well as in its other consequences, can be an irreversible harm.").

IV. INSTIGATION

A. *Actus Reus*

Instigation's jurisprudential roots at the ad hoc Tribunals go back as far as the first judgment regarding the guilt or innocence of a defendant for international crimes post–World War II—*Prosecutor v. Dusko Tadić* (1997). In that decision, the ICTY Trial Chamber took a broad view of Article 7(1) for purposes of outlining general culpability. It ruled:

> [The] accused will be found criminally culpable for any conduct where it is determined that he knowingly participated in the commission of an offence that violates international humanitarian law and his participation directly and *substantially affected the commission of that offence* through supporting the actual commission before, during, or after the incident.[238]

The following year, the *Akayesu* Trial Chamber, with this baseline understanding of the individual responsibility portion of the ICTY Statute, began the task of fleshing out the instigation aspect of the identical ICTR statutory provision (found at Article 6(1)). The judges found that instigation "involves prompting another to commit an offence; but this is different from incitement in that it is punishable only where it leads to the actual commission of an offence desired by the instigator."[239] In *Prosecutor v. Semanza* (2003), another panel of ICTR judges considered the scope of conduct that could satisfy the crime and explained that its *actus reus* encompassed "urging" or "encouraging."[240] While yet another specified that this could come about "verbally or by other means of communication."[241] And an ICTY Trial Chamber, in *Prosecutor v. Blaškić* (2000) elaborated further in this regard: "Instigation can be performed by any means, both by express or implied conduct. . . ."[242] That said, the instigation must be "specific enough to constitute instructions . . . to the physical perpetrators to commit" the target offense.[243]

238. Prosecutor v. Tadić, Case No. IT-94-1-T, Opinion and Judgment, ¶ 692 (Int'l Crim. Trib. for the Former Yugoslavia May 7, 1997) (emphasis added).

239. Prosecutor v. Akayesu, Case No. ICTR-96-4-T, Judgement, ¶ 482 (Sept. 2, 1998).

240. Prosecutor v. Semanza, Case No. ICTR-97-20-T, Judgement and Sentence, ¶ 555 (May 15, 2003).

241. Prosecutor v. Ndindabahizi, Case No. ICTR-2001-71-I, Judgement and Sentence, ¶ 456 (July 15, 2004).

242. Prosecutor v. Blaškić, Case No. IT-95-14-T, Judgement, ¶ 280 (Int'l Crim. Trib. for the Former Yugoslavia Mar. 3, 2000).

243. Prosecutor v. Brđanin, Case No. IT-99-36-T, Judgement, ¶¶ 468, 527, 662 (Int'l Crim. Trib. for the Former Yugoslavia Sept. 1, 2004).

Further, looking beyond mere affirmative acts, the *Blaškić* Chamber ruled that the wording in Article 7(1) regarding instigation "is sufficiently broad to allow for the inference that both acts and omissions may constitute instigating" and that "this notion covers both express and implied conduct."[244] In this sense, context is crucial to determining liability. As explained by the ICTY Trial Chamber in *Prosecutor v. Brđanin* (2004):

> The Trial Chamber is . . . satisfied that the ARK Crisis Staff's decisions of 28 and 29 May 1992 prompted the municipal authorities and the police, who implemented them, to commit the crimes of deportation and forcible transfer after those dates. Although the two decisions are, not disingenuously, framed in terms of voluntary compliance, to the municipal authorities and the police they could have only meant a direct incitement to deport and forcibly transfer non-Serbs from the territory of the ARK. This is the only reasonable conclusion that may be drawn when the terms of the decisions are considered in the light of the Accused's unambiguous public statements, made repeatedly from early April 1992 onwards, calling upon the non-Serb population to leave the Bosnian Krajina and stating that only a small percentage of non-Serbs would be allowed to stay.[245]

In cases of omission, the prosecutor bears the burden of proving the instigator was "under a duty to prevent the [target] crime from being brought about."[246] Moreover, assuming the duty is established, omissions "amount to instigation in circumstances where a commander has created an environment permissive of criminal behavior by subordinates."[247]

That said, the Trial Chamber in *Prosecutor v. Orić* (2006) laid out certain boundaries regarding the scope of instigation's *actus reus*. First, while instigation may entail "prompting" another to commit an offense, this has to be more than merely facilitating the commission of the principal offence, as it may suffice for aiding and abetting."[248] The judgment went on to elaborate:

> It requires some kind of influencing the principal perpetrator by way of inciting, soliciting or otherwise inducing him or her to commit the crime. This

244. *Blaškić*, Case No. IT-95-14-T, ¶ 280. Presumably, this would mean instigation could be effectuated via images or nonverbal movements. *See* Jerry Kang, *Trojan Horses of Race*, 118 Harv. L. Rev. 1489, 1524 (2005) (noting that "nonverbal behavior can instigate retaliatory responses . . .").

245. *Brđanin*, Case No. IT-99-36-T, ¶¶ 468, 527, 662.

246. Prosecutor v. Orić, Case No. IT-03-68-T, Judgement, ¶ 273 (Int'l Crim. Trib. for the Former Yugoslavia June 30, 2006).

247. Prosecutor v. Galić, Case No. IT-98-29-T, Judgment, ¶ 168 (Int'l Crim. Trib. for the Former Yugoslavia Dec. 5, 2003).

248. *Id.* ¶ 271.

> does not necessarily presuppose that the original idea or plan to commit the crime was generated by the instigator. Even if the principal perpetrator was already pondering on committing a crime, the final determination to do so can still be brought about by persuasion or strong encouragement of the instigator. However, if the principal perpetrator is an "*omnimodo facturus*" meaning that he has definitely decided to commit the crime, further encouragement or moral support may merely, though still, qualify as aiding and abetting.[249]

At the other end of the spectrum, however, notwithstanding "a certain capability to impress others," instigation is different from "ordering," which "implies at least a factual superior-subordinate relationship. . . ."[250] Instigation, on the other hand, "does not presuppose any kind of superiority."[251] Although there is still doctrinal confusion on this point, which will be discussed later in this book, instigation need be neither direct nor public. There is similarly no requirement that the instigator be present at the scene of the crime. Thus, instigating influence can be generated "both face to face and by intermediaries as well as exerted over a smaller or larger audience, provided that the instigator has the corresponding intent."[252]

B. *Mens Rea*

The instigation *mens rea* standard eventually emerged after a lack of consensus among trial chambers from the two ad hoc tribunals. At various points, "knowledge," "intent," "indirect intent," and "intent with awareness" were adopted by different panels of the ICTR and ICTY. For example, the Trial Chamber in *Prosecutor v. Kamuhanda* (2004) held that the instigator's "knowledge" that his acts assisted in the commission of the crime could satisfy the prosecution's *mens rea* burden.[253] But *Prosecutor v. Bagilishema* (2001) had mandated that the instigator "intend" that the crime be committed; while *Prosecutor v. Kordić* (2001) held that the instigator must have "directly intended" to provoke the crime's commission.[254]

To confuse matters even more, yet another ICTR Trial Chamber, in *Prosecutor v. Semanza* (2003), required the participant to act both "intentionally and with the awareness" that he is influencing the principal perpetrators to commit the crime. And a string of ICTY judgments, from 2001 through 2005, found it sufficient that the instigator either "intended to provoke or induce the commission

249. *Id.*

250. *Id.* ¶ 272.

251. *Id.*

252. *Id.* ¶ 273.

253. Prosecutor v. Kamuhanda, Case No. ICTR-95-54A-T, Judgement, ¶ 599 (Jan. 22, 2004).

254. Prosecutor v. Bagilishema, Case No. ICTR-95-1A-T, Judgement, ¶ 31 (June 7, 2001); Prosecutor v. Kordić, Case No. IT-95-14/2-T, Judgement, ¶ 387 (Int'l Crim. Trib. for the Former Yugoslavia Feb. 26, 2001).

of the crime or was aware of the substantial likelihood that the commission of the crime would be a probable consequence of his acts."[255]

Then, in *Prosecutor v. Orić* (2006), the Trial Chamber, after considering the previous muddled jurisprudence and the nature of the liability at issue, embraced an "intent" standard and set out its parameters:

> Considering this development in the interpretation of the instigator's *mens rea* in light of the type and seriousness of crimes over which the Tribunal has jurisdiction, the Trial Chamber holds that individual criminal responsibility both for the commission of, and the participation through, instigation requires intention. The Trial Chamber further holds that intention contains a cognitive element of knowledge and a volitional element of acceptance, and that this intention must be present with respect to both the participant's own conduct and the principal crime he is participating in. This means that, first, with regard to his own conduct, the instigator must be aware of his influencing effect on the principal perpetrator to commit the crime, as well as the instigator, even if neither aiming at nor wishing so, must at least accept that the crime be committed. Second, with regard to the principal perpetrator, the instigator must be both aware of, and agree to, the intentional completion of the principal crime. Third, with regard to the volitional element of intent, the instigator, when aware that the commission of the crime will more likely than not result from his conduct, may be regarded as accepting its occurrence. Although the latter does not require the instigator precisely to foresee by whom and under which circumstances the principal crime will be committed nor that it would exclude indirect inducement, the instigator must at least be aware of the type and the essential elements of the crime to be committed.[256]

Thus, the instigator must have a "double intent"—the intent to utter the speech and the intent for the target crime to be committed (in other words, two layers of intent).[257] Moreover, the intention is bifurcated into cognitive and volitional elements. Regarding the first layer (intent to utter the speech), the instigator must want to exert, and be aware of, his influencing effect on the principal perpetrator to execute the target crime (or accept that the crime be carried out). As for

255. *See* Prosecutor v. Kvocka, Case No. IT-98-30/1-T, Judgement, ¶ 252 (Int'l Crim. Trib. for the Former Yugoslavia Nov. 2, 2001); Prosecutor v. Naletilić, Case No. IT-98-34-T, Judgement, ¶ 60 (Int'l Crim. Trib. for the Former Yugoslavia Mar. 31, 2003); Prosecutor v. Brđanin, Case No. IT-99-36-T, Judgement, ¶ 269 (Int'l Crim. Trib. for the Former Yugoslavia Sept. 1, 2004); Prosecutor v. Limaj, Case No. IT-03-66-T, Judgment, ¶ 514 (Int'l Crim. Trib. for the Former Yugoslavia Nov. 30, 2005).

256. Prosecutor v. Orić, Case No. IT-03-68-T, Judgement, ¶ 279 (Int'l Crim. Trib. for the Former Yugoslavia June 30, 2006).

257. *See* Wibke Timmermann, Incitement in International Law 242 (2014) ("The intention has to be 'present with respect to both the participant's own conduct and the principal crime he is participating in,' that is, the instigator must have a 'double intent.'").

the second layer (intent to have the target crime committed), this encompasses awareness of and agreement to intentional commission of the target crime. The agreement element can be satisfied by a heightened awareness, that is, knowledge that the crime's commission will more likely than not result from the principal perpetrator's conduct.[258]

C. Contribution

As we have seen, instigation is punishable only when the speech is in fact followed by subsequent related criminal conduct.[259] In effect, there must be established a connection between the instigation and commission of the target crime.[260] Nevertheless, in principle, that does not inevitably signify proof of "but for" causation. In other words, it has been held that "it is not necessary to prove that the crime would not have been perpetrated without the accused's involvement."[261] Instead, it need only be demonstrated that "that the contribution of the accused in fact had an effect on the commission of the crime."[262]

In various decisions, this has been formulated in different fashions. For example, certain ad hoc tribunal judges have ruled that the prosecution must marshal evidence that the defendant's conduct constituted "a clear contributing factor"[263] or "substantially contributed"[264] to the conduct of the principal perpetrator. And two ICTR Trial Chambers have found that, in addition to "substantial," the instigator's contribution must be "direct."[265] Given these different formulations, there is confusion regarding the exact standard, as will be demonstrated in Chapter 6.

V. ORDERING

A. Overview

Although, as we saw in Chapter 3, the Nuremberg Charter did not contain an explicit "ordering" mode of liability, the responsibility of certain Nuremberg defendants was

258. *Id.*

259. Prosecutor v. Akayesu, Case No. ICTR-96-4-T, Judgement, ¶ 482 (Sept. 2, 1998).

260. Prosecutor v. Blaskić, Case No. IT-95-14-T, Judgement, ¶ 278 (Int'l Crim. Trib. for the Former Yugoslavia Mar. 3, 2000).

261. Prosecutor v. Kordić, Case No. IT-95-14/2-T, Judgment, ¶ 387 ((Int'l Crim. Trib. for the Former Yugoslavia Feb. 26, 2001).

262. *Id.*

263. Prosecutor v. Kvocka, Case No. IT-98-30/1-T, Judgement, ¶ 252 ((Int'l Crim. Trib. for the Former Yugoslavia Nov. 2, 2001).

264. *Kordić*, Case No. IT-95-14/2-A, Judgement, ¶ 27.

265. Prosecutor v. Ndindabahizi, Case No. ICTR-2001-71-1, Judgement and Sentence, ¶ 463 (July 15, 2004); Prosecutor v. Mpambara, Case No. ICTR-2001-65-A, Judgement, ¶ 18 (Sept. 11, 2006).

clearly predicated on the functional equivalent of "ordering." For example, Hermann Göring's guilt for war crimes and crimes against humanity was grounded, in part, on the fact that he "signed a directive concerning the treatment of Polish workers in Germany" and "directed Himmler and Heydrich to 'bring about a complete solution of the Jewish question in the German sphere of influence in Europe.'"[266]

We saw that "ordering" was embedded into the individual responsibility provisions of the ad hoc tribunal statutes as well as the Rome Statute.[267] And the jurisprudence setting forth the elements of ordering are found in judgments issued by the ICTY and ICTR.

The essence of the offense, as reflected in these judgments, is that a "person in a position of authority uses it to convince another to commit an offence."[268] This breaks down into three separate components: a circumstance element (a superior/subordinate relationship); an *actus reus* element (the transmission of an order); and a *mens rea* element (awareness of a substantial likelihood that a crime will be committed in execution of the order). We shall consider each of these in turn.

B. Superior-Subordinate Relationship

With respect to the first element, there is no need for the prosecution to establish a formal superior-subordinate relationship.[269] Instead, proof of the defendant's authority such that he could compel another to commit a crime in following his order will suffice.[270] In fact, the requirement boils down to "the *implied* existence of a superior-subordinate relationship"[271] and, distinguishing it from command responsibility, there is no need to establish effective control.[272] This permits establishing liability for ordering in the context of civilian superior-subordinate relationships.[273]

266. United States v. Goering, Judgment, Streicher (Int'l Mil. Trib. Sept. 30, 1946), *reprinted in* 6 F.R.D. 69, 147–148 (1946).

267. Statute of the International Criminal Tribunal for the Former Yugoslavia, S.C. Res. 827, art. 2(3)(c), U.N. Doc. S/RES/827 (May 25, 1993), *amended by* S.C. Res. 1166, annex, U.N. Doc. S/RES/116 (May 13, 1998) [hereinafter ICTY Statute]. *See also* Statute of the International Criminal Tribunal for Rwanda, S.C. Res. 955, art. 6(1), U.N. Doc. S/RES/955 (Nov. 8, 1994) [hereinafter ICTR Statute]; Rome Statute of the International Criminal Court art. 25(3)(b), July 17, 1998, 2178 U.N.T.S. 3 (entered into force July 1, 2002) [hereinafter Rome Statute].

268. Prosecutor v. Akayesu, Case No. ICTR-96-4-T, Judgement, ¶ 483 (Sept. 2, 1998).

269. *Kordić*, Case No. IT-95-14/2-A, Judgement, ¶ 28.

270. *Id.*

271. Prosecutor v. Semanza, Case No. ICTR-97-20-T, Judgement and Sentence, ¶ 342 (May 15, 2003) (emphasis added).

272. Prosecutor v. Kamuhanda, Case No. ICTR-99-54A-A, Judgement, ¶ 75 (Sept. 19, 2005).

273. *See* Ilias Bantekas & Susan Nash, International Criminal Law 24 (2007) ("An order is a command for action or omission that is issued by a superior to a subordinate, irrespective of whether the relationship is military or civilian.").

C. *Actus Reus*

1. Transmission

Ordering's *actus reus* consists of transmitting an unlawful command to one or more subordinates.[274] An order is unlawful if it violates general international criminal law or international humanitarian law, "even if it is in conformity with the domestic law of the State of the person who issued it."[275] The order may be written or oral and directed either at a specific individual or individuals or to unknown recipients.[276] And the order itself need not be prima facie illegal for liability to attach.[277] It may also be channeled to its intended recipients through a number of intermediaries.[278] In this regard, it is important to note that an individual does not have to be the original author of the order to be assigned responsibility—passing it to the next link in the chain of command may be sufficient.[279]

2. Proof of Transmission

The *actus reus* can be proved through circumstantial evidence.[280] For instance, transmission of an order can be established by demonstrating a significant number of similar actions over disparate locations within a compressed time frame.[281] Moreover, the order need not be in writing or tape-recorded to sustain a conviction—testimony or other secondary evidence can be enough.[282]

3. The Target Crime: Omission, Commission, and Causal Link

Pursuant to the Appeals Chamber judgment in *Prosecutor v. Galić* (2006), a superior's omission to act cannot result in the superior incurring ordering liability.[283] That stripe of culpability is covered under Article 7(3) of the ICTY Statute (Article 6(3) of the ICTR Statute and Article 28 of the Rome Statute) under the

274. Prosecutor v. Brđanin, Case No. IT-99-36-T, Judgement, ¶ 270 (Int'l Crim. Trib. for the Former Yugoslavia Sept. 1, 2004).

275. Bantekas & Nash, *supra* note 273, at 24.

276. *Id.*

277. Prosecutor v. Blaškić, Case No. IT-95-14-T, Judgement, ¶ 281 (Int'l Crim. Trib. for the Former Yugoslavia Mar. 3, 2000).

278. *Id.* ¶ 282.

279. Prosecutor v. Kupreškić, Case No. IT-95-16-A, Judgement, ¶ 566 (Int'l Crim. Trib. for the Former Yugoslavia Jan. 14, 2000).

280. *Blaškić*, Case No. IT-95-14-T, Judgement, ¶ 281.

281. Robert Cryer et al., An Introduction to International Criminal Law and Procedure 375 (3d ed. 2014).

282. *Id.*

283. Prosecutor v. Galić, Case No. IT-98-29-A, Appeals Judgement, ¶¶ 90, 103–104 (Int'l Crim. Trib. for the Former Yugoslavia Nov. 30, 2006).

rubric of superior responsibility.[284] Ad hoc tribunal jurisprudence has specified that responsibility for ordering will lie only when the ordered crime is actually consummated.[285] And the order must substantially contribute to the commission of the crime (but need not be a *sine qua non*)—thus, there must be a causal link.[286] The Rome Statute is no different, also treating ordering as a form of secondary liability triggered uniquely if the target offense "occurs or is attempted."[287]

D. *Mens Rea*

The Appeals Chamber judgment in *Prosecutor v. Blaskič* reflects the ad hoc tribunal consensus regarding the mental element for the crime of ordering: "the awareness of the substantial likelihood that a crime will be committed in the execution of that order. . . ."[288] The *Blaškić* Appeals Chamber concluded: "Ordering with such awareness has to be regarded as accepting that crime."[289] Still, as noted previously, an order need not be illegal on its face to secure a conviction.[290] Cryer observes that this is "consonant with the point that a mistake of law that does not affect *mens rea* is not exculpatory, and a mistake about whether certain conduct is criminal does not per se affect *mens rea*."[291] Responsibility is measured according to the *mens rea* of the person who issued (or passed on) the order, not the *mens rea* of the person who carried it out.[292]

VI. CONCLUSION

By the start of the new millennium, the ad hoc tribunals had created a foundational body of jurisprudence for the speech-related criminal modalities of incitement, persecution, instigation, and ordering. Upon this edifice, not perfect by any means, one could nevertheless have imagined the further construction of a body of law that developed the aspects that worked and discarded and/or remedied those that did not. But that is not what happened. As we shall see in Part II, "Fragmentation,"

284. ICTY Statute, *supra* note 267, art. 7(3); ICTR Statute *supra* note 267, art. 6(3). *Blaškić*, Case No. IT-95-14-T, Judgement, ¶ 282 (Int'l Crim. Trib. for the Former Yugoslavia Mar. 3, 2000).

285. *Blaškić*, Case No. IT-95-14-T, Judgement, ¶ 282.

286. Prosecutor v. Milutinović, Case No. IT-05-87-T, Judgement, ¶ 1213 (Int'l Crim. Trib. for the Former Yugoslavia Feb. 26, 2009).

287. Rome Statute, *supra* note 267, art. 6(3).

288. *Blaškić*, Case No. IT-95-14-A, Judgement, ¶ 42 (Int'l Crim. Trib. for the Former Yugoslavia July 29, 2004).

289. *Id.*

290. *Id.*

291. Cryer, *supra* note 281, at 376.

292. *Blaškić*, Case No. IT-95-14-T, Judgement, ¶ 282.

the tribunals, as well as certain domestic jurisdictions, where relevant, refused to exercise any kind of stewardship role toward the emerging framework.

Instead, at most, they paid lip service to certain elements, let the bad tendencies in the law become ingrained, and never seemed to consider the possibility of holistic doctrinal development or policy course corrections. The pernicious effects of this approach shall now be considered.

PART TWO

Fragmentation

5

Problems Regarding the Crime of Direct and Public Incitement to Commit Genocide

"[The] text has disappeared under the interpretation."

—FRIEDRICH NIETZSCHE[1]

I. INTRODUCTION

As we have seen, by 2003 the crime of direct and public incitement to commit genocide had been analyzed in several International Criminal Tribunal for Rwanda (ICTR) decisions. And, on the surface at least, it appeared as if a workable and coherent set of elements had been identified and fleshed out. In particular, the *Akayesu* and *Media Case* Trial Chamber judgments had ostensibly elucidated and defined the following requisite criteria of the incitement offense: (1) "direct" (whether the persons for whom the message was intended immediately grasped the implication thereof—from this one can deduce that the message can be implicit); (2) "public" (a call for criminal action to a number of individuals in a public place or to members of the general public via mass media); (3) incitement (illegal urging to commit genocide parsed by reference to purpose and context); and (4) *mens rea* (the intent to destroy, in whole or in part, a national, ethnic, racial, or religious group, as such). Causation, the ICTR seemed to rule, was not an element of the crime.

But, as revealed in this chapter, all was not as it seemed. In fact, there was much intrinsic ambiguity and incoherence within the framework. In certain instances, skeletal definitions or analysis did not go far enough. In others, enunciation of rules was accompanied by impliedly inconsistent doctrinal suggestions.

1. FRIEDRICH NIETZSCHE, BEYOND GOOD AND EVIL 37, ¶ 38 (Rolf-Peter Horstmann & Judith Norman eds., Cambridge University Press 2002) (1895).

Atrocity Speech Law. Gregory S. Gordon.

And while the cases decided between *Akayesu* and the *Media Case* implied an enlarged scope for the notion of incitement, these conceptual advances were not processed in any sort of doctrine-development-conscious, systematic or consistent manner. They were more like free-floating suggestions untethered from *Akayesu*'s nascent doctrinal moorings.

And while the *Media Case* judgment might have consolidated some of the learning of the previous judgments and advanced the doctrinal enterprise to a certain extent, the cases decided after it similarly came up short in terms of systematic application or further explication of the elements. As a result, a chaotic and ill-defined jurisprudence developed. And, as demonstrated in this chapter, the resulting confusion has helped give license to repressive regimes to suppress legitimate speech. As well, given the uncertain parameters, it has sapped incitement of its preventive force—its chief value from a policy perspective.

II. PROBLEMS WITHIN THE BASIC FRAMEWORK

In general, there are four primary problems with the framework as laid out in the ICTR foundational cases: (1) inadequate explanation of the scope of the "direct" element; (2) a similarly deficient definition of the "public" criterion; (3) failure to identify the essential components of "incitement"; and (4) an inconsistent and incoherent treatment of "causation." Each of these shall be treated in turn.

A. Problems Regarding the "Direct" Element

Much of the doctrinal confusion that bedevils the incitement framework stems from its original source—the *Akayesu* Trial Chamber judgment. Starting with the gloss the Chamber put on the first descriptor of incitement—"direct"—the language proved equivocal and confusing. The muddle, here and elsewhere, can be traced in no small part to the Chamber's efforts to reconcile Common Law and Civil Law permutations of the relevant rules. For example, with respect to the "direct" element, the Trial Chamber began its analysis by seemingly endorsing the Civil Law interpretation:

> The "direct" element of incitement implies that the incitement assume a direct form and specifically provoke another to engage in a criminal act, and that more than mere vague or indirect suggestion goes to constitute direct incitement. Under Civil law systems, provocation, the equivalent of incitement, is regarded as being direct where it is aimed at causing a specific offence to be committed. The prosecution must prove a definite causation between the act characterized as incitement, or provocation in this case, and a specific offence.[2]

2. Prosecutor v. Akayesu, Case No. ICTR-96-4-T, Judgement ¶ 557 (Sept. 2, 1998).

Of course, in Common Law contexts, as considered in the previous chapter, "provocation" is tantamount to "instigation" and does carry a causation requirement. Was the *Akayesu* Chamber adopting the Civil Law standard for this element in respect of "incitement"? The subsequent text was not entirely clear in this regard. Although the next sentence began with the qualifier "however," it is difficult to read into the words that followed a rejection of the Civil Law standard. More specifically, the Chamber then stated:

> However, the Chamber is of the opinion that the direct element of incitement should be viewed in the light of its cultural and linguistic content. Indeed, a particular speech may be perceived as "direct" in one country, and not so in another, depending on the audience. The Chamber further recalls that incitement may be direct, and nonetheless implicit. Thus, at the time the Convention on Genocide was being drafted, the Polish delegate observed that it was sufficient to play skillfully on mob psychology by casting suspicion on certain groups, by insinuating that they were responsible for economic or other difficulties in order to create an atmosphere favourable to the perpetration of the crime. The Chamber will therefore consider on a case-by-case basis whether, in light of the culture of Rwanda and the specific circumstances of the instant case, acts of incitement can be viewed as direct or not, by focusing mainly on the issue of whether the persons for whom the message was intended immediately grasped the implication thereof.[3]

In point of fact, viewing a speech "in the light of its cultural and linguistic content" does not necessarily foreclose treatment of causation. The same is true of knowing whether "the persons for whom the message was intended immediately grasped the implication thereof." If anything, the Trial Chamber arguably suggested a two-part inquiry: (1) consideration of audience understanding, followed by (2) consideration of causation. Thus, for example, postspeech violence would not necessarily be attributed to the speech if the listener did not grasp its meaning. Also, per that interpretation, even assuming listener comprehension, the speech would not be direct if violence did not ensue. So even if the *Akayesu* judgment text can arguably be read to elevate "listener comprehension" as being the sole dispositive consideration, another credible interpretation, not foreclosed given the Chamber's failure to disavow the Civil Law position, is that a causation requirement was adopted.

This is especially true in light of the Chamber's next pronouncement, a noncommittal sentence as to the relevant legal tradition that seems an equivocal coda for the preceding two paragraphs on the nature of the "direct" element: "In light of the foregoing, it can be noted in the final analysis that *whatever the legal system*, direct and public incitement must be defined for the purposes of interpreting Article 2(3)(c), as directly provoking the perpetrator(s) to commit

3. *Id.* ¶¶ 557–558.

genocide. . . ."[4] With respect to opting for the Civil Law versus Common Law interpretation, the Chamber is simply punting. And thus "direct" might still imply a showing of causation.

At the same time, in commenting on what form "speech" could take such that it might be considered "direct," the Chamber noted that it could consist of "speeches, shouting or threats uttered in public places or at public gatherings, or through the sale or dissemination, offer for sale or display of written material or printed matter in public places or at public gatherings, or through the public display of placards or posters, or through any other means of audiovisual communication."[5] This is problematic as it is so general. In other words, it would have been helpful to know the nature of the "communication" at issue, as opposed to a merely superficial description of its potential dissemination media.

By way of example, for a speech to be considered direct, is it limited to certain grammatical tenses? Does it have to be in the imperative—for instance, "Attack the traitors now"? If not, is it limited to declarations or statements made in the affirmative (i.e., "Attacking the traitors is necessary")? Or does it extend to negative statements as well ("Do not pity the traitors")? Might it apply to statements about the future (i.e., "The traitors will be wiped out") or words of praise regarding past action ("You have acted valiantly in dealing with the traitors")? For that matter, what about statements in the conditional tense ("If you don't kill the traitors, they will kill you")? Given that use of metaphors can amount to "direct" incitement, how abstract can those metaphors be ("Kiss a wet red sky and you will set yourself free")?

Simply stating that such analytical details do not matter given that the ultimate inquiry is whether the listener readily grasped the statement's significance is beside the point. Providing future courts with guidance regarding the scope of readily graspable phraseology would have advanced the doctrinal development significantly. Judgments such as *Kambanda* (e.g., "You refuse to give your blood to your country and the dogs drink it for nothing"), *Ruggiu* ("The 1959 revolution ought to be completed"), and *Niyitegeka* (thanking the militia for "work" they had done) involved unusual variations in grammar. Not creating a lexicon to classify such categories of speech as techniques of incitement was certainly a lost opportunity that would have brought additional clarity to a burgeoning and still largely amorphous jurisprudence.

B. Problems Regarding the "Public" Element

Once again, problems regarding the meaning of another key element of the incitement offense, "public," go back to the element's definitional DNA, as laid out in the *Akayesu* Trial Chamber judgment. Already, the relevant prefatory language establishes the judgment's expository opaqueness. The Trial Chamber begins by noting that "the public element of incitement to commit genocide may be better appreciated in light of two factors: the place where the incitement occurred and

4. *Id.* ¶ 559 (emphasis added).

5. *Id.*

whether or not assistance was selective or limited."[6] The first part of the Chamber's analysis, regarding "the place where the incitement occurred," appears relevant on its face. But the second part—"whether or not assistance was selective or limited" seems like a non sequitur. There is no antecedent reference to "assistance" so its use here is rather baffling. How is "assistance" naturally or logically related to whether speech is "public" or not?[7] That is not clear. Then, injecting the notion of whether the already-mysterious "assistance" is "selective" or "limited" manages to obscure even further an aspect of the analysis that is already cloudy. And there is no citation, footnote or other parenthetical language that helps clarify.[8]

The sentence that follows does not shed any light on the meaning of "selective" or "limited" assistance either. Instead, it seemingly introduces a new piece of the conceptual puzzle: "A line of authority commonly followed in Civil Law systems would regard words as being public where they were spoken aloud in a place that were [*sic*] public by definition."[9] Apart from being grammatically suspect, the sentence is not very helpful in explaining the law. In particular, there is no insight as to what is meant by a place that is "public by definition." According to what definition? Would an example have been possible? Although perhaps more forgivable, the failure to define "aloud" also gives jurists little to work with. It would seem the speech would need to be audible to listeners. But listeners located within what proximity to the speaker? How many meters or yards away could they be? Or, alternatively and more flexibly, would it how make more sense to introduce a standard of "reasonable proximity"? There is no guidance at all in this regard.

And, once again, the subsequent sentence offers nothing of value in terms of explaining what directly precedes it. More specifically, the Chamber seemes to jump to yet another definition of "public," although one more self-evident and internally coherent: "According to the International Law Commission, public incitement is characterized by a call for criminal action to a number of individuals in a public place or to members of the general public at large by such

6. *Id.* ¶ 556.

7. *See Assistance*, Merriam-Webster, http://www.merriam-webster.com/dictionary/assistance (last visited Sept. 18, 2016) (defining assistance as "the act of helping or assisting someone: help or support").

8. Given that the Trial Chamber was working with French materials, is it possible that the reference is related to the French verb "assister," which means "to be present at" "to attend" or "to witness" (in the sense of attendance at an event)? *See Assister*, Collins English-French Electronic Dictionary, http://www.wordreference.com/fren/assister (last checked Sept. 19, 2016). In that sense, it could be that "selective or limited assistance" refers to whether the audience was gathered for a specific purpose or was limited to a certain category of persons listening to the speech in relation to their status. Of course, this is merely speculation as the Trial Chamber provided no inkling whatsoever as to what this terminology actually means in English. Subsequent jurisprudence suggests this is the correct interpretation. *See* Prosecutor v. Kalimanzira, Case No. ICTR-05-88-T, Judgment ¶ 515 (June 22, 2009) ("[The] public element should be appreciated in light of the place where the incitement occurred and whether or not *attendance was selective or limited*.") (emphasis added).

9. Prosecutor v. Akayesu, Case No. ICTR-96-4-T, Judgement, ¶ 556.

means as the mass media, for example, radio or television."[10] Still, language such as "a number of individuals" and "in a public place" once again leaves open various questions. How many individuals does it take before reaching critical mass? What makes a place "public"? Moreover, three different sentences with three different conceptions of "public" were provided. Which one takes precedence? That is not clear. And what is "mass media"? Does it include print media? Or, more modernly, social media (subsequent cases might have fleshed this out but, as we shall see, have failed to build on the definition)?

The subsequent sentence, the paragraph's final one, offers nothing helpful either. It merely emphasizes that the drafters of the Genocide Convention meant for incitement to be "public," not "private" (a term simply utilized but not defined): "It should be noted in this respect that at the time Convention was adopted, the delegates specifically agreed to rule out the possibility of including *private* incitement to commit genocide as a crime, thereby underscoring their commitment to set aside for punishment only the *truly public* forms of incitement."[11] This might explain the policy choice made but not the definitions of "public" or "private" that underlie it. Simply to offer that a speech cannot constitute incitement if it is "private" begs the question entirely of what constitutes "private" versus "public." Does that mean the speech cannot be in an enclosed space? What if the speech is given to a relatively small gathering but on a "public" road at a time when members of the general public are not in the vicinity (for any number of reasons, including the lateness of the hour)? Does "public" mean the audience must be persons with whom the speaker is unacquainted? How many of them should there be? And so the lexical boundaries of a key element—"public"—remained underdeveloped.

Unfortunately, this doctrinal lapse engenders more than just academic lament, as demonstrated by the facts and application of the rule in *Akayesu* itself. There, in the early morning hours of April 19, 1994, Akayesu, joined a group "of over 100 people" who had gathered around the dead body of a young member of the *Interahamwe* in Gishyeshye.[12] He then urged the gathering "to unite in order to eliminate what he termed the "sole enemy: the accomplices of the *Inkotanyi*."[13] In finding Akayesu guilty of incitement, the Chamber did not specify the size of the assembly—only noting that it was "over 100 people" (i.e., it is possible it could have been 101) or its specific location (other than saying it was in Gishyeshye "in a public place"[14]) and noting that he was speaking during a "meeting."[15] Thus, the judgment left much ambiguity in terms of the meaning of "public."

10. *Id.*

11. *Id.* (emphasis added).

12. *Id.* ¶ 673.

13. *Id.* ¶ 673 (iii).

14. *Id.* ¶ 674.

15. *Id.* ¶ 673 (v) ("*During the said meeting*, Akayesu received from the Interahamwe documents which included lists of names, and read from the lists to the crowd by stating, in particular, that the names were those of RPF accomplices.") (emphasis added).

As a result, in a string of cases decided after *Akayesu*, a wildly inconsistent jurisprudence developed. That started to become apparent in the first major incitement judgments after *Akayesu*. More specifically, in the *Media Case* (2003), in convicting Jean-Bosco Barayagwiza of direct and public incitement to commit genocide, the Trial Chamber implicitly found that, *inter alia*, speeches he made at roadblocks urging militia to commit violence against Tutsis satisfied the "public" element.[16]

However, in the subsequent Appeals Chamber judgment of 2007, the judges found that any such speeches made by Barayagwiza at roadblocks were not sufficiently "public" because:

> [The] supervision of roadblocks cannot form the basis for the Appellant's conviction for direct and public incitement to commit genocide; while such supervision could be regarded as instigation to commit genocide, it cannot constitute public incitement, since *only the individuals manning the roadblocks would have been the recipients of the message and not the general public.*[17]

But this ruling flies in the face of one limb of *Akayesu*'s definition of "public"—that the speech may be deemed "public" if made "in a public place." *Oxford Dictionaries* defines "roadblock" as "a barrier or barricade on a road, especially one set up by the authorities to stop and examine traffic . . ."[18] It also defines "traffic" as "vehicles moving on a *public* highway."[19] Using these common definitions, then, a roadblock can reasonably be interpreted as being a "public" place. And, thus, pursuant to the second limb of the *Akayesu* definition, Barayagwiza's roadblock speeches should have been deemed "public" for purposes of the crime of direct and public incitement to commit genocide.

This point was underscored when the *Media Case* Appeals Chamber ruling was arguably contradicted a year later. In *Prosecutor v. Bikindi* (2008),[20] another set of judges found that the defendant's speech, in a remarkably similar setting, was sufficiently "public." In that case, the Trial Chamber found that Bikindi, on a rural road and using a car's loudspeaker, directed a group of militia on assignment to kill Tutsis. This was held to satisfy the "public" element notwithstanding the defendant's traveling on a road between two small, rural towns in a convoy of militia assigned to a killing operation—the kind of situation in which the *Media*

16. Prosecutor v. Nahimana, Judgement and Sentence, ICTR-Case No. 99-52-T ¶ 1035 (Dec. 3, 2003) (in convicting Barayagwiza of direct and public incitement to commit genocide, noting that he "was also on site at the meetings, demonstrations and roadblocks that created an infrastructure for the killing of Tutsi.").

17. *Nahimana*, Case No. ICTR-99-52-A, Judgement, ¶ 862 (Nov. 28, 2007) (emphasis added).

18. *Roadblock*, Oxford Dictionaries, http://www.oxforddictionaries.com/definition/english/roadblock (last visited Sept. 18, 2016).

19. *Traffic*, Oxford Dictionaries, http://www.oxforddictionaries.com/definition/english/traffic (last visited Sept. 18, 2016) (emphasis added).

20. Prosecutor v. Bikindi, Case No. ICTR-01-72-T, Judgement ¶ 281 (Dec. 2, 2008).

Case Appeals Chamber would find a speech not to be "public" because the recipients of the message were not "members of the general public" (akin to the roadblocks in the *Media Case*). Nor was this the sort of "whipping up the anonymous masses"-style of oration seemingly implicated by the other branch of *Akayesu*'s "public" definition and endorsed by the *Media Case* Appeals Chamber judgment.

So then how can Bikindi's roadblock utterances be distinguished from Barayagwiza's *Media Case* locutions in a comparable venue? Was it use of the vehicle's loudspeaker that permitted the Chamber to distinguish Bikindi's vocalizations from Barayagwiza's? If so, no explanation of how this would be justified from a policy perspective was offered. If, to quote the *Media Case* Appeals Chamber judgment, the recipients of the message were not members of the "general public," it is hard to see why mere electronic voice amplification should change the analysis.

Additional confusion was sown via a pair of judgments decided after *Bikindi*. In the Trial Chamber judgment in *Prosecutor v. Kalimanzira* (2009),[21] the panel convicted the minister of interior during the genocide, of, *inter alia*, direct and public incitement to commit genocide in connection with speeches made to an indeterminate number of militia members manning roadblocks. With respect to one count of the incitement, focusing on the defendant's statements at the "Jaguar" roadblock, where the defendant ostensibly only spoke directly to one militia member, the Chamber nevertheless focused on the "public" nature of his exhortation:

> The Chamber therefore finds that sometime in mid to late April 1994, Kalimanzira stopped at the Jaguar roadblock and handed a rifle to Marcel Ntirusekanwa in the presence of several others who were also manning the roadblock. Upon giving the rifle, he told everyone present that the gun was to be used to kill Tutsis. Though the wording of paragraph 21 of the Indictment could imply that Marcel alone was present at the roadblock and received instructions from Kalimanzira, the Prosecution Pre-Trial brief clarified the more public quality of the alleged incitement. The rifle was not intended to be distributed to Marcel in particular or to be used by him only; the gun and the instructions were disseminated to the group. The incitement to kill Tutsis was clear, direct, and in a *public place*, to an *indeterminate group of persons*.[22]

Regardless, given the vague contours of the law, it is not surprising to see the *Kalimanzira* Appeals Chamber arrive at a vastly different conclusion the following year.[23] Even though, as in *Bikindi*, the defendant's words did not constitute a "private" conversation and they were directed to a group of persons doing "public" work on behalf of the genocidal rump government in a "public" place

21. Prosecutor v. Kalimanzira, Case No. ICTR-05-88-T, Judgement (June 22, 2009).

22. *Id.* ¶¶ 560–561.

23. *Kalimanzira*, Case No. ICTR-05-88-A, Judgement, ¶¶ 151–161 (Oct. 20, 2010).

(a roadblock), the Chamber overturned the conviction related to this speech. Its reasoning suggests the "public element" was not satisfied given that Kalimanzira's speech was not delivered to a sufficiently large audience or via mass media or via electronic volume enhancement (such as a loudspeaker system or bullhorn).[24]

In justifying its departure from the Trial Chamber in the case before it, as well as the one in *Bikindi*, the *Kalimanzira* Appeals Chamber did not directly rely on the language regarding "public" spelled out in *Akayesu*. This led it to look for guidance from other sources and arrive at erroneous conclusions. For example, it relied on the portion of the IMT judgment related to defendants Julius Streicher and Hans Fritzsche to find that only speeches made to the public at large could be considered "incitement."[25] Unfortunately, as we saw in Chapter 3, those defendants were convicted of crimes against humanity (persecution), not direct and public incitement to commit genocide, which was not even a charging option at that time.

Further, in distinguishing *Bikindi*, the Appeals Chamber reasoned: "Finally, the *Bikindi* Trial Chamber held Simon Bikindi responsible for direct and public incitement based on its determination that he had used a public address system to disseminate messages inciting the commission of genocide when travelling on a *public road* to address the population [citation]. These findings were upheld on appeal [citation]." But this reasoning does not withstand scrutiny. As already established through common dictionary definitions, the roadblocks at issue in *Kalimanzira* were arguably also on "public" roads. Moreover, as regards "public," nothing meaningful distinguishes an address made to members of a militia assigned to a killing mission merely because, in one case (*Bikindi*), electronic volume enhancement was used but not in the other (*Kalimanzira*). In other words, by 2010, the ICTR had created a definitional quagmire in regard to the "public" element of the incitement offense.

And its effects were felt again two years later in *Prosecutor v. Ngirabatware* (2012).[26] In that case, the Trial Chamber convicted the defendant, minister of planning during the genocide, of direct and public incitement to commit genocide based on a speech he gave at a roadblock on the Cyanika-Gisa road in Nyamyumba commune (Gisenyi Prefecture) on February 22, 1994.[27] In particular, the Trial Chamber found that, after the killing of Martin Bucyana, the chairman of the extremist Hutu Coalition for the Defense of the Republic (CDR) political party, Ngirabatware told a group of approximately 150 to 250 persons at the roadblock to kill Tutsis.[28] Even though the Trial Chamber acknowledged ICTR precedent establishing that instructions given at roadblocks cannot rise to the level of "public" incitement, the speech's audience consisted of as many as

24. *Id.* ¶ 156.

25. *Id.* ¶ 157.

26. Prosecutor v. Ngirabatware, Case No. ICTR-99-54-T, Judgement and Sentence (Dec. 20, 2012).

27. *Id.* ¶¶ 1366–1370.

28. *Id.* ¶ 1366.

150–250 persons, and thus, the Chamber indicated, it was not delivered strictly to persons manning the roadblock.[29] The Appeals Chamber affirmed that reasoning[30] and, via reference to the prosecution's arguments, alluded to the "publicly accessible location at which Ngirabatware made the inciting statement . . . ."[31]

But further probing reveals specious reasoning in both decisions. In finding that some of those present were not there in relation to various functions of the roadblock, the Chambers merely supposed that a roadblock would not be manned by as many as 150–250 persons. But nothing backs up that assumption. A particularly large roadblock, for example, could conceivably be staffed by such a large number, especially if personnel were needed around an expansive perimeter. This seems plausible given that roadblocks were "a key element of the Hutu campaign of mass murder" and that "the construction of such roadblocks had been carefully planned and coordinated some time before the actual outbreak of the genocide."[32] In light of the central role played by roadblocks in the genocide, Linda Melvern describes their numerical "reinforcement" after the initial round of killing after Habyarimana's plane was shot down. Thus, in *Prosecutor v. Ntagerura*, et al. (2004), for example, one witness testified about a significant roadblock staffed by two hundred persons who, for a time, were joined by an additional one hundred to discuss plans for an imminent mass killing operation.[33]

So large numbers at a roadblock do not necessarily signify the presence of mere bystanders or passersby. And roadblocks, places where organized killing operations were carried out, cannot plausibly be characterized as public, social gathering places, even in a milieu as warped as genocidal Rwanda. Consequently, a superficial head count, just like electronic voice amplification and public road accessibility, was being used to save an incitement conviction from what had become a nonsensically construed requirement. Or, alternatively, it sought to make an intellectually dishonest end-around in respect of a requirement that, from a policy perspective, was perhaps not even justified in the first place.

C. Problems Regarding the "Incitement" Element

As we have seen, the *Media Case* Trial Chamber explicitly identified two analytic criteria to determine whether discourse could be categorized as either legitimate

29. *Id.* ¶ 1367.

30. *Ngirabatware*, Case No. MICT-12-29-A, Judgement, ¶¶ 53–54 (Dec. 18, 2014).

31. *Id.* ¶ 51.

32. 2 Samuel Totten & Paul R. Bartrop, Dictionary of Genocide 370 (2008).

33. Prosecutor v. Ntagerura, Case No. ICTR-99-46-T, Judgement and Sentence, ¶ 448 (Feb. 25, 2004). The witness's testimony indicated that one hundred militia arrived at a roadblock where there were two hundred persons in order to recruit a portion of the two hundred to join a killing operation. *Id.* Although the Trial Chamber did not accept the witness's testimony because he was an accomplice, it lacked credibility, and it was not corroborated, the Trial Chamber did not question the witness's reliability in respect of the number of persons at the roadblock. *Id.* ¶ 484.

expression or criminal advocacy: its purpose and its context.[34] These two criteria were discussed under two separate subheadings in the judgment—"Purpose" and "Context." As we have also seen, however, there were two additional criteria implicitly used by the *Media Case* Trial Chamber in formulating its analysis: text and the relationship between speaker and subject.[35]

These last two criteria are very important. The former suggests that scrutiny of the phraseology itself has much inherent value in terms of evaluating the speech's legitimacy. In the words of the *Media Case* Trial Chamber:

> The actual language used in the media has often been cited as an indicator of intent. For example, in the *Faurisson* case, the term "magic gas chamber" was seen by the UN Human Rights Committee as suggesting that the author was motivated by anti-Semitism rather than pursuit of historical truth. In the *Jersild* case, the comments of the interviewer distancing himself from the racist remarks made by his subject were a critical factor for the European Court of Human Rights in determining that the purpose of the television program was the dissemination of news rather than propagation of racist views.[36]

The other arguably separate analytic criterion, not properly recognized as such by the *Media Case* Trial Chamber judgment, speaker-subject relationship, is crucial for assessing the minority-dissent versus the establishment-bludgeon character of the speech. The analysis should be more speech-protective when the speaker is part of a minority criticizing the government or the country's majority:

> The dangers of censorship have often been associated in particular with the suppression of political or other minorities, or opposition to the government. The special protections developed by the jurisprudence for speech of this kind, in international law and more particularly in the American legal tradition of free speech, recognize the power dynamic inherent in the circumstances that make minority groups and political opposition vulnerable to the exercise of power by the majority or by the government. . . . The special protections for this kind of speech should accordingly be adapted, in the Chamber's view, so that ethnically specific expression would be more rather than less carefully scrutinized to ensure that minorities without equal means of defence are not endangered.[37]

34. Prosecutor v. Nahimana, Case No. ICTR-99-52-T, Judgement and Sentence, ¶¶ 1000–1006, 1022.

35. *See* Gregory S. Gordon, *"A War of Media, Words, Newspapers, and Radio Stations": The ICTR Media Trial Verdict and a New Chapter in the International Law of Hate Speech*, 45 Va. J. Int'l L. 139, 172–174 (2004) (discussing the four elements of incitement and how the Chamber treated each element).

36. *Nahimana*, Case No. ICTR-99-52-T, ¶ 1001.

37. *Id.*

In burying these two discrete and vital criteria within the larger mass of the "incitement" analysis, the Trial Chamber further contributed to a murky jurisprudence. At least the judgment alluded to these two criteria. But were other potentially valuable ones ignored altogether? Might the medium of transmission—print versus broadcast, for example—have a bearing on the analysis? Should the individual history of the speaker, in terms of previous speeches, for example, be taken into account? What about the political situation of the country where the speech takes place or the demographic/educational makeup of the audience (beyond the narrow inquiry of whether the listeners immediately grasped the import of the message)? Should one consider the existence of armed conflict, or the imminent outbreak of armed conflict, when there seems to be an empirical link between armed conflict and mass atrocity?[38] How about periods of political transition, such as elections, implementation of power-sharing agreements or withdrawal of occupying powers? Such events, if they constitute tectonic shifts in governance, have often empirically augured paroxysms of violence.[39]

The point is that merely asking the finder of fact to examine the "context," would appear not to go far enough. And although the *Media Case* Trial Chamber provided certain limited insights into the specifics of the context inquiry, this preliminary reflection suggests it could have gone much further. Again, the jurisprudence seems inadequate on this score and solutions for fixing it will be explored in Chapter 8.

D. Problems Related to Causation

In Chapter 4, we could discern a nearly schizophrenic quality to the International Criminal Tribunal for Rwanda's jurisprudence regarding causation. Although it technically recognized incitement's inchoate nature—in other words, it is a speech crime that is consummated regardless of whether the speech actually provokes genocide[40]—mass murder connected to incitement appeared in the factual findings of its incitement judgments. Once again, the chief culprit in sowing confusion is the *Akayesu* Trial Chamber judgment.

38. Scott Straus calls "the empirical connection between genocide and war . . . arguably the most robust empirical finding in the most recent literature." Scot Straus, *"Destroy Them to Save Us": Theories of Genocide and the Logics of Political Violence*, 24 Terrorism & Pol. Violence 544, 546 (2012). He goes on to specify that "genocides generally occur in wartime or in response to the threat of armed conflict; most major cases of genocide, such as the Herero genocide, the Armenian genocide, the Holocaust, Rwanda and Bosnia, all take place in wartime." *Id.*

39. *See, e.g.*, David Gillies & Gerald J. Schmitz, *Conclusion: An Ounce of Prevention: Preliminary Implications for Policy and Practice*, *in* Elections in Dangerous Places: Democracy and the Paradoxes of Peacebuilding 249 (David Gillies ed., 2011) (referring to mass violence after recent elections in Kenya, Côte d'Ivoire, and Haiti).

40. *See, e.g.*, Prosecutor v. Akayesu, Case No. ICTR-96-4-T, Judgement, ¶ 562.

Revealingly, before its analysis of the incitement charges, the judgment cited approvingly to the International Law Commission (ILC)'s 1996 Draft Code of Crimes against the Peace and Security of Mankind, which, as we saw in Chapter 3, included a causation requirement for the incitement crime. In particular, the *Akayesu* Trial Chamber noted that Article 2(3) of the Draft Code "reaffirmed the principle of individual responsibility for the five forms of participation deemed criminal referred to in Article 6(1) [which includes incitement] and consistently included the phrase "which in fact occurs . . ."[41] Moreover, as we saw earlier in this chapter, the Chamber's analysis of "direct," which wove in aspects of the Civil Law, invited speculation as to whether an implied causation requirement was embedded into the element.

But the Chamber went beyond merely endorsing the ILC Draft Code and alluding to causation in parsing the "direct" element. Given its acknowledgment that incitement is an inchoate crime, it inexplicably went so far as to suggest in its factual finding section that causation could be an element of the incitement crime: "the Chamber feels that it is not sufficient to simply establish a possible coincidence between the Gishyeshye meeting and the beginning of the killing of Tutsi in Taba, but that *there must be proof of a possible causal link* between the statement made by the Accused during the said meeting and the beginning of the killings."[42] Then, as if to affirm causation as a requirement, in finding Akayesu guilty of incitement in connection with his April 19, 1994, speech to the gathering at Gishyeshye, the Chamber explicitly made a finding that Akayesu's words were responsible for the subsequent bloodshed:

> The Chamber is of the opinion that there is a causal relationship between Akayesu's speeches at the gathering of 19 April 1994 and the ensuing widespread massacres of Tutsi in Taba. . . . [The] Chamber finds that the direct and public incitement to commit genocide as engaged in by Akayesu, was indeed successful and did lead to the destruction of a great number of Tutsi in the commune of Taba.[43]

The *Media Case* Trial Chamber judgment, although similarly stressing the inchoate nature of incitement, also made factual findings regarding the murderous impact of the two relevant media outlets' inflammatory rhetoric. These findings were made at the macro level, as we have seen, with the Trial Chamber generally imputing a causation role to "the media"[44] and observing that, while the downing of the Rwandan president's plane may have triggered the genocide, "RTLM, *Kangura*, and CDR were the bullets in the gun."[45]

41. *Id.* ¶ 475.

42. *Id.* ¶ 349.

43. *Id.* ¶¶ 673, 675.

44. Prosecutor v. Nahimana, Case No. ICTR-99-52-T, Judgement and Sentence, ¶ 952.

45. *Id.* ¶ 953.

At the same time, as chronicled in Chapter 4, the Chamber devoted a portion of its analysis establishing the link on the micro level between the murder of individual Tutsis and their being specifically mentioned by name in broadcasts both before and after the commencement of the Rwandan Genocide on April 6, 1994.[46] If causation is irrelevant to proving the crime, why devote so much energy and space chronicling it?[47]

More recently, in *Prosecutor v. Bikindi* (2008),[48] the Trial Chamber found "beyond a reasonable doubt" that the defendant, a famous Rwandan songwriter and performer, addressed an audience at a political rally advocating that those gathered must kill Tutsis, to whom he referred as "serpents," and his music was played on cassette.[49] One commentator has noted that the Trial Chamber seems to have discounted Bikindi's Kivumu rally speech in assessing his liability for incitement because "it has not been established that anti-Tutsi violence occurred in the vicinity of the rally either immediately before or after it."[50] And in *Prosecutor v. Nyiramasuhuko*, et al. (2015), in finding the defendant guilty of incitement to commit genocide, the Trial Chamber noted that "after both megaphone announcements searches were conducted and more Tutsis were killed . . ."[51]

46. *Id.* ¶ 478.

47. Richard Wilson speculates the preoccupation with causation stems from the Tribunal wanting a degree of comfort in certifying compliance with genocide's draconian *mens rea* requirement. *See* Richard Wilson, *Inciting Genocide with Words*, 36 MICH. J. INT'L L. 295–298 (2015). Susan Benesch questions whether the causation analysis is meant to compensate for a poorly developed test for determining incitement. *See* Susan Benesch, *The Ghost of Causation in International Speech Crime Cases, in* PROPAGANDA, WAR CRIMES TRIALS AND INTERNATIONAL LAW 257 (Predrag Dojčinović ed., 2012) (examining the relevance of causation in the ICTR judgments) [hereinafter *The Ghost of Causation*].

48. Prosecutor v. Bikindi, Case No. ICTR-01-72-T, Judgement (Dec. 2, 2008).

49. *Id.* ¶ 141.

50. Susan Benesch, *Song as a Crime against Humanity: The First International Prosecution of a Pop Star, in* TRIALS AND TRIBULATIONS OF INTERNATIONAL PROSECUTION 67–68, 70 (Henry F. Carey & Stacey M. Mitchell eds., 2013) [hereinafter *Song as a Crime*]; *Bikindi*, Case No. ICTR-01-72-T, ¶ 183 ("The Prosecution has not proven, however, that this meeting led to anti-Tutsi violence immediately thereafter."). That said, quite schizophrenically, the Chamber did reaffirm in its legal analysis that causation is not an element of incitement. *Id.* ¶ 419 ("As an inchoate crime, public and direct incitement to commit genocide is punishable even if no act of genocide has resulted therefrom."). Moreover, because this rally took place in 1993, Bikindi's speech during it could not have factored into his liability for incitement as it was outside the Tribunal's temporal jurisdiction, which was limited to the calendar year 1994. Statute of the International Criminal Tribunal for Rwanda, S.C. Res. 955, art. 1, U.N. Doc. S/RES/955 (Nov. 8, 1994) [hereinafter ICTR Statute].

51. Prosecutor v. Nyiramasuhuko, et al., Case No. ICTR-98-42-T, Judgement and Sentence ¶ 6010 (June 24, 2011). On appeal, however, the Appeals Chamber sought to justify inclusion of this factual analysis including this factual analysis by noting "that in determining whether a speech constitutes direct and public incitement to commit genocide, it may be helpful to examine how the speech was understood by its intended audience in order to determine its true message." Prosecutor v. Nyiramasuhuko, et al., Case No. ICTR-98-42-A, Judgement ¶ 2678 (Dec. 14, 2015). Nevertheless, as discussed in Chapter 11, pursuant to this

This factual fixation on causation, along with *Akayesu*'s partially cloaking it in the mantle of quasi-legal element, has led some experts to speculate whether it constitutes a *de facto* requirement. One scholar has referred to these allusions to causation in the ICTR judgments as "the ghost of causation."[52] Another one opines: "Reviewing the entire corpus of ICTR case law in incitement to commit genocide, one might reasonably ask whether the ICTR judges' attention to causation in adjudicating ICG [incitement to commit genocide] has elevated it to the level of a requisite element of the crime."[53] And thus, yet another aspect of the incitement framework leaves jurists befuddled.

That said, a basic framework for incitement had been constructed. Figure 5.1 below sets out that framework, including its seeming lacuanae and question marks. Would future judicial decisions avail themselves of the framework? And, if so, would they do so in a systematic, rigorous and fruitful way? The section that follows is devoted to answering those questions.

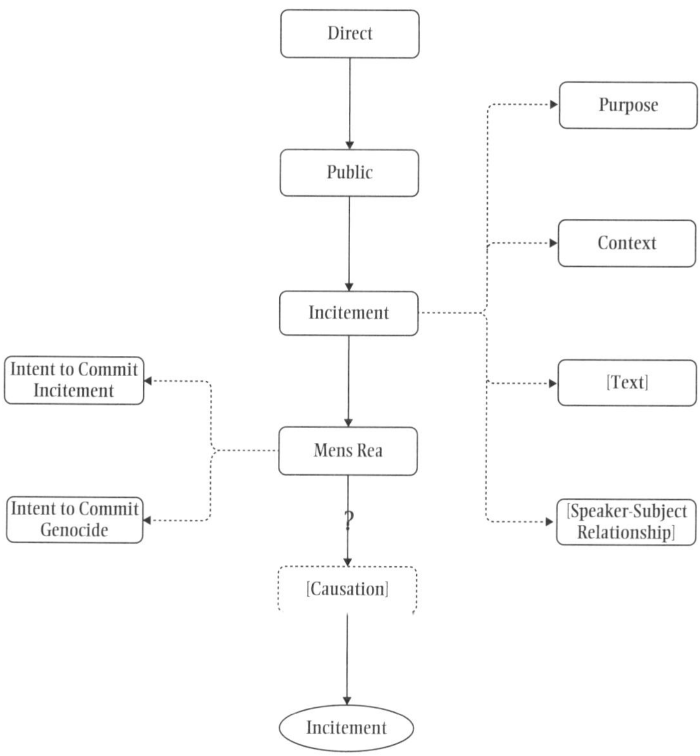

Figure 5.1 Elements of the Crime of Incitement under the *Akayesu/Media Case* Framework.

book's proposed "Unified Field Theory," if the speech resulted in violence, it should not even be charged as incitement. Rather, the charge should be instigation.

52. Benesch, *The Ghost of Causation, supra* note 47, at 262.

53. Richard Wilson, *supra* note 47, at 277, 287. *See also* Toby Mendel, *Study on International Standards Relating to Incitement to Genocide or Racial Hatred*, UN Special Adviser on the

III. FAILURE TO APPLY THE BASIC FRAMEWORK

Although, as we have seen, aspects of it are problematic, the ICTR's *Media Case* Trial Chamber judgment offered an elemental doctrinal base to which, in theory, future decisions could return as a point of repair and build on as a platform for incitement's normative development. Unfortunately, subsequent jurisprudence has failed to do that. Starting with the *Media Case* Appeals Chamber judgment, the ICTR's judicial output has failed systematically or rigorously to apply, much less develop, the basic incitement framework. Even an important incitement decision handed down by municipal judges, the Canadian Supreme Court judgment in *Mugesera v. Canada* (2005),[54] ignored the basic incitement framework established by the ICTR. Proceeding in chronological order, this chapter will now examine those cases and explain how adjudicators gave short shrift to the elements laid out in the ICTR precedents and thereby left the jurisprudence in a shambles.

A. *Mugesera v. Canada* (2005)

1. Background: An Infamous Speech

Léon Mugesera served as vice president of the Gisenyi Province branch of Habyarimana's MRND Party.[55] In November 1992, during the intercommunal violence that eventually culminated in the 1994 genocide, Mugesera gave an infamous oration, commonly understood at the time by his compatriots as urging the liquidation of Rwanda's Tutsis.[56] What follows are the relevant excerpts from that speech, delivered to a gathering of about one thousand at a political meeting in Kabaya, Gisenyi Prefecture:

> You know there are "Inyenzis" [cockroaches] in the country who have taken the opportunity of sending their children to the front, to go and help the "Inkotanyis". . . . Why do they not arrest these parents who have sent away their children and why do they not exterminate them? Why do they not arrest the people taking them away and why do they not exterminate all of them? . . . [We] must do something ourselves to exterminate this rabble . . . . Recently, I told someone who came to brag to me that he belonged to the P.L.—I told him "The mistake we made in 1959, when I was still a child, is to let you leave." I asked if he had not heard of the story of the Falashas, who returned

Prevention of Genocide (Apr. 2006), at 49, http://www.concernedhistorians.org/content_files/file/TO/239.pdf (offering that "causation is an appropriate concept in analysing incitement, if understood as the creation of the potential for genocide or hatred").

54. Mugesera v. Canada, [2005] 2 S.C.R. 100, 2005 SCC 40 (Can.).

55. *See* Joseph Rikhof, *Hate Speech and International Criminal Law: The Mugesera Decision by the Supreme Court of Canada*, 3 J. Int'l Crim. Just. 1121, 1121–1122 (2005).

56. *Id.*

> home to Israel from Ethiopia? He replied that he knew nothing about it! . . . "I am telling you that your home is in Ethiopia, that we will send you by the Nyabarongo so you can get there quickly." [Another] important . . . point is that we must all rise, we must rise as one man . . . if anyone touches one of ours, he must find nowhere to go.[57]

2. The Arrest Warrant, Flight to Canada, and Removal Case Process

Based on the seemingly genocidal urgings of the speech, Rwandan authorities soon issued what amounted to an arrest warrant against Mugesera. But they were unable to serve it on him as he had slipped out of out of the country and made his way to Canada.[58] By 1995, though, Canadian officials had learnt of the incitement allegations against Mugesera and initiated legal proceedings to have him deported. The grounds for removal were illegal entry based on human rights violations (in connection with his speech) and misrepresentations regarding his personal history (primarily related to the outstanding Rwandan criminal charges).[59] The Canadian charging instrument, using local nomenclature, included a charge for the crime of direct and public incitement to commit genocide.[60]

3. The Canadian Supreme Court Decision

a. Introduction

After nearly a decade of the case glacially moving through a labyrinthine appeals process, the Canadian Supreme Court finally upheld a 1996 lower court judgment that had ordered Mugesera's removal from Canada.[61] In conducting its analysis, the Court was called on to consider Mugesera's liability for direct and public incitement to commit genocide. The Canadian municipal statute that criminalized genocide was based on Article II of the Genocide Convention. Logically then, the decision looked to international law in parsing the elements of the incitement crime.[62] And the incitement legal structure put in place from

57. *Mugesera*, [2005] 2 S.C.R. 100 app. III, ¶¶ 15–29.

58. *Id.* ¶ 3; Gerard Prunier, The Rwanda Crisis: History of a Genocide 171–172 (1995).

59. Rikhof, *supra* note 55, at 1123.

60. *Id.* The allegations were fivefold: (1) "counseling" to commit murder; (2) advocating or promoting genocide (equivalent to incitement to genocide); (3) public incitement of hatred; (4) committing a crime against humanity; and (5) misrepresenting his background when applying for permanent residence. *Id.*

61. *Id.*

62. *Mugesera*, [2005] 2 S.C.R. 100, ¶ 82 ("International law is thus called upon to play a crucial role as an aid in interpreting domestic law, particularly as regards the elements of the crime of incitement to genocide.").

Akayesu through the *Media Case* was the obvious point of reference. But while the decision paid lip service to some of the ICTR elements (but not others), it failed to apply those elements thoroughly or systematically.

In particular, the portion of the decision dedicated to direct and public incitement to commit genocide is contained in Paragraphs 81 through 98.[63] In this textual sequence, the first three paragraphs are merely introductory in nature and situate the crime both historically and in terms of international and domestic law.[64]

b. Causation

By Paragraphs 84 and 85, the decision cites to the *Akayesu* and *Media Case* Trial Chamber judgments.[65] But it does so for purposes of determining whether causation is an element—this is somewhat unusual given that the ICTR decisions typically deal with causation last, which is logical considering that it is a nonelement. And, in fact, the Canadian Supreme Court affirmed the principle that incitement is an inchoate crime and that no proof is necessary of speech as a catalyst for actual violence.[66] Still, the Court's decision to take the elements out of order is an unfortunate harbinger of its inadequate treatment of the balance of the incitement framework.

c. *Actus Reus*: "Direct" and "Public" Only

That becomes apparent in the next Paragraph, 86, wherein the Court considers the *actus reus* of the crime and declares: "The criminal act requirement for incitement to genocide has two elements: the act of incitement must be direct and it must be public."[67] Curiously, in light of the *Media Case*'s focus on the element of "incitement" itself, the Court omits reference to that criterion altogether (this will be discussed in greater depth below). With regard to the "public" element, the Court provides no breakdown of it whatsoever, merely noting: "The speech was public. We need only consider the meaning of the requirement that it be direct."[68]

And indeed, although the Court set forth *Akayesu*'s bare-bones phraseology regarding "direct" (i.e., "more than mere vague or indirect suggestion goes to constitute direct incitement"), it failed to clarify some of the more difficult line-drawing issues raised earlier in this chapter.[69] In particular, as inciting language

63. *Id.* ¶¶ 81–98.

64. *Id.* ¶¶ 81–83.

65. *Id.* ¶¶ 83–85.

66. *Id.* ¶ 85.

67. *Id.* ¶ 86.

68. *Id.* That is unfortunate given that, as we saw earlier in this chapter, there are issues regarding the exact definition and scope of "public."

69. *Id.* ¶ 87.

can be incredibly abstract, are there grammatical or metaphorical vanishing points in terms of the "direct" boundaries? This is especially relevant in the *Mugesera* case, where, in seemingly urging violence, the speaker alludes to fairly abstract tropes such as rivers, insects, and historical events.

d. *Mens Rea*

The decision does go on to devote two paragraphs to a discussion of *mens rea*.[70] But that is easily the most straightforward of the incitement elements. A lengthy explanation for why "the person who incites must also have the specific intent to commit genocide" and a reminder that "intent can be inferred from the circumstances" are not of great utility in light of the cursory treatment of the other elements. This is especially true since the other elements tend to furnish collateral, if not direct, proof of *mens rea*.

e. Omitting the *Media Case*'s "Incitement" Analysis

The balance of the Court's incitement examination involves an application of the elements to the facts before it.[71] And while it finds there was incitement, the Court's analysis is deficient from a doctrinal standpoint. Most glaringly, as noted previously, there is no reference to, or application of the *Media Case* judgment's breakdown of "incitement" itself. It will be recalled that the *Media Case* Trial Chamber explicitly identified two analytic criteria to determine whether discourse could be categorized as either legitimate expression or criminal advocacy: its purpose and its context. This portion of the *Media Case* was not even cited by the *Mugesera* Court, much less applied or further elucidated.

And the facts of *Mugesera* presented a golden opportunity to do so. In particular, explicitly using the *Media Case* criteria, an exegetical review of the speaker's precise words (such as "Nyabarongo," "Falasha," and "Inyenzi") as revelatory of his purpose, as well as a breakdown and application of the surrounding factual circumstances (the hate speech and inter-ethnic violence directed against Tutsis in the early 1990s) would have gone a long way toward systematizing and regularizing the analysis for the crime of direct and public incitement to commit genocide.

To be fair, the Canadian Supreme Court did, in a desultory way, provide insights in certain passages regarding the significance of Mugesera's words. It pointed out, for example, that the "P.L." person with whom Mugesera described having a conversation in his speech (where he referenced the "Falashas" or "Ethiopians") was a Tutsi.[72] Also, the Court shed light on the reference to the year 1959, explaining that was when many Tutsis were massacred.[73] The

70. *Id.* ¶¶ 88–89.

71. *Id.* ¶¶ 90–98.

72. *Id.* ¶ 91.

73. *Id.*

Court also noted that a stereotypical view in Rwanda was that the Tutsis had their origins in Ethiopia, and this belief was even taught in public schools. Finally, related to that, the Court explained that Mugesera's allusion to the "Nyabarongo River" was meant to suggest that Tutsi corpses be "returned" to Ethiopia—the river runs through Rwanda toward Ethiopia, is non-navigable (i.e., Tutsis could not arrive there via watercraft) and, in earlier massacres, Tutsi corpses had been dumped in the Nyabarongo.[74] But all this analysis was simply extracted from the Immigration Appeal Division's decision below (authored by adjudicator Pierre Duquette), presumably in applying the "direct" element (although there is no looping back to the *Akasyesu* phraseology in the Court's analysis). In other words, the Canadian Supreme Court's examination of the speech was not broken down via, or explicitly filtered through, a precise legal elements analysis.

The context element (in terms of surrounding factual circumstances), although not explicitly identified as such, is indirectly touched on in the *mens rea* portion of the analysis! To wit, the Court writes: "On the issue of whether Mr. Mugesera had the requisite mental intent, Mr. Duquette found that '[s]ince he knew approximately 2,000 Tutsis had been killed since October 1, 1990, the context leaves no doubt as to his intent' (para. 323), and that 'he intended specifically to provoke citizens against one another' (para. 324)."[75] Thus, overall, the Court correctly found that Mugesera had committed the crime of direct and public incitement to commit genocide.[76] But it used the incitement framework criteria in a desultory, almost haphazard, manner. For purposes of firming up the jurisprudence, expanding it where necessary, and putting it in a good position going forward, the Canadian Supreme Court did not achieve the necessary level of rigor or systematicity in its application of the elements. And thus a bad precedent had been established.

74. *Id.* ¶ 92.

75. *Id.* ¶ 96.

76. It should be noted that, not long after its issuance, I viewed the *Mugesera* decision as a salutary addition to the growing body of incitement jurisprudence. *See* Gregory S. Gordon, *From Incitement to Indictment? Prosecuting Iran's President for Advocating Israel's Destruction and Piecing Together Incitement Law's Emerging Analytical Framework*, 98 J. Crim. L. & Criminology 853 (2008) (praising the decision for dealing with the various "strands of analysis from the ICTR incitement cases"). At that time, my view of the case was affected more by the fact that the decision covered the crucial points regarding context, even if that element was not explicitly identified as such or applied in an orderly or rigorous manner vis-à-vis the other elements. *Mugesera* also explicitly rejected causation as a required element and that made a valuable contribution. But as subsequent incitement decisions were being published, it became clear that the Canadian Supreme Court's haphazard handling of the elements, as well as its lack of doctrinal rigor, had set a bad precedent that was being repeated in other decisions. And it was having a deleterious effect on the development of incitement law. So my position on *Mugesera* has evolved. *See* Gregory S. Gordon, *Music and Genocide: Harmonizing Coherence, Freedom and Nonviolence in Incitement Law*, 50 Santa Clara L. Rev. 607 (2010)

B. The *Serugendo* and *Muvunyi* Decisions (2006)

One year later, two incitement cases were decided that could have helped compensate for *Mugesera*'s lapses. Unfortunately, that did not happen. In *Prosecutor v. Serugendo*,[77] the Trial Chamber delivered a judgment and sentence in the course of accepting the guilty plea of Joseph Serugendo, Radio Télévision Libre des Milles Collines (RTLM)'s chief technician, who was also a founding member of the radio station.[78] In convicting Serugendo of, among other charges, direct and public incitement to commit genocide, it directly cited the *Media Case* Trial Chamber decision but merely noted that incitement's elements consisted of "[inciting] others to commit genocide; [the] incitement was direct; [the] incitement was public; and [the] accused had the specific intent to commit genocide . . ."[79] There was absolutely no reference to the crime's "incitement" criterion and only cursory acknowledgment of its other criteria.

Prosecutor v. Muvunyi,[80] decided later that year, was little more palliative than *Serugendo*. In that case, the defendant, the most senior military officer in the Butare Prefecture during the genocide, was charged with incitement based on the following incidents: (1) at a meeting in April or May of 1994, Muvunyi addressed a crowd of Hutu male civilians during which he equated Tutsis to "snakes" that should be killed; (2) at the same meeting, he chastised the *bourgmestre* of Gikonko for hiding a Tutsi and then asked the *bourgmestre* to produce the Tutsi so that he could be killed (the man was then brought to the meeting and murdered); and (3) at a different public meeting held in May 1994, Muvunyi made a speech in which he called for the killing of Tutsis, the destruction of Tutsi property, associated Tutsis with the enemy at a time of war, and denigrated Tutsi people by associating them with snakes and poisonous agents.[81]

The Trial Chamber's incitement analysis began rather inauspiciously. It noted that previous ICTR judgments "considered the International Military Tribunal (IMT) cases of *Streicher* and *Fritzsche* which dealt with incitement to murder and extermination as crimes against humanity."[82] Then, indicative of the muddled mess that the incitement jurisprudence was becoming, the Trial Chamber added

(noting that "the criteria were being used in a desultory manner—not sufficiently rigorous or systematic in application".).

77. Prosecutor v. Serugendo, Case No. ICTR-2005-84-I, Judgement and Sentence (June 12, 2006).

78. *Id.* ¶¶ 22–30.

79. *Id.* ¶ 9.

80. Prosecutor v. Muvunyi, Case No. ICTR-2000-55A-T, Judgement and Sentence (Sept. 12, 2006).

81. *Id.* ¶¶ 507–510.

82. *Id.* ¶ 500. This was true as far as it went but, for greater analytical clarity, the Chamber might have noted that the specific crime at issue was persecution—the references to "murder" and "extermination" give the impression that the crimes against humanity at issue were for those enumerated offenses, instead of persecution.

that "the IMT cases could not deal with direct and public incitement because that conduct was first criminalized by the *Geneva Conventions of 1948*."[83] Of course, the Trial Chamber mistook the Geneva Conventions of 1949 (not 1948) for the Genocide Convention of 1948!

From this *faux pas*, the Trial Chamber did recover somewhat. Even though the balance of its incitement examination was, in the main, a carbon copy of that in *Mugesera* and *Serugendo*, it dug a little more deeply than its immediate predecessors in one important respect. It actually cited to *Nahimina*'s "incitement" element, pointing to the decision's teaching that "context is equally important in considering the potential impact of expression."[84] It then went on to examine the context for Muvunyi's second speech, including "the inter-ethnic killings prevalent in Rwanda in 1994, the war between the Tutsi-dominated Rwandan Patriotic Front rebels and the Hutu-dominated Rwandan Army, as well as the culture and language of Rwanda . . ."[85]

This was the extent of the judgment's consideration of the "incitement" element. Unfortunately, its treatment of this element is nowhere close to being adequate. First, it limited the analysis to "context" alone and ignored "purpose." Second, its treatment of the element was very parenthetical—it was alluded to very cursorily in a footnote with no acknowledgment of the element above the line. Third, and most problematically, it conflated the "incitement" and "direct" elements, discussing the former only in the context of the latter. Thus, for example, in reference to Muvunyi's first speech referring to Tutsis as "snakes," the Chamber considered "the context of the language and culture of Rwanda" only in reference to whether Muvunyi's "audience immediately understood the genocidal implication of his words . . ."

This is not an insignificant error. The "direct" calculus is geared strictly toward assessing the audience's understanding of the speech's genocidal implications. The "incitement" element goes beyond mere listener comprehension and provides an objective assessment of whether speech should be characterized as illicit advocacy. That the Trial Chamber conflated the two is revealing—it demonstrates a core lack of appreciation and understanding for the Tribunal's incitement framework. Thus, even though *Muvunyi* at least included the "incitement" element in its analysis, it was not enough to clean up the sloppy jurisprudence of *Mugesera* and *Serugendo*, and it demonstrated a flawed appreciation of the basic criteria.

C. The *Media Case* Appeals Chamber Judgment (2007)

1. General Affirmation of the Trial Chamber

The following year, the ICTR Appeals Chamber published its judgment in the *Nahimana* case (or the *Media Case*), and left undisturbed those sections of the

83. *Id.* n.701 (emphasis added). In fairness to the Trial Chamber, the erroneous reference to the Geneva Conventions was in a footnote, not above the line.

84. *Id.* ¶ 502, n.705.

85. *Id.* ¶ 509.

Trial Chamber decision analyzing the elements of direct and public incitement to commit genocide.[86] In the most germane portion of the ruling, the panel generally affirmed the approach taken by the judges below with respect to incitement:

> The Appeals Chamber considers that the Trial Chamber did not alter the constituent elements of the crime of direct and public incitement to commit genocide in the media context (which would have constituted an error).... Furthermore, the Appeals Chamber notes that several extracts from the [Trial Chamber] Judgment demonstrate that the Trial Chamber did a good job of distinguishing between hate speech and direct and public incitement to commit genocide.... The Appeals Chamber will now turn to the Appellants' submissions that the Trial Chamber erred (1) in considering that a speech in ambiguous terms, open to a variety of interpretations, can constitute direct incitement to commit genocide, and (2) in relying on the presumed intent of the author of the speech, on its potential dangers, and on the author's political and community affiliation, in order to determine whether it was of a criminal nature. The Appellants' position is in effect that incitement to commit genocide is direct only when it is explicit and that under no circumstances can the Chamber consider contextual elements in determining whether a speech constitutes direct incitement to commit genocide. For the reasons given below, the Appeals Chamber considers this approach overly restrictive.[87]

2. Overturning Portions of the Incitement Convictions

Of note, given the beyond a reasonable doubt standard, the Appeals Chamber ruled that certain pre-genocide speech that had factored into the Trial Chamber's verdict could not be deemed incitement.[88] It also found that the defendants' pre-1994 conduct, which had also factored into the Trial Chamber's finding of liability for incitement, was beyond the ICTR's temporal jurisdiction. This, in turn, resulted in a reduction of the defendants' respective sentences.[89]

Related to this, it should be noted that the prosecution had attempted to shoehorn Hassan Ngeze's 1990–1993 *Kangura* pieces into the Tribunal's 1994 temporal jurisdiction by connecting them to a 1994 RTLM radio contest that involved listeners searching *Kangura* back issues to locate certain identified information.[90] Disallowing incitement counts based on these older issues of

86. Prosecutor v. Nahimana, Case No. ICTR-99-52-A, Judgement, ¶¶ 695–697 (Nov. 28, 2007).

87. *Id.* ¶¶ 695–697. Susan Benesch has written that the Appeals Chamber "rebuked" the Trial Chamber for "not drawing a clear line between hate speech and incitement to genocide." Susan Benesch, *Vile Crime or Inalienable Right: Defining Incitement to Genocide*, 48 Va. J. Int'l L. 485, 489 (2008) [hereinafter *Vile Crime*]. As indicated clearly by ¶¶ 696–697, however, her assertion is simply not backed up by the actual text of the judgment.

88. *See, e.g., Nahimana*, Case No. ICTR-99-52-A, ¶¶ 740–751.

89. *See, e.g., id.* ¶ 314.

90. *Id.* ¶ 410.

Kangura, the Appeals Chamber tacitly suggested two new potential elements for the incitement framework: temporality (the allegedly inciting articles were not written contemporaneous with their republication), and instrumentality (it was RTLM, not Ngeze, who was responsible for or instrumental in their publication).[91]

The Appeals Chamber found as well that the "republication" impacted the directness assessment: "Even if, in attempting to find the answers to the questions asked in the competition, the participants happened to re-read certain extracts from *Kangura* capable of inciting the commission of genocide, this could only constitute an indirect incitement to genocide."[92]

3. Failure to Develop the Doctrine

Apart from the temporality issues, in the main, the Appeals Chamber endorsed the legal analysis formulated by the relevant ICTR Trial Chambers in their incitement decisions to that time.[93] The Appeals Chamber, however, could have done so much more to advance the doctrinal enterprise. The *Media Case* represented an ideal chance to appraise the components of the incitement framework in a thorough manner, and illuminate their model application in more precise detail. Instead, the Chamber merely signed off on the status quo and added little of jurisprudential value.[94] Thus, another occasion to augment and standardize the incitement framework was squandered. And this anemic approach would give rise to a comparably flaccid analytic exercise the following year in the *Bikindi* judgment.

D. *Prosecutor v. Bikindi* (2008)

1. Background

The ICTR indicted Rwandan pop singer Simon Bikindi on June 15, 2005. The charging instrument consisted of six counts for crimes perpetrated in 1994, including one charge of direct and public incitement to commit genocide under Articles 2(3)(c) and 6(1) of the ICTR Statute.[95] The incitement count was predicated on the performance and broadcast of the defendant's extremist Hutu songs at pre-killing-operation meetings, during radio broadcasts and at political rallies. It also stemmed from Bikindi's orations urging extremist Hutu party activists and militia to liquidate the Tutsi population.[96]

91. *Id.*

92. *Id.*

93. *Id.* ¶ 314.

94. *Id.* ¶ 316.

95. Prosecutor v. Bikindi, Case No. ICTR-01-72-T, Judgement, ¶ 5 (Dec. 2, 2008).

96. *Bikindi*, Case No. ICTR-01-72-T, Amended Indictment, ¶¶ 31–41 (June 15, 2005) [hereinafter Amended Indictment].

In the journalistic and scholarly coverage of the case pre-verdict, the analysis centered primarily on the defendant's music.[97] Bikindi was a famous pop tune-smith in Rwanda and director of the *Irindiro Ballet*, a dance troop whose performances were choreographed to traditional Rwandan rhythms.[98] He also worked for the Rwandan government, serving in the Ministry of Youth and Sports and was a member of Habyarimana's MRND Party. It was chiefly as a music star, however, that Bikindi rose to fame and prominence in pre-genocide Rwanda.[99] His tunes were piped into bars, buses, salons, and offices;[100] certain well-heeled patrons even booked his band for their children's wedding receptions.[101]

During this period, Bikindi wrote the now infamous standard *Njyewe nanga Abahutu* ("I Hate the Hutu") as well as other jingles, including *Bene Sebahinzi* ("Descendants of the Father of Farmers") and *Twasezereye ingoma ya cyami* ("We Said Goodbye to the Monarchy").[102] These recordings supposedly demonized Tutsis as "Hutu enslavers, enemies or enemy accomplices by blaming the enemy for the problems of Rwanda, by continuously making references to the 1959 Revolution and its gains by the *rubanda ngamwinshi* [Hutus] and by supporting the Bahutu Ten Commandments, and inciting ethnic hatred and people to attack and kill Tutsi."[103]

In light of the potential speech-chilling consequences of interdicting works of art in a genocidal context, international hate speech law pundits keenly awaited the *Bikindi* Trial Chamber's decision. Hassan Ngeze's *Media Case* attorney, John Floyd, voiced serious trepidations regarding Bikindi's music-based incitement charges. He likened prosecuting the Rwandan composer to "putting Bob Dylan on trial for protest songs."[104] Robert Snyder observed that the charges against Bikindi:

> [C]ould lead to a backlash against musicians who arguably support one ethnic, political, or social group over another. Considering that Bikindi's songs are characterized by the prosecution as only songs of Hutu solidarity and not

97. *See, e.g.*, Benesch, *Vile Crime*, *supra* note 87, at 490 ("The ICTR is now set to sail further into uncharted waters, since it is conducting the trial of a Hutu pop star, Simon Bikindi, whose elliptical lyrics and catchy tunes—officially banned in Rwanda since 1994—incited genocide, according to the ICTR prosecutors.").

98. Amended Indictment, *supra* note 96, ¶¶ 3–13.

99. *See Singer Bikindi: From Defence Witness to the Dock over "Genocide Music,"* Rwanda News Agency (Sept. 18, 2006), http://www.rwandagateway.org/article.php3?id_article=2947.

100. *Id.*

101. *Id.*

102. Prosecutor v. Bikindi, Case No. ICTR-01-72-T, Judgement, ¶ 187.

103. *Id.*

104. Dina Temple-Raston, *Radio Hate*, Legal Affairs (Sept.–Oct. 2002), https://www.legalaffairs.org/issues/September-October-2002/feature_raston_sepoct2002.msp.

> direct calls for the killing of Tutsis, a large range of potential music could be affected.[105]

Nevertheless, Snyder noted as well the case's promise for buttressing free expression prerogatives:

> By stressing the context in which Bikindi wrote and performed these songs and his position of influence with Rwandans, the Tribunal can limit the potential impact of any conviction. It was not the fact that Bikindi merely wrote and performed this music that made his actions potentially criminal. Rather, it was the message of the songs, combined with their presentation amidst calls for outright genocide on the airwaves of RTLM and at gatherings of the Interahamwe that made Bikindi's music so deadly.[106]

2. The Trial Chamber Judgment

After all the First Amendment hysteria it generated preceding its issuance, the *Bikindi* decision ended up being rather underwhelming in terms of its freedom of expression impact. In effect, the Trial Chamber sidestepped the issue. It did find that Bikindi's songs "advocated Hutu unity against a common foe and incited ethnic hatred"[107] and that they were "deployed in a propaganda campaign in 1994 in Rwanda to incite people to attack and kill Tutsi"[108] (in effect finding they could have constituted incitement to genocide). But the Trial Chamber thought the evidence lacking to find beyond a reasonable doubt "that Bikindi composed these songs with the specific intention to incite such attacks and killings, even if they were used to that effect in 1994."[109] Further, the Chamber ruled that not enough proof was marshaled to establish that Bikindi "played a role in the dissemination or deployment of his . . . songs in 1994."[110]

In arriving at this decision, the Trial Chamber failed to consider explicitly in its analysis the *Media Case* incitement elements of purpose, text, context, and the relationship between speaker and subject. It paid minimal lip service to context, conflating it with the "direct" element and merely observing that:

> To determine whether a speech rises to the level of direct and public incitement to commit genocide, context is the principal consideration, specifically: the cultural and linguistic content; the political and community affiliation of the

105. Robert H. Snyder, *"Disillusioned Words Like Bullets Bark": Incitement to Genocide, Music, and the Trial of Simon Bikindi*, 35 Ga. J. Int'l & Comp. L. 645, 673–674 (2007).

106. *Id.* at 674.

107. *Bikindi*, Case No. ICTR-01-72-T, ¶ 249.

108. *Id.* ¶ 255.

109. *Id.*

110. *Id.* ¶ 263.

> author; its audience; and how the message was understood by its intended audience, i.e., whether the members of the audience to whom the message was directed understood its implication.[111]

The Trial Chamber recognized that a "direct appeal to genocide may be implicit; it need not explicitly call for extermination, but could nonetheless constitute direct and public incitement to commit genocide in a particular context."[112] It therefore found that "depending on the nature of the message conveyed and the circumstances," it could not "exclude the possibility that songs may constitute direct and public incitement to commit genocide."[113]

However, the Trial Chamber pinned Bikindi's liability for incitement exclusively to an incident that happened in late June 1994 on a road between the Rwandan villages of Kivumu and Kayove, where Tutsis were being slaughtered. One witness reported that during his outbound travel to Kivumu, Bikindi, riding in a truck with a loudspeaker, made statements to the *Interahamwe* engaging in the murder operation.[114] Bikindi supposedly declared: "You sons of *Sebahinzi*, who are the majority, I am speaking to you, you know that the Tutsi are minority. Rise up and look everywhere possible and do not spare anybody."[115] The witness construed this to signify that while certain Tutsis had already been murdered, others were hiding and Bikindi was urging his audience to do whatever necessary to eliminate the remaining Tutsi survivors.[116]

Moreover, the witness gave evidence that during the return trip, "Bikindi stopped at a roadblock and met with leaders of the local *Interahamwe* where he insisted, 'you see, when you hide a snake in your house, you can expect to face the consequences.'"[117] Afterward, the Trial Chamber recounted, citizens in the area and the militia intensified their hunt for Tutsis, employing scent hounds and entering residences to sniff out any Tutsis still hiding. The witness affirmed that, soon thereafter, several Tutsis were murdered.[118]

Another witness swore that, on Bikindi's coming back from Kayove, he heard the singer ask members of the *Interahamwe* over a truck's public address system whether they had "killed the Tutsis" there, and whether they had killed the "snakes."[119] The witness also recounted hearing Bikindi's music being broadcast

111. *Id.* ¶ 387. This seems primarily like a reprise of the "direct" analysis.

112. *Id.*

113. *Id.* ¶ 389.

114. *Id.* ¶ 268.

115. *Id.*

116. *Id.*

117. *Id.*

118. *Id.*

119. *Id.* ¶ 269.

as the convoy of vehicles moved on.[120] On the strength of these statements, the Trial Chamber ruled that Bikindi had made an explicit call to eliminate the Tutsis. Therefore, such speech constituted direct and public incitement to commit genocide:

> Bikindi's call on "the majority" to "rise up and look everywhere possible" and not to "spare anybody" immediately referring to the Tutsi as the minority unequivocally constitutes a direct call to destroy the Tutsi ethnic group. Similarly, the Chamber considers that Bikindi's address to the population on his way back from Kayove, asking "Have you killed the Tutsis here?" and whether they had killed the "snakes" is a direct call to kill Tutsi, pejoratively referred to as snakes. In the Chamber's view, it is inconceivable that, in the context of widespread killings of the Tutsi population that prevailed in June 1994 in Rwanda, the audience to whom the message was directed, namely those standing on the road, could not have immediately understood its meaning and implication. The Chamber therefore finds that Bikindi's statements through loudspeakers on the main road between Kivumu and Kayove constitute direct and public incitement to commit genocide.[121]

3. Another Squandered Opportunity

Unfortunately, yet again, the ICTR wasted a perfect chance both to concretize and expand on the analytic incitement law structure set forth in its previous decisions. The Trial Chamber's omitting to ground itself on that precedent and build on it added significantly to the risk of completely squandering the jurisprudential gains made in incitement jurisprudence. This half-hearted approach, which even confused the elements of "direct" and "incitement," left the body of law vulnerable to claims that it is capricious and inimical to healthy free expression. Bikindi's lyrics should have been systematically filtered through the purpose, text, context, and speaker-subject crucible.

That exercise would have bestowed the test with superior interpretive power and greater normative coherence. And the Trial Chamber's rulings thus might have been regarded as resting on less slender of a reed. As one commentator has noted in reference to the *Bikindi* Trial Chamber judgment:

> Therefore the Trial Chamber missed an opportunity to interpret Bikindi's speech uttered *before* the genocide—which may have been catalytic of genocide and therefore should be of greater interest than speech that came only in the wake of the slaughter. Bikindi left Rwanda just before the carnage started on April 4, 1994, and did not return until it was almost over. It is only happenstance that the ICTR was able to convict him for a speech act after his return, and in the end Bikindi was convicted for a few words shouted over a loudspeaker, without music, although the ICTR clearly selected him from

120. *Id.*

121. *Id.* ¶ 423.

> among hundreds of possible defendants because of his songs.... [Since] the tribunal convicted Bikindi only on one unambiguous charge of incitement to genocide, this case left much work undone. Even in light of the ICTR's body of jurisprudence on speech, it remains difficult to distinguish rigorously between speech that is "merely" hateful, repugnant, or discriminatory, and speech that is criminal—and dangerous to restrict or punish speech. It is critical for courts to determine, and explain well, how to draw the line.[122]

4. Collateral Positive Developments

Despite its jurisprudential weaknesses, the *Bikindi* Trial Chamber judgment did have some positive collateral aspects, even if their inclusion was not a conscious choice made by the judges. More specifically, the decision indirectly suggested the formation of two new analytic criteria: temporality and instrumentality. The judgment also reaffirmed the critical role played by indirect incitement techniques and the irrelevance of causation.

a. Temporality and Instrumentality

First, the *Bikindi* Trial Chamber appeared to develop the *Media Case* Appeals Chamber's suggestion of two new analytic criteria, temporality and instrumentality, to resolve whether a speaker is liable for genocidal incitement.[123] These criteria are germane in instances where speech is republished by a third party after initially being uttered by the original speaker.[124]

With respect to temporality, the Trial Chamber wrote that, given its conclusion that Bikindi penned the songs well before they were employed strategically during the genocide, he could not have had the necessary genocidal intent.[125] Thus, the Chamber impliedly incorporated a "temporality" criterion—the offensive words must have been uttered at or near the time of the contextual violence that renders them genocidal.[126] Here, Bikindi composed his songs well before the 1994 killing operations.

Moreover, the Trial Chamber seemed to attribute importance to the way the songs were disseminated in relation to the genocidal violence. Even if recordings of the songs might have been transmitted as a run-up to and in unison with the massacres, those electronic reproductions were not within Bikindi's control.[127] Thus, an implied "instrumentality" criterion can be gleaned from the decision

122. Susan Benesch, *Song as a Crime, supra* note 50, at 67–68, 70.

123. This is consistent with the *Media Case* Appeals Chamber analysis regarding Ngeze's pre-1994 *Kangura* writings. *See* Prosecutor v. Nahimana, Case No. ICTR-99-52-A, Judgement, ¶ 410 (considering Ngeze's "republished" 1990–1993 articles).

124. *Id.*

125. Prosecutor v. Bikindi, Case No. ICTR-01-72-T, Judgement, ¶ 421.

126. The analogy with republication of Ngeze's pre-1994 articles is apt except that music is routinely rebroadcast, whereas written text is more likely to be published on one occasion.

127. *Bikindi*, Case No. ICTR-01-72-T, ¶ 263.

as well. Put another way, when recordings are involved, the recorded would-be inciter must be responsible for actual contemporaneous dissemination of the criminal speech (i.e., the playing of the recording) that is charged.[128]

b. Reaffirming the Jurisprudence on Indirect Incitement Techniques and Dismissing Causation

Even without these implied doctrinal advances, the decision is useful in that it helps affirm important ancillary points established in previous judgments. For instance, in referencing Bikindi's use of code words, such as "snakes" and "work" as part of the incitement,[129] the Trial Chamber reaffirmed the pivotal role played by euphemisms and metaphors in incitement. Additionally, since the Chamber classified Bikindi's roadside inquiry as to whether Tutsis had been eliminated as incitement, it gave its imprimatur to the principle that questions can constitute a form of incitement.

This signifies a beneficial extension of what may be deemed potential indirect incitement techniques. Moreover, the judgment can be extolled for confirming the inconsequence of causation in incitement law: "As an inchoate crime, public and direct incitement to commit genocide is punishable even if no act of genocide has resulted therefrom."[130]

But the overall value of these unintentional contributions is sadly limited. Ironically, in not consciously announcing their formulation and/or systematically and explicitly incorporating them into the analysis, the Trial Chamber reinforced the sloppy practices that have led to the law's much-too-imperfect development.

E. Incitement Cases Post-*Bikindi*

1. *Prosecutor v. Kalimanzira* (2009)

As discussed previously in this chapter, in *Prosecutor v. Kalimanzira* (2009),[131] the Trial Chamber convicted the genocide rump government's minister of interior, Calixte Kalimanzira, of, among other charges, direct and public incitement to commit genocide in connection with speeches made to militia manning roadblocks. In its judgment, the Trial Chamber did not even allude to the "incitement" criterion

128. As noted in the *Media Case* Appeals Chamber judgment with regard to Ngeze's republished 1990–1993 articles, the republication in *Bikindi* (i.e., the replaying of the songs) would likely also entail a finding that the alleged incitement was not sufficiently direct. *See Nahimana*, Case No. ICTR-99-52-A, ¶ 410. Unfortunately, once again, the *Bikindi* Trial Chamber is guilty of merely skimming the surface of the analysis and wasting an opportunity to delve into and develop this important issue.

129. *Bikindi*, Case No. ICTR-01-72-T, ¶ 269.

130. *Id.* ¶ 419. As noted earlier in this chapter, though, despite finding his speech otherwise amounted to incitement, the Trial Chamber refused to assign incitement liability to Bikindi for the speech because the "Prosecution has not proven, however, that this meeting led to anti-Tutsi violence immediately thereafter." *Id.* ¶ 183.

131. Prosecutor v. Kalimanzira, Case No. ICTR-05-88-T, Judgement (June 22, 2009).

announced in the *Media Case* Trial Chamber decision.[132] This criterion was similarly ignored in the Appeals Chamber judgment overturning Kalimanzira's incitement conviction. There, the judges merely noted, laconically, that "a person may be found guilty of direct and public incitement to commit genocide . . . if he or she directly and publicly incited the commission of genocide (*actus reus*) and had the intent to directly and publicly incite others to commit genocide (*mens rea*)."[133]

2. *Prosecutor v. Ngirabatware* (2012)

As we have seen previously in this chapter, Augustin Ngirabatware, minister of planning for Rwanda's genocidal rump government, was convicted, *inter alia*, of direct and public incitement to commit genocide in connection with a speech made to militia members at a roadblock.[134] Neither the Trial Chamber, nor the 2014 Appeals Chamber that affirmed his conviction,[135] made reference to the "incitement" element set out in the *Media Case*. Thus, in its most recent incitement judgments, the Tribunal missed a last chance to take control of and reorient a jurisprudential ship that had strayed off course.[136]

IV. THE RISKS OF DILUTED DETERRENCE AND GOVERNMENT SUPPRESSION

As the *Kalimanzira* Trial Chamber itself noted: "The inchoate nature of the crime [of direct and public incitement to commit genocide] allows intervention at an earlier stage, with the goal of preventing the occurrence of genocidal acts."[137] But for such intervention to be possible, the crime must be well defined—so as to deter would-be offenders and properly notify law enforcement. In this regard, it is axiomatic that

> [A] criminal statute must clearly define exactly what act is deemed "guilty"—that is, the exact behavior that is being prohibited. This is done so that all persons are put on notice that if they perform the guilty act, they will be liable

132. *Id.* ¶¶ 510–515. In fairness, the Trial Chamber's treatment of the "direct" and "public" elements is better than average, which makes its complete disregard of the "incitement" analysis utterly perplexing.

133. Prosecutor v. Kalimanzira, Case No. ICTR-05-88-A, Judgement, ¶ 155 (Oct. 20, 2010).

134. Prosecutor v. Ngirabatware, Case No. ICTR-99-54-T, Judgement and Sentence (Dec. 20, 2012).

135. Prosecutor v. Ngirabatware, Case No. MICT-12-29-A, Judgement (Dec. 18, 2014).

136. Similar anemic analysis is provided in two other recent cases. *See* Prosecutor v. Nyiramasuhuko, et al., Case No. ICTR-98-42-T, Judgement and Sentence, ¶¶ 5985–5987 (June 24, 2011) (ignoring the *Media Case*'s "incitement" element); Prosecutor v. Nzabonimana, Case No. ICTR-98-44D-T, Judgement and Sentence, ¶¶ 1751–1755 (May 31, 2012) (also leaving out the *Media Case*'s "incitement" element).

137. Prosecutor v. Kalimanzira, Case No. ICTR-05-88-T, Judgement, ¶ 510 (June 22, 2009).

> for criminal punishment. . . . Unless the [offense] is clearly defined, one might not know whether or not one's behavior is illegal.[138]

The current iteration of the incitement offense arguably fails at this task. As we have seen, there are too many confusing arroyos and fissures in the crime's elemental topography to give adequate notice to either the general public or justice officials as to what behavior is being proscribed or permitted. And the problem is only exacerbated given that the object of regulation, speech, is foundationally abstract and fluid.

And, as a result, there are potentially troubling second- and third-order consequences. That control of speech is involved necessarily means the boundaries of free expression are also implicated. In well-functioning liberal democracies this may be of lesser import. But for inherently repressive regimes, a vaguely defined speech crime is an invitation to snuff out political dissent. Justin La Mort warns that "a vague or overly expansive interpretation of incitement will be abused and misused by dictators in silencing artists, journalists, and genuine political opposition."[139] That sentiment is echoed by Joel Simon, executive director of the Committee to Protect Journalists, who summarizes the problem as follows:

> Within the contours of the global freedom of expression movement, there must be zero tolerance for speech that incites violence. The problem is that international law is a muddle on this issue. The vagueness of the standards not only makes it difficult for well-intentioned governments to understand and act on their responsibilities; they also make it easier for repressive leaders to justify suppression of speech that is merely critical by citing their obligation to stem incitement.[140]

And, for this purpose, certain strong men have already exploited the vague contours of the incitement offense. In an article published in the *Columbia Review of Journalism*, Simon specified:

> The practice of casting the suppression of critical media as a legitimate effort to fight . . . incitement is now distressingly common. . . . Since 2002, the Committee to Protect Journalists has documented nearly fifty such cases in at least a half-dozen countries. In Chad, for instance, four journalists were recently sentenced to jail terms ranging from three months to three years on

138. James V. Calvi & Susan Coleman, American Law and Legal Systems 178 (2016).

139. Justin La Mort, *The Soundtrack to Genocide: Using Incitement to Genocide in the Bikindi Trial to Protect Free Speech and Uphold the Promise of Never Again*, 4 Interdisc. J. Hum. Rts. L. 43, 44 (2010).

140. Joel Simon, The New Censorship: Inside the Battle for Media Freedom 185 (2015).

> incitement charges. . . . All four journalists had criticized the government and one had reported on an alleged massacre.[141]

V. CONCLUSION

So the stakes are high—effective genocide prevention and protection of free speech. The incitement crime is an essential implement in law enforcement's genocide prevention toolkit. But in its current form, it cannot fulfill the function for which it was promulgated. The tribunals have failed to clarify or flesh out certain foundational elements—the "direct," "public," and "incitement" elements of the offense. And this has left a confused jurisprudence regarding the causation element. Moreover, even the workable parts of the incitement framework have not been applied consistently or systematically in the most recent decisions. This has yielded an inadequate jurisprudence and a fragmented legal landscape. In the words of former Canadian Minister of Justice Irwin Cotler, juridical efforts to give teeth to the Genocide Convention's incitement prohibition "have proven manifestly inadequate."[142] Thus, the crime of direct and public incitement to commit genocide is doctrinally broken. It needs to be fixed, and this book will explain how to do so in Chapter 8.

141. Joel Simon, *Of Hate and Genocide: In Africa, Exploiting the Past*, Colum. Journalism Rev. 9 (Jan.–Feb. 2006) (also noting that "the misuse of hate-speech laws by repressive African governments may well be a greater threat right now than hate speech itself.").

142. Irwin Cotler, *State-Sanctioned Incitement to Genocide, in* The Content and Context of Hate Speech: Rethinking Regulation and Responses 454 (Michael Herz & Peter Molnar eds., 2012) (noting the ongoing collective failure to end genocide in Darfur).

6

Problems Regarding Persecution, Instigation, and Ordering

"Harmony makes small things grow, lack of it makes great things decay."
—Gaius Sallustius Crispus[1]

"Just because two variables have a statistical relationship with each other does not mean that one is responsible for the other."
—Nate Silver[2]

I. INTRODUCTION

The problems that have developed regarding the crime of direct and public incitement to commit genocide, as we have seen, stem primarily from internal incoherence within a framework developed by the International Criminal Tribunal for Rwanda (ICTR). For hate speech as the crime against humanity of persecution (often abbreviated herein as CAH-persecution), the problem is not lack of intra-tribunal consistency but rather a divergent approach between the ICTR and the other global judicial institution that has issued jurisprudence on the issue: the International Criminal Tribunal for the former Yugoslavia (ICTY). In Chapter 4, we saw that the ICTR, in *Prosecutor v. Ruggiu*,[3] found that hate-speech radio broadcasts not necessarily calling for action blatantly deprived the target ethnic

1. *Gaius Sallustius Crispus*, Brain Quote, http://www.brainyquote.com/quotes/authors/s/sallust.html (last visited Sept. 18, 2016).

2. Nate Silver, The Signal and the Noise: Why So Many Predictions Fail—But Some Don't 183 (2012).

3. Prosecutor v. Ruggiu, Case No. ICTR-97-32-I, Judgement and Sentence, ¶ 17 (June 1, 2000).

Atrocity Speech Law. Gregory S. Gordon.

group of fundamental rights and thus, even without proof of causally related violence, could be the basis for charging persecution as a CAH. This approach was also adopted, as described in this chapter, by other cases arising out of the Rwandan genocide, including the *Media Case* Trial Chamber judgment and the Canadian Supreme Court's opinion in *Mugesera v. Canada*. But, as this chapter demonstrates, the ICTY arrived at a diametrically opposed result, finding that hate speech not directly advocating violence could not serve as the *actus reus* for CAH-persecution. And that injected dissonance and confusion into this area of the law, which the *Media Case* Appeals Chamber judgment failed to clear up in 2007.

With respect to instigation, the muddle created by the ICTR's variously alluding to it with reference to both its Civil Law and Common Law roots, as well as its lexical blurring in the ad hoc tribunals' two official languages—English and French—has left jurists puzzled as to its relationship to incitement. Among other problems, this means that each offense has overlapping elements and there is unnecessary conflation and, thus, doctrinal disorder. Thus, for example, the limitation of instigation to private speech and incitement to public speech is untenable both conceptually and from a policy perspective. Moreover, recent jurisprudence has appended a new, unprecedented, and doctrinally indefensible element to instigation's base *actus reus* of "prompting": a "different forms of persuasion" requirement (such as use of threats, seduction, or promises). In addition, the ad hoc tribunals' vague pronouncements in terms of the causal relationship between instigation's speech acts and resulting violence (via discussion of the "contribution" requirement) has clouded the jurisprudence further. This chapter explores the problems the persecution and instigation decisions have caused with respect to the development of both crimes against humanity (persecution) and instigation.

Finally, with respect to the crime of ordering, this chapter explains that it is doctrinally deficient because it criminalizes commands by a superior only if a subordinate carries them out. When the target crime is not committed, the superior does not face criminal consequences, in spite of the fact that a superior-subordinate relationship signifies a greater likelihood of the target crime's being executed. This is in contrast to incitement, where lack of commission results in criminal liability for the speaker, despite the absence of a superior-subordinate relationship.

II. CRIMES AGAINST HUMANITY (PERSECUTION)

A. Background

In Chapter 4, we reviewed the origin and development of crimes against humanity. And we saw how its subcategory of persecution became a vehicle through which to prosecute hate speech. The main charges against Julius Streicher, Hans Fritzsche, and Otto Dietrich at Nuremberg were all tied to this offense. And other persecution cases before the International Military Tribunal (IMT) and Nuremberg Military Tribunals, whose gravamen was something other than hate speech, contributed toward the doctrinal development of the offense. In fact, as we have seen, the potential acts covered were rather variegated and the crime sufficiently elastic so as to create an expansive ambit. Actionable conduct under this rubric included enacting discriminatory laws, enforcing forms of social, political, and economic apartheid based on ethnicity or religion and/or segregating target groups by placing them in ghettos.

We also saw that, post–Cold War, the ICTY continued the mapping project for this crime. *Prosecutor v. Tadić* (1997), for example, delineated three baseline elements: (1) the occurrence of a discriminatory act or omission; (2) a discriminatory basis for that act or omission on one of the listed grounds, specifically race, religion, or politics; and (3) the intent to cause and a resulting infringement of an individual's enjoyment of a basic or fundamental right.[4] And *Prosecutor v. Kupreškić* (2000) laid out the *actus reus* criteria: (1) a gross or blatant denial; (2) on discriminatory grounds; (3) of a fundamental right, laid down in international customary or treaty law; and (4) reaching the same level of gravity as the other crimes against humanity enumerated in Article 5 of the ICTY Statute.[5]

It will be recalled that the *Kupreškić* Chamber included a set of guidelines to help interpret the offense: (a) "a narrow definition of persecution is not supported in customary international law"[6] and was understood by the IMT to "include a wide spectrum of acts . . . ranging from discriminatory acts targeting . . . general political, social and economic rights, to attacks on [the] person";[7] (b) persecution encompasses conduct such as murder and other serious acts on the person; (c) it is "commonly used to describe a series of acts rather than a single act," as "[a]cts of persecution will usually form part of . . . a patterned practice, and must be regarded in their context"; and (d) "[a]s a corollary to [(c)], discriminatory acts charged as persecution must not be considered in isolation" and "may not, in and of themselves, be so serious as to constitute a crime against humanity"—for example, curtailing rights to participate in social life (such as visits to public parks, theaters, or libraries) must not be considered in isolation but examined in their context and weighed for their cumulative effect.[8] In light of these yard markers, the Trial Chamber in *Prosecutor v. Brđanin* ruled that "'the denial of fundamental rights to Bosnian Muslims and Bosnian Croats, including the . . . right to proper judicial process, or right to proper medical care' [constitute] persecutions."[9]

All this helps put into context the ICTR's judgment regarding persecution based on hate speech in *Prosecutor v. Ruggiu* (2000). There, the Trial Chamber held

4. Prosecutor v. Tadić, Case No. IT-94-1-T, Opinion and Judgment, ¶ 715 (Int'l Crim. Trib. for the Former Yugoslavia May 7, 1997).

5. Prosecutor v. Kupreškić, Case No. IT-95-16-T, Judgement, ¶ 621 (Int'l Crim. Trib. for the Former Yugoslavia Jan. 14, 2000).

6. *Id.* ¶ 615.

7. *Id.* ¶ 597.

8. *Id.* ¶ 615.

9. Prosecutor v. Brđanin, Case No. IT-99-36-T, Judgement, ¶¶ 1029–1031 (Int'l Crim. Trib. for the Former Yugoslavia Sept. 1, 2004).

that hate speech could qualify as the *actus reus* for CAH-persecution. It began by embracing the liberal interpretation of persecution adopted by the tribunals at Nuremberg and relying on the similarly supple tests laid out in the ICTY cases. In applying this jurisprudence to Ruggiu's Radio Télévision Libre des Milles Collines (RTLM) broadcasting career, the Chamber was clear that CAH-persecution via speech can be effectuated without the speaker directly calling for violence. More specifically, the judges explained that the words on their own attacked the victims and thus whether they inspired others to engage in violence was beside the point. The venomous verbal volleys in themselves worked a deprivation of the victims' fundamental rights, such as liberty and humanity.

Moreover, consistent with the crime's chapeau requirement, the Trial Chamber pointed out that that the speaker must unleash his tirades with awareness that they are "part of a widespread or systematic attack on a civilian population and pursuant to some kind of policy or plan." So this necessarily means the verbal conduct is linked to organized and/or large-scale mistreatment of civilians—not the sort of run-of-the-mill municipal-scale hate speech uttered on park soapboxes or talk-radio programs in non-mass-violence settings.

B. The ICTR's Treatment of Persecution in the *Media Case*

The ICTR's next significant hate speech as persecution decision was handed down in the *Media Case*. Defendants Ferdinand Nahimana, Jean-Bosco Barayagwiza, and Hassan Ngeze were each charged, *inter alia*, with CAH-persecution in connection with running their hate media enterprises, RTLM and *Kangura*. In considering CAH-persecution, the Trial Chamber initially zeroed in on *Kupreškić*'s requirement of a "gross or blatant denial of a fundamental right reaching the same level of gravity" as the other acts enumerated as "crimes against humanity under the Statute."[10] The Chamber then found that "hate speech targeting a population on the basis of ethnicity, or other discriminatory grounds, reaches this level of gravity and constitutes persecution under Article 3(h) of its Statute."[11] The judges then expounded:

> In *Ruggiu*, the Tribunal so held, finding that the radio broadcasts of RTLM, in singling out and attacking the Tutsi ethnic minority, constituted a deprivation of "the fundamental rights to life, liberty and basic humanity enjoyed by members of the wider society." Hate speech is a discriminatory form of aggression that destroys the dignity of those in the group under attack. It creates a lesser status not only in the eyes of the group members themselves but also in the eyes of others who perceive and treat them as less than human. The denigration of persons on the basis of their ethnic identity or other group

10. Prosecutor v. Nahimana, Case No. ICTR-99-52-T, Judgement and Sentence, ¶ 1072 (Dec. 3, 2003) (quoting Prosecutor v. Kupreškić, Case No. IT-95-16-T, Judgement, ¶ 627 (Int'l Crim. Trib. for the Former Yugoslavia Jan. 14, 2000)).

11. *Id.*

> membership in and of itself, as well as in its other consequences, can be an irreversible harm.
>
> . . . .
>
> Unlike the crime of incitement, which is defined in terms of intent, the crime of persecution is defined also in terms of impact. It is not a provocation to cause harm. It is itself the harm. Accordingly, there need not be a call to action in communications that constitute persecution.

Of crucial importance in this passage is the Chamber's observation that, in all circumstances, hate speech is the equal of the other enumerated CAH crimes in terms of gravity. In so finding, it cited the prohibitions on hate advocacy enshrined in the International Covenant on Civil and Political Rights (ICCPR) and the Convention on the Elimination of All Forms of Racial Discrimination (ICERD). And it concluded that hate speech is not a protected form of communication under international law.[12] This conclusion was bolstered, the judges noted, in light of analogous proscriptions in a plethora of municipal jurisdictions, including Rwanda, Vietnam, Russia, Finland, Ireland, Ukraine, Iceland, Monaco, Slovenia, and China.[13]

The Chamber also noted that this approach was harmonious with the IMT's *Streicher* decision. There, the defendant's CAH-persecution conviction was "for anti-Semitic writings that significantly predated the extermination of Jews in the 1940s."[14] And, the Chamber explained, they were tantamount to "a . . . poison that infected the minds of the German people and conditioned them to follow the lead of National Socialists in persecuting the Jewish people."[15] In consideration of all these sources, then, the panel could comfortably conclude that "hate speech that expresses ethnic or other forms of discrimination violates the norm of customary international law prohibiting discrimination."[16]

With these considerations in mind, the judges then analyzed the culpability of the *Media Case* defendants. Its overall conclusion was that:

> In Rwanda, the virulent writings of *Kangura* and the incendiary broadcasts of RTLM functioned in the same way, conditioning the Hutu population and creating a climate of harm, as evidenced in part by the extermination and genocide that followed. Similarly, the activities of the CDR, a Hutu political party that demonized the Tutsi population as the enemy, generated fear

12. *Id.* ¶ 1074.

13. *Id.* ¶ 1075. As discussed later in this chapter, and in Chapter 9, in the CAH context, analyzing hate speech in terms of its treatment in the garden-variety domestic criminal statutes is misplaced. Such advocacy is criminal in the special CAH context because, by definition, it has to be yoked to a widespread or systematic attack directed against a civilian population.

14. *Id.* ¶ 1073.

15. *Id.*

16. *Id.* ¶ 1076.

and hatred that created the conditions for extermination and genocide in Rwanda.[17]

Specific instances of hate speech as persecution were then enumerated.[18] The Chamber began by referencing a pre-genocide February 1993 *Kangura* piece with the title "A Cockroach Cannot Give Birth to a Butterfly,"[19] which it characterized as "brimming with ethnic hatred but [that] did not call on readers to take action against the Tutsi population."[20] The judges also observed that "[t]he RTLM interview broadcast on June 1994, in which Simbona interviewed by Gaspard Gahigi, talked of the cunning and trickery of the Tutsi, also constitutes persecution."[21] Per the Chamber, misogynistic hate speech also constituted persecution: "The portrayal of the Tutsi woman as a *femme fatale*, and the message that Tutsi women were seductive agents of the enemy was conveyed repeatedly by RTLM and *Kangura*."[22]

In summing it all up, the Chamber cited the words of a prosecution witness who related that the defendants' hate rhetoric "spread petrol throughout the country little by little, so that one day it would be able to set fire to the whole country."[23] Per the Chamber, this was the equivalent of "the poison described in the *Streicher* judgment."[24]

C. The ICTY's Different Treatment of Persecution in *Kordić*

In 2001, an ICTY Trial Chamber issued its judgment in the case of *Prosecutor v. Kordić*,[25] which has been the sole ICTY decision to consider the issue of whether hate speech can constitute the *actus reus* for CAH-persecution. The charges in that case stemmed from an ethnic-cleansing campaign carried out by Bosnian Croats who sought to remove Muslims from an area of central Bosnia-Herzegovina with a view to incorporating the region into greater Croatia.[26]

The defendant, Dario Kordić, had become a prominent Bosnian-Croat politician by the time the former Yugoslavia was dissolving.[27] He was president of

17. *Id.* ¶ 1073.

18. *Id.* ¶ 1078.

19. *Id.*

20. *Id.* ¶ 1037.

21. *Id.* ¶ 1078.

22. *Id.* ¶ 1079.

23. *Id.* ¶ 1078 (internal quotation marks omitted).

24. *Id.*

25. Prosecutor v. Kordić, Case No. IT-95-14/2-T, Judgement, ¶ 209 (Int'l Crim. Trib. for the Former Yugoslavia Feb. 26, 2001).

26. *Id.* ¶¶ 5, 9.

27. *Id.* ¶ 5.

the Croatian Democratic Union of Bosnia and Herzegovina, and vice president/member of the Presidency of the Croatian Community of Herzeg-Bosnia (later the Croatian Republic of Herzeg-Bosnia) during the early- to mid-1990s.[28] Count One of the indictment specified that Kordić and others prosecuted the ethnic-cleansing plan by, among other things, "encouraging, instigating and promoting hatred, distrust and strife on political, racial, ethnic or religious grounds, by propaganda, speeches and otherwise."[29]

Oddly, at no point did the decision specify which speeches were the object of the persecution charge or engage in any legal analysis regarding the content of any such communications. Paragraph 522 (under the subheading "The Role of Dario Kordić") chronicled various acts by the defendant that happened to include certain statements. Paragraph 521, which was at the beginning of this section, declared: "This period also saw the emergence of Dario Kordić as a key Bosnian Croat negotiator and his assumption of the rank of 'Colonel'."[30]

At Paragraph 522, the Chamber related: "The events of the late summer [of 1992] show Dario Kordić being as active as ever. . . ."[31] The judges then provided details regarding the previously referenced activities (this boiled down to Kordić's taking part in meetings and participating in press conferences) and associated statements made by the defendant. The latter, which as explained above, the judges failed to cite explicitly as the basis for the persecution charge, comprised the following:

> (a) On 28 July 1992 the first HVO [Croatian Defense Council—the military arm of the Republic of Herzeg-Bosnia or HZ H-B] press conference was held in Busovaca. Kordić was introduced as Vice-President of the HVO. He greeted the conference on behalf of the regional HVO of Central Bosnia and reported that there had been "certain misunderstandings within the military section" of Busovaca municipal HVO. The misunderstandings had been cleared up.
>
> . . . .
>
> (c) [On 18 August 1992 i]n Novi Travnik he was escorted by soldiers and in a speech said that Novi Travnik would be a Croatian town. . . . In Travnik, Kordić and Koctroman addressed the troops: the text of a proposed speech states that those who do not wish to live in the Croatian provinces of HZ H-B are all enemies and must be fought with both political and military means. In Vitez, the gist of Kordić's speech was a statement to the Muslims of the Lacva Valley

28. *Kordić, Dario*, The Hague Justice Portal, http://www.haguejusticeportal.net/index.php?id=6014 (last visited Sept. 18, 2016).

29. *Kordić*, Case No. IT-95-14/2-T, Annex V, ¶ 37.

30. *Kordić*, Case No. IT-95-14/2-T, ¶ 521.

31. *Id.* ¶ 522.

> that this was Croat land and that they had to accept that this was Herceg Bosna.
>
> ....
>
> (e) On 30 September 1992 Kordić, as Vice-President of HZ H-B, was present at a meeting of the Presidency of the Kakanj HVO, a neighboring municipality to Varec. The minutes of the meeting record Kordić as saying that the HVO was the government of the HZ H-B and what they were doing with the HZ H-B was the realization of a complete political platform: they would not take Kakanj by force but "it is a question of time whether we will take or give up what is ours. It has been written down that Varec and Kakanj are in HZ H-B. The Muslims are losing morale and then it will end with 'give us what you will'".[32]

Strangely, the decision omitted any reference to the prosecution's stance in respect of these statements, or any of the defendant's speech for that matter, which could be considered as supporting the CAH-persecution charge. Rather, in the subsequent paragraph, the judges alluded to the *defense* position regarding the defendant's discourse:

> The defence evidence on this topic[33] dealt with Kordić's speeches and the terms used in them. For instance, that he always attended areas when things were critical (for instance Jajce, Vitez and Travnik), that he provided political and moral support; and gave a morale-raising speech to soldiers defending Jajce, saying "we have to defend Jajce and I will go with you to defend Jajce". As to the terms used, the defence evidence was to the effect that Kordić's political speeches were never racially inflammatory nor were they intended to foment hatred of Bosnian Muslims by Bosnian Croats. Kordić was portrayed by many witnesses as a moderate, caring person with a strong sense of responsibility. His was not a vehement personality. One witness, who had worked with him for many years prior to the conflict and who claimed to have heard many of his political speeches, testified that she never heard Kordić use derogatory terms with respect to Muslims, publicly or privately, and furthermore that his speeches were never racially inflammatory or incited violence. He did not use derogatory terms for other ethnic groups, apart from extremists about whom he was very sharp. Brigadier Cekerija testified in similar terms and said that in his public appearances, which the witness often saw, Mr. Kordić often stated that Bosnian Croats were one of the constituent peoples in BiH as well as Bosnian Muslims and Bosnian Serbs. Several witnesses involved

32. *Id.* (footnotes omitted).

33. The wording "the defence evidence on this topic" insinuates that the paragraph before considered the prosecution's submissions on this "topic"—in other words, evidence regarding Kordić's speeches and the nomenclature used in them.

in the political process at the time testified that they never heard Kordić, in meetings or at press conferences, refer pejoratively to other ethnic groups.[34]

This paragraph is inexplicably on an island—conceptually and narratively apart from the rest of the judgment—with the judges providing no commentary on it whatsoever. There was no prosecution response included in the judgment either. Ostensibly, this indicated the prosecution's approving the defense portrayal of statements as not deprecating or animosity-inducing and therefore not persecutory.

By the same token, this imbalanced account of the evidence was in harmony with the panel's previous examination of hate speech and CAH-persecution. The judges had earlier emphasized the significance of the Latin aphorism *nullum crimen sine lege*. In other words, so as to uphold the norm respecting legality, conduct charged as "persecution" must be deemed criminal under international law at the time the offense is committed.[35] Still, the panel allowed that "the *actus reus* for persecution requires no link to crimes enumerated elsewhere in the Statute."[36]

So, to the speech at issue, the Chamber then applied the four-prong *actus reus* test formulated in *Kupreškić*: "(1) a gross or blatant denial; (2) on discriminatory grounds; (3) of a fundamental right, laid down in international customary or treaty law; (4) reaching the same level of gravity as the other crimes against humanity enumerated in Article 5 of the [ICTY] Statute."[37] The Chamber then ruled that "acts which meet the four criteria set out above, as well as the general requirements applicable to all crimes against humanity, may qualify as persecution without violating [the *nullum crimen* principle]."[38] Thus, the Chamber was not swayed by Kordić's argument that, in light of Article 7(1)(h) of the Rome Statute, persecutory conduct had to be linked to other offenses within the International Criminal Court (ICC)'s jurisdiction.[39] Accepting the defense position, the judges found, would be too constricting and they stressed "the unique nature of the crime of persecution as a crime of cumulative effect."[40] Citing *Kupreškić*, they observed:

> [A]cts of persecution must be evaluated not in isolation but in context, by looking at their cumulative effect. Although individual acts may not be inhumane, their overall consequences must offend humanity in such a way that they may be termed "inhumane".[41]

34. *Kordić*, Case No. IT-95-14/2-T, ¶ 523.

35. *Id.* ¶ 192.

36. *Id.* ¶ 193.

37. *Id.* ¶ 195.

38. *Id.*

39. *Id.* ¶¶ 191, 197.

40. *Id.* ¶ 199.

41. *Id.* (quoting Prosecutor v. Kupreškić, Case No. IT-95-16-T, Judgement, ¶ 622 (Int'l Crim. Trib. for the Former Yugoslavia Jan. 14, 2000)) (first level of internal quotation marks omitted).

Moreover, the Chamber reviewed other ICTY cases where defendants were convicted of CAH-persecution. In those instances, the Chamber observed, the conduct amounted to physical attacks on the victims and/or their property.[42] And so the Chamber was able to conclude that the persecution offense "encompasses both bodily *and mental harm* and infringements upon individual freedom."[43]

Still, in administering the *Kupreškić actus reus* test, the *Kordić* Chamber concluded the relevant speech could not constitute persecution. That analysis was contained in Paragraph 209, which began with language that could not have been very encouraging to the prosecution: "the Indictment against Dario Kordić is the first indictment in the history of the International Tribunal to allege this act [encouraging and promoting hatred on political, racial, ethnic, or religious grounds]."[44] The rest of the paragraph then set out the Chamber's decision on the issue:

> The Trial Chamber, however, finds that this act, as alleged in the Indictment, does not by itself constitute persecution as a crime against humanity. It is not enumerated as a crime elsewhere in the International Tribunal Statute, but most importantly, it does not rise to the same level of gravity as the other acts enumerated in Article 5. Furthermore, the criminal prohibition of this act has not attained the status of customary international law. Thus to convict the accused for such an act as is alleged as persecution would violate the principle of legality.[45]

Intended to buoy the Chamber's conclusion was footnote number 272, which was affixed to Paragraph 209.[46] The judges were seemingly mindful that, with one pithy paragraph, they might have broken with settled views regarding the *Streicher* decision. Thus, the footnote started by claiming that "criminal

42. *Id.* ¶ 198.

43. *Id.* (emphasis added).

44. *Id.* ¶ 209. That statement is misleading as the Chamber failed to acknowledge several other non-ICTY judicial decisions that had also dealt with this topic.

45. *Id.* (footnotes omitted).

46. *Id.* ¶ 209 n.272. Also of note is the *Kordić* Chamber's finding that terminating the employment of Bosnian Muslims was similarly not of the same gravity level as the other ICTY Article 5 enumerated acts. *Id.* ¶¶ 209–210. This squarely flies in the face of the Nuremberg and ICTY precedents. *See, e.g.*, United States v. von Weizsaecker (*Ministries Case*), Judgment, *in* 14 Trials of War Criminals: "The Ministries Case," 308, 471 (1951) (characterizing job removals as constituting a part of Nazi persecution of Jews); *see also* Prosecutor v. Brđanin, Case No. IT-99-36-T, Judgement, ¶ 1041 (Int'l Crim. Trib. for the Former Yugoslavia Sept. 1, 2004) (holding that ethnic-based employment termination equates to persecutory conduct). Thus, the *Kordić* judgment took employment termination out of context, as it did with speech, and treated it independently, thereby neutering its effect in relation to other acts and detaching it from the overarching aggregate impact of the persecutory campaign. *See* Fausto Pocar, *Persecution as a Crime Under International Criminal Law*, 2 J. Nat'l Sec. L. & Pol'y 355, 359 (2008) (concluding, given the relevant precedents, that "one must consider policies such as

prosecution of speech acts falling short of incitement finds *scant* support in international case law"[47] (suggesting that there is *some* support for such prosecutions—even if the *Kordić* judges omitted to define the key term *incitement*). In light of the subsequent sentence, the implied small modicum of support would seem to come from *Streicher*, whose scope the *Kordić* Chamber tried to circumscribe. In *Streicher*, the *Kordić* panel offered, "the International Military Tribunal convicted the accused of persecution because he 'incited the German people to active persecution,'" which amounted to "incitement to murder and extermination."[48]

The Chamber then referenced the ICTR's *Prosecutor v. Akayesu* judgment,[49] which entailed a low-level official coordinating a genocide operation with local militia in his commune.[50] The gravamen of the charges against him was genocide, but a collateral incitement count was included in the indictment.[51] In focusing on the paucity of hate speech-based CAH-persecution charges in international criminal law cases, the *Kordić* Chamber simply noted that Akayesu—who was not a media personality or national official but a low-level commune figure whose guilt was only obliquely linked to speech—was convicted of direct and public incitement to commit genocide, not CAH-persecution.[52]

Interestingly, the *Kordić* Chamber made no reference to the *Ruggiu* judgment, which had been issued by an ICTR Trial Chamber the previous year and affirmed the CAH-persecution guilty plea of a radio announcer.[53] Curiously as well, considering it totally ignored instigating and ordering, the *Kordić* Chamber nakedly asserted that "the only speech act explicitly criminalised under the statutes of the International Military Tribunal, Control Council Law No. 10, the ICTY, ICTR and ICC Statute, is the direct and public incitement to commit genocide."[54]

discriminatory employment dismissals, denial of public services, and denials of justice as persecutory acts, particularly when committed in conjunction with one another" (emphasis added)).

47. *Kordić*, Case No. IT-95-14/2-T, ¶ 209 n.272 (emphasis added).

48. *Id.* The *Kordić* Chamber omitted, *inter alia*, the following language in *Streicher*: "In his speeches and articles, week after week, month after month, he infected the German mind with the virus of anti-Semitism and incited the German people to active *persecution*." United States v. Goering, Judgment, Streicher (Int'l Mil. Trib. Sept. 30, 1946), *reprinted in* 6 F.R.D. 69, 161–163 (1946) (emphasis added).

49. Prosecutor v. Akayesu, Case No. ICTR-96-4-T, Judgement (Sept. 2, 1998).

50. *See* Gregory S. Gordon, *"A War of Media, Words, Newspapers and Radio Stations": The ICTR Media Trial Verdict and a New Chapter in the International Law of Hate Speech*, 45 VA. J. INT'L L. 139, 149–153 (2004) (summarizing the ICTR's case and the guilty verdict rendered against Mayor Akayesu for genocide and CAH).

51. *Id.* at 149–150.

52. *Kordić*, Case No. IT-95-14/2-T, ¶ 209 n.272.

53. Gordon, *supra* note 50, at 153.

54. *Kordić*, Case No. IT-95-14/2-T, ¶ 209 n.272. "Instigating" and "ordering" are other speech acts explicitly criminalized in the ICTY and ICTR statutes. *See, e.g.*, Statute of the

The Chamber also tried to validate its decision by alluding to certain state reservations to human rights treaty provisions that prohibit incitement to impermissible discrimination and hatred (such as that contained in the ICCPR).[55] This resulted in a split on the issue, the Chamber pointed out, between the United States, which is extremely speech-protective, and the majority of other states (such as Germany, Canada, France, and South Africa), which focus more on protecting the victims of hate speech.[56] In light of this doctrinal divergence, the *Kordić* Chamber asserted, "[T]here is no international consensus on the criminalisation of this act [incitement] that rises to the level of customary international law."[57]

D. The Canadian Supreme Court Adopts the ICTR Approach in *Mugesera*

In the last chapter, we looked at the *Mugesera v. Canada* decision in the context of incitement to commit genocide. But the Canadian Supreme Court also dealt with the topic of CAH-persecution in its judgment. In particular, the Court was called on to decide whether hate speech charged as persecution was equal in gravity to the other enumerated CAH bad acts. It will be recalled that Mugesera,

International Criminal Tribunal for the Former Yugoslavia, S.C. Res. 827, art. 2(3)(c), U.N. Doc. S/RES/827 (May 25, 1993), *amended by* S.C. Res. 1166, annex, U.N. Doc. S/RES/116 (May 13, 1998) [hereinafter ICTY Statute] ("A person who planned, instigated, ordered, committed or otherwise aided and abetted . . . a crime referred to in articles 2 to 5 . . . shall be individually responsible for the crime."); *see also* Rome Statute of the International Criminal Court art. 25(3)(b), July 17, 1998, 2178 U.N.T.S. 3 (entered into force July 1, 2002) [hereinafter Rome Statute] (fixing criminal liability for one who "[o]rders, solicits or induces the commission of . . . a crime"). In addition, the *Kordić* Chamber refused to recognize that, even if not explicit, these statutes, including the IMT Charter and Control Council No. 10, allow proscription of other speech-related conduct, including CAH-persecution.

55. *Kordić*, Case No. IT-95-14/2-T, ¶ 209 n.272.

56. *Id.*

57. *Id.* As we saw in Chapter 2, this is arguably specious reasoning as the United States is essentially isolated in terms of its extremely zealous protection of speech. So the fact that the rest of the world differs in its stance does not indicate a "split"—rather it signifies that the United States is an outlier. So there is arguably international consensus on this issue. Even were that not the case, as will be discussed in greater depth in Chapter 9, the *Kordić* Chamber basing its analysis on these international conventions and municipal statutes is independently problematic because those laws are not meant to deal with the CAH precondition of a widespread or systematic attack directed against a civilian population. Additionally, as already demonstrated herein, persecution's constituent units of conduct need not be criminal in and of themselves. *See* Prosecutor v. Kvočka, Case No. IT-98-30/1-T, Judgement, ¶ 186 (Int'l Crim. Trib. for the Former Yugoslavia Nov. 2, 2001) ("[A]cts that are not inherently criminal may nonetheless become criminal and persecutorial if committed with discriminatory intent.").

an extremist Hutu politician, made a notorious November 1992 speech wherein he sought to vilify and debase the Tutsis.[58]

In that infamous oration, he denigrated Tutsis as cockroaches (*inyenzi*) and equated them to serpents and thieves.[59] He implored those in attendance to shun them and treat them as aliens, not as citizens of Rwanda. He then reached a crescendo in which he advocated for the "cockroaches" (Tutsis) to "be leaving . . . instead of living among us . . . . Let them pack their bags, let them get going, so that no one will return here. . . ."[60] Based on the speech, the Rwandan authorities filed criminal charges against him, but he escaped to Canada before they could arrest him. Once there, the Canadians learnt of the Rwandan indictment and instituted an illegal-entry immigration case against him.[61]

The case eventually reached the Canadian Supreme Court, which had to rule, *inter alia*, whether there were reasonable grounds to conclude Mugesera was guilty of CAH-persecution and thus not eligible for entry into Canada per its immigration laws.[62] In tackling this issue, the Court specifically considered whether "a speech that incites hatred, which as we have seen Mr. Mugesera's speech did, [can] meet the initial criminal act requirement for persecution as a crime against humanity."[63] The justices then reviewed relevant ICTY and ICTR cases, and explicitly considered the divergence in approach between the judgments in the *Ruggiu/Media Case* and *Kordić*. Based on this analysis, it found that Mugesera's November 1992 oration could qualify as CAH-persecution.[64] It started by examining the connection between Mugesera's speech and the widespread or systematic attack against the civilian population:

> [T]he attack must be directed against a relatively large group of people, mostly civilians, who share distinctive features which identify them as targets of the attack. A link must be demonstrated between the act and the attack. In essence, the act must further the attack or clearly fit the pattern of the attack, but it need not comprise an essential or officially sanctioned part of it. A persecutory speech which encourages hatred and violence against a targeted group furthers an attack against that group. In this case, in view of the [lower court's] findings, [Mugesera's] speech was a part of a systematic attack that was occurring in Rwanda at the time and was directed against Tutsi and moderate Hutu. . . .[65]

58. Mugesera v. Canada, 2005 SCC 10, [2005] 2 S.C.R. 100, ¶¶ 65–73 (Can.).

59. *Id.* app. III, ¶¶ 13, 17, 28. As we saw in the last chapter, those who heard the speech also understood that parts of it called for Tutsis to be exterminated.

60. *Id.* app. III, ¶ 28.

61. *Id.* ¶¶ 3–5.

62. *Id.* ¶¶ 1–5, 112.

63. *Id.* ¶ 137.

64. *Id.* ¶¶ 146–147.

65. *Id.* at 10.

With this in mind, the Court could conclude that "the harm in hate speech lies not only in the injury to the self-dignity of target group members but also in the credence that may be given to the speech, which may promote discrimination and even violence."[66] As a result, the Court held that Mugesera's speech met the elements of CAH-persecution.[67]

E. The Appeals Chamber Judgment in the *Media Case* Fails to Resolve the ICTR/ICTY Split

The 2007 Appeals Chamber judgment in the *Media Case* represents the next important milestone in the doctrinal development of speech as CAH-persecution. On appeal, the media executive defendants contended that hate speech could not satisfy CAH-persecution's *actus reus* element.[68] Relying on Paragraph 209 and footnote 272 of the *Kordić* decision, Nahimana, Barayagwiza, and Ngeze advanced, *inter alia*, the following arguments: (1) "hate speech is not regarded as a crime under customary international law (except in the case of direct and public incitement to commit genocide)" and so defendants' convictions violated the principle of legality; (2) "hate speech does not fall within the definition of the crime against humanity of persecution, because it does not lead to discrimination in fact and is not as serious as other crimes against humanity"; and (3) "the Trial Chamber erred in relying on the *Ruggiu* Trial Judgment to conclude that hate speech targeting a population by reason of its ethnicity is sufficiently serious to constitute a crime against humanity, because that judgment was not the result of a real trial."[69]

The American nongovernmental organization Open Society Institute filed an *amicus curiae* brief on behalf of the defendants, which maintained that Streicher's conviction for CAH-persecution was based entirely on his "prompting 'to murder and extermination at the time when Jews in the East were being killed under the most horrible conditions.' "[70] This position was supported, the brief argued, by the IMT's acquittal of Hans Fritzsche "on grounds that his hate-laced rhetoric did not seek 'to incite the Germans to commit atrocities against the conquered people.' "[71] The brief found fault with the *Media Case* Trial Chamber judgment because it failed to adopt the *Kordić* approach, which, as we have seen, deemed mere hate speech, not accompanied by calls for violence, as an insufficient basis for bringing persecution charges.[72]

66. *Id.* ¶ 147. But the court also emphasized that "hate speech always denies fundamental rights. The equality and the life, liberty and security of the person of target-group members cannot but be affected." *Id.*

67. *Id.* ¶ 148.

68. Prosecutor v. Nahimana, Case No. ICTR-99-52-A, Judgement, ¶¶ 970–972 (Nov. 28, 2007).

69. *Id.* ¶ 972.

70. *Id.* ¶ 979 (quoting United States v. Goering, Judgment, Streicher (Int'l Mil. Trib. Sept. 30, 1946), *reprinted in* 6 F.R.D. 69, 163 (1946)).

71. *Id.* (quoting *Goering*, Judgment, Streicher, 6 F.R.D. at 163).

72. *Id.*

So that sets the context for the Appeals Chamber judgment. The judges began their analysis by laying out the relevant doctrine, which affirmed that "the crime of persecution consists of an act or omission which discriminates in fact and which: denies or infringes upon a fundamental right laid down in international customary or treaty law (the *actus reus*); and was carried out deliberately with the intention to discriminate on one of the listed grounds, specifically race, religion or politics (the *mens rea*)."[73] But the Chamber observed that "not every act of discrimination will constitute the crime of persecution: the underlying acts of persecution, whether considered in isolation or *in conjunction with other acts*, must be of a gravity equal to the crimes listed under Article 3 of the [ICTR] Statute."[74]

The panel also pointed out, though, that "it is not necessary that these underlying acts of persecution amount to crimes in international law."[75] Thus, it was not persuaded by the defendants' arguments that hate speech on its own cannot amount to a criminal offense at international law.[76]

Similarly, the Appeals Chamber verified that "hate speech targeting a population on the basis of ethnicity, or any other discriminatory ground, violates the right to respect for the dignity of the members of the targeted group as human beings and therefore constitutes 'actual discrimination.'"[77] Justification for this principle was found in the Universal Declaration of Human Rights, whose preamble "expressly refers to the recognition of dignity inherent to all human beings, while the Articles set out its various aspects."[78] The Chamber further affirmed that "speech inciting to violence against a population on the basis of ethnicity, or any other discriminatory ground, violates the right to security of the members of the targeted group and therefore constitutes 'actual discrimination.'"[79]

However, the judges also acknowledged limits on the regulation of hate speech, finding that they were not "satisfied that hate speech alone can amount to a violation of the rights to life, freedom, and physical integrity of the human being."[80] Consequently, they found that "other persons need to intervene before such violations can occur; a speech cannot, in itself, directly kill members of a group, imprison or physically injure them."[81]

The panel then grappled with an associated but independent issue: whether infringements of essential rights at issue in CAH-persecution cases (i.e., the right to respect for human dignity and the right to security) are as grave as when

73. *Id.* ¶ 985 (quoting Prosecutor v. Krnojelac, Case No. IT-97-25-A, Judgement, ¶ 185 (Int'l Crim. Trib. for the Former Yugoslavia Sept. 17, 2003)).

74. *Id.* (emphasis added).

75. *Id.*

76. *Id.*

77. *Id.* ¶ 986.

78. *Id.* ¶ 986 n.2256.

79. *Id.* ¶ 986.

80. *Id.*

81. *Id.*

fundamental rights are violated in the case of the commission of the other crimes against humanity listed in Article 3 of the ICTR Statute.[82] Here, in respect of an issue at the heart of the split between the ICTR and ICTY regarding hate speech and persecution, a juncture so obviously crucial to the development of the jurisprudence, the Chamber essentially punted:

> The Appeals Chamber is of the view that it is not necessary to decide here whether, in themselves, mere hate speeches not inciting violence against the members of the group are of a level of gravity equivalent to that for other crimes against humanity. As explained above, it is not necessary that every individual act underlying the crime of persecution should be of a gravity corresponding to other crimes against humanity: *underlying acts of persecution can be considered together. It is the cumulative effect of all the underlying acts of the crime of persecution which must reach a level of gravity equivalent to that for other crimes against humanity.* Furthermore, the context in which these underlying acts take place is particularly important for the purpose of assessing their gravity.[83]

Having sorted through the various legal tenets, the Chamber then connected them to the case *sub judice*. It ruled that the post-genocide rhetoric at issue, that is, speech uttered after April 6, 1994, was accompanied by calls for genocide and was delivered in the context of a massive persecution campaign against Rwanda's Tutsi population.[84] That campaign was characterized, the Chamber pointed out, by both violent crimes and property destruction.[85] As a result, in this environment, the speeches at issue were of an equivalent gravity to that of the other enumerated crimes against humanity.[86] According to the Chamber:

> [T]he hate speeches and calls for violence against the Tutsi made after 6 April 1994 (thus *after the beginning of a systematic and widespread attack against the Tutsi*) themselves constituted underlying acts of persecution. In addition . . . some speeches made after 6 April 1994 did in practice substantially contribute to the commission of other acts of persecution against the Tutsi; these speeches thus also instigated the commission of acts of persecution against the Tutsi.[87]

Based on Article 3 of the ICTR Statute, the Chamber further found that any pre-genocide speech, for which the defendants might bear liability, did not

82. *Id.* ¶ 987.

83. *Id.* (emphasis added).

84. *Id.* ¶ 988.

85. *Id.*

86. *Id.*

87. *Id.* (emphasis added) (footnotes omitted).

amount to the crime of persecution as the speech was not uttered as part of a widespread or systematic attack against the Tutsi population.[88] The Chamber added, however, that pre-genocide speech could be considered to have "instigated the commission of acts of persecution."[89] Still, with respect to both RTLM's radio transmissions and *Kangura*'s written pieces, the Chamber found that the pre–April 6, 1994, speech did not, as a matter of fact, catalyze the commission of chargeable persecutory conduct.[90]

Three of the Appeals Chamber judges issued partly dissenting opinions dealing with the question of persecution. Only American judge Theodor Meron, however, found fault with the majority approach because it was *too* permissive regarding hate speech as the foundation for a valid persecution charge. Judge Meron opined that, in absolutely all situations, "mere hate speech may not be the basis of a criminal conviction."[91] Uniquely in circumstances where hate speech "rises to the level of inciting violence or other imminent lawless action" should it be subject to criminal prosecution.[92]

To justify this stance, Judge Meron alluded to a supposed absence of global consensus with respect to municipal criminalization of hate speech. From this, he asserted that such speech being the basis for a criminal conviction in the case *sub judice* contravened the principle of legality.[93] He then cited with approval the *Kordić* decision ruling that hate speech not directly urging violence was not of comparable gravity to the other listed CAH acts (such as deportation or imprisonment).[94] He went on to assert that *Kordić* must perfectly embody the customary norms concerning hate speech because, "the Prosecution did not appeal this important determination, and the Appeals Chamber did not intervene to correct

88. *See id.* ¶¶ 993 (referring to the RTLM broadcasts), 1013 (analyzing the *Kangura* publications). This is an erroneous description of the situation pre–April 6, 1994, and not consistent with what was happening on the ground during that period. An International Commission of Investigation on Human Rights Violations in Rwanda, for example, found that as early as 1993, "the Rwandan state committed acts of genocide, and its violations were massive and systematic, with the deliberate intent to attack the Tutsi ethnic group, as well as opponents of the regime." *See Commission of Inquiry: Rwanda 93*, United States Institute of Peace, http://www.usip.org/publications/commission-inquiry-rwanda-93 (last visited Sept. 18, 2016).

89. Prosecutor v. Nahimana, Case No. ICTR 99-52-A, Judgement, ¶ 993 (Nov. 28, 2007).

90. *See id.* ¶¶ 994 (reviewing the RTLM broadcasts), 1014 (considering the *Kangura* publications). The Chamber backed up its findings related to RTLM by stating "it has not been established that the broadcasts prior to 6 April 1994 substantially contributed to the murder of Tutsi after 6 April 1994." *Id.* This is a strange observation, and not dispositive of the issue, since the Chamber had already granted that persecutory conduct could be wider in scope than just murder. Consequently, the Chamber did not take into account speech uttered before April 6, 1994, that might have victimized Tutsis short of resulting in their murder.

91. *Id.* ¶ 13 (Meron, J., partly dissenting).

92. *Id.* ¶ 12.

93. *Id.* ¶ 5.

94. *Id.* ¶ 7.

a perceived error. . . ."[95] Judge Meron also waxed rhapsodic about the existential importance of protecting hate speech, referring to the United States' elevation of political dissent as a core value.[96] Invoking the American Constitution and related Supreme Court jurisprudence, he noted: "[T]he government may not prohibit the expression of an idea simply because society finds the idea itself offensive or disagreeable. . . . [U]nder the rubric of persecution, to criminalize unsavory speech that does not constitute actual imminent incitement might have grave and unforeseen consequences."[97]

The other two partial dissents adopted a contrary stance, finding that the majority opinion's approach to hate speech and persecution was too restrained. In particular, without qualification, they reasoned that hate speech on its own ought to be the basis for a valid persecution charge. In his partial dissent, Judge Fausto Pocar initially explained that the majority decision "does not appear to rule definitively on the question whether hate speech can per se constitute an underlying act of persecution."[98] Judge Pocar then offered his personal view on this issue: "In my opinion, the circumstances of the instant case are, however, a perfect example where hate speech fulfils the conditions necessary for it to be considered as an underlying act of persecution."[99]

Filtering the facts before him from this perspective, Judge Pocar found that RTLM's hate screeds clearly targeted Tutsis on discriminatory grounds and caused Hutus to discriminate against them, "thus violating their basic rights."[100] He then definitively pronounced the legal ramifications: "Taken together and in their context, these speeches amounted to a violation of equivalent gravity as the other crimes against humanity [and thus] were per se underlying acts of persecution."[101]

Judge Mohamed Shahabuddeen's partial dissent was on all fours with Judge Pocar's, only more in-depth. He pointed out that Nahimana, Barayagwiza, and Ngeze were essentially contending that only certain "inciting" speech—that calling for genocide or extermination—could be deemed as grave as the other listed acts in the crimes against humanity provision.[102] Judge Shahabuddeen dismissed this argument through simple logic—persecution as a crime against humanity is larger in its range than incitement to commit genocide—thus, the former cannot be limited in scope to the latter.[103]

95. *Id.*

96. *Id.* ¶¶ 7, 11.

97. *Id.* ¶¶ 11–12 (citing Texas v. Johnson, 491 U.S. 397, 414 (1989); Brandenburg v. Ohio, 395 U.S. 444, 447 (1969); Watts v. United States, 394 U.S. 705, 708 (1969)).

98. *Id.* ¶ 3 (Pocar, J., partly dissenting).

99. *Id.*

100. *Id.*

101. *Id.*

102. *Id.* ¶ 7 (Shahabuddeen, J., partly dissenting).

103. *Id.* ¶ 9.

Judge Shahabuddeen then clarified why the IMT's *Fritzsche* judgment, cited by the appellants, did not cast doubt on his conclusion. Fritzsche was found not guilty since "he did not take part 'in originating or formulating propaganda campaigns.'"[104] Further, while the IMT mentioned in *dictum* that Fritzsche had not intended "to incite the German people to commit atrocities on conquered people," that does not indicate the Tribunal enshrined genocidal incitement as a required element "for persecution (by making public statements) as a crime against humanity."[105]

Indeed, Shahabuddeen explained that other Nuremberg jurisprudence demonstrated that "a more satisfactory test is that an allegation of persecution as a crime against humanity has to show harm to 'life and liberty'" or "acts committed in the course of wholesale and systematic violation of life and liberty."[106] The other Nuremberg judgments teach that this may include economic (except for expropriation of industrial property) and political discrimination.[107] Consequently, "it is not necessary to prove a physical attack."[108] Shahabuddeen thusly summarized: "In my argument, the court may well regard the 'cumulative effect' of harassment, humiliation, and psychological abuse as impairing the quality of 'life', if not 'liberty', within the meaning of the tests laid down in *Einsatzgruppen*."

He did not stop there, however, critically evaluating the more circumscribed formulation of persecution championed by the *Kordić* Trial Chamber. The *Kordić* decision, he began, seemed to suggest that, shorn of context (in other words, removed from consideration as part of a wider persecution cabal or a widespread or systematic attack against a civilian population), a naked allegation of "encouraging, instigating and promoting hatred, distrust and strife on political, racial, ethnic or religious grounds, by propaganda, speeches or otherwise" cannot be the cornerstone of a persecution charge.[109] But when considered in the proper context, he clarified, hate speech could very well support a doctrinally sound persecution allegation:

> In my opinion, the Trial Chamber's judgment in that case overlooked the fact that it is not possible fully to present a campaign as persecutory if integral allegations of hate acts are excluded. What is pertinent to such a case is the general persecutory campaign, and not the individual hate act as if it stood alone. The subject of the indictment is the persecutory campaign, not the particular hate act. This was why non-crimes were included with crimes in the *Ministries* case. It may be said that an act, which is ordinarily a non-crime, can no longer be treated as a non-crime if it can be prosecuted when committed in a special context. But the possibility of the act being regarded as

104. *Id.* ¶ 10.

105. *Id.* ¶¶ 10–11.

106. *Id.* ¶ 12 (citing the decisions in *Flick* and *Einsatzgruppen*).

107. *Id.*

108. *Id.*

109. *Id.* ¶ 15.

> criminal if committed in a certain context only reinforces the proposition that the Trial Chamber's exclusion of it in *Kordić and Čerkez* is not consistent with the *Ministries* case, or with other cases of the ICTY; the exclusion is contrary to customary international law and is incorrect.[110]

Judge Shahabuddeen had another key illuminating point to make—his brethren on the Appeals Chamber should not have paid attention to the Trial Chamber's emphasis on certain international human rights instruments, such as the ICCPR, which mandate states parties to criminalize hate speech that incites to racial hatred or discrimination.[111] These hate speech-criminalization requirements in the treaties demonstrated, per the Trial Chamber, that the prohibited discourse could be the object of a persecution count.[112] The Appeals Chamber went one step further in the analysis, however, pointing out that certain signatories had issued reservations to those treaty provisions and that meant the prohibitions had not attained the status of customary international law. As a result, the Appeals Chamber reasoned, the associated prohibited conduct, could not, when considered on its own, be the basis of a persecution count.[113] Judge Shahabuddeen deftly shot holes in that reasoning:

> These instruments operate on the basis that a mere hate speech could be criminalised in domestic law: freedom of expression is not absolute. But the Trial Chamber did not mean that the fact that a prosecution could be brought domestically by virtue of legislation enacted pursuant to these instruments necessarily showed that a similar prosecution could be brought internationally. Those instruments were illustrative, not foundational; they were used by the Trial Chamber to illustrate the nature of the rights breached at international law, not to found a right to complain of a breach at international law.[114]

With all this taken into account, Judge Shahabuddeen was able to synthesize his views as follows:

> All that can be legitimately extracted from the post-World War II jurisprudence, including *Fritzsche*, is that the underlying acts must be sufficiently grave to affect the "life and liberty" of the victims—though not necessarily by a physical act against them. It is for an international court to exercise its powers of clarification by explaining what concrete cases will satisfy that criterion. It may be recalled that the ICTY Appeals Chamber, in its discussion

110. *Id.* ¶ 16 (footnotes omitted).

111. *Id.* ¶ 18.

112. *Id.* ¶ 5.

113. *Id.*

114. *Id.* ¶ 18 (footnote omitted).

> of customary international law, unanimously held that "where a principle can be shown to have been so established, it is not an objection to the application of the principle to a particular situation to say that the situation is new if it reasonably falls within the application of the principle". A new case, thus decided, is not an extension of customary international law; it is a further illustration of the workings of that law. This at the same time answers criticisms that the principle of legality was breached in this case. In holding that proof of extermination or genocide is not required, a Trial Chamber is not making new law with retrospective application, or at all.
>
> To respond to what I believe to be the position of the appellants, I am of the view that, where statements are relied upon, the gravity of persecution as a crime against humanity can be established without need for proof that the accused advocated the perpetration of genocide or extermination.[115]

Thus, despite the strong dissents, the *Media Case* Appeals Chamber left the issue unresolved. And so the now-entrenched discrepancy between the two ad hoc tribunals is seen in Table 6.1.

Table 6.1 Split between the ICTR and ICTY in Approaches to Persecution

<table>
<tr><th>*Ruggiu/Media Case*
Trial Chamber Judgement</th><th>*Kordić*</th></tr>
<tr><td colspan="2">Both applied the four-prong *Kupreškić actus reus* test:
(1) a gross or blatant denial;
(2) on discriminatory grounds;
(3) of a fundamental right, laid down in international customary or treaty law;
(4) reaching the same level of gravity as the other crimes against humanity enumerated in the statutes</td></tr>
<tr><td>Non-advocacy hate speech can qualify as persecution's *actus reus* as it satisfies all four prongs of the *Kupreškić* test.</td><td>Non-advocacy hate speech cannot qualify as persecution's *actus reus* as it does not satisfy prongs (3) and (4) of the *Kupreškić* test.</td></tr>
<tr><td colspan="2">*Media Case* Appeals Chamber Judgement fails to resolve the split.</td></tr>
</table>

F. The *Šešelj* Trial Chamber Judgment Skirts the Issue Altogether

Arguably the last ad hoc tribunal case capable of bridging the gap between the ICTR and the ICTY on the issue of hate speech and CAH-persecution, *Prosecutor*

115. *Id.* ¶¶ 19–20 (footnotes omitted).

v. Vojislav Šešelj, completely skirted the issue in its first opportunity, the March 2016 Trial Chamber judgment acquitting the defendant of all charges.[116] In Chapter 1, we saw that Šešelj, through fiery and noxious hate sermons delivered during the early-1990s Balkan wars, urged Serb ultranationalist militias to kill and ethnically cleanse non-Serbs in portions of Croatia, Bosnia, and the Serbian province of Vojvodina.[117] In connection with his speeches, *inter alia*, the ICTY charged him with individual (via direct commission, instigation and aiding and abetting) and joint criminal enterprise (JCE) responsibility for commission of war crimes and crimes against humanity, including persecution.[118]

Regarding speech as contributing to the JCE, Paragraph 10(b) of the Third Amended Indictment (Indictment) alleged that Šešelj "made inflammatory speeches in the media, during public events, and during visits to the volunteer units and other Serb forces in Croatia and Bosnia and Herzegovina, instigating those forces to commit crimes in violation of Articles 3 and 5 of the Statute of the Tribunal."[119] Paragraph 10(c) claimed that the defendant "espoused and encouraged the creation of a homogeneous 'Greater Serbia', encompassing the territories specified in this indictment, by violence, and thereby participated in war propaganda and incitement of hatred towards non-Serb people."[120] Finally, Paragraph 10(d) charged that he "called for the expulsion of Croat civilians from parts of the Vojvodina region in Serbia (namely, Hrtkovci, Nikinci, Ruma, Šid, and other places bordering Croatia) and thus instigated his followers and the local authorities to engage in a persecution campaign against the local Croat population."[121]

Count One of the Indictment, styled "Persecutions," stated in Paragraph 15 that they were committed against Croat, Muslim, and other non-Serb civilian populations in the territories of the SAO SBWS (Slavonia, Baranja, and Western Srem), and in the municipalities of Zvornik, "Greater Sarajevo," Mostar, and Nevesinje in Bosnia and Herzegovina and parts of Vojvodina in Serbia."[122] Paragraph 17 declared that "these persecutions were committed on political, racial and religious grounds and included . . . (k) direct and public denigration through 'hate speech' of the Croat, Muslim and other non-Serb populations in Vukovar, Zvornik, and Hrtkovci on the basis of their ethnicities as described in paragraphs 20, 22, and 23

116. Prosecutor v. Šešelj, Case No. IT-03-67-T, Judgement (Int'l Crim. Trib. for the Former Yugoslavia Mar. 31, 2016).

117. *See supra* Chapter 1, IV.E.1; Marlise Simons, *Tribunal Acquits Serbian Nationalist of War Crimes*, N.Y. Times, Mar. 31, 2016, at A9.

118. *Šešelj*, Case No. IT-03-67, Third Amended Indictment, ¶¶ 5, 10(b), 17(k) (Int'l Crim. Trib. for the Former Yugoslavia Dec. 7, 2007). The speeches, including some characterized as "instigation," were also relevant in the indictment insofar as they constituted part of Šešelj's contribution to the JCE to commit war crimes and crimes against humanity.

119. *Id.* ¶ 10(b).

120. *Id.* ¶ 10(c).

121. *Id.* ¶ 10(d).

122. *Id.* ¶ 15.

[detailing persecutions or instigations of persecutions against victims in, respectively, Vukovar, Zvornik, and certain small towns around Sarajevo]."[123]

These were the charges on which evidence was presented at trial regarding hate speech as persecution (and instigation to persecution). Thus, another perfect opportunity to clarify the law regarding CAH-persecution was presented. And it was completely squandered. The judgment is riddled with misunderstandings of the law and fact, specious reasoning, and faulty use of terminology. It is one of the worst judicial opinions this author has ever read—in any jurisdiction or in any context. What follows is a brief resume of the decision and its deficiencies, many of which are linked to the confusion in terminology regarding atrocity speech that this book seeks to clear up.

One of the central flaws of the judgment lies in its baseline analysis of the situation in the former Yugoslavia. For purposes of this book, one of the Trial Chamber's key conclusions doctrinally renders irrelevant any analysis regarding the persecution offense. In particular, flying in the face of well-settled ICTY precedent, the *Šešelj* Chamber found that extremist Serbs did not carry out a widespread or systematic attack against non-Serb civilians in that region during the time in question.[124] Instead, the Chamber would have us believe, the milieu was strictly one of garden-variety armed conflict where civilians from all ethnic groups participated in "street fighting" over contested territory, but no criminal actions were directed toward civilians.[125] And rather than engaging in ethnic cleansing, the Chamber found that the Serb militias provided safe convoy:

> The majority cannot, in these circumstances, reject the defense argument—amply supported in certain selected witness accounts—that explains that civilians were fleeing combat zones to seek refuge in localities where they could find members of the same ethnic or religious group; that the buses chartered in this context were not for purposes of forced population transfers, but rather for humanitarian assistance for non-combatants who were fleeing areas where they did not feel safe anymore.[126]

123. *Id.* ¶¶ 17, 17(k), 20, 22, & 23.

124. *Šešelj*, Case No. IT-03-67-T, ¶ 192 ("The majority considers that insufficient evidence was offered to establish irrefutably that a widespread or systematic attack was directed against civilian populations . . .").

125. *Id.* ("[Rather than a widespread or systematic attack against a civilian population] the evidence proffered and examined reveals an armed conflict between opposing military factions with some civilian elements involved."). The Trial Chamber added: "The presence of an indeterminate portion of civilian combatants, within the context of confrontations that many witnesses described as street fights wherein every square inch of territory, every house was fought over, provides a perspective that forecloses the view that an attack was directed against a civilian population." *Id.*

126. *Id.* ¶ 193.

Thus, absurdly, the two majority judges found that armed Serb extremists were essentially operating a form of gratuitous Greyhound bus service for non-Serb residents of the areas they attacked, which excluded the possibility of their committing a widespread or systematic attack against those civilians. As a result, with a CAH chapeau element remarkably found missing, the majority obviated the need to discuss Šešelj's liability for CAH-persecution. Apart from the obvious injustice of this bizarre ruling, it also signified another wasted chance to clarify the law regarding persecution.[127] And it served as a segue to the next portion of the Trial Chamber's decision, which revealed some of the serious deficits in the law of instigation. That will be the object of the section that follows.

III. INSTIGATION

A. Conflating Instigation with Incitement

As we have seen from analyzing the *Akayesu* case, the first ad hoc tribunal post-trial decision analyzing the role of hate speech in relation to mass atrocity, the jurisprudence was marred from the outset by a blurring of the line between the concepts of incitement, on one hand, and instigation (or provocation), on the other. Part of this fuzziness stemmed from reliance on Civil Law, as opposed to Common Law, conceptions of these crimes. Another aspect of the problem related to the linguistic overlap between French, one of the two official languages of the ad hoc tribunals, and English, their other official language.

In Chapter 5, we noticed the Civil Law versus Common Law dimension of the problem from the perspective of incitement. More specifically, in considering the first key element of that crime, the *Akayesu* Trial Chamber noted that under "Civil law systems, provocation, the equivalent of incitement, is regarded as being direct where it is aimed at causing a specific offence to be committed."[128] This intermingling of terminology is apparent when one considers that "provocation" is synonymous with "instigation."[129] Thus, as we have seen, *Akayesu*, also in conformance with the Civil Law tradition's conflation of incitement and instigation, is thought by some possibly to have imported a causation requirement into incitement.

Further, and related, confusion is due to the influence of the French language on the jurisprudence of the ad hoc tribunals. As was noted previously, French

127. *Id.* ¶ 293. In the words of the majority: "As a threshold matter, given that the majority has not affirmed the existence of crimes against humanity, the analysis that follows will be limited to determining whether the accused is liable for instigating commission of violations of the laws or customs of war." *Id.*

128. Prosecutor v. Akayesu, Case No. ICTR-96-4-T, Judgement ¶ 557 (Sept. 2, 1998).

129. Avitus A. Agbor, Instigation to Crimes against Humanity: The Flawed Jurisprudence of the Trial and Appeal Chambers of the International Criminal Tribunal for Rwanda 69 n.168 (2013).

is one of the two official languages of the ICTY and ICTR. Thus, the works of French jurists and statutes from francophone jurisdictions, most prominently Rwanda, have exerted an important influence on the development of the ICTR jurisprudence. And *Akayesu* is where all that began.

If the Trial Chamber's analysis of incitement verged on a Civil Law exegesis of instigation, then its take on instigation was plainly informed by French linguistic considerations that implicated incitement. In the Gallic tongue, the word *incitation* can denote both "incitement" *and* "instigation." Similarly, the verb *inciter* means both "to incite" and "to instigate." This seems to have influenced *Akayesu*'s view of the two terms in English. According to the Trial Chamber:

> The second form of liability is "incitation" (in the French version of the Statute) to commit a crime, reflected in the English version of Article 6 (1) by the word *instigated.* In English, it seems the words incitement and instigation are synonymous. Furthermore, the word "instigated" or "instigation" is used to refer to incitation in several other instruments.[130]

The end of the first sentence in this quotation is followed by a footnote, 82, which cites the "Lexique Anglais-Français (principalement juridique) of the Council of Europe, Strasbourg, January 1997."[131] The *Akayesu* Trial Chamber then offered some grammatically-challenged gloss, noting that the lexicon "translates 'incitement' by incitation, instigation ou provocation or the "Dictionnaire Français/ Anglais" Larousse, or the 'Dictionnaire Français/ Anglais' Super Senior Robert Collins."[132] Unfortunately, this prose is about as clear as the Chamber's messy admixture of French and English language and legal concepts.

The overall confusion is summed up well by the Trial Chamber in *Prosecutor v. Kalimanzira*:

> The distinction between committing direct and public incitement and committing genocide by means of instigation often seems blurred. The term "incitement" is synonymous with "instigation", "provocation", and "encouragement", all of which are used interchangeably when describing the conduct underlying certain modes by which genocide may be committed.[133]

This doctrinal disorder surfaces in both the relevant jurisprudence and expert commentary. With respect to the former, for example, in *Prosecutor v. Rutaganda* (1999), the Trial Chamber's conflation of incitement and instigation was demonstrated by its noting that Article 6(1) of the ICTR Statute criminalizes

130. *Akayesu*, Case No. ICTR-96-4-T, ¶ 481 (emphasis added).

131. *Id.* ¶ 481 n.82.

132. *Id.*

133. Prosecutor v. Kalimanzira, Case No. ICTR-05-88-T, Judgement ¶ 511 (June 22, 2009).

"incitement."[134] Unfortunately, Article 6(1), which assigns individual responsibility to persons who "planned, instigated, ordered, committed or otherwise aided and abetted in the planning, preparation or execution of a crime . . ." does not even contain the word "incite" or any variation thereof.[135] The Trial Chamber then did a terminology flip-flop, observing that "instigation" (not "incitement") requires proof of the "direct" and "public" elements.[136] As previously demonstrated, "direct" and "public" are elements of "incitement," not instigation.[137]

From its doctrinal-linguistic origins, the confusion regarding instigation versus incitement has arguably been exacerbated by more specific conceptual boundary-bleeding. For example, perhaps because, in the popular imagination, incitement is elementally limited to "public" speech, that is speech presumably directed at members of the public in general—conventional wisdom reserves instigation for "private" speech, in other words, speech presumably directed at specifically identified individuals.[138] But, as ad hoc tribunal judges have held that "instigation" can consist of speech directed at members of the public at large, certain international judges have confused matters even more by arguably incorporating a "direct" element into instigation.

In *Prosecutor v. Brđanin* (2004), for instance, an ICTY Trial Chamber held that when instigation's *actus reus* consists of public statements, they must be "specific enough to constitute instructions . . . to the physical perpetrators to commit" the target offense.[139] Wibke Timmermann notes that this requirement "appears to be similar to the interpretation which the Rwanda Tribunal has given to the qualification 'direct' in the crime of 'direct and public incitement to commit genocide.'" Seemingly supporting this analysis, in *Prosecutor v. Ndindabahizi* (2004), where the charged speech was uttered in a public space (a roadblock), the Trial Chamber held that "[i]n order to be guilty of instigating . . . genocide, the acts constituting the encouragement must *directly* and substantially contribute to the perpetration of genocide by another person."[140]

134. Prosecutor v. Rutaganda, Case No. ICTR-96-3, Judgement and Sentence, ¶ 458 (Dec. 6, 1999).

135. Statute of the International Criminal Tribunal for Rwanda, S.C. Res. 955, art 6(1), U.N. Doc. S/RES/955 (Nov. 8, 1994) [hereinafter ICTR Statute].

136. *Rutaganda*, Case No. ICTR-96-3, ¶ 458.

137. *See also* Prosecutor v. Musema, Case No. ICTR-96-13-T, Judgement and Sentence, ¶ 120 (Jan. 27, 2000) (going back and forth in using the terms and elements of "incitement" and "instigation" in discussing the same count of the indictment).

138. Wibke Timmermann, Incitement in International Law 234 (2014) ("Instigation or solicitation are directed at a specific, identifiable group of individuals and aim at the commission of particular criminal acts.").

139. Prosecutor v. Brđanin, Case No. IT-99-36-T, Judgement, ¶¶ 468, 527, and 662 (Int'l Crim. Trib. for the Former Yugoslavia Sept. 1, 2004).

140. Prosecutor v. Ndindabahizi, Case No. ICTR-2001-71-1, Judgement and Sentence, ¶ 466 (July 15, 2004).

Surveying these cases, Timmermann concludes that it is "difficult to understand how 'specific enough to constitute instructions' would be a very different, let alone less strict requirement than 'direct.'"[141] And, thus, she laments how "confusing" this "state of affairs has become."[142]

Arguably reflecting that confusion, in the original version of the *Šešelj* Trial Chamber judgment, written in the French language, at Paragraphs 293–296, the majority provided analysis regarding the term "incitation" (e.g., "Pour qu'une Chambre puisse conclure à l'existence d'une *incitation* à commettre des crimes . . .").[143] The doctrinal analysis clearly supports the inference that the Chamber is discussing what in English would be described as "instigation." For example, it alluded to a "substantial contribution" requirement ("[les] actes constitutifs de l'incitation . . . doivent avoir *substantiellement contribué* à la commission des crimes . . .").[144]

And yet, the English summary of the judgment, in referring to the same passage, referred to the crime of "incitement." For example, in roughly the same portion of the analysis as the full judgment, the summary states: "I will now summarise the findings of the Chamber regarding the Prosecution's allegations of *incitement* to commit crimes with which Vojislav Šešelj is charged."[145] That section was then bookended by the following text: "[The] Majority [does not] find that there was *incitement to war crimes* . . ."[146]

Perhaps the admixing of terminology is not strictly a function of poor foreign language transliteration. In discussing *incitation* in the original French text (doubtless, given the contextual discussion in the judgment, meaning "instigation" in English), the *Šešelj* majority cited to that portion of the ICTR Trial Chamber and Appeals Chamber judgments in the *Media Case* dealing with direct and public incitement to commit genocide.[147] For example, in discussing causation in reference to Šešelj's liability for acts of instigation, the two majority judges cited Paragraphs 1011 and 1020–1022 of the *Media Case* Trial Chamber judgment and Paragraphs 698–703 of the corresponding Appeals Chamber judgment.

Those paragraphs, in each *Media Case* judgment, are explicitly related to the crime of direct and public incitement to commit genocide, not instigation. For example, Paragraph 1011 of the *Media Case* Trial Chamber judgment

141. Wibke Timmermann, *supra* note 138, at 24.

142. *Id.*

143. Prosecutor v. Šešelj, Case No. IT-03-67-T, Judgement, ¶ 294 (Int'l Crim. Trib. for the Former Yugoslavia Mar. 31, 2016) (emphasis added).

144. *Id.* (emphasis added).

145. *Šešelj*, Case No. IT-03-67-T, Judgment Summary (Mar. 31, 2016), http://www.icty.org/x/cases/seselj/tjug/en/160331_judgement_summary.pdf.

146. *Id.*

147. *Id.* ¶ 300, n.343.

begins: "The ICTR jurisprudence provides the only direct precedent for the interpretation of 'direct and public incitement to genocide.'"[148] And the first sentence of Paragraph 698 states explicitly that it is engaged in "determining whether a speech constituted direct incitement to genocide."[149] We can conclude, then, that the jurisprudential boundary between "incitement" and "instigation" is quite amorphous.

Not surprisingly, this has sown confusion in the scholarly commentary as well. The clearest proof of this is found in the work of Avitus A. Agbor of the University of Witwatersrand School of Law. In a 2012 article titled "The Substantial Contribution Requirement: The Unfortunate Outcome of an Illogical Construction and Incorrect Understanding of Article 6(1) of the Statute of the ICTR," Agbor seriously conflates the crimes of instigation and incitement by arguing that instigation is an inchoate crime and the ICTR's jurisprudence in relation to it is flawed because it has included a contribution requirement.[150]

Again, Agbor's objection to the contribution requirement is premised on his understanding that instigation is an inchoate crime.[151] This argument is then reprised in two more scholarly pieces—another article that appeared the following year titled "The Problematic Jurisprudence on Instigation under the Statute of the ICTR: The Consistencies, Inconsistencies and Misgivings of the Trial and Appeal Chambers of the ICTR"[152] and a book from the same year, *Instigation to Crimes against Humanity: The Flawed Jurisprudence of the Trial and Appeal Chambers of the International Criminal Tribunal For Rwanda (ICTR).*[153]

Of course, notwithstanding its being the premise of three separate academic works, this argument is entirely flawed. As Wibke Timmermann writes: "Instigation under Article 6(1) of the Rwanda Tribunal Statute and Article 7(1) of the Yugoslavia Tribunal Statute, as well as solicitation and inducement under Article 25(3)(b) of the Rome Statute, are forms of participation in another person's crime or accessory liability and therefore *not inchoate*."[154] But the point is not the merits of the argument per se. It is the false *perception*, arguably owing to the sloppy jurisprudence, that incitement and instigation share qualities that they do not in fact share. Perhaps, looking at this from the other

148. Prosecutor v. Nahimana, Case No. ICTR-99-52-T, Judgement and Sentence, ¶ 1011 (Dec. 3, 2003).

149. *Nahimana*, Case No. ICTR-99-52-A, Judgement, ¶ 862 (Nov. 28, 2007).

150. Avitus A. Agbor, *The Substantial Contribution Requirement: The Unfortunate Outcome of an Illogical Construction and Incorrect Understanding of Article 6(1) of the Statute of the ICTR*, 12 Int'l Crim. L. Rev. 155 (2012).

151. *Id.* at 156 (indicating that his chief premise "is the inchoate nature of instigation . . .").

152. Avitus A. Agbor, *The Problematic Jurisprudence on Instigation under the Statute of the ICTR: The Consistencies, Inconsistencies and Misgivings of the Trial and Appeal Chambers of the ICTR*, 13 Int'l Crim. L. Rev. 385 (2013).

153. Agbor, *supra* note 129.

154. Wibke Timmermann, *supra* note 138, at 222 (emphasis added).

end of the telescope, this has helped contribute to the confusion regarding causation in incitement jurisprudence.

B. The New and Unsupported "Different Forms of Persuasion" Requirement

As we learnt in Chapter 4, *Prosecutor v. Akayesu* held that instigation's *actus reus* consists of *prompting* another to commit an offense; but this is different from incitement in that it is punishable only where it leads to the actual commission of an offence desired by the instigator."[155] Thus "prompting," or equivalent language such as "urging," "encouraging," or other similar words, has been the standard applied in numerous cases since.[156]

However, like a bolt out of the blue, the Trial Chamber in *Prosecutor v. Šešelj* added a new requirement, namely, proof that the instigator used different forms of persuasion, such as threats, seduction, or promises, toward the perpetrator of the target crime.[157] The Trial Chamber cited no legal authority in support of this proposition and simply created a new requirement out of whole cloth.

At most, the Trial Chamber cited to the prosecution's Pre-Trial Brief, which in turn relied on the Rwandan Criminal Code.[158] However, in its Pre-Trial Brief, the prosecution alluded to "promises, threats or abuse of power" merely as illustrative examples of types of instigation, noting that "instigation may take many forms."[159] This new requirement, being without support in law, policy, or logic, cannot be considered legitimate and now represents another doctrinal glitch in the law of instigation.

C. Ambiguity in the Contribution Requirement

In discussing the basic elements of instigation in Chapter 4, we saw that perhaps the central characteristic that distinguishes it from incitement is actual postspeech commission of the target offense. But the jurisprudence has equally mandated that prosecutors establish a link, specifically in the form of a "contribution," to execution of the underlying offense.

155. Prosecutor v. Akayesu, Case No. ICTR-96-4-T, Judgement ¶ 482 (Sept. 2, 1998).

156. *See, e.g.*, Prosecutor v. Semanza, Case No. ICTR-97-20-T, Judgement and Sentence, ¶ 555 (May 15, 2003) (using the verbs "urging" and "encouraging"); Prosecutor v. Ndindabahizi, Case No. ICTR-2001-71-I, Judgement and Sentence, ¶ 456 (July 15, 2004); Prosecutor v. Krstić, Case No. IT-98-33-T, Judgement ¶ 601 (Int'l Crim. Trib. for the Former Yugoslavia Aug. 2, 2001); Prosecutor v. Blaškić, Case No. IT-95-14, Judgement, ¶ 280 (Int'l Crim. Trib. for the Former Yugoslavia Mar. 3, 2000).

157. Prosecutor v. Šešelj, Case No. IT-03-67-T, Judgement, ¶ 295 (Int'l Crim. Trib. for the Former Yugoslavia Mar. 31, 2016).

158. *Id.* n.325.

159. *Šešelj*, Case No. IT-03-67-T, Prosecution-Pre-Trial Brief, ¶ 146.

Unfortunately, the nature of this "contribution" has varied considerably in the relevant case law. For example, in *Prosecutor v. Kordić*, the Trial Chamber held that it is sufficient to show "that the contribution of the accused in fact had an effect on the commission of the crime."[160] Other ICTY judges have found that the instigator's communication must constitute "a clear contributing factor to the conduct of the other person(s)."[161] And panels from the ICTR—in *Prosecutor v. Ndindabahizi* and *Prosecutor v. Mpambara*—have ruled that prosecutors must prove a "direct . . . and substantial . . . contribut[ion]" to the target crime.[162] Yet other ad hoc tribunal judges have mandated a "substantial contributing factor" as adequate proof of instigation.[163]

Once again, the confusion has arguably led to anomalous results in the most recent instigation case. In *Prosecutor v. Šešelj*, as we saw earlier in this chapter, the two-judge majority considered whether the defendant was guilty of instigation to war crimes. In analyzing liability in relation to these charges, the Trial Chamber began with an exposition of the law governing the crime of instigation. It observed, in relevant part:

> For a Chamber to conclude there has been instigation to commit crimes, it must find the existence of a material element or *actus reus* in relation to the instigation that must have substantially contributed to the commission of crimes . . . the material element entails provoking someone to commit an offense. It is not necessary to prove the crime would not have been committed without the involvement of the accused, but it must be shown that the incitement was a contributing factor in the behavior of another person who committed the crime.[164]

But the Trial Chamber failed to hew to this standard. In particular, in relation to a speech given by the accused in Hrtkovci, the judges set out the allegation:

> According to the indictment, on 6 May 1992, the Accused would have given an "incendiary" speech in the village of Hrtkovci during which he would have

160. Prosecutor v. Kordić, Case No. IT-95-14/2-T, Judgement, ¶ 387 (Int'l Crim. Trib. for the Former Yugoslavia Feb. 26, 2001).

161. *See, e.g.*, Prosecutor v. Kvočka, Case No. IT-98-30/1-T, Judgement, ¶ 252 (Int'l Crim. Trib. for the Former Yugoslavia Nov. 2, 2001); Prosecutor v. Naletilić, Case No. IT-98-34-T, Judgement, ¶ 60 (Int'l Crim. Trib. for the Former Yugoslavia Mar. 31, 2003); Prosecutor v. Galić, Case No. IT-98-29-T, Judgement and Opinion (Int'l Crim. Trib. for the Former Yugoslavia Dec. 5, 2003); Prosecutor v. Brđanin, Case No. IT-99-36-T, Judgement, ¶ 269 (Int'l Crim. Trib. for the Former Yugoslavia Sept. 1, 2004).

162. Prosecutor v. Ndindabahizi, Case No. ICTR-2001-71-I, Judgement and Sentence, ¶ 463 (July 15, 2004); Prosecutor v. Mpambara, Case No. ICTR-01-65-T, Judgement, ¶ 18 (Sept. 11, 2006).

163. Prosecutor v. Orić, Case No. IT-03-68-T, Judgement, ¶ 276 (Int'l Crim. Trib. for the Former Yugoslavia June 30, 2006).

164. Prosecutor v. Šešelj, Case No. IT-03-67-T, Judgement, ¶¶ 294–295 (Int'l Crim. Trib. for the Former Yugoslavia Mar. 31, 2016).

> called for the expulsion of the Croats of that sector. A good number of Croat residents would have decided to leave the village because of this speech.[165]

The Trial Chamber then laid out, and unequivocally credited, the specific evidence adduced by the prosecution in support of the charge:

> 330. The Chamber can rely on the testimony of a number of witnesses, as well as documentary evidence, establishing the content of the speech given by the Accused on 6 May 1992 in Hrtkovci, especially Exhibits P547 and P548, to which the Chamber accords great probative value.
>
> 331. According to Exhibit P547, a written transcription of speeches of the "Campaign Rally of the Radical Serbian Party [SRS]" held on 6 May 1992 in Hrtkovci, published in his book *The Devil's Apprentice*, the Accused notably declared that the SRS "was fighting for the rebuilding of an independent and free Serbian State" comprising the Serb territories designated by the Karlobag-Karlovac-Mitrovica Line at the heart of Yugoslavia, and in which was located in the Serb sector the village of Hrtkovci. He expressed his wish that democratic, multiparty elections be quickly held. He also declared that that there was no place for Croats in Hrtkovci; that only Croats having spilled blood at the side of Serbs, designated as "Catholic Serbs," could remain; that Croats had to leave Serbia and that Serb "refugees" in Hrtkovci were going to move into the abandoned Croat houses, whose addresses would be disseminated by the police . . . that those Croats who had not already left would be taken in buses to the border; he stated his conviction that the Serbs of Hrtkovci and surrounding villages would know how to preserve their unity and they would "quickly rid themselves of any remaining Croats in their village and its surroundings."
>
> 332. The nature of this speech is confirmed by Exhibit P548, through which it is established, among other things, that subsequent to the speech being given, slogans such as "Ustachi get out" and "Croats, go to Croatia" and "This is Serbia" were chanted by the crowd.[166]

Following from this, the Trial Chamber concluded there was proof beyond a reasonable doubt that Šešelj called for the expulsion of Croats, who were indeed subsequently expelled: "Based on the evidence marshalled, a majority of the Chamber can conclude, with Judge Antonetti dissenting, that the Accused's speech on this occasion constituted a clear call for expulsion or forced transfer of Croats from the locality."[167]

165. *Id.* ¶ 329.

166. *Id.* ¶¶ 330–332.

167. *Id.* ¶ 333.

But the Trial Chamber then ruled that Šešelj could bear no liability for instigation flowing from this speech because "the Prosecution was not able to marshal evidence that this speech would have been *at the root of the departure* of the Croats or the persecution campaign alleged by the Prosecution that was supposedly carried out in the locality after the speech."[168] To "be at the root" of an occurrence smacks of a "but for" causation standard.

Similarly, the Trial Chamber found that two additional speeches, given before the Serb Parliament, on April 1 and 7, respectively, "constituted clear calls for the expulsion and forcible transfer of Croats."[169] And, yet again, the Chamber refused to assign liability to the defendant given an insufficient "impact" of the defendant's speeches in reference to the war crimes alleged in the indictment. But this seems at odds with the Chamber's acknowledging, a couple of paragraphs later, "the reality of a certain influence and aura of the Accused, notably with respect to members of his own party and certain combatants."[170] The Chamber elaborated further regarding the impact of Šešelj's words on those who carried out the target crimes linked to his speeches:

> One of [the Serb combatants]—VS-002—affirmed that the Accused "was a Voïvode Serb. We would never have refused his orders." Other witnesses specified that the Accused was the ideological leader of the volunteers and that they considered the Accused as a god. The Chamber also heard several witnesses who testified that the Accused's speeches had an important impact on those who were listening.[171]

As Šešelj was exhorting his listeners, the Serb combatants at issue, to remove Croats forcibly, and in light of his influence on those combatants, it seems implausible to exclude his speeches as making some kind of important contribution to the forcible removals that followed them. The Chamber's doing so seems tantamount to imposing a "but for" causation standard. And that is arguably owing to the confusion regarding the precise parameters of instigation's "contribution" requirement.

IV. ORDERING

As we saw in Chapter 4, the elements of ordering were rather straightforward—superior-subordinate relationship, transmission of an illegal command to a subordinate, awareness of the substantial likelihood that a crime will be committed in the execution of the order, and subsequent commission of a related crime. But one element of the crime stands out. As Michael Karnavas points out: "A causal link

168. *Id.* (emphasis added).

169. *Id.* ¶ 335.

170. *Id.* ¶ 341.

171. *Id.*

must be shown between the order and the actual commission of the crime."[172] He goes on:

> Ordering should be considered as being "closely associated" with instigating and so it is necessary to show that the order was a substantial factor in the commission of the crime. Indeed, the ICTR Appeals Chamber in *Kamuhanda* set out an even stricter standard of a "direct and substantial effect on the commission of the illegal act".[173]

But does it make sense to consider ordering as akin to instigation and thus in need of a causal link between the relevant speech and commission of a crime? It is submitted that in terms of both logic and policy, the answer is clearly no. What is the difference between ordering and instigation? Instigation involves the defendant's mere exhortation of another person—it could be anyone—to commit a crime. But ordering necessarily involves speech issued within the context of a superior-subordinate relationship. And it entails not mere "advocacy" but actual "issuance of a command."

Although ordering does not necessarily implicate the same degree of authority exerted over the superior by the subordinate as the doctrine of command responsibility, the latter serves as a helpful point of reference. If the superior-subordinate relationship can lead to *omission* liability of the latter for the crimes of the former, then it is perhaps logical to postulate that *commission* (via ordering an illegal act) should incur liability for the superior in case of the subordinate's *omission*.

Yet another doctrine sheds light on this. Consider the crime of incitement. As with instigation, it entails exhortation of another to commit a crime. Again, the nature of the relationship between the speaker and the listener does not factor into the elements of the offense. And yet incitement incurs inchoate liability. In other words, even if the crime urged is not committed, criminal responsibility will be assigned to the speaker.

However, in the case of ordering, where the speaker exercises a position of control over the listener, it makes no sense for speech *commanding* commission of crimes not to incur inchoate liability as well. Put another way, pursuant to its current formulation, a mere *request* to commit crime with no follow-up may result in penal sanction but a *command* to do so will lead to none. Thus, there exists another significant lacuna in the law and an inconsistency in policy vis-à-vis incitement/instigation. As Robert Cryer reasons:

> The first point is that is that by ordering an offence, the superior creates a very significant risk of the harm (the offence ordered) occurring. This is more

172. Michael G. Karnavas, *Forms of Perpetration*, *in* Elements of Genocide 104 (Paul Behrens & Ralph Henham eds., 2013).

173. *Id.* (quoting Prosecutor v. Kupreškić, Case No. IT-95-16-T, Judgement, ¶ 567 (Int'l Crim. Trib. for the Former Yugoslavia Jan. 14, 2000) and Prosecutor v. Kamuhanda, Case No. ICTR-95-54A-T, Judgement, ¶ 75 (Jan. 1, 2004)).

> pronounced in the case of ordering offences than simple incitement because of the superior-subordinate relationship that must be proved. . . . The relationship . . . is important . . . because it makes the likelihood of the occurrence of the ordered offence high. . . . Indeed, there is often criminal liability for failure to obey orders. As a result, ordering, per se creates a significant risk of commission of an offence, probably more so than simple instigation or encouragement.[174]

V. CONCLUSION

Much of the existing scholarship on speech and atrocity has focused on issues related to the crime of direct and public incitement to commit genocide. But as this chapter has demonstrated, there are glaring problems elsewhere. Crimes against humanity (persecution) is plagued by a rift between the ICTR and the ICTY in terms of whether hate speech not directly calling for action, a significant and potentially lethal portion of discourse in persecution campaigns, can satisfy the *actus reus* element of the crime.

And instigation often suffers from a doctrinally messy conflation/confusion with incitement, an unsupported and unjustified *actus reus* add-on, and a schizophrenically formulated contribution element that has resulted in the offense's arguably being saddled with a "but for" causation requirement. Ordering, for its part, as presently formulated, permits absolving superiors for commanding crimes such as genocide, crimes against humanity, and war crimes merely because the subordinate did not carry out the offense. Given the nature of the superior-subordinate relationship, where speech in the form of a directive is inherently likely to be complied with, this creates a significant liability gap in the law. But, as we shall see in Chapter 9, these problems are far from insoluble. And that chapter will propose doctrinally feasible solutions in due course.

174. Robert Cryer, *General Principles of International Criminal Law*, *in* THE PERMANENT INTERNATIONAL CRIMINAL COURT: LEGAL AND POLICY ISSUES 246 (Dominic McGoldrick et al. eds., 2004).

7

The Liability Gap in Reference to Hate Speech and War Crimes

> "Loose and violent talk by an officer of high rank is always likely to excite to wrongdoing those among his subordinates whose wills are weak or whose passions are strong. . . ."
>
> —Theodore Roosevelt[1]

I. INTRODUCTION

If the hate speech–core crime relationship is plagued by internal incoherence with respect to incitement to genocide and instigation and institutional incompatibility as concerns persecution, the problem in reference to war crimes is quite different. In effect, the issue is a relative absence of law. Remarkably, given the inherently violent nature of the battlefield, with the exception of directly ordering grave breaches, international humanitarian law contains no hate speech provisions. This chapter explores the deadly implications of that normative vortex and details the relevant legal instruments that evidence it.

II. SPEECH AND MILITARY PERSONNEL IN THE ATROCITY CONTEXT

A. Military Commanders Inciting Their Subordinates

For laypersons, the term "incitement" betokens fiery rhetoricians publicly igniting the passions of their listeners in large civic gathering places or through mass

1. Gary D. Solis, The Law of Armed Conflict: International Humanitarian Law in War 65 (2010).

media. Reality is often at odds with that popular conception, however. Instead, the prime instigators of civilian atrocities are typically found in structured military and/or paramilitary groups.[2] As will be demonstrated below, in the course of communicating with their charges as part of entirely licit campaigns, officers may so viciously denigrate protected persons—civilians or prisoners of war, for example—that the aspersions are perceived as exhortations to violence. Alternatively, this type of suggestive rhetoric can be an integral component of patently illegal attacks, such as being part of an ethnic cleansing operation, civilian retaliation killings, or collective hostage taking.

And incitement of this stripe has an ancient lineage. As we saw in Chapter 1, Egyptian Pharaoh Amenemhet I exhorted his troops to commit war crimes by characterizing their battlefield opponents as nonhuman predators.[3] As will be recalled, he is supposed to have bragged: "I subdued lions, I captured crocodiles. I repressed those of Wawat, I captured the Medjai, I made the Asiatics do the dog walk."[4]

More recently, superiors interacting with subordinates in martial contexts have employed comparable rhetorical strategies with similarly destructive consequences. In the twentieth and twenty-first centuries, commanders in the US military, and those of armed forces in other parts of the world, have violently whipped up their soldiers in this manner. The remainder of this section will provide illustrative examples.

1. United States Military

a. General Jacob Smith in the Philippine-American War

Modern war crimes incitement can be traced as far back as 1901, during the Philippine-American War. On the heels of a surprise guerilla attack in the town of Balangiga, during which more than forty American soldiers were killed, US Army Brigadier General Jacob Smith addressed his underlings as follows: "I wish you to kill and burn. The more you kill and burn, the better you will please

2. *See, e.g.*, Natasha Razak, Book Note, 48 Osgoode Hall L. J. 379, 380 (2010) (reviewing Ryan Goodman & Mindy Jane Roseman, Interrogations, Forced Feedings, and the Role of Health Professionals (2009)) ("Military policies and group psychology work in concert in the military environment to create an 'atrocity-producing situation . . . .' ").

3. *See* Mu-Chou Poo, Enemies of Civilization: Attitudes towards Foreigners in Ancient Mesopotamia, Egypt and China 74 (2005) (chronicling the Egyptian approach to foreigners as manifested in Pharaonic propaganda); David Livingstone Smith, Less than Human: Why We Demean, Enslave, and Exterminate Others 109 (2011) (showing Amenemhet I's dehumanization of Egypt's enemies).

4. Poo, *supra* note 3, at 74. Nubian people, the Wawat and the Medjai, occupied the region of what is today Sudan, to the immediate south of Egypt. *See* William James Hamblin, Warfare in the Ancient Near East: Holy Warriors at the Dawn of History 416 (2006) (discussing Egyptian execration texts and describing particular enemies of Egypt, including the Medjai and the "Nubians of Wawat"); Richard A. Lobban, Jr., Historical Dictionary of Ancient and Medieval Nubia 404 (2004) (defining "Wawat" as a "sometimes independent polity in Lower Nubia"). Amenemhet I's pledge to make "the Asiatics do the dog walk" is eerily reminiscent of the inhuman treatment suffered by prisoners of the US military at Abu Ghraib almost two millennia later: *see infra* notes 14–18 and accompanying text.

me. . . . The interior of Samar must be made a howling wilderness."[5] Granted, Smith's words did not amount to direct orders to murder innocent civilians. But US soldiers, whipped into a frenzy by his rhetoric, acted on it by setting fire to Filipino villages, pillaging them, and slaughtering scores of civilians who were supposed to be immune from violence according to the most rudimentary principles of international humanitarian law.[6]

In connection with uttering those words, General Smith was charged by the US Army with "the relatively benign offence of 'conduct to the prejudice of good order and military discipline.'" In 1902, in Manila, he was tried before a general court-martial.[7] At the end of the proceeding, he was given the proverbial slap on the wrist—his conviction merely resulted in the sixty-two-year-old walking away from the army through "early" forced retirement.[8]

b. General George S. Patton in World War II

On June 27, 1943, on the eve of the Allied invasion of Sicily, General George S. Patton shouted to the officers of his 45th US Infantry Division:

> When we land against the enemy, don't forget to hit him and hit him hard. We will bring the fight home to him. When we meet the enemy, we will kill him. We will show him no mercy. He has killed thousands of your comrades, and must die. . . . You will tell your men that. They must have the killer instinct. . . . We will get the name of killers and killers are immortal.[9]

Soon thereafter, in attempting to capture airfields around Biscari on the south end of the island, soldiers of the 45th US Infantry Division slaughtered, without any ostensible justification, close to one hundred German and Italian prisoners of war.[10] Two courts-martial took place in the wake of the massacres. Sgt. Horace T. West of A Company, 180th Infantry Regiment, 45th Infantry Division,

5. *See* Guénaël Mettraux, *US Courts-Martial and the Armed Conflict in the Philippines (1899–1902): Their Contribution to National Case Law on War Crimes*, 1 J. Int'l Crim. Just. 135, 136–137, 139 (2003) (giving the details of the incident involving Gen. Smith and his subsequent court-martial).

6. Paul A. Kramer, The Blood of Government: Race, Empire, the United States & the Philippines 145 (2006) (examining letters penned by US Marines that implied their violence was in response to Gen. Smith's rhetoric).

7. Mettraux, *supra* note 5, at 139 (detailing the court-martial of Gen. Smith).

8. *Id.* at 143 (explaining Gen. Smith's sentence).

9. Joanna Bourke, An Intimate History of Killing: Face-to-Face Killing in Twentieth-Century Warfare 171–172 (1999) (discussing Patton's words and how his officers interpreted these words as exhortations to slaughter prisoners "en masse"). *See generally* Solis, *supra* note 1, at 385–386 (discussing the Sicilian attack and subsequent court-martial of Gen. Patton's subordinates).

10. Peter Lieb, *Biscari Massacre (1943)*, *in* 1 Atrocities, Massacres, and War Crimes: An Encyclopedia 67–69 (Alexander Mikaberidze ed., 2013) (the actual number of victims connected to the subsequent courts-martial was eighty. But Peter Lieb explains that "the total

was convicted, but Capt. John C. Compton, who commanded C Company of the same regiment, was acquitted.[11]

Both men testified during their respective trials that their actions were carried out in accordance with General Patton's June 27 speech.[12] Patton himself, however, despite the related atrocities, was never even so much as reprimanded for the inflammatory speech to his troops.[13]

c. General Geoffrey D. Miller at Abu Ghraib

Fast-forwarding to the post–World War II era, members of the US military notoriously tortured and sexually assaulted detained Iraqis at Abu Ghraib Prison in 2003.[14] Criminal justice professor Adam Lankford observes: "The military . . . endorsed the notion that prisoners were mere animals."[15] General Geoffrey D. Miller, the highest-ranked officer at Abu Ghraib, is supposed to have said to those he commanded, "You have to treat the prisoners like dogs. If . . . they believe that they're any different than dogs, you have effectively lost control of your interrogation from the very start. . . . And it works. This is what we do down at Guantánamo Bay."[16]

Lankford describes the effect of General Miller's rhetoric on the Military Police guards he commanded: "[A]t different times, they rode the prisoners around like animals, made them bark like dogs, and led them around on leashes."[17] And what became of General Miller? Like General Smith after the atrocities in the Philippines, he simply went on to retire from the army, never having been prosecuted or punished in relation to his statements.[18]

number of victims . . . remains unknown as other murderous incidents around the airfield were not brought to court." *Id.* at 68.

11. *Id.* West was sentenced to life imprisonment but, incredibly, was released the following year and restored to duty with the rank of private. *Id.*

12. Solis, *supra* note 1, at 386 (explaining how the court-martialed subordinates of Gen. Patton "raised as their defense the 'orders' issued by Patton in his June 27 speech").

13. *Id.* (explaining how a "Washington-initiated inquiry into Patton's remarks exonerated the general").

14. Adam Lankford, *Promoting Aggression and Violence at Abu Ghraib: The U.S. Military's Transformation of Ordinary People into Torturers*, 14 Aggression & Violent Behav. 388, 389 (2009).

15. *Id.* at 394.

16. Philip Zimbardo, The Lucifer Effect: Understanding How Good People Turn Evil 414 (2007) (reporting certain statements that Brig. Gen. Janis Karpinsky attributed to Gen. Miller).

17. Lankford, *supra* note 14, at 394.

18. Josh White, *General Who Ran Guantanamo Bay Retires*, Wash. Post, Aug. 1, 2006, at A6 (chronicling Gen. Miller's retirement and pointing out that "[m]ilitary commanders twice have cleared Miller of wrongdoing").

d. Colonel Harry Tunnell in Afghanistan

More recently, connected to US military involvement in Afghanistan, yet another American commander communicated with his troops in a similarly incendiary fashion. Various sources reported that Colonel Harry Tunnell "was seriously at odds with the counterinsurgency strategy of outreach favored by the military brass in Afghanistan. His proclivities apparently ran more to 'search and destroy' than 'hearts and minds.'"[19]

In discussing the Taliban with his troops, he emphasized that the soldiers "must stay focused on the destruction of the enemy" and that the enemy "must be attacked relentlessly."[20] Tunnell indicated to his charges that dealing with enemy Afghans in this way entailed taking actions "political correctness dictates that we cannot talk about."[21] One report states that "Tunnell also pushed his men to go after 'guerrilla hunter killers . . .'"[22]

Soldiers under Tunnell's command in the 5th Stryker brigade of the 2nd Infantry Division, inspired in part by his murderous promptings, were charged with forming a "kill team" that randomly executed innocent Afghan civilians for sport and amputated their fingers as war trophies.[23] These were referred to as "the Maywand District murders."[24]

At the court-martial of one of the convicted soldiers, an expert witness testified that Col. Tunnell set an example that resulted in his troops committing the underlying war crimes.[25] A senior US military official, who worked with the brigade in early 2009 at the National Training Center before it deployed to Afghanistan, stated:

> When you feel violent intent coming down from the command and into the culture of the brigade, that's when you end up with things like the rogue

19. Anne Mulrine, *Pentagon Had Red Flags about Command Climate in "Kill Team" Stryker Brigade*, Christian Sci. Monitor (Oct. 28, 2010), http://www.csmonitor.com/USA/Military/2010/1028/Pentagon-had-red-flags-about-command-climate-in-kill-team-Stryker-brigade (describing the Pentagon's alarm at Col. Tunnell's approach and the manner in which the soldiers under Col. Tunnell's command were reacting to his fiery rhetoric).

20. *Id.*

21. *Id. See also* Mark Boal, *The Kill Team: How US Soldiers in Afghanistan Murdered Innocent Civilians*, Rolling Stone (Mar. 27, 2011), http://www.rollingstone.com/politics/news/the-kill-team-20110327 ("Tunnell, who at the time was the commander of 5th Stryker Brigade, openly mocked the military's approach to counterinsurgency—which emphasizes the need to win the support of local civilians—as better suited to a 'social scientist.'").

22. *Id.*

23. *Id.*

24. Gillie Collins, *The "Kill Team" Provides Slanted Account of Maywand District Murders*, The Stanford Daily (Aug. 1, 2014), http://www.stanforddaily.com/2014/08/01/the-kill-team-provides-slanted-account-of-maywand-district-murders/.

25. Mary Sanchez, *Rogue Soldiers Stain Military Reputations*, Kan. City Star, Mar. 29, 2011, at A11.

> platoon. . . . He established a culture that allowed that kind of mindset to percolate. And there are second- and third-order effects that come with that.[26]

In spite of this, Tunnell has faced no criminal charges.[27] In the words of one expert: "[T]he Army has no interest in moving the court-martial proceedings up the chain of command."[28]

2. Beyond the US Military

a. The Rape of Nanking

This sort of incitement extends beyond the US military and has been responsible for criminal conduct committed by armies around the globe, with prominent examples in Asia, Europe, Latin America, and Africa. One of the most chilling instances of such incitement occurred in the 1930s, during Japan's aggressive war against China in the run up to the Second World War. For a hellish month and a half at the end of 1937 and the beginning of 1938, in capturing the Chinese city of Nanking, Japanese troops perpetrated among the most horrific war crimes in the annals of modern combat operations.[29] Forever seared in the popular imagination as the "Rape of Nanking," it involved soldiers relentlessly committing sexual assaults, mutilations, torture, and murder of thousands of innocent Chinese civilians in the most brutal manner.[30]

Leading up to this unimaginable orgy of violence, and even during it, Japanese commanders dehumanized would-be victims through inflammatory rhetoric that often invoked beasts or vermin.[31] In particular, Japanese officers ingrained in their charges that that the Chinese were *chancorro*, or subhumans.[32] They became convinced that these civilians were "below human, like bugs or animals" and that "[t]he Chinese didn't belong to the human race."[33]

In describing how he bayoneted unarmed Chinese civilians, one of the Japanese invaders acknowledged: "If I'd thought of them as human beings I couldn't have done it. But because I thought of them as animals or below human beings, we did it."[34] Another perpetrator recounted that, because of this indoctrination, when the soldiers were killing women they thought they were

26. Mulrine, *supra* note 19.

27. *See id.* (describing the communications between Col. Tunnell and his superiors, including a video teleconference during which Col. Tunnell was reprimanded, but also noting that Tunnell remains in the army).

28. Sanchez, *supra* note 25.

29. Smith, *supra* note 3, at 17.

30. *Id.*

31. Laurence Rees, Horror in the East: Japan and the Atrocities of World War II 28 (2002).

32. *Id.*

33. *Id.*

34. *Id.*

killing "pigs."[35] No Japanese commanders were ever prosecuted for conditioning their soldiers to engage in such horrors.[36]

b. The Holocaust

Not long after the bloodbath of Nanking, as the Nazis were making military incursions throughout Europe, German commanders in Poland were denigrating Jews and thereby inspiring violence against them at the hands of their subordinates. In his book *Ordinary Men*, Christopher Browning gives an unsettling account of one such speech and its aftermath.

On the morning of July 13, 1942, German Major Wilhelm Trapp addressed his battalion in the Polish village of Jósefów.[37] In an oration brimming with emotion, he informed his underlings that Jews were responsible for the boycott that had damaged Germany, whose women and children were being killed by Allied bombings.[38] And he said to them that Jews had been collaborating with partisans.[39] Having been whipped up by Trapp's words, his men stormed Jósefów and slaughtered 1,500 Jews.[40] As with the other commanders whose rhetoric inspired atrocities, as chronicled elsewhere in this chapter, Trapp evaded justice in respect of this speech.

c. Guatemala during the 1980s

Approximately forty years later, the Guatemalan military was attacking civilians of the Mayan ethnic minority during that country's early 1980s civil war. Military commanders incited much of the violence.[41] They told their subordinates that the

35. David Andrew Schmidt, Ianfu—The Comfort Women of the Japanese Imperial Army of the Pacific War: Broken Silence 87 (2000).

36. *See* M. Cherif Bassiouni, *Justice and Peace: The Importance of Choosing Accountability over Realpolitik*, 35 Case W. Res. J. Int'l L. 191, 197 (2003) (noting that at the International Military Tribunal for the Far East not a single person was indicted or prosecuted specifically "for the horrific violations that have come to be known as the 'Rape of Nanking'").

37. Christopher R. Browning, Ordinary Men 1–2 (1991). Even though Trapp's unit was technically referred to as a battalion of the "Order Police," the Order Police was deployed after being given "military training and equipment" and it was thought of as a "police army" or "large military formations within the police." *Id.* at 3–4. Browning compares the Order Police to "U.S. National Guard units" and reports that certain units "fought in the Ardennes . . . and took part in the attack on Leningrad. . . ." *Id.* at 5.

38. *Id.* at 2.

39. *Id.*

40. *Id.* at 2–3. Technically it could be argued that the men were actually ordered to kill the innocent Jewish civilians. But Trapp notified them they did not have to take part in the massacre. In other words, it was entirely voluntary. *Id.* at 2.

41. *See generally* Frank Smyth, *Painting the Maya Red: Military Doctrine and Speech in Guatemala's Genocidal Acts*, United States Holocaust Memorial Museum Symposium: Speech, Power, Violence (2009), at 2–4, 12–13, http://www.ushmm.org/genocide/spv/pdf/smyth_frank.pdf (explaining the role that speech played in Guatemalan human rights violations).

Mayans living in the remote highlands were "pro-guerilla."[42] And their speeches to the soldiers also contained the message that "[t]he innocent must pay for the sins of the guilty."[43] Yet another crucial method of indoctrinating the troops was invoking the metaphor that the sea was to the fish what the population was to the guerrilla and thus they needed "to drain the sea to kill the fish."[44]

From early 1982 until mid-1983, owing in part to this sort of poisonous language, Guatemalan troops murdered thousands of innocent Mayan civilians.[45] Guatemala set up a truth commission to memorialize what happened and to provide catharsis to the victims. But the officers responsible for the hate speech that gave rise to much of the violence were not brought to justice.[46]

d. The Democratic Republic of the Congo

Incitement in the war context has also factored into sexual crimes committed in the Democratic Republic of the Congo. Testimony at the International Criminal Court (ICC) trial of former Congolese warlord Thomas Lubanga, revealed that rebel officers communicating with subordinates, but not issuing orders to them, contributed to the mass rape phenomenon in that war-torn country.[47]

One former child soldier swore under oath, for instance, that during military operations in Congo's Ituri region, officers in Lubanga's Union of Congolese Patriots informed young recruits that they could engage in sexual relations with females in their camp—young girls who had been abducted from their families.[48] Commanders supposedly told them: "You're free to take any of the girls and sleep with her."[49]

42. *Id.* at 3–4 (explaining that the Guatemalan military officer corps used language that "in each case served to dehumanize civilians especially ethnic Mayans suspected of supporting the nation's Marxist guerrillas").

43. *Id.* at 14–15.

44. *Id.* at 9 (discussing how the Guatemalan military inverted the Maoist metaphor that "the guerrilla must move among the people as a fish swims in the sea" to justify killing civilians).

45. *Id.* at 5 ("More than 200,000 people were killed or forcibly disappeared in Guatemala, largely back in the late 1970s and early 1980s . . . .").

46. *See* Matt Halling, *A Law of No Gods, No Masters—Developing and Defending a Participatory Legal System*, 32 Hastings Int'l & Comp. L. Rev. 237, 254 (2009) (contrasting "the work done by the International Criminal Tribunal for Rwanda with the absent accountability for genocide in Guatemala"); Ming Zhu, *Power and Cooperation: Understanding the Road Towards a Truth Commission*, 15 Buff. Hum. Rts. L. Rev. 183, 195 (2009) (chronicling the history of the truth commission in Guatemala).

47. *See* Jeanine Oury, Comment, *The Rape Epidemic in the Congo: Why Impunity in the Congo Can Be Solved by International Intervention*, 6 Loy. U. Chi. Int'l L. Rev. 421, 424, 426 (2009) (explaining that in October 2008 there were up to fifty rapes committed daily in the Congo and concluding that "impunity to perpetrators of sexual violence is the primary cause of the mass rape epidemic in the Congo").

48. Rachel Irwin, *Court Hears Rape Allegations*, AllAfrica.com (Feb. 27, 2009), http://allafrica.com/stories/200904280753.html (reporting on the testimony of a former child soldier with the Union of Congolese Patriots at the trial of Thomas Lubanga at The Hague).

49. *Id.*

The young male soldiers perceived this as urging them to rape the girls.[50] And, in fact, mass sexual assault of the girls ensued.[51] The ICC convicted Lubanga for recruitment of child soldiers, but his subordinate officers and their acts of incitement are not the specific object of ICC criminal proceedings.

B. Civilians Inciting Military Personnel

1. During the Rwandan Genocide

Contemporary noninternational armed conflicts often entail participation by persons whose status as military versus civilian can be blurred. Especially in reference to the 1994 Rwandan civil war—inextricably linked to the Rwandan Genocide—civilians routinely directed military and paramilitary squads in perpetrating crimes against humanity, genocide, and war crimes against other civilians. The radio announcers of the Radio Télévision Libre des Milles Collines (RTLM) are among the most prominent actors in this regard. Cassandra Cotton explains:

> Many such broadcasts were directed to the militiamen manning "each roadblock [where] portable radios blasted the music and exhortations of RTLM" so that any Tutsi trying to escape would be captured and promptly exterminated, as those fleeing were targeted by RTLM as traitors and RPF accomplices. A well-documented example, popularized in the film *Hotel Rwanda*, involved RTLM broadcasting the names of sixty-two evacuees on a convoy authorized by the interim government; both vehicles were stopped at roadblocks after the radio directed the militia to attack. As several survivors have said, listening to RTLM was the most accurate method of determining if one was being targeted by the militias.[52]

50. *Id.* (explaining that "[r]ape was . . . encouraged in the camp").

51. *Id.*

52. Cassandra Cotton, *Where Radio Is King: Rwanda's Hate Radio and the Lessons Learned*, Atlis J.: Gender, Env't & Hum. Rts. (Spring 2007) (internal citations omitted), http://atlismta.org/online-journals/0607-journal-gender-environment-and-human-rights/whereradio-is-king/. During the Rwandan Genocide, militias were considered part of the Rwandan armed forces. *See* Sonja Boelaert-Suominen, *Prosecuting Superiors for Crimes Committed by Subordinates: A Discussion of the First Significant Case Law Since the Second World War*, 41 Va. J. Int'l L. 747, 763 (2001) (noting that "paramilitary and irregular militia" were operating during the conflict in Rwanda, and also discussing the commanders' potential for criminal liability); Chi Mgbako, *Ingando Solidarity Camps: Reconciliation and Political Indoctrination in Post-Genocide Rwanda*, 18 Harv. Hum. Rts. J. 201, 205 (2005) (describing how Rwandan Armed Forces and militia death squads "formed a nucleus of Armed Groups"). In these circumstances, militia forces are subject to the same law of war requirements as regular forces. *See* Christiane Amanpour, *Paramilitaries*, *in* Crimes of War (Roy Gutman, David Rieff, & Anthony Dworkin eds., rev. & expanded ed. 2007) (stating that paramilitaries, including militia, may qualify as lawful combatants as long as they are under responsible command, carry distinctive signs, carry arms openly, and obey the laws and customs of war and noting that paramilitaries "may be tried for war crimes they commit").

Also during the Rwandan Genocide, civilians not connected to the media similarly urged militia to commit atrocities. A prominent example in this regard is Rwandan singer Simon Bikindi. As we saw in Chapter 5, while transiting between two small towns in a truck, Bikindi—a prominent member of the extremist Hutu ruling party—exhorted *Interahamwe* militias on an attached public address system to "[r]ise up" and not to "spare" any Tutsi.[53] On the return trip, Bikindi asked the *Interahamwe* whether they had killed the "snakes."[54] Even though Bikindi was convicted of direct and public incitement to commit genocide, the military aspect of his transgressions was essentially overlooked.[55]

2. Postelection Violence in Côte d'Ivoire

Outside of Rwanda, another illustrative example arises in relation to the fall of Côte d'Ivoire's President Laurent Gbagbo in the spring of 2011. As Gbagbo would not give up the presidency after losing the Ivoirian November 2010 election, radio broadcasters loyal to him used the airwaves to demonize the supporters of Gbagbo's victorious opponent, Alassane Ouattara.[56] Owing in part to such incendiary rhetoric, the Ivoirian military inflicted violence on civilians viewed as enemies of Gbagbo. And in March 2011, "Ivoirian troops machine-gunned a group of women marching peacefully in favor of Ouattara in Abidjan."[57] In light of the limited scope of current atrocity speech law, these Ivoirian journalists cannot be prosecuted for incitement to commit war crimes and may escape liability altogether.

3. Donald Trump and the War against ISIS

As this book has demonstrated, those who incite to violence often do so obliquely. The most prominent recent example of potential liability for incitement to war crimes has been fairly explicit, however. Its origin was a civilian figure who, at the time, was seeking to become commander-in-chief of US armed forces, Republican presidential candidate Donald Trump. He stated as part of the 2016 primary-season debate process that, in order to minimize American civilian casualties in the war

53. Prosecutor v. Bikindi, Case No. ICTR-01-72-T, Judgement, ¶ 268 (Dec. 2, 2008).

54. *Id.* ("The witness also testified that on the way back . . . Bikindi stopped at a roadblock and met with leaders . . . where he insisted, 'you see, when you hide a snake in your house, you can expect to face the consequences.' After Bikindi left the roadblock, members of the surrounding population . . . intensified their search for Tutsi[s] . . . ."). As we saw in Chapter 5, Bikindi was later convicted of direct and public incitement to commit genocide based on this conduct. A conviction for incitement to commit war crimes would have had important expressive value with respect to the military nature of the crime.

55. *Bikindi*, Case No. ICTR-01-72-T, ¶ 441 (stating the crimes for which Bikindi was convicted and those for which he was not convicted).

56. *Ivory Coast in Speech-Fueled Catastrophe*, Voices that Poison (Apr. 2, 2011), http://voicesthatpoison.wordpress.com/2011/04/02/ivory-coast-in-speech-fueled-catastrophe/ (noting Gbagbo's use of "inflammatory speech to frighten the population and incite his supporters").

57. *Id.*

against the Islamic State of Iraq and Al-Sham (ISIS), the United States "should hit the kin of enemy fighters."[58] Similarly, in that same context, Trump also said:

> You have to take out their families, when you get these terrorists, you have to take out their families. When they say they don't care about their lives, you have to take out their families.[59]

During the campaign, Trump encouraged the US military to use torture against captured ISIS soldiers:

> Don't tell me [torture] doesn't work. Torture works, OK folks? I think we should go much stronger than waterboarding, that's the way I feel. They're chopping off heads, believe me, we should go much stronger.[60]

Assuming the US war with ISIS is considered a noninternational armed conflict, pursuant to Common Article 3 of the Geneva Conventions, the underlying activity Trump has advocated—murdering ISIS soldiers' kin and torturing captured ISIS soldiers—would clearly amount to war crimes. Common Article 3 counsels that persons not directly participating in hostilities:

> [Shall] in all circumstances be treated humanely. . . . To this end, the following acts are and shall remain prohibited at any time and in any place whatsoever . . . *violence to life and person, in particular murder* of all kinds, mutilation, cruel treatment and *torture*.[61]

58. Gregory Krieg, *Israeli Expert: Trump's Call to Kill Terrorists' Families Immoral, Ineffective*, CNN.Com (Dec. 3, 2015), http://edition.cnn.com/2015/12/03/politics/donald-trump-kill-terrorist-families-war-crime/.

59. *Id.*

60. Felicia Schwartz, *Donald Trump Calls for Use of Torture, Resumption of Waterboarding*, Wall St. J. (Feb. 17, 2016), http://blogs.wsj.com/washwire/2016/02/17/donald-trump-calls-for-use-of-torture-resumption-of-waterboarding/.

61. *See, e.g.*, Convention (III) relative to the Treatment of Prisoners of War. Geneva art. 3, Aug. 12, 1949, 6 U.S.T. 3316 [hereinafter Common Article 3]. This has been incorporated into the United States Code as a "grave breach" via 18 U.S.C. § 2441, which provides, in relevant part:

> **(d) Common Article 3 Violations.**
>
> **(1) Prohibited conduct.** In subsection (c)(3), the term "grave breach of common Article 3" means any conduct (such conduct constituting a grave breach of common Article 3 of the international conventions done at Geneva August 12, 1949), as follows:
>
> **(A) Torture.**
> The act of a person who commits, or conspires or attempts to commit, an act specifically intended to inflict severe physical or mental pain or suffering (other than pain or suffering incidental to lawful sanctions) upon another person within his custody

Although this remains in the realm of the hypothetical, assuming no jurisdictional issues, if it were determined that Trump's words encouraged or gave comfort to soldiers contemplating commission of the crimes he advocated in his public remarks (but not to the point of a causal relationship), Trump could not be prosecuted.[62] Such impunity would be the result of a complete absence of law criminalizing incitement to commit war crimes. That normative void will be detailed in the section that follows.

III. MILITARY SPEECH IN INTERNATIONAL LAW

The law of armed conflict (LOAC, or international humanitarian law, or IHL) has taken a fairly restrictive approach to the phenomenon of criminal speech. As set forth below, some very limited normative guidelines touching on speech are found in the Geneva and Hague Conventions. But those provisions do not give rise to liability for incitement. This section will consider IHL's anemic response to the problem of illegal speech. By extension, it will examine international criminal law's comparable dearth of rules in respect of war crimes and illegal advocacy.

A. International Humanitarian Law and Criminal Speech

One point bears mentioning at the outset—there is a striking paucity of IHL principles or rules dealing with speech. What little there is focuses on direct orders tied to grave breaches. For instance, Article 49 of the First Geneva Convention (for the Amelioration of the Condition of the Wounded in Armies in the Field), Article 50 of the Second Geneva Convention (for the Amelioration of the Condition of Wounded, Sick and Shipwrecked Members of Armed Forces at Sea), Article 129 of the Third Geneva Convention (relative to the Treatment of Prisoners of War), and Article 146 of the Fourth Geneva Convention (relative to the Protection of Civilian Persons in Time of War) each have identical introductory language with respect to grave breaches: "The High Contracting Parties undertake to enact any legislation necessary to provide effective penal sanctions

> or physical control for the purpose of obtaining information or a confession, punishment, intimidation, coercion, or any reason based on discrimination of any kind.
> ....
> **(D) Murder.**
> The act of a person who intentionally kills, or conspires or attempts to kill, or kills whether intentionally or unintentionally in the course of committing any other offense under this subsection, one or more persons taking no active part in the hostilities, including those placed out of combat by sickness, wounds, detention, or any other cause.

18 USC. § 2441 (a) & (d) (2008).

62. Of course, by winning via a razor-thin margin in the Electoral College (despite losing the popular vote by nearly 3 million votes), Trump has been elected. As president, if Trump were to utter comparable rhetoric, he would be doing so as the commander-in-chief of US armed forces. Thus, the case for incitement to war crimes would be exponentially stronger.

for persons committing, *or ordering to be committed*, any of the grave breaches of the present Convention defined in the following Article."[63]

Likewise, Article 40 of Additional Protocol I to the Geneva Conventions, covering the Protection of Victims of International Armed Conflicts, declares in relevant part: "It is prohibited *to order* that there shall be no survivors [or] to threaten an adversary therewith. . . ."[64] A similar provision is found in Additional Protocol II, which is concerned with the Protection of Victims of Non-International Armed Conflicts. Article 4(1) of APII provides: "It is prohibited *to order* that there shall be no survivors."[65]

In all four Geneva Conventions and their Additional Protocols, the aforementioned provisions are the only ones touching on criminal speech.

Of the 1899 and 1907 Hague Conventions with Respect to the Laws and Customs of War on Land, and their annexes,[66] only a single provision governs criminal speech. Article 23 of the Annex to the 1907 Convention Respecting the Laws and Customs of War on Land (Hague IV) declares: "In addition to the prohibitions provided by special Conventions, it is especially forbidden. . . . To *declare* that no quarter will be given . . ."[67]

B. Military Speech in International Criminal Law

1. Nuremberg

The foundational statutes of international criminal law (ICL) similarly lacked rules regarding illicit military speech. The equivalent of ICL's birth certificate,

63. Geneva Convention for the Amelioration of the Condition of the Wounded and Sick in Armed Forces in the Field art. 49, Aug. 12, 1949, 6 U.S.T. 3114, 75 U.N.T.S. 31 [hereinafter First Geneva Convention] (emphasis added); Geneva Convention for the Amelioration of the Condition of Wounded, Sick and Shipwrecked Members of Armed Forces at Sea art. 50, Aug. 12, 1949, 6 U.S.T. 3217, 75 U.N.T.S. 85 [hereinafter Second Geneva Convention] (emphasis added); Geneva Convention Relative to the Treatment of Prisoners of War art. 129, Aug. 12, 1949, 6 U.S.T. 3316, 75 U.N.T.S. 135 [hereinafter Third Geneva Convention] (emphasis added); Geneva Convention Relative to the Protection of Civilian Persons in Time of War art. 146, Aug. 12, 1949, 6 U.S.T. 3516, 75 U.N.T.S. 287 [hereinafter Fourth Geneva Convention] (emphasis added).

64. Protocol Additional to the Geneva Conventions of 12 August 1949, and Relating to the Protection of Victims of International Armed Conflicts art. 40, June 8, 1977, 1125 U.N.T.S. 3 [hereinafter Protocol I] (emphasis added).

65. Protocol Additional to the Geneva Conventions of 12 August 1949, and Relating to the Protection of Victims of Non-International Armed Conflicts art. 4(1), June 8, 1977, 1125 U.N.T.S. 609 [hereinafter Protocol II] (emphasis added).

66. Convention (II) with Respect to the Laws and Customs of War on Land, July 29, 1899, 32 Stat. 1803, 187 Consol. T.S. 410 [hereinafter 1899 Hague Convention]; Convention (IV) Respecting the Laws and Customs of War on Land, Oct. 18, 1907, 36 Stat. 2277, 205 Consol. T.S. 277 [hereinafter 1907 Hague Convention]. Regulations Respecting the Laws and Customs of War on Land were attached as Annexes to each Convention.

67. Annex to 1907 Hague Convention, *supra* note 66, art. 23 (emphasis added).

the Nuremberg International Military Tribunal Charter, introduced a "War Crimes" provision at Article 6(b). And the concluding words of Article 6, the umbrella liability provision under which the war crimes provision was situated, announced liability for conspiracy to commit the crimes set forth in Article 6 that could be attributed to, among others, "instigators."[68] That is the full extent of the Charter's explicitly criminalizing incendiary speech connected to grave IHL violations.

2. The Ad Hoc Tribunals

Criminal military speech provisions are similarly sparse in the statutes for the ad hoc tribunals for the former Yugoslavia and Rwanda. International Criminal Tribunal for Yugoslavia (ICTY) Statute Article 2 (Grave Breaches of the Geneva Conventions of 1949) states that the "International Tribunal shall have the power to prosecute persons committing or *ordering to be committed* grave breaches. . . ."[69] Moreover, Article 7 (Individual Criminal Responsibility), which is explicitly linked to Article 2 (Grave Breaches) and Article 3 (Violations of the Laws or Customs of War), provides that "a person who planned, *instigated, ordered*, committed, or otherwise aided and abetted in the planning, preparation or execution of a crime referred to in articles 2 to 5 of the present Statute, shall be individually responsible for the crime."[70]

International Criminal Tribunal for Rwanda (ICTR) Statute Article 4 (Violations of Article 3 Common to the Geneva Conventions and of Additional Protocol II) contains an analogous provision governing noninternational armed conflict. It declares that the "International Tribunal for Rwanda shall have the power to prosecute persons committing or *ordering to be committed* serious violations" of Common Article 3 and Additional Protocol II.[71] Also parallel to the ICTY "Individual Criminal Responsibility" provision, Article 6 of the ICTR Statute provides that a "person who planned, *instigated, ordered*, committed or otherwise aided and abetted in the planning, preparation or execution of a crime

68. Charter of the International Military Tribunal art. 6, Aug. 8, 1945, 59 Stat. 1544, 1547, 82 U.N.T.S. 279 [hereinafter IMT Charter] ("Leaders, organizers, *instigators* and accomplices participating in the formulation or execution of a common plan or conspiracy to commit any of the foregoing crimes are responsible for all acts performed by any persons in execution of such plan." (emphasis added)).

69. Statute of the International Criminal Tribunal for the Former Yugoslavia, S.C. Res. 827, art. 2(3)(c), U.N. Doc. S/RES/827 (May 25, 1993), *amended by* S.C. Res. 1166, annex, U.N. Doc. S/RES/116 (May 13, 1998) [hereinafter ICTY Statute] (emphasis added).

70. *Id.* art. 7(1) (emphasis added).

71. Statute of the International Criminal Tribunal for Rwanda, S.C. Res. 955, art. 4, U.N. Doc. S/RES/955 (Nov. 8, 1994) [hereinafter ICTR Statute].

referred to in articles 2 to 4 of the present Statute, shall be individually responsible for the crime."[72]

3. The Hybrid Tribunals

As regards the hybrid tribunals, the statute of the Special Court for Sierra Leone (SCSL) had the same provisions as the ICTR Statute regarding violations of Common Article 3 and Additional Protocol II (SCSL Statute Article 3) and Individual Responsibility (SCSL Statute Article 6).[73] Article 6 of the Law on the Establishment of the Extraordinary Chambers in the Courts of Cambodia (ECCC) declares that "[t]he Extraordinary Chambers shall have the power to bring to trial all Suspects who committed or *ordered the commission of* grave breaches of the Geneva Conventions."[74] The statute for the ECCC also deals with speech in connection with individual criminal responsibility at Article 29 as follows: "Any Suspect who planned, *instigated, ordered*, aided and abetted, or committed the crimes referred to in article 3 new, 4, 5, 6, 7 and 8 of this law shall be individually responsible for the crime."[75]

4. The International Criminal Court

As the founding statute of the sole *permanent* court among the current array of ICL institutions, perhaps the most revealing document concerning military speech in international criminal law is the Rome Statute of the International Criminal Court.[76] In line with the other constituent instruments, there is a dearth of relevant text. Within Article 8 ("War Crimes"), there are two provisions related to speech. Articles 8(2)(b)(xii) (relating to international armed conflicts) and 8(2)(e)(x) (relating to non-international armed conflicts) describe as a serious violation of "the laws and customs applicable in international armed conflict, within the established framework of international law" any act of "*Declaring* that no quarter will be given . . ."[77]

72. *Id.* art. 6 (emphasis added).

73. *See* Statute of the Special Court for Sierra Leone arts. 3, 6, Jan. 16, 2002, 2178 U.N.T.S. 137 [hereinafter SCSL Statute] (emphasis added).

74. Law on the Establishment of the Extraordinary Chambers in the Courts of Cambodia for the Prosecution of Crimes Committed during the Period of Democratic Kampuchea, Royal Decree No. NS/RKM/1004/006, art. 6 (Oct. 27, 2004) [hereinafter ECCC Law] (emphasis added), http://www.eccc.gov.kh/sites/default/files/legal-documents/KR_Law_as_amended_27_Oct_2004_Eng.pdf.

75. *Id.* art. 29 (emphasis added).

76. *See generally* Rome Statute of the International Criminal Court art. 1, July 17, 1998, 2187 U.N.T.S. 3, *reprinted in* 1 United Nations Diplomatic Conference of Plenipotentiaries on the Establishment of an International Criminal Court, Official Records (1998) [hereinafter Rome Statute] ("[The International Criminal Court] is hereby established. It shall be a permanent institution and shall have the power to exercise its jurisdiction over persons for the most serious crimes of international concern . . . .").

77. *Id.* arts. 8(2)(b)(xii) and 8(2)(e)(x) (emphasis added). As seen *supra*, this is identical to the language used in Article 23 of the Annex to the 1907 Hague Convention.

Otherwise, the Rome Statute configures its ordering and instigating provisions differently from the other ICL foundation documents. Instead of appending language directly onto particular war crimes articles and then laying out a separate, and redundant, individual responsibility article, the Rome Statute fuses all substantive war crimes provisions into a unified Article 8 and then deals with individual criminal responsibility exclusively in Articles 25 and 28.[78] Subsection (3)(b) of Article 25 declares that "a person shall be criminally responsible and liable for punishment for a crime within the jurisdiction of the Court if that person . . . orders, solicits or induces the commission of such a crime which in fact occurs or is attempted. . . ."[79]

Relative to the other ICL individual responsibility provisions previously analyzed, Article 25(3)(b) enlarges the ambit of culpable acts by adding "soliciting" and "inducing" to simple "ordering."[80] Nevertheless, at the same time, it also constricts its breadth by assigning liability only when an offense actually takes place or is attempted.[81] As will be discussed in Chapter 10, this is unduly restrictive and could be easily remedied with an incitement provision for war crimes, which, in light of its emphasis on inchoate liability, would assign liability arising exclusively from the speaker's words themselves.

To summarize, then, the current law on criminal speech in the military context deals with only a very limited range of actions, mainly direct orders to commit war crimes. Even with respect to the Rome Statute, which includes "soliciting" and "inducing" commission of war crimes, actual consummation or attempt to commit the target crime is mandatory for inculpating a defendant who does not issue an order. There is no liability for incitement. And this squarely undermines the potential early enforcement benefit of inchoate liability as law enforcement may not act precommission to prevent war crimes after the violence-conditioning process commences. Only once the slaughter begins could liability attach for solicitation/inducement. This represents a gaping normative hole that must be filled by including an incitement offense in relation to war crimes, as will be suggested in Chapter 10.

IV. CONCLUSION

From a policy perspective, the absence of criminal provisions in the military context for inflammatory speech not leading to actual commission of war crimes is baffling. The battlefield is perhaps the most inherently violent locale in human affairs. And yet, for example, rhetoric that would arouse giving no quarter or indiscriminate killing of persons *hors de combat* is essentially permissible as long as it does not rise to the level of a direct order. History has seen the consequences of this normative void. Throughout the twentieth century alone, commission of

78. *Id.* arts. 8, 25, and 28.

79. *Id.* art. 25(3)(b).

80. *Id.*

81. *Id.*

terrible war crimes around the world has arguably been the result of hate speech uttered by both military commanders and civilians placed in positions of authority vis-à-vis soldiers or militia. And that conduct has gone entirely unpunished. Pursuant to the Geneva Conventions and their Additional Protocols, as well as the Hague Conventions and provisions of the various international criminal law constituent instruments, there are no legal bars to such speech. And, thus, we are confronted with more evidence of a fragmented international doctrinal approach toward hate speech in relation to atrocity crimes.

PART THREE

Fruition

8

Fixing Incitement to Commit Genocide

"The goal is nothing other than the coherence and completeness of the system . . ."

—MAX PLANCK[1]

I. INTRODUCTION

Chapter 5 exposed the shortcomings—both in structure and in application—of the existing jurisprudential framework of the incitement offense. This chapter now considers and proposes remedies for these problems. As a threshold matter, perhaps scuttling the framework altogether would be the preferred approach. In fact, certain experts have recommended doing just that. And so that is this chapter's point of departure. It begins by considering proposed alternative standards and discovers that, while making important contributions to the analytical exercise, these proposed frameworks have faults of their own and thus are not suitable as wholesale replacements.

As a result, the chapter then turns to potential ways to overhaul the existing framework. The problems in the current structure include glitches with respect to the "direct," "public," and "incitement" (or "content") elements as well as the looming and ambiguous presence and impact of causation. Potential approaches to dealing with these issues are explored and solutions identified. Finally, the desultory efforts of courts in applying the current framework are considered. In the end, this chapter demonstrates that, even if the doctrinal discombobulation can be straightened out, it avails justice little if courts fail to apply the new standards consistently and thoroughly.

1. J. L. HEILBRON, THE DILEMMAS OF AN UPRIGHT MAN: MAX PLANCK AS SPOKESMAN FOR GERMAN SCIENCE 51 (1986).

II. DISCARDING THE EXISTING FRAMEWORK AND ADOPTING A NEW ONE?

In light of the issues detailed in Chapter 5, alternative incitement tests have been proposed. Two in particular are worthy of serious consideration: Susan Benesch's "Reasonably Probable Consequences" test,"[2] and Carol Pauli's "Communications Research Framework" test.[3] Analysis of each test follows.

A. The "Reasonably Probable Consequences" (or "Vile Crime") Test

1. Formulation of the Test

In her thought-provoking and much cited 2008 article, "Vile Crime or Inalienable Right: Defining Incitement to Genocide," Susan Benesch proposed the Reasonably Probable Consequences test (also referred to herein as the "Vile Crime" test) to ascertain if hate speech legally amounts to direct and public incitement to commit genocide.[4] Her six-limbed analytical framework breaks down as follows:[5]

1. [Nature of Message and Audience Understanding:]
   Was the speech understood by the audience as a call to genocide? Did it use language, explicit or coded, to justify and promote violence?
2. [Speaker Authority and Audience Capacity:]
   Did the speaker have authority or influence over the audience and did the audience have the capacity to commit genocide?
3. [Recent Violence:]
   Had the victims-to-be already suffered an outbreak of recent violence?
4. [Survival of Marketplace of Ideas:]
   Were contrasting views still available at the time of the speech? Was it still safe to express them publicly?

2. *See* Susan Benesch, *Vile Crime or Inalienable Right: Defining Incitement to Genocide*, 48 Va. J. Int'l L. 485, 491 (2008) (explaining that the ICTR elements should be rejected and formulating this alternative test) [hereinafter *Vile Crime*]. I have previously referred to Benesch's proposed framework as the "Reasonably Probable Consequences" test in previous scholarship. *See* Gregory S. Gordon, *Music and Genocide: Harmonizing Coherence, Freedom and Nonviolence in Incitement Law*, 50 Santa Clara L. Rev. 607, 609 (2010) [hereinafter *Music and Genocide*].

3. *See* Carol Pauli, *Killing the Microphone: When Broadcast Freedom Should Yield to Genocide Prevention*, 61 Ala. L. Rev. 665 (2010) (proposing the Communications Research Framework test). Again, I have previously referred to Pauli's evaluative factors as the "Communications Research Framework" in previous scholarship. *See* Gordon, *Music and Genocide, supra* 2, at 609.

4. Benesch, *Vile Crime, supra* note 2, at 498.

5. As the reader can see, the six-prong inquiry consists of nine questions. But some of these fit under the umbrella of one prong and thus the prongs add up to six.

5. [Dehumanization and Audience Conditioning:]
   Did the speaker describe the victims-to-be as subhuman, or accuse them of plotting genocide? Had the audience been conditioned by the use of these techniques in other, previous speech?
6. [Prior Similar Messages:]
   Had the audience received similar messages before the speech?[6]

2. Issues with the Test

This test has undoubtedly exerted a significant impact in debates regarding the viability of the existing incitement framework. But it is submitted that there are three reasons why it does not work as a wholesale substitute: (1) it is too rigid in its proposed application; (2) parts of it are ambiguous; and (3) it appears too fixed in scope. Each of these issues shall be treated in turn.

a. Rigidity

Unfortunately, as proposed in "Vile Crime or Inalienable Right", Benesch's proposed test is absolute. As she writes: "In my view, all six prongs must be satisfied for a court to find that incitement to genocide has been committed by a defendant."[7] Benesch's criteria certainly have much utility in determining if permissible hate speech has transformed into illegal incitement. But her approach here

6. *Id.* at 498. Benesch has since refined and added evaluative factors to the test, but the same conceptual parameters are in place. Now there are five criteria: speaker (authority, influence over audience); audience (target audience, capacity to commit violence, experiencing fearful emotions, access to alternative forms of information); content (understood by audience, use of dehumanization, use of fear, use of coded words, repeat of previous similar message); sociohistorical context (intergroup conflicts, recent outbreaks of violence after hate speech, audience facing economic insecurity); and mode of transmission (speech transmitted in a way that would reinforce its capacity to persuade—influential media outlet or accompanied by music?). *See, e.g.*, Susan Benesch, *The Ghost of Causation in International Speech Crime Cases*, *in* Propaganda, War Crimes Trials and International Law 257, 262–264 (Predrag Dojčinović ed., 2012) [hereinafter *Ghost of Causation*]. This set of evaluative factors has some overlap with a set I proposed (along with a typology of genocide techniques) two years earlier in *Music and Genocide*, *supra* note 2, at 635–644.

7. Benesch, *Vile Crime*, *supra* note 2, at 520. My critique here was originally expressed in the *Music and Genocide* article. *See* Gordon, *Music and Genocide*, *supra* note 2, at 625–628 (setting out the critique). Subsequently, Benesch modified the proposed test such that the criteria are no longer mandatory. *See* Benesch, *Ghost of Causation*, *supra* note 6, at 262 ("No single indicator or criterion is required, since none is an element of the crime of incitement to genocide."). Although Benesch has changed her position on this issue, given the influence and high citation rate of her *Vile Crime* article, where the test is the piece's conceptual fulcrum, I am still addressing it here as a viable proposed alternative test. *See, e.g.*, Article 19, *Policy Brief: Prohibiting Incitement to Discrimination, Hostility or Violence*, at 29 n.64 (Dec. 2012), https://www.article19.org/data/files/medialibrary/3548/ARTICLE-19-policy-on-prohibition-to-incitement.pdf (relying explicitly on the *Vile Crime* test); Pauli, *supra* note 3, at 668 (using the *Vile Crime* test as a conceptual point of repair for formulation of yet another proposed alternative framework). In essence, the *Vile Crime* article and the test it showcases have taken

is too lockstep and rigid. And, arguably, it fully jettisons, or, at the very least, does not explicitly incorporate, the International Criminal Tribunal for Rwanda (ICTR) framework.[8] What could be the negative consequences of this approach?

A hypothetical might help illustrate. We can posit, for instance, in a setting of large-scale inter-ethnic violence of several days' duration, an influential member of the government belonging to the country's ethnic majority delivering an address via the radio metaphorically advocating liquidation of the ethnic minority. In particular, he says to the ethnic majority audience that they should "go to work" in reference to dealing with problems caused by the minority group. The broadcast represents a coded message encouraging and vindicating violence toward the minority group and is immediately understood by listeners as a call to genocide. Imagine as well that the citizens who are the target of this speech have been subjected to ethnically motivated violence for the better part of a week, and the government has sole access to media outlets.

Under the "Reasonably Probable Consequences" test, the speech at issue could not be considered direct and public incitement to commit genocide simply because: (1) the speaker did not characterize the targeted population as specifically subhuman or accuse them of plotting genocide (and listeners had not been previously "conditioned" through these rhetorical strategies in previous orations); and (2) the listeners had not heard similar messages before this particular address.

However, in light of the widespread ethnically motivated violence, and considering that the listeners instantly grasped the rhetoric's meaning and were willing to act on it, it is difficult to square such a result with the law's penal mainsprings. Significantly, as we are in the realm of comparative analysis, exoneration would not be the likely outcome of filtering this scenario through the ICTR test. That conclusion is all the more resonant since, as demonstrated in this book, incitement's chief policy lodestar is prospective *prevention*, not retrospective punishment. Benesch's proposed hairsplitting in her "Vile Crime" article risks chilling meaningful preventive enforcement.

b. Ambiguity

Additionally, considering the strict nature of the test as proposed in "Vile Crime," it is of concern that some of its terminology seems vague. For instance, what constitutes "an outbreak of recent violence"? How "recent" must it be? Must it be

on a life of their own. Nevertheless, even if that iteration of the test were entirely moribund, it serves as an excellent conceptual counterpoint to the existing ICTR framework and so, in this independent sense, it has value in being analyzed here.

8. Possibly in response to *Music and Genocide*, or perhaps for other reasons, Benesch claimed that her test only supplemented the existing framework, noting: "This framework is not intended to displace the existing requirements for incitement to genocide: that it be direct and public, and that the speaker act with specific intent." *See* Benesch, *Ghost of Causation, supra* note 6, at 262. It should be noted that, significantly, Benesch completely ignored the ICTR's inclusion of the "incitement" prong of the existing framework. *Id.* In any event, she did not specify how her criteria fit into, or interact with, the existing ICTR framework.

violence on a certain scale—as calibrated in numbers of dead or wounded—or can it be radical, concentrated violence visited on fewer victims?

How should one ascertain if listeners had been previously "conditioned" through employment of similar speech techniques? What constitutes "conditioning"? How can one measure it? How can one establish if the "conditioning" has a causal relationship with those techniques? Considering the draconian nature of the test, this lack of precision is troubling.

c. Finality

In her "Vile Crime" article, one can infer that Benesch views the "Reasonably Probable e Consequences" test as a self-contained universe. I do not question the depth of her research and thinking, but her distilling of six elements constitutes no more than her personal insights regarding the relationship between rhetoric and bloodshed from historic fact patterns. It is entirely conceivable that other criteria might be gleaned.[9]

It could be helpful, for instance, to determine if the speaker in question has previously incited to mass violence. Of value as well could be a consideration of the channels of communication utilized—some arguably have a greater propensity for inciting lawless violence more rapidly than others (radio or television, for instance, as opposed to newspapers or pamphlets).

Genocide experts have also alluded to the observed link between genocide and war.[10] Benesch might have appended the existence or imminent outbreak of international or noninternational armed conflict as an additional criterion of her test, for example (indeed, that will be explicitly proposed below). It indicates that the "Reasonably Probable Consequences" test, while of considerable conceptual and interpretive value, does not work as a wholesale substitute for the existing framework. Nevertheless, as will be demonstrated below, much of it can be folded into the current jurisprudential structure.[11]

B. The "Communications Research Framework"

1. Background and Statement of the Test

Professor Carol Pauli has proposed an alternative test that employs a "communications research framework" for ascertaining if instances of burgeoning

9. *See, e.g.*, Pauli, *supra* note 3, at 4–5 (noting that the Reasonably Probable Consequences test excludes some factors "that may prove decisive in determining prospectively when a broadcast or other mediated speech is dangerous enough to justify intervention").

10. *See* Martin Shaw, What Is Genocide? 28 (2007) ("[The] major, commonly recognized instances of genocide—not only the Holocaust, but also Armenia and Rwanda—have been clearly connected with war contexts, and this is an overwhelming empirical trend."); Paul Bartrop, *The Relationship Between War and Genocide in the Twentieth Century: A Consideration*, 4 J. Genocide Res. 519, 524 (2002) ("[For] regimes committing [genocide] the presence of war can play a vital role in masking genocidal activities.").

11. Again, Benesch later acknowledged as much.

incitement to genocide should trigger application of prior restraint by such methods as jamming broadcast signals.[12] Thus, she considers communications research postulates such as the "ritual model,"[13] "the spiral of silence,"[14] and "dependence theory."[15] Pauli posits that the analytic structure culled from these theories should consist of the following factors:

1. Media Environment:
   Finding incitement more likely in a coercive media environment with an absence of competing messages and frequent message repetition;
2. Political Context:
   Postulating that incitement is more likely when political instability heightens audience dependence on the communication media and thereby strengthens the influence of the hate messages on audience members;
3. Audience Characteristics:
   Finding the impact of a message may be stronger where the audience is young or unsophisticated, already inclined toward prejudiced views or highly networked along such lines as tribal membership and religion;
4. Authority of Message Source:
   Concluding that speech will more likely be restricted as dangerous where the source of an incendiary statement is a person of authority in the eyes of the audience;
5. Content of Message:
   Focusing on text appealing to base emotions and communicating recourse to violence as indicative of incitement;
6. Channel of Communication:
   Positing that written text is less likely than broadcast media to lead to violence—distinguishing a "book from a bullhorn," as it were; and
7. Overt Acts:
   Opining that overt acts, such as stockpiling weapons, help gauge the immediacy and degree of physical danger posed by the inflammatory speech.[16]

2. Relationship to the "Reasonably Probable Consequences" Test

In comparison to Benesch, Pauli deals with incitement from the other end of the telescope. The Reasonably Probable Consequences test was proposed from a

12. Pauli, *supra* note 3, at 669 ("[This paper] proposes a framework, based on research in the field of communication, to determine when a message constitutes incitement to genocide so as to justify international prior restraint through measures such as jamming of broadcast signals.").

13. *Id.* at 673 n.52.

14. *Id.* at n.51.

15. *Id.* at n.56.

16. *See id.* at 674–677.

retrospective vantage point out of concern for the potential of hate speech being too freely pegged as incitement. In contrast, the Communications Research Framework takes a prospective view of the problem and seeks rather to nip hate speech in the bud before it can contribute toward the blossoming of genocidal violence.

Still, a good number of Pauli's elements correlate with those of Benesch.[17] For instance, Benesch's "Nature of Message and Audience Understanding" element is analogous to Pauli's "Content of Message" and "Audience Characteristics" criteria. The "Speaker Authority and Audience Capacity" factors in the Benesch framework overlap considerably with the "Authority of Message Source" and the "Audience Characteristics" in Pauli's analytic grid. Benesch's "Survival of the Marketplace of Ideas" prong is akin to Pauli's "Media Environment." But Benesch's "Recent Violence" and "Prior Similar Messages," and Pauli's "Political Context" and "Channel of Communication," respectively, appear to have no equivalent criteria in the other test.

3. Issues with the "Communications Research Framework"

While there is much overlap between the Reasonably Probable Consequences and Communications Research Framework tests, the latter can be distinguished in respect of two key characteristics that raise concerns. First, on a procedural level, the test is strictly focused on ascertaining if speech should be subject to prior restraint and does not directly consider liability for criminal incitement.[18] Second, the test seems to contemplate a standard of proof less exacting than beyond a reasonable doubt (see below), and would filter it through a more stripped-down procedure likely presided over not by courts but by administrative bodies, such as the International Telecommunications Union (ITU).[19]

Moreover, Pauli problematically modifies the substantive burden of establishing incitement. First, as other scholars have, she speciously reckons the ICTR test includes a causation requirement: "Since speech does no physical harm, the ICTR convictions required a finding of an additional proximate cause in order to link incitements to genocide."[20] Based on this, she finds doctrinal justification in

17. *Id.* at 668 (noting that the Benesch test's "elements overlap and support several that are also proposed here").

18. *Id.* at 699 ("This Article has proposed a framework of seven factors that can be used to determine when media messages constitute incitement to genocide and may legally be disrupted.").

19. Pauli observes that the "ITU constitution prohibits harmful interference to radio signals of other states or recognized broadcast agencies, whether from competing radio signals or other 'electrical apparatus.'" *Id.* at 695.

20. *Id.* at 686. Pauli deduces this by reading out of context a passage from the *Media Case* Trial Chamber judgment: "The nature of media is such that causation of killing and other acts of genocide will necessarily be effected by an immediately proximate cause in addition to the communication itself." *Id.* at n.73 (quoting Prosecutor v. Nahimana, Case No. ICTR-99-52-T, Judgement and Sentence, ¶ 952 (Dec. 3, 2003)). In the following sentence, though, the judgment goes on to clarify: "In the Chamber's view, this does not diminish the causation to

appending an "overt acts" criterion to her framework.[21] This arguably amounts to a "causation-light" requirement, which is clearly at odds with the foundationally inchoate character of the offense.[22]

Second, her framework entirely excludes the intent element—the crucial legal component in any genocide case.[23] Pauli acknowledges that "because the framework focuses on prevention rather than culpability, it does not . . . include the criminal element of purpose or intent."[24] Hence, eliminating intent creates a fatal doctrinal lacuna and reinforces the conclusion that the Communications Research Framework is not a suitable replacement for the existing ICTR test.

C. The Relationship between the Two Proposed Alternative Tests and the Existing ICTR Framework

It is important to realize that the Benesch "Vile Crime" and Pauli Communications Research tests share many elements with the ICTR framework. Benesch's "Audience Understanding" criterion, for instance, tracks perfectly the ICTR framework's "Direct" analysis, which inquires, as we have seen, whether the message recipient immediately grasped the message's significance. Likewise, Benesch's "Nature of Message" and Pauli's "Content of Message" elements largely correspond with the

be attributed to the media, or the criminal accountability of those responsible for the communication." *Id.* In point of fact, the *Media Case* Trial Chamber decision explicitly rejected a causation requirement for incitement in this paragraph.

21. Pauli, *supra* note 3, at 686. Regrettably, this is inimical to the crime-prevention aspirations of Pauli's proposed framework. Including a physical conduct prerequisite (overt acts) where there was formerly none merely adds weight to the prosecution's already heavy burden of making out a prima facie case of incitement and pursuing enforcement at a preliminary juncture that could facilitate effective prevention, instead of punishment alone postcommission.

22. *See* Prosecutor v. Musema, Case No. ICTR-96-13-A, Judgement and Sentence, ¶ 193 (Jan. 27, 2000) (explaining that inchoate offenses (conspiracy, in that case) are "punishable by virtue of the criminal act as such and not as a consequence of the result of that act."). *See also* Ira P. Robbins, *Double Inchoate Crimes*, 26 HARV. J. ON LEGIS. 1, 3 (1989) ("Indeed, the main purpose of punishing inchoate crimes is to allow the judicial system to intervene before an actor completes the object crime."); Nick Zimmerman, *Attempted Stalking: An Attempt-to-Almost-Attempt-to-Act*, 20 N. ILL. U. L. REV. 219, 222 (2000) ("Crimes that are punished before the harm that is the ultimate concern of society occurs are called inchoate crimes.").

23. *See* Louis Rene Beres, *After the Gulf War: Israel, Pre-emption, and Anticipatory Self-Defense*, 13 HOUS. J. INT'L L. 259, 271 (1991) ("The key to understanding and identifying genocide lies in the 'intent to destroy.'"); Mark A. Bland, *An Analysis of the United Nations International Tribunal to Adjudicate War Crimes Committed in the Former Yugoslavia: Parallels, Problems, Prospects*, 2 IND. J. GLOBAL LEGAL STUD. 233, 255 (1994) ("The word 'intent' is key: without the requisite intent to destroy a group, the heinous act cannot qualify as genocide."); Walter Gary Sharp, Sr., *The International Criminal Tribunal for the Former Yugoslavia: Defining the Offenses*, 23 MD. J. INT'L L. & TRADE 15, 25 (1999) ("The key distinction between genocide and similar crimes . . . is that a conviction of genocide requires proof that the act was committed with the intent to take part in a plan to destroy a particular national, ethnical, racial, or religious group.").

24. Pauli, *supra* note 3, at 676.

"Text" and "Purpose" criteria of the "incitement" element in the ICTR framework (although, as explained in Chapter 5, the "text" criterion was not explicitly teased out by the ICTR in the *Media Case* Trial Chamber judgment). Similarly, Benesch's reference to "Speaker Authority" and Pauli's to "Authority of Message Source" and "Audience Characteristics," both seem to implicate the ICTR's "Relationship between the Speaker and Subject" criterion of the "incitement" element (again, as pointed out in Chapter 5, this criterion was not featured as such in the *Media Case* decision but was nevertheless embedded in the Trial Chamber's analysis).

In the main, though, the other Benesch/Pauli elements can be situated in the "Context" criterion of the "incitement" element of the existing ICTR test. Thus, evaluative factors such as "Political Context," "Media Environment," "Recent Violence," and "Prior Similar Message" are quite helpful guiding the adjudicator in ascertaining if hate speech rises to the level of direct and public incitement to commit genocide.

However, unlike the Benesch approach in "Vile Crime," which mandates that, without exception, each element of the test be met or there can be no incitement conviction, employing the factors strictly for analytical purposes would provide needed interpretive guidance and adjudicative flexibility. It would allow judges to conduct a nuanced contextual evaluation to determine if the speech has reached inchoate genocidal critical mass.[25] If, for instance, "recent violence" or "prior similar messages" were lacking, that should not necessarily prevent an incitement finding if other contextual factors are present in large quantities or in high degrees (a position Benesch herself ultimately came to embrace). In effect, this approach would permit a "totality of the circumstances" analysis that would better respect liberty of expression (considering the wealth of evaluative factors) while allowing adequate flexibility for the incitement offense to accomplish its crucial preventive goal. Adopting this methodology is strongly recommended in the next section of this chapter, where proposals are advanced for strengthening the existing framework.

III. FIXING THE EXISTING FRAMEWORK

A. Introduction

So if the current ICTR framework is to be salvaged, what fixes are in order? In Chapter 5, issues with respect to three different elements and one "nonelement" were discerned. The specific flawed elements were "direct," "public," and "incitement." The "nonelement," causation, has been treated ambiguously in the jurisprudence,

25. *See* Vihar R. Patel, *Are Patented Research Tools Still Valuable? Use, Intent, and a Rebuttable Presumption: A Proposed Modification for Analyzing the Exemption from Patent Infringement under 35 USC. § 271(E)(1)*, 47 Idea 407, 447 (2007) ("Despite the illusory attractiveness of precise rules, 'nuanced and flexible standards are generally more appropriate for [a legally] dynamic innovation environment . . . .'" (quoting Janice E. Mueller, *The Evanescent Experimental Use Exemption from United States Patent Infringement Liability: Implications for University and Non Profit Research and Development*, 56 Baylor L. Rev. 917, 965 (2004))).

ostensibly excluded from the framework but then indirectly handled as an element all the same. As it turns out, part of the problem with the "direct" element entails confusion regarding whether causation is integrated into it. As a result, approaches to repairing the "direct" and "causation" elements are considered together. That is followed by analysis regarding the "public" and "incitement" criteria.

B. Fixing the Direct and Causation Elements

1. Clearing Up the Confusion Regarding Causation

As we have seen, the source of incitement law's "Original Sin"—the polluted well from which many of its problems spring—can be traced to the ICTR's 1997 Trial Chamber judgment in *Prosecutor v. Akayesu*. Starting with the first word of the offense's full name, "direct," red flags were raised regarding the quality of the judicial analysis. Chapter 5 revealed that much of the problem stemmed from a fundamental and inherent pitfall in the early development of any sub-branch of international law—reconciling the principles of competing legal cultures and the terminology of different linguistic traditions.

Regarding legal culture, as will be recalled, the *Akayesu* Trial Chamber equivocated in terms of adopting a Civil Law versus Common Law standard for purposes of defining "direct." There is an easy explanation for this. In terms of early-phase parsing of rules that are the product of transnational cooperation, international criminal law guru Roger Clark has bemoaned "the subtle differences in legal culture—even within a particular family of legal systems—that bedevil the achievement of consensus, let alone understanding . . . it is difficult to communicate across different systems."[26]

With regard to incitement's "direct" element, in terms of reconciling the Common Law versus the Civil Law paradigms, the *Akayesu* Trial Chamber was put in a thorny position, both politically and normatively. In the first place, this was the first substantive judgment of the ICTR, whose statute incorporated both Civil and Common Law rules that were often in discord with one another.[27] The ICTR Statute was a product of the Common Law tradition.[28] But, at the same time, it was designed to permit adjudication of guilt arising from criminal

26. Roger Clark, *Epilogue*, *in* Mohamed Elewa Badar, The Concept of *Mens Rea* in International Criminal Law: The Case for a Unified Approach 433 (2013).

27. *See* Nigel Eltringham, *"A War Crimes Community?": The Legacy of the International Criminal Tribunal for Rwanda Beyond Jurisprudence*, 14 New Eng. J. Int'l & Comp. L. 309 (2008) (referring to "clashes in common and civil law practices" as contributing to "routine frustrations of those who work at the ICTR as they negotiate the novel characteristics of an international criminal tribunal . . .").

28. José E. Alvarez, *Trying Hussein: Between Hubris and Hegemony*, 2 J. Int'l Crim. Just. 319, 326 (2004) (noting that reports indicate the ICTR statute was drafted by the United States, a Common Law jurisdiction).

activity that took place on the territory of Rwanda, a Civil Law jurisdiction.[29] In this schizophrenic context, the Trial Chamber rendering judgment after the ICTR's first full trial seemed torn between the two opposing normative gravitational pulls. And its decision to pay obeisance to both legal traditions did nothing but engender confusion.

Thus, the Trial Chamber noted, clearly channeling the Civil Law perspective, that "incitement" is the same as "provocation" (synonymous for "instigation," which implies subsequent causal violence) and then left no doubt regarding the causal implications of this:

> Under Civil law systems, provocation, the equivalent of incitement, is regarded as being direct where it is aimed at causing a specific offence to be committed. The prosecution must prove a definite causation between the act characterized as incitement, or provocation in this case, and a specific offence.[30]

So this is where causation insinuates itself into the framework. The Trial Chamber then doubled down on this Civil Law approach by conducting a causation analysis in the factual section and alluding to causation as a legal requirement separately from the "direct" criterion. Of course, at the same time, the Tribunal announced that causation was not an element of the crime. So how should this equivocation resolve itself? Put another way, how can international courts going forward put in order the current legal latticework?

First, future courts need to reaffirm in very decisive and bold language that causation is not an element of the crime. In doing so, they must spell out why—the incitement crime is inchoate and geared toward prevention. That means early intervention. Having a causation requirement would be inimical to that goal.

Second, future courts should, at least until the lingering confusion is dispelled, explain the initial bad decisions made in *Akayesu* and, to a certain extent, renounce them. There must be some affirmative acknowledgment of the problem and a frank expression of a desire to fix it. The confusion that has come in the wake of those poor jurisprudential choices calls for that kind of explicit course-correction.

Third, there must never be analyses of causation in the fact sections of future incitement judgments. This does nothing but perpetuate the confusion and create the impression that courts are speaking out of both sides of their mouths.[31] This jurisprudential hedging reveals doctrinal cowardice and obfuscates proper policy orientation.

29. Paul Christoph Bornkamm, Rwanda's Gacaca Courts: Between Retribution and Reparation 61 (2012) ("Traditionally, Rwanda's legal system is a civil law system . . .").

30. Prosecutor v. Akayesu, Case No. ICTR-96-4-T, Judgement ¶ 557 (Sept. 2, 1998).

31. Moreover, as will be explained in Chapter 11, pursuant to the Unified Liability Theory, if the crime that is the object of the incitement is actually carried out, the proper charge is instigation, not incitement.

Finally, and quite connected to the previous point, if the right case presents itself, prosecutors should be prepared to charge incitement for otherwise qualifying speech even when there is no subsequent genocidal violence. And judges should be prepared to convict if prosecutors can sustain their burdens of pleading and proof. This would be the most effective manner of clearing up the causation confusion issue in incitement law and calibrating enforcement to satisfy more effectively the offense's policy priorities.

2. Fleshing Out the Scope of "Direct"

Another issue exposed in Chapter 5 related to the "direct" element was the lack of precision regarding its scope. As we saw, the ICTR has only offered barebones guidance regarding speech's medium of dissemination, explaining that "direct" speech could consist of shouting or threats uttered in public places or at public gatherings, or through the sale or dissemination, offer for sale, or display of written material or printed matter in public places or at public gatherings, or through the public display of placards or posters, or through any other means of audiovisual communication.[32] But what about content?

After nearly two decades, a wide range of judges have scrutinized myriad fact patterns wherein toxic rhetoric prodded ordinary citizens to murder their fellow citizens on unimaginable scales. Regrettably, no judicial body, including, most glaringly, the ICTR, has methodically classified these incitement techniques or elucidated their legal import. This endeavor should be undertaken in court decisions going forward.[33]

More specifically, such jurisprudence should explicitly identify the following as normatively actionable types of incitement: (1) direct calls for destruction; (2) predictions of destruction; (3) verminization, pathologization, demonization, and other forms of dehumanization; (4) accusation in a mirror; (5) euphemisms and metaphors; (6) justification during contemporaneous violence; (7) condoning and congratulating past violence; (8) asking questions about violence; (9) conditional calls for incitement; and (10) victim-sympathizer conflation.[34]

32. *Id.* ¶ 559.

33. This is a project I have proposed since the issuance of the *Media Case* Trial Chamber judgment. *See, e.g.*, Gregory S. Gordon, *"A War of Media, Words, Newspapers and Radio Stations": The ICTR Media Trial Verdict and a New Chapter in the International Law of Hate Speech*, 45 Va. J. Int'l L. 139, 186–187 (2004) [hereinafter *A War of Media*] ("Incitement can take many forms and this might have been a golden opportunity for international law to recognize them explicitly."). *See also* Gordon, *Music and Genocide, supra* note 2, at 638.

34. As noted in the Introduction, it must be acknowledged that, standing alone, certain of the less direct techniques, such as asking questions or victim-sympathizer conflation, might not be sufficient to support an independent incitement count. That said, when manifold statements are at issue, the less direct techniques could be the basis for separate incitement charges if anchored to more egregious speech in the same indictment. And so, depending on the facts, congratulating past violence, on its own, may not rise to the level of incitement. But when evaluated in the context of direct calls and dehumanization, for example, it might be

a. Direct Calls for Destruction

Direct calls for destruction are relatively rare, but they should be classified as a separate incitement technique. Examples would include the June 4, 1994, broadcast of Radio Télévision Libre des Milles Collines (RTLM) announcer Kantano Habimana, wherein he implored his audience to exterminate the "Inkotanyi," or Tutsis, discernible by height and physical appearance.[35] He chillingly concluded: "Just look at his small nose and then break it."[36] Another notable instance was arguably Iranian President Mahmoud Ahmadinejad's call for Israel's destruction when he told a gathering in October 2005 that Israel "must be wiped off the map."[37]

b. Predictions of Destruction

Prophesying destruction constitutes a less direct form of incitement. In the *Media Case* Trial Chamber judgment, for instance, certain RTLM broadcasts that foretold elimination of the *inyenzi* or cockroaches (i.e., Tutsis) were among those transmissions held to meet the legal definition of incitement, including the following:

> I think we are fast approaching what I would call dawn . . . dawn, because—for the young people who may not know—dawn is when the day breaks. Thus when day breaks, when that day comes, we will be heading for a brighter future, for the day when we will be able to say "There isn't a single *Inyenzi* left in the country." The term *Inyenzi* will then be forever forgotten, and disappear for good. . . .[38]

included as a separate incitement charge. Likewise, a combination of less direct techniques, when considered as a whole, might be the basis for incitement charges, even absent instances of the more direct techniques. Finally, at the very least, if evidence of an indirect technique is not sufficiently strong for charging purposes, it could still serve as excellent evidence of *mens rea* or context.

35. Prosecutor v. Nahimana, Case No. ICTR-99-52-T, Judgement and Sentence, ¶ 396.

36. *Id. See also* Prosecutor v. Kajelijeli, Case No. ICTR 98-44A T, Judgment and Sentence, ¶ 856 (Dec. 1, 2003) (defendant implored a gathering to "[k]ill and exterminate all those people in Rwankeri" and to "exterminate the Tutsis.").

37. *See* Nazila Fathi, *Iran's New President Says Israel Must Be "Wiped Off the Map,"* N.Y. TIMES, Oct. 27, 2005, at A8. *See generally* Gregory S. Gordon, *From Incitement to Indictment? Prosecuting Iran's President for Advocating Israel's Destruction and Piecing Together Incitement Law's Emerging Analytical Framework*, 98 J. CRIM. L. & CRIMINOLOGY 853 (2008) (explaining how Ahmadinejad's statement might have been prosecuted as direct and public incitement to commit genocide). Certain commentators have disputed that this constitutes direct and public incitement to commit genocide. *See, e.g.*, Benesch, *Vile Crime, supra* note 2, at 490–491 ("Ahmadinejad's speech was reprehensible and perhaps even dangerous, but did not constitute incitement to genocide, in my view.").

38. *Nahimana*, Case No. ICTR-99-52-T, ¶ 405 (internal quotation marks omitted).

Former Iranian President Mahmoud Ahmadinejad was also responsible for what could perhaps be classified as the same sort of incitement. In 2008, for example, as Israel celebrated its sixtieth anniversary, Ahmadinejad said to a gathering that the Jewish state was "dying" and that its statehood anniversary celebrations were an attempt to prevent its "annihilation."[39]

c. Verminization, Pathologization, Demonization, and Other Forms of Dehumanization

Respectively, verminization, pathologization, and demonization are methods by which speakers try to dehumanize their would-be victims and thereby advocate their liquidation. Verminization caricatures victims as vile, pestilent creatures, such as lice, whose extermination would be considered normal and desirable.[40] During the Rwandan Genocide, for instance, extremist Hutu propagandists called the Tutsis *inyenzi*, the Kinyarwanda word for "cockroach."[41] RTLM journalist Georges Ruggiu's guilty plea was accompanied by a confession that the word *inyenzi*, as employed in the sociopolitical context of 1994 Rwanda, signified designating the Tutsis as "persons to be killed."[42]

In the same vein, pathologization, or depiction of an object as a disease, is a comparable means of urging out-group destruction.[43] According to a prominent alliance of medical doctors and legal scholars, pathologization "expropriates pseudo-medical terminology to justify massacre [and it] dehumanizes the victims as sources of filth and disease, [propagating] the reversed social ethics of the perpetrators."[44] As alluded to in Chapter 1, in Nazi Germany, for instance, Jews were the targets of pathologization:

> [F]rom the inception of the regime, there is a continuous stream of metaphors equating Jews with disease. Respirologist Kurt Klare, co-founder of the Nazi Physicians' League . . . communicated . . . about the "decomposing influence of Jewry" within the German organism, as if Jewry were a sickness. This theme of Jewish "racial decomposition" and the consequent "cleansing of our *völkisch* body," was graphically reiterated by Dr. [Gerhard] Wagner and his

39. Ali Akbar Dareini, *Iranian Leader Marks Israeli Anniversary with Menace*, H ERALD SCOT. (May 15, 2008), http://www.theherald.co.uk/news/foreign/display.var.2272254.0.0.php#comments. Of course, this assumes that the other elements of incitement could be proved, which, in this case, is not entirely clear.

40. *See* Benesch, *supra* note 2, at 503.

41. *Nahimana*, Case No. ICTR-99-52-T, ¶ 179.

42. Prosecutor v. Ruggiu, Case No. ICTR-97-32-I, Judgement and Sentence, ¶ 44(iii) (June 1, 2000).

43. Rony Blum et al., *"Ethnic Cleansing" Bleaches the Atrocities of Genocide*, 18 EUR. J. PUB. HEALTH 204, 204 (2007), http://eurpub.oxfordjournals.org/cgi/reprint/18/2/204.

44. *Id.*

> medical aides on the occasion of the Nazi party rally in fall 1935—the fatal rally that introduced the anti-Jewish race laws.[45]

Demonization employs similarly sinister figurative speech but is more phantasmagorical and/or anthropocentric in nature. In particular, its slanders center on devils, malefactors, and other nefarious personages.[46] Mahmoud Ahmadinejad, for instance, once asked an audience if Israeli Jews were human beings, and responded to his own query in the negative: "'They are like cattle, nay, more misguided.' A bunch of bloodthirsty barbarians. Next to them, all the criminals of the world seem righteous."[47] During the same time period, he similarly described the Israeli people to partisans at a political gathering as "filthy bacteria," a "wild beast," and a "scarecrow."[48]

Of course, other forms of dehumanization are possible. In *Prosecutor v. Nyiramasuhuko*, et al. (2015), for example, two of the accused told an audience to "sweep the dirt outside."[49] In finding that this constituted incitement to commit genocide, the Trial Chamber found that the audience "understood the words . . . 'sweeping dirt', to mean they needed to kill Tutsis."[50] Thus, the intended victims could also be rhetorically linked to, and thereby dehumanized by, other abhorrent objects, such as garbage, scum, poison, or feces.

d. Accusation in a Mirror

"Accusation in a mirror" is a genocidal speech technique that entails accusing the victim of a plan to commit the identical offenses that the actual perpetrator seeks to commit or has already committed.[51] In an infamous mimeographed document found in the wake of the Rwandan Genocide and titled *Note Relative à la Propagande d'Expansion et de Recrutement* an anonymous Rwandan

45. Michael H. Kater, Doctors under Hitler 178 (1989).

46. *See* David Luban, *A Theory of Crimes against Humanity*, 29 Yale J. Int'l L. 85, 120–121 (2004).

47. Middle E. Media Research Inst., *Iranian President Ahmadinejad Addresses Rally & Warns the US & England*, 1229 Special Dispatch Series (Aug. 3, 2006), http://www.memri.org/reports/iranian-president-ahmadinejad-addresses-rally-warns-us-england-fire-wrath-peoples-about. The example is apt to the extent Ahmadinejad could be held to have satisfied incitement's other requirements.

48. Michal Lando et al., *Ahmadinejad: Israel Filthy Bacteria*, Jerusalem Post (Feb. 20, 2008), http://www.jpost.com/servlet/Satellite?cid=1203343707673&pagename=JPost%2FJPArticle%2FShowFull.

49. Prosecutor v. Nyiramasuhuko, et al., Case No. ICTR-98-42-T, Judgement and Sentence ¶ 6026 (June 24, 2011).

50. *Id.* ¶ 6027.

51. *See* Kenneth L. Marcus, *Accusation in a Mirror*, 43 Loy. U. Chi. L.J. 357, 358 (2012) ("AiM [accusation in a mirror] is a rhetorical practice in which one falsely accuses one's enemies of conducting, plotting, or desiring to commit precisely the same transgressions that one plans to commit against them.").

propagandist praised this technique.[52] Drawing on the ideas of notable previous propagandists, including Joseph Goebbels and Vladimir Lenin, he observed that "the party which is using terror will accuse the enemy of using terror" which will "persuade listeners and 'honest people' that they are being attacked and are justified in taking whatever measures are necessary 'for legitimate [self-]defense.'"[53] Kenneth Marcus provides an excellent illustration of how this represents a perversion of the Golden Rule:

> For example, if one plans to kill one's adversaries by drowning them in a particular river, then one should accuse one's adversaries of plotting precisely the same crime. As a result, one will accuse one's enemies of doing the same thing despite their plans. It is similar to a false anticipatory *tu quoque*: before one's enemies accuse one truthfully, one accuses them falsely of the same misdeed.[54]

Léon Mugesera availed himself of this mendacious agitprop strategy in his infamous 1992 speech, in which he accused the *inyenzi* ("cockroaches") at several reprises of plotting to perpetrate genocide against the Hutus:

> These people called *Inyenzis* are now on their way to attack us. . . . I am telling you, and I am not lying, it is . . . they only want to exterminate us. They only want to exterminate us: they have no other aim. Are we really waiting till they come to exterminate us?[55]

Regarding this insidious technique, Catherine MacKinnon notes: "This infamous 'accusation in a mirror'—the propaganda technique in which one side falsely attributes attacks to the other in order to justify retaliation in kind, casting aggression as self-defense—was especially causally potent."[56] Kenneth Marcus elaborates on this observation and puts it into better historical context:

> AiM's [accusation in a mirror] directness can be seen in both its widespread usage by genocidaires and its effectiveness. First, AiM has historically been an almost invariable harbinger of genocide. [It] has been commonly used in atrocities committed by Nazis, Serbs, and Hutus, among others. . . . Second, AiM is extraordinarily effective as a means of facilitating genocide and other forms of persecution. This is largely because of the manner in which it legitimizes

52. Alison Des Forges, "Leave None to Tell the Story": Genocide in Rwanda 75–76 (1999).

53. *Id.* at 76.

54. Marcus, *supra* note 51, at 359.

55. Mugesera v. Canada, [2005] 2 S.C.R. 100, 2005 SCC 40 app. III, ¶ 18.

56. Catherine MacKinnon, *International Decision*: Prosecutor v. Nahimana, Barayagwiza & Ngeze, 98 Am. J. Int'l L. 325, 330 (2004).

the crimes it describes, but also because AiM serves at least five other functions, both in genocidal and non-genocidal contexts: to shock, to silence, to threaten, to insulate, and, finally, to motivate or incite. The extraordinary efficacy of this method, combined with the great frequency of its usage, suggests that it should raise the same flags as the more commonly discussed methods of demonization and dehumanization. In contrast to these techniques, however, AiM is more direct in the sense that it communicates a specific message to its listeners (i.e., do unto others as they would do unto you).[57]

e. Euphemisms and Metaphors

Conflict entrepreneurs seldom employ explicit terminology to tempt their murderous minions to act. Rather, they tend to speak in coded language, and this can be classified as a separate incitement technique.[58] During the Rwandan Genocide, for instance, "go to work," seemingly the most common massacre directive, connoted "kill Tutsis."[59] William Schabas has perspicaciously commented: "[t]he history of genocide shows that those who incite the crime speak in euphemisms."[60]

f. Justification during Contemporary Violence

Describing atrocities already occurring in an effort to persuade listeners that the crimes are morally justified can also be categorized as a separate incitement technique. W. Michael Reisman explains that "in many of the most hideous international crimes, many of the individuals who are directly responsible operate within a cultural universe that inverts our morality and elevates their actions to the highest form of group, tribe, or national defense."[61]

By way of example, RTLM announcer Georges Ruggiu would ascribe positive virtues to violence (e.g., by stating that the population is having a "good time" killing).[62] Several decades earlier, Nazi leaders went to great pains to stress to potentially complicit Germans the "humaneness" of their massacres, torture, death marches, slavery, and other atrocities.[63]

57. Marcus, *supra* note 51, at 361–362.

58. Benesch, *Vile Crime, supra* note 2, at 506.

59. *See, e.g.*, Prosecutor v. Ruggiu, Case No. ICTR-97-32-I, Judgement and Sentence, ¶ 44(iv) (June 1, 2000).

60. William A. Schabas, *International Decision*: Mugesera v. Minister of Citizenship and Immigration, 93 Am. J. Int'l L. 529, 530 (1999).

61. W. Michael Reisman, *Accountability for International Crime and Serious Violations of Fundamental Human Rights: Legal Responses to Genocide and Other Massive Violations of Human Rights*, 59 Law & Contemp. Probs. 75, 77 (1996).

62. *Ruggiu*, Case No. ICTR-97-32-I, ¶ 44(v).

63. *See* Raul Hilberg, The Destruction of the European Jews 1010 (3d ed. 2003).

g. Condoning or Congratulating Past Violence

Publicly admiring murderers for previous genocidal violence is yet another technique that has been used to great effect. So, for example, RTLM announcers, such as Georges Ruggiu, congratulated the "valiant combatants" who engaged in a "battle" against Tutsi civilians.[64] Rwandan Transportation Minister Eliézer Niyitegeka similarly gave thanks to the militias for their "good work."[65]

h. Asking Questions

The *Bikindi* decision confirmed that posing questions can qualify as an incitement technique.[66] It will be recalled that on Simon Bikindi's return trip from Kayove, he broadcast the following question to militia over a truck loudspeaker: "[H]ave you killed the Tutsis here?" And he went on to ask the militia if they had killed the "snakes."[67] These questions were among the factual findings contributing toward Bikindi's criminal responsibility for direct and public incitement to commit genocide.[68]

i. Conditional Calls for Destruction

In the *Media Case* Appeals Chamber judgment, the panel referred to a January 1994 *Kangura* article written by Hassan Ngeze and titled "The Last Lie." In it, Ngeze wrote that if "the *Inyenzi*" made a "small mistake," they would be exterminated, and if they made the mistake of attacking once again, there would be "none of them left in Rwanda, not even a single accomplice. All the Hutu are united."[69] The Appeals Chamber found that this qualified as a call for incitement to commit genocide, even if the appeal was conditional on the Rwandan Patriotic Front initiating an attack, as the condition was satisfied.[70] Thus, incitement may be predicated on conditional calls for eliminationist violence and this should be recognized as a discrete incitement technique.[71]

64. *Ruggiu*, Case No. ICTR-97-32-I, ¶ 44(v).

65. Prosecutor v. Niyitegeka, Case No. ICTR-96-14-T, Judgement and Sentence, ¶ 142 (May 16, 2003).

66. Prosecutor v. Bikindi, Case No. ICTR-01-72-T, Judgement, ¶ 423 (Dec. 2, 2008).

67. *Id.* ¶ 269.

68. *Id.* ¶ 423.

69. Prosecutor v. Nahimana, Case No. ICTR-99-52-A, Judgement, ¶ 771 (Nov. 28, 2007).

70. *Id. See also* Wibke Timmermann & William A. Schabas, *Incitement to Genocide*, *in* Elements of Genocide 164 (Paul Behrens & Ralph Henham eds., 2013) ("According to the Appeals Chamber, the fact that the appeal to exterminate the Tutsi was conditional on the occurrence of an attack by the RPF did not change the directness of the call for the commission of genocide if the condition was realized.").

71. *Cf.* Model Penal Code § 2.02(6), titled "Requirement of Purpose Satisfied if Purpose Is Conditional," which declares that if "a particular purpose is an element of an offense, the

j. Conflating Victims and Sympathizers

It has been observed that "inciters intentionally conflate victims-to-be and members of the dominant group who sympathize with them, preparing the audience for the killing of both."[72] Thus, in the Third Reich, non-Jews who protected Jews were the victims of brutal attacks. Or they were sent to concentration camps and murdered simply owing to their sympathy for Jewish people. Likewise, Hutus in genocidal Rwanda who were considered sympathetic to Tutsis were labeled as "traitors," conflated with Tutsis or "the enemy," and slaughtered as if they had been Tutsi themselves.[73] In the following decade, Iranian President Mahmoud Ahmadinejad, who, as we saw at the beginning of this section, had threatened to "wipe Israel off the map" also made threats against those who would come to Israel's defense, warning: "Anybody who recognizes Israel will burn in the fire of the Islamic nation's fury."[74]

These incitement techniques are described in Figure 8.1.

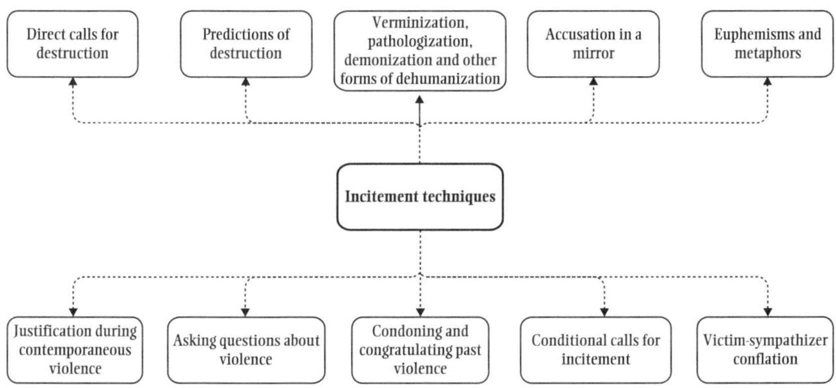

Figure 8.1 Incitement Techniques.

element is established although such purpose is conditional, unless the condition negatives the harm or evil sought to be prevented by the law defining the offense." Model Penal Code § 2.02(6) (1985). Query whether this would constitute incitement if the condition were not satisfied. It is beyond the scope of this discussion to contemplate the doctrinal implications of that scenario.

72. Benesch, *Vile Crime, supra* note 2, at 506.

73. *See, e.g.*, Thomas Kamilindi, *Journalism in a Time of Hate Media*, *in* The Media and the Rwandan Genocide 136, 138–139 (Allan Thompson ed., 2007) (featuring a Hutu journalist who describes how he became "one of the targets of the Hutu militia" because he was perceived as sympathetic to Tutsis).

74. *Ahmadinejad Quotes*, Jerusalem Post Online Ed. (May 16, 2006), http://www.jpost.com/servlet/Satellite?cid=1145961353170&pagename=JPost%2FJPArticle%2FPrinter.

C. Fixing the "Public" Element

1. The Current Definition and Nature of the Problem

Chapter 5 also revealed issues concerning the "public" element. Once again, the source of the glitches can be traced back to the original gloss put on the term by the *Akayesu* Trial Chamber judgment. It will be recalled that the Chamber held that "the public element of incitement to commit genocide may be better appreciated in light of two factors: the place where the incitement occurred and whether or not assistance was selective or limited."[75]

The notion of "assistance," given the common English definition—along the lines of "help," "aid," "reinforcement," "succor," "relief"[76]—seemed preposterous. As we saw, it is possible that "assistance" is a direct transposition and conjugation of the French verb *assister*, meaning to "to be present at," "to attend," or "to witness" (in the sense of attendance at an event).[77] But that is pure speculation—the Trial Chamber never even hinted at this as a possible explanation. Thus, confusion still reigned.

The Chamber then offered additional insight into the definition of "public"—once again injecting the Civil Law perspective into the mix: "A line of authority commonly followed in Civil law systems would regard words as being public where they were spoken aloud in a place that were [*sic*] public by definition."[78] Apart from the grammatical flaw, the big issue here was the lack of guidance as to what was meant by a place that is "public by definition." There was also a failure to define "aloud" in reference to the proximity of any would-be auditors.

Rather than clarify, the Chamber lurched toward another possible definition: "According to the International Law Commission, public incitement is characterized by a call for criminal action to a number of individuals in a public place or to members of the general public at large by such means as the mass media, for example, radio or television." This one also leaves readers scratching their heads. How many individuals? How does one define "public"? And what is the scope of "mass media"? No answers were forthcoming.

Not surprisingly, in light of this confusion, we saw that an inconsistent jurisprudence sprang up regarding the meaning of "public." The gist of the problem was revealed in the cases involving road blocks. As detailed in Chapter 5, the decisions veered wildly—some decisions finding that roadblocks were "public" places because located on "public" roads and others reaching the opposite conclusion because members of the "public" were not present. Some judgments concluded that if the number of persons at the roadblock was sufficiently large, any speech to those persons otherwise hewing to the legal definition constituted incitement. Others reached the opposite conclusion. From a policy perspective,

75. Prosecutor v. Akayesu, Case No. ICTR-96-4-T, Judgement, ¶ 556.

76. *See Assistance*, Merriam-Webster, http://www.merriam-webster.com/dictionary/assistance (last visited Sept. 18, 2016).

77. *See Assister*, Collins English-French Electronic Dictionary, http://www.wordreference.com/fren/assister (last visited Sept. 18, 2016).

78. *Akayesu*, Case No. ICTR-96-4-T, ¶ 556.

there was no principled distinction between or among these decisions. In other words, what was the essence of "public" such that we could define it in a way that justified including the element in the first place?

2. Reconsidering the Necessity of the "Public" Element

So perhaps it is worth digging more deeply and inquiring why incitement to commit genocide carries a "public" element in the first place. One source explains that "its 'public' nature distinguishes it from an act of private incitement (which could be punishable under the Genocide Convention as 'complicity in genocide' or possibly not punishable at all)."[79] But why should "private" incitement not be criminalized at all? Perhaps inciting a smaller number of persons could be reflected in less severe sentencing, but why not assign the properly tailored category of individual criminal responsibility to such conduct in the first place? As suggested, charging it as complicity in genocide would be an option, but that would be a viable strategy only if the target crime were committed or attempted. So it would not offer the distinct advantage of incitement's inchoate nature. And even if the target crime were committed or attempted (and charged as complicity and/or attempt), complicity/attempt would not capture the speech-related nature of the crime. That has very important expressive and normative value that would be lost.[80]

Wibke Timmermann argues that "private" incitement is merely solicitation and involves a speaker who exerts control over his listeners—thus his capacity to impede is in equal measure to his capacity to instigate. "Public" incitement, on the other hand, implicates a kind of passion—a genie let out of a bottle that takes on a life of its own, as it were—that merits a separate kind of criminalization. As explained by Timmermann:

> It is further submitted that *public* incitement and solicitation/instigation present very different dangers. Incitement involves the stirring up of uncontrollable anger and passion; once the masses are incited, the inciter is unable to stop them. It is therefore properly characterized as an inchoate offence. By contrast, the danger of solicitation lies in the control that the solicitor exercises over the minds of the specific individuals solicited. This control is only apparent and punishable once the crime has at least been attempted.[81]

With all due respect to Ms. Timmermann, the distinction she is trying to draw seems to be more one of scale than substance. It is not clear why "private"

79. United States Holocaust Memorial Museum, *Incitement to Genocide in International Law*, Holocaust Encyclopedia, http://www.ushmm.org/wlc/en/article.php?ModuleId=10007839 (last updated Jan. 29, 2016).

80. Alexander K. A. Greenawalt, *International Criminal Law for Retributivists*, 35 U. Pa. J. Int'l L. 969, 1036 (2014) (discussing the "great expressive value" in expanding ICL).

81. Wibke Timmermann, Incitement in International Law 16 (2014). Of course, apart from the issue of the harm in "public" versus "private" incitement, Timmermann's reference to solicitation/instigation is misplaced. Solicitation/instigation applies to speech that has

incitement is not capable of whipping up "uncontrollable anger and passion" just as easily as the "public" variety. If anything, close physical proximity to the speaker would arguably arouse more of an emotional response than merely hearing a disembodied voice faintly crackling over the airwaves of a radio transmission. Thus, if immediate presence in a more intimate setting is logically more likely to inflame listeners' emotions, would it not reasonably follow that the speaker would be less likely to exert a Svengali-like control over the listeners? Timmermann's conceit of a hypnotic control that can easily be turned on and off in a "private" setting does not withstand scrutiny.

In fact, there is nothing inherently "public" about incitement. The *Oxford English Dictionary* defines "incitement" as "the action of provoking unlawful behavior or urging *someone* to behave unlawfully."[82] Similarly, *Black's Law Dictionary* describes "incitement" as "the act or an instance of provoking, urging on, or stirring up . . . the act of persuading *another person* to commit a crime. . . ."[83] As these definitions suggest, "incitement is a speech act"[84] and, in the abstract, contemplates one listener at a minimum. In his seminal treatise *On Liberty*, John Stuart Mill indicated incitement consists of a speech intended by the speaker to provoke lawless action in a context conducive to such action being taken.[85] Moreover, Mill would consider such speech to be incitement regardless of whether it actually provoked the intended criminal conduct.[86] In other words, he confirms that it is an inchoate crime.

Thus, incitement's distinguishing characteristic, apart from its being speech intended to provoke lawless action, is its inchoate nature—but there is nothing inherently "public" about it. We know this from the Genocide Convention's *travaux préparatoires*, as discussed in Chapter 3, given that "private" incitement was seriously considered before being rejected at the eleventh hour.

3. Eliminating the "Public" Element

So how can the jurisprudence regarding the "public" element be fixed? The answer is simple: by discarding the requirement altogether. That would obviate the necessity of unprincipled line-drawing exercises seeking to determine, for example, if an audience over or under one hundred means a speech was "public"

its intended effect—commission of the crime. Incitement, on the other hand, is an inchoate crime that necessarily implies that the target crime has not been committed.

82. *Incitement*, Oxford Dictionaries, http://www.oxforddictionaries.com/definition/english/incitement (last visited Sept. 18, 2016) (emphasis added).

83. Black's Law Dictionary 86 (5th ed. 1979).

84. Raphael Cohen-Almagor, *Boundaries of Freedom of Expression before and after Prime Minister Rabin's Assassination*, *in* Liberal Democracy and the Limits of Tolerance: Essays in Honor and Memory of Yitzhak Rabin 82 (Raphael Cohen-Almagor ed., 2000).

85. John Stuart Mill, On Liberty, 107–108 (2d ed. 1863). *See also* Cohen-Almagor, *supra* note 84, at 82.

86. Cohen-Almagor, *supra* note 84.

versus "private." And it would eliminate hairsplitting determinations about whether speeches on a "public" road can be considered "incitement" if only a few persons were addressed.

The fact is that small, medium, and large groups can be incited to commit genocide. Their exact numbers should not determine the existence or not of the inciter's criminal liability—even if they might sensibly affect the scope of his sentence. By way of example, in a posited genocidal context, consider the person whose rhetoric in a large room in a mansion (a large "private" residence) seeks to inspire eighty listeners present in the room to murder hundreds of members of the victim group. If the listeners do not go on to commit the desired murder, the speaker should nevertheless be charged with incitement. That the room in the private residence was not accessible to the general public and was filled with fewer than one hundred persons should be of no moment. The serious potential for bringing about, through speech, the mass murder of the genocide's victim group should be enough to trigger viable incitement charges.

Similarly, toward the end-phases of a genocidal campaign, a speech broadcast on a radio with a limited transmission range that narrowly reaches an area where only a handful of persons hear it and where there are no out-group survivors left in the immediate vicinity, would ostensibly satisfy the "public" element. Why should that speech, which is arguably of less concern than in the preceding example's "private" speech, be chargeable while the "private" speech, much more dangerous in light of the context, fail to qualify as incitement because it is not "public"?

There is no compelling articulable reason. In essence, the distinction is problematic and should be excised. It is noteworthy, in this regard, that the International Law Commission's original Draft Code of Offences against the Peace and Security of Mankind criminalized "direct incitement to commit any of the offences in the preceding paragraphs of this article."[87] Public was not an element.

D. Fixing the "Incitement" Element

1. Establishing "Text" and "Speaker-Subject Relationship" as Distinct Criteria

The final element that needs fixing, and arguably the most important, is the "incitement" element itself. To begin, Chapters 4 and 5 revealed that, even though the *Media Case* Trial Chamber overtly identified two analytic criteria to determine if speech should be deemed legitimate expression versus criminal advocacy—purpose and context[88]—there were two additional elements tacitly incorporated into the analysis: text and the relationship between speaker and subject.[89]

87. Draft Code of Offenses against the Peace and Security of Mankind, art. 2(13)(i), [1954] 1 Y.B. Intl' L. Comm'n 1, U.N. Doc. A/CN.4/R.6.

88. Prosecutor v. Nahimana, Case No. ICTR-99-52-T, Judgement and Sentence, ¶¶ 1000–1006, 1022 (Dec. 3, 2003).

89. *See* Gordon, *A War of Media*, *supra* note 33, at 172–174 (2004) (examining these elements and the Chamber's treatment of them).

Chapter 5 considered the advantages of these two additional criteria. First, exegetical treatment of the words themselves lends much to the exercise. In particular, it permits inter- and intra-textual comparative analysis as well as hermeneutic scrutiny of empirically verifiable coded language or catchphrases, such as "magic gas chamber," "go to work," or "find the cockroaches." Second, examining the speaker-subject relationship goes a long way toward revealing the social utility of the speech. There are discernable benefits to providing greater protection to minority or dissenting speech, which can help stimulate robust discussion in the public sphere and/or expose problematic or deleterious establishment policies. By the same token, in mass atrocity contexts, speech issued as the mouthpiece of the governing power or majority group is most likely linked to persecutory or dissent-chilling objectives. According greater protection to the former and less to the latter makes good sense, then, from a policy perspective.

So the first fix is an easy one—extract these two important ingredients from the larger analytic stew of the "incitement" examination and make them full-fledged criteria in their own right.

2. Fleshing Out the Context Criterion: Ethos, Logos, and Pathos

a. Background

I consider the "context" criterion the most important of the "incitement" components. From the literature and discussions about this topic over the years, I have found that the most fundamental inquiry in this area, both from lay and expert perspectives, relates to what distinguishes common hate speech from incitement to genocide. And of all the elements we have considered, context is by far the most vital. The ICTR decisions—most prominently the *Media Case* Trial Chamber judgment—certainly identify it as a mandatory element. Unfortunately, however, as seen in Chapter 5, the jurisprudence has left it underdeveloped. Thus, there are some proposals here for providing courts with greater guidance and, generally, they encompass Aristotle's classification of rhetoric into the categories of ethos, logos, and pathos—that is, an analysis of the speaker (ethos) and the words themselves (logos), including any potentially intense emotional impact on the listeners given audience characteristics and surrounding circumstances (pathos).[90]

b. Internal Context ("Ethos")

First, it would be helpful to bifurcate "context" into two separate sub-limbs—internal and external.[91] Per this proposal, "internal" context would embrace aspects of

90. Magedah E. Shabo, Rhetoric, Logic & Argumentation: A Guide for Student Writers 8 (2010) ([Aristotle's] fourth-century B.C. *Treatise on Rhetoric* . . . describes three different modes of persuasion. . . . The first kind depends on the ***personal character of the speaker*** [ethos]; the second on ***putting the audience into a certain frame of mind*** [pathos]; **the third on the proof, or apparent *proof, provided by the words of the speech itself*** [logos].") (emphasis in the original).

91. *See* Lawrence Schlam, *Legislative Term Limitation under a "Limited" Popular Initiative Provision*, 14 N. Ill. U. L. Rev. 1, 60 (1993) (explaining the significance of distinguishing

the speaker herself: her background and professional profile, her previous publication/broadcast history, and her personal manner of transmission (including tone of voice).[92] It would also include the authority of the speaker. Are we dealing with a high-level government official (or even lower-ranking but with sufficient stature to have a significant impact on public opinion) or a private person with other indicia of authority, such as media personality, tycoon, or political activist?

c. External Context ("Pathos")

External context would comprise the environment and circumstances surrounding the speech. In this regard, as alluded to earlier in this chapter, it would be helpful to fold in the factors identified by Benesch and Pauli, including political/social context (has the government or armed nonstate group been exercising strong or absolute authority and/or engaging in a persecutory campaign against a victim group that has included recent violence against members of that group and/or violence on the heels of hate speech?); media environment (does the government exercise a monopoly over media outlets and/or does the audience have access to alternative or competing messages?); and audience characteristics (have the message recipients been subjected to previous similar messages and/or are they experiencing economic difficulties and/or do they have a history of committing violence against the victim group?).[93]

These internal and external factors are summarized in Figure 8.2.

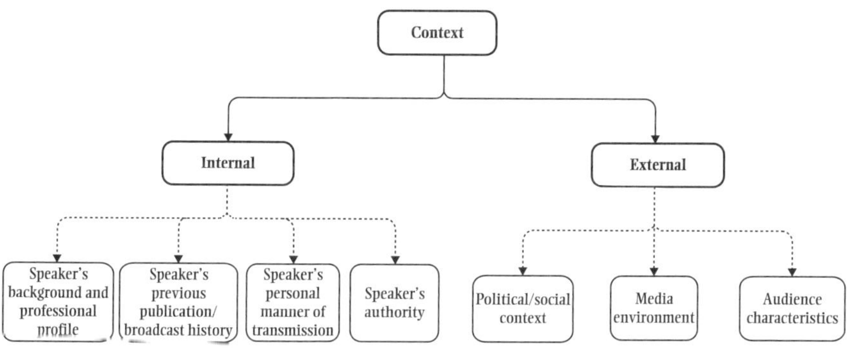

Figure 8.2 Evaluative Factors for the "Context" Element.

between internal and external context in statutory interpretation and concluding that "[w]hen ambiguity exists . . . both internal and external context usually must be taken into account to weigh the chances of absurd, unfair or unreasonable results should one interpretation be adopted as compared to another").

92. As indicated in Chapter 4, tone of voice has already been flagged by the ICTR as a significant evaluative factor for the contextual consideration of whether licit hate speech has eroded into illicit incitement. *See Nahimana* Case No. ICTR-99-52-T, ¶ 1022 ("The tone of the statement is as relevant to this determination as is its content.").

93. Benesch has organized these factors into a set of draft guidelines for monitoring inflammatory speech and evaluating its dangerousness, that is, the capacity to catalyze violence by

d. Evaluating the Context Factors

Again, these evaluative factors are not exhaustive and others could be conceived/considered through additional research or case law development or via various other inductive or deductive processes. For example, as suggested previously, another factor could be "international situation," including external pressure from other states (such as threats of embargoes or withholding aid) and/or outbreak or imminent outbreak of armed conflict.

Yet another evaluative factor could be a period of elections or other political transition. It will be recalled that the Rwandan Genocide took place in the context of implementation of the Arusha Accords, which would have reduced the power of the sitting government and ceded some authority to the Rwandan Patriotic Front (RPF) Tutsi rebels. We also saw in Chapter 1 that mass violence erupted in and around elections and/or transfers of power in Kenya in 2007–2008 and in Côte d'Ivoire in 2010–2011. Finally, and perhaps most obviously, the provable falsity of a statement could be another factor taken into consideration.[94]

And there is no formula for determining how the configuration of the factors could result in a determination or not of incitement. The easy situation is speech uttered in the context of a government campaign against a minority victim group. The speech contains code words identifiable as calls for mass murder of the victim group. There has been previous violence against the victim group following comparable hate speech. The speaker at issue has been responsible for that previous hate speech and the government monopolizes all channels of communication, including mass and social media. The intended audience understands the message, has been provided with weapons by the government and is facing an economic crisis. At the same time, the state is involved in an armed conflict with a neighbor state. This would be a clear case of incitement.

But if only some of the factors are present, but not others, the judges will have to exercise their discretion and come to a conclusion based on the totality of circumstances. If only a small number of factors are present, but they are

one group against another. She refers to such inflammatory rhetoric as "dangerous speech" and distinguishes it from "hate speech," which she describes as "too broad for successful early warning of mass atrocities . . ." Susan Benesch, *Dangerous Speech: A Proposal to Prevent Group Violence*, World Policy Institute (Jan. 12, 2012), http://www.worldpolicy.org/sites/default/files/Dangerous%20Speech%20Guidelines%20Benesch%20January%202012.pdf. As suggested in this section, in conducting the overall analysis, some of the evaluative factors may be considered in reference to more than one element. But it is still important to maintain discrete analytic boundaries between and among the elements to achieve the greatest degree of conceptual clarity and doctrinal rigor.

94. *See* Toby Mendel, *Study on International Standards Relating to Incitement to Genocide or Racial Hatred*, UN Special Adviser on the Prevention of Genocide (Apr. 2006), at 61, http://www.concernedhistorians.org/content_files/file/TO/239.pdf (noting that falsehoods may be indicative of incitement).

extremely strong, they could militate in favor of an incitement finding. Thus, if there has been previous violence as part of a persecutory campaign against the same victim group following similar speech, that situation would likely compel an incitement conclusion. On the other hand, if the only factors present are that the government is rather authoritarian and exercises a media monopoly, the listening audience is experiencing economic difficulties, and the victim group is being dehumanized in speech uttered by someone with little authority, then perhaps this would not qualify as incitement. But add in the fact that there had been recent violence against the victim group and that could be enough to tilt the balance the other way. Again, the determinative test will be the totality of circumstances.

3. Adding New Criteria

At the same time, based on the analysis in Chapter 5, three new criteria should be added to the "incitement" element framework: (1) channel of communication; (2) temporality; and (3) instrumentality. Each of these will be considered in turn.

a. Channel of Communication

One of the factors identified in Carol Pauli's Communications Research Framework, "Channels of Communication," deserves to be a separate element. First, from a chronological standpoint, written communication media are much less apt to incite to mass violence than broadcast media.[95] For instance, Pauli differentiates between "the impact of a book from that of a bullhorn."[96] What is more, certain of the non-international-criminal-law decisions on which the *Media Case* Trial Chamber formulated its test distinguishing between hate speech and incitement also appear to differentiate between written and broadcast materials. A case in point is *Arslan v. Turkey*, where the European Court of Human Rights (ECtHR) threw out the conviction of a journalist who had been found guilty because his prizewinning book, *History in Mourning, 33 Bullets*, described the Turks as invaders who had slaughtered peasants and meant to exterminate the Kurds.[97]

Pauli homed in on the Court's differential treatment of written media:

> The [*Arslan*] Court was more forgiving toward a book than it apparently would have been toward other channels of communication. It found a literary work to be less likely than the mass media (presumably meaning the broadcast media) to disturb national security and public order. In this case, the

95. *See* Scott Hamack, *The Internet Loophole: Why Threatening Speech On-Line Requires a Modification of the Courts' Approach to True Threats and Incitement*, 36 Colum. J.L. & Soc. Probs. 65, 100 (2002) ("[A] written, as opposed to spoken, medium . . . will be less likely to give rise to an imminent lawless action.").

96. Pauli, *supra* note 3, at 670.

97. Arslan v. Turkey, 31 Eur. Ct. H.R. 264, 286 (2001).

Court overturned speech restrictions placed on a book that painted a negative picture of Turks and their treatment of Kurds.[98]

In a similar vein, "the United States has not criminalized or prosecuted the mere publication of written materials as incitement"[99] because "[t]he root of incitement theory appears to have been grounded in concern over crowd behavior."[100] The availability and circulation of the material should also be considered. In regards to the *Media Case*, for instance, American First Amendment attorney Floyd Abrams has remarked that Hassan Ngeze's newspaper, *Kangura*, was distributed in a milieu where "only [30 percent] of Rwandans are literate, [so] the paper was never widely read."[101]

This contrasts with *Zana v. Turkey*,[102] where the ECtHR affirmed the conviction of a former mayor who spoke favorably of Kurdish Worker Party violence in a major national daily newspaper.[103] Pauli writes that "the resulting prominence of the statement [given its placement in a major daily national newspaper] was a factor as the Court upheld the speaker's conviction."[104]

Of course, a speech made directly to an audience that is physically present before the speaker is extremely impactful, as discussed in connection with the "public" element. Even though it may not be as capable of being disseminated beyond the immediate vicinity of the listeners, it will arguably exert more influence over those listeners than dissemination through the indirect channels of various media.

b. Temporality

It will be recalled that, in *Prosecutor v. Bikindi*, the defendant's songs were recorded before the genocide and disseminated by persons other than the defendant during the ensuing orgy of violence. Temporality and instrumentality are germane in instances where speech is republished by a third party after initially being uttered by the original speaker.[105]

98. Pauli, *supra* note 3, at 686.

99. Elizabeth M. Renieris, *Combating Incitement to Terrorism on the Internet: Comparative Approaches in the United States and United Kingdom and the Need for International Solution*, 11 Vand. J. Ent. & Tech. L. 673, 682 (2009).

100. Herceg v. Hustler Magazine, Inc., 814 F.2d 1017, 1023 (5th Cir. 1987).

101. Judith Miller, *Killing Again*, N.Y. Post (Jan. 29, 2007), http://www.nysun.com/opinion/killing-again/47538/ ("[Simon] has documented nearly [fifty] such cases in Burundi, the Central African Republic, Togo, Gabon, Zimbabwe, and sadly, Rwanda . . . .").

102. Zana v. Turkey, 27 Eur. Ct. H.R. 667, 673 (1999).

103. *Id.* at 691.

104. Pauli, *supra* note 3, at 686.

105. This is consistent with the *Media Case* Appeals Chamber analysis regarding Ngeze's pre-1994 *Kangura* writings. *See* Prosecutor v. Nahimana, Case No. ICTR-99-52-A, Judgement, ¶ 410 (Nov. 28, 2007) (considering Ngeze's "republished" 1990–1993 articles).

First, the *Bikindi* Trial Chamber held that, in light of its finding that the defendant composed his tunes well in advance of their being disseminated during the 1994 cataclysm, he could not have had the requisite genocidal intent.[106] In essence, the Trial Chamber tacitly incorporated a "temporality" criterion. In other words, the judges indicated that the offensive words must have been spoken at or near the time of the contextual violence that renders them genocidal.

c. Instrumentality

Likewise, the *Bikindi* Trial Chamber seemed to find relevant the method in which the songs were disseminated in relation to the genocidal killings. Even if the songs were played as a prelude to and in chorus with the slaughter, these were electronic reproductions that were not within the defendant's control.[107] Therefore, an implicit "instrumentality" criterion can be gleaned from the decision. Put another way, when a recording is disseminated, the recorded would-be inciter must be responsible for actual contemporaneous dissemination of the illicit rhetoric (i.e., the playing of the recording) that is charged—the antecedent conduct of making the recording will not be chargeable.[108]

4. Putting All the Criteria Together and Conceptualizing Them

In the end, with the additions and refinements, the existing framework for determining whether hate speech constitutes direct and public incitement to commit genocide should consist of seven criteria (with context being bifurcated): (1) purpose; (2) text; (3) context (both internal and external, with the latter involving consideration of the evaluative factors discussed in this chapter); (4) relationship between speaker and subject; (5) channel of communication; (6) temporality; and (7) instrumentality.

Additionally, these criteria can be conceptualized as falling roughly into three separate categories: (1) content; (2) circumstances; and (3) medium. "Content" would cover the first two criteria—purpose and text. Purpose is embedded and manifested in the content of the speech itself—the text is a mirror of the speaker's motivation. And the text itself, of course, is the actual lexical material of the speech. Reference to this category helps answer the questions: "What has been said and why has it been said?"

106. Prosecutor v. Bikindi, Case No. ICTR-01-72-T, Judgement, ¶ 421 (Dec. 2, 2008).

107. *Id.* ¶ 263.

108. As explained in the *Media Case* Appeals Chamber judgment regarding Ngeze's republished 1990–1993 articles, the republication in *Bikindi* (i.e., the replaying of the songs) would likely also involve a finding that the alleged incitement was not sufficiently direct. *See Nahimana*, Case No. ICTR-99-52-A, ¶ 410. Unfortunately, once again, the *Bikindi* Trial Chamber is guilty of merely skimming the surface of the analysis and missing the opportunity to delve into this important issue.

The "circumstances" conceptual category encompasses the "context" criterion itself as well as the relationship between speaker and subject. Given that it captures what surrounds the speech, it is exogenous to content itself and thus merits its own conceptual category. And it has independent conceptual heft being that the context criterion bifurcates into internal and external branches and is fleshed out through numerous evaluative factors. Moreover, it implicates the freedom of expression calculus that inheres in situating the relationship between the speaker and subject of the speech. It helps answer the questions: "Who said it and where was it said?" (Note that "where" is not narrowly geographic but also encompasses "under what circumstances"?)

Finally, "medium" is also a distinct conceptual bellwether for determining whether speech can be deemed incitement. It considers the means, timing, and agency of disseminating the speech, including the inherent propensity of certain outlets to trigger inflammatory chain reactions.[109] And it helps answer the question: "How was the speech delivered?"

The matrix of these categories, and their relationship to one another, can be seen in Figure 8.3.

E. Consideration of the Elements as a Whole and in Relation to One Another

Again, as within the evaluation of factors within the "context" criterion, there is no precise formula for how the elements must align with one another or be weighted collectively or individually to achieve critical mass in terms of a finding of direct and public incitement to commit genocide. Certain of the elements are straightforward in terms of the element being satisfied or not—public, direct, intent, temporality, and instrumentality. Others add or subtract to an incitement finding depending on how factors within them are evaluated—context, relationship between speaker and subject, and channel of communication. One could envisage, for example, that the first five elements were satisfied but a serious nonincitement skewing of evaluative factors within context, speaker-subject relationship, and communication channel could nevertheless result in a "nonincitement" finding. In this regard, context is arguably the most important single element, and its bifurcation into "internal" and "external" yields a more refined, free-speech-friendly analysis and thus more authoritative, policy-sensitive, and doctrinally sound conclusions.

109. Again, of course, one could credibly contend that there is overlap between and among these conceptual categories. "Medium," for example, could arguably be folded into the "Circumstances" category. But considering "Medium" on its own is useful as it draws attention to the significance of dissemination as a function of communications efficacy and individual criminal responsibility. Thus, in general, these conceptual categories strike the right balance between providing broad parameters of understanding and focusing on certain narrow characteristics that are distinct from one another.

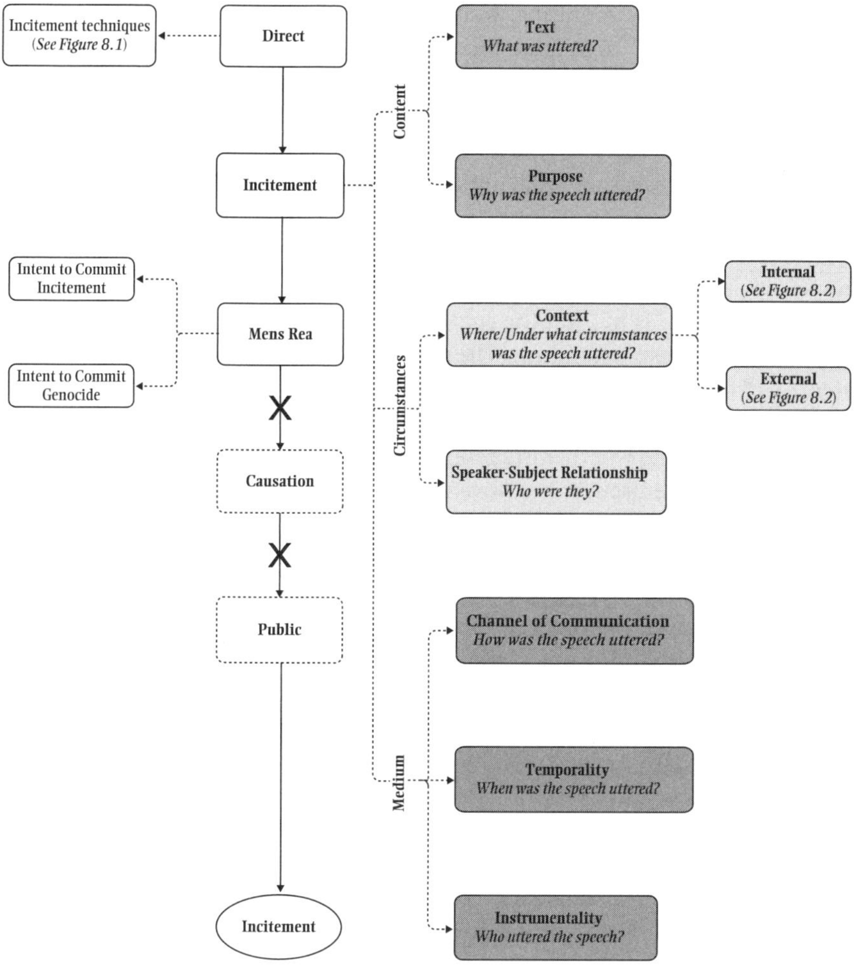

Figure 8.3 Elements of Incitement and Conceptual Categories under the Proposed Framework.

IV. APPLYING THE FRAMEWORK

Of course, the most policy-sensible and logically constructed framework will be of little value unless applied by courts. Apart from potential cases brought by the Residual Mechanism, the ICTR's work has concluded. But additional incitement prosecutions arising out of the Rwandan Genocide may still be pursued by Rwandan courts or domestic courts from other jurisdictions exercising universal jurisdiction.[110]

110. *Rwanda: International Criminal Tribunal Closing Its Doors: Governments Should Bring Remaining Genocide Suspects to Justice*, Human Rights Watch (Dec. 23, 2015), https://www.hrw.org/news/2015/12/23/rwanda-international-tribunal-closing-its-doors.

With respect to the municipal courts in Rwanda, the pending *Mugesera* case (currently on appeal) highlights the need for systematic and principled application of the recommended framework. And, appropriately enough, that case brings into relief many of the issues discussed in this chapter. For example, as seen in Chapter 5, Mugesera gave his infamous speech in November 1992. But the Rwandan Genocide did not begin until April 1994. Certain critics have argued that the gap in time between the late 1992 speech and the spring 1994 outbreak of genocide precludes a finding of incitement. But application of the elements in the ICTR framework, as set out in this book, reveals that approach would be misguided.[111]

The question is "What was the context *contemporaneous with* the speech?"—this should not entail examining the context on the ground seventeen months later. As chronicled in Chapter 1, there was arguably a genocidal environment in Rwanda in November 1992. We must consider both the internal context analysis (e.g., examining whether Mugesera had made similar previous speeches, as well as the tone he used in his November 1992 speech) as well as the external context evaluative factors (considering the government's contemporaneous persecutory campaign against the Tutsis, previous, but recent, outbreaks of violence following similar speech, and the capacity of his audience to commit genocidal violence). Of course, the court should not consider whether causal violence followed the speech (and, in fact, should explicitly renounce that approach). In short, this case calls for the kind of disciplined, step-by-step analysis and in-depth contextual parsing that complete and rigorous application of the framework entails.[112]

And, going forward, cases will certainly arise outside the Rwandan context and require the same approach. Whether those cases are heard by domestic courts via universal jurisdiction, by new ad hoc international or regional courts, or by the International Criminal Court itself, consistent application of the framework across national and international court systems will be paramount. And it will promote fairness, deterrence, and greater respect and understanding for this body of law.

V. CONCLUSION

While the types of incitement to genocide may be protean in nature, there is an elemental underlying nature of the offense that courts and experts have sought

111. And, in fact, Mugesera was convicted of incitement on April 15, 2016. *See* Stevenson Mugisha, *Mugesera Sent to Prison for Life*, THE RWANDA FOCUS (Apr. 15, 2016), http://www.focus.rw/wp/2016/04/mugesera-sent-to-prison-for-life/. But as the written decision is not available in English, the details regarding the exact grounds for conviction are not apparent. We will consider this further in the Conclusion.

112. As will be seen in the Conclusion, based on press accounts, in convicting Mugesera of incitement to genocide, among other crimes, it would appear that the Rwandan High Court did not take this approach. *See* Mugisha, *supra* note 111 (in announcing Mugesera's conviction, the judge noted that the defendant's incitement "*led to the 1994 genocide against the Tutsi.*") (emphasis added).

to define for nearly two decades. A notion as elusive as incitement should not be dealt with consistent with US Supreme Court Justice Potter Stewart's oft-quoted approach toward pornography: "I know it when I see it."[113] Nor can it be processed through a Procrustean analytic exercise that glosses over the unique traits and nuances of each exhortation and its contextual setting. The ICTR framework has instead adopted a Solomonic approach that mandates examination of certain core elements (purpose, text, context, and relationship between speaker and subject), but also allows jurists a relatively wide berth in applying them to each distinct fact pattern.

At the same time, further elucidation of certain elements will be essential for encouraging judges and other participants in the international legal system to perceive the framework's fundamental fairness and workability. This means clarifying the clash-of-legal-systems ambiguity that currently inheres in the "direct" element and incorporating the typology of incitement techniques outlined above. It also requires strongly explicit abandonment of the quasi-implied causation element that involves explaining why it was treated ambiguously in earlier jurisprudence. It equally demands refraining, in a very strict manner, from causation consideration in the factual analysis section of judicial opinions. Removing the indefinable "public" element, which has been applied inconsistently and runs afoul of incitement's fundamental policy concerns, would be a welcome development too.

As well, much can be done to fix the critical "incitement" element. First, consistent with the *Media Case* Trial Chamber's implicit suggestion in its judgment, "text" and "subject-speaker relationship" should be treated as separate, explicit criteria. Moreover, the evaluative factors examined earlier, such as political context, media environment, recent violence, and existence or imminent outbreak of armed violence, should be folded into the existing framework under the "external context" rubric. At the same time, the new criteria of channels of communication, temporality, and instrumentality will go a long way toward ensuring more refined and legally coherent analysis consistent with incitement's policy objectives of prevention, deterrence, punishment, and protection of free speech. Overall, these "incitement" element criteria can be understood as fitting with the larger conceptual categories of "content," "circumstances," and "medium," which help us answer the what, why, who, where, when, and how questions related to the speech so we can understand whether it should legally qualify as incitement.

Normative coherence, free expression, and nonviolence can certainly be harmonized within a maturing incitement framework. None of the nascent problems identified in Chapter 5 is by any means intractable or deep-seated. But the bad habits must be corrected now lest they become ingrained and incitement law degenerate permanently into a doctrinal tea-leaf-reading exercise. Under that scenario, repressive governments will continue to exploit incitement law for

113. Jacobellis v. Ohio, 378 U.S. 184, 197 (1964) (Stewart, J., concurring).

purposes of stifling legitimate speech, and would-be defendants will not be put on notice as to what constitutes incitement. Nor will lawyers or judges know how to apply the law. Neither free expression nor genocide prevention goals would be well served under such a scenario. There is still time to course-correct. It is hoped the suggestions in this chapter will serve as a roadmap for doing so promptly and effectively.

9

Fixing Persecution, Instigation, and Ordering

"From discord make harmony."

—Albert Einstein[1]

I. INTRODUCTION

Chapter 6 considered the jurisprudential disconnect between the International Criminal Tribunal for Rwanda (ICTR) and the International Criminal Tribunal for the former Yugoslavia (ICTY) regarding hate speech as the crime against humanity of persecution. Trial courts for the former took the position that crimes against humanity (persecution) could be committed even if the speaker did not explicitly call for violence against the victim group and there was no causally related subsequent violence (the Canadian Supreme Court in *Mugesera v. Canada* adopted the same approach). A trial court for the ICTY, in *Prosecutor v. Kordić*, however, rejected that position, holding that hate speech not directly calling for violence could not constitute persecution because it did not rise to the same level of gravity as the other enumerated crimes against humanity (CAH) acts, such as murder and rape. Then, in the *Media Case* Appeals Chamber judgment, the majority found that pure hate speech, if accompanied by separate calls for violence or actual violence, could give rise to CAH-persecution liability, but declined to rule on whether nonadvocacy hate speech, standing alone, is of a level of gravity equivalent to that of the other enumerated CAH crimes.

This chapter will consider the rift between the two ad hoc tribunals and opine as to which position makes better sense from a doctrinal and policy point of

1. William Safire & Leonard Safir, Words of Wisdom: More Good Advice 213 (1989) (citing Einstein's "Three Rules of Work").

view. Consistent with logic, good policy, and the relevant precedents, as well as the base requirements for crimes against humanity, it concludes that hate speech not directly calling for action should qualify as persecution.

We also saw in Chapter 6 that instigation has been plagued by some of the same linguistic and legal-culture-confusion problems as certain aspects of incitement. In particular, given a definitional overlap between French and English regarding the words "incitement" and "instigation," the two concepts, as well as their requirements, are often conflated in both the published judicial decisions and scholarly commentary. Moreover, recent jurisprudence has attempted to graft an unsupported, and unprecedented, "different forms of persuasion" requirement onto the crime's *actus reus* element. Further, the sloppy jurisprudence has allowed the offense's "contribution" requirement seemingly to be interpreted as a "but for" causation element, which runs afoul of the early cases that held no such absolute criterion attached to the offense.

This chapter will explain how the confusion between instigation and incitement can be cleared up. Essentially, as with the misperceived causation requirement in incitement, the decisions need to be explicit in acknowledging the problems, painstakingly distinguishing between incitement and instigation, and explaining how the policy concerns of the latter offense militate against saddling it with a draconian causation requirement. Similarly, the chapter will demonstrate that the new and illegitimate "different forms of persuasion" *actus reus* requirement can be cleanly excised with no adverse doctrinal consequences.

We also saw in Chapter 6 that ordering's restrictive target-crime-commission requirement unduly hampers the crime's enforcement potential. Based on sound policy and precedent, this chapter will explain why this requirement should be jettisoned so as to include inchoate liability within the offense's ambit.

II. FIXING HATE SPEECH AS CAH-PERSECUTION

A. Unresolved Issues from the Existing Jurisprudence

As we saw in Chapter 6, by the concluding lines of the *Media Case* Appeals Chamber judgment majority opinion, which could have resolved the ICTR-ICTY rift regarding the relationship between hate speech and CAH-persecution, mystery remained on various levels. True, some of the tricky issues had been resolved. For example, the Appeals Chamber had adopted the *Kupreškić* formulation of persecution as comprising "an act or omission which discriminates in fact and which: [(1)] denies or infringes upon a fundamental right laid down in international law or treaty law (the *actus reus*); and [(2)] was carried out deliberately with the intent to discriminate on one of the enumerated grounds, i.e., race, religion, or politics (the *mens rea*)."[2]

And in line with the ICTY jurisprudence, the *Media Case* Appeals Chamber held that not necessarily every discriminatory act, in itself, can constitute

2. Prosecutor v. Nahimana, Case No. ICTR-99-52-A, Judgement, ¶ 985 (Nov. 28, 2007).

persecution.[3] In particular, any underlying persecutory act, whether considered in isolation or in conjunction with other acts, must be equivalent in gravity to the other crimes enumerated in Article 3 of the ICTR Statute (equivalent to Article 5 of the ICTY Statute).[4] Still, the Chamber found, the underlying persecutory conduct does not have to equate to "crimes" as such in international law.[5]

Further, the Appeals Chamber ruled that "hate speech targeting a population on the basis of ethnicity, or any other discriminatory ground, violates the right to the respect for dignity of the targeted group as human beings, and therefore constitutes 'actual discrimination.'"[6] It also held that speech inciting to violence against a victim group on the enumerated discriminatory grounds violates the group members' right to security. So this also represents actual discrimination.[7] The Appeals Chamber acknowledged, however, that it was "not satisfied" that "hate speech alone can amount to a violation of the rights to life, freedom, and physical integrity of the human being."[8] That is to say that other persons must intervene before such violations can take place. In other words, in itself, a speech cannot "directly kill members of a group, imprison or physically injure them."[9] This seems somewhat of a truism—speech *qua* speech does not result in direct *physical* harm to listeners.

Yet while speech in itself does not visit physical harm on those who hear it, it may nonetheless, the Chamber allowed, lead to infringements of the rights of dignity or security.[10] Unfortunately, though, as we saw in Chapter 6, that was as far as the Chamber was prepared to go. In other words, at this critical point of the judgment's reasoning, the Appeals Chamber essentially punted. In particular, it offered no guidance as to whether "mere hate speeches not inciting violence against members of a group are of a level of gravity equivalent to that for other crimes against humanity."[11] Nevertheless, the judges suggested such speeches, in the proper context, could be considered equally grave:

> [I]t is not necessary that every individual act underlying the crime of persecution should be of a gravity corresponding to other crimes against humanity: underlying acts of persecution can be considered together. It is the cumulative effect of all the underlying acts of the crime of persecution which must reach a level of gravity equivalent to that for other crimes against

3. *Id.*

4. *Id.*

5. *Id.*

6. *Id.* at 986.

7. *Id.*

8. *Id.*

9. *Id.*

10. *Id.* ¶ 987.

11. *Id.*

humanity. Furthermore, the context in which these underlying acts take place is particularly important for the purpose of assessing their gravity.[12]

Apart from the explicitly unresolved issue of whether "hate speeches" not "inciting" violence are of a level of gravity comparable to the other CAH enumerated offenses, other implicit, but equally important, questions were yet to be resolved. Most crucially, and foundationally, what exactly is "hate speech" in the first place? Or, equally essential, what precisely does "incite" mean? To provide the proper analytic resolution, these bedrock issues must be addressed. And the next subpart will do that.

B. The Spectrum of Speech at Issue

1. Overview

The cases dealing with speech and persecution tend to bifurcate the former into two broad categories: (1) hate speech; and (2) speech that incites violence.[13] To the extent the distinction is meaningful, perhaps classifying either type of speech into finer analytic categories is called for. And this raises some threshold questions. Is it even proper to have two general but distinct groupings? Or might there be a spectrum of speech wherein, depending on other contextual factors, various points thereon might decide persecution liability? Given the capacious range of persecutory speech, the latter approach seems preferable. As one commentator has noted:

> [A] wide definition of hate speech would include group libel, or an attack on the dignity or reputation of a given group or individual. This would cover speech that is considered offensive regardless of whether it would lead to harmful results. A narrower definition of hate speech, however, would limit speech "that is intended to incite hatred or violence" against certain groups or individuals.[14]

For purposes of this analysis, let us begin with a bird's-eye view and posit that all relevant speech should be considered "hate speech." The free-expression-focused nongovernmental organization "Article 19" defines "hate speech" as "expression which is abusive, insulting, intimidating, harassing and/or which incites violence, hatred or discrimination against groups identified by a specific

12. *Id.*

13. *See* Gregory S. Gordon, *From Incitement to Indictment? Prosecuting Iran's President for Advocating Israel's Destruction and Piecing Together Incitement Law's Emerging Analytical Framework*, 98 J. Crim. L. & Criminology 853, 886–90 (2008) [hereinafter *From Incitement to Indictment*] (analyzing this in the context of the *Ruggiu* case and the *Media Case*).

14. Onder Bakircioglu, *Freedom of Expression and Hate Speech*, 16 Tulsa J. Comp. & Int'l L. 1, 4 (2008).

set of characteristics."[15] The Council of Europe's Committee of Ministers has indicated that the term "hate speech" includes: "All forms of expression which spread, incite, promote or justify racial hatred, xenophobia, anti-Semitism or other forms of hatred based on intolerance, including intolerance expressed by aggressive nationalism and ethnocentrism, discrimination and hostility towards minorities, migrants and people of immigrant origin."[16]

Thus, incitement can be logically classified as a subset of hate speech falling on a certain point along the spectrum of hate speech, and not a completely separate conceptual category of speech in itself.[17] It would behoove us, then, to consider exactly where we would find the major points, including incitement, along this gamut of speech.

2. General Hate Speech

As a starting point, we would find the mildest forms of hate speech—broad forms of discourse generally casting aspersions on a group.[18] Such expression could be effectuated via repetition of rhetoric that conveys stereotypical racial, ethnic, or religious denigration. This could include group libel, that is, verbally assaulting or slandering a vulnerable minority and thereby likely subjecting its members to enhanced levels of rancor and/or physical aggression.[19] Such expression would consist of general statements not necessarily targeting one specific person. Within its ambit, one could find more diluted forms of verminization (characterizing group members as parasitic, pestilent subhuman creatures such as lice or locusts or similar creatures), pathologization (equating the group with disease), demonization (associating the group with satanic or other comparably evil qualities), or other forms of dehumanization (such as describing the group as dirt, scum, excrement, or other repulsive substances).[20]

15. Article 19, *Policy Brief: Prohibiting Incitement to Discrimination, Hostility or Violence*, at 5 (Dec. 2012), https://www.article19.org/data/files/medialibrary/3548/ARTICLE-19-policy-on-prohibition-to-incitement.pdf.

16. Committee of Ministers Recommendation, Oct. 30 1997. This definition was referred to by the European Court of Human Rights in Gündüz v. Turkey, Application No. 35071/97, Judgement, ¶¶ 43, 22 (Dec. 4, 2004).

17. *See* Michael Rosenfeld, *Hate Speech in Constitutional Jurisprudence*, *in* Content and Context of Hate Speech: Rethinking Regulation and Responses 242, 281 (Michael Herz & Peter Molnar eds., 2012) ("Not all hate speech is alike, and its consequences may vary from one setting to another.").

18. *See* Phyllis B. Gerstenfeld, Hate Crimes: Causes, Controls and Controversies 35 (2010) (defining hate speech as "words or symbols that are derogatory or offensive on the basis of race, religion, sexual orientation, and so on").

19. *See* Kent Greenfield, *Group Libel Laws*, *in* Dictionary of American History (Stanley I. Kutler ed., 3d ed. 2003).

20. *See* Chapter 8, Section III.B.2 (setting forth typology of incitement techniques); Gregory S. Gordon, *Music and Genocide: Harmonizing Coherence, Freedom and Nonviolence in Incitement Law*, 50 Santa Clara L. Rev. 607, 639–41 (2010) [hereinafter *Music and Genocide*] (categorizing incitement techniques).

3. Harassment

Positioned further toward the other end of the range, speech voiced *directly* at out-group members can be classified as "harassment."[21] These communications would target the group as a whole (e.g., "You have no reason to exist in this society," or, "You are hated demons") or to particular individuals (e.g., "You bloodthirsty animals of the Kicukiro neighborhood belong in a zoo, not walking freely on our streets. You are ruining our city").[22] A good example of this was featured in this book's Introduction, which chronicled the Janjaweed militia chanting to victims in Darfur lines such as

> "You make this area dirty; we are here to clean the area."
> "You blacks are like monkeys. You are not human."[23]

4. Incitement

Moving along the same trajectory on the spectrum, the next significant demarcation point would be incitement, that is, advocacy directed toward third persons.[24] This is communication meant to inspire listeners to take action against the

21. *See* Norman E. Bowie & Robert L. Simon, The Individual and the Political Order: An Introduction to Social and Political Philosophy 136 (4th ed. 1998) (labeling speech at specifically targeted persons as a type of harassment).

22. As Chapter 2 suggests, even in the world's most speech-protective country, the United States, such speech might be deemed "fighting words," not meriting First Amendment protection. Per the US Supreme Court:

> There are certain well-defined and narrowly limited classes of speech, the prevention and punishment of which has never been thought to raise any Constitutional problem. These include . . . the insulting or "fighting" words . . . . It has been well observed that such utterances are no essential part of any exposition of ideas, and are of such slight social value as a step to truth that any benefit that may be derived from them is clearly outweighed by the social interest in order and morality.

Beauharnais v. Illinois, 343 U.S. 250, 255–57 (1952). Likewise, speech urging third parties to engage in illicit acts in the United States is not afforded First Amendment protection if its goal is "imminent" lawless action and it is reasonably likely to provoke such lawless action imminently. *See* Brandenburg v. Ohio, 395 U.S. 444, 447 (1969) (ruling that speech exhorting lawless action is protected unless it is "directed to inciting or producing imminent lawless action and is likely to incite or produce such action"). As a result, considering the parallel to municipal laws, it makes sense that incitement, next along the spectrum after harassment, should also be deemed more grave than general hate speech. Staying within the US framework, of these categories of communication, only general hate speech would most likely find complete constitutional protection.

23. David Livingstone Smith, *Dehumanization, Genocide, and the Psychology of Indifference*, Psychology Today (Dec. 2, 2011), http://www.psychologytoday.com/blog/philosophy-dispatches/201112/dehumanization-genocide-and-the-psychology-indifference-0.

24. *See* Ian Leigh, *Homophobic Speech, Equality Denial, and Religious Expression*, *in* Extreme Speech and Democracy 375, 379 (Ivan Hare & James Weinstein eds., 2010).

out-group.[25] We can bifurcate this sort of speech into two categories: (1) incitement toward nonviolent action; and (2) incitement toward violent action.[26] With respect to the former, three types of relevant, general nonviolent speech categories can be discerned: (1) incitement to hatred; (2) incitement to discrimination; and (3) incitement to persecution.[27]

a. Incitement to Hatred, Discrimination, and Persecution

Incitement to hatred means exhorting listeners or readers to cultivate a general opprobrium for the target group.[28] It is akin to group libel but takes a more active tone in urging audience contempt for the intended victims.[29] Simon Bikindi's song *Njyewe Nanga Abahutu* ("I Hate the Hutu"), for instance, pointedly urged extremist Hutus to cultivate extreme contempt for moderate Hutus who gave encouragement and assistance to Tutsis in the lead-up to the genocide (both moderate Hutus and Tutsis were victim groups during this period).[30]

Incitement to discrimination consists of beseeching listeners or readers to oppress the victim group in certain nonviolent ways.[31] Examples include calling on the audience to refuse providing the target group with medical treatment or service in restaurants or to discourage marriage with target group members. Illustrative, in this regard, is a Nazi pamphlet disseminated to German adolescents cautioning them not to "mix" with Jewish people or marry them for fear of race "defilement."[32]

Incitement to persecution is incitement to discrimination in a more intensified and methodical form.[33] It is speech seeking blanket exclusion of the target group from enjoyment of economic, social, cultural, and civil rights.[34] In the early 1990s, on the eve of the Rwandan Genocide, for instance, Hassan Ngeze

25. *Id.*

26. *Id.*

27. *Id.* (analyzing the divisions of incitement category within the framework of the Netherlands Criminal Code).

28. *See* Wibke Timmermann, *The Relationship Between Hate Propaganda and Incitement to Genocide: A New Trend in International Law toward Criminalization of Hate Propaganda*, 18 LEIDEN J. INT'L L. 257, 276 (2005).

29. *Id.*

30. *See* Gordon, *Music and Genocide*, *supra* note 20, at 618 ("These songs allegedly characterized Tutsis as 'Hutu enslavers, enemies or enemy accomplices.'").

31. *See* Wibke Timmermann, *supra* note 28, at 575–76 (explaining how incitement dehumanizes out-groups and excludes the possibility of empathy with such groups).

32. *See You and Your People: Your Marriage and Your Children*, GERMAN PROPAGANDA ARCHIVE, http://www.calvin.edu/academic/cas/gpa/du.htm (last visited Sept. 18, 2016).

33. *See* David L. Neressian, *Comparative Approaches to Punishing Hate: The Intersection of Genocide and Crimes Against Humanity*, 43 STAN. J. INT'L L. 221, 263 (2007) (describing persecution as discrimination on a widespread or systematic basis).

34. *Id.*

published in *Kangura* the infamous "Ten Commandments of the Hutu" in a 1990 issue of *Kangura*. One expert has characterized this tract as a call for "Hutus to separate themselves from the Tutsis."[35] In fact, it was an appeal for complete marginalization of Tutsis in Rwanda: (1) Hutu males must not have close personal or work relations with Tutsi women; (2) Hutu women are superior to Tutsi women; (3) Hutu women must fraternize only with Hutu men; (4) Tutsis are dishonest, and no Hutu should conduct business with them; (5) all high-level positions in society should be occupied by Hutus only; (6) the education sector should be majority Hutu; (7) the military must be exclusively Hutu; (8) the Hutus should stop having mercy on the Tutsis; (9) all Hutus must have unity and solidarity; and (10) the ideology of the 1959 and 1961 revolution (when many Tutsis were disenfranchised, forced to leave Rwanda, or massacred) must be taught to Hutus at all levels.[36]

b. Incitement to Violence

Incitement to violence is yet another important subcategory. There are two kinds—explicit and nonexplicit.[37]

i. Nonexplicit

As incitement to violence is routinely accomplished via code, nonexplicit calls are rather ordinary.[38] William Schabas has noted that inciters "speak in euphemisms."[39]

These nonexplicit techniques, largely overlapping with the nonovert incitement methods considered in Chapter 8, can be protean in nature and include: (1) predictions of destruction (in the *Media Case* Trial Chamber judgment, for example, certain Radio Télévision Libre des Milles Collines (RTLM) broadcasts that prophesied destruction of the Tutsis were among those transmissions found to constitute incitement);[40] (2) so-called "accusation in a mirror" (i.e., imputing to the victim the desire to perpetrate the same offenses that the actual criminal is perpetrating, as in Léon Mugesera's November 1992 speech: "These people called *Inyenzis* are now on their way to attack us." "They

35. *The Path to Genocide*, United Nations, http://www.un.org/en/preventgenocide/rwanda/text-images/Panel%20Set%202%20Low%20Res.pdf.

36. *See* 1 Samuel Totten & Paul Bartrop, Dictionary of Genocide 200 (2008).

37. *See* Gordon, *Music and Genocide, supra* note 20, at 638–39 (noting the difference between explicitly calling for violence and more indirect methods of predicting violence).

38. *Id.* at 638–44.

39. William A. Schabas, *Mugesera v. Minister of Citizenship and Immigration*, 93 Am. J. Int'l L. 529, 530 (1999) (speaking of incitement to genocide).

40. Prosecutor v. Nahimana, Case No. ICTR-99-52-T, Judgement and Sentence, ¶ 405 (Dec. 3, 2003) ("Thus when day breaks, when that day comes, we will be heading for a brighter future, for the day when we will be able to say 'There isn't a single *Inyenzi* left in the country.'").

only want to exterminate us.");[41] (3) euphemisms and metaphors (during the Rwandan Genocide, for instance, "go to work," a typical extermination directive, meant "kill Tutsis");[42] (4) justification during contemporaneous violence (i.e., characterizing atrocity already under way such that it persuades listeners the crimes are morally defensible—to potentially complicit German citizens, for instance, Hitler's henchmen emphasized the "humaneness" of their extermination, torture, death marches, slavery, and other mass crimes);[43] (5) condoning and congratulating past violence (Georges Ruggiu, taking a page from the standard RTLM playbook, would congratulate the "valiant combatants" who engaged in a "battle" against Tutsi civilians);[44] (6) posing questions about violence (for example, Simon Bikindi asked Hutu militia over a truck loudspeaker if they had killed Tutsis and whether they had killed the "snakes");[45] and (7) more virulent forms of verminization, pathologization, demonization, or other forms of dehumanization (Ruggiu acknowledged, for instance, that the term *inyenzi*, as employed in reference to Tutsis within genocidal Rwanda's sociopolitical context, took on the meaning of "persons to be killed").[46]

ii. Explicit

Reaching the far end of the spectrum, explicit appeals for violence represent the most dangerous type of incitement. Although somewhat rare in the mass-atrocity context, in the popular imagination this is the archetypal speech responsible for fomenting mass murder. A chilling instance is Kantano Habimana's June 4, 1994, RTLM broadcast during which he asked the audience to exterminate the "Inkotanyi," or Tutsis, who would be known by height and physical appearance.[47] Habimana then concluded: "Just look at his small nose and then break

41. Mugesera v. Canada, 2005 SCC 40, [2005] 2 S.C.R. 100, ¶¶ 18, 69; Kenneth L. Marcus, *Accusation in a Mirror*, 43 Loy. U. Chi. L.J. 357, 359 (2012); *see also* Gordon, *Music and Genocide, supra* note 20, at 641–42.

42. *See, e.g.*, Prosecutor v. Ruggiu, Case No. ICTR-97-32-I, Judgement and Sentence, ¶ 44(iv) (June 1, 2000) (noting that over the passage of time, "go to work" meant "go kill the Tutsis and Hutu political opponents of the interim government"); *see also* Gordon, *Music and Genocide, supra* note 20, at 642 (noting that "go to work" meant "go kill the Tutsis").

43. *See* 3 Raul Hilberg, The Destruction of the European Jews 1010 (1961); Gordon, *Music and Genocide, supra* note 20, at 642.

44. *Ruggiu*, Case No. ICTR-97-32-I, ¶ 44(v); Prosecutor v. Niyitegeka, Case No. ICTR-96-14-T, Judgement and Sentence, ¶ 142 (May 16, 2003); *see also* Gordon, *Music and Genocide, supra* note 20, at 642–43.

45. Prosecutor v. Bikindi, Case No. ICTR-01-72-T, Judgement, ¶ 423 (Dec. 2, 2008); *see also* Gordon, *Music and Genocide, supra* note 20, at 643.

46. *Ruggiu*, Case No. ICTR-97-32-I, ¶ 44(iii); *see also* Gordon, *Music and Genocide, supra* note 20, at 639–41.

47. Prosecutor v. Nahimana, Case No. ICTR-99-52-T, Judgement and Sentence, ¶ 396 (Dec. 3, 2003).

it."[48] Iranian President Mahmoud Ahmadinejad furnished another ominous example. It will be recalled that in October 2005 he advocated Israel's destruction, telling the Iranian people that Israel "must be wiped off the map."[49]

The gradations of inflammatory rhetoric just described are summarized in Figure 9.1, "The Spectrum of Hate Speech," found at the end of this chapter, on page 347.

C. Hate Speech as an *Actus Reus* for CAH-Persecution

Now equipped with a more granular and accurate hate speech typology, we can better consider the question the *Media Case* Appeals Chamber judgment failed to tackle: may hate speech not explicitly calling for violence constitute the *actus reus* for CAH-persecution? Based on a review of CAH's chapeau elements, as well as the relevant jurisprudence and characteristics of the persecution offense itself, that question must be answered in the affirmative.

1. Considering the CAH Chapeau

a. Widespread or Systematic Attack

It is in the chapeau of crimes against humanity that one finds the most compelling grounds for concluding that speech alone could qualify as CAH-persecution. The chief consideration here is that a precondition for CAH is a "*widespread* or *systematic attack* against any *civilian* population."[50] Therefore, it is a nonstarter to consider whether any underlying actions can be the basis of crimes against humanity charges unless those actions link to a situation where civilians are being victimized by large-scale or well-planned lawlessness. ICTY jurisprudence instructs that an "attack" is a "course of conduct involving the commission of acts of violence."[51] Even if those attacks are not characterized by

48. *Id.*

49. *See* Nazila Fathi, *Iran's New President Says Israel Must Be "Wiped off the Map,"* N.Y. Times, Oct. 27, 2005, at A8. Some analysts have noted that this does not rise to the level of direct and public incitement to commit genocide. *See, e.g.*, Susan Benesch, *Vile Crime or Inalienable Right: Defining Incitement to Genocide*, 48 Va. J. Int'l L. 485, 490–91 (2008) ("Ahmadinejad's speech was reprehensible and perhaps even dangerous, but did not constitute incitement to genocide, in my view."). But given Iran's support of terrorist attacks against Israel during that time, it may have constituted CAH-persecution. *See, e.g.*, Gordon, *From Incitement to Indictment, supra* note 13, at 880–82 (2008).

50. *See* Stuart Ford, *Is the Failure to Respond Appropriately to a Natural Disaster a Crime Against Humanity? The Responsibility to Protect and Individual Criminal Responsibility in the Aftermath of Cyclone Nargis*, 38 Denv. J. Int'l L. & Pol'y 227, 255 (2010) ("It is now generally agreed that the customary international law definition of crimes against humanity requires that crimes against humanity take place in connection with a widespread or systematic attack on a civilian population.").

51. Prosecutor v. Limaj, Case No. IT-03-66-T, Judgement, ¶ 182 (Int'l Crim. Trib. for the Former Yugoslavia Nov. 30, 2005); Prosecutor v. Blagojević, Case No. IT-02-60-T, Judgement, ¶ 543 (Int'l Crim. Trib. for the Former Yugoslavia Jan. 17, 2005); Prosecutor v. Brđanin, Case No. IT-99-36-T, Judgement, ¶ 131 (Int'l Crim. Trib. for the Former Yugoslavia Sept. 1, 2004); Prosecutor v. Galić, Case No. IT-98-29-T, Judgement, ¶ 141 (Int'l Crim. Trib. for the Former Yugoslavia Dec. 5, 2003).

physical violence, they will, at a minimum, entail "inhumane mistreatment of the civilian population."[52]

b. State Agency or the Equivalent

And, from an empirical perspective, state agents, or the equivalent, tend to be the perpetrators of the attack.[53] As William Schabas has observed in respect of the cases before the international tribunals: "Essentially all prosecutions have involved offenders acting on behalf of a State and in accordance with a State policy, or those acting on behalf of an organization that was State-like in its attempts to exercise control over territory and seize political power . . . ."[54] Additionally, the International Criminal Court (ICC) Statute unambiguously requires that the wider attack be in accordance with or in furtherance of a state or organizational policy involving the multiple commission of enumerated CAH acts.[55]

c. The Defendant's Knowledge

Moreover, as is true for other crimes against humanity, making out a successful prima facie case of persecution implicitly requires meeting the chapeau element

52. *Galić*, Case No. IT-98-29-T, ¶ 257.

53. Even if the ICTY Statute, for instance, "implicitly requires that crimes against humanity arise from an official state action or policy," that Tribunal has concluded that *state* policy is not a requirement of crimes against humanity. Cristin B. Coan, *Rethinking the Spoils of War: Prosecuting Rape as a War Crime in the International Criminal Tribunal for the Former Yugoslavia*, 26 N.C. J. INT'L L. & COM. REG. 183, 200 (2000); *see also* Prosecutor v. Jelisić, Case No. IT-95-10-T, Judgement, ¶ 100 (Int'l Crim. Trib. for the Former Yugoslavia Dec. 14, 1999), *aff'd*, Case No. IT-95-10-A, Judgement (Int'l Crim. Trib. for the Former Yugoslavia July 5, 2001).

54. William A. Schabas, *State Policy as an Element of International Crimes*, 98 J. CRIM. L. & CRIMINOLOGY 953, 954 (2008). *But see* Prosecutor v. Kunarac, Case No. IT-96-23/1-A, Judgement, ¶ 98 n.114 (Int'l Crim. Trib. for the Former Yugoslavia June 12, 2002) (defendant found guilty of crimes against humanity related to the detention and rape of female civilians, where the *chapeau* attack was carried out by members of an organized paramilitary group, not state agents per se); Situation in the Republic of Kenya, Situation No. ICC-01/09, Decision Pursuant to Article 15 of the Rome Statute on the Authorization of an Investigation into the Situation in the Republic of Kenya, ¶¶ 116–128, ICC Doc. ICC-01/09-19 (Mar. 31, 2010) (post-election violence was committed not by "an organization with state-like qualities" but by "an amorphous or private group of individuals whose principal distinguishing feature . . . turned on its ability to perpetrate vile acts."). But even when non-state actors are involved, the perpetrators may exercise authority in the immediate local sphere where the attack occurs. Thus, in the Kenya matter just cited to, the attack involved participation of local political and business leaders). *Id.* The point is that, as will be discussed in the next subsection, in the area where the attack is taking place, its perpetrators, even if non-state actors, may have control of media outlets such that the marketplace of ideas ceases to function. But, if that is not true, the case for prosecuting the speech at issue may be less compelling. This potential scenario will be discussed in Section II.D of this chapter.

55. Rome Statute of the International Criminal Court art. 7(2)(a), July 17, 1998, 2178 U.N.T.S. 3 (entered into force July 1, 2002) [hereinafter Rome Statute].

that the defendant was *aware* that his conduct was part of the widespread or systematic attack.[56] In accord with the relevant jurisprudence, then, any speech that is the basis of a CAH-persecution charge must be consciously uttered in service of a state, or state-like, campaign to subject a civilian population to violence or other types of inhumane treatment. This point must be underscored in relation to cases before the ICC, as the Rome Statute specifies that persecution must be perpetrated in connection with any other enumerated CAH act or any crime within the jurisdiction of the Court.[57]

d. Elimination of the Marketplace of Ideas and Other Free-Speech Rationales

In state-initiated or state-endorsed persecution programs, such as those carried out in 1994 Rwanda or in the early-1990s Balkans, the media are almost always government-monopolized and are not available to air victim- or minority-group dissent. Joseph Keeler notes that, as regards both the Rwandan and Balkan 1990s paroxysms of violence, "the head of state either had complete or at least significant control over the media."[58] In such situations, government-controlled media represent just one more weapon in a managed campaign directed at the victim civilian population.

As another commentator points out, mass-atrocity perpetrators "typically have overwhelming, state-sponsored access to the means of broadcasting or other media distribution. This sort of access would be impossible for an individual with a soapbox or even a website."[59] While this is globally true in respect of crimes against humanity, it is particularly true of persecution, which, based on the genesis and development of the offense, Cherif Bassiouni has characterized as "*State action or policy* leading to the infliction upon an individual of . . . physical or mental suffering."[60]

Even the most zealous guardians of free expression would likely shrink at the prospect of condoning this sort of state-manufactured speech in service of mass-atrocity campaigns (even if only generalized hate speech or harassment were at

56. *See* Mikol Sirkin, *Expanding the Crime of Genocide To Include Ethnic Cleansing: A Return to Established Principles in Light of Contemporary Interpretations*, 33 Seattle U. L. Rev. 489, 499 (2010).

57. Rome Statute, *supra* note 55, art. 7(1)(h).

58. Joseph A. Keeler, *Genocide: Prevention through Nonmilitary Measures*, 171 Mil. L. Rev. 135, 184 (2002); *see also* Ameer F. Gopalani, *The International Standard of Direct and Public Incitement To Commit Genocide: An Obstacle to U.S. Ratification of the International Criminal Court Statute?*, 32 Cal. W. Int'l L.J. 87, 97 (noting that in Rwanda, "the government controlled the media").

59. Benesch, *supra* note 49, at 496. As the title of this article suggests, it focused on the particular characteristics of incitement to commit genocide. But the same logic applies with equal force to the context of a widespread or systematic attack against a civilian population.

60. M. Cherif Bassiouni, Crimes against Humanity in International Criminal Law 327 (2d rev. ed. 1999).

issue, and not direct appeals to inflict physical harm on the victim group). Judge Theodore Meron's partial dissent in the *Media Case* Appeals Chamber judgment, as we saw in Chapter 6, was premised almost exclusively on an American doctrinal ethos that promotes the "benefit of protecting political dissent."[61] Alluding to the US Constitution and decisions putting gloss on its First Amendment, Judge Meron stressed that the "government may not prohibit the expression of an idea simply because society finds the idea itself offensive or disagreeable."[62]

But the normative underpinnings of the American jurisprudence relied on by Judge Meron assume the existence of a society with open and accessible channels of communication or, put in slightly different words, that allows dissemination of minority or antiestablishment discourse. Regarding open channels of communication, as we saw in Chapter 2, Justice Oliver Wendell Holmes Jr. postulated in his seminal dissent in *Abrams v. United States*[63] that "the theory of our Constitution" is "that the ultimate good desired is better reached by free trade in ideas [because] the best test of truth is the power of the thought to get itself accepted in the competition of the market."[64] As for the tolerance-of-dissent rationale, in *Texas v. Johnson*[65] the US Supreme Court "reaffirmed that the core purpose of the First Amendment is to protect political dissent."[66] One commentator has observed that "U.S. free-speech doctrine" is not germane in the mass-atrocity context because the "marketplace of ideas" theory loses its currency.[67] "U.S. law protects odious and even violent speech," this commentator continues, "in the belief that 'bad' speech will eventually be neutralized by 'good' speech."[68] But by the time mass atrocity is unfolding, she concludes, "there is such a disproportion in access to the means of disseminating information that protests by the targeted group, or even by sympathizers among the audience, would be extremely unlikely" to stop the bad speech.[69]

Similarly, other rationales proffered in defense of the most vigorous free-speech protections, and explored in depth in Chapter 2, are not implicated in the sociopolitical or communications landscape of the crimes against humanity context. For instance, logic and common sense dictate that "free speech as an essential element of democratic governance, providing citizens with the necessary

61. *See* Prosecutor v. Nahimana, Case No. ICTR-99-52-A, Judgement, ¶ 11 (Nov. 28, 2007) (Meron, J., partly dissenting).

62. *Id.* (citing Texas v. Johnson, 491 U.S. 397, 414 (1989); Brandenburg v. Ohio, 395 U.S. 444, 447 (1969); Watts v. United States, 394 U.S. 705, 708 (1969)).

63. Abrams v. United States, 250 U.S. 616, 630 (1919) (Holmes, J., dissenting).

64. *Id.*

65. *Johnson*, 491 U.S. 397 (1989).

66. United States v. Haggerty, 731 F. Supp. 415, 422 (W.D. Wash. 1990).

67. Benesch, *supra* note 49, at 496.

68. *Id.*

69. *Id.*

information to exercise their civic duties,"[70] or making "a vital contribution to personal autonomy, individual self-expression, and diversity of lifestyle"[71] will not be present in a society suffering a government-sponsored, widespread, or systematic attack against a civilian population.[72] This is speech stripped entirely of Meiklejohnian trappings.

As Faustin Pocar has noted with regard to "limitations on freedom of expression":

> It has been argued that [hate speech as a basis for persecution] conflates hate speech with incitement to violent crimes and makes protected speech an element of the crime of persecution. I disagree with such a view. With all due respect, I believe that this approach does not, among other things . . . adequately address the power of propaganda to incite when it takes place in situations of extended discrimination with an ethnic component. . . .
>
> . . .
>
> [Moreover,] *the existence of stringent general requirements for crimes against humanity, such as the need for a widespread or systematic attack against the civilian population*, warrants the conclusion that offensive or otherwise disagreeable speech will generally not form the basis for a conviction of this type.

70. Robert Wheeler Lane, Beyond the Schoolhouse Gate: Free Speech and the Inculcation of Values 50 (1995). This is consistent with the views of philosopher Alexander Meiklejohn that we examined in Chapter 2. *Id.* Justice Brandeis also conveyed this view in his *Whitney v. California* concurrence, also considered in Chapter 2:

> Those who won our independence believed that the final end of the state was to make men free to develop their faculties, and that in its government the deliberative forces should prevail over the arbitrary. . . . They believed that freedom to think as you will and to speak as you think are means indispensable to the discovery and spread of political truth . . . .

Whitney v. California, 274 U.S. 357, 375 (1927) (Brandeis, J., concurring).

71. Lane, *supra* note 70, at 51.

72. In dissecting the *Media Case* Trial Chamber judgment, Diane Orentlicher implicitly made common cause with Judge Meron's position in his partial dissent in the *Media Case* Appeals Chamber judgment. *See* Diane E. Orentlicher, *Criminalizing Hate Speech in the Crucible of Trial*: Prosecutor v. Nahimana, 12 New Eng. J. Int'l & Comp. L. 17, 39–40 (2005). Unfortunately, Professor Orentlicher grounded her conclusions on the same flawed assumption as Judge Meron: that the ICTR was adjudicating the issue of whether hate speech not explicitly calling for violence, *in the abstract*, should be proscribed. Even though she acknowledged that the case for criminalization makes "powerful and deeply compelling claims," *id.* at 43, she rejected the ICTR's approach because, in her view, mere hate speech not calling for violence signifies that no international crime is implicated. And therefore an international court should not entertain charges arising out of such speech. Given that the speech is the basis for crimes against humanity charges, however, Professor Orentlicher fails to recognize that the speech must be linked to a widespread or systematic attack directed against a civilian population. Thus, an international crime is, by definition, implicated and is appropriately the object of international adjudication. Relatedly, it takes the contention concerning free expression out of the realm of American assumptions related to exercise of disagreeable

Only in extreme situations will some types of speech be considered underlying acts of persecution.[73]

2. The Elements of Persecution

The elements of persecution itself similarly lend credence to the idea that speech can serve as its *actus reus*. It will be recalled that per the *Kupreškić* test, persecution's *actus reus* must consist of (1) a gross or blatant denial; (2) on discriminatory grounds; (3) of a fundamental right, laid down in international customary or treaty law; and (4) reaching the same level of gravity as the other crimes against humanity enumerated in Article 5 of the ICTY Statute.[74] We saw in Chapter 6 that the *Kordić* judgment found speech wanting with respect to the third and fourth limbs of this test (and arguably, by implication, the first limb).[75]

a. Prong 3 of the *Kupreškić* Test

In respect of the third limb of the *Kupreškić* test, the *Kordić* Chamber found that hate speech not explicitly urging violence did not rise to the level of a fundamental rights infringement based entirely on a review of some treaties that regulate speech on a *domestic* level.[76] Because, as seen in Chapter 2, a very small number of nations, most prominently the United States, have voiced reservations in terms of criminalizing mere hate speech in their municipal statutes, *Kordić* deduced from the lack of unanimity that infringement of a fundamental right was not implicated.[77] But grounding the analysis on lack of consensus regarding *domestic* speech laws in the *garden-variety* crime context was entirely misplaced.[78] To be precise, persecution does not entail criminalization of hate speech

expression—persecutory hate speech charged in ICL cases is typically government-initiated and -controlled rhetoric and in service of a criminal enterprise. Therefore, it should not be lumped in with the sort of speech that gave rise to the great Holmes/Brandeis dissents/concurrences or the Nazi speech at issue in the *Brandenburg* decision.

73. Fausto Pocar, *Persecution as a Crime under International Criminal Law*, 2 J. Nat'l Sec. L. & Pol'y 355, 360–61 (2008).

74. Prosecutor v. Kupreškić, Case No. IT-95-16-T, Judgement, ¶ 621 (Int'l Crim. Trib. for the Former Yugoslavia Jan. 14, 2000).

75. Prosecutor v. Kordić, Case No. IT-95-14/2-T, Judgement, ¶ 209 n.272 (Int'l Crim. Trib. for the Former Yugoslavia Feb. 26, 2001).

76. *Id.*

77. *Id.*

78. To be fair, the ICTR has taken the same flawed approach by observing generally that hate speech is not protected speech under international law (referring to the International Covenant on Civil and Political Rights and the International Convention on the Elimination of All Forms of Racial Discrimination) or in most domestic criminal codes such as those of Rwanda, Vietnam, Russia, Finland, Ireland, Ukraine, Iceland, Monaco, Slovenia, and China. *See* Prosecutor v. Nahimana, Case No. ICTR-99-52-T, Judgement and Sentence, ¶¶ 1075–76 (Dec. 3, 2003). Again, considering such garden-variety domestic criminal laws without regard to the chapeau elements of crimes against humanity terribly skews the analysis.

in the everyday municipal setting. Rather, as explained in Chapters 4 and 6, its focus is hate speech uttered as part of a widespread or systematic attack directed against a civilian population.

And the *Kordić* adjudicators exacerbated the ills of this flawed approach by examining "speech" alone—in a vacuum, in the abstract: "The Trial Chamber, however, finds that this act, as alleged in the Indictment, does not by itself constitute persecution as a crime against humanity."[79] Incongruously though, the *Kordić* Chamber elsewhere noted "the unique nature of the crime of persecution as a crime of cumulative effect."[80] Citing *Kupreškić*, it pointed out that "acts of persecution must be evaluated not in isolation but in context, by looking at their cumulative effect. Although individual acts may not be inhumane, their overall consequences must offend humanity in such a way that they may be termed 'inhumane.'"[81]

Further, in any case before the ICC, pursuant to Article 7(1)(h) of that Court's statute, persecution must take place "in connection with any act referred to in this paragraph or any crime within the jurisdiction of the Court."[82] Hence, on top of the chapeau's already tethering the speech to a widespread or systematic attack against a civilian population involving the multiple commission of enumerated CAH acts and pursuant to a state or organizational policy, Article 7(1)(h) yokes the speech even more closely to inhumane treatment by grafting it onto yet another offense within the ICC's subject-matter jurisdiction. This could be either another enumerated crime against humanity, such as murder, extermination, enslavement, torture, or rape, or another major core offense, such as genocide or war crimes. Discourse in service of such crimes unmistakably involves violation of a fundamental right, laid down in international customary or treaty law. This conclusion is all the more forceful since "the Rome Statute is widely accepted and was intended to provide a collation of existing customary international law prohibitions, [and] so 'represents compelling evidence of the customary international law of crimes against humanity'."[83]

79. Prosecutor v. Kordić, Case No. IT-95-14/2-T, Judgement, ¶ 209 (Int'l Crim. Trib. for the Former Yugoslavia Feb. 26, 2001).

80. *Id.* ¶ 199.

81. *Id.*

82. Rome Statute, *supra* note 55, art. 7(1)(h).

83. Adriaan Barnard, *Slegs Suid Afrikaners—South Africans Only? A Review and Evaluation of the International Crime of Apartheid*, 7 N.Z. J. Pub. & Int'l L. 317, 355 (2009) (citations omitted). Professor Margaret deGuzman observes that, although the Rome Statute "does not purport to crystallize the international law of crimes against humanity," "[n]onetheless, [its] definition is the only one that has been adopted by a large segment of the world's states." Margaret M. deGuzman, *Crimes against Humanity*, *in* Routledge Handbook of International Criminal Law 126 (William A. Schabas & Nadia Bernaz eds., 2011); *see also* William J. Fenrick, *The Crime against Humanity of Persecution in the Jurisprudence of the ICTY*, 22 Neth. Y.B. Int'l L. 81, 95 (2001) ("The ICC elements [for the crime of persecution] will be used as a template."). Still, the *Kordić* Chamber would not accept the defense contention that the prosecution needed to demonstrate, per the Rome Statute requirement, that persecution be linked

b. Prong 4 of the *Kupreškić* Test

Regarding the fourth limb of the *Kupreškić actus reus* test—that persecution attain a level of gravity comparable to the other enumerated CAH offenses—the *Kordić* Chamber found hate speech wanting as (1) "[it] is not enumerated as a crime elsewhere in the International Tribunal Statute";[84] and (2) the only speech explicitly and separately criminalized in international law is direct and public incitement to commit genocide.[85] As before, the reasoning in *Kordić* is flawed.

To begin, nothing supports the proposition that enumeration elsewhere in the ICTY Statute[86] represents a definitive gravity litmus test. The judges on the *Kordić* bench simply asserted this without any citation or reasoning to back it up. However, in framing its *actus reus* test, *Kupreškić* plainly refused to include this as an evaluative criterion: "A persecutory act need not be prohibited explicitly in Article 5 or elsewhere in the Statute."[87]

Even had *Kupreškić* not registered an opinion on this issue, consideration of enumeration elsewhere would still be problematic. While this criterion could notionally claim analytic value, it would be outweighed by anomalous statutory interpretation consequences. More specifically, if a persecutory act were symbiotically attached to another explicitly prohibited act in the ICTY Statute (as *Kordić* necessarily suggests), then the separate offense of persecution as contained in Article 5(h) would be rendered a nullity. It would make no sense for the Statute's framers to include it as a separate enumerated act within the provision because, in effect, it would only be repeating another act with the inclusion

to another crime in the ICTY Statute. The Chamber held that Kordić's take on the provision was too limiting and was not consistent with customary international law. *Kordić*, Case No. IT-95-14/2-T, ¶ 197. It is possible the Chamber refused to link it to another offense so it could more easily examine hate speech in a vacuum so as to reject it as an *actus reus* for persecution.

84. *Kordić*, Case No. IT-95-14/2-T, ¶ 209. The phraseology of the decision appears to suggest that this does not back up the Chamber's conclusion in respect of the fourth limb of the *Kupreškić actus reus* test. It reads:

> The Trial Chamber, however, finds that this act [encouraging and promoting hatred on political, etc. grounds], as alleged in the Indictment, does not by itself constitute persecution as a crime against humanity. It is not enumerated as a crime elsewhere in the International Tribunal Statute, but most importantly, it does not rise to the same level of gravity as the other acts enumerated in Article 5.

Id. Nevertheless, this text appears in the same sentence as the gravity observation and does not otherwise fit into the four-prong *actus reus* test. So it is assumed that it informs a portion of the "gravity" analysis.

85. *Id.* ¶ 209 n.272.

86. *See* Statute of the International Criminal Tribunal for the Former Yugoslavia, S.C. Res. 827, art. 5, U.N. Doc. S/RES/827 (May 25, 1993), *amended by* S.C. Res. 1166, annex, U.N. Doc. S/RES/116 (May 13, 1998) [hereinafter ICTY Statute].

87. Prosecutor v. Kupreškić, Case No. IT-95-16-T, Judgement, ¶ 614 (Int'l Crim. Trib. for the Former Yugoslavia Jan. 14, 2000).

of the discriminatory grounds cited in Article 5(h) (i.e., political, racial, or religious).[88] Put another way, this would arguably transform persecution into little more than a sentence enhancement more appropriately placed in a different section of the Statute. That does not square with its being separately enumerated as an offense in its own right within Article 5, as it appears in the actual structure and context of the Statute.

Moreover, there are indications the Statute contemplates that nonenumerated acts could be sufficiently grave to constitute a crime against humanity. That explains the inclusion of Article 5(i), alluding to "other inhumane acts"—a catch-all section necessarily signifying that nonlisted conduct may be sufficiently grave for CAH purposes, despite its not being otherwise specifically enumerated in Article 5[89]

Further, the *Kordić* Chamber offered nothing to back its assertion that hate speech on its own cannot satisfy the gravity prong because the only speech act explicitly outlawed elsewhere in international law is direct and public incitement to commit genocide. *Kupreškić* flatly rejected this as a relevant evaluative factor, holding that "whether or not such acts are legal . . . is irrelevant."[90] And, in any event, the *Kvočka* decision qualified the implications of the *Kordić* dictum as follows:

> The *Kordić* Trial Chamber Judgement stated that "in order for the principle of legality not to be violated, acts in respect of which the accused are indicted under the heading of persecution must be found to constitute crimes under international law at the time of their commission." The Trial Chamber reads this statement as meaning that jointly or severally, the acts alleged in the Amended Indictment must amount to persecution, not that each discriminatory act alleged must individually be regarded as a violation of international law.[91]

More importantly, though, the *Kordić* judges disregarded the *Kupreškić* Chamber's well-articulated analysis, amply backed by precedent, in elucidating

88. Still, persecution interpreted this way does not necessarily preclude the possibility that conduct that happens to be enumerated in the statute, such as murder or rape, may serve as the basis for a persecution charge. So long as the crime was committed with the necessary requisite discriminatory intent, the conduct should qualify. But that should not be the *sole* source of persecutory acts—put another way, nonenumerated acts should also be eligible for qualifying as the basis for a persecution charge.

89. ICTY Statute, *supra* note 86, art. 5.

90. *Kupreškić*, Case No. IT-95-16-T, ¶ 614. Despite the fact that *Kupreškić* offered this dictum within a domestic law context, the same logic applies at the international level. Either way, this interpretation of the law is found elsewhere in the relevant jurisprudence. *See, e.g.*, Prosecutor v. Kvočka, Case No. IT-98-30/1-T, Judgement, ¶ 186 (Int'l Crim. Trib. for the Former Yugoslavia Nov. 2, 2001) ("Thus, acts that are not inherently criminal may nonetheless become criminal and persecutorial if committed with discriminatory intent.").

91. *Kvočka*, Case No. IT-98-30/1-T, ¶ 186 (footnote omitted).

the gravity element of the test's fourth limb. To wit, in announcing the gravity requirement, the judges explicitly quoted the Nuremberg Military Tribunal (NMT) *Flick* decision. As explained in Chapter 4,[92] *Kupreškić* featured *Flick*'s teaching that expropriation of *industrial* property was not sufficiently grave to amount to CAH-persecution.[93] We saw in Chapter 4, though, that *Kupreškić* then cited the *I.G. Farben Case* decision,[94] suggesting that, in contrast to *Flick*, crimes involving *personal* property, such as dwellings, household furnishings, and food supplies, could be deemed of sufficient gravity for CAH purposes.[95] One can infer from this that crimes directly against the *person*, in contrast to those involving commercial property, should be considered of sufficient gravity for purposes of prong four of the *Kupreškić actus reus* test. By extension, as hate speech is directed against, and directly impacts, *persons*, as opposed to mere property, it should, contrary to *Kordić*, satisfy the *Kupreškić* test's gravity prong.

c. Other Analysis of Persecution

Lastly, the root characteristics ascribed to persecution by publicists and jurists since 1946 reinforce the proposition that hate speech can serve as the crime's *actus reus*. International tribunals have taken an extremely broad view of conduct that may constitute this offense. Reviewing the relevant jurisprudence, Cherif Bassiouni suggests persecution be defined as "'*State action or policy*' leading to the infliction upon an individual of *harassment*, torment, oppression, or discriminatory measures, designed to or likely to produce physical or mental suffering or economic harm, because of the victim's beliefs, views, or membership in a given identifiable group (religious, social, ethnic, linguistic, etc.)."[96]

In light of this consensus regarding its ample scope, certain cardinal principles may be gleaned regarding the crime: (1) physical injury is not persecution's sole harm—mental or economic injury may also be its object;[97] (2) a multitude of connected persecutory acts should not be examined separately—instead, all such acts arising from a common nucleus of operative facts in a case should be taken into account *cumulatively* and within the appropriate *context*;[98] (3) conduct that is not intrinsically or legally criminal may still be deemed persecutory and illicit in the proper context if carried out with the requisite discriminatory

92. For this discussion, *see* Chapter 4, Section III.A.

93. *See Kupreškić*, Case No. IT-95-16-T, ¶ 619 n.897.

94. *See* United States v. Krauch (*I.G. Farben Case*), Testimony of Defense Witness Huenermann, *in* 7 Trials of War Criminals: "The I.G. Farben Case" 1122, 1129–30 (1952).

95. *Kupreškić*, Case No. IT-95-16-T, ¶ 619 n.897.

96. Bassiouni, *supra* note 60, at 327 (emphasis added).

97. Prosecutor v. Tadić, Case No. IT-94-1-T, Judgement, ¶ 695 (Int'l Crim. Trib. for the Former Yugoslavia May 7, 1997) ("Throughout history . . . the terms 'persecute' and 'persecution' have come to be understood to refer to discriminatory practice resulting in physical or mental harm, economic harm, or all of the above . . . ." (quoting Bassiouni, *supra* note 60, at 327)).

98. *Kupreškić*, Case No. IT-95-16-T, ¶ 622.

intent;[99] and (4) in light of the foregoing, a restricted definition of persecution is not consistent with customary international law.[100]

Consequently, "jurisprudence from World War II trials found acts or omissions such as denying bank accounts, educational or employment opportunities, or choice of spouse to Jews on the basis of their religion, constitute persecution."[101] In a similar vein, ICTY decisions have described as persecution tortious or criminal conduct directed against property, as opposed to persons, including destruction of dwellings and personal property,[102] as well as demolition and damage of religious or educational institutions.[103] Consistent with this capacious construal of conduct that may amount to persecution in general, hate speech ought to be included within its ambit.

3. The Jurisprudence and Commentary on Hate Speech as Persecution

a. The Nuremberg Cases

i. The Streicher *Case*

Case law and expert analysis specifically treating speech and persecution reinforce this conclusion. Both Nuremberg and ICTR/ICTY precedents are instructive in this regard. With respect to Nuremberg, a good portion of the scholarly insight has centered on the International Military Tribunal (IMT)'s *Streicher* and *Fritzsche* decisions.

Ardent defenders of free expression attempt to quell any alarm raised by the potential speech-chilling effects of *Streicher*'s persecution conviction by citing the IMT's concluding words in its decision: "Streicher's incitement to murder and extermination at the time when Jews in the East were being killed under the most horrible conditions clearly constitutes persecution on political and racial grounds in connection with war crimes, as defined by the Charter, and constitutes a crime against humanity."[104] Based on this lone sentence, they contend that the conviction was premised exclusively on Streicher's urging violence contemporaneous with the Final Solution being carried out in the East.[105]

99. Prosecutor v. Kvočka, Case No. IT-98-30/1-T, Judgement, ¶ 186 (Int'l Crim. Trib. for the Former Yugoslavia Nov. 2, 2001).

100. *Kupreškić*, Case No. IT-95-16-T, ¶ 605.

101. *Kvočka*, Case No. IT-98-30/1-T, ¶ 186.

102. *See Kupreškić*, Case No. IT-95-16-T, ¶ 631 ("The Trial Chamber finds that attacks on property can constitute persecution.").

103. *See* Prosecutor v. Kordić, Case No. IT-95-14/2-T, Judgement, ¶¶ 206–07 (Int'l Crim. Trib. for the Former Yugoslavia Feb. 26, 2001). Importantly, the *Kordić* judges took a broader view of persecution when speech was not involved.

104. United States v. Goering, Judgment, Streicher (Int'l Mil. Trib. Sept. 30, 1946), *reprinted in* 6 F.R.D. 69, 163 (1946).

105. *See, e.g.*, Orentlicher, *supra* note 72, at 40–41.

But there is more than this one sentence. The decision equally emphasized criminal responsibility for general hate speech that conditioned German citizens to persecute Jews. In fact, the "Crimes against Humanity" section of the judgment stated:

> For his twenty-five years of speaking, writing, and preaching hatred of the Jews, Streicher was widely known as "Jew-Baiter Number One". In his speeches and articles week after week, month after month, he infected the German mind with the virus of anti-Semitism, and incited the German people to active persecution. Each issue of "*Der Sturmer*", which reached a circulation of 600,000 in 1935, was filled with such articles, often lewd and disgusting.[106]

And then, two paragraphs on, the IMT plainly specified that Streicher's criminal responsibility was based, at least in part, in general hate speech that poisoned German feelings toward Jews and aimed at *persecution* of the Jews, not merely their physical liquidation: "Such was the poison Streicher injected into the minds of thousands of Germans which caused them to follow the National Socialist policy of Jewish *persecution* and extermination."[107] One commentator helps put this into perspective:

> Nuremberg judges followed the prosecution's lead in the *Streicher* decision, converging on the psychology and mental states of the German populace. They eschewed identifying a specific causal connection between Streicher's speeches or publications and any particular criminal acts, but rather

106. *Goering*, Judgment, Streicher, 6 F.R.D. at 162.

107. *Id.* (emphasis added). Professor Orentlicher believes the Tribunal restricted Streicher's speech-related persecution liability to the World War II years given CAH's required nexus to war crimes and crimes against peace in the London Charter. Regarding his prewar speech, Orentlicher claims it would be impossible to prove the nexus. *See* Orentlicher, *supra* note 72, at 40–41. That may be true as far as it goes, but the *Streicher* decision can be interpreted as folding into its analysis wartime discourse not necessarily calling for destruction of the Jews. In fact, as noted, the decision's CAH section started by temporally framing his writings and speeches within a span of a quarter of a century. Those twenty-five years necessarily included both the prewar and war periods. During that quarter-century, enveloping the war years, according to the decision's introductory paragraph on Crimes against Humanity, Streicher "infected the German mind with the virus of anti-Semitism, and incited the German people to active *persecution*." *Goering*, Judgment, Streicher, 6 F.R.D. at 161–63. As demonstrated above, "persecution" is not limited to physical violence against the victim group. Likewise, later in the judgment, the Tribunal referred to an article published by Streicher in 1940 (during World War II) comparing the Jews to locusts. After alluding to this text, the Tribunal declared: "Such was the poison Streicher injected into the minds of thousands of Germans which caused them to follow the National Socialist policy of Jewish *persecution* and extermination." *Id.* at 162 (emphasis added). Thus, Streicher's speech during the war plainly called for persecution, not merely liquidation. That said, the decision is not a model of clarity and there is admittedly support for both Orentlicher's contention and the one asserted here.

emphasized the relationship between his propaganda and the broader anti-Semitic mindset of Germans . . ."[108]

Seen within this context, the prosecution's opening statement is illuminating. It indicates that the gravamen of the persecution case is *conditioning* German citizens to being open to carrying out a mass violence campaign against a victim population, not direct calls for imminent commission of such violence:

> It may be that this defendant is less directly involved in the physical commission of crimes against Jews. The submission of the prosecution is that his crime is no less the worse for that reason. No government in the world, before the Nazis came to power, could have embarked upon and put into effect a policy of mass extermination without having a people who would back them and support them. It was to the task of educating people, of producing murderers, educating them and poisoning them with hate, that Streicher set himself. In the early days he was preaching persecution. As persecution took place he preached extermination and annihilation . . . .
>
> . . .
>
> It is the submission of the prosecution that he made these things possible—made these crimes possible—which could never have happened had it not been for him and for those like him. Without him, the Kaltenbrunners, the Himmlers, the General Stroops would have had nobody to carry out their orders. The effect of this man's crimes, of the poison that he has injected into the minds of millions and millions of young boys and girls and young men and women lives on. He leaves behind him a legacy of almost a whole people poisoned with hate, sadism, and murder, and perverted by him.[109]

Behind-the-scenes chronicling of the prosecution's trial preparations leaves no doubt, in this regard. An internal American memorandum alluding to the strategy developed by Robert Jackson's team against the editor-in-chief of *Der Stürmer* explains the theory of the case in unmistakable terms: "Streicher helped to create, through his propaganda, the psychological basis necessary for carrying through *a program of persecution* which culminated in the murder of six million men, women, and children."[110]

108. Richard Wilson, *Inciting Genocide with Words*, 36 Mich. J. Int'l L. 278, 285 (2015).

109. Robert E. Conot, Justice at Nuremberg 384–85 (1983) (quoting Lieutenant Colonel J. M. Griffith-Jones of the British prosecution) (internal quotation marks omitted).

110. Thomas J. Dodd, *Defense of Streicher*, University of Connecticut: Archives & Special Collections at the Thomas J. Dodd Research Center, at 1, http://archives.lib.uconn.edu/islandora/object/20002%3A1953#page/1/mode/2up.

ii. The Fritzsche *Case*

Free-speech advocates also put much stock in the Tribunal's *Fritzsche* decision.[111] They emphasize the following language as suggesting the Tribunal exclusively took into account direct appeals for violence as the basis for the persecution charges:

> It appears that Fritzsche sometimes made strong statements of a propagandistic nature in his broadcasts. But the Tribunal is not prepared to hold that they were intended to incite the German people to commit atrocities on conquered peoples, and he cannot be held to have been a participant in the crimes charged. His aim was rather to arouse popular sentiment in support of Hitler and the German war effort.[112]

As previously explained, though, portions of the *Fritzsche* decision also support the inference that speech not calling for violence could constitute persecution. The decision explains that the foundation of the persecution count is "deliberately falsifying news to arouse in the German people those passions which led them to the commission of atrocities."[113] Fabricating news to arouse passions is not necessarily the same thing as direct calls for violence. In the same vein, the decision alluded to Fritzsche's link to "propaganda campaigns"—this sort of terminology betokens rhetoric that would *condition* civilians to perpetrate violence rather than directly calling on them to do so.[114]

As Judge Shahabuddeen observed in his *Media Case* Appeals Chamber partial dissent, even if the IMT happened to point out that Fritzsche apparently did not intend "to incite the German people to commit atrocities on conquered people," this does not demonstrate that the Tribunal thereby sought to make advocacy to genocide or extermination an essential element "to the success of a charge for persecution (by making public statements) as a crime against humanity."[115] This is all the more true since, by definition, CAH-persecution is not the same as incitement to genocide. Thus, as Judge Shahabuddeen has explained: "[W]here statements are relied upon, the gravity of persecution as a crime against humanity can be established without need for proof that the accused advocated the perpetration of genocide or extermination."[116]

111. *See* Orentlicher, *supra* note 72, at 39 (distinguishing Fritzsche's speech from Streicher's).

112. United States v. Goering, Judgment, Fritzsche (Int'l Mil. Trib. Oct. 1, 1946), *reprinted in* 6 F.R.D. 69, 187 (1946).

113. *Id.*

114. *Id.* Of course, explicit appeals to violence could form part of a greater propaganda campaign. But the IMT language suggests they were not the sole method of manipulating the population to inspire violence against the Jewish people.

115. Prosecutor v. Nahimana, Case No. ICTR-99-52-A, Judgement, ¶¶ 10–11 (Nov. 28, 2007) (Shahabuddeen, J., partly dissenting).

116. *Id.* ¶ 20.

And Judge Shahabuddeen's thinking is corroborated, as before, by the Nuremberg prosecutors' view of the *Fritzsche* case. Significantly, American prosecutor Drexel Sprecher argued in the courtroom that Fritzsche's "propaganda diatribes" helped "fashion the psychological atmosphere of utter and complete unreason and . . . hatred."[117]

iii. The Dietrich *Case*

Granted, the *Streicher* and *Fritzsche* judgments provide no definitive answers with respect to this issue. There is another case, however, that does. Incredibly, experts have somehow ignored a vital piece of the Nuremberg jurisprudential mosaic: the *Ministries Case* decision regarding Nazi Press Chief Otto Dietrich. That opinion's germane text treating the criminal responsibility of Hitler's newspaper czar for speech is shorn of any reference to direct appeals for violence. Rather, it centers on the defendant's part in acculturating Germans to a climate of pervasive persecution against Jews. In this regard, recall from Chapter 6 that the crux of the opinion finds:

> It is thus clear that a well thought-out, oft-repeated, persistent campaign to *arouse the hatred* of the German people against Jews was fostered and directed by the press department and its press chief, Dietrich. . . . The only reason for this campaign was to blunt the sensibilities of the people regarding the campaign of persecution and murder which was being carried out. . . .
>
> . . .
>
> [The] clear and expressed purpose [of this speech] was to enrage Germans against the Jews, to justify the measures taken and to be taken against them, and to subdue any doubts which might arise as to the justice of measures of racial persecution to which Jews were to be subjected. By them Dietrich consciously implemented, and by furnishing the excuses and justifications, participated in, the crimes against humanity regarding Jews . . . .[118]

117. International Military Tribunal, Nuremberg Trial Proceedings Volume 6, Forty-First Day, Wednesday, 23 January 1946, Morning Session, Capt. Drexel Sprecher (Counsel for the Prosecution), 68, http://avalon.law.yale.edu/imt/01-23-46.asp (last visited Dec. 14, 2016).

118. United States v. von Weizsaecker (*Ministries Case*), Judgment, *in* 14 Trials of War Criminals: "The Ministries Case" 308, 575 (1952) (emphasis added). Count Five of the Indictment, on which Dietrich was convicted, is styled "War Crimes and Crimes against Humanity: Atrocities and Offenses Committed against Civilian Populations"—the word "persecution" is not explicitly used there. And despite the NMT's not employing the term persecution in the last sentence of the cited language, there is no doubt that the finding of guilt against Dietrich nevertheless embraced CAH-persecution. In its decision against Dietrich, the NMT alluded explicitly to "persecution" against the Jews in three different passages. If that does not erase all doubt, the prosecution's opening statement, clarifying the indictment charges, does:

> The war crimes and crimes against humanity charged in the indictment fall into three broad categories. First, there are war crimes committed in the actual course of hostilities or against members of the armed forces of countries at war with Germany. These are set forth in count three of the indictment. Second, there are crimes committed,

This quotation plainly evinces the Tribunal's view that Dietrich's criminal liability hinged on speech seeking to "enrage the Germans," "justify persecutory measures," and "subdue doubts" about persecution. This was discourse aimed at brainwashing and establishing a foundation for eventual embrace of Adolf Hitler's monstrous policies. There were no direct appeals to take up violence against the Jews. Hence, while language in *Streicher* and *Fritzsche* might leave the issue unresolved, the *Dietrich* judgment crucially dispels any doubts and teaches that rhetoric not calling for violence may nonetheless satisfy the *actus reus* element for the crime against humanity of persecution.

b. The Rwandan Cases before the *Media Case* Appeal

The ICTR Trial Chamber judgments, as well as the *Mugesera v. Canada* decision from the Canadian Supreme Court, unambiguously confirm this. *Ruggiu* emphasized that, within the framework of an official widespread or systematic attack against a civilian population, rhetoric spouted, sponsored, or sanctioned by that government, which targets an out-group, amounts to a deprivation of fundamental rights, including liberty and humanity.[119] The words are not merely proxies via which others are motivated to engage in violence separate from the words. The verbal volleys themselves are, within that lethal context, the actual violation. Put another way, they effectuate the violation.

Likewise, the *Media Case* Trial Chamber held that the extremist writings of *Kangura* and the inflammatory transmissions of RTLM groomed Hutus to persecute Tutsis. Fear and hatred, natural byproducts of this persecution campaign, ultimately paved the way for genocide against the Tutsis in 1994. And

> chiefly against civilians, in the course of and as part of the German occupation of countries overrun by the Wehrmacht. These include various crimes set forth in count five of the indictment, the charges of plunder and spoliation in count six, and the charges pertaining to slave labor in count seven. Many of the crimes in this second category constitute, at one and the same time, war crimes as defined in paragraph 1 *(b)* and crimes against humanity as defined in paragraph 1 *(c)* of Article II of Law No. 10. *Third, there are crimes committed against civilian populations in the course of persecution on political, racial, and religious grounds. Such crimes, when committed prior to the actual initiation of Germany's invasions and aggressive wars, are set forth in count four of the indictment; when committed thereafter, they are charged in count five.* The crimes described in count four accordingly, are charged only as crimes against humanity; those charged in count five, for the most part, constitute at one and the same time war crimes and crimes against humanity.

Id. at 167–68 (emphasis added). *See also* Gregory S. Gordon, *The Forgotten Nuremberg Hate Speech Case: Otto Dietrich and the Future of Persecution Law*, 75 Ohio St. L.J. 571 (2014) (providing an even deeper examination of the *Dietrich* case and aspects of the proceedings (including the prosecution's closing argument) that demonstrate he was in fact convicted of persecution, despite no allegations of explicit calls for violence).

119. Prosecutor v. Ruggiu, Case No. ICTR-97-32-I, Judgement and Sentence, ¶¶ 19–21 (June 1, 2000).

the *Kangura*/RTLM speech gave rise to persecution liability at the ICTR, just as Dietrich's press directives did at Nuremberg.[120]

In keeping with this, Canada's *Mugesera* decision also found that hate speech, on its own, can satisfy persecution's *actus reus* requirement, even if it does not bring about causally related violence. The Supreme Court stressed the demonstrable connection between Mugesera's hate-laced discourse and the widespread or systematic attack against a significant segment of the civilian population in Rwanda at that time. [121]

c. The *Kordić* Case

This survey of post–World War II cases unequivocally demonstrates that hate speech not advocating imminent violent conduct may satisfy persecution's *actus reus* element. Of all the court decisions that have grappled with this issue, *Kordić* is the outlier. As was suggested in Chapter 6, however, that judgment is deeply flawed. Its mangling of the *Kupreškić actus reus* test was covered earlier in this chapter. But *Kordić* suffers from other deficiencies too.

i. Gratuitous and Artificial Analysis

To begin, the judgment's overall treatment of the persecution question seems forced, contrived, and hollow. In connection with an ethnic-cleansing campaign, prosecutors had charged Kordić with persecution effectuated by, *inter alia*, "encouraging, instigating and promoting hatred, distrust, and strife on political, racial, ethnic or religious grounds, by propaganda, speeches and otherwise."[122] The indictment itself, however, had not identified a single speech to back up the charge. And the Trial Chamber did not come to the rescue in its judgment. To be blunt, there is absolutely no evidence of any Kordić statements the prosecution might have marshaled to support the count at trial. At Paragraph 522, the judgment alludes to certain Kordić statements uttered in connection with various political events and meetings.[123] But they are not cited as support for the persecution count (the subsection containing this paragraph is generically titled "The Role of Dario Kordić"). On the other hand, Paragraph 523 relates a defense depiction of Kordić's statements as never ethnically divisive or in any way derogatory.[124] Oddly, no prosecution rebuttal is referenced by the Chamber to counter this. It follows, then, that no witnesses were led or documents offered into evidence at trial regarding speeches as persecution. Quite simply, it seems not to have been a contested issue at trial.

120. *Nahimana*, Case No. ICTR-99-52-T, Judgment and Sentence, ¶¶ 1072–1073, 1092 (Dec. 3, 2003).

121. Mugesera v. Canada, 2005 SCC 40, [2005] 2 S.C.R. 100, ¶¶ 146–47 (Can.).

122. Prosecutor v. Kordić, Case No. IT-95-14/2-T, Annex V, ¶ 37 (Int'l Crim. Trib. for the Former Yugoslavia Feb. 26, 2001).

123. *Id.* ¶ 522.

124. *Id.* ¶ 523.

This is why the analysis in Paragraph 209 of *Kordić*, the key passage on persecution and hate speech, seems so gratuitous and artificial. The Chamber's contrived injection of the speech and persecution issue into its opinion smacks of a ploy to gut the latter as a viable charge. The Chamber's analysis seems generated in a conceptual bubble with little or no regard to the facts in the case at hand. One wonders how to reconcile this exercise in abstraction with an evidentiary record replete with details of a massive ethnic-cleansing campaign, which, as noted in Chapter 6, the Trial Chamber delved into liberally elsewhere.

ii. Internal Inconsistency

The ills of this decontextualized and superficial analysis regarding speech and persecution are further exacerbated by various internal inconsistencies in the judgment. As noted in Chapter 6, the decision stressed the importance of examining acts of alleged persecution cumulatively and in context.[125] But in reference to the alleged persecutory speech in the case before it, the Chamber inexplicably sheared it of context and considered it "on its own." In effect, there is no reference to the related persecutory conduct or violence that forms the overarching widespread or systematic attack against the civilian population.[126] The judges then conveniently rejected, perhaps so as to avoid cumulative/contextual assessment, the defense request that the ICC "connected-to-other-crimes" requirement be adopted.[127] This is especially strange as the whole case stemmed from a massive, elaborate, and violent ethnic-cleansing campaign otherwise referenced throughout the decision. The Chamber's antiseptic consideration of the speech charges, without even so much as a mention of the relationship between the charged speech conduct and the ethnic cleansing, could not be more removed from the called-for contextual/cumulative analysis. And given the resulting thin reed on which the examination rests, it could not be less convincing.

To make matters worse, *Kordić* acknowledged that CAH-persecution "encompasses both bodily and *mental* harm and infringements upon individual freedom."[128] But its end analysis on this issue as regards speech is contrary to this foundational observation.[129] Once again, an internal inconsistency calls the decision's legitimacy and persuasive authority into question.

125. *See Kordić*, Case No. IT-95-14/2-T, ¶ 199 ("Although individual acts may not be inhumane, their overall consequences must offend humanity in such a way that they may be termed 'inhumane.'").

126. *See id.* ¶ 209 ("[T]his act, as alleged in the Indictment, does not by itself constitute persecution as a crime against humanity.").

127. *See id.* ¶ 199 (asserting that persecution can consist of one act if evidence of discriminatory intent exists).

128. *Id.* ¶ 198.

129. *See id.* ¶ 209 (stating that a conviction for hate speech as persecution would "violate the principle of legality").

iii. Erroneous Coverage of Previous Cases

But the decision is not just problematic internally. It also botched its coverage of existing legal precedent on speech and persecution. For starters, it simply ignored the passages in *Streicher*, directly and conspicuously cited by the ICTR judgments, which imply that speech not advocating imminent violence may amount to persecution.[130] Moreover, the decision bungled its account of ICTR precedent. First, it nakedly asserted that the sole previous ICTR *conviction* for crimes arising from speech was the *Akayesu* finding of guilt for direct and public incitement to commit genocide.[131] Based on that, it inexplicably suggested that only direct and public incitement to commit genocide was chargeable as a speech crime.[132] This was not only doctrinally incoherent but factually wrong. Just the previous year, the ICTR had convicted RTLM broadcaster Georges Ruggiu for *CAH-persecution* based on his anti-Tutsi/Belgian hate screeds within Rwanda's 1994 widespread and systematic attack directed against the civilian population. And the ICTR's opinion in that case left no doubt that Ruggiu's culpability was not derived uniquely from explicit appeals for violence. Inexplicably, *Kordić* did not even mention *Ruggiu*.

iv. Misplaced Reliance on the Ordinary Domestic Context

Finally, the *Kordić* decision made much of the alleged absence of consensus as to criminalization of hate speech in international instruments and garden-variety laws in domestic jurisdictions.[133] Owing to this asserted lack of uniformity concerning criminalization (primarily on account of the United States), it concluded that hate speech was not as grave as the other enumerated CAH offenses and thus not suitable as the *actus reus* for CAH-persecution[134] (diametrically opposed to the ICTR's conclusion, which found consensus on this issue[135]).

130. *Kordić* allows that "criminal prosecution of speech acts falling short of incitement finds *scant* support in international case law" (implying that there is *some* precedent in favor of such prosecutions (i.e., *Streicher*)—even if *Kordić* omitted to define the critical term "*incitement*"). *Kordić*, Case No. IT-95-14/2-T, ¶ 209 n.272 (emphasis added).

131. *Id.*

132. *Id.* It should be noted that the *Kordić* Chamber also asserted, without further elaboration, that "the only speech act explicitly criminalised under the statutes of the International Military Tribunal, Control Council Law No. 10, the ICTY, ICTR and ICC Statute, is direct and public incitement to commit genocide." *Id.* ¶ 209 n.272. First, this is not true with respect to the IMT and CCL No. 10 instruments, as "incitement" was not a crime at international law at the time of their drafting. Moreover, it conveniently excludes the fact that all these instruments implicitly provide for prosecution of other speech crimes, including CAH-persecution.

133. *See id.* ¶ 209 n.272 (considering various sources including the US First Amendment and the International Covenant on Civil and Political Rights).

134. *See id.* ("The sharp split over treaty law in this area is indicative that such speech may not be regarded as a crime under customary international law.").

135. *See, e.g.*, Prosecutor v. Nahimana, Case No. ICTR-99-52-T, Judgement and Sentence, ¶¶ 1074–75 (Dec. 3, 2003) ("A great number of countries around the world, including Rwanda,

As noted previously, though, it is problematic to use garden-variety municipal laws as a point of repair as they do not take into account the contextual *sine qua non* of CAH, the widespread or systematic attack directed against a civilian population. It is in *that* context that hate speech must be assessed. Further, whether hate speech might otherwise be criminalized or not, the jurisprudence is unambiguous that underlying acts of persecution need not be criminal to satisfy the *actus reus* element.[136] So *Kordić*'s reliance on the described lack of consensus regarding criminalization of hate speech outside the CAH framework is entirely misplaced.[137]

v. *Rejected by* Brđanin

Damningly, the approach to persecution in *Kordić* was subsequently rejected by implication in *Prosecutor v. Brđanin*.[138] Although the latter ICTY case did not involve speech per se, the conduct at issue arose from nonviolent conduct—specifically, discriminatory denial of employment, freedom of movement, proper judicial process, and proper medical care. Unlike *Kordić*, the *Brđanin* judges analyzed these acts through the filter of the wider ethnic cleansing campaign against Bosnian Muslims and Croats.[139] And they held that, when considered in context, each of these acts could give rise to persecution charges.[140] Significantly, *Kordić* had deemed denial of employment analogous to hate speech in concluding that neither act amounted to violation of a fundamental right.[141] In ruling that denial of employment *does* constitute a sufficiently serious violation when viewed in context, the *Brđanin* Chamber syllogistically disavowed *Kordić*'s related ruling concerning hate speech.

d. The *Media Case* Appeals Chamber Judgment

To round out our analysis of the relevant jurisprudence, as we considered in Chapter 6, the *Media Case* Appeals Chamber judgment is nearly on all fours with

have domestic laws that ban advocacy of discriminatory hate, in recognition of the danger it represents and the harm it causes.").

136. *See, e.g.*, Prosecutor v. Kvočka, Case No. IT-98-30/1-T, Judgement, ¶ 186 (Int'l Crim. Trib. for the Former Yugoslavia Nov. 2, 2001) (citing the World War II trials that found the denial based on religion to Jews of bank accounts, educational or employment opportunities, or the freedom to choose one's spouse constituted persecution).

137. This is true as well of the ICTR's same reliance on it to reach the opposite conclusion—the crimes against humanity context cannot be ignored.

138. Prosecutor v. Brđanin, Case No. IT-99-36-T, Judgement, ¶¶ 1029–1031 (Int'l Crim. Trib. for the Former Yugoslavia Sept. 1, 2004).

139. *See id.* (holding that tribunals should evaluate whether rights are fundamental on a case-by-case basis).

140. *See id.* ("The Trial Chamber considers that it is not necessary to examine the fundamental nature of each right individually, but rather to examine them as a whole.").

141. *See* Prosecutor v. Kordić, Case No. IT-95-14/2-T, Judgement, ¶¶ 209–10 (Int'l Crim. Trib. for the Former Yugoslavia Feb. 26, 2001) (stating that such speech "does not rise to the same level of gravity as the other crimes against humanity").

that Tribunal's lower court decisions in respect of hate speech and persecution. In general, it agreed that speech can serve as the *actus reus* for a CAH-persecution count. Although it concluded that speech on its own does not amount to a violation of the rights to life, freedom, and physical integrity of the human being, it still reasoned that hate speech alone may violate victims' rights of dignity or security.[142] It nevertheless refused to weigh in on whether, absent a call for action, such violations are as grave as the other enumerated crimes against humanity.

But as this book has shown, that is essentially an academic point. Because the CAH chapeau mandates the speech be linked to a widespread or systematic attack against a civilian population, by definition, the speech could never be hermetically sealed and isolated from the attack on civilians. This point has even greater resonance at the ICC, where persecution must be tethered to another of the Rome Statute's offenses. Still, could the connection between the hate speech and the civilian attack be so attenuated as to cast doubt on whether the speech truly qualifies as persecution? The next section of this chapter grapples with that prospect.

D. Limits on Speech as the Basis for CAH-Persecution?

As we have seen, the relationship between hate speech and the crimes against humanity chapeau furnishes the most persuasive justification for allowing speech to serve as persecution's *actus reus*. But this is not a blank check, as speech can vary in its characteristics. Similarly, widespread or systematic attacks directed against civilian populations, as well as individual conduct in relation to those attacks, can be quite different in light of diverse features. Given the free-speech concerns explored throughout this book, should certain speech in certain contexts be considered exempt from persecution charges?

1. Possible Limitations Related to the CAH Chapeau

The first potential limitation to charging hate speech as persecution could arise when: (1) the speech is not strongly connected to the widespread or systematic attack; or (2) the nature of the attack itself does not support a finding of liability. Each of these should be considered. Regarding the first scenario, the nexus between the speech and the attack may be attenuated in both manner and extent. So, for instance, although the attack may meet the minimum connectivity threshold, it may be somewhat remote geographically.[143] As for temporal considerations, the attack may only be at its embryonic stage.[144] Again, it may be

142. *See* Prosecutor v. Nahimana, Case No. ICTR-99-52-A, Judgement, ¶ 986 (Nov. 28, 2007) (finding that violations of dignity and security constitute discrimination).

143. *See* deGuzman, *supra* note 83, at 70 ("[T]he attack need not cover a very large geographic area."); *see also id.* at 73 ("It is not necessary that the entire population of a particular geographic area be attacked.").

144. *See id.* at 133 (alluding to responsibility for "emerging attacks").

true that an incipient attack could technically satisfy the chapeau requirement, but its "emerging" nature might also mean, from a policy perspective, that any related speech should not be prosecuted.[145]

As well, the specific characteristics of the widespread or systematic attack should be dissected. An important consideration in this regard is the absence of a legal requirement that the attack be violent. The *Akayesu* Trial Chamber clarified that "attack" straightforwardly denotes an "unlawful act of the kind enumerated" in the ICTR statute, which can be non-violent in nature, like imposing a system of apartheid."[146] In the same vein, the Special Court for Sierra Leone Trial Chamber in *Prosecutor v. Fofana* explained that an attack consists of a "campaign, operation, or course of conduct . . . not limited to the use of armed force, but also encompasses any mistreatment of the civilian population."[147] One commentator has similarly observed that "the concept of mistreatment might well cover acts that could not be underlying crimes . . . [and] mistreatment generally means 'to treat badly,' which does not seem to require severe suffering."[148]

Those responsible for the widespread or systematic attack should also be put under the microscope. Even if, to date, mostly states have been the authors of such attacks, the responsible culprits might also be nongovernmental agents. Thus, ICTY jurisprudence is clear that no state plan or policy is necessary for crimes against humanity.[149] The defendant in *Prosecutor v. Kunarac*, for example, was found guilty of crimes against humanity related to the detention and rape of female civilians, but the chapeau attack was carried out by members of an organized paramilitary group, not state agents.[150]

Likewise crimes against humanity may flow from a state *or* organizational policy at the ICC and the "organizational" descriptor has been very liberally construed.[151] To illustrate, an ICC Pre-Trial Chamber in *Situation in the Republic of Kenya*, held that the 2007–2008 postelection violence in that country was committed not by "an organization with state-like qualities" but by "an amorphous

145. Significantly, the Rome Statute's Elements of Crimes demand a more rigorous mental element "[in] case of an emerging widespread or systematic attack against a civilian population." International Criminal Court [ICC], *Elements of Crimes*, art. 7, Intro., ¶ 2, ICC Doc. ICC-ASP/1/3 (Sept. 9, 2002).

146. Prosecutor v. Akayesu, Case No. ICTR-96-4, Judgement, ¶ 581 (Sept. 2, 1998).

147. Prosecutor v. Fofana, Case No. SCSL-04-14-T, Judgement, ¶ 111 (Aug. 2, 2007).

148. Ford, *supra* note 50, at 258.

149. *See* Prosecutor v. Kunarac, Case No. IT-96-23/1-A, Judgement, ¶ 98 n.114 (Int'l Crim. Trib. for the Former Yugoslavia June 12, 2002) (noting that sources cited in support of the policy requirement "merely highlight the factual circumstances of the case at hand, rather than . . . an independent constitutive element").

150. *See id.* ¶¶ 1–4 (approving the Trial Chamber's findings); *see also* Schabas, *supra* note 54, at 960 ("These were crimes committed by members of an organized paramilitary group, but they were not necessarily attributable to a State plan or policy.").

151. Rome Statute, *supra* note 55, art. 7(2)(a).

or private group of individuals whose principal distinguishing feature . . . turned on its ability to perpetrate vile acts."[152]

One commentator explains the significance of this ruling is that "the policy brains behind crimes against humanity need not be part of an organization as such, as opposed to being merely organized and systematic in executing their criminal activities."[153] Thus, liability may attach to a well-organized clique of private persons, without state-like qualities, who mastermind the widespread or systematic attack. This has profound repercussions for hate speech and persecution jurisprudence. Why? The analysis herein has proceeded on the assumption that, in the majority of crimes against humanity situations, the chapeau attack will be perpetrated by a government. Were that not the case, then safeguarding free expression could assume greater weight in the calculus.

The link between the speaker and the chapeau attack should be scrutinized too. As we have seen, the defendant's charged conduct must be "part of" a widespread or systematic attack. This bifurcates into objective and subjective elements.[154] Regarding the former, "by its nature or consequences," the defendant's actions must objectively be part of the attack.[155] Meg deGuzman elaborates:

> The objective component does not require, however, that the act was committed in the midst of the attack. A crime can be part of an attack even if it is geographically or temporally distant from the attack as long as it is connected in some manner. Judges take into account the particular circumstances involved in determining whether an act can "reasonably be said to have been part of the attack."[156]

Peering at it from the other side of the telescope, then, the individual criminal conduct may be geographically or temporally removed from the broader attack.

Further, the subjective element presupposes the defendant's acting with knowledge that his conduct is part of a widespread or systematic attack against a civilian population.[157] Ad hoc and hybrid tribunal jurisprudence has adopted a

152. Situation in the Republic of Kenya, Situation No. ICC-01/09, Decision Pursuant to Article 15 of the Rome Statute on the Authorization of an Investigation into the Situation in the Republic of Kenya, ¶¶ 116–128, ICC Doc. ICC-01/09-19 (Mar. 31, 2010) (alluding to the participation of political and business leaders).

153. Charles C. Jalloh, *International Decision: Situation in the Republic of Kenya. No. ICC-01/09-19. Decision on the Authorization of an Investigation*, 105 Am. J. Int'l L. 540, 544–45 (2011).

154. *See* Prosecutor v. Kunarac, Case No. IT-96-23/1-A, Judgment, ¶ 99 (Int'l Crim. Trib. for the Former Yugoslavia June 12, 2002) (ruling that the defendant must both play a role in the attack and know that his or her conduct constitutes part of the chapeau attack).

155. *Id.*

156. deGuzman, *supra* note 83, at 74–75 (footnotes omitted) (quoting *Kunarac*, Case No. IT-96-23/1-A, ¶ 100).

157. *Id.* at 75.

flexible approach to this requirement, allowing the knowledge to be constructive, not merely actual.[158] The ICC does have a more restrictive *mens rea* requirement that consists of "awareness that a circumstance exists or a consequence will occur in the ordinary course of events . . ."[159] But deGuzman observes that "[a] question remains whether, under customary international law, crimes against humanity require actual knowledge that one's act is part of a widespread or systematic attack . . . ."[160] Consequently, the lower *mens rea* standard may also sanction a more attenuated connection between the speech at issue and the wider attack.

2. Possible Limitations Related to Speech

The character of the charged speech may similarly impact the persecution analysis. As elucidated above in Section II.B of this chapter ("The Spectrum of Speech at Issue"), "hate speech" should not be viewed monolithically. That section presented a hierarchy. General hate speech, which is group-focused and broadly derisive, is relatively less grave than harassment and incitement. In order of gravity, next on the spectrum is harassment, rhetoric voiced directly to the victims and more susceptible to persecution charges. At the far end of the spectrum, speech addressed to third parties and exhorting them to take action against victims is incitement, which represents the most serious category of hate speech. And even incitement gets parsed. Incitement to persecution, for example, is less severe than incitement to violence. And, as we have seen, the latter bifurcates into direct and indirect forms.

At the same time, it is advisable that the particular words and their quantity, in addition to their medium of dissemination, also be taken into account.[161] Even general hate speech, if particularly dehumanizing or inflammatory and broadcast at frequent intervals through mass media outlets, could inflict much more serious harm than, say, a milder form of indirect incitement to persecution delivered at a modest gathering.[162]

The take-away from all this is that the nature of the chapeau attack vis-à-vis the type of speech should be evaluated on a case-by-case basis. A persecution charge may be unfounded, for example, when less grave hate speech is coupled with a distant widespread or systematic attack directed against a civilian population

158. *See, e.g.*, Prosecutor v. Fofana, Case No. SCSL-04-14 T, Judgement, ¶ 110 (Aug. 2, 2007) (holding that the mental element is satisfied if the accused "had reason to know" his act was part of the wider attack); Prosecutor v. Blaškić, Case No. IT-95-14-T, Judgement, ¶ 251 (Int'l Crim. Trib. for the Former Yugoslavia Mar. 3, 2000) (finding that *mens rea* is established if the accused "took the risk" that his conduct was part of a widespread or systematic attack).

159. Rome Statute, *supra* note 55, art. 30(3).

160. deGuzman, *supra* note 83, at 75.

161. *See* Gordon, *Music and Genocide, supra* note 20, at 635–36 (explaining that "from a temporal perspective, written communication media are much less apt to incite to mass violence than broadcast media").

162. *See* Pocar, *supra* note 73, at 361 (discussing "the power of propaganda to incite when it takes place in situations of extended discrimination with an ethnic component").

that is not initiated or sanctioned by the state. That conclusion would be even more compelling if the attack itself were nonviolent or temporally attenuated.

3. Possible Scenarios

So, more tangibly, what kind of speech linked to civilian-directed, nongenocidal mass violence could be exempted from CAH-persecution charges? Different scenarios could play out. For instance, members of a minority ethnic group in one section of a country could spontaneously establish a militia to facilitate carving out a separate state in that region.[163] The militia start to exercise control over the region by subjecting the civilian population to threats, segregation, and violence. At the same time, a member of the same minority ethnic group, in a corner of the country far removed from the uprising, begins to broadcast hate speeches over a private radio station that attempt to dehumanize members of the majority ethnic group. If the burgeoning attack in the breakaway region is stymied early on but progressed sufficiently to support CAH charges against its authors, may the private radio announcer in the geographically distant part of the country, a member of the attacking ethnic minority, be charged with CAH-persecution?

In light of the criteria considered, this seems like a rather weak case. The attack may technically qualify as "widespread" or "systematic," but apparently had only just crossed that threshold and never got past the incipient phase. Further, the attack was not government-initiated, so the free-expression concerns are amplified as a minority, acting against the state's interests, is criticizing the majority.[164]

Other considerations could further tilt the balance against CAH-persecution charges in this fact pattern. Since the widespread/systematic attack was "emerging" when the speech was broadcast, we could imagine imposing a higher *mens rea* requirement—intent, for instance, instead of mere knowledge. That elevated standard may be tricky to prove beyond a reasonable doubt. Likewise, the chapeau attack could be the imposition of a temporary apartheid regime in the region, an arguably nonviolent attack.[165] It is submitted that speech in the service of such a nonviolent attack, uttered by a member of the nation's minority group, should be treated much more deferentially. This seems like archetypal dissenting discourse that should be tolerated within Justice Holmes's marketplace of ideas metaphor.[166] On the other hand, if the speech were more egregious, such as

163. Nonstate armed groups made up of disenfranchised minority group members and perpetrating large-scale violence have been the object of CAH prosecutions. *See, e.g.*, Prosecutor v. Kony, Case No. ICC-02/04-01/05, Decision on the Prosecutor's Application for Warrants of Arrest Under Article 58, ICC Doc. ICC-02/04-01/05 (July 8, 2005) (calling for the arrests of Joseph Kony and other leaders of the Lord's Resistance Army in Uganda charged with CAH).

164. *See generally* Texas v. Johnson, 491 U.S. 397, 399 (1989) (finding that the First Amendment protects one's right to burn an American flag in protest against government policies).

165. *See* Rome Statute, *supra* note 55, art. 7(1)(j) (including apartheid as an enumerated act).

166. *See* Abrams v. United States, 250 U.S. 616, 630 (1919) (Holmes, J., dissenting).

virulently dehumanizing harassment of, or incitement to persecute, members of the victim group, then persecution charges become more viable.

Conversely, prosecutors could bring a much stronger persecution case if the speech appealed for violence, even in indirect or coded language, and was voiced in the locality where the chapeau attack was unfolding. The case would be even more robust if the wider attack were extremely violent, had been in progress for some time, and were being carried out by an organization that had asserted iron-fisted control over the region. In that scenario, a nongovernmental chapeau attack is far outweighed by other relevant considerations, especially verbally abetting ethnic violence perpetrated by the local *de facto* authority that also monopolizes the region's channels of communication. The persecution charge would be even stronger still if, exploiting the communications monopoly, the chapeau attackers were to hinder dissemination of opposition viewpoints. On those facts, we have a clear deterioration of the metaphorical marketplace and the most significant policy hurdles to mounting a worthwhile CAH-persecution case would be removed.

Other scenarios could be envisaged. For example, the nature of the attack itself, even if government-sponsored, could affect how the speech is evaluated. Stuart Ford contends, for instance, that government refusal to furnish disaster relief to civilians may satisfy the CAH chapeau requirements.[167] Given such a chapeau attack by *omission*, connected speech charged as persecution might take on a different cast. So a radio broadcaster announcing his spiritual conviction that doling out humanitarian aid is sinful and would be received not by human beings, but by parasitic vermin, would still be a tough case to prosecute, notwithstanding the level of vitriol in the discourse. If this truly did qualify as a widespread or systematic attack against a civilian population, its relative lack of gravity would dampen the prospects for successfully charging related speech as persecution.

Clearly, the potential scenarios are protean in nature. The key is to analyze every situation individually pursuant to the nature of the attack, the identity of the parties, and the category of speech. Empirically, the chapeau attack in persecution cases has been state-initiated and the hate speech intimately linked to the attack. But, as we have seen, the formula may vary. And in those cases we need to undertake a reasoned analysis sensitive to the germane policy considerations as well as the special social value of free expression.

III. FIXING INSTIGATION

We saw in Chapter 7 that instigation has suffered from a lexical/doctrinal blurring between that offense and incitement, as well as a raft of inconsistent pronouncements from the ad hoc tribunals regarding the nature and scope of the "contribution" requirement. The latter problem has arguably created a slippery slope

167. Ford, *supra* note 50, at 255.

permitting incorporation of a "but for" causation requirement that is at odds with instigation's doctrinal moorings and policy objectives. Fortunately, each of these problems is easily fixed, as set forth in the two subsections that follow.

A. Disambiguating Instigation from Incitement

This problem goes back to *Akayesu*'s "Original Sin" of commingling the terms "inciting" and "instigating" (or "incitement and "instigation"),[168] which, as we have seen, has had negative ripple effects throughout this area of the law. How did this problem arise? Chapter 7 explained how, in Civil Law jurisdictions, the two terms may be considered synonymous. And the same is true of the two terms in the French language, one of the two official languages of the ad hoc tribunals.

Among other things, this admixing of terminology has contributed to the perception among academics that incitement has a causation requirement. From the perspective of instigation, it has sown confusion in the jurisprudence that has, at times, unjustifiably saddled the offense with some of incitement's doctrinal burden, such as demonstrating the speech was sufficiently "direct."[169] It has also caused confusion in the academic literature, as evidenced by Avitus Agbor's work, which goes so far as to assert, erroneously, that instigation is an inchoate crime.[170]

How can the problem be fixed? The solution is rather simple and akin to the recommendations offered in the previous chapter to clear up the muddle regarding causation in relation to the crime of incitement. Future decisions must explicitly acknowledge the initial ambiguity in *Akayesu* and affirmatively disavow it. They must explain why the confusion was created in the first place, recognizing the French/English and Civil Law/Common Law overlap. And they should then embrace the Common Law version of the crime that has been largely accepted by the international criminal law jurisprudence. Any lingering theoretical discussion comparing the French and English terms, as well as the Civil Law versus Common Law conceptions, has no place in judicial decisions meant to put potential future defendants on notice of the law's requirements and promote deterrence.

168. Prosecutor v. Akayesu, Case No. ICTR-96-4-T, Judgement ¶ 481 (Sept. 2, 1998) ("The second form of liability is 'incitation' (in the French version of the Statute) to commit a crime, reflected in the English version of Article 6 (1) by the word *instigated*.").

169. *See, e.g.*, Prosecutor v. Ndindabahizi, Case No. ICTR-2001-71-1, Judgement and Sentence, ¶ 466 (July 15, 2004) ("[I]n order to be guilty of instigating . . . genocide, the acts constituting the encouragement must *directly* and substantially contribute to the perpetration of genocide by another person.") (emphasis added).

170. *See, e.g.*, Avitus A. Agbor, *The Substantial Contribution Requirement: The Unfortunate Outcome of an Illogical Construction and Incorrect Understanding of Article 6(1) of the Statute of the ICTR*, 12 Int'l Crim. L. Rev. 155 (2012) (erroneously arguing that the ICTR's instigation jurisprudence is flawed because it has included a contribution requirement when the offense is inchoate).

The designation of the crime in the Rome Statute of the International Criminal Court will also help clear up some of the confusion. Rather than assign criminal liability to a defendant who "instigates" an offense, Article 25 of the statute does so in reference to a defendant who "solicits or induces the commission of such a crime which in fact occurs or is attempted . . . ."[171] This move away from the term "instigate" should help refocus judicial pronouncements and academic commentary toward the distinct doctrinal attributes of "instigation" versus "incitement."

B. Eliminating the "Different Forms of Persuasion" *Actus Reus* Requirement

Chapter 6 discussed the *Šešelj* Trial Chamber judgment's gratuitously shoehorning into instigation's *actus reus* element a "different forms of persuasion" requirement. That requirement would oblige the prosecutor to prove that the instigator used different forms of persuasion, such as threats, seduction, or promises, toward the perpetrator of the target crime.[172] As we saw in Chapter 6, however, the Trial Chamber cited nothing in support of imposing this additional burden. Prompting, urging, or its variants, should be sufficient for the *actus reus*. Quite simply, from doctrinal and policy perspectives, this unprecedented and unnecessary burden cannot be justified and should be abandoned. Thus, its complete excision is recommended here.

C. Clarifying the Contribution Requirement

As we have seen, the key aspect that differentiates instigation from incitement is actual postspeech perpetration of the target crime. Moreover, instigation requires a certain connection between the speech and the subsequent offense. Chapter 4 made clear that the connection does not rise to the level of "but for" causation. Instead, a prima facie case entails proving that the instigator "contributed" to execution of the target offense.

But Chapter 6 explained how this "contribution" requirement has been formulated inconsistently in the ad hoc tribunal jurisprudence. The description of this element has ranged from being a plain "contribution" that merely "had an effect on the commission of the crime"[173] to "a clear contributing factor to the conduct of the other person(s)"[174] to a "direct and substantial contribution" to the target

171. Rome Statute, *supra* note 55, art. 25(3)(b).

172. Prosecutor v. Šešelj, Case No. IT-03-67-T, Judgement, ¶ 295 (Int'l Crim. Trib. for the Former Yugoslavia Mar. 31, 2016).

173. Prosecutor v. Kordić, Case No. IT-95-14/2-T, Judgement, ¶ 387 (Int'l Crim. Trib. for the Former Yugoslavia Feb. 26, 2001).

174. *See, e.g.*, Prosecutor v. Kvočka, Case No. IT-98-30/1-T, Judgment, ¶ 252 (Int'l Crim. Trib. for the Former Yugoslavia Nov. 2, 2001).

crime.[175] As we saw in Chapter 6, arguably due to the schizophrenic nature of these rulings, the most recent case to interpret the element has applied it as if it carried a "but for" causation requirement. In *Prosecutor v. Šešelj*, the majority reviewed speeches given by the defendant that were followed by commission of war crimes related to the speech. In particular, the evidence was quite strong that Šešelj's speeches played an important role in the subsequent ethnic cleansing of Croats that followed them. But the Trial Chamber found the contribution requirement was not satisfied because it held the speeches were not "at the root of the departure of the Croats or the persecution campaign."[176] Again, this smacks of a "but for" causation requirement.

So how can this situation be rectified? Judges need to settle on one standard and apply it clearly and consistently. It is submitted that "substantial" contribution should be that standard. In this regard, reference to accomplice liability standards is useful. After all, "instigating [is a form] of accomplice liability in the ad hoc tribunals' Statutes."[177] And for purposes of accomplice liability, the commentary suggests "substantial contribution" is the appropriate standard. According to James G. Stewart:

> For many, the causal contribution an accomplice makes to an offense must be "substantial" in order to implicate her in the consummated crime. By insisting on substantial contributions, we erect a threshold that excludes *de minimis* assistance, *viz.* conduct that had little more than a trivial impact on a crime's occurrence. [The goal is to avoid extending] accomplice liability beyond the point of plausibility, to an extreme where it chills normal social interaction . . . .[178]

From a policy perspective, this makes sense as applied to instigation. The point is to exclude from its ambit speech that has only a trivial impact on a target crime's commission. Adopting a "substantial contribution" standard achieves this. This is a sensible solution and, if applied consistently, will lend coherence to this aspect of instigation law.

175. *See, e.g.*, Prosecutor v. Mpambara, Case No. ICTR-01-65-T, Judgement, ¶ 18 (Sept. 11, 2006).

176. *Šešelj*, Case No. IT-03-67-T, ¶ 333.

177. James L. Bischoff, *Reception of Common Law in Substantive International Criminal Law*, *in* The Diversification and Fragmentation of International Criminal Law 542 (Larissa van den Herik & Carsten Stahn eds., 2012). *See* ICTY Statute, *supra* note 86, art. 7(1) ("A person who planned, instigated, ordered, committed or otherwise aided and abetted . . . a crime referred to in articles 2 to 5 . . . shall be individually responsible for the crime."); Statute of the International Criminal Tribunal for Rwanda, S.C. Res. 955, art. 6(1), U.N. Doc. S/RES/955 (Nov. 8, 1994).

178. James G. Stewart, *Complicity*, *in* The Oxford Handbook of Criminal Law 549 (Markus D. Dubber & Tatjana Hörnle eds., 2014).

IV. FIXING ORDERING

We saw in Chapter 6 that the crime of ordering required a causal link between the command and the commission of the target offense. This had two doctrinal implications that we saw were problematic. First, even if the target offense were committed, ad hoc tribunal jurisprudence has found that the order must have "a direct and substantial effect on the commission of the illegal act."[179] So a perceived attenuated connection between the order and the commission of the substantive crime could absolve the superior of all liability. Second, *a fortiori*, if the target offense is not subsequently carried out, the superior would be similarly exonerated.[180] Why is this problematic? Given the required element of the superior-subordinate relationship, where failure to obey orders is normatively unacceptable, "the likelihood of the occurrence of the ordered offence [is] high."[181] And thus ordering "per se creates a significant risk of commission of an offense, probably more so than simple instigation or encouragement."[182]

As we saw in Chapter 6, this creates a knotty doctrinal issue since incitement carries inchoate liability notwithstanding the lack of formal relationship between speaker and listener while ordering, necessarily within the superior-subordinate context, does not. The solution to this problem is simple: convert ordering into an inchoate offense. As explained by Robert Cryer:

> It is the hierarchical relationship that provides us with an insight into the special harm of ordering, and thus why there is a strong case for a separate inchoate crime of ordering. The Rome Statute . . . contains a lacuna in this regard . . . There is also a further cumulative form of harm that argues in favour of an inchoate crime of ordering. This is that, unlike incitement . . . ordering offenses against international law also involves an abuse of authority.[183]

And there is precedent for ordering as an inchoate crime. For example, General Nickolaus von Falkenhorst, Commander-in-Chief of the German Armed Forces in Norway, was charged with ordering his troops to transfer Jewish prisoners

179. Prosecutor v. Kamuhanda, Case No. ICTR-99-54A-A, Judgment, ¶ 75 (Sept. 19, 2005). A somewhat softer standard of the order having a "substantial factor" in the commission of the crime had been applied previously. *See, e.g.*, Prosecutor v. Kupreškić, Case No. IT-95-16-T, Judgment, ¶ 862 (Int'l Crim. Trib. for the Former Yugoslavia Jan. 14, 2000).

180. Michael G. Karnavas, *Forms of Perpetration*, *in* Elements of Genocide 104 (Paul Behrens & Ralph Henham eds., 2013) ("A causal link must be shown between the order and the actual commission of the crime.").

181. Robert Cryer, *General Principles of International Criminal Law*, *in* The Permanent International Criminal Court: Legal and Policy Issues 246 (Dominic McGoldrick et al. eds., 2004).

182. *Id.*

183. *Id.*

of war to the Security Police for execution.[184] The order was not carried out. Nevertheless, a British Military Court convicted von Falkenhorst of war crimes for issuing the order.[185] Thus, per Antonio Cassese and Paula Gaeta:

> Although the ICTY and ICTR have treated ordering ... exclusively as [a mode] of liability for participating in a completed crime, there is considerable historical authority supporting ordering ... as [an inchoate crime]. When ordering is conceived of as an inchoate offence, an authority figure issuing an illegal order may be found guilty even if the order is not carried out by the subordinates.... Ordering makes most sense as an inchoate crime....[186]

V. CONCLUSION

As pointed out in Chapter 6, persecution, instigation, and ordering have been largely shunted to the side in terms of expert commentary regarding the shortcomings of international hate speech law. Most handwringing, and any proposed nostrums, center on the offense of direct and public incitement to commit genocide. But genocide, and any speech connected to it, is more rarely charged given a lower empirical incidence and the higher *mens rea*. In the meantime, the sister crimes of persecution, instigation, and ordering are far more useful arrows in the prosecutor's quiver. Government-sponsored attacks against a civilian population, if not qualifying as genocide, can nearly always be charged as crimes against humanity. And, given the law's current form, hate speech on the battlefield that contributes to the commission of war crimes can be charged as

184. Trial of Generaloberst Nickolaus Von Falkenhorst (Brunswick, Brit. Milit. Ct., July 29th–Aug. 2d, 1946), XI L. Rpt. Trials War Crim. 29 (US War Crimes Comm'n, 1949).

185. *Id.*

186. Antonio Cassese & Paula Gaeta, Cassese's International Criminal Law 204 (3d ed. 2013). Cassese and Gaeta also cite the case of General Jacob A. Smith, the US commander we considered in Chapter 7 in connection with inciting his troops during counterinsurrectionary operations in the Philippines. Apart from his incitement, Cassese and Gaeta point out that in 1902 "a US Court Martial held that General Smith was guilty of ordering that no quarter should be given to the enemy in the Philippines, even though in fact his troops did not comply with the order." *Id.* It should be noted that Cassese and Gaeta suggest that, for inchoate liability to attach, the *mens rea* of the crime should be "the superior intended the order to be executed and knew that the order was illegal, or else the order was manifestly illegal." *Id.* Such liability, they opine, should also be limited to situations of "formal authority, such as the military context." *Id.* The position of this book, impliedly accepted by Cryer, is that inchoate liability should attach consistent with the current *mens rea* standard and formulation of the superior-subordinate relationship requirement. Cryer, *supra* note 181, at 246. And Elies van Sliedregt is in accord, noting that the *dolus eventualis* standard is sufficient. She explicitly points out that it is appropriate to impose liability if the result was foreseen and accepted even in "situations where there is divergence between the order and the executed offence." Elies van Sliedregt, Individual Criminal Responsibility in International Criminal Law 106 (2012).

instigation. Certainly, ordering easily covers all the core crimes and often is all that is available factually. Incitement to commit genocide may be viewed as a more "sexy" crime in the eyes of the public, but persecution, instigation, and ordering have far more utility.

And yet the efficacy of all three of them is currently hindered by problems that need fixing. This chapter has demonstrated how the repairs can be made. Hate speech uttered in service of a widespread or systematic attack directed against a civilian population should be chargeable as persecution, regardless of whether it directly calls for violence. Its connection to the attack, which is mandated by the crime's chapeau elements, justifies criminalization. And this is consistent with the great weight of precedent, including, most compellingly, the *Otto Dietrich* decision at Nuremberg.

Absent such a fix in the law, ongoing instances of hate speech not calling for action but nevertheless contributing to violence in places such as Sudan and Burma, as chronicled in Chapter 1, will go unpunished. And unless the nature and requirements of instigation are better defined, there will be no justice for the victims of hatemongers such as Vojislav Šešelj, whose recent acquittal on instigation charges can be chalked up, in part, to a bogus "different forms of persuasion" requirement that was read into the *actus reus* and essentially a conversion of the contribution requirement into a "but for" causation requirement. Moreover, quite simply, ordering should carry inchoate liability. The problems can be fixed. But the international legal community has to muster the collective will to implement and secure the needed remedies. It is hoped this chapter will contribute toward that result.

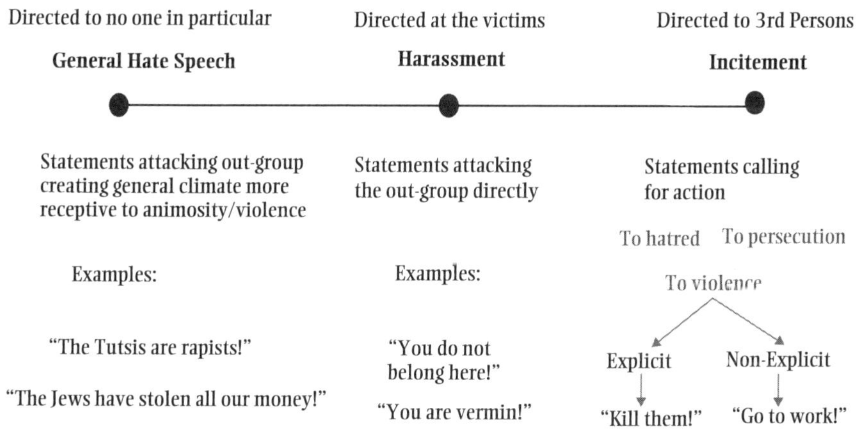

Figure 9.1 The Spectrum of Hate Speech.

10

Adopting Incitement to Commit War Crimes

> "The general, unable to control his irritation, will launch his men to the assault like swarming ants . . ."
>
> "But when the army is restless and distrustful, trouble is sure to come . . ."
>
> "He will win whose army is animated by the same spirit throughout all its ranks."
>
> —SUN TZU[1]

I. INTRODUCTION

Chapter 7 was devoted to highlighting the historical relationship between speech and war crimes and a concomitant dearth of normative options to curb or punish such transgressions. Every law of armed conflict (LOAC) instrument over the past 150 years, from the Lieber Code to the Geneva Convention to the Hague Conventions to the Additional Protocols, has given short shrift to the problem of hate rhetoric on the battlefield. The same is true of international criminal law charters from the London Agreement to the Rome Statute. And the pernicious effects of this legal void have meant impunity for offenses as varied as no quarter, civilian slaughter, POW torture, and sexual assault. But is there a viable doctrinal solution?

This chapter proposes one—incitement to commit war crimes. And it demonstrates that any imagined ills related to this proposed expansion of speech criminalization in the military context—from supposed chilling effects to drags on operational efficacy—are easily outweighed by the salutary impact of wider proscription. It is submitted that exposing intraforce military relations to the

1. SUN TZU, THE ART OF WAR 48, 51 (Lionel Giles trans., 1910).

Atrocity Speech Law. Gregory S. Gordon.

specter of greater verbal regulation will promote LOAC compliance and esprit de corps, thereby ultimately enhancing broader functional objectives. And it is high time to enact such reform. As the twenty-first century passes the midpoint of its second decade, war weapons have become more lethal and war tactics more savage. At the same time, the incitement offense has fossilized as a penal option within the narrow target-crime confines of genocide. As the international legal imagination has begun to visualize its utility in relation to other global crimes, most prominently terrorism, its adaption for LOAC violation purposes seems prudently incremental and normatively sound.

II. EXTENDING INCITEMENT'S REMIT

As we saw in Chapter 7, superiors in the armed forces and civilians in the media have employed toxic rhetoric to motivate troops to perpetrate war crimes. Regarding military leaders, the current legal regime centers uniquely on responsibility for *ordering* subordinates to commit crimes against troops *hors de combat* or against civilians. As for civilians, urging troops to violate humanitarian law currently implicates no LOAC prohibition whatsoever. Thus, formulation of a new offense—direct incitement to commit war crimes—is called for. But how would such an offense be formulated? Where would it be codified? The next subsections offer proposals.

A. Amending the Geneva Conventions or Other LOAC Instruments

As a starting point, integrating this new norm into LOAC should entail modifying the Geneva Conventions.[2] To wit, the article immediately preceding the grave breaches provision of each Geneva Convention should be amended as follows (the language to be added appears in italics): "The High Contracting Parties undertake to enact any legislation necessary to provide effective penal sanctions for persons committing, ordering, *or directly inciting to be committed*, any of the grave breaches of the present Convention defined in the following Article."[3]

2. *See* Sarah M. Buel, *Putting Forfeiture to Work*, 43 U.C. Davis L. Rev. 1295, 1347 n.282 (2010) ("The main source of international humanitarian law is the four Geneva Conventions of 1949 . . . ."). Granted, certain contemporary LOAC norms, such as proscribing forced marriages, have arisen external to the Geneva Conventions. *See, e.g.*, Wanda M. Akin, *Justice on the Cheap*, 28 T. Jefferson L. Rev. 19, 27 (2005) (observing that the Special Court for Sierra Leone's "forced marriage" counts against accused from the Revolutionary United Front broke new ground in LOAC). This book postulates, however, that an amendment of the Geneva Conventions would promote greater textual and institutional coherence and compliance.

3. This supplemental text thereby inserts language criminalizing direct incitement into each of the four Geneva Conventions. *See* Geneva Convention for the Amelioration of the Condition of the Wounded and Sick in Armed Forces in the Field art. 49, Aug. 12, 1949, 6 U.S.T. 3114, 75 U.N.T.S. 31 [hereinafter First Geneva Convention] (emphasis added); Geneva Convention for

Likewise, Article 40 of Additional Protocol I should be modified to read as follows (suggested new language again in italics): "It is prohibited to order *or directly incite* that there shall be no survivors [or] to threaten an adversary therewith. . . ."[4] Along the same lines, Additional Protocol II should undergo a comparable revision: "It is prohibited to order *or directly incite* that there shall be no survivors."[5] To the extent that any other LOAC instruments prohibit *orders* to commit war crimes, those should also be amended to include incitement provisions comparable to those just proposed for the Geneva treaties.

B. Amending the Rome Statute or Other ICL Instruments

In the same vein, the incitement to commit genocide provision of the Rome Statute, Article 25(3)(e), should be expanded. At present, that section reads: "[A] person shall be criminally responsible and liable for punishment for a crime within the jurisdiction of the Court if that person . . . in respect of the crime of genocide, directly and publicly incites others to commit genocide . . . ."[6] For purposes of covering war crimes, the provision should be expanded as follows (once again, the supplemental language is in italics):

> [A] person shall be criminally responsible and liable for punishment for a crime within the jurisdiction of the Court if that person . . . in respect of the crime of genocide *or war crimes*, directly and publicly incites others to commit genocide *or directly incites others to commit war crimes. . . .*

Since they cover only offenses that have already taken place, as well as fixed temporal jurisdictions, there is no need to consider amending the constituent instruments for the International Criminal Tribunal for the former Yugoslavia

the Amelioration of the Condition of Wounded, Sick and Shipwrecked Members of Armed Forces at Sea art. 50, Aug. 12, 1949, 6 U.S.T. 3217, 75 U.N.T.S. 85 [hereinafter Second Geneva Convention] (emphasis added); Geneva Convention Relative to the Treatment of Prisoners of War art. 129, Aug. 12, 1949, 6 U.S.T. 3316, 75 U.N.T.S. 135 [hereinafter Third Geneva Convention] (emphasis added); Geneva Convention Relative to the Protection of Civilian Persons in Time of War art. 146, Aug. 12, 1949, 6 U.S.T. 3516, 75 U.N.T.S. 287 [hereinafter Fourth Geneva Convention].

4. Similarly, this means incorporating language into Protocol I criminalizing direct incitement. *See* Protocol Additional to the Geneva Conventions of 12 August 1949, and Relating to the Protection of Victims of International Armed Conflicts art. 40, June 8, 1977, 1125 U.N.T.S. 3 [hereinafter Protocol I].

5. As before, the necessary language regarding incitement would be placed within the text of Protocol II. *See* Protocol Additional to the Geneva Conventions of 12 August 1949, and Relating to the Protection of Victims of Non-International Armed Conflicts art. 4(1), June 8, 1977, 1125 U.N.T.S. 609 [hereinafter Protocol II].

6. Rome Statute of the International Criminal Court art. 25(3)(e), July 17, 1998, 2187 U.N.T.S. 3 (entered into force July 1, 2002), *reprinted in* 1 United Nations Diplomatic Conference

(ICTY) or other extant hybrid tribunals.[7] To the extent new tribunals are created going forward, their constituent instruments should model the suggested amended provision of the Rome Statute.

III. FORMULATING THE ELEMENTS OF THE CRIME

A. The "Public" Component

Of course, to give these amendments teeth, adjudicators will need a roadmap to help navigate the elements of the new offense. One element is conspicuous by its absence—"public." Why is the proposed offense not styled "direct and *public* incitement to commit war crimes"—consistent with "direct and *public* incitement to commit genocide"? First, as we saw in Chapter 8, this book calls for elision of the "public" element in respect of genocide given its questionable utility and unreasonable constriction of the crime.

Nevertheless, even if, *arguendo*, the public element makes sense for genocide, war crimes are quite distinct offenses. Those who support the "public" requirement for genocide can point out that, on its widest scale, genocide may implicate mass mobilization and involvement of the entire spectrum of society. As James Hughes observes:

> [Genocide,] whether perpetrated by a technologically advanced modern bureaucratic state like Nazi Germany or a relatively undeveloped rural society like Rwanda, requires mass mobilisation. It is the mass of "ordinary" citizens that become engaged. This may generally involve assisting the state with the process of identification, exclusion, dehumanisation, and ultimately extermination.[8]

Given this dynamic, supporters of the "public" element can argue, it makes sense that incitement to *genocide* would include a "public" element involving, as described in the Genocide Convention's *travaux préparatoires*, "direct appeals to the public by means of speeches, radio or press inciting it to genocide . . . ."[9]

of Plenipotentiaries on the Establishment of an International Criminal Court, Official Records (1998) [hereinafter Rome Statute].

7. The International Criminal Tribunal for Rwanda shut down in December of 2015. *See* Jeffrey Gettleman, *Special UN Court on Rwandan Genocide Closes Its Doors after 21 Years*, N.Y. Times, Dec. 15, 2015, at A6.

8. James Hughes, *Genocide*, *in* Routledge Handbook of Ethnic Conflict 122, 123 (Karl Cordell & Stefan Wolff eds., 2011) (citation omitted).

9. Hirad Abtahi & Philippa Webb, The Genocide Convention: The Travaux Préparatoires 238 (2008). On the other hand, as pointed out in Chapters 5 and 8, direct and public incitement to commit genocide has been established at the International Criminal Tribunal for Rwanda (ICTR) in cases of individuals directing a discrete group of militia to kill Tutsis. This did not involve a general broadcast to a large segment of the public. *See* Prosecutor

War crimes are easily differentiated in this regard.[10] They are routinely "committed by soldiers acting on their own rather than according to a larger policy," and they do not mandate "an illegal collective action."[11] Additionally, they are perpetrated in the context of a "chain of command or formal hierarchical ordering that characterizes armed conflict as such."[12] In large part, incitement to commit war crimes entails superiors speaking to subordinates. Thus, enormous public gatherings or mass media transmissions to anonymous throngs are not implicated. So a "public" element need not be incorporated.

B. The "Direct" Element

On the other hand, the "direct" element of the crime should be retained. Effective limits on preventive enforcement overreach, and concomitant protection of free speech, necessitate restricting liability to situations where the words are understood as advocating perpetration of war crimes.[13] Otherwise, hate rhetoric

v. Bikindi, Case No. ICTR-01-72-T, Judgement, ¶ 268 (Dec. 2, 2008). The Appeals Chamber in Prosecutor v. Kalimanzira, Case No. ICTR-05-88-A, Judgement, ¶ 155 n.409 (Oct. 20, 2010), has opined that Bikindi's incitement was nevertheless sufficiently "public" because he used a "public address system" while traveling on a "public road." We saw in Chapter 5 that this reasoning is specious. Merely because Bikindi used a voice-amplification tool on a thoroughfare not located on private property does not change the fact that he addressed himself to a discrete group of militia. The PA system may have been used because, for example, the truck from which Bikindi make his remarks was, due to the terrain perhaps, located at a distance from the militia members.

10. Significantly, the United States Army Field Manual on the Law of Land Warfare criminalizes "direct incitement to commit war crimes," not direct *and public* incitement to commit war crimes. US Dep't of the Army, Field Manual 27-10, The Law of Land Warfare, ¶ 500 (1956) [hereinafter FM 27-10].

11. Allison Marston Danner, *Constructing a Hierarchy of Crimes in International Criminal Law Sentencing*, 87 Va. L. Rev. 415, 472 (2001). However, it bears mention that Article 8 of the Rome Statute provides: "The Court shall have jurisdiction in respect of war crimes in particular when committed as part of a plan or policy or as part of a large-scale commission of such crimes." Rome Statute, *supra* note 6, art. 8. But this has been found to be a jurisdictional prerequisite versus an element of the crimes. *See* Beth Van Schaack, *Obstacles on the Road to Gender Justice: The International Criminal Tribunal for Rwanda as Object Lesson*, 17 Am. U. J. Gender Soc. Pol'y & L. 361, 385 n.105 (2009) (referring to this text as "soft threshold language").

12. Catharine A. MacKinnon, *The ICTR's Legacy on Sexual Violence*, 14 New Eng. J. Int'l & Comp. L. 211, 217 (2008) (distinguishing war crimes from genocide on this point).

13. Abtahi & Webb, *supra* note 9, at 1160; *see also* A.J.P., Jr., *Constitutional Law—Due Process—Freedom of Speech*, 15 Tex. L. Rev. 373, 374 (1937) ("The early test as applied to *limitations on federal power to abridge free speech* under the Espionage Act, enacted during the war, *required a direct incitement* to violent resistance to the government.") (emphasis added); Robert Cryer, *Incitement*, Enotes.Com, http://www.enotes.com/genocide-encyclopedia/incitement (last visited June 25, 2011) ("To be prosecuted as criminal, the incitement must also be direct. Vague suggestions or hints are not enough. One reason for this limitation is the need to strike a balance between criminalizing incitement and preserving freedom of speech.").

emanating from military superiors, however abhorrent, should be protected from prosecution. And the proverbial wheel need not be reinvented—the definition of "direct" employed for incitement to genocide should be incorporated into the proposed new crime. That means the message is "direct" if, when viewing the language in the light of its cultural and linguistic content, the persons for whom the message was intended immediately grasped the implication thereof.[14] This assures needed suppleness related to the interlocutor's specific military and/or national culture. And yet it also allows for fact and/or expert witnesses to establish use of code words or other veiled incitement methods.

C. *Mens Rea*

The *mens rea* formulation should also hew to that of incitement to genocide, consisting of a dual intent: (1) to provoke another to commit war crimes; and (2) to commit the underlying war crime itself. Regarding the latter, in contrast to genocide's *dolus specialis*, war crimes typically carry a simple intentionality or willfulness *mens rea*.[15]

D. Incitement

Similarly, with respect to the "incitement" element itself, borrowing from the genocide context is again quite helpful. In adjusting for the war crimes situation, we can distill three relevant criteria: purpose, text, and context.[16] Purpose here would entail, at one end of the gamut, valid aims such as superiors enlightening subordinates regarding the nature of a counterinsurgency operation, for instance. On the opposite end of the spectrum, explicit calls for civilian massacres would evince a patently illicit objective. More involved judicial probing, pursuant to the totality of the circumstances (including all the contextual evaluative factors discussed below), will be required in more "grey-zone" cases.

Consideration of "text" replicates the incitement to genocide drill. Language is parsed to reveal, for example, use of code words or, to the contrary, legitimate contextual explanations. Thus, an officer instructing his charges to *conquer the*

14. *See* Prosecutor v. Akayesu, Case No. ICTR-96-4-T, Judgement, ¶ 556 (Sept. 2, 1998).

15. *See* William Schabas, *Mens Rea and the International Criminal Tribunal for the Former Yugoslavia*, *in* War Crimes and Human Rights: Essays on the Death Penalty, Justice and Accountability 467, 472–74 (2008).

16. The most prominent missing criterion here would be the relationship between speaker and subject. But in the military setting, whether the speaker is a member of a "majority" or "minority" group criticizing or not the powers that be or disenfranchised minorities is of no moment. Likewise, channel of communication as well as temporality and instrumentality are not as critical to the analysis as any potential incitement to war crimes would likely be limited to nonrecorded, person-to-person communications. That said, if recorded statements or broadcast media were implicated (especially the latter, in cases where civilians are inciting military personnel), then these criteria could certainly be consulted.

hearts and minds of the villagers probably signifies that he wishes his soldiers to win the villagers over with kindness, not subject them to physical violence (notwithstanding the vagueness of the word "conquer").[17]

The most significant of these criteria is "context." As with incitement to genocide, the examination bifurcates into internal and external inquiries. Internal contextual analysis covers factors such as the speaker's personal and professional history (including rank and previous communications with troops), and the tone, cadence, and volume of the relevant communication. Another potentially relevant indicator could be means of transmission and location. For example, did the commander communicate via a public address system to a large assembly of troops, or did he make statements to a smaller gathering in the barracks?[18] Rank differential between the speaker and listener could also be taken into account. Greater rank disparity, for instance, could help militate in favor of an incitement finding. As within the genocide context, external context for incitement to war crimes examines the factual landscape surrounding the speech, which could embrace previous related messages within the same military but by other commanders as well as recent perpetration of war crimes by the same unit or military force.

E. Causation

In the realm of incitement, from both policy and doctrinal perspectives, war crimes should be no different from genocide in relation to causation. More specifically, it is recommended that causation not be included as an element of the offense. This is just as much an inchoate crime with a unique enforcement imperative. As elucidated by David Brody and James Acker:

> [The] criminal law typically concerns itself with the harms associated with illegal acts that are consummated. With inchoate crimes . . . the law criminalizes behaviors that have not yet necessarily culminated in a tangible social harm. . . . [I]nchoate crimes deal with conduct that is designed to culminate in the commission of a substantive offense but . . . has not yet achieved its culmination because there is something the actor or another still must do. . . . Society feels justified in stepping in to assure that the target of the inchoate offense . . . does not occur.[19]

17. It is quite possible, of course, that this could entail a battle of experts concerning the meaning of code words within that military in that specific time and place.

18. In the same vein, an electronically volume-enhanced oration to a division may resemble incitement more than a less official conversation, spoken in a relatively hushed voice in a comparatively private setting.

19. David C. Brody & James R. Acker, Criminal Law 368 (2d ed. 2010).

Therefore, if the other prima facie elements are made out, once an inciting message is communicated in the military context, as in the genocidal realm, liability attaches. It does not hinge on the perpetration of causally related post-speech war crimes.

IV. PUTTING THE NEW OFFENSE IN PERSPECTIVE

A. Other Calls for Expanding Incitement

This book urges broadening the ambit of incitement—a crime that tends to alarm both free speech advocates as well as those wary of inchoate liability's license for more intrusive law enforcement.[20] But proposals for expanding the scope of incitement to encompass more than just genocide certainly predate this book. For instance, according to Robert Cryer:

> [Incitement] to particular examples of war crimes and crimes against humanity may be as serious as some instances of incitement to genocide. If a sadistic person sought to persuade others to drop a nuclear device on a city which would kill 100,000 people, for motives of personal pleasure or in order to persecute, rather than eliminate, a group, the act he or she seeks to incite would not meet the formal definition of genocide. Yet the act being encouraged is not much less serious than certain examples of genocide.[21]

Beyond the core mass atrocity crimes covered in the Rome Statute, there have been efforts to criminalize incitement to terrorism.[22] Article 5 of the 2005 Council of Europe Convention on the Prevention of Terrorism obliges state parties to enact domestic legislation outlawing incitement to terrorism.[23] Daphne Barak-Erez and David Scharia explain that the Convention "regards the prevention of incitement to terrorism as one of the main elements of an effective

20. Ameer F. Gopalani, *The International Standard of Direct and Public Incitement to Commit Genocide: An Obstacle to U.S. Ratification of the International Criminal Court Statute?*, 32 CAL. W. INT'L L.J. 87, 88 (2001) (pointing out that the US representative for negotiation of the Genocide Convention "declared the [incitement provision] was a plain infringement on the guarantees of free speech protected by the First Amendment"); JAY M. FEINMAN, LAW ONE HUNDRED ONE 289 (3d ed. 2010) ("The use of inchoate crimes as a law enforcement tool raises the central problem in this area . . . . If we define it too broadly, we will criminalize behavior that is far removed from causing harm.").

21. Cryer, *supra* note 13.

22. *See generally* Ben Saul, *Speaking of Terror: Criminalising Incitement to Violence*, 28 U. NEW S. WALES L.J. 868 (2005) (discussing how the law does, and should, respond to incitement to violence).

23. *Council of Europe Convention on the Prevention of Terrorism*, C.E.T.S. 196, art. 5 (May 16, 2005), http://conventions.coe.int/Treaty/en/Treaties/html/196.htm.

counter-terrorism strategy."[24] And a number of European states have made it a crime to incite to terrorism.[25] On the transnational plane, in 2005 the UN Security Council issued Resolution 1624, which "calls upon all states to adopt such measures as may be necessary and appropriate and in accordance with their obligations under international law to . . . prohibit by law incitement to commit a terrorist act or acts."[26]

B. Existing Domestic Incitement to Commit War Crimes Provision

Incitement to commit war crimes has also been codified in at least one domestic jurisdiction. United States Army Field Manual 27–10 (The Law of Land Warfare), Article 500 defines as criminal: "Conspiracy, *direct incitement*, and attempts *to commit*, as well as complicity in the commission of, crimes against peace, crimes against humanity, and *war crimes* . . . ."[27] Research does not reveal this provision having been used to prosecute incitement to commit war crimes or as the subject of expert commentary.[28] Importantly, it is found in Section II of the Manual, titled "Crimes under International Law." Thus, from the American perspective, the offense is already part of the global legal order.[29]

24. Daphne Barak-Erez & David Scharia, *Freedom of Speech, Support for Terrorism, and the Challenge of Global Constitutional Law*, 2 Harv. Nat'l Sec. J. 1, 9 (2011).

25. *See, e.g.*, Terrorism Act 2006, c. 11, § 1(1) (United Kingdom), Loi du 29 juillet 1881 sur la liberté de la presse [Law of July 29, 1881 on the Freedom of the Press], http://www.legifrance.gouv.fr/affichTexte.do?cidTexte=LEGITEXT000006070722&dateTexte=20110918.

26. S.C. Res. 1624, ¶ 1, U.N. Doc. S/RES/1624 (Sept. 14, 2005), http://www.securitycouncilreport.org/atf/cf/%7B65BFCF9B-6D27-4E9C-8CD3-CF6E4FF96FF9%7D/IP%20SRES%201624.pdf.

27. FM 27-10, *supra* note 10, ¶ 500.

28. At least one article refers to the provision. In a piece criticizing the administration of George W. Bush for its policies in the Middle East, Francis A. Boyle refers to the provision and generally states:

> Furthermore, various members of the Bush Jr. administration have committed numerous inchoate crimes incidental to these substantive offences that under the Nuremberg Charter, Judgment, and Principles as well as U.S. Army Field Manual 27-10 (1956) are international crimes in their own right: planning, and preparation—which they are currently doing today against Iran—solicitation, incitement, conspiracy, complicity, attempt, aiding and abetting.

Francis A. Boyle, *Law and Resistance: The Republic in Crisis and the People's Response*, 2 Crit. 154, 155–56 (2009). Apart from my article, *Formulating a New Atrocity Speech Offense: Incitement to Commit War Crimes*, 43 Loy. U. Chi. L. J. 281 (2012), extensive research failed to unearth any application of, or commentary on, this provision. Nor have any additional insights concerning the provision been forthcoming based on discussions with various LOAC experts.

29. The US Army's basis for concluding that incitement to commit war crimes is already an offense under international law is not apparent. Perhaps it derives from a liberal reading

C. Situating the New Crime Conceptually

1. Commission and Omission Liability

The advantages of adding the new incitement offense are apparent from both a practical and conceptual perspective. At present, an officer's responsibility for war crimes perpetrated by one of his soldiers can be categorized as either commission or omission liability. With respect to the former, as described in Chapter 7, current international humanitarian law (IHL) and international criminal law (ICL) treaties and statutes criminalize a superior's *ordering* perpetration of war crimes.[30] Likewise, commission liability would encompass a military actor's *instigating* perpetration of a war crime to a person with whom he was not in a superior-subordinate relationship when the war crime is subsequently committed.[31]

of the Nuremberg jurisprudence. More specifically, Article 6 of the Nuremberg Charter required showing a nexus between crimes against humanity and war crimes or crimes against peace. *See* Darryl Robinson, *Defining "Crimes against Humanity" at the Rome Conference*, 93 Am. J. Int'l L. 43, 46 n.16 ("The Nuremberg Charter stated that crimes against humanity could occur 'before or during the war,' but a nexus was indirectly introduced by the requirement that the crime be connected to war crimes or a crime against peace."). In light of the required nexus, might it be argued that incitement charged as a crime against humanity was seen as encompassing incitement to commit war crimes? *See, e.g.*, Charity Kagwi-Ndungu, *The Challenges in Prosecuting Print Media for Incitement to Genocide*, *in* The Media and the Rwanda Genocide 330, 337 (Allan Thompson ed., 2007) ("The International Military Tribunal at Nuremberg linked Streicher's propaganda with the war crimes that had been carried out . . . and implicitly linked the alleged crimes against humanity with war crimes."); Robert H. Snyder, *Disillusioned Words Like Bullets Bark: Incitement to Genocide, Music, and the Trial of Simon Bikindi*, 35 Ga. J. Int'l & Comp. L. 645, 654 n.72 (2007) ("Even though the Nuremberg Charter did not set out incitement to commit crimes against humanity or war crimes as a separate offense, the International Military Tribunal (IMT) had little trouble convicting Streicher of the charge.").

30. *See, e.g.*, First Geneva Convention, *supra* note 3, art. 49 ("The High Contracting Parties undertake to enact any legislation necessary to provide effective penal sanctions for persons committing, *or ordering to be committed*, any of the grave breaches of the present Convention defined in the following Article." (emphasis added)); Statute of the International Criminal Tribunal for the Former Yugoslavia, S.C. Res. 827, art. 2, U.N. Doc. S/RES/827 (May 25, 1993), *amended by* S.C. Res. 1166, annex, U.N. Doc. S/RES/116 (May 13, 1998) [hereinafter ICTY Statute] (emphasis added) ("The International Tribunal shall have the power to prosecute persons committing or *ordering to be committed* grave breaches . . . ." (emphasis added)).

31. *See, e.g.*, Statute of the International Criminal Tribunal for Rwanda, S.C. Res. 955, art. 6(1), U.N. Doc. S/RES/955 (Nov. 8, 1994) [hereinafter ICTR Statute] ("A person who planned, instigated, ordered, committed or otherwise aided and abetted in the planning, preparation or execution of a crime referred to in Articles 2 to 4 of the present Statute, shall be individually responsible for the crime."). As the text of ICTR Statute Article 6(1) reveals, commission liability in this area also includes planning and aiding and abetting.

With respect to *omission* liability, the doctrine of "command responsibility" has developed. Article 7(3) of the ICTY Statute, for example, declares:

> The fact that any of the acts . . . was committed by a subordinate does not relieve his superior of criminal responsibility if he knew or had reason to know that the subordinate was about to commit such acts or had done so and the superior *failed* to take the necessary and reasonable measures to prevent such acts or to punish the perpetrators thereof.[32]

To make out a case of command responsibility, the relevant case law requires proof of the following three elements: (1) the existence of a superior-subordinate relationship of effective control; (2) the existence of the requisite *mens rea*, namely, that the commander knew or had reason to know of his subordinates' crimes; and (3) that the commander failed to take the necessary steps to prevent or punish the offenses.[33] Command responsibility is categorized as a type of *omission* liability, as responsibility centers on the commander's *failure* to act.[34]

2. Inchoate Liability

Incitement to commit war crimes would add a third, intermediary mode of liability within the realm of grave LOAC violations: inchoate liability. Not exactly commission liability, as culpability does not hinge on the subordinate's consummation of the target crime, and distinguishable from omission liability because it involves the commander's affirmative conduct, it criminalizes an act based on its likely *potential* to cause harm. And so, theoretically, if not practically, it provides law enforcement with the chance of *preventing* mass violence before it takes place. This preemptive capability is what makes the proposed new offense an invaluable addition to commander-subordinate modes of criminal liability.

One possible objection may be that "instigation" already proscribes the felonious behavior contemplated in the proposed new crime as it consists of "prompting another to commit an offence"[35] or "urging, encouraging, or prompting"

32. ICTY Statute, *supra* note 30, art. 7(3) (emphasis added). The ICTR and Special Court for Sierra Leone (SCSL) have identical provisions. *See also* ICTR Statute, *supra* note 31, art. 6(3); Statute of the Special Court for Sierra Leone art. 6 (3), Jan. 16, 2002, 2178 U.N.T.S. 137 [hereinafter SCSL Statute] (emphasis added).

33. *See, e.g.*, Prosecutor v. Akayesu, Case No. ICTR-96-4-T, Judgement, ¶ 486 (Sept. 2, 1998); Prosecutor v. Brima, Case No. SCSL-04-16-T, Judgement, ¶¶ 760–62 (June 20, 2007); Prosecutor v. Delalić, Case No. IT-96-21-T, Judgement, ¶ 346 (Int'l Crim. Trib. for the Former Yugoslavia Nov. 16, 1998).

34. *See* Alexander Zahar & Göran Sluiter, International Criminal Law 259 (2008) ("Command responsibility is a form of omission liability, for it is based on proof of failure to restrain the actions of others.").

35. Prosecutor v. Blaškić, Case No. IT-95-14-T, Judgement, ¶ 280 (Int'l Crim. Trib. for the Former Yugoslavia Mar. 3, 2000); *see also* Prosecutor v. Krstić, Case No. IT-98-33-T, Judgement, ¶ 601 (Int'l Crim. Trib. for the Former Yugoslavia Aug. 2, 2001).

another to commit a transgression.[36] There is a critical distinction, though, as clarified by Wibke Timmermann:

> Instigation has been considered to be punishable only where it leads to the commission of the substantive crime, which means that it is not an inchoate crime; the instigation must be causally connected to the substantive crime in that it must have contributed significantly to the commission of the latter, the instigator must act intentionally or be aware of the substantial likelihood that the substantive crime will be committed, and he must intend to bring about the crime instigated. By contrast, direct and public incitement has been held to be an inchoate crime, which is applicable only in connection with the crime of genocide.[37]

Moreover, this additional level of preventive enforcement would apply to the battlefield, a space more fundamentally violent in nature than any other and more inherently vulnerable to the eruption of mass violence. Why should incitement charges be possible within the civilian realm, a much less intrinsically violent dimension, and not within the military environment, where the normative baseline objective is homicide? Incitement as a speech-regulator in armed conflict stands to incentivize more reflective and responsible use of speech among superiors and more vigilance among subordinates in terms of reporting seemingly illicit rhetoric. Presumably, this helps foster overall heightened cognizance of LOAC and deterrence of war crimes throughout the ranks.

D. Extending Liability to Cover Civilians

Further, the suggested new law would permit bringing *civilians* to justice for incitement to war crimes. As we saw in Chapter 7, civilians—including media personalities and other prominent figures (presidential candidate Donald Trump, for example!)—may leverage their position and/or authority to goad soldiers and militia to slaughter innocent civilians. This recommended extension of incitement would subject their appeals to breach the laws of war to criminal liability before their ultimate objectives could be attained. Even if this conduct could be prosecuted as a different offense, such as incitement to genocide or crimes against humanity (persecution), incitement to commit war crimes helps emphasize the singular military nature of the speech and thus carries more expressive value and deterrence potential in the LOAC milieu.

36. Prosecutor v. Semanza, Case No. ICTR-97-20-T, Judgement and Sentence, ¶ 381 (May 15, 2003).

37. Wibke Timmermann, *Incitement in International Criminal Law*, 88 Int'l Rev. Red Cross 823, 839 (2006).

E. Comparing the New Offense to Incitement to Commit Genocide and Crimes against Humanity (Persecution)

1. Incitement to Commit Genocide

Incitement to commit war crimes may lend greater normative coherence to atrocity speech law in other respects as well. First, as amply demonstrated at various points in this book, the sole "incitement" offense prosecutors can currently charge is direct and public incitement to commit genocide. But that crime is not likely to cover battlefield atrocities. Even if it could, as has been stressed throughout this volume, genocide poses formidable prosecution challenges. Stuart Ford notes that "genocide is exceptionally difficult to prove because of the specific intent requirement and genocide convictions are relatively rare."[38] Since direct and public incitement to commit genocide features an identical *mens rea*, the hurdles that must be overcome in prosecuting it are equally daunting.

2. Crimes against Humanity (Persecution)

Crimes against humanity (persecution) could be another potential charge, but it is of questionable utility. Why? Given its chapeau characteristics, it applies uniquely to offenses committed against civilians.[39] That would mean no justice for a sizable portion of incitement's victim class in the military milieu, that is, fighters *hors de combat*. Nevertheless, even if civilians could be confirmed as the exclusive target, it may be well-nigh impossible to prove the requisite "widespread or systematic attack." Imagine the scenario of a captain who, although not giving an official order, urges his company via coded terminology to murder unarmed women and children in a small village his troops were about to enter? Let us posit further that this conduct takes place on the fringes of an armed conflict sector wherein battlefield atrocities are ultimately prosecuted as war crimes? In respect of the village atrocities, proving a widespread or systematic attack against a civilian population is not viable. That would also be the case if a private radio station broadcasts an appeal to soldiers to perpetrate precision assaults on the inhabitants of a tiny, undefended hamlet.

Even if the chapeau requirement could be easily satisfied, prosecuting the speech as incitement to war crimes offers more policy advantages. First, it more effectively captures the transgression's military nature and better promotes deterrence among officers and rank-and-file soldiers. It also better sensitizes civilians, such as Simon Bikindi, who would egg on criminal-propensity soldiers, to their own possible liability for incitement to war crimes. Finally, charging these delicts

38. Stuart Ford, *Is the Failure to Respond Appropriately to a Natural Disaster a Crime against Humanity? The Responsibility to Protect and Individual Criminal Responsibility in the Aftermath of Cyclone Nargis*, 38 Denv. J. Int'l L. & Pol'y 227, 275 (2010).

39. *See, e.g.*, Rome Statute, *supra* note 6, art. 7 ("For the purpose of this Statute, 'crime against humanity' means any of the following acts when committed as part of a widespread or systematic attack directed against any *civilian* population . . . ." (emphasis added)).

as crimes of "incitement" stresses the *speech* aspect of the crime in a way that the generic charge of persecution cannot.

F. Potential Concerns

1. Infringing Free Speech Rights

The new offense raises concerns, though. Of these, the specter of unduly constraining legitimate expression is the most worrisome. As one expert puts it: "[Service] personnel are citizens and voters, and insulating them from the discussion of controversial public issues could result in a military cut off from societal concerns and values, itself a threat to a democracy."[40]

From both self-actualization and operational standpoints, officers ought to enjoy the right to air their opinions to soldiers who serve under them. This could logically and strategically include offering views as to the nature of the enemy. Casting the adversary in an extremely negative light may certainly be defensible given the need to prepare troops psychologically for battle. That said, if the speech is motivated by illicit aims, for example, inspiring troops to kill civilians or take no prisoners, no operational rationale can condone it—such rhetoric must be enjoined and prosecuted under all circumstances.

This would be consistent even with the extreme American libertarian speech values, according to which incitement is not unconditionally safeguarded expression. As we saw in Chapter 2, pursuant to *Brandenburg v. Ohio*, speech will not be protected if it "is directed to inciting or producing imminent lawless action and is likely to produce such action."[41] It is submitted that this standard may be consistent with the test proposed herein for incitement to commit war crimes: depending on the circumstances, fulfilling the crime's "context" element (which could, hypothetically, situate the speech within a pattern of unlawful attacks against civilians, for example) may satisfy *Brandenburg*'s imminence requirement; if so, the *mens rea* requirement is likely parallel to *Brandenburg*'s intent limb; and since war crimes is the object of the relevant incitement, *Brandenburg*'s "lawless action" prong is easily satisfied.[42]

40. Edward F. Sherman, *A Special Kind of Justice*, 84 Yale L.J. 373, 386 (1974) (reviewing Joseph W. Bishop, Jr., Justice under Fire: A Study of Military Law (1974)).

41. Brandenburg v. Ohio, 395 U.S. 444, 447 (1969).

42. Arguably, even the current international test for incitement to genocide may be consistent with the *Brandenburg* standard. *See* Gregory S. Gordon, *From Incitement to Indictment? Prosecuting Iran's President for Advocating Israel's Destruction and Piecing Together Incitement Law's Emerging Analytical Framework*, 98 J. Crim. L. & Criminology 853, 911 (2008) (suggesting that Iranian President Mahmoud Ahmadinejad's advocacy for Israel's destruction would not qualify for American Constitutional protection under *Brandenburg*). *But see* Justin La Mort, *The Soundtrack to Genocide: Using Incitement to Genocide in the Bikindi Trial to Protect Free Speech and Uphold the Promise of Never Again*, 4 Interdisc. J. Hum. Rts. L. 43, 52, 62 (2010) (explaining that the international test for incitement to genocide is not as exacting as *Brandenburg*). *See also* Audrey Golden, Comment, *Monkey Read, Monkey Do: Why*

Regardless, even in the United States, *Brandenburg* is limited to civilians and does not extend to soldiers.[43] Moreover, significantly, "the standard for First Amendment protections applied to military personnel is lower than that applied to civilians."[44] To wit, military courts eschew the *Brandenburg* test and "in applying the [less strict] clear and present danger test, have virtually excluded any requirement of proof by the military of an immediate likelihood that adverse conduct will result from the speech . . . . Those cases . . . leave servicemen's First Amendment rights largely dependent upon the indulgence of the military."[45]

2. Institutional Concerns

Apart from free expression concerns, incitement to commit war crimes presents possible institutional problems. From a practical perspective, would soldiers agree to testify against their officers?[46] Any reluctance on the part of subordinates, in this regard, would likely be heightened as the offense is inchoate and only punishes speech, as opposed to a more tangible, less abstract transgression. In the same vein, should one expect that the military brass, answerable only to their own courts, would be willing to prosecute a fellow officer in connection with this new offense? Such authorities are typically loath to bring their own to justice, even in cases where atrocities take place. As one expert has observed:

> Beyond the text of the various instruments, the key impediment to successful invocation of the humanitarian law of international armed conflict is likely to be the attitude of the combatants toward prosecutions. States have proved

the First Amendment Should Not Protect the Printed Speech of an International Genocide Inciter, 43 Wake Forest L. Rev. 1149, 1171–73 (2008) (speculating that Nazi propaganda would have qualified for First Amendment protection under the *Bradenburg* test). This all presupposes that reference would be had to the US First Amendment, but, as explained in Chapter 2, international law has not embraced the exceptional American framework. *See, e.g.*, Prosecutor v. Nahimana, et al., Case No. ICTR-99-52-A, Judgement, ¶ 1010 (Nov. 28, 2007) ("The Chamber considers international law, which has been well developed in the areas of freedom from discrimination and freedom of expression, to be the point of reference for its consideration of these issues, noting that domestic law varies widely while international law codifies evolving universal standards.").

43. *See* Jeffrey Lakin, *Atheists in Foxholes: Examining the Current State of Religious Freedom in the United States Military*, 9 First Amend. L. Rev. 713, 727 (2011).

44. *Id.*

45. Sherman, *supra* note 40, at 387; *see also* Dale Carpenter, Response, *The Value of Institutions and the Values of Free Speech*, 89 Minn. L. Rev. 1407, 1414 n.23 (2005) (describing *Brandenburg* standard as "stricter standard" than clear and present danger test of Schenck v. United States, 249 U.S. 47, 52–53 (1919)); Danley K. Cornyn, Note, *The Military, Freedom of Speech, and the Internet: Preserving Operational Security and Servicemembers' Right of Free Speech*, 87 Tex. L. Rev. 463, 471 (2008) ("[T]he 'clear and present danger' standard applies to service members' speech . . . .").

46. *See* Samuel Brenner, *"I Am a Bit Sickened": Examining Archetypes of Congressional War Crimes Oversight after My Ly and Abu Ghraib*, 205 Mil. L. Rev. 1, 73–74 (2010) (explaining

reluctant to prosecute their own soldiers for war crimes unless they are especially heinous and publicized, thereby justifying impunity, or a small administrative punishment, on the exigencies of warfare.[47]

But it would be hard to justify scuttling the incitement to war crimes proposal in light of these concerns. These potential hurdles are not unique to the proposed new offense—they are institutional impediments related to any attempt to prosecute military higher-ups for war crimes in courts-martial. While the challenges may be more imposing as the charged conduct is merely speech, Chapter 7 demonstrated the overwhelming normative necessity for it. And this chapter has proved that it is doctrinally feasible. While the new offense may end up having more aspirational than enforcement value, its potential second- and third-order salutary effects more than justify its adoption.[48]

V. CONCLUSION

Throughout this tome, we have seen that speech and atrocity are constant companions. That reality is all the more apparent on the battlefield, where homicide is normatively sanctioned. The international community has outlawed hate speech that calls for or results in genocide and crimes against humanity. Sound logic and compelling policy dictate that war crimes advocacy be criminalized too. Conditioning soldiers to breach the law of armed conflict is socially undesirable conduct but not the same as "ordering" them to do so, for which superiors can be brought to book. Nor is it akin to "instigating" them to engage in such conduct, another potential crime under current law, but only chargeable if there is no superior-subordinate relationship between the speaker and listener and the latter consequently commits the target offense. Direct incitement to commit war crimes would permit punishment of atrocity-conditioning and atrocity-persuading agents *before* law of armed conflict violations occur. And it would extend LOAC's writ to *civilians* who incite armed forces—a reality of mass-mobilization modern warfare.

The incitement to genocide framework, suitably altered, furnishes a ready template for gleaning the elements of this new offense. And those elements, as well as attendant regulations and relevant jurisprudence, should be whetted so

the difficulties experienced by subordinates testifying against their superiors and focusing on the ordeals of soldiers forced into that role in connection with the My Ly massacre and the Abu Ghraib prison scandal).

47. John F. Murphy, *Civil Liability for the Commission of International Crimes as an Alternative to Criminal Prosecution*, 12 Harv. Hum. Rts. J. 1, 15 (1999).

48. *See* Ryan Goodman & Derek Jinks, *Incomplete Internalization and Compliance with Human Rights Law*, 19 Eur. J. Int'l L. 725, 735 (2008) ("The legitimating effect may result from the 'expressive function' of law—an effect that is operative notwithstanding a lack of enforcement of the law.").

as to abate any possible free expression chilling effects or substantial operational hindrances. Officers should be able to exercise the prerogative of educating their troops and inspiring them before leading them into battle. But that should not include verbally whipping them up so as to commit grave breaches of the Geneva Conventions or other serious violations of the laws and customs of war. Adopting the crime of incitement to commit war crimes will help assure that does not happen.

11

Restructuring: A Unified Liability Theory for Atrocity Speech Law

"Out of clutter, find simplicity."

—Albert Einstein[1]

"Law develops according to its own logic."

—Enrico Pattaro[2]

I. INTRODUCTION

If the goals of this book were to be realized, would discrete fixes of individual atrocity speech modalities suffice? The answer is an emphatic no. Adjusting the individual offenses to achieve internal consistency and doctrinal efficacy still leaves each one conceptually siloed and normatively disconnected from one another. As this chapter will demonstrate, such macro dissonance would thwart the drive toward effective deterrence, ample doctrinal coverage and speech-specific expressive justice. How is this true?

We have seen the preventive value of the inchoate incitement crime, which permits early intervention based on initial conduct posing a credible threat. Why has it been limited to genocide when the other horrific atrocity offenses—crimes against humanity and war crimes—equally call for preventive action? Additionally, persecution based on speech conduct entails rhetoric uttered

1. William Safire & Leonard Safir, Words of Wisdom: More Good Advice 213 (1989) (citing Einstein's "Three Rules of Work").

2. 1 Enrico Pattaro, A Treatise of Legal Philosophy and General Jurisprudence: The Law and the Right 168 (2005).

Atrocity Speech Law. Gregory S. Gordon.

contemporaneously with the chapeau violence. However, there is arguably no speech-specific offense that criminalizes comparable rhetoric when voiced during the occurrence of genocidal bloodshed or war-related depredations. Why should such "egging-on" speech, or "speech abetting," as it will be termed here, be exempted from a speech-specific criminal prohibition?

In fact, it is hard to imagine any good policy reasons for these doctrinal deficits. Rather, as reflected in Chapter 3, it would seem the current legal landscape is the result of a complete lack of global vision or intentionality in formulating the various modalities that comprise atrocity speech law. This chapter will consider the history of those formulations from the perspective of the systemic incoherence in the ensemble of atrocity speech crimes. From there, it will consider how certain structural changes can be made to realize the crucial speech-specific prevention, systematization, and expressive goals emphasized throughout this book. In the end, it will propose a "Unified Liability Theory" for atrocity speech law. That theory posits that the core atrocity offenses—genocide, crimes against humanity, and war crimes—should be methodically attached to each type of liability—inciting, speech abetting, instigating, and ordering.[3] And this proposed change can be operationalized via treaty and a modification of the Rome Statute of the International Criminal Court (ICC), as well as any other relevant international or domestic instruments. The chapter will conclude with consideration of the theoretical and practical implications of this change.

II. THE HAPHAZARD FORMULATION OF THE ATROCITY SPEECH CRIMES

A. At Nuremberg

The reactive and doctrinally haphazard manner in which atrocity speech law has been framed was apparent from its earliest origins. We saw in Chapter 3 that Chief US Prosecutor Robert Jackson, in reference to Nazi crimes, stressed the central role of "incitement" during the summer 1945 negotiations in London for what would become the International Military Tribunal (IMT) at Nuremberg.[4] Jackson was perhaps the single most important figure who exerted an individual impact on those negotiations.[5] But despite his views regarding the significance of incitement, the term never even found its way into the Nuremberg IMT Charter, as demonstrated in Chapter 3.

3. Of course, the core crimes could eventually be expanded to include aggression or possibly terrorism, as will be discussed in Section IV.A of this book's Conclusion.

4. *See* Robert H. Jackson, Report of Robert H. Jackson, United States Representative to the International Conference on Military Trials (Dept. of State 1945) 376 (emphasizing, in reference to Nazi crimes, "The knowing incitement and planning is as criminal as the execution.").

5. *See generally* Henry T. King, Jr., *Robert Jackson's Transcendent Influence over Today's World*, 68 ALB. L. REV. 23, 23 (2004) (noting Jackson's "preeminence in the development and implementation of war crimes concepts . . .").

In fact, save for reference to the lone word "instigators," in connection with conspiracy to commit any of the three principal offenses (crimes against peace, war crimes, and crimes against humanity), no language regarding speech appears in the key subject matter jurisdiction provision of the Charter, Article 6:

> **Article 6.**
> The Tribunal established by the Agreement referred to in Article 1 hereof for the trial and punishment of the major war criminals of the European Axis countries shall have the power to try and punish persons who, acting in the interests of the European Axis countries, whether as individuals or as members of organizations, committed any of the following crimes.
>
> The following acts, or any of them, are crimes coming within the jurisdiction of the Tribunal for which there shall be individual responsibility:
>
> (a) **CRIMES AGAINST PEACE**: namely, planning, preparation, initiation or waging of a war of aggression, or a war in violation of international treaties, agreements or assurances, or participation in a common plan or conspiracy for the accomplishment of any of the foregoing;
>
> (b) **WAR CRIMES**: namely, violations of the laws or customs of war. Such violations shall include, but not be limited to, murder, ill-treatment or deportation to slave labor or for any other purpose of civilian population of or in occupied territory, murder or ill-treatment of prisoners of war or persons on the seas, killing of hostages, plunder of public or private property, wanton destruction of cities, towns or villages, or devastation not justified by military necessity;
>
> (c) **CRIMES AGAINST HUMANITY**: namely, murder, extermination, enslavement, deportation, and other inhumane acts committed against any civilian population, before or during the war; or persecutions on political, racial or religious grounds in execution of or in connection with any crime within the jurisdiction of the Tribunal, whether or not in violation of the domestic law of the country where perpetrated.
>
> Leaders, organizers, *instigators* and accomplices participating in the formulation or execution of a common plan or conspiracy to commit any of the foregoing crimes are responsible for all acts performed by any persons in execution of such plan.[6]

Moreover, notwithstanding this omission at the trial itself, hate speech was the focal point of two different prosecutions—that of tabloid publisher Julius

6. Charter of the International Military Tribunal at Nuremberg, Agreement for the Prosecution and Punishment of the Major War Criminals of the European Axis, Art. 6, Aug. 8, 1945, 59 Stat. 1544, 3 Bevans 1238, 82 U.N.T.S. 279 (emphasis added).

Streicher and Nazi Radio Chief Hans Fritzsche.[7] But instigation, explicitly enshrined in the Charter, was not charged. Nor was incitement.[8] Instead, a provision that did not even explicitly reference speech—persecution as a crime against humanity—was the object of charges against both Streicher and Fritzsche. But, as we have seen in the IMT's judgments in these cases, in discussing the speech at issue, the judges variously referred to "incitement," thus confusing matters even more.[9]

A similar approach was adopted in respect of Control Council Law No. 10, which governed subsequent prosecutions against lesser Nazi officials in the American zone (and, in particular, in the case brought against Nazi Press Chief Otto Dietrich).[10] In the end, the doctrinal and penal implications of Nuremberg's oblique and fuzzy treatment of speech crimes would have ripple effects on the law's subsequent development.

B. During the Cold War Period

Indeed, nowhere is speech even mentioned in the General Assembly's 1946 "Affirmation of the Principles of International Law Recognized by the Charter of the Nuremberg Tribunal"[11] or the International Law Commission's subsequent enshrinement of those tenets in the 1950 "Principles of International Law Recognized in the Charter of the Nuremberg Tribunal and in the Judgment of the Tribunal."[12]

7. MICHAEL SALTER, NAZI WAR CRIMES, US INTELLIGENCE AND SELECTIVE PROSECUTION AT NUREMBERG 7 (2007) ("Nazi propagandists were also targeted as defendants, including radio broadcaster Hans Fritzsche and the anti-Semitic publisher Julius Streicher.").

8. WILLIAM A. SCHABAS, GENOCIDE IN INTERNATIONAL LAW: THE CRIME OF CRIMES 332 (2d ed. 2009) (noting that incitement to genocide "did not exist in international law at that time [i.e., the time of the IMT trial at Nuremberg] . . .").

9. *See, e.g.*, United States v. Goering, Judgment, Streicher (Int'l Mil. Trib. Sept. 30, 1946), *reprinted in* 6 F.R.D. 69, 161–63 (1946) ("Streicher's *incitement* to murder and extermination at the time when Jews in the East were being killed under the most horrible conditions clearly constitutes persecution on political and racial grounds in connection with war crimes as defined by the Charter, and constitutes a crime against humanity.") (emphasis added).

10. Allied Control Council Law No. 10, Punishment of Persons Guilty of War Crimes, Crimes against Peace and Against Humanity, Dec. 20, 1945, *reprinted in* Telford Taylor, Final Report to the Secretary of the Army on the Nuremberg War Crimes Trials Under Control Council Law No. 10, at 250 (1949) [hereinafter CCL No. 10]; United States v. Ernst Weizsaker (*Ministries Case*), *in* 12 TRIALS OF WAR CRIMINALS BEFORE THE NUERNBERG MILITARY TRIBUNALS UNDER CONTROL COUNCIL LAW NO. 10, 498 (1951) [hereinafter *Ministries Case*].

11. Affirmation of the Principles of International Law Recognized by the Charter of the Nuremberg Tribunal, G.A. Res. 95(1), U.N. GAOR, 1st Sess., U.N. Doc. A/236 at 1144 (Dec. 11, 1946).

12. Principles of International Law Recognized in the Charter of the Nuremberg Tribunal and in the Judgment of the Tribunal, Documents of the Second Session Including the Report

Speech plays a role in the 1948 "International Convention on the Prevention and Punishment of the Crime of Genocide" (Genocide Convention).[13] As we have seen, Article III of the Convention requires states parties to punish "[d]irect and public incitement to commit genocide."[14] But the Genocide Convention centers on "genocide" and treats incitement only incidentally. This is the first international legal codification of "incitement" as an offense, and it would be the blueprint for future formulations of incitement in the major international criminal law instruments, including the ad hoc tribunal statutes and the statute for the International Criminal Court.[15]

In the meantime, as revealed in Chapter 7, the 1949 Geneva Conventions ignore speech as a crime almost entirely—with the exception of "ordering" grave breach conduct.[16] Incitement does not find its way into the Geneva Conventions at all. And crimes against humanity have not been the subject of an international convention—*a fortiori* incitement to commit crimes against humanity has been similarly overlooked in terms of treaty law.[17]

C. During the Post–Cold War Period

Rather, as dealt with in Chapter 3, hate speech as a crime against humanity was charged at Nuremberg in the cases of defendants Streicher, Fritzsche, and Dietrich. And as we saw in Chapters 3, 4, and 6, that template was uncritically reproduced for the post–Cold War ICL constituent instruments. Chapter 3 demonstrated that the ICTY Statute was drafted in great haste and in an effort to deal with an unfolding crisis. So the Nuremberg model came in handy. Thus, as at Nuremberg, ICTY Statute Article 5 (ICTR Statute Article 4), the provision covering crimes against humanity, has no explicit reference to speech. Rather, taking a page out of the Nuremberg playbook, following the chapeau, one of the

of the Commission to the General Assembly, [1950] 2 Y.B. INT'L L. COMM'N 13, U.N. Doc. A/CN.4/SER.A/1950/Add.1.

13. International Convention on the Prevention and Punishment of the Crime of Genocide, Dec. 9, 1948, 78 U.N.T.S. 277 [hereinafter Genocide Convention].

14. *Id.* art. III.

15. *See* David Scheffer, *The International Criminal Court*, *in* ROUTLEDGE HANDBOOK OF INTERNATIONAL CRIMINAL LAW 70 (William Schabas & Nadia Bernaz eds., 2010). (noting that the text of the Genocide Convention was used for the ad hoc tribunals and the ICC and the Convention was the first to codify the crime of incitement).

16. *See, e.g.*, Geneva Convention for the Amelioration of the Condition of the Wounded and Sick in Armed Forces in the Field art. 49, Aug. 12, 1949, 6 U.S.T. 3114, 75 U.N.T.S. 31 ("The High Contracting Parties undertake to enact any legislation necessary to provide effective penal sanctions for persons committing, *or ordering to be committed*, any of the grave breaches of the present Convention defined in the following Article.") (emphasis added).

17. JOHN QUIGLY, THE GENOCIDE CONVENTION: AN INTERNATIONAL LAW ANALYSIS 13 (2006) (noting that "crimes against humanity are not the subject of a treaty comparable to the Genocide Convention.").

enumerated acts is "persecutions on political, racial and religious grounds . . ."[18] And as explained in Chapter 4, in prosecuting atrocity firebrands from both Rwanda and the former Yugoslavia, each tribunal charged the hate speech at issue pursuant to this provision.

The ICC has not deviated from this modus operandi. Once again, the relevant crimes against humanity provision, Article 7, contains no explicit reference to speech. Rather, as before, in the enumerated acts following the chapeau (in Article 7(1)), one finds subsection (h) "persecution," against "any identifiable group or collectivity on political, racial, national, ethnic, cultural, religious, gender . . . or other grounds that are universally recognized as impermissible under international law . . ."[19] This provision is being used to prosecute atrocity rabble-rousers. For example, the Court charged Joshua arap Sang with crimes against humanity (persecution) in connection with hate speech broadcast on Kenyan radio after the disputed 2007 elections (although that case has since been dropped after prosecution claims that key witnesses were intimidated).[20]

A similar cut-and-paste approach was taken with respect to incitement. As that offense had historically been attached only to genocide, the ad hoc tribunal and ICC statutes simply aped their international lawmaking predecessors. Thus, the ICTY/ICTR, in the relevant genocide provision for each statute, simply reproduced wholesale Articles II and III of the Genocide Convention. It will be recalled that, after a definition of genocide in Article II, Article III(c) of the Genocide Convention states that "the following acts shall be punishable . . . (c) direct and public incitement to commit genocide."[21]

Thus, in an entirely parallel structure, ICTY Statute Article 4(2)/ICTR Statute Article 2(2) define genocide precisely as it is defined in the Genocide Convention.[22] And ICTY Statute Article 4(3)/ICTR Statute Article 2(3) declare that "the following acts shall be punishable."[23] And then, at subsection (c) this

18. Statute of the International Criminal Tribunal for the Former Yugoslavia, S.C. Res. 827, art. 5(h), U.N. Doc. S/RES/827 (May 25, 1993), *amended by* S.C. Res. 1166, annex, U.N. Doc. S/RES/116 (May 13, 1998) [hereinafter ICTY Statute]. *See also* Statute of the International Criminal Tribunal for Rwanda, S.C. Res. 955, art. 3(h), U.N. Doc. S/RES/955 (Nov. 8, 1994) [hereinafter ICTR Statute].

19. Rome Statute of the International Criminal Court art. 7(1)(h), July 17, 1998, 2178 U.N.T.S. 3 (entered into force July 1, 2002) [hereinafter Rome Statute].

20. *See* Gregory S. Gordon, *Setting the Record Straight on International Speech Crime Law*, Jurist (May 24, 2011), http://jurist.org/forum/2011/05/gregory-gordon-arap-sang.php (explaining that the alleged persecution does not stem directly from radio hate speech targeting ethnic minorities but is based on acts of murder and forcible transfer of population where the hate speech supposedly supported the murders and deportations).

21. Genocide Convention, *supra* note 13, arts. II, III(c).

22. ICTY Statute, *supra* note 18, art. 4(2); ICTR Statute, *supra* note 18, art. 2(2).

23. ICTY Statute, *supra* note 18, art. 4(3); ICTR Statute, *supra* note 18, art. 2(3).

language is included: "direct and public incitement to commit genocide."[24] And no other provision in either ad hoc tribunal statute alludes to incitement in connection with any other offense.

Similarly, although the Rome Statute separates the provisions defining genocide and its modes of liability—in Articles 6 and 25, respectively—the same essential approach is taken by the ICC. Article 6 once again incorporates wholesale the definition of genocide from Article II of the Genocide Convention. And Article 25(3)(e) states that a person shall be criminally responsible if that person, "in respect of the crime of genocide, directly and publicly incites others to commit genocide . . ."[25] "Incitement" appears nowhere else in the statute.

And although in each of these statutes instigation (or solicitation/inducement in the Rome Statute) evidently applies to each of the core crimes of genocide, crimes against humanity, and war crimes, it is a free-floating mode of liability not in any way linked to the other speech-related crimes, to wit, incitement and persecution. Thus, Articles 7/6 (1) of the ICTY/ICTR statutes state that "a person who . . . instigated in the planning, preparation or execution of a crime referred to in . . . the present Statute, shall be individually responsible for the crime."[26] And, along the same lines, pursuant to Article 25(3)(b) of the Rome Statute, "a person shall be criminally responsible . . . if that person . . . orders, solicits or induces the commission of such a crime which in fact occurs or is attempted . . ."[27]

D. Reflections on the Current Legal Landscape

1. Political Realities

That atrocity speech law grew this way—in a piecemeal, disconnected fashion with no teleological guideposts—is in many ways understandable as "any legal system arises and develops in specific historical circumstances."[28] And thus, "the content of rules [and] their particular development [are] the unintended outcome of historical development."[29] In the case of atrocity speech law, the choices made at Nuremberg may seem logical based on the exigencies facing Allied lawyers at the time. International criminal law was in its infancy and had to be applied conservatively to eschew charges of overreaching. Crimes against humanity, the newest and least embraced of the Nuremberg crimes, was reined in via the armed conflict nexus. Thus, if crimes against humanity were already considered

24. ICTY Statute, *supra* note 18, art. 4(3)(c); ICTR Statute, *supra* note 18, art. 2(3)(c).

25. Rome Statute, *supra* note 19, arts. 6, 25(3)(e).

26. ICTY Statute, *supra* note 18, art. 7(1); ICTR Statute, *supra* note 18, art. 6(1).

27. Rome Statute, *supra* note 19, arts. 6, 25(3)(b).

28. Sudha R. Shenoy, Towards a Theoretical Framework for British and International Economic History 335 (2001).

29. *Id.*

controversial, any connected inchoate speech offense would have been considered especially taboo. In this context, one can easily understand the absence of an incitement to crimes against humanity charge. Even incitement to war crimes seems like a stretch. And genocide had not even been officially formulated as a legal concept—as we have seen—the Genocide Convention was not adopted until December 1948.

But post–Cold War qualms regarding development of this body of law are harder to understand. Certainly, achieving accord among a diverse group of diplomats is no easy feat. And the desire to manufacture consensus arguably tends to promote conservatism. In that context, cutting and pasting is clearly the path of least resistance. That is especially true in the situation the ICTY Statute framers found themselves in—having to react quickly to an unfolding crisis.[30]

Then, the ICTR largely reproduced the ICTY template. Former US Foreign Service Officer Dr. Gregory Stanton, who drafted UN Security Council Resolution 955 (1994), which contained the ICTR Statute, reveals:

> The US State Department Office of the Legal Advisor wanted the ICTR Statute to directly reflect the ICTY Statute in order to create a consistent body of international criminal law. Lawyers rely on precedent. Convincing the legal advisors to the Security Council members would be easier if the ICTR statute copied the ICTY statute, which the Security Council had already adopted. It's why every UN Security Council Resolution begins with citations to previous ones.[31]

The drafters of the ICC Statute found themselves similarly constrained. According to Roger Clark, one of the document's key framers:

> The essential approach to drafting the substantive criminal law and general part provisions of the Rome Statute was a conservative one. With few exceptions, there was no disposition to tread new ground. The reference to incitement was found in the Genocide Convention and the Statutes of the *ad hoc* tribunals. But the latter referred to incitement in the context of genocide

30. *See* Theodor Meron, The Making of International Criminal Justice: A View from the Bench 117 (2011) (indicating that the ICTY Statute was "drafted quickly").

31. E-mail from Dr. Gregory Stanton, Research Professor in Genocide Studies and Prevention, George Mason University School of Conflict Analysis and Resolution, and President, Genocide Watch, to author (Aug. 19, 2016) (on file with author). Stanton was able to insert two key substantive changes, so that the ICTR Statute includes violations of Common Article 3 and Optional Protocol 2 of the Geneva Conventions in its subject matter jurisdiction, eliminating the "war nexus" and creating jurisdiction over nonstate actors. *Id.* "At first," he says, "some pointed out that the US was not even a state-party to Optional Protocol 2. But they conceded that the UN Security Council could make law and that the US could vote for this expansion of the ICTR's jurisdiction. However, no thought was given to changing international criminal law." *Id.*

> alone. A few of us suggested that, since we had an opportunity to draft for the future, incitement should apply to all four crimes within the jurisdiction of the Court. No formal amendment was ever made and the idea gained little traction.[32]

And thus a series of golden opportunities were squandered. Penal treatment of weaponized words in the context of atrocity, a body of law misshapen and riddled with gaping holes thanks to diplomacy trumping legislative reason, simply calcified.

2. Broadening Incitement and Adding Speech Abetting

Thus, from the perspective of logic and good policy, inclusion of incitement to commit crimes against humanity or war crimes could have been possible. It will be recalled, as seen in Chapter 3, the International Law Commission's 1954 draft Code of Offences against the Peace and Security of Mankind, as well as its updated 1996 version, criminalized incitement to commit genocide, crimes against humanity and war crimes.[33] We saw in Chapter 10 that formulation of the crime of incitement to commit war crimes makes sense from both doctrinal and policy perspectives. So does the prospect of codifying incitement to commit crimes against humanity. In reference to that offense, Elies van Sliedregt, in a treatise meant to advise the International Law Commission on drafting a possible Convention on Crimes against Humanity, has advised that "inclusion of [incitement to commit crimes against humanity] seems useful and desirable."[34] And Wibke Timmermann and William Schabas have noted: "The same reasons for criminalizing direct and public incitement to commit genocide are equally valid in the case of other mass crimes such as crimes against humanity,

32. E-mail from Roger Clark, Board of Governors Professor of Law, Rutgers Law School, to author (Aug. 9, 2016) (on file with author). Clark also noted: "The Genocide Convention's reference to (inchoate) conspiracy, incidentally, simply got lost in the shuffle." *Id.*

33. Draft Code of Offenses against the Peace and Security of Mankind, [1950] 1 Y.B. Int'l L. Comm'n 1, U.N. Doc. A/CN.4/R.6, art. 2(13)(ii); Rep. of the Int'l Law Comm'n, *Draft Code of Crimes against the Peace and Security of Mankind*, 48th Sess., July 17, 1996, U.N. Doc. A/CN.4/L.532; U.N. GAOR 51st Sess., Supp. No. 10, art. 2.3(f), *reprinted in* [1996] 2 Y.B. Int'l L. Comm'n 17.

34. Elies van Sliedregt, *Modes of Participation*, *in* Forging a Convention for Crimes against Humanity 254 (Leila Nadya Sadat ed., 2011) (noting as well that, in contrast to conspiracy to commit crimes against humanity, incitement "is more acceptable as an inchoate offense . . ."). Curiously, however, the International Law Commission's current draft articles in respect of a potential Crimes against Humanity Convention contain no incitement provision. *See* First Report of the International Law Commission on the Work of Its Sixty-Seventh Session, [2015] 2 Y.B. Int'l L. Comm'n pt. 2; Second Report of the International Law Commission on the Work of Its Sixty-Seventh Session, [2016] 2 Y.B. Int'l L. Comm'n pt. 2.

especially extermination or persecution, or aggression, and it would appear desirable to extend the applicability of incitement to those offences."[35]

ICL legislators might have also considered the basic nature of crimes against humanity (persecution) and whether it might have broader application. It is submitted that hate speech as persecution has been grossly undertheorized. What is it in essence? It is speech that is part of a widespread or systematic attack directed against a civilian population and is uttered knowing that it is part of that attack.[36] As noted earlier, it could aptly be described as "egging-on" speech—it provides support to the attack while it is taking place. Thus it is speech that lends aid synchronously with violence. It is not clear why it should be criminalized uniquely with respect to crimes against humanity. Why not apply it to genocide or war crimes?

And in structuring international criminal statutes, why not take into account that a series of speech crimes have developed and are related to one another? A speech-dedicated provision in the ICL constituent instruments could have gathered these offenses together, more effectively structured them, demonstrated their relationship to one another, and, given the central role of speech in mass atrocity, served as a strong reminder to prosecutors that, as part of charging strategy, speech crimes should always be considered in their own right. They are central to the etiology of pernicious discrimination-focused out-group mass violence.[37]

As the framers of the ICL charters and statutes have overlooked the utility of a doctrinal expansion and structural consolidation of international speech crimes, this book will urge amending extant instruments to do so and/or drafting future ones in the same mold. In the section that follows, consistent with the proposed Unified Liability Theory, the necessary blueprint will be laid out.

III. EXPANDING AND CONSOLIDATING ATROCITY SPEECH CRIMES

A. Doctrinal Expansion

In fact, the underlying conceptual/structural conceit in all this is a matrix with four types of liability along the horizontal axis (five if ordering is bifurcated into

35. Wibke Timmermann & William A. Schabas, *Incitement to Genocide*, *in* Elements of Genocide 173 (Paul Behrens & Ralph Henham eds., 2013).

36. Gregory S. Gordon, *Hate Speech and Persecution: A Contextual Approach*, 46 Vand. J. Transnat'l L. 303, 310 (explaining the relationship between the speaker's knowledge and the widespread or systematic attack).

37. *See* Susan Benesch, *Dangerous Speech Along the Path to Mass Violence*, World Policy Institute, http://www.worldpolicy.org/content/dangerous-speech-along-the-path-to-mass-violence (last visited Sept. 18, 2016) ("Inflammatory public speech rises steadily before outbreaks of mass violence, suggesting that it is a precursor or even a prerequisite for violence, which makes sense: groups of killers do not form spontaneously.").

non-inchoate and inchoate) and three types of liability along the vertical (four if one includes aggression—see discussion below). The core crimes are genocide, crimes against humanity, and war crimes (and, again, possibly aggression). The types of liability are incitement, "speech abetting," instigation, and ordering (with the latter bifurcated into non-inchoate and inchoate varities). Of these, only "speech abetting" is new. But it corresponds to speech uttered contemporaneously with existing, ongoing violence. In other words, it is the "egging-on" type of rhetoric that roughly corresponds with hate speech currently charged as crimes against humanity (persecution).[38]

But the proposal here is to liberate this sort of liability from its crimes against humanity silo and apply it to genocide and war crimes, when appropriate.[39] Similarly, incitement should be untethered in its exclusive pairing with genocide and be available for application to all the core crimes, consistent with the ILC's 1954 and 1996 versions of its Draft Code of Offences/Crimes against the Peace and Security of Mankind.[40]

If this approach were taken, speech connected to each core crime could be charged as a function of timing and impact. Incitement would apply to speech urging, but not resulting in, causally related violence. Instigation would be charged when causally related violence followed the verbal act. Speech abetting would be charged if the expression at issue were voiced contemporaneously with acts that could be characterized as genocide, crimes against humanity, or war crimes. Ordering would apply to speech commanding commission of an atrocity crime, whether it is committed or not, if there were a superior-subordinate relationship between speaker and listener. This way, pursuant to the Unified Liability Theory, the entire range of potential criminal speech could be charged in connection with each offense and in a more granular, and accurate, fashion. This can be seen in Figure 11.1 below.

38. It should be noted that "abetting" has a different connotation from its constant companion "aiding." According to the ICTR, aiding is defined as providing assistance to someone, while abetting entails facilitating the commission of an act by being sympathetic thereto. Prosecutor v. Akayesu, Case No. ICTR-96-4-T, Judgement, ¶ 123 (Sept. 2, 1998). According to Smith and Hogan, "the natural meaning of 'to aid' is 'to give help, support, or assistance to'; and of 'to abet', 'to incite, instigate or encourage.'" J.C. Smith & Brian Hogan, Criminal Law (7th ed. 1992).

39. In theory, this could extend to aggression. If, for example, State A were in the process of launching an invasion of State B, if leaders of State C made radio broadcasts applauding State A, one could imagine a possible charge of speech abetting in reference to State A's act of aggression.

40. Draft Code of Offenses against the Peace and Security of Mankind, art. 2(13)(i) [1950] 1 Y.B. Int'l L. Comm'n 1, U.N. Doc. A/CN.4/R.6; Rep. of the Int'l Law Comm'n, *Draft Code of Crimes against the Peace and Security of Mankind*, 48th Sess., July 17, 1996, U.N. Doc. A/CN.4/L.532; U.N. GAOR 51st Sess., Supp. No. 10, art. 2.3(f), *reprinted in* [1996] 2 Y.B. Int'l L. Comm'n 17.

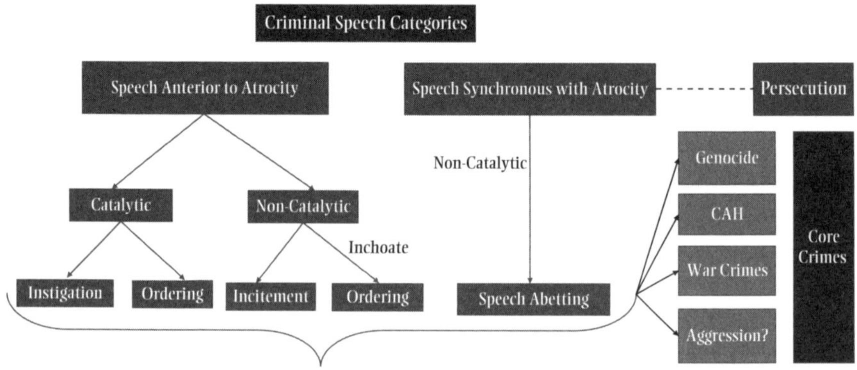

Figure 11.1 Unified Liability Theory.

B. Operationalization

1. By Treaty

So how can this doctrinal expansion be put into practice? Two potential initiatives come to mind. First, a treaty might be a good initial approach. A "Convention on the Classification and Criminalization of Atrocity Speech Offenses," for example, could, in its preamble, explain the current deficit in the law and the need to address it. The body of the treaty could then set out the relevant offenses and definitions. Thus, one could imagine a treaty looking roughly as follows:

a. Text of the Proposed Treaty

CONVENTION ON THE CLASSIFICATION AND CRIMINALIZATION OF ATROCITY SPEECH OFFENSES

The Contracting Parties to this Convention,

Recognizing the well-documented historical link between hate speech and mass atrocity that has inflicted great suffering and losses on humanity;

Noting that four forms of liability related to hate speech and mass atrocity have been developed in the jurisprudence since the trial before the International Military Tribunal at Nuremberg—ordering, instigation, incitement, and persecution as a crime against humanity;

Considering that incitement, which applies to hate speech that is intended to result in, but does not result in, subsequent violence, has until now, only been criminalized in connection with genocide;

Taking into account that hate speech charged as persecution entails verbal expression uttered contemporaneously with violence and thus can otherwise be referred to as "speech abetting";

Acknowledging the fact that the equivalent of "speech abetting" (i.e., persecution) has, until now, only been criminalized in connection with crimes against humanity;

Recognizing that provisions related to hate speech and atrocity core crimes have traditionally been scattered in various parts of international criminal law instruments and never assembled in one unified, organized provision;

Being convinced that hate speech, as such an essential precondition for mass atrocity, should be singled out for separate doctrinal treatment and criminalization;

Have agreed as follows:

Article 1

The Contracting Parties confirm that hate speech, when uttered for purposes of triggering or supporting atrocity crimes, should be accurately categorized in its different penal forms and criminalized and punished according to the actual form it takes. Such speech shall be considered to give rise to what is known as "atrocity speech liability."

Article 2

For purposes of this Convention, "atrocity crimes" means genocide, crimes against humanity, and war crimes, as defined respectively in Articles 6, 7, and 8 of the Rome Statute of the International Criminal Court [hereinafter "Rome Statute"].[41]

Article 3

For purposes of this Convention, "victim group" refers to a group that is the object of persecution, as defined by Articles 7(1)(h) and 7(2)(g) of the Rome Statute, by one or more other groups in society.

41. The list of target offenses could eventually be expanded to include aggression. Article 5(1)(d) of the Rome Statute includes aggression among the crimes within the jurisdiction of the Court. Rome Statute, *supra* note 19, art. 5(1)(d). Article 5(2) states that the Court would only exercise jurisdiction over the aggression offense "once a provision is adopted in accordance with articles 121 and 123 defining the crime and setting out the conditions under which the Court shall exercise jurisdiction with respect to this crime." *Id.* art. 5(2). Pursuant to Articles 121 (concerning amendment of the statute) and 123 (concerning a review conference in relation to the crimes in Article 5), a review conference was held in Kampala, Uganda, in the summer of 2010 and amendments related to the crime of aggression were adopted. These included defining "aggression" and making the jurisdiction available even without a Security Council referral. *See* Sean D. Murphy, *The Crime of Aggression at the International Criminal Court*, *in* The Oxford Handbook of the Use of Force in International Law 539 (Marc Weller ed., 2015). At the same time, it was decided that jurisdiction over the crime would not become operative until sometime after January 1, 2017. *Id.* at 534. As of the printing of this book, such jurisdiction is not yet operative. But should it become so, Article 2 of the Convention on the Classification and Criminalization of Atrocity Speech Offenses could be amended to include aggression. The conceptual ramifications of such an expansion are considered later in this book. *See* Conclusion, Section IV.A.

Article 4

For purposes of this Convention, “hate speech” consists of:

1. “General Hate Speech,” which is defined as broad forms of speech generally casting aspersions on a victim group, effectuated via statements of stereotypical racial, ethnic, or religious denigration, including group libel and other general statements not necessarily targeting one specific person or specific persons within the group;
2. “Harassment,” which is defined as general hate speech voiced directly at a person or persons belonging to a victim group; and
3. “Incitement,” which is defined as urging or provoking another to mistreat members of a victim group and does not carry the legal significance of the word used in Article 5(1) herein, which refers to the “incitement” form of liability.[42]

Article 5

For purposes of this Convention, atrocity speech liability arises from incitement, speech abetting, instigation, and ordering, which are defined as follows:

1. “Incitement” means, with the intent of causing another to commit an atrocity crime as defined herein, and having the same *mens rea* as the atrocity crime, urging another to commit the atrocity crime, when the crime is not subsequently perpetrated.
2. “Speech abetting” means, with knowledge of the ongoing commission of an atrocity crime, and with intent to encourage or assist the commission of that crime, uttering hate speech during the commission and in the presence of that crime, when the hate speech is heard by other persons and has no causal relationship to that crime.
3. “Instigation” means, with the intent of causing another to commit an atrocity crime as defined herein, and having the same *mens rea* as the atrocity crime, urging another to commit the atrocity crime, when the crime is subsequently perpetrated and the urging made a substantial contribution thereto.
4. “Ordering” means, with awareness of the substantial likelihood that an atrocity crime will be committed in the execution of an order, the transmission of an order by a superior to a subordinate to commit that crime, regardless of whether or not the crime is subsequently committed.

42. As has been explained throughout this book, “incite” has both lay and legal meanings. As used in this portion of the proposed treaty, there is reference to its lay definition. Of course, a primary objective of this book is to clear up confusion regarding use of the legal and lay terms but somctimes reference to the lay meaning of “incite” may be necessary in a legal document. In such cases, there should be clear language distinguishing the one from the other.

Article 6

The Contracting Parties undertake to enact the necessary legislation to give effect to the provisions of the present Convention, and, in particular, to provide effective penalties for persons found guilty pursuant to the types of liability enumerated in Article 5. The types of liability and definitions set forth in Article 5 shall be the object of a separate provision in any such legislation and shall be titled "Liability Related to Speech."

Article 7

Persons charged pursuant to the types of liability enumerated in Article 5 shall be tried by a competent court or tribunal as may have jurisdiction pursuant to the laws of the relevant Contracting Parties.

Article 8

The original of the present Convention shall be deposited in the archives of the United Nations. A certified copy of the Convention shall be transmitted to each Contracting Party. The present Convention shall be registered by the Secretary-General of the United Nations on the date of its coming into force.

b. Application of the Treaty

Of course, the treaty would obligate states parties to amend their domestic laws to achieve compliance. But it could also serve as a template for statutory change for non-states parties.[43] Similarly, it could serve as a blueprint for newly created ad hoc international courts or tribunals.

2. By Amendment of the Rome Statute

In practical terms, probably the most important application of the Unified Liability Theory would be in reference to the International Criminal Court. In the case of the ICC, it is recommended that this be effected through amendment of the institution's Rome Statue.[44] In particular, the Assembly of States Parties could add an Article 25*bis*, titled "Liability Related to Speech."[45] Pursuant to this amendment, Articles 25(3)(b) (covering orders and instigation (i.e., "soliciting"

43. *See* Bertram Ramcharan, *The Law-Making Process: From Declaration to Treaty and Custom*, *in* The Oxford Handbook of International Human Rights Law 513 (Dina Shelton ed., 2013) (referring to treaties catalyzing changes in domestic laws to ensure conformity with the treaty).

44. It should be noted that amending the statute via its Article 121 is an involved process requiring an initial adoption by two-thirds of the members of the Assembly of States Parties (ASP), as well as subsequent ratification by seven-eighths majority of all ASP members. Rome Statute, *supra* note 19, art. 121 (3) & (4).

45. 25*bis* has been selected here as the proposed new Rome Statute article notwithstanding the Kampala aggression amendments' addition of 3*bis* to Article 25. Rome Statute, *supra* note 19, art. 25(3*bis*). Article 25(3*bis*) declares: "In respect of the crime of aggression, the provisions

and "inducing," the words used in the Rome Statute) and (e) (covering incitement to genocide) would be removed from Article 25 of the existing statute and incorporated into Article 25*bis*.[46]

Additionally, incitement would be expanded consistent with Article 5 of the proposed Convention on the Classification and Criminalization of Atrocity Speech Crimes. Also, consistent with Article 5 of the Convention, speech abetting would be added and the scope of ordering would be expanded to encompass inchoate liability.

IV. THEORETICAL AND PRACTICAL ISSUES RAISED BY THE UNIFIED LIABILITY THEORY

The content and mechanics related to implementing the Unified Liability Theory have now been discussed. It remains to consider the theoretical and practical implications of such implementation. These issues bifurcate into matters related to both the theoretical and practical. From a theoretical perspective, it is important to understand the conceptual parameters and consequences of implementation. For example, what impact would the proposal have on substantive law provisions as well as other modes of liability and inchoate crimes? In particular, if speech abetting is adopted, what happens to the crime of persecution? What are the larger policy implications of this? Is it doctrinally feasible to fuse modes of liability and inchoate crimes into a single unified provision? And why is there a need for a separate liability provision dedicated entirely and uniquely to speech?

From a practical point of view, what would be the specific elements of the crimes? How would those elements affect charging decisions? Thus, if a complicated set of facts seemed to implicate incitement and speech abetting at the same time, how would that be charged? And in presenting a prima facie case of speech abetting, for example, what elements would have to be proved by the prosecution at trial? How do those elements relate to those of the other liability types? And how should charging ordering be handled, given that, per this book's proposal, it be treated as both a mode of liability and an inchoate crime? The subsection that follows will engage with these issues.

A. Theoretical Issues

1. Situating the Reconfigured Body of Law Conceptually

In conceptual terms, this new doctrinal flexibility and expansion would provide greater coverage in terms of potential liability scenarios. Thus, freeing incitement from its traditional doctrinal moorings would expand inchoate liability to

of this article shall apply only to persons in a position effectively to exercise control over or to direct the political or military action of a State." *Id.* As this only covers a subprovision of Article 25, 25*bis* is still available.

46. *Id.* arts. 25(3)(b) (covering ordering and instigation) and (3)(e) (covering incitement to genocide).

criminalize speech urging, but not resulting in, crimes against humanity and/or war crimes. Moreover, in contrast to the current state of the law, inchoate liability would be available to criminalize orders that do not result in commission of offenses (clearly in the military context but possibly as well in the civilian context).

"Speech abetting," the proposed new form of liability, would also enlarge the scope of verbal criminality connected to atrocity offenses. In particular, rhetoric with no causal relation to atrocity violence, but uttered simultaneously to it, would be extended beyond crimes against humanity and attach to both genocide and war crimes (and even with regard to crimes against humanity, it would impose less rigorous requirements than persecution). At the same time, instigation, and ordering, to the extent applicable, would still be available as forms of liability (while ordering would be expanded to include inchoate liability).

Overall, then, this newly configured set of speech crimes would fill gaps within the existing doctrinal landscape. In relation to war crimes, for example, as we saw in Chapter 10, an officer's culpability for offenses committed by other military personnel can be currently classified as either commission or omission liability. In terms of commission liability, there is ordering or instigation (to the extent the superior-subordinate relationship cannot be established—if, for example, the listener were of comparable rank). As for omission liability, there is the doctrine of command responsibility.[47] But by extending responsibility for ordering that does not result in commission of crimes and adding incitement, inchoate liability would be well covered.

As for crimes against humanity, rather than exclusively affixing liability for speech *qua* speech to persecution, the Unified Liability Theory opens up numerous possibilities. For one, we should not think of "incitement to crimes against humanity" monolithically. More specifically, each enumerated crimes against humanity offense can now be the target crime for incitement. Thus, incitement to murder or extermination as a crime against humanity would be possible. Jens Ohlin suggests that Streicher's conviction at Nuremberg was the functional equivalent of this: "At Nuremberg, Julius Streicher was convicted for incitement to commit murder and extermination for articles published in *Der Stürmer*."[48]

Similarly, speech abetting could apply to the whole gamut of sub-chapeau offenses as well. For example, speech abetting in reference to deportation, imprisonment, torture, rape, and enforced disappearance would all be in play.

47. *See, e.g.*, ICTY Statute Article 7(3), which states: "The fact that any of the acts . . . was committed by a subordinate does not relieve his superior of criminal responsibility if he knew or had reason to know that the subordinate was about to commit such acts or had done so and the superior *failed* to take the necessary and reasonable measures to prevent such acts or to punish the perpetrators thereof." ICTY Statute, *supra* note 18, art. 7(3).

48. Jens David Ohlin, *Inchoate Crimes*, *in* The Oxford Companion to International Criminal Justice 373 (Antonio Cassese ed., 2009).

In the same vein, verbal liability would now extend to speech uttered simultaneously with genocidal violence, not merely preexisting the violence, and with no causal relationship thereto. In considering this possibility, one realizes the inadequacy of cabining speech related to genocide to instances of strict temporal anteriority or catalytic connection. As the United States Holocaust Memorial Museum (USHMM) observes: "Genocide is often . . . *accompanied* by widespread hate speech."[49] The doctrinal modifications suggested herein will unyoke speech offenses from their traditional and artificial penal associations and make them work to better capture the full range of verbal liability.

2. The Value of a Separate "Liability Related to Speech" Provision

It could be argued that there is current coverage for the liability gaps just detailed. Generic accomplice liability, for example, already theoretically covers speech abetting.[50] Moreover, why is it necessary to create a separate speech-crime provision, cannibalizing the existing ancillary rules? The answer is simple—speech plays an extremely important role in catalyzing and fueling atrocity. *The Diplomat* refers to hate speech as one of "the starkest early warning signs of mass atrocity."[51] More specifically, the USHMM notes that "Genocide is often preceded . . . by widespread hate speech."[52] And Lynn Tirrell warns that "a steady, deep and widespread derogation is not only an antecedent to genocide; it becomes part of the genocide itself."[53] Thus, for expressive and educational purposes, in addition to highlighting it as an enforcement priority and promoting deterrence, it should be the object of a separate provision. As Thomas Davies notes in relation to the *Media Case*, for example:

> All three defendants were, of course, convicted of other crimes as well. But, considering the particularly important role of the media in the Rwandan genocide, the convictions of Nahimana and Ngeze for incitement are arguably of special significance for the purpose of establishing the truth about how the genocide came about.[54]

49. *Hate Speech and Incitement to Genocide*, United States Holocaust Memorial Museum, https://www.ushmm.org/confront-genocide/how-to-prevent-genocide/hate-speech-and-incitement-to-genocide (last visited Sept. 18, 2016) (emphasis added).

50. *See* Dennis J. Baker, Reinterpreting Criminal Complicity and Inchoate Participation Offences 11 n.30 (2016) (indicating that verbal encouragement may give rise to accomplice liability).

51. Prashanth Parameswaran, *Is Myanmar Approaching Genocide?*, May 4, 2015, The Diplomat, http://thediplomat.com/2015/05/is-myanmar-approaching-genocide/.

52. United States Holocaust Memorial Museum, *supra* note 49.

53. Lynn Tirrell, *Studying Genocide: A Pragmatist Approach to Action-Engendering Discourse*, *in* Pragmatism, Law and Language 153 (Graham Hubbs & Douglas Lind eds., 2014).

54. Thomas E. Davies, Note, *How the Rome Statute Weakens the International Prohibition on Incitement to Genocide*, 22 Harv. Hum. Rts. J. 245, 251 n.22 (2009).

Further, folding all speech-related delicts into a single provision provides for a better organized exposition of the law and calls greater attention to speech as a potent factor in provoking and fueling atrocity. As a practical matter, rather than having a fragmented collection of rules scattered in different parts of a statute, the proposed consolidated provision puts the proper emphasis on speech crimes and facilitates simultaneous consideration of the offenses so that prosecutors can make more efficient and effective charging decisions.[55]

3. Placement within the Statute and Relationship among the Offenses

a. Incitement within the Statutory Framework

Another conceptual issue raised by the Unified Liability Theory relates to the nature and statutory placement of the offenses, particularly with respect to incitement and persecution. As enshrined in the statutes of the ad hoc tribunals, direct and public incitement to commit genocide is found as part of the crime of "Genocide" under Article 2 of the ICTR Statute and Article 4 of the ICTY Statute.

In contrast, the proposed "Convention on the Classification and Criminalization of Atrocity Speech Offenses" and Rome Statute Article 25*bis* place incitement within the more general "Individual Criminal Responsibility" section of the statute, arguably attenuating its connection to the crime of genocide itself. One could conceivably contend that this has the effect of diluting the potency of incitement's liability.[56] But this concern seems misplaced as the difference amounts to more of an optical perception than anything else.

Whether it is placed in the portion of the statute setting out the institution's subject matter jurisdiction offenses or part of its "individual criminal liability" section, it is still an inchoate offense carrying the same elements. It is not clear how its relative placement in a statute would affect the stigma it carries on conviction or the attendant punishment it would yield.[57]

55. *See* Victor Thuronyi, 1 Tax Law Design and Drafting 81 (1996) (in the context of tax law, noting the greater efficacy, awareness, and application of the law when statutory provisions are concentrated and well-organized).

56. Davies, for instance, contends that the Rome Statute treats incitement as a mode of liability and thus "renders the prohibition . . . far less effective than it has been in the jurisprudence of the ICTR." Davies, *supra* note 54, at 246. But this argument is specious. Davies erroneously concludes that the ICC has converted incitement to a mode of liability. Thus, making out a prima facie case of it, he concludes, obligates a prosecutor "to perform the sometimes difficult task of showing a causal link between the incitement and a subsequent act of genocide." *Id.* at 245. But that is not true—as it remains an inchoate crime regardless of its placement in the Rome Statute, subsequent violence does not have to be proved. Incitement has not become a mode of liability.

57. Inchoate crimes are considered "substantive" crimes. *See* Ira P. Robbins, *Double Inchoate Crimes*, 26 Harv. J. on Legis. 1, 3 (1989) (noting the widespread treatment of inchoate offenses as substantive crimes).

If anything, incitement was always a poor fit under the substantive genocide provisions of the ad hoc tribunal statutes, which simply cut-and-pasted Articles II (genocide) and III (punishable acts of genocide) of the Genocide Convention and shoehorned them into Articles 2 and 4, respectively, of the ICTR and ICTY statutes.[58] In that sense, Articles 2(3) and 4(3) of the ICTR/ICTY statutes, which reproduced the Genocide Convention's criminal responsibility provision (Article III), always seemed as if they should have been placed in Articles 6/7 of the ICTR/ICTY statutes,[59] which generally handled individual criminal responsibility (and covered crimes against humanity and war crimes as these did not have separate criminal responsibility sections embedded in the substantive provisions).

Indeed, the ICC took a much more logical approach. Rather than creating a repetitive "individual criminal liability" subsection within its genocide provision (Article 6), it limited that provision to the basic elements of the core genocide offense. Then, as with all the other core crimes, it located related modes of liability, such as attempt, complicity, or solicitation (i.e., instigation) in Article 25, the "Individual Criminal Responsibility" section. That was the logical place for incitement as well and so it was inserted as Article 25(3)(e).

b. Persecution or Speech Abetting?

With regard to hate speech as persecution, on the surface, the Rome Statute technically treats it as a substantive crime, as opposed to a mode of liability. But on deeper analysis, that is arguably a superficial conclusion. It will be recalled that, per Article 7(1)(h) of the Rome Statute, to prove persecution, the prosecution must link it to "any act referred to in this paragraph or any crime within the jurisdiction of the Court."[60] In this sense, as it exists only as an adjunct provision symbiotically attached to other substantive provisions, one could say that it is already the functional equivalent of a mode of criminal liability.

Moreover, in any event, the proposed changes that would result in implementing the Unified Liability Theory would not eliminate charging hate speech as the crime against humanity of persecution. It must be emphasized that these are two different types of liability, even if both of them involve hate speech uttered contemporaneously with the commission of atrocity. In addition to knowledge of a widespread or systematic attack, persecution necessarily entails discriminatory animus against a prescribed set of groups based on the group's identity. As noted by the Trial Chamber in *Prosecutor v. Kupreškić*:

> The *mens rea* requirement for persecution is higher than for ordinary crimes against humanity, although lower than for genocide. . . . Persecution as a crime against humanity is an offence belonging to the same *genus* as genocide. . . . In both categories what matters is the intent to discriminate. [F]rom

58. ICTY Statute, *supra* note 18, art. 4(3); ICTR Statute, *supra* note 18, art. 2(3).

59. ICTY Statute, *supra* note 18, art. 7(1); ICTR Statute, *supra* note 18, art. 6(1).

60. Rome Statute, *supra* note 19, art. 7(1)(h).

> the viewpoint of *mens rea*, genocide is an extreme and most inhuman form of persecution. [W]hen persecution escalates to the extreme form of wilful and deliberate acts designed to destroy a group or part of a group, it can be held that such persecution amounts to genocide.[61]

As a mode of liability, speech abetting does not carry this elevated *mens rea* requirement and only obliges the prosecutor to prove the speaker had knowledge of commission of the underlying crime. Thus, speech abetting in relation to the crime against humanity of extermination, in addition to the intent to abet, only requires knowledge that the crime is being committed.[62] The ICTR has held that, for purposes of accomplice liability, although it is not necessary to know the precise criminal conduct the principal engaged in, an accomplice must be aware of its essential elements.[63] From this, one can infer that this includes knowledge that the crime being committed is international in nature. Thus, in the case of crimes against humanity, this would include knowledge that the crime was part of a widespread or systematic attack directed against a civilian population.[64]

As opposed to charging persecution, prosecutors may simply find it more convenient, and logical, to focus on speech abetting in connection with an enumerated offense, such as murder or extermination that fits the facts more squarely and carries a less onerous *mens rea* standard. Additionally, as we have considered previously, prosecutors could charge in the alternative and seek to prove both persecution (connected to murder or extermination, for instance) and speech abetting (connected to the same crimes). The point is that one charge does not necessarily exclude the others. And, theoretically, persecution and speech abetting should be able to coexist without creating any meaningful doctrinal problems.

61. Prosecutor v. Kupreškić, Case No. IT-95-16-T, Judgement, ¶ 636 (Int'l Crim. Trib. for the Former Yugoslavia Jan. 14, 2000).

62. Even if the prosecutor had to prove the accused had the *mens rea* of the target crime, in the case of extermination, it would be a less onerous burden. The *mens rea* for that crime is that the accused acted with the intent to kill persons on a large scale or in knowledge that the deaths of a large number of people were a probable consequence of the act. Prosecutor v. Lukić, Case No. IT-98-32/1-T, Judgement, ¶ 939 (Int'l Crim. Trib. for the Former Yugoslavia July 20, 2009).

63. Prosecutor v. Nahimana, et al., Case No. ICTR-99-52-A, Judgement, ¶ 482 (Nov. 28, 2007).

64. Margaret deGuzman notes that "culpability for crimes against humanity does not require that the perpetrator have any specific knowledge about the contents of the attack" as "the elements elaborated in paragraph 2(a) of Article 7 are jurisdictional elements intended to aid judges in determining whether an attack reaches the level required for a crime of universal jurisdiction." Margaret McAuliffe deGuzman, *The Road to Rome: The Developing Law of Crimes Against Humanity*, 22 Hum. Rts. Q. 335, 380 (2000). Of course, outside the context of crimes against humanity, the knowledge regarding the nature of the crime as international would also apply. Thus, for genocide, this would include the knowledge that the criminal act arose from an intent to destroy, in whole or in part, the victim group. And for war crimes, it would include the knowledge of a nexus between the crime committed and an armed conflict.

c. Mixing Crimes and Modes of Liability in One Provision

Another potential objection to Article 25*bis* is that it would represent a forced fusion of substantive crimes (incitement and ordering as an inchoate crime) with modes of liability (instigation, speech abetting, and ordering where the target crime is completed). According to Michael Karnavas:

> There has been some discussion within the jurisprudence on genocide as to the relationship between "instigating" and "incitement to commit genocide". Nonetheless, it should be noted that the two concepts are necessarily distinct: "instigating" is a mode of liability while "incitement" is a substantive, albeit inchoate, crime.[65]

Similarly, the Unified Liability Theory proposes that ordering be treated as an inchoate crime (when the target offense is not carried out) and a mode of liability (when it is perpetrated). And speech abetting is also a mode of liability (in reference to the charged defendant, serving as a liability-connecter in reference to the atrocity crime).

Thus, the proposed Article 25*bis* would indeed combine modes and substantive offenses. But it is hard to see why this is problematic. The Rome Statute's Article 25 itself represents a collection of modes of liability (e.g., aiding in 25(3)(c) and contributing in 25(3)(d)) and inchoate crimes (e.g., incitement in 25(3)(e) and attempt in 25(3)(f)). Article 25*bis* would merely be a smaller version of Article 25 but organized around the principle of liability for speech. Again, it would emphasize the importance of speech as a catalyst for and accompaniment to international crimes. And it would provide better coherence and organization to the overall "individual criminal responsibility" section of any international criminal law statute.

4. The Utility of a Separate Speech Abetting Provision

Some might question whether a *sui generis* speech-related form of accomplice liability is necessary. Accomplice liability (and conspiracy liability, for that matter) frequently consists of speech only. So, those critics might contend, a separate speech-related form of liability is redundant.

But such skepticism would be unwarranted. Although accomplice liability may consist of speech only, its forms are protean. Thus, liability for aiding and abetting routinely consists of nonspeech acts that range from supplying tools precrime to serving as a lookout during the crime's commission to disposing of evidence and covering up postcommission.

Even were that not the case, in the context of mass atrocity (as opposed to the garden-variety setting), speech plays a distinctive function that deserves particular attention. In relation to genocide, conspiracy's essence is an agreement, which typically implicates speech (although not necessarily). And yet tribunal statutes have

65. Michael G. Karnavas, *Forms of Perpetration*, *in* Elements of Genocide 101–02 (Paul Behrens & Ralph Henham eds., 2013).

included the offense of "conspiracy to commit genocide" alongside "incitement to commit genocide," an implicit recognition of the special power of speech in the mass atrocity context. The Unified Liability Theory merely posits that it should be applied to crimes against humanity and war crimes too.

Moreover, some might argue that the notion of simultaneity in reference to international speech crimes is illusory. For them, simultaneity could be perceived as nothing more than a crude proxy for causation. But why would it be difficult to fathom speech that is uttered simultaneously with mass violence, but does not necessarily *cause* or *contribute toward causing* it?

By way of example, one could imagine a person at home aware that a campaign of violence is being perpetrated against an out-group by the in-group. This homeowner is a member of the in-group and is aware of the government campaign. He bears no animosity toward the out-group (meaning persecution would not apply) but hates women in general. One day, a group of policemen arrive at a park across the street from the homeowner. The police begin raping female members of the out-group and the homeowner can hear the sexual violence taking place. He walks across the street to the park and sees the police raping the women. The homeowner then stands on a park bench close to the sexual violence and begins screaming at the police to continue the attack and encourages them to humiliate the women. He then screams vulgarities at the women, calling them "animals," who are "getting what they deserve."

In this case, the homeowner's speech is clearly noncatalytic—the violence had begun before he uttered the speech at issue. But the speech was simultaneous with the violence and had the effect of encouraging and/or sustaining it. It could be charged as speech abetting with respect to rape as a crime against humanity. The *mens rea* of knowledge of the widespread or systematic attack, as well as the defendant's intent to abet the crime of rape, could both be established. And persecution as a crime against humanity would not be a viable charge as it is posited the defendant does not have animus toward the out-group—an essential component of persecution. Rather, his hatred is toward women in general. So a charge of speech abetting would permit the possibility of punishing the crime.

B. Practical Issues

1. Multiple and Alternative Charging

In terms of practical issues that could arise, the prospect of multiple charging must be considered. In particular, one speech could give rise to charges with respect to more than one mode of criminal liability.[66] For example, a speaker present during a genocidal murder operation who thanks perpetrators for their

66. Christine Bishai, *STL in the Year 2011: Atrocity Crime Litigation Review in the Year 2011*, 11 Nw. J. Int'l Hum. Rts. 271, 303 (2011) (noting that international criminal law allows multiple charging); James Nicholas Boeving, Note, *Aggression, International Law, and the ICC: An Argument for the Withdrawal of Aggression from the Rome Statute*, 43 Colum. J. Transnat'l L. 557, 594 n.217 (observing that alternative charges may be possible at the ICC).

"good work" while they are killing victims and has the requisite *mens rea* could certainly be liable for genocidal "speech abetting" in reference to the contemporaneous genocidal violence. However, if the expression of thanks can be proved to have provoked subsequent fresh acts of genocidal violence, it could also be charged as "instigation" to genocide. If the speech were uttered in a genocidal environment with the proper *mens rea* but did not result in violence, then it could be charged as incitement to genocide. If the environment were not genocidal, it could be charged as incitement to crimes against humanity.

Similarly, taking the same fact scenario, if the relationship between the speaker and listener were one of superior-subordinate in a military hierarchy, the speech, slightly modified to suggest a command, could be charged as ordering. On the other hand, if the superior-subordinate relationship were factually in doubt, it could be charged as incitement. And if evidence of genocidal intent were not terribly strong, the speech could be charged as incitement to commit war crimes.

Overall, then, one of the clear advantages of the Unified Liability Theory is its flexibility and breadth of coverage. With alternative charging, prosecutors can adduce evidence regarding the crimes and the judges can evaluate how the evidence comes in at trial. This should lead to more complete and accurate justice.[67]

2. Charging in Connection with Other Modes of Liability or Inchoate Crimes

Related to this, to the extent applicable, prosecutors will be able to charge these categories of liability related to speech with other modes of liability or crimes. Thus, if a speechwriter provides a text to an atrocity agitator who knowingly spews his venomous rhetoric in the presence of an atrocity that is taking place, the scribe could presumably be charged with complicity in speech abetting.[68] Similarly, if the context were genocidal and the speech did not lead to atrocity, an amanuensis who knowingly helped draft the speech might be similarly charged with accomplice liability in relation to incitement.[69] Moreover, charging

67. *See Kupreškić*, Case No. IT-95-16-T, Judgement, ¶ 727(b) (explaining that prosecutors may charge in the alternative "whenever an offence appears to be in breach of more than one provision, depending on the elements of the crime the Prosecution is able to prove."). The *Kupreškić* Trial Chamber went on to provide an example. Murder, for instance, could be charged as a crime against humanity. However, to the extent it might not be clear if the element of a widespread or systematic attack can be satisfied, it could also be charged as a war crime. *Id. See also* Antonio Cassese & Paula Gaeta, Cassese's International Criminal Law 370 n.28 (3d ed. 2013) (discussing the viability of alternative charging).

68. The law permits charging complicity in reference to another mode of liability. Thus, for example, a charge of complicity in planning is possible. *See* Bakhtiyar R. Tuzmukhamedov, *Preemption by Armed Force of Trans-Boundary Terrorist Threats: The Russian Perspective*, 83 Int'l L. Stud. 83, 87 (2014); (referring to complicity in planning a terrorist act); Ian M. Ralby, *Joint Criminal Enterprise Liability in the Iraqi High Tribunal*, 28 B.U. Int'l L.J. 281, 303 (2010) (noting that aiding and abetting of planning has been criminalized in international criminal law).

69. *See* Prosecutor v. Nyiramasuhuko, et al., Case No. ICTR-98-42-A, Judgement ¶ 3345 (Dec. 14, 2015) (indicating that aiding and abetting direct and public incitement to commit

a double-inchoate offense, such as attempted incitement, should not render the charge any less viable.[70] Thus, a person who records a speech urging atrocity and attempts to broadcast it via a radio station, but the station's transmitter is not functioning properly, should be liable for attempted incitement.

In a related vein, one might imagine a group of demagogues collaborating on a speech or series of speeches that one or more of them would subsequently deliver. Pursuant to Rome Statute Article 25(3)(a), this could trigger co-perpetrator liability in relation to incitement, speech abetting, or instigation with respect to one or more of the core crimes.[71] Or for those with lesser roles, contribution liability could be envisaged via Article 25(3)(d).[72] The point is that the crimes in the proposed Article 25*bis* could work in perfect tandem with the other modes of individual criminal responsibility and inchoate crimes enumerated in Article 25. Their placement in a new, dedicated provision changes nothing.

3. The Elements of the Crimes

a. Incitement

i. *Direct and Public*

As the text of the proposed Convention on the Classification and Criminalization of Atrocity Speech Offenses indicates, the crime of "incitement" has shed the words "direct" and "public." A bit of explanation is in order. Regarding "direct," there is no substantive change, as that element would remain. In Chapter 10, that was made explicitly clear in respect of incitement to commit war crimes and was never in doubt as to incitement to commit genocide. The same is true for crimes against humanity. "Direct" is simply being taken out of the title, which makes it less cumbersome.

ii. *Elements of Incitement to Crimes against Humanity*

At this juncture, for the same reasons previously articulated regarding war crimes and genocide, as just noted, incitement to commit crimes against humanity should also carry the "direct" element. We have seen in the Convention that, consistent with the target crime, the offense's *mens rea* is knowledge (along with intent to incite). Moreover, incitement to commit crimes against humanity should have the same "content" element as incitement to commit genocide

genocide is a viable charge). *See also* 1 Gideon Boas et al., Forms of Responsibility in International Criminal Law 303 (2007) (noting that "there is theoretically no bar to the imposition of accomplice liability for an inchoate crime" but adding that certain combinations would "lead to absurd results, such as planning a conspiracy or instigating incitement."). Presumably, liability for assistance in drafting a speech meant to spur mass murder would not yield an "absurd result."

70. *See* Robbins, *supra* note 57, at 6 (arguing that double inchoate offenses may "serve important purposes of the criminal law").

71. Rome Statute, *supra* note 19, art. 25(3)(a).

72. *Id.* art. 25(3)(d).

and incitement to commit war crimes. In other words, content should be examined with respect to "text," "purpose," "context" (both internal and external—including all the evaluative factors considered in Chapter 8), the "relationship between the speaker and subject," and channel of communication. In cases of recordings and republications, the elements of "temporality" and "instrumentality" must be considered. As always, given that we are dealing with an inchoate crime, causation cannot be a requirement.

The other element to consider is "public." Chapter 8 demonstrated why it was a problematic mandatory criterion for incitement to genocide.[73] The same is true for incitement to crimes against humanity. As we saw, incitement projected on smaller groups, where there is more person-to-person contact, is logically more lethal. Still, if "public" incitement can be shown to have more of a potentially pernicious impact in terms of its capacity to generate large-scale violence, it should be considered as an aggravating sentencing factor. That applies to incitement to genocide and war crimes as well.[74]

b. The Presence and Hearing Requirements of Speech Abetting

Article 5 of the proposed "Convention on the Classification and Criminalization of Atrocity Speech Offenses" provides that speech abetting means "with knowledge of the ongoing commission of an atrocity crime, and with intent to encourage or assist the commission of that crime, uttering hate speech during the commission and in the presence of that crime, when the hate speech is heard by other persons." Two aspects of the elements require some explanation.

With respect to the "in the presence" requirement, the idea is to criminalize hate speech that is physically proximate to the atrocity crime. In essence, this amounts to speech uttered within earshot of either the perpetrators or victims of the crime. It should be noted that there is important wiggle room within the requirement. Thus, speech enhanced electronically, via bullhorn for example, would satisfy the requirement if it nevertheless reached the ears of the perpetrator or victim. One could easily imagine such a scenario.

In the Simon Bikindi case, for example, it will be recalled that the singer was shouting on the truck's public address system while passing the *Interahamwe*

73. We also saw in Chapter 10 why, for different reasons, it was problematic to have it as an element for incitement to commit war crimes.

74. An analogy might be between public versus private incitement and principal versus accessory liability. Nonprincipal status should not negate liability, just as "nonpublic" incitement should not negate incitement liability (although, depending on the circumstances, "nonpublic" incitement is arguably more potent than public incitement, which is more impersonal, less direct). However, to the extent that "public" incitement can, in any individual case, be shown to be more incendiary, that could result in an enhanced sentence upon conviction (or a lesser sentence if the "public" incitement appears less virulent in a given fact scenario). The same is true of principal versus accessory liability. *See* Paul S. Davies, *Complicity*, *in* UNRAVELLING TORT AND CRIME 301 (Matthew Dyson ed., 2014) ("[The] criminal law is more flexible in tailoring the punishment of the defendant . . . it will often be the case . . . that the accessory will receive a more severe or more lenient sentence than the principal . . .").

militia. If the militia were murdering Tutsis as Bikindi drove by and he were congratulating them or praising them on the public address system, his conduct would qualify as speech abetting, despite the greater physical distance between the speaker and the crime scene. Even more attenuated, but still possible, if the speaker's voice were broadcast over a stadium's public address system while mass executions were taking place at the stadium, that could constitute speech abetting too. Of course, it would still require the appropriate knowledge and intent, and the words would have to encourage. But this does suggest a certain breadth with respect to the "presence" requirement.

In the same vein, the "hearing" requirement assures that the speaker is not giving a speech in isolation. She could have the requisite intent and be in the presence of the crime's commission but only whisper such that the speech was inaudible. That would not qualify for liability. Nor would the person with similar knowledge and intent but speaking alone in her residence at the top of her lungs. If no one else heard the speech, it would not be actionable. In any event, this is only a rough guide—these elements of speech abetting, as well as the other new types of liability, will have to be fleshed out and interpreted by subsequent jurisprudence.

c. Speech Abetting and Genocide

The other issue to consider is speech abetting in relation to the crime of genocide. As we have seen, one of genocide's key defining traits is its *mens rea* of *dolus specialis*. As explained by William Schabas:

> [Article II] of the 1948 Genocide Convention, which describes genocide as one of five punishable acts, including killing "committed with intent to destroy, in whole or in part, a national, ethnical, racial or religious group, as such." These words distinguish genocide from garden-variety killing. Judgments of the international criminal tribunals are replete with declarations that the defining element of genocide is this "specific intent" or "special intent" or, for continental jurists, its *dolus specialis*.[75]

The International Commission of Inquiry on Darfur further elaborated that it entails that "the perpetrator consciously desired the prohibited acts he committed to result in the destruction, in whole or in part, of the group as such, and knew that his acts would destroy in whole or in part, the group as such."[76]

However, as previously considered, speech abetting's *mens rea* is characterized by a "knowledge" standard in reference to the underlying atrocity offense. In other words, the defendant must be aware of the ongoing commission of the

75. William A. Schabas, *State Policy as an Element of International Crimes*, 98 J. Crim. L. & Criminology 953, 968 (2008).

76. Int'l Comm'n of Inquiry on Darfur, Report of the International Commission of Inquiry on Violations of International Humanitarian Law and Human Rights Law in Darfur, ¶ 518, U.N. Doc. S/2005/60 (Jan. 25, 2005).

atrocity crime but not necessarily intend for the crime to be committed—rather, he must only intend to encourage or assist the commission of the crime. So it might appear that there is an incompatibility between the *mens rea* for the speech offense (knowledge) and the more exacting standard for the underlying atrocity crime (intent to destroy).

But this does not, in fact, represent a doctrinal incongruity. And one need only consider "aiding and abetting" genocide, speech abetting's doctrinal cousin, to understand why. In *Prosecutor v. Ntakirutimana* (2004), reflecting the consensus at the ad hoc tribunals, the ICTR found that the *mens rea* of knowledge is sufficient for aiding and abetting genocide.[77] As Jens Ohlin notes: "The tension between the *mens rea* for aiding and abetting (knowledge) and the *mens rea* for genocide as a principal perpetrator (special intent) is not as worrisome, since aiding and abetting represents an inherently lower form of criminal participation."[78] It is submitted that the same is true for speech abetting in relation to genocide.

4. Statutory and Charging Treatment of Ordering

The final practical consideration relates to the ordering offense. It will be recalled that, while ordering has traditionally been limited as a mode of liability, this book proposes that it be chargeable as an inchoate crime. There are two practical, and related, considerations to deal with here. First, Article 25*bis* refers to "ordering" monolithically, in other words, it does not explicitly distinguish between ordering as a mode of liability and as an inchoate offense (although it does declare that it creates liability "regardless of whether or not the crime is subsequently committed"). For the ICC, the Elements of the Crimes should reflect the differences between the two types of liability. And, related to this, prosecutors charging the crime should be sure to distinguish carefully between the mode-type and inchoate-type of ordering liability. This will be especially true in non-ICC jurisdictions, which are not likely to append a separate "Elements of the Crimes" document for purposes of breaking down the particulars of provisions in their criminal statutes.

V. CONCLUSION

The importance of fixing the individual atrocity speech offenses cannot be overstated. On a micro level, the viability of each liability category hinges on internal coherence, doctrinal logic, policy prudence, and systematic application. The bulk of this tome has been devoted to explaining why and showing how such objectives can be accomplished. But if significant energy and resources are invested

77. Prosecutor v. Ntakirutimana, Case Nos. ICTR-96-10-A and ICTR-96-17-A, Appeals Judgement, ¶ 501 (Dec. 13, 2004).

78. Jens David Ohlin, *Joint Intentions to Commit International Crimes*, 11 Chi. J. Int'l L. 693, 710 n.89 (2011).

in fixing micro-level problems, it would seem reasonable, and indeed desirable, to resolve the macro-level issues too and put the overall system in order. Failing that, inconsistencies and doctrinal gaps would continue to thwart the aims of atrocity speech law. By adopting the proposed Unified Liability Theory, those problems can be resolved.

It is hard to argue against applying incitement to the other core offenses of crimes against humanity and war crimes. Adopting the new delict of "speech abetting" fills an important gap so that noncatalytic, synchronous speech that gives comfort and encouragement to genocide, war crimes, and crimes against humanity perpetrators can be punished in its own right. And placing the liability categories of incitement, speech abetting, instigation, and ordering into a single provision would promote greater doctrinal cohesion and organization as well as streamline and systematize prosecutorial charging considerations. More importantly, it would serve the educational and expressive function of underscoring speech's central role in sparking, sustaining, and aggravating organized, large-scale, and severe human rights and humanitarian law violations.

While certain practical and theoretical questions may arise in considering such an approach, they should not hinder adoption of this proposal. Elements for the speech offenses (i.e., incitement, speech abetting, instigation, and ordering) can be formulated in harmony with the underlying core crimes (i.e., genocide, crimes against humanity, and war crimes). And the migration of incitement and a more expansive form of persecution (speech abetting) from the substantive law section of the ad hoc tribunal statutes to the "individual criminal responsibility" section of the Rome Statute—an approach consistent with Article 25 of the Rome Statute—in no way diminishes the potential penal or stigmatic implications of a conviction pursuant to the proposed Article 25*bis*.

The change in doctrinal approach can be operationalized through adoption of a treaty and/or inclusion in future statutes or amendment of existing instruments, including the Rome Statute. This, in turn, would promote greater consistency in prosecuting atrocity speech in both municipal and transnational fora around the world. And it would more effectively put would-be verbal hatemongers on notice that speech in atrocity contexts will not be the collateral postscript to filling the mass graves. Rather, it will serve as humanity's alarm bell, auguring justice and triggering punishment before it is too late.

Conclusion

> "Kind words can be short and easy to speak, but their echoes are truly endless."
>
> —Mother Teresa[1]

I. INITIAL REFLECTIONS: MUGESERA'S CONVICTION

On April 15, 2016, in relation to his infamous November 1992 speech, a Rwandan High Court found Léon Mugesera guilty of incitement to commit genocide, inciting ethnic hatred and persecution as a crime against humanity.[2] He was sentenced to life in prison. Per press accounts, the decision was announced via the reading of a "four hour verdict" by Presiding Judge Antoine Muhima.[3] Rendered in Kinyarwanda, the jurisdiction's national tongue, the written judgment has yet to be translated into English. But, as predicted in Chapter 8, news reports suggest it runs afoul of many of the foundational principles of the incitement framework elucidated in this book. According to one source, Judge Muhima declared: "Due to the fact that Léon Mugesera used the authority he had as a leader *to incite hatred among the population which led to the 1994 genocide against the Tutsi* and failure to show any remorse of the crimes he committed ever since he was arrested, the court finds him guilty of genocide crimes and has sentenced him to life imprisonment."[4]

1. Sam Majdi, The Wisdom of the Great 436 (2012).

2. Stevenson Mugisha, *Mugesera Sent to Prison for Life*, The Rwanda Focus (Apr. 15, 2016), http://www.focus.rw/wp/2016/04/mugesera-sent-to-prison-for-life/. He was acquitted of conspiracy to commit genocide and planning genocide. *Id.*

3. *Id.*

4. *Id.*

Even based on this limited press account, we see a reprise of familiar leitmotifs from previous jurisprudence. First, there is the old reliance on causation in convicting a defendant of incitement. It has been well established in this tome that causation is not an element of incitement. But the *Mugesera* verdict is only the latest evidence that judges, not sufficiently secure with this facet of the offense, feel obliged to allude to causation's factual occurrence. Interestingly, given that Mugesera's sinister speech was in November 1992 and the Rwandan Genocide started in April 1994, it seems a stretch to assert a causal link, in any event.

Significantly, another press account of the *Mugesera* verdict notes that evidence was adduced at trial that "killings broke out shortly in the Kamonyi and Bigogwe areas after [Mugesera's] speech."[5] Even if the Court found it was necessary to establish causation factually, why not cite to this evidence? If it were because the Court was concerned that postspeech violence in 1992 would not be considered sufficiently "genocidal," there was ample evidence available to the Court that it was. Ben Kiernan notes that "State-sponsored genocidal massacres of Tutsi began in 1990–91."[6] And, more specifically, Gérard Prunier refers to genocidal massacres in 1992 being perceived by Hutu perpetrators as "collective work, chopping up men was 'bush clearing' and slaughtering women and children was 'pulling out the roots of the bad weeds.'"[7] Thus, a proper application of the "context" criterion, including all the evaluative factors considered in Chapter 8, seemingly could have supported a finding of incitement to genocide in relation to Mugesera's 1992 speech without reference to subsequent causally related crime.

Further, considering that violence erupted in Kamonyi and Bigogwe soon after Mugesera's speech, prosecutors could have charged instigation to genocide (or to crimes against humanity) with respect to those massacres. But they did not. And the Court would seem to have made no reference to it either. Again, this omission is further proof of an absence of systematic consideration of the evidence in relation to the law as it has been formulated.

And accounts of the *Mugesera* verdict provide glimpses of conceptual and linguistic muddle as well. Another media source, referring to the verdict, quoted Judge Muhima as declaring that Mugesera was guilty of having "directly incited commission of genocide and torture, which constitutes a crime against humanity."[8] Crimes against humanity (persecution), to which the judge reportedly referred in

5. Robert Muriisa, *Rwanda: Suspect Gets Life Imprisonment for Genocide Related Crimes*, Imirasire (Apr. 16, 2016), http://eng.imirasire.com/news/top-news/in-rwanda/article/genocide-suspect-gets-life.

6. Ben Kiernan, Blood and Soil: A World History of Genocide and Extermination from Sparta to Darfur 566 (2007).

7. Gérard Prunier, The Rwanda Crisis: History of a Genocide 139–42 (1995).

8. *Génocide au Rwanda: Léon Mugesera, un ex-responsable du parti d'Habyarimana, condamné à perpétuité*, Jeune Afrique (Apr. 15, 2016), http://www.jeuneafrique.com/318427/societe/genocide-rwanda-leon-mugesera-ex-responsable-parti-dhabyarimana-condamne-a-perpetuite/ (translation into English by the author). The original text reads: "La Cour estime

this bit of text and of which Mugesera was convicted, has entirely different elements from incitement to commit genocide, to which the judge also alluded in the same sentence. Without the precise text to consider, we cannot know for sure. But this appears to be yet another instance of loose language sowing confusion.

II. A SUMMARY OF THE BOOK'S CONCLUSIONS

So we have another snapshot of a broken body of law. Can the situation be remedied? The prognosis, it is submitted, should remain sanguine. This book has demonstrated that a logical, coordinated, and rigorous approach to the law of speech and atrocity would take care of the problems. Let us consider again what that might consist of. First, in reference to each crime individually, a simple inventory and housecleaning are in order.

A. Direct and Public Incitement to Commit Genocide

What ails the crime of direct and public incitement to commit genocide? To begin, we need further clarification regarding the "direct" element, including a clean break with all Civil Law (and French language) references as well as a clear directive from courts that causation is not an element of the crime. Incitement's "Original Sin" from *Akayesu* must be expiated once and for all via pellucid and authoritative judicial prose.

Related to that, jurists should discontinue the practice of factual consideration of causation in incitement cases. And if causation can be proved, as just considered in connection with *Mugesera*, the more appropriate charge is instigation. Given that instigation necessarily entails resultant violence, it should be perceived as the more stigmatic, and relevant, count. Perhaps, for the average citizen or nonspecialist lawyer, "incitement" carries more weight as a basis for conviction given its totemic association with "genocide," a word brimming with a dark power of its own. Regardless, we simply have to get over our obsession with the popularly perceived condemnatory power of the word "incitement." It has muddied up the law for long enough.

Further, the conceptual parameters of "direct" need further elaboration. Thus, as recommended in Chapter 8, the assiduous compilation of a glossary of incitement techniques should be woven into judicial pronouncements. This volume has demonstrated that the naked imperative voice is rarely employed to urge slaughter. Rather, such advocacy is often effected via interrogation, prediction, condition, congratulations, scare tactics, metaphors, and dehumanization, among others. And it must be stressed that the called-for glossary would have equal utility in parsing the verbal conduct of defendants charged with persecution,

que M. Mugesera est coupable. Il est un complice de ceux qui ont commis le génocide car il a directement incité à commettre le génocide et la torture constitutive de crime contre l'humanité, et incité à la haine ethnique." *Id.*

instigation, and even, to a lesser extent, ordering.[9] Verbal strategies for realizing atrocity may be protean but their potency as applied across the spectrum of different speech offenses is often lethally uniform.

At the same time, the "public" element has proved to be unworkable and unnecessary. It is resistant to mathematical formulae and dependent on arbitrary line-drawing exercises. One person's perceived public frontage road could be another person's perceived private residential access point. How can we distinguish whether that same road is "public" or "private" in a principled manner? And why should we have to suffer through that ridiculous drill? At the same time, the advocate's voice in closer proximity to the listener is arguably more compelling than from a distance. Private incitement can be just as lethal, if not more, than public. So there is simply no good rationale for retaining "public" as an element. If necessary or appropriate, it could serve as a sentencing consideration. Otherwise, it should be jettisoned.

The "incitement" element of the crime also needs work. The exposition of its criteria has been deficient and that has also hindered reasoned and persuasive judicial craft. The yard markers explicitly identified in the *Media Case* Trial Chamber judgment—purpose and context—make for a solid enough foundation but are inadequate signposts for a complete analytic roadmap. As it happens, in that very same decision, the Trial Chamber made allusion to two other relevant criteria—text and the relationship between the speaker and subject. Those provide, respectively, a more focused exegetical depth of perception and an added safeguard against illegitimate speech-suppression. They should be added to the mix as well.

Moreover, loosely tracking Aristotelian classifications of rhetoric, "context" should be bifurcated into "internal" (consistent with Aristotle's "*ethos*"—i.e., focusing on the speaker) and "external" prongs (consistent with Aristotle's *logos*—i.e., focusing on the speech itself—and *pathos*—i.e., focusing on audience characteristics and surrounding circumstances). The former (internal) should take into account the orator's personal history and career background, her publication/transmission résumé, and her individual broadcast style (including tone of voice). The latter (external) would encompass considerations such as speech placement/timing and externally verifiable falsity (*logos*) as well as the political/social and media environments (*pathos*). It would also include audience features, such as cognitive and affective capacities as well as previous indoctrination. Overall, judicial flexibility in considering these factors should be the order of the day. In other words, a totality of the circumstances approach should be taken and a Procrustean approach strictly eschewed.

Deeper reflection regarding the "incitement" element also suggests the addition of three new criteria: (1) channel of communication; (2) temporality; and (3) instrumentality. The first gives due weight to Marshall McCluhan's

9. In explicating the meaning of a command, one could imagine the use of metaphor, for example. Equally, in theory, an interrogation could, in context and when viewed holistically, amount to an order.

iconic observation that "the medium is the message."[10] Quite simply, swifter and more dynamic modes of dissemination, such as electronic, in contrast to print, or social media, as opposed to word-of-mouth, are more susceptible to be adjudged a form of incitement. The second two of the three new proposed criteria acknowledge the reality that messages are often disseminated as recordings or repeated in a removed temporal sequence. In other words, the toxic speech must have been uttered at or near the time of the contextual violence that renders it genocidal. And any recordings of such speech must be the direct product of the defendant's own instrumentality. Put another way, the defendant himself must hit the play button within the genocidal time frame, not merely record the speech in advance of it and let others unleash it on the world, without the defendant's agency.

In the end, seven criteria emerge as necessary for "incitement" consideration: (1) purpose; (2) text; (3) context (both internal and external, with the latter involving consideration of the evaluative factors discussed in Chapter 8); (4) relationship between speaker and subject; (5) channel of communication; (6) temporality; and (7) instrumentality. Further, these criteria can be placed within the larger conceptual classifications of "content," "circumstances," and "medium," which assist in answering the what, why, who, where, when, and how questions related to the speech so we can better appreciate whether it should be punished as incitement.

This analysis may seem complex, but it is reflective of the critical role played by this element. A more granular examination is called for to properly protect exercise of legitimate expression and accurately mete out punishment for verbal transgression. Perhaps to the chagrin of those who cherish free speech (including this author), such analysis does not lend itself to mathematic precision. And supple judicial discernment, guided by the evaluative factors spelled out in detail in Chapter 8, should be the preferred approach.

At the same time, all of the elements of the incitement framework must be applied consistently and rigorously if they are to have any juridical utility. Merely trotting out a select few of them according to the whim of the judicial scrivener will no longer do. We have seen that such an approach has been corrosive of well-reasoned and tempered justice. And it has given rise to a mottled set of doctrinal pronouncements that sap incitement law of both its deterrent and expressive power. Mugesera has appealed his conviction for incitement to Rwanda's Supreme Court.[11] Perhaps the jurists on that bench can render a judgment that pays heed to all the relevant elements and applies them systematically and rigorously.

10. J. Hillis Miller, The Medium Is the Maker: Browning, Freud, Derrida and the New Telepathic Ecotechnologies 24 (2009).

11. Rodrigue Rwirahira, *Leon Mugesera Gets Life Term for Genocide Crimes*, The New Times (Apr. 16, 2016), http://www.newtimes.co.rw/section/article/2016-04-16/199005/.

B. Persecution, Instigation, and Ordering

Notwithstanding the talismanic significance of the "incitement" offense in the popular imagination, the other speech crimes considered in this tome—persecution, instigation, and ordering—are equally, if not more, deserving of our consideration. Given genocide's high intent threshold, these sister modalities are charged more frequently and have a greater chance of securing a conviction.

1. Persecution

Unfortunately, though, as we have seen, persecution is in a state of gridlock. The split between the International Criminal Tribunal for Rwanda (ICTR) and International Criminal Tribunal for the former Yugoslavia (ICTY) occludes proper application and development of the law governing speech in service of widespread or systematic attacks directed against civilian populations. Speech of this stripe not calling directly for action should nevertheless be criminalized. It cannot wrap itself in the mantle of democracy-promotion, self-governance, diversity-enhancement, community-building, or individual-empowerment in light of its link to a pervasive or well-organized attack on ordinary citizens in a community. The American rationales for hypervigilance in defense of hate speech, which we explored in Chapter 2, do not apply here. The "marketplace of ideas" has been likely shut down or is not functioning properly. Not surprisingly then, interdicting such discourse finds support in the wider persecution jurisprudence, as well as the speech-focused persecution precedents, including the overlooked *Dietrich* judgment at Nuremberg.

Only the ICTY's *Kordić* decision deviates from this great weight of authority. But we have seen that it is deeply flawed—internally inconsistent, at odds with existing ICTY precedent, less than forthcoming about existing ICTR precedent, and promptly repudiated by ICTY follow-on cases. And *Kordić*, as well as the American approach to hate speech in general, is the outlier in a world where international human rights treaties and most nonauthoritarian domestic jurisdictions have no compunction outlawing virulent forms of out-group-focused hate speech. At the same time, not all toxic rhetoric uttered in hotspots rife with ethnic tension or nascent intercommunal violence merits persecution charges. As Chapter 9 emphasizes, specific attention must be paid to a whole host of factors, including the extent of the widespread or systematic attack, its physical proximity to the speech (or vice versa), and the nature of the speech itself. The paramount policy consideration of protecting treasured free expression rights must remain an integral part of the analysis.

2. Instigation

But incitement and persecution are not the only offenses in need of judicial tinkering. As we saw in Chapter 6, instigation suffers from doctrinal malaise as well. Its blurring with incitement has stripped it of an independent penal identity and led to conceptual and jurisprudential muddle. As a threshold matter, it must be disambiguated from the French verb *inciter* (which encompasses both the English words "incitement" and "instigation"). And it should be cleanly cut loose from the Civil Law conception while being firmly, and exclusively, situated in the Common Law domain, where it finds its true ad hoc tribunal roots.

At the same time, it needs clarity in terms of its "contribution" element. A confusing smorgasbord of formulations over the years has arguably saddled it with a "but for" causation requirement as suggested in the *Šešelj* Trial Chamber judgment. That is contrary to its jurisprudential and policy wellsprings. As Chapter 9 demonstrated, based on analogous criminal law concepts and sound policy considerations, a "substantial contribution" standard should be adopted. The majority on the *Šešelj* trial bench also grafted a new and unsupported "different forms of persuasion" requirement onto incitement's *actus reus*. That unsightly excrescence should be removed.

3. Ordering

With respect to ordering, given the required superior-subordinate relationship, which permits a reasonable inference of substantial likelihood of order execution, the lack of inchoate liability is surprising. Incitement is characterized by this sort of liability but contains no such inbuilt listener-to-speaker deference in its elemental DNA. Thus, if a stranger *importuning* commission of atrocities can be found guilty by virtue of the verbal conduct alone, then logically a superior *commanding* the same should also be legally responsible for the utterance itself. Also, ordering should carry inchoate liability.

C. The Unified Liability Theory

But what about the ensemble of atrocity speech modalities? From a bird's-eye perspective, they look like an unshapely, disjointed mess. We might analogize the state of affairs to pipes in a plumbing system that do not connect. Incitement does not link to war crimes or crimes against humanity. No synchronous speech offense attaches to genocide or war crimes. When speech is causally connected to genocide, it is typically charged as incitement instead of instigation. So what can be done to connect the joints and make the system work on the wider level? This book has proposed a Unified Liability Theory that would create macro-coherence within this category of law.

How does it work? It is important to realize that, in tracking the systemic interaction of these offenses, there are temporal, catalytic, and status considerations. As concerns the temporal, it is necessary to inquire whether the speech was uttered before or during the violence. If before, then we know we are dealing with incitement, instigation, or ordering. In cases where the speech is noncatalytic and there is no preexisting status link between speaker and listener, then we look at incitement as the appropriate charge (assuming all required elements can otherwise be proved). But if the speaker and listener have a superior-subordinate relationship, then the correct charge is ordering—in line with this book's proposal that ordering liability extend to the inchoate. On the other hand, if speech has a causal tie to subsequent violence, with no status relationship implicated, then the appropriate charge is instigation. Once again, in cases of a superior-subordinate connection, then ordering would be the applicable delict—ordering being the one previolence speech offense that should cover both target-crime commission and non-target-crime commission.

The temporal alternative is speech synchronous with violence. For this we have the charge of speech abetting. And persecution as a crime against humanity is still available to prosecutors. Of course, as considered in Chapter 11, one common nucleus of operative facts can give rise to different charges. Speeches given within a compressed time frame to a multitude of listeners could sustain or fuel existing violence with respect to certain listeners (giving rise to speech abetting charges (or persecution too, for crimes against humanity only)) and/or spawn new violence with respect to others (yielding potential incitement, instigation, or ordering charges). As well, all the core offenses should now be in play. Chapters 7 and 10 made the case for conjoining war crimes and incitement into a single new delict. Chapter 11 explained why crimes against humanity and incitement should be similarly fused to expand charging options. Speech abetting should apply to genocide and war crimes, not just crimes against humanity.

And all of these reforms can be operationalized through promulgation of a new treaty, "The Convention on the Classification and Criminalization of Atrocity Speech Offenses," and/or through amendment of the Rome Statute to include Article 25*bis*—"Liability Related to Speech." That new provision, whose equivalent could also be placed in domestic statutes as well as the constituent instruments of existing and/or new ad hoc international tribunals, would contain all four types of speech liability—incitement, speech abetting, instigation, and ordering—connected to all three core international offenses—genocide, crimes against humanity, and war crimes.

III. THE IMPORTANCE OF REMEDYING THE LAW GOING FORWARD

The stakes in enacting these proposed reforms are high. The *Mugesera* conviction in Rwanda is being appealed, and so an ideal opportunity arises to clarify the law regarding incitement and persecution.[12] At the ICTY, the prosecution has appealed the *Šešelj* Trial Chamber judgment, permitting possible clarifications and rectifications regarding persecution (assuming a reversed finding regarding crimes against humanity) and instigation.[13] Similarly, Laurent Gbagbo and Charles Blé Goudé have been charged with persecution (in relation to hate speech) and soliciting/inducing/ordering in connection with postelection violence in Côte d'Ivoire in 2010 and are currently on trial before the International Criminal Court (ICC).[14] Joshua arap Sang's case before the same body was dismissed, but his role as a radio announcer in connection with 2007–2008

12. *Id.*

13. *Prosecutor to Appeal UN Tribunal's Acquittal of Vojislav Šešelj of War Crimes in the Balkans*, UN News Centre (Apr. 6, 2016), http://www.un.org/apps/news/story.asp?NewsID=53625#.V8BZoTVHaA0.

14. Prosecutor v. Gbagbo, Case No. ICC-02/11-01/11-656-Red, Decision on the Confirmation of Charges ¶¶ 167, 226 (June 12, 2014); Prosecutor v. Blé Goudé, Case No. ICC-02/11-02/11-186, Decision on the Confirmation of Charges ¶¶ 192(d), 194 (Dec. 11, 2014).

postelection violence in Kenya is illustrative of analogous cases that will call on the ICC to get the law of atrocity speech right.

Other cases pending at the ICC involve charges of soliciting/inducing and/or ordering. Dominic Ongwen, a brigadier general of the Lord's Resistance Army (LRA) rebel group in Uganda, is charged with, *inter alia*, soliciting or inducing crimes against humanity and war crimes.[15] The trial in his case began on December 6, 2016.[16] Meanwhile, an ICC Pre-Trial Chamber has found reasonable grounds to believe that Ongwen's LRA superior, Joseph Kony, the rebel group's leader, induced the commission of rape.[17] Another ICC Pre-Trial Chamber concluded there were reasonable grounds to believe that Sudanese leader Ahmad Harun solicited Janjaweed militia to attack civilians and pillage shops, houses, and livestock in Darfur.[18]

And that list merely represents those cases already the subject of arrest warrants or confirmed charges. Earlier sections of this book have referred to ongoing government-sponsored or -tolerated hate speech precipitating mass violence in Myanmar (against Rohingya Muslims), South Sudan (Dinka versus Nuer and vice versa), and in areas controlled by ISIS (against Yazidis and others).[19] All of these cases could eventually result in criminal charges stemming, in part, from use of speech to provoke, assist, or sustain mass violence.

So a finely calibrated but fulsome approach to the law, which strikes the proper balance between upholding liberty of expression and tamping atrocity-friendly rhetoric, has been the goal of this book. It has concentrated on surveying and diagnosing the individual atrocity speech modalities of direct and public

15. Open Society Justice Initiative, *Briefing Paper, Dominic Ongwen at the ICC: Confirmation of Charges*, Open Society Foundations (Jan. 2016), https://www.opensocietyfoundations.org/sites/default/files/briefing-ongwen-icc-confirmation-charges%2020160120_0.pdf.

16. Tom Maliti, *Defense Argues Ongwen Unfit as ICC Trial Opens*, International Justice Monitor (Dec. 6, 2016), https://www.ijmonitor.org/2016/12/defense-argues-ongwen-mentally-unfit-as-icc-trial-opens/

17. As of the time this book is going to print, the arrest warrant has yet to be executed. Prosecutor v. Kony, Case No. ICC-02/04-01/05, Warrant of Arrest for Joseph Kony Issued on 8 July 2005 as Amended on 27 September 2005, ¶ 13 (Sept. 27, 2005). The same was true of Kony's second-in-command, Vincent Otti, but he has since been confirmed dead. *See Uganda's LRA Confirm Otti Death*, BBC News (Jan. 28, 2008), http://news.bbc.co.uk/2/hi/africa/7204278.stm.

18. Prosecutor v. Harun, Case No. ICC-02/05-01/07-1-Corr, Decision of the Prosecution Application under Art. 58(7) of the Statute, ¶¶ 90–91, 94 (Apr. 27, 2007), *id*. Warrant of Arrest for Ahmad Harun (Apr. 27, 2007).

19. *See, e.g.*, Annie Gowen, *New Concerns Rise over Burmese Treatment of Rohingya Muslims*, Wash. Post (Nov. 11, 2014), https://www.washingtonpost.com/world/asia_pacific/new-concerns-rise-over-burmese-treatment-of-rohingya-muslims/2014/11/11/4c0f42fe-5947-11e4-9d6c-756a229d8b18_story.html ("Every day, the trapped people could hear a Buddhist monk exhorting people over a loudspeaker to keep up the blockade to starve the Muslims to death."); Anna Therese Day, *From Hate Speech to Rape Speech: Women in South Sudan Are Targets of Sexual Violence*, N.Y. Times (July 9, 2015), http://nytlive.nytimes.com/womenintheworld/2015/07/09/from-hate-speech-to-rape-speech-women-in-south-sudan-are-targets-of-sexual-violence/ ("Their dispatches quickly escalated from hate speech to rape speech, with opposition fighters calling on men to commit acts of sexualized violence against the women and girls of their rival ethnicities.").

incitement to commit genocide, hate speech as a crime against humanity (persecution), instigation, and ordering. In the process, it has offered ways to remedy various problems within each offense and proposed a global restructuring of the crimes to eliminate gaps in coverage and promote strategic coherence in charging strategy. It is hoped that this has laid the preliminary groundwork for a new discipline in international criminal law (ICL): atrocity speech law.

IV. FUTURE AREAS OF EXPLORATION

A. Expansion of the Target Crimes

But it is also hoped that work in this area will continue; that this book may be a springboard for additional research and development in the subgenre. What might that work consist of? For one, it is clear that ICL speech liability may extend to target crimes beyond those already covered in this book. An obvious example is terrorism. In Chapter 10, we briefly alluded to existing law criminalizing incitement to terrorism. Of course, speech abetting, instigation, and ordering could also apply.

Another obvious possibility is incitement to aggression. In my piece "Of War-Councils and War-Mongering: Considering the Viability of Incitement to Aggression," I have already undertaken a preliminary examination of this potential offense.[20] That paper concludes that incitement to aggression can be a viable crime but with certain limitations.

In particular, it posits that aggression-related discourse can theoretically be bifurcated between "war-council" speech and "war-mongering" speech.[21] With respect to the former, it considers that aggression is a leadership-oriented crime with an *in personam* jurisdiction limited to an individual exercising control over the political or military action of a state.[22] But such a person, even if the most powerful dictator, is not capable of carrying out himself the multitude of simultaneous and multilevel tasks necessary to plan and launch a modern aggressive war. He will operate within some sort of bureaucratic framework and/or military hierarchy that will necessarily require communication with other government/military officials as part of such an enterprise.[23]

Such communications, the paper notes, are tantamount to "councils of war" conducted in the relatively insular corridors of power. With respect to such "war-council" aggression speech, the utility of any corollary incitement provision is questionable—those who would act—the controllers of the government/military apparatus—need no exhorting as they monopolize agency.[24] Moreover,

20. Gregory S. Gordon, *Of War-Councils and War-Mongering: Considering the Viability of Incitement to Aggression*, *in* FOR THE SAKE OF PRESENT AND FUTURE GENERATIONS: ESSAYS ON INTERNATIONAL LAW, CRIME AND JUSTICE IN HONOUR OF ROGER S. CLARK (Brill-Nijhoff, S. Linton, G. Simpson, & W. Schabas eds., 2015).

21. *Id.* at 422–23.

22. *Id.* at 415–16.

23. *Id.* at 424.

24. *Id.*

unlike the other core crimes, any theoretical "inciting" speech connected to war-council aggression conduct does not as directly entail dehumanization or marginalization of an out-group being targeted for violence or inhumane treatment.[25]

But the paper concludes that the other variety of aggression-related discourse that a theoretical incitement crime implicates, "war-mongering," is quite different. It implicates government leaders conditioning their citizens to support illegal war campaigns through speeches and mass media.[26] It is not always a *sine qua non* for perpetrating the crime of aggression (as war-council conduct is), but, in cases of controversial war campaigns, it is sometimes needed to assure sufficient troop morale and civilian cooperation.[27] And it empirically entails speech dehumanizing the enemy population.[28] Further, it has historically been recognized as an offense—including at the International Military Tribunal at Nuremberg (as to defendants Rudolf Hess, Wilhelm Keitel, and Alfred Rosenberg) and at the International Military Tribunal for the Far East (IMTFE) at Tokyo (with respect to defendants Sadao Araki and Kingoro Hashimoto).[29]

So criminalizing such speech via incitement makes more sense and, indeed, fills important gaps within the aggression offense's definitional and operational framework. Thus, the paper concludes, the crime of direct and public incitement to commit aggression, the "public" element implicitly excluding "war-council" communication, is viable. Given aggression's role as the breeding ground for the other core ICL crimes, I argue that qualifiedly including it within the envelope of incitement achieves the proper balance between sound policy and doctrinal coherence.[30] Still, this is only a preliminary analysis. It is hoped that it can stimulate additional research and reflection.

B. Other Aspects of Speech and Atrocity

One can also envisage work on the following related aspects, including nonlegal ones, that would help advance the atrocity speech law project: (1) historical research; (2) sentencing; (3) denial; and (4) sociological research. Each of these shall now be considered in sequence.

1. Historical Research

A thumbnail sketch of the history of speech and atrocity was provided in Chapter 1. But the purpose of that chapter was to put into context the legal analysis that would follow. Conducting research in preparation for writing this book

25. *Id.*

26. *Id.* at 425.

27. *Id.*

28. *Id.*

29. *Id.* at 423.

30. *Id.* at 427–28.

revealed that a treasure trove of information is out there for legal scholars looking to fill in large gaps in the literature related to the history of speech and atrocity.

For example, there is no definitive book on the role of propaganda in fomenting the Armenian Genocide. And the literature on speech and gross human rights violations is even sparser when it comes to other early twentieth-century atrocities. Germany has acknowledged that it committed the twentieth century's first genocide by massacring the Herero people, who had tried to resist German colonial rule in what was then German South-West Africa.[31] Herero civilians were initially massacred in the thousands by the Germans, with many being "driven into the Namibian desert to die of starvation and dehydration."[32] Then survivors were "herded into concentration camps and given as slave labour to German businesses, where many died of overwork and malnutrition."[33] And hate speech factored prominently into the Second Reich's genocidal campaign against the Herero. According to Karl Yambert:

> German propaganda . . . utilized inflammatory, racially charged disinformation [interweaving] two thematic strands. One was that . . . of a race war between civilized Germans and barbarous, even brutish and sub-human Negroes. . . . A second theme was that of claiming that horrific atrocities were perpetrated by the Herero against the settlers, particularly the mutilation and butchering of German men and women. German officialdom ensured that reports of such atrocities were published in Germany's newspapers, despite efforts by some in the colonies to disprove these reports as fabrications.[34]

Ten years later, during World War I, at roughly the same time as the Ottoman Empire was exterminating Armenians, it was also engaging in genocidal campaigns against two other Christian minority groups within its territory: the Greeks and the Assyrians.[35] Approximately 350,000 Greeks resident in Turkey, nearly the entire Greek population at that time, were killed—many on forced marches between Anatolia and the Syrian Desert.[36] The Assyrians, an ancient people living in modern-day southeastern Iraq and northwestern Iran, were also victims of an Ottoman extermination campaign. Through death marches in the Syrian Desert, as well as massacres, torture, and other atrocities committed

31. Justin Huggler, *Germany to Recognise Herero Genocide and Apologise to Namibia*, The Telegraph (July 14, 2014), http://www.telegraph.co.uk/news/2016/07/14/germany-to-recognise-herero-genocide-and-apologise-to-namibia/.

32. *Id.*

33. I. I. Isaac, Inter-African Development and Development Fund (IADF): With Alternative Strategies toward Sustainable Economic Development for Africa, Vol. 1, 71 (2009).

34. Karl A. Yambert, *Role of Propaganda in the Herero Genocide*, *in* 1 Modern Genocide: The Definitive Resource and Document Collection 1043 (Paul R. Bartrop & Steven Leonard Jacobs eds., 2015).

35. Paul R. Bartrop, Genocide: The Basics 34–35 (2014).

36. *Id.* at 34–35.

in towns and villages, approximately one-quarter million Assyrians lost their lives.[37] Hate speech helped fuel these atrocities, but there is a paucity of scholarly analysis on this subject.[38]

Another pre–World War II hidden genocide, Stalin's 1932–1933 starvation of the Ukrainians that resulted in the death of an estimated 3.3 million people, was supported by a Soviet hate speech campaign.[39] But there has been no scholarly coverage of it in ICL literature. And although there has been much coverage of the Third Reich's weaponized words used against the Jews, no in-depth ICL study has been conducted focusing specifically on the life, work, and trials of the Nazis' Holocaust propagandists.

This is a particularly glaring omission in the case of Nazi Radio Section Chief Hans Fritzsche, whose atrocity-focused body of work should be explored in greater depth given his acquittal before the International Military Tribunal (IMT) at Nuremberg. As suggested in Chapter 3, given that the Allies later found very incriminating evidence against him, Fritzsche's acquittal can in large part be explained by a rush to judgment in light of incipient Cold War political considerations.[40] As I have noted elsewhere:

> But Fritzsche was put in the dock at the IMT at the insistence of the Soviet Union, which had in its custody significantly fewer IMT defendants than the other allies, especially the Americans. Fritzsche was one of only two high-ranking Nazis captured by the Soviets (the other being Raeder). They felt Fritzsche's inclusion would help balance the inequality regarding IMT defendants vis-a-vis the other allies. So his prosecution before the IMT, as opposed to a subsequent trial in the Russian zone, was motivated largely by incipient Cold War political considerations.[41]

Similarly, from a legal-historical perspective, there appears to be no ICL-focused academic study specifically concentrating on the propaganda work of IMTFE defendants Sadao Araki and Kingoro Hashimoto.

37. *Id.*

38. *See* David Gaunt, *The Assyrian Genocide of 1915*, Seyfo Center (Apr. 18, 2009), http://www.atour.com/history/1900/20140424a.html (noting that Ottoman hate speech directed against the Armenians was understood as a call for violence against all Christians in the Empire, including the Assyrians and Greeks).

39. *Holodomor: Memories of Ukraine's Silent Massacre*, BBC News (Nov. 23, 2013), http://www.bbc.com/news/world-europe-25058256 (noting that the Soviets confiscated all grain supplies and closed off the Ukrainian border); Liudmyla Hrynevych, *The Holodomor and the Language of Hate in Stalinist Propaganda*, Holodomor Research and Education Consortium (Oct. 29, 2016), https://www.eventbrite.ca/e/the-holodomor-and-the-language-of-hate-in-stalinist-propaganda-tickets-27260968290.

40. *See How Did Hans Fritzsche Avoid the Noose?*, Propagander FAQ, http://grwa.tripod.com/050.html (last visited Aug. 28, 2016).

41. Gregory S. Gordon, *The Forgotten Nuremberg Hate Speech Case, Otto Dietrich and the Future of Persecution Law*, 75 Ohio St. L.J. 571, 583 n.88 (2014).

Finally, within the area of ICL, one also encounters a dearth of propaganda-focused research on the Khmer Rouge's genocidal hatemongers. And it is clear that other, more recent, atrocity-focused propaganda could be the subject of future scholarly studies, including the genocide in Darfur and the ongoing massacres being perpetrated by ISIS.

2. Sentencing

A key issue, which is outside the scope of this book, is sentencing. We have seen a wide disparity in sentencing outcomes based on atrocity speech convictions to date. We can start with convictions for direct and public incitement to commit genocide (DPICG), where the defendants were also convicted of other crimes, such as genocide itself or murder/extermination as a crime against humanity (CAH). These would include: (1) ICTR defendants Jean-Paul Akayesu (mayor of Taba commune during the genocide—convicted of genocide, several counts of CAH (murder, extermination, torture, rape, inhumane acts), and DPICG—sentenced to life in prison);[42] (2) Jean Kambanda (prime minister of the genocidal rump government—genocide, conspiracy to commit genocide, complicity in genocide, CAH (murder and extermination), and DPICG—life in prison);[43] (3) Hassan Ngeze (founder and editor-in-chief of *Kangura*—aiding and abetting genocide, aiding and abetting CAH (extermination), and DPICG—thirty-five years in prison);[44] and (4) Eliezer Niyitegeka (minister of information for the rump government—genocide, conspiracy to commit genocide, CAH (murder, extermination, and other inhumane acts), and DPICG—life in prison).[45] With the exception of Ngeze, whose individual criminal responsibility, apart from the DPICG count, was limited to complicity, each defendant received a life sentence.

This stands in contrast to ICTR sentences based uniquely on speech-related convictions: Ferdinand Nahimana (founder/executive of Radio Télévision Libre des Milles Collines (RTLM)—convicted of DPICG and CAH (persecution)—sentenced by the ICTR to thirty years in prison);[46] Georges Ruggiu (RTLM announcer—DPICG and CAH (persecution)—ICTR sentence of twelve years in prison);[47] Juvénal Kajelijeli (mayor of Mukingo commune—DPICG—ICTR

42. *Akayesu, Jean Paul*, The Hague Justice Portal, http://www.haguejusticeportal.net/index.php?id=8778 (last visited Aug. 28, 2016).

43. Kambanda, Jean, The Hague Justice Portal, http://www.haguejusticeportal.net/index.php?id=8872 (last visited Aug. 28, 2016).

44. *Ngeze, Hassan*, The Hague Justice Portal, http://www.haguejusticeportal.net/index.php?id=8415 (last visited Aug. 28, 2016).

45. *Niyitegeka, Eliezer*, The Hague Justice Portal, http://www.haguejusticeportal.net/index.php?id=9217 (last visited Aug. 28, 2016).

46. *Nahimana, Ferdinand*, The Hague Justice Portal, http://www.haguejusticeportal.net/index.php?id=8412 (last visited Aug. 28, 2016).

47. *Ruggiu, George*, The Hague Justice Portal, http://www.haguejusticeportal.net/index.php?id=9164 (last visited Aug. 28, 2016).

sentence of forty-five years in prison);[48] Tharcisse Muvunyi (most senior military officer in the Butare Prefecture and commander of the *École des sous-officiers* (ESO) in Butare—DPICG—ICTR sentence of fifteen years in prison);[49] and Léon Mugesera (regional vice chairman of the pre-genocide ruling party, the Mouvement Révolutionnaire pour le Développement (MRND) and university professor—DPICG, incitement to hatred, and CAH (persecution)—Rwandan High Court sentence of life in prison).

What do these results tell us? Frankly, it is hard to say. All of these sentences, except for one, were issued by the ICTR. And the ICTR Statute and Rules of Procedure and Evidence do not offer much guidance. Article 23 of the ICTR Statute (Penalties) states, in relevant part:

> 1. The penalty imposed by the Trial Chamber shall be limited to imprisonment. In determining the terms of imprisonment, the Trial Chambers shall have recourse to the general practice regarding prison sentences in the courts of Rwanda.
> 2. In imposing the sentences, the Trial Chambers should take into account such factors as the gravity of the offence and the individual circumstances of the convicted person.[50]

And Rule 101 (Penalties) of the ICTR Rules of Procedure and Evidence (RPE) provides, in pertinent part:

> (A) A person convicted by the Tribunal may be sentenced to imprisonment for a fixed term or the remainder of his life.
> (B) In determining the sentence, the Trial Chamber shall take into account the factors mentioned in Article 23 (2) of the Statute, as well as such factors as:
>   (i) Any aggravating circumstances;
>   (ii) Any mitigating circumstances including the substantial cooperation with the Prosecutor by the convicted person before or after conviction;
>   (iii) The general practice regarding prison sentences in the courts of Rwanda . . .[51]

48. *Kajelijeli, Juvénal*, The Hague Justice Portal, http://www.haguejusticeportal.net/index.php?id=8414 (last visited Aug. 28, 2016).

49. *Muvunyi, Tharcisse*, The Hague Justice Portal, http://www.haguejusticeportal.net/index.php?id=8411 (last visited Aug. 28, 2016).

50. Statute of the International Criminal Tribunal for Rwanda, S.C. Res. 955, art. 23, U.N. Doc. S/RES/955 (Nov. 8, 1994) [hereinafter ICTR Statute].

51. Int'l Crim. Trib. for Rwanda, Rules of Procedure and Evidence, adopted July 5, 1995, amended Feb. 21, 2000 (7th rev.), U.N. Doc. ITR/3/REV.7 Rule 101 (2000), http:// www.unictr.org/Portals/0/English/Legal/Evidence/English/210200.pdf.

The ICTR Statute emphasizes gravity of the offense and the individual circumstances of the convicted person, and the RPE stresses consideration of aggravating and mitigating circumstances. Although these may account for some of the differences in sentencing outcomes above, it is significant that both the ICTR Statute and RPE have one factor in common: the general practice regarding prison sentences in the courts of Rwanda. And consideration of this factor, in reference to the speech-liability-alone sentences considered above, is striking. The one sentence issued by a Rwandan court for strictly speech-related crimes—life imprisonment for Léon Mugesera—indicates a great discrepancy between sentencing practices in Rwanda and at the ICTR as regards strictly speech-liability defendants. In that regard, it should be noted that Valerie Bemeriki, one of RTLM's most infamous broadcasters, was sentenced to life in prison by a local Rwandan *gacaca* court.[52]

Even within the group of ICTR speech-liability-alone defendants, there are various kinds of discrepancies regarding sentencing. In contrast to the speech-offense-only defendants, the first group of defendants received life sentences with the exception of the sole media figure Hassan Ngeze, who was only sentenced to thirty-five years imprisonment. Apart from complicity in reference to his nonspeech crimes, why was Ngeze, a key propagandist in the Rwandan Genocide, sentenced to a discernably lower sentence than the other defendants? How much did his speech crimes factor into his sentence? How much did they factor into the life sentences of the other defendants in that group? That is not clear from the record because the speech crimes were not given dedicated consideration.

Regarding the ICTR defendants sentenced strictly in reference to speech offenses, other issues are raised. RTLM founder Ferdinand Nahimana, convicted of DPICG and CAH (persecution), the person most responsible for the creation and initial management of "Radio Machete," the genocide's media command post, received only a thirty-year prison sentence. In contrast, a small-town mayor, Juvénal Kajelijeli, who was convicted of DPICG only, got forty-five years. RTLM announcer Georges Ruggiu, the station's French-speaking firebrand, got only twelve years, while a local military officer, Tharcisse Muvunyi, received fifteen.

But the most glaring discrepancy is that between the roles and conduct of the speech-crime-only defendants sentenced in Rwandan courts versus the roles and conduct of those sentenced by the ICTR. The former include a university

52. *Rwanda Jails Journalist Valerie Bemeriki for Genocide*, BBC News (Dec. 14, 2009), http://news.bbc.co.uk/2/hi/africa/8412014.stm (Bemeriki was also convicted of "planning genocide" and complicity in several murders). Literally meaning "small grass" (referring to the lawn where communities sat in mediation), *gacaca* is a traditional Rwandan dispute resolution mechanism that had traditionally been used to settle small-scale civil disputes, such as land, personal injury, and inheritance claims. Timothy Longman, *Justice at the Grassroots? Gacaca Trials in Rwanda*, *in* Transitional Justice in the Twenty-First Century: Beyond Truth versus Justice 209–10 (Naomi Roht-Arriaza & Javier Mariezcurrena eds., 2006). It was modified by the Rwandan government to adjudicate lower-level perpetrator cases arising from the 1994 genocide. *Id.*

professor (Mugesera) whose sentence was based almost entirely on a single speech that was given a year and a half before the outbreak of genocide as well as another RTLM radio announcer (Bemeriki). Both were sentenced to life in prison, while Nahimana, the founder of RTLM, the vocal-engine of the genocide (and Bemeriki's former boss), got less than fifty. And the ICTR's RTLM radio announcer defendant, Ruggiu, was sentenced to twelve years as opposed to the one sentenced by a Rwandan court to incarceration in perpetuity. The contrasts, as seen in Tables 1 and 2 below, are stark and, it is submitted, merit more fulsome scholarly consideration.

Table 1 Sentencing Outcomes based on Convictions for Speech Crimes and other References for Rwandan Gencoide Hate Speech Defendants

Defendant	**Profile**	**Conviction**	**Sentence**
1. Jean-Paul Akayesu	Mayor of Taba commune during the genocide	Genocide, several counts of CAH (murder, extermination, torture, rape, inhumane acts) and DPICG	Life in prison
2. Jean Kambanda	Prime minister of the genocidal rump government	Genocide, conspiracy to commit genocide, complicity in genocide, CAH (murder and extermination), and DPICG	Life in prison
3. Hassan Ngeze	Founder and editor-in-chief of *Kangura*	Aiding and abetting genocide, aiding and abetting CAH (extermination), and DPICG	35 years in prison
4. Eliezer Niyitegeka	Minister of Information for the rump government	Genocide, conspiracy to commit genocide, CAH (murder, extermination, and other inhumane acts), and DPICG	Life in prison

With the exception of Ngeze, whose individual criminal responsibility, apart from the DPICG count, was limited to complicity, each defendant received a life sentence.

This stands in contrast to ICTR sentences based uniquely on speech-related convictions shown in Table 2.

Table 2 Sentencing Outcomes based on Convictions for Speech Crimes Only

Defendant	Position	Conviction	Sentence
1. Ferdinand Nahimana	Founder/executive of Radio Télévision Libre des Milles Collines (RTLM)	DPICG and CAH (persecution)	30 years in prison
2. Georges Ruggiu	RTLM announcer	DPICG and CAH (persecution)	12 years in prison
3. Juvénal Kajelijeli	Mayor of Mukingo commune	DPICG	45 years in prison
4. Tharcisse Muvunyi	Most senior military officer in the Butare Prefecture and Commander of the *École des sous-officiers* (ESO) in Butare	DPICG	15 years in prison
5. Léon Mugesera	Regional vice chairman of the pre-genocide ruling party, the Mouvement Révolutionnaire pour le Développement (MRND) and university professor	DPICG, incitement to hatred, and CAH (persecution)	Life in prison **(Rwandan High Court)**
6. Valérie Bemeriki	RTLM announcer	DPICG, planning genocide	Life in prison (Gacaca Court)

Of course, other factors affected punishment level in these cases, including the aforementioned aggravating and mitigating circumstances as well as offense gravity and individual circumstances. But the judges involved in formulating these sentences did not specify any "nature-of-speech-crime factors" that could be consulted to better understand the calculation of the prison terms. But we could imagine what those might have been.

In particular, how should incitement be punished vis-à-vis persecution? Or in relation to instigation or ordering? With reference to consideration of incitement in its own right, what weight should be given to the various incitement techniques that were employed? All things being equal, should indirect techniques yield shorter prison sentences than direct ones? Should the relative degree of the "public" nature of the crime result in upward or downward adjustments? And should resultant violence, including consideration of violence scale and severity, be taken into account (not as a condition of liability but strictly as a sentencing factor)? Related to that, all things being equal, should large genocidal media outlet executives be punished more severely than local government administrators? If so, based on which criteria? Finally, should the context evaluative factors considered in Chapter 8 as part of the "incitement" analysis for liability purposes (such as the speaker's personal history, previous acts of violence, audience vulnerability, etc.) be reconsidered so as to arrive at a more just sentence? These are just some of the incitement-dedicated considerations one could imagine.

Others could be postulated for persecution. In particular, should the nature of the hate speech (group libel versus harassment versus incitement) inform the sentencing calculus? How about spatial and/or temporal proximity between the widespread or systematic attack and the hate speech? Should the scale of the attack impact the sentencing decision? Or should the identity or historic vulnerability of the victim group be taken into account? And, of course, other sentencing factors could be tailored specifically for the crimes of instigation and ordering, including the fact that causal violence is an element of each of these speech crimes.

Overall, then, given that "the principle of uniformity and proportionality [are extremely] compelling in the international criminal law context,"[53] it would be best if those tenets could be more consciously and systematically incorporated into atrocity speech law. It is hoped that future scholarly work in this area take on this important project.

3. The Special Case of Denial: Speech after Atrocity

According to Professor Gregory Stanton's atrocity prediction/prognosis model titled "The 10 Stages of Genocide," the genocidal process unfolds as follows: (1) classification (use of categories to distinguish those discriminating and those discriminated against (target group) into "us and them" by ethnicity, race, religion, or nationality—e.g., German and Jew, Hutu, and Tutsi); (2) symbolization (assigning symbols to the classification—i.e., associating with or foisting upon a target group certain colors or apparel, such as the golden Star of David patch for Jews in Nazi Germany or the blue scarf for Eastern Zone residents in Khmer Rouge Cambodia); (3) discrimination (denying basic rights of the victim group, such as the Nazi Nuremberg Laws of 1935 stripping Jews of citizenship and other fundamental rights); (4) dehumanization (equating the target group with animals, vermin, insects, or diseases); (5) organization (e.g., establishing militia and drawing up lists); (6) polarization (e.g., broadcasting hate propaganda or forbidding social, civic, or economic interaction with the target group); (7) preparation (the target group is segregated, its property expropriated, and death lists are drawn up); (8) persecution (stripping group members of their property, identifying them via forcing them to wear symbols, such as the Star of David in Nazi Germany, and putting their names on death lists); (9) extermination (the actual killing of the dehumanized victims begins); and (10) denial (it always follows a genocide and is a signal that additional killings of the victim group are intended).[54]

53. Jennifer J. Clark, Note, *Zero to Life: Sentencing Appeals at the International Criminal Tribunals for the Former Yugoslavia and Rwanda*, 96 Geo. L.J. 1685, 1690 (2008).

54. Gregory H. Stanton, *The Ten Stages of Genocide*, Genocide Watch, http://www.genocidewatch.org/genocide/tenstagesofgenocide.html (last visited Aug. 29, 2016).

From an atrocity speech law perspective, should denial be criminalized? This is a question I considered preliminarily in my article "Speech Along the Atrocity Spectrum."[55] To answer that question properly, I suggested in that piece, the specific context of the denial should be taken into account. Denial by direct perpetrators or their confederates as the end-phase of a genocidal cabal must be dealt with as a function of conspiracy law, not ordinary hate speech regulation. As Professor Stanton observes:

> The perpetrators of genocide dig up the mass graves, burn the bodies, try to cover up the evidence and intimidate the witnesses. They deny that they committed any crimes, and often blame what happened on the victims. They block investigations of the crimes, and continue to govern until driven from power by force, when they flee into exile. There they remain with impunity, like Pol Pot or Idi Amin, unless they are captured and a tribunal is established to try them.[56]

That said, once the conspiracy has run its course, denial rhetoric must be seen in a different light. It is not part of a cover-up. And it is less likely to provoke fresh violence in the short term. In light of this more tenuous connection to the original atrocity, free speech advocates oppose criminalizing denial.[57]

And there may be good policy justifications for that. Letting deniers vent their lies, the argument would go, reveals their inanity. And it gives legitimate historians the chance to republish the legitimate narrative, further validating it in the public imagination and reinforcing the truth.[58] Similarly, if certain atrocity-related particulars have remained more obscure, denial has the unintended effect of bringing them to light and better burnishing the historical record.[59] And, from a Meiklejohnian perspective, allowing deniers to promote their theories, however spurious, fortifies the public perception that persons are autonomous and empowered to make significant individual choices.[60] Finally, giving free rein to deniers furnishes society with a mirror by which to inspect itself and understand whether, and to what extent, education may

55. Gregory S. Gordon, *Speech Along the Atrocity Spectrum*, 42 GA. J. INT'L & COMP. L. 425, 452 (2014).

56. *Id.*

57. *See* Russell L. Weaver, *Brandenburg and Incitement in a Digital Era*, 80 MISS. L.J. 1263, 1288 (2011) ("For example, even though countries like France and Germany prohibit Holocaust denial, the United States does not (and probably cannot) impose criminal restrictions on Holocaust denials because of the First Amendment to the United States Constitution's guarantee of free speech.").

58. *See generally* Robert Post, *Hate Speech*, *in* EXTREME SPEECH AND DEMOCRACY 123–38 (Ivan Hare & James Weinstein eds., 2009) (pointing out the problems with genocide denial laws).

59. *Id.*

60. *Id.*

be wanting or extremist groups may be growing and/or gaining traction.[61] Such intelligence is crucial for effective and efficient governance and policy prioritization.

On the other hand, not all countries are the same. Certain ones have particular histories that make criminalizing denial much more palatable, if not necessary. Germany, for instance, grappling with the heavy burden of the Shoah, had powerful justifications for enacting Holocaust-denial laws.[62] And few would quibble when Rwanda's new leaders, taking power after four months of unimaginable Tutsi mass slaughter, criminalized denial of the 1994 genocide.[63] The directly culpable and traumatized genocide forum country has a special and historic interest in outlawing related mendacity.[64]

Even the most zealous guardians of free speech voice sympathy for such prohibitions within post-genocidal societies themselves.[65] But they draw the line there. American First Amendment expert Floyd Abrams, for instance, frowns on Holocaust denial laws for countries such as the United States and Canada, which are not the loci of the original atrocities at issue.[66] Still, both of these nations have given refuge to large numbers of victims, and antidenial laws may be warranted to protect them. As Katharine Gelber observes:

> [In] the act of denying this historical truth [of the Holocaust], the deniers denigrate the Jewish people and memories of historical occurrences, suggest that those who accept the truth of the Holocaust lie, and relativize the suffering incurred. Thus, the act of Holocaust denial is not simply an expression of belief in what did or did not happen historically, given that the Holocaust has been historically verified. It is an act of vilification that denigrates and harms.[67]

61. *Id.*

62. *See* Gordon Butler, *The Essence of Human Rights: A Religious Critique*, 43 U. Rich. L. Rev. 1255, 1300–01 (2009) (noting that Holocaust denial in Germany threatens democratic stability while that may not be the case in the United States).

63. *See* Jennifer M. Allen & George H. Norris, *Is Genocide Different? Dealing with Hate Speech in a Post-Genocide Society*, 7 J. Int'l L. & Int'l Rel. 146, 172 (2011) ("Given the short passage of time and the existence of militant groups that deny the genocide, a statute specifically outlawing genocide denial, similar to those found in Germany, Israel, and the EU, would be an important tool to help Rwanda overcome the racist attitudes that have fueled its violent past."). However, as discussed *infra*, one may wonder whether, over time, such denial laws might outlive their original justification. *Id.*

64. *Id.*

65. *See, e.g.*, Floyd Abrams, *On American Hate Speech Law*, *in* The Content and Context of Hate Speech: Rethinking Regulations and Responses 116, 118 (Michael Herz & Peter Molnar eds., 2012).

66. *Id.* at 125.

67. Katharine Gelber, *Reconceptualizing Counterspeech in Hate Speech Policy*, *in* The Content and Context of Hate Speech: Rethinking Regulation and Responses 198, 210–11 (Michael Herz & Peter Molnar eds., 2012).

Notwithstanding these considerations, though, criminalizing denial raises other problematic issues. In particular, even if denial prohibitions are justified in the immediate aftermath of atrocity, while survivors remain among us, might they eventually outlive their utility?[68] Should they ultimately be phased out? If so, when? Moreover, assuming such laws are on balance still beneficial, can they be (or are they being) effectively enforced? If not, there could be compelling reasons to jettison them or refrain from enacting them in the first place.

Then again, if a legislative void permits denial to flourish at some point in the more distant future, could it eventually help fertilize new outgrowths of atrocity? Professor Stanton notes that denial "is among the surest indicators of future genocidal massacres."[69] And even if insufficient on its own, denial can often be mixed with other, more direct, methods of incitement capable of conconcting potent verbal cocktails that foment violence against victim groups. So definitive answers about the best methods for dealing with denial are elusive indeed. And further research in this area is strongly recommended.

4. Empirical Research on the Relationship between Speech and Violence

This book has proceeded from the well-supported premise that hate speech is a causal factor in mass atrocity campaigns. And there is certainly compelling anecdotal evidence to that effect. In the words of one Rwandan genocidaire: "Killing[,] . . . if you are adequately conditioned, . . . [y]ou do it without shame . . . we were efficiently conditioned by radio broadcasts . . ."[70] But the precise nature and extent of this phenomenon merits further study. And various scholars have been doing that. Research such as social psychologist Stanley Milgram's early 1960s "obedience to authority" experiments at Yale and Phillip Zimbardo's Stanford Prison Experiment a decade later, have demonstrated how speech, in tandem with other conduct, can be used to develop a perpetrator mindset in ordinary citizens.[71]

But can such a link be demonstrated in actual situations of mass atrocity? Political scientist Scott Straus has raised doubts, in this regard. Using a mix of empirical data, including radio transmission range calculations, broadcast

68. *See* Jennifer M. Allen & George H. Norris, *Is Genocide Different? Dealing with Hate Speech in a Post-Genocide Society*, 7 J. Int'l L. & Int'l Rel. 146, 172 (2011).

69. Stanton, *supra* note 54.

70. Jean-Pierre Chrétien, *RTLM Propaganda: The Democratic Alibi*, *in* The Media and the Rwandan Genocide 55, 55 (Allan Thompson ed., 2007).

71. *See* Stanley Milgram, Obedience to Authority, at xi–xvii (1973) (experiments inspired, in part, by the trial of Nazi war criminal Adolf Eichmann were set up to show a subject obeying an authority figure despite believing that obeying would cause pain to a third person); Philip Zimbardo, The Lucifer Effect: Understanding How Good People Turn Evil 263 (2007) (arriving at similar conclusions after conducting an experiment with simulated guard-prisoner interactions).

content statistics, and responses from interviews with confessed killers, he has concluded that RTLM's impact on the Rwandan Genocide was more limited than commonly supposed. Straus specifies:

> There appears to be a substantial gap between RTLM's broadcast range and where genocidal violence took place; there is little positive and much negative evidence that broadcast range corresponds to where violence started earliest in different regions; the bulk of violence appears to have occurred before the most inflammatory broadcasts aired; most perpetrators in a survey say face-to-face mobilization, not radio, led them to join attacks; and, when asked, no respondent identified radio as the primary determinant of the genocide. Each piece of evidence has limits. RTLM's range is not conclusively known; a full transcript record of RTLM broadcasts does not exist; convicted perpetrators may not tell the truth. But together, the evidence amounts to a persuasive refutation of the commonly-held beliefs that radio had widespread, direct effects and that hate radio was the primary driver of the genocide and participation in it.[72]

That said, Straus acknowledges that RTLM still played an important role in facilitating the genocide:

> In the capital, RTLM's broadcasting of names and locations, as well as its generally hostile tone, inspired attacks and were a factor in the hardliners' ability to assert dominance. . . . By broadcasting a belligerent and jingoistic tone and catalyzing acts of violence, RTLM signaled that hardliners had power and reinforced hardliners' messages. . . . Hate radio constituted one dimension by which hardliners achieved dominance and persuaded individuals to join attacks against Tutsi civilians.[73]

But Straus has also conceded that he was working with a limited data set.[74]

Economist and public policy professor David Yanagizawa-Drott has reached different conclusions, however, with a larger set of data. His 2010 statistical study of the effects of RTLM indicates that, during the 1994 genocide, murders were 65–77 percent higher in Rwandan villages that received the full RTLM signal, versus those that did not receive the signal for exogenous reasons, such as hills in the line-of-sight between radio transmitters and villages or other topographical

72. Scot Straus, *Rwanda and RTLM Radio Media Effects*, United States Holocaust Memorial Museum, at 10 (2009), https://www.ushmm.org/confront-genocide/speakers-and-events/all-speakers-and-events/speech-power-violence [hereinafter *Media Effects*] (last visited Aug. 29, 2016). *See also* Scott Straus, *What Is the Relationship between Hate Radio and Violence? Rethinking Rwanda's "Radio Machete,"* 35 Pol. & Soc. 609, 612–13 (2007).

73. Straus, *Media Effects*, *supra* note 72, at 10.

74. *Id.* at 1–2 (noting that the existing data was "limited in important ways . . .").

obstructions.[75] Further, through additional statistical analysis, Yanagizawa-Drott has more recently calculated that an estimated 51,000 perpetrators, or approximately 10 percent of the overall violence, can be attributed to the station.[76]

Even more recently, in empirical analysis of the psychological effects of speeches given by extreme Serbian nationalist politician Vojislav Šešelj, a team of researchers led by psychologist Christine Lillie and anthropology/law professor Richard Wilson, considered which types of propaganda are most likely to instigate mass atrocities.[77] They coded 242 actual public speeches given by Šešelj for references to revenge, nationalism, stereotyping, dehumanization, justice, victimization, past atrocities, politics, and direct threats.[78] Participants read either one of the speeches or a control speech and were then asked questions about empathy, perception of intent, and whether violence is morally justifiable.[79] Only speeches focusing on revenge and past atrocities intensified the participants' propensity to morally justify violence.[80] Contrary to conventional wisdom, the researchers concluded, that sort of speech, as opposed to speech dehumanizing the out-group, has the most potential for spurring atrocity.[81]

Although research in this area is burgeoning, it is still only preliminary. Much more needs to be conducted. The results to date raise important questions about the relationship between speech and atrocity. One thing remains clear, however—to varying degrees, all the current research suggests an important link between these two phenomena. The nature of that link merits further scholarly exploration. But the need for the law to punish those who exploit that link for political, personal, or social advantage remains unchanged.

C. Further Multidisciplinary Inquiries

This book has considered the analysis of speech from an almost exclusively legal perspective. That said, it has at times delved into philosophy, including consideration of Aristotle's theories of rhetoric. This too is fertile ground for further exploration

75. David Yanagizawa-Drott, *Propaganda and Conflict: Theory and Evidence from the Rwandan Genocide*, The Bureau for Research and Economic Analysis of Development (Dec. 6, 2010), at 27–28, http://ibread.org/bread/sites/default/files/0511conf/Yanagizawa-Drott.pdf.

76. David Yanagizawa-Drott, *Propaganda and Conflict: Evidence from the Rwandan Genocide*, Q. J. Econ. 4 (2014) (showing that RTLM had a direct effect on the level of violence, which increased in radio coverage areas, and an indirect effect as broadcasts exhibited positive spillover effects in militia violence).

77. Christine M. Lillie, Brock Knapp, Lasana T. Harris, & Richard Ashby Wilson, *This Is the Hour of Revenge: The Psychology of Propaganda and Mass Atrocities*, SSRN (Mar. 18, 2015), http://ssrn.com/abstract=2580521 or http://dx.doi.org/10.2139/ssrn.2580521.

78. *Id.* at 5.

79. *Id.* at 5–6.

80. *Id.* at 17.

81. *Id.* at 18.

of the relationship between discourse and mass violence. "Foucauldian Discourse Analysis," for example, an outgrowth of Michele Foucault's philosophy, focuses on power relationships in society as expressed through language and practices.[82] This could help deepen our understanding of atrocity-speech environments, boundaries of free expression, and the social dynamic behind them. Similarly, sociologist Jürgen Habermas's theories on communicative rationality and the public sphere could make an important contribution to such an inquiry from a different perspective.[83] In particular, his concept of "Ideal Speech," which posits that an "ideal speech situation" is found when communication between individuals is governed by basic, implied rules, could help us better distinguish between viable communications ecosystems and toxic discourse spheres that could usher in atrocity.[84]

Linguistics could also be a helpful added area of study. Thus, cross-pollinating the kind of speech analysis called for in Chapters 8 and 9 of this book with semiotics, for example, could be quite fruitful. Consideration of Ferdinand de Saussure's concepts of sign/signifier/signified/referent or syntagmatic and paradigmatic axes of linguistic description could advance incitement's contextual inquiry significantly.[85] In this regard the work of other, more modern, semioticians, such as Roland Barthes and Jacques Derrida, could further enrich the exegetical enterprise. Finally, J. L. Austin's scholarship on speech act theory, with its breakdown of performative utterances into locutionary (meaning), illocutionary (providing force in utterance), and perlocutionary aspects (*the achieving of* certain *effects* by speech), could help develop more satisfying theories of actionable rhetoric, including greater insight into the thorny issue of causation.[86] It is beyond the scope of this book to pursue these lines of thinking further here. But it is hoped that other scholars will take the baton.

V. FINAL REFLECTIONS

In regulating human decency, the law's writ is circumscribed. It cannot legislate civic grace or decorum. It cannot enjoin hate. But it still has a role to play

82. *See* Mary M. Talbot, Language and Gender 119 (2010) ("Discourses are constituted in history and society; what is included as truth, access to that truth, who may determine it, all depend on relations of power in institutions.").

83. Michael Pusey, Jürgen Habermas 104 (1987) (explaining the rational potential of ideal speech and the public sphere but explaining Foucault's criticism of this notion given that they are subject to forms of power).

84. *Id.*

85. Chris Barker, The SAGE Dictionary of Cultural Studies 181–82 (2004) (discussing the theories of the founder of semiotics, Swiss linguist Ferdinand de Saussure).

86. J. L. Austin, How to Do Things with Words 94–101 (1975). *See also* Richard Wilson, *Inciting Genocide with Words*, 36 Mich. J. Int'l L. 277, 305 (2014) ("The thesis advanced here is that Austin provides us with a theory of speech acts that, if applied in international criminal law, would advance a coherent development of ICG [incitement to commit genocide] jurisprudence.").

in regulating verbal conduct that helps foment the most unspeakable crimes. That its impact may be limited does not mean that its potential to maximize its utility should be ignored. In preventing and punishing atrocity speech, we need rules that are understandable, workable, and consistent with one another. We need to avoid fetishizing certain concepts, such as "incitement" and "genocide" so that we may fashion an effective penal approach to all actionable rhetoric. This book has suggested such an approach. Even if it only stimulates discussion and prompts limited positive changes at first, it will have been worth the effort. It will have left a template for more meaningful reform that may yet be enacted. We must continue to work toward full doctrinal efficacy.

At the same time, we must understand the need for a much wider-ranging, holistic approach. Statutes and international criminal charters can only go so far. The emerging norm of Responsibility to Protect must be developed and given teeth.[87] Preempting rants that would spur bloody uprisings means much more than punishing them after the streets are stained red. Early warning protocols and rapid response systems must be prioritized to obviate criminal judgments years after the fact. Even better, the effort to instill in young people an appreciation for diversity and an abhorrence of violence will be the most effective antidote to the atrocity speech phenomenon. Education and the flourishing of reasoned public discourse through civil society and media engagement will be the best bulwark against any future rising tide of hate.

87. At the UN 2005 World Summit, global leaders made a "soft-law" commitment to protect vulnerable populations from atrocity crimes, including genocide, by adopting the "Responsibility to Protect" principle, which authorizes military intervention via Security Council resolution to prevent such crimes. *See* Responsibility to Protect Populations from Genocide, War Crimes, Ethnic Cleansing, and Crimes against Humanity, 2005 World Summit Outcome Document, G.A. Res. 60/1, ¶¶ 138–40, U.N. GAOR, 60th sess., U.N. Doc. A/Res/60/1 (Oct. 24, 2006).

Index